P9-DVY-441

Laurie J. & Lee Bowers
PO Box 173
Silver Lake, OR 97638-0173

John G. Lake

His Life, His Sermons, His Boldness of Faith

KCP

KENNETH COPELAND PUBLICATIONS
FORT WORTH, TEXAS

John G. Lake His Life, His Sermons, His Boldness of Faith

ISBN 0-88114-962-4 30-0802

Library of Congress Catalog Card Number: 94-72505

All scripture is from the *King James Version* unless otherwise noted.

Kenneth Copeland Publications
Fort Worth, Texas 76192-0001

Most of the sermons in this work are previously unpublished. The following is a list of works previously printed in whole or in part and are included herein with permission of the publishers:

Harrison House Publishers, Tulsa, Oklahoma
"Adventures in God" in *Adventures in God* (1981).

"Triune Salvation," "A Reply to Dr. Elwood Bulgin," "Spiritualism," "Reign as Kings" in *John G. Lake: A Man Without Compromise* (1989).

Christ for the Nations, Dallas, Texas
"The Baptism of the Holy Ghost—2," "Have Christians a Right to Pray 'If it be Thy Will,'" "The Power of Divine Healing," "Second Crowning" and "Sin in the Flesh" in *The New John G. Lake Sermons* (1986).

"Christ Liveth in Me," "Compassion," "The Habitation of God," "Sanctification," "Spiritual Hunger" and "The Strong Man's Way to God" in *Spiritual Hunger and Other Sermons* (1987).

Sacramento Union
"The Truth About Divine Healing"

In Appreciation

Through the months of preparation for this manuscript many people gave their time and care to make it possible. A very special thank you from Kenneth Copeland Ministries to...

Betty Oaks

Billye Brim

Sue Stone

Timothy Reidt

Roberts Lairdon Ministries

Mrs. Freda Lindsay and Christ for the Nations

Harrison House Publishers

Olean Taylor

Table of Contents

Foreword

Many years ago someone gave me a notebook full of John Lake's sermons. I read each one carefully and joyfully. Through the years, as I have read and reread them many times, I have continued to receive more revelation and understanding. These sermons have imparted something in my life that I would not exchange for anything in the world. Probably more than anything, I have received a greater understanding of my dominion as a believer which encourages increased boldness in my life.

Some years ago, I was at a time in my life when I needed to lay aside natural weights that were holding me back spiritually. As I made a fresh commitment to run the race God set before me, the Lord led me to read one of these sermons every day. I did just that and it changed my life forever! I believe you will experience the same stirring I did. This is wonderful material to stir yourself up as Paul exhorted Timothy to do.

Because these messages have been such a blessing and have made such an impact on both Kenneth and me, I have desired for years to make them available to you.

These sermons helped teach me and train me. I believe they'll be just as great a blessing to you and cause you to increase spiritually. You will want to feed on them for the rest of your days here on earth. I know as I go over them again and again, they *always* stir me to new heights.

Also desiring to share these rich truths, John Lake's grandchildren have given us permission to share his anointed life and ministry with you. I am so grateful for their father, Wilford Reidt, who edited and preserved these wonderful messages for us. Before he went to be with the Lord he gave my friend, Betty Oaks, stewardship over these sermons. He asked her to see to it that they were not altered in any way. Because they are so powerful that's the way I've always wanted them to be offered. I feel it would be wrong to change them in any way.

There are some things I might have said differently. For instance, he uses some terms concerning the races that today are considered improper. However, in his day those were the common terms used. He was a man of great love for all races, so don't let anything like that hinder your receiving him as a man through whom God speaks.

There are some things I might not have said at all. One thing I recall is about going to doctors. The Pentecostal people (or at least many) didn't believe in going to the doctor under any circumstances. John Lake and his family adhered to that.

We don't tell people not to go to the doctor. Many people aren't developed in their faith. You have to do according to what direction you get and according to your faith level. But whatever you do, believe God.

So enjoy this bold man's gospel. Ask the Holy Spirit to impart to you insight and revelation. He did it for John Lake, He did it and is still doing it for us, and He'll do it for you. Study these words from heaven—we have kept them intact, just the way they were preached.

Gloria Copeland

A Strong Man's Gospel

John G. Lake

1870-1935

From the time he was a boy, John Graham Lake always seemed to be busy trying to get someone healed—if not himself, then someone else. His own struggle for life began the day he was born—March 18, 1870.

Born in Ontario, Canada, Lake was one of 16 children. And like many of his brothers and sisters, he grew up with a strange digestive disease that nearly killed him. For nine years he suffered with the disease and the unpleasant treatments that were necessary to keep him alive.

While Lake managed to somehow survive, eight of his siblings didn't. One by one they died and funerals, tears and grief eventually overshadowed his childhood. Lake's memories were filled with the cries of his parents. The sorrow intensified as even his extended family seemed unusually plagued with sickness and death.

All this heartache only made Lake more painfully and keenly aware of the fact that sickness was something bad, something evil. In all his life he never saw *any* good come out of it. As Lake grew older this overexposure to sickness and sorrow sparked in him a rare and intense desire for the power of God. It was this driving passion that would not let John G. Lake rest until he had found a way to beat sickness, disease...and even death itself.

God's Lightning Rod

As a child, Lake had seen enough to know that he and his family needed a miracle. What he didn't know was how to get one.

In the church where he grew up, miracles and supernatural healing never seemed much of an option. If anything, the church people to whom he looked for help spent a lot of time trying to convince him that God meant life's traumas and tragedies for his good. Somehow, Lake could never quite see the *good* for all the suffering around him. So he kept looking for his miracle.

At age 16, Lake moved with his family to the United States and settled in northern Michigan. It was there that he was saved as a result of a Salvation Army meeting and joined the Methodist Church. But still, sickness would not loosen its death grip on Lake and his family.

Finally, he could wait no longer—something had to be done. And it looked like it would be up to him to do it. He later wrote, "There was nobody to pray for me...As I sat alone, I said, 'Lord, I am finished with the world and the flesh, with the doctor and with the devil. From today, I lean on the arm of God.'"

At that moment, there was no evident sign of healing or any other manifestation of God's power in his body. Yet, one thing was certain, Lake had consecrated himself to God. And though it may not have looked like it on the outside, he knew on the inside that the disease was gone. He was that determined.

But while the disease was gone, the struggle wasn't over.

As Lake grew to be a young man, he suffered yet another ailment. Rheumatism was causing his legs to grow out of shape and distort his body.

Again, his church couldn't offer him the results that he passionately sought. His pastor told him, "Brother, you are glorifying God." Other church people said, "Brother, be patient and endure it." And for a while, Lake believed them—but he was still deformed. *What Good News was there in that?* Where was the powerful gospel that had been able to save him?

What Lake really wanted was another miracle. So again, his heart stretched toward God. As he did, a flash of truth pierced the deception of his mind, and in the light of God's Word, Lake caught a glimpse of God's will.

"I discovered that [disease] was not the will of God at all, but the will of the dirty, crooked-legged devil that wanted to make me like himself.

"I laid down everything and went to Chicago, to the only place where I knew that a man could get healed. I went to John Alexander Dowie's Divine Healing Home."

There in Chicago, the power of God surged through Lake's body and straightened his legs. Lake caught hold of the power of God, and the fact that Christianity is *"a strong man's gospel."* For the first time he saw how God wanted a race of people who are bold, strong, pure, good and blessed. He saw how the signs and wonders of the New Testament were meant for his day—and every day!

John Lake left Chicago healed. He also left with a bold gospel that declared *healing for everyone*—even the unsaved and the unchurched. This was the gospel that sparked astounding passion and boldness in his soul.

Though Lake had been born a sickly child in the 19th century, he now stood boldly at the threshold of the 20th century as a lightning rod stretched between heaven and earth, just waiting to be struck by the very *"lightning of God,"* as he later called it. And with each release of God's power that eventually charged his life, Lake in turn electrified the modern world. Time after time he jolted Christians and non-Christians alike by showing them the true heart and power of God.

Unraveling the Curse of Death

As far back as Lake could remember, his mind had always been buzzing with ideas, always thinking and wondering—especially about science.

He had focused a lot of his formal education and studies on chemistry and electricity; he had even gained somewhat of a reputation as a pioneer in those fields. But by age 21, Lake had redirected his studies and become a Methodist minister. With that, he began aiming his tireless curiosity at the supernatural power of God—and how it connected to the natural realm.

So, for Lake's curious and scientific mind, it wasn't enough just to know that God healed, he had to know *how.*

The answer to *"How?"* started coming when God began unraveling all the sickness and death that had bound Lake's family for 32 years...

In February 1891, Lake married Jennie Stevens of Newberry, Michigan. They adored each other and eventually had seven children. But less than five years into their marriage, several well-known physicians diagnosed Jennie with tuberculosis and an incurable heart disease. Soon after that, she became an invalid. Sorrow was back—and it didn't let up.

At the doctors recommendation, Lake moved his young family back to Sault Sainte Marie, Michigan, where he had grown up as a teenager. The northern climate was supposed to ease his wife's condition. But for Lake, it seemed that nothing could ease the rising grief, which had nearly reached flood stage.

Again Lake was surrounded by sickness and disease—an invalid brother, a sister dying from breast cancer, another sister slowly bleeding to death and now...his dear Jennie. He stood by helplessly. Where was his strong man's gospel? And was it strong enough to hold back this tide of oppression?

More desperate than ever before, Lake fell back on what had worked for him in the past—Dowie's Healing Home in Chicago.

Lake and his family decided their brother would be first. He had been an invalid for 22 years, so they carefully loaded him up and took him to Chicago. In a matter of just moments after healing ministers laid their hands on him, he was healed—he got up and walked out!

Next, the Lakes took their 34-year-old sister who was dying from breast cancer. She had been operated on five times and had to be carried on a stretcher. She too was healed!

Then there was the sister who was bleeding to death. Her case was perhaps more trying for Lake because, being only about a year apart in age, they had grown up especially close to each other.

One night, Lake's phone rang—it was his mother. She was calling to let him know that his sister was nearly dead, and that if he wanted to see her alive, he'd have to hurry. When he arrived, she was unconscious and had no pulse. *Now what could he do?* Lake wrestled deep within his soul.

And then it came to him!

He rushed a telegram to Dowie in Chicago. The message read: "My sister has apparently died, but my spirit will not let her go. I believe if you will pray, God will heal her."

Dowie's reply came: "Hold on to God. I am praying. She will live." And she did! Within the hour, the whole family rejoiced—another Lake had been snatched from death!

That left only Jennie.

A 9:30 Appointment With Healing

On the heels of all the family celebration came the evening when death seemed to settle in heaviest over Jennie. But why? So much had happened—such wonderful displays of God's healing power had moved through the other three. Somehow they had tapped into the very life force of God. But how did healing really work—what made it happen?

On this particular evening, a minister friend of Lake's stopped by to visit. After standing for a while beside Jennie's bed, the two men stepped outside for a walk. As they made their way through the moonlit night, the minister spoke up out of a heart of compassion: "Brother Lake, be reconciled to the will of God."

In contrast to the stillness of night, those words hit Lake like a slap in the face. The more he thought about those words the angrier he became. He realized that what this minister was really saying was, "Be reconciled to let your wife die."

Let her die? He couldn't do that! Where was the *strength* in that kind of gospel?

Suddenly, wind kicked up in Lake's soul—and a storm blew in with a vengeance. Surely, God had been insulted by such a suggestion!

Then the storm turned to rage, and Lake headed for home. When he got there, he walked up to the fireplace, took a Bible off the mantelpiece, and threw it on a table. *So, where was the power...especially now, when he needed it most?*

The book fell open to Acts 10—verse 38 caught his eyes: *"God anointed Jesus of Nazareth with the Holy Ghost and with power: who went about doing good, and healing all that were OPPRESSED OF THE DEVIL; for God was with him."*

There it was—Lake saw it! The light of the Word shone brightly into his soul, revealing the truth *and* the power: Jesus is the Healer and *Satan is the oppressor.* Satan was the one who had been dousing Lake and his family with oppression and sorrow, sickness and death. Satan was the problem—Jesus was the solution. It was so clear!

In the past, though Lake clearly saw that sickness, disease and death were obviously not from God, he still had not fully understood that behind all these tragedies was the devil. And just as importantly, he saw that *God was with him.* God was not just with Jesus, John Dowie and other famous healing evangelists and preachers, but God—and His power—was with John Lake. John Lake could pray and the sick would recover. He had the same faith and the same Holy Spirit available to him.

Well, that changed everything. He had stumbled onto a powder keg of boldness that was about to explode.

Now the winds really blew, and a fury of faith churned deep inside Lake.

Yes! Jennie *was* going to be healed. He was sure of it. And it was up to him to do something about it. Now Lake knew who he was dealing with—Satan. And he also knew that he had every right to do something about it. Jesus had given him that right—and the power to go with it...

Yes, healing was coming, but this time, Lake decided it would be different. This time, *he* was setting the time for it.

The time—9:30 a.m., April 28, 1898.

Lake called and telegraphed friends, instructing them to pray at the appointed time, because at precisely 9:30 a.m., he would lay his hands on his wife and she would be healed. It was that simple.

The appointed time for healing came—and with it—the power of God!

Lake put his hands on Jennie and the paralysis left, the coughing left, her heart became normal, her temperature normal and her breathing regular. Then, with a voice as big as her husband's boldness, Jennie cried out—"Praise God! I am healed!" Lake was startled. He had not heard such a powerful voice from her in years.

Jennie's resounding praise echoed throughout the city, across the state and around the nation. Newspapers heralded the event as well: "Jennie Lake had been healed!" And from that morning on, the letters and people never stopped pouring in to the Lakes' once private lives. There were hundreds of other families who were just as desperate as John and Jennie had been for the lightning of God to flash through their lives. From miles and miles they came, people who wanted what the Lakes had—their faith, their boldness, their strong man's gospel.

A healing ministry was born. As Lake put it, "We were forced into it. God answered, and many were healed."

From the time he was a boy, Lake had pushed and shoved and twisted his way through the darkness of sickness and disease just to get a grip on the power of God—the lightning of God. And now the struggle seemed over. Now Lake had gotten hold of enough of that power for himself, his family, and thousands more. But as he took hold of it, suddenly, another struggle stared him square in the face.

Getting Down to Business

With sure-footed stride, Lake boldly crossed into a new threshold of success. A strong anointing to heal the sick had come upon him. And while he handled this anointing with great success on the outside, on the inside, it only intensified the struggle that had been going on for years.

The struggle? Choosing between getting down to business with God, or getting down to business with the world. It started back in October 1891.

Eight months after Lake had married Jennie, the Methodist Church appointed him to be pastor of a church in Wisconsin. But for some reason, instead of taking the pastorate, Lake decided to go into business for himself.

It wasn't long before Lake's success in the business world equaled his passion for God. After all, he was an intense and determined man. Whatever he went after, he got—and a lot of it too!

One of Lake's first business ventures was to start a newspaper, *The Harvey Citizen,* in Harvey, Illinois. Then, after making the move to Michigan because of Jennie's failing health, Lake dove into real estate. On the first day of business alone, he earned $2500. And within two years he had amassed nearly $250,000 in personal wealth, which around the turn of the century was a fortune.

By the time Lake was 30, he had helped start another newspaper—the *Soo Times*—and some of the wealthiest men in North America were courting him for his expertise in managing people and money. He later bought a seat on the Chicago Board of Trade, and was reported to have become a millionaire.

In the height of Lake's financial success, from 1900 to 1907, he was hired by a group of investors to form and manage one of the country's largest life insurance companies. Part of his job included managing the company's agents. By simply advising an agent just 20 to 30 minutes, Lake could earn hundreds of dollars in commission. That was in addition to a salary already set at about $50,000 a year.

But in the middle of all this financial success, something richer was happening in the heart and soul of John Lake. He was beginning to see—and count—the value of men's souls.

Since that glorious morning when Jennie was healed in 1898, Lake had started preaching and holding healing meetings in the Chicago area. By 1901, he and his family had moved 40 miles north to Zion City, Illinois—where John Dowie had moved his ministry headquarters—so Lake could study divine healing up close, as well as teach it, until 1904.

In all, Lake ministered part time for a period of 10 years, and during that time, hundreds of people were saved and healed.

"But at the end of that 10 years," Lake wrote, "I believe I was the hungriest man for God that ever lived. My friends would say, 'Mr. Lake, you have a beautiful Baptism in the Holy Ghost.' Yes, it was nice as far as it went, but it was not answering the cry of my heart."

How could that have been? How could such a glorious display of God's power through Lake's life not have satisfied the cry of his heart?

Simple. Many of Lake's friends and associates assumed that he had received the Baptism in the Holy Spirit, when in fact, he had not. Actually, he had never fully understood it, though many had talked to him about it. Meanwhile, people who saw him minister with such success were indeed judging him by his works—and certainly, he had been wonderfully anointed by the Spirit to minister. Yet, there was more for Lake to learn, more for him to receive. And deep in his heart he knew it.

A New Power

Oh, Lake's heart cried out for the Baptism in the Spirit. He was so determined to receive.

For the first nine months of 1907, Lake fasted, prayed and cried out to God. He just had to have all of God that he could get. Finally, in the tenth month, he got what he was after—and a big dose of it too.

On one October day, Lake accompanied his preaching partner and friend Tom Hezmalhalch to the home of an invalid woman. They were going to pray for her healing. As Tom instructed the woman about healing before they prayed, Lake sat comfortably in a deep leather chair across the room. His mind soon drifted, and again he was thinking about the Baptism in the Spirit.

Suddenly, a great calm invaded the restlessness of Lake's soul. And for the first time in his life—that he could remember—his mind became still. Something like a warm, tropical rain shower began bathing his soul. Oh, it was so peaceful. Then, out of the calm of that moment, Lake heard the Lord say, *I have heard your prayers, I have seen your tears. You are now baptized in the Holy Spirit.*

Finally, it was his—something more precious, more beautiful, more personal...the baptism of his spirit into God's Spirit. Now, his own heart was full; it was complete; it was satisfied.

That's when the power came—a power like never before.

Lake was still sitting in the chair when a downpour of electrical-like currents surged through his body, causing him to convulse nearly out of control. And moments later, he began speaking in tongues.

"When the phenomena had passed," Lake wrote, "the glory of it remained in my soul. I found that my life began to manifest in the varied range of the gifts of the Spirit. Healings were of a more powerful order.

"My nature became so sensitized that I could lay my hands on any man or woman and tell what organ was diseased, and to what extent."

Lake tested this new wonder by going to hospitals and touching patients to determine what their ailments were. And to make it even more challenging, most of them were cases that even the physicians could not diagnose. Nevertheless, time after time, Lake's diagnoses were proven to be correct. But for him personally, the ultimate test was to demonstrate before the eyes of medical science just how the power of God affected the human body.

So at one point, Lake submitted himself to a series of experiments at a well-known research clinic. It was because of his formal education in science and medicine that he was even allowed access to such clinics.

During one of these experiments Lake told the professors, "'Gentlemen, go down in your hospital and bring back a man who has inflammation in the bone. Take your instrument [a powerful X-ray machine with microscopic attachments] and attach it to his leg. Leave enough space to get my hand on his leg.'"

Lake reported that "When the instrument was ready, I put my hand on the man's shin and prayed, 'God, kill the devilish disease by Your power. Let the Spirit move in him; let It live in him.'

"Then I asked, 'Gentlemen, what is taking place?'

"They replied, 'Every cell is responding.'"

The scientists were astounded at what they saw. For, as best as they could tell, they were witnessing some sort of re-creative process that was taking place in the leg of a dying man—and it was happening right there under their own microscope!

With such manifestations of supernatural power in his ministry, it wasn't long before Lake spent more and more time in healing meetings at night. By now he was preaching to crowds of thousands, instead of hundreds.

Meanwhile, Lake was still trying to carry on his daytime business as usual. And that was becoming difficult in an unusual way.

Lake had proven to be a sharp businessman and now he was successfully managing agents for the large life insurance company. But almost overnight he discovered that he could no longer concentrate on business—at least not on man's business. It wasn't that his mind drifted, rather, he only seemed able to focus on God's business. And God was in the business of men's souls. During this time, it was typical for Lake to be in the middle of a business deal and hear the Spirit say, *How about his soul? How about his soul?*

"After a little bit," Lake said, "I had to stop and say, 'Brother, are you a Christian? If not, kneel down.'"

Right there in his office, Lake would kneel down and pray with men and lead them to the Lord.

"I saw them come to God every day for six months. But O, I forgot about the insurance—and the company was paying me to [sell] insurance."

Finally, in April 1907, Lake's long and intense struggle came to an end when he decided to follow his heart. "I was compelled to abandon my business and turn all my attention to bringing men to the feet of Jesus," he wrote. And in a dramatic move, he and Jennie disposed of all their wealth and possessions and began seeking God's purpose for their lives. They even decided never to disclose their personal needs to anyone—but instead, trust God as never before.

Lake cut his ties to the business affairs of men, rolled up his sleeves and prepared to do business for God—full time. The last move he made like that got him charged with the very lightning of God. But this time, he was headed for something that even his exceptionally active mind could not imagine. He was about to step into the fire of God.

Liquid Fire Falls on South Africa

The next item of business came as no surprise to Lake.

One day in the closing months of 1907, while he was out chopping down a tree, Lake distinctly heard the Holy Spirit say, *Go to Indianapolis. Prepare for a winter campaign. In the spring you will go to Africa.*

Lake's heart didn't skip a beat when he heard the part about going to Africa—if anything, it raced with excitement. From the time he was a boy, Lake had dreamed of going to Africa. Even as a young man, the idea just wouldn't go away. So Lake didn't waste any time. He moved his family to Indianapolis, joined up again with his friend Tom Hezmalhalch to preach a series of meetings, and planned the trip of a lifetime.

But Lake needed a lot more than childhood imagination to get himself, his wife, seven children and a group of missionaries to Africa.

In February 1908, Lake and Hezmalhalch—who also had decided to go to Africa—prayed and asked the Lord for $2,000. That's what they figured it would cost for their party of 17 to travel from Indiana to Johannesburg, South Africa. Four days later, they had the money to buy all the tickets. And on April 19, 1908, the small group of missionaries left for Africa.

As far as personal expenses and needs, Lake boarded ship with only $1.25 in his pockets for his family of nine to travel halfway around the world. Furthermore, once they got there, he didn't have a clue as to where they would live. But by the time he and his family stepped off the ship in Cape Town, South Africa—about two weeks later—Lake had been given $200 plus a fully furnished house in Johannesburg. This journey of faith had turned into a trail of miracles.

The next miracle Lake needed was a place to preach. He was, after all, a stranger to these people, dream or no dream, and he needed some sort of introduction.

The Lakes barely had time to settle in to their new home when, just days after they arrived in Johannesburg, God opened the first door to Lake's ministry. A South African pastor was taking a leave of absence for a few weeks and Lake was asked to fill in while he was gone. Lake jumped at the offer.

His first Sunday in the pulpit, with the aid of an interpreter, Lake preached to a congregation of 500 Zulus.

The service started out quiet that morning...unusually quiet. Lake wasn't sure what was about to happen, but he recognized that uneasy silence that fills the air just minutes before a storm hits. He sensed the Spirit was about to do something. So he waited.

What happened that day was like watching a volcano erupt. In both morning and evening services, as the Spirit fell, signs and wonders began showering the congregation. But it didn't stop there. In the days that followed, spectacular displays of God's power spilled out into the community like lava. A fiery trail of revival cut through the hearts of people desperate for a strong man's gospel. Within weeks, scores of people in Johannesburg and surrounding areas were saved and filled with the Holy Spirit—hundreds were supernaturally healed.

News of this supernatural outburst quickly spread across the nation and crowds flocked in from even remote parts of the country. The small door that God had opened for Lake became the doorway to five years of powerful ministry in all of South Africa.

The anointing that fell on Lake while he was in South Africa astounded even Lake himself. It was far beyond his wildest imagination. The only way he could described it was as *"liquid fire"* pumping through his veins. But of course, this kind of *fire-power* did come in handy.

In one meeting, a man kept getting up and interrupting Lake. When Lake finally had enough, he pointed his finger at the man and told him to sit down. Instantly the man fell to the floor and lay there for two hours. After the meeting, the man described what happened and said it was as though he had been shot down by a bullet.

Then, there were the times that this anointing seemed to have its disadvantages.

Lake was a real hands-on type of person and he really enjoyed greeting people as they came into his meetings. Often, however, when he could get close enough and shake people's hands, they would fall under the power of the Spirit and block the entrances to his meetings. At other times the anointing on him became so strong that people would fall under its power simply by coming within six feet of him.

Since Lake was not affiliated with any existing church or mission organization (though he later established his own), he rented halls to hold his meetings in the Johannesburg area.

It wasn't long before the growing crowds outgrew the halls, and he had to use a different approach. That's when he started holding "cottage meetings" in people's homes scattered throughout a town or city. In these cottage meetings, Lake and his partner Hezmalhalch would go from house to house, preaching as a team and speaking as many as five or six times each in just one meeting.

Meanwhile, at the Lake's home, the steady flow of sick people never let up. In fact, so many kept coming to the Lakes for prayer that Jennie usually had to give up preparing dinner so she could direct the flow of people into and out of the house while John prayed for them.

Within 18 months after stepping foot onto South African soil, Lake had established his own "tabernacle"—a main church and congregation—in Johannesburg, and had started and was overseeing 100 other churches in surrounding areas. And that was just the beginning.

The Price of Boldness

If John Lake ever lacked boldness, he certainly made up for it in South Africa. The strong man's gospel that he preached had by now invaded and cut through nearly every wall of religious, racial and political prejudice. And that took boldness.

But Lake's reputation for boldness soon stirred up controversy.

Perhaps one of the most shocking and intense controversies Lake faced during his South Africa mission was his outward love for the black nationals.

This controversy over racism seemed to hit its boiling point in early 1909, when Lake greeted Elias Letwaba, a black South African national, on the platform during a meeting. With a heart full of love, Lake put his arm around Letwaba's neck, kissed him and called him "my brother." This infuriated some of the unconverted white men in the audience to the point that they hissed at and booed Lake.

At that, Lake turned and shouted, "My friends, God has made of one blood all nations of men. If you do not want to acknowledge them as your brothers, then you'll have the mortification of going away into eternal woe, while you see many of these black folk going to eternal bliss."

Then he quoted 1 John 3:15: *"Whosoever hateth his brother is a murderer: and ye know that no murderer hath eternal life abiding in him."*

Still, many in the audience started shouting that the "black devils" should be kicked into the streets. But Lake didn't back down. He welcomed Letwaba, and with his hand on the man's shoulder, said, "If you turn out these men, then you must turn me out too, for I will stand by my black brethren."

The crowd eventually quieted down...such love was new to South Africa.

Meanwhile, race wasn't the only wave of controversy that came crashing against Lake's ministry.

Back in the United States, wave after wave of rumors rolled in from South Africa, rumors that Lake was misusing the ministry's money. But by the time Lake caught wind of these rumors, he seemed caught in the backlash of accusation. Though the accusations were later proven false, trust in Lake had eroded, and the flow of financial gifts to his ministry dwindled to a trickle. Sadly, this was the man who had gone to Africa without any support from mission organizations, who never took collections in his meetings, and who had stuck to his decision to never make his personal needs known.

Now Lake's young mission, which had grown to 125 ministers in the field, began to suffer even more as difficult circumstances got worse. Ironically, while thousands of South Africans were being saved and healed, Lake, his staff and their families were often in dire need.

Then came another pounding wave of controvesy—"the masterstroke of Satan," as Lake called it.

Not even a full year into his ministry, Lake returned home from a preaching tour in the Kalahari Desert and found that his dear Jennie had died—and just 12 hours before his return. He was nearly devastated.

Sources do not agree on the date of Jennie Lake's death, but Lake recorded that she died of a stroke on December 22, 1908. Some say she died as late as 1912. Nevertheless, most accounts agree that Jennie Lake died from malnutrition and physical exhaustion. The reason being, while Lake was away on preaching tours such as this one to the Kalahari, scores of sick people would show up at his home and wait for him to return. Most were poor and without provisions and slept in the Lakes' yard. Jennie would usually take what little food she and her seven children could afford and share it with them.

In 1910, two years after Jennie's death—and still grieving—Lake wrote:

"As I look back over the terrible struggles of planting this work in Africa, I now really feel God in His mercy permitted her to escape this awful time of sorrow, trials and fighting by taking her on to heaven. Lies, blackmail, suggestion of evil of every kind. They say I am possessed of a devil; that's how people are saved and healed."

But when it seemed that *Satan the oppressor* had whipped Lake and his strong man's gospel, Lake came back with even more boldness and more passion for souls.

Mission to America

In late 1909, about a year after Jennie's death, Lake returned to America—but not for good, and not defeated. His purpose was to get more workers and money for South Africa.

He returned to Johannesburg in 1910 with $3,000 and eight more missionaries. And for the next three years, he worked fiercely. He founded the Apostolic Church which developed into two large churches in South Africa—the Apostolic Faith Mission (which is not part of the Apostolic Faith Church in the United States) and the Zion Christian Church. By 1913, Lake's ministry totaled 1,250 preachers, 625 congregations, 100,000 converts—and countless miracles.

Furthermore, Lake's public display of affection toward Elias Letwaba back in 1909 was probably more significant than Lake himself realized at the time. For as Lake left South Africa, God was raising up Letwaba to build a Bible school—Patmos Bible School—which later turned out thousands of trained workers who evangelized *all* of Africa. Like no one else, Letwaba carried on the work that Lake had begun.

Lake compared his work in South Africa to what David said about Moses in Psalm 103:7: *"He made known his ways unto Moses, his acts unto the children of Israel."*

"The people of Africa seemed to behold the phenomena of what God did," Lake wrote, "but God took my spirit behind the scenes and let me see *how* [He] did them."

"How?" is what Lake had been asking for years. And even in South Africa, he was just as much a student as he was teacher and preacher. When Lake boarded ship with his seven children for the final return trip to America in 1913, he took with him the priceless understanding of how God's power worked.

Lake was tired when he left South Africa. He even may have appeared to be drifting aimlessly back across the Atlantic, with boldness no longer filling his sails. But nothing could have been further from the truth. As Lake departed, he set course for yet another mission. Armed with the experience *and* understanding of God's power, he returned to America to launch his fiercest attack ever against the kingdom of darkness. His plan? Teach the next generation how to grab onto and skillfully wield the power of God.

His first year back in America, Lake and his children leisurely traveled from city to city, renewing old friendships and resting. During that time Lake married Florence Switzer, and together they eventually had five more children. But by the end of 1914, he was ready to get back to work. So he moved his growing family to Spokane, Washington, and got started.

The first thing Lake did was rent a suite of rooms in an old office building. Then, with the power of God and a lot of hard work, Lake transformed everyday office space into the Divine Healing Institute. What were once offices, now became classrooms filled with men and women who wanted to learn how to apply God's healing power to their everyday lives. And for the next six years, Lake trained the next generation of "healing technicians," as he called them.

Healing technician meant you didn't stay in the classroom and read textbooks all day—Lake was, after all, a hands-on type of person.

After sufficient teaching from God's Word and his own revelation knowledge, Lake usually assigned each technician to the home of a sick person. His instructions to them: *Don't come back to class until that person is healed.* Of course some might be gone an hour, some a day and some for weeks, but they came back understanding what it took to get someone healed. Actually, what the students learned was to spend time with the sick, teach them the Word, and become sensitive to each one's specific needs.

Lake's plan worked! So well, in fact, that Lake and his healing technicians were now ministering to as many as 200 sick people a day, and of those, only one fourth were members of a church. Also, many of the people were coming from as far away as 5,000 miles to be healed. Before long, Lake's Divine Healing Institute became known around the world as the famous "Healing Rooms."

With so many sick people to treat, Lake and his team of technicians came across just about every known form of disease—and saw it healed. Furthermore, most of the cases were ones that physicians had pronounced hopeless.

One such case was a 35-year-old woman who had a 30-pound fibroid tumor in her abdomen. Lake described the tumor as "a twisted mass of muscle and sinew, arteries and veins, teeth and hair...equal [in weight] to three and a half large babies."

Then one day, out of the agony of not being able to sit or lie down because of pain, Lake said the woman "threw her hands to heaven and cried out, 'Jesus, heal me now!'

"The power of God struck her. That mass began to twist and crunch and wither and diminish, and the action was so terrific that she cried out at the top of her voice, 'Oh, Jesus, not that way, not that way!' But in three minutes the thing was totally gone. It had absolutely dematerialized—no blood, no puss, no substance."

Clear Vision

As busy as Lake was during those six years, he still found time to start the Apostolic Church in Spokane and oversee the International Apostolic Congress—the parent organization to his church, which was moved to Spokane from England at the outbreak of World War I.

That meant, at age 50, Lake was an apostle and bishop over a denomination, pastor of a church and thriving ministry that was internationally known, and teacher of an institute that trained healing technicians. Most people, perhaps, would have been content to take it easy from then on.

But not John Lake—he had a vision.

Lake's vision was to establish a chain of healing missions all across the country. And that meant getting back out on the road.

So in May 1920, Lake moved to Portland, Oregon, to start and oversee another Apostolic Church, as well as a ministry similar to the one in Spokane. These too became just as outstanding as the ones in Spokane.

During this time that Lake was pastoring in Portland, he had a vision of an angel. And in this vision, the angel opened a Bible to the book of Acts, drawing Lake's attention to the outpouring of the Spirit on Pentecost and to the entire book of Acts itself. Then the angel spoke to him:

"This is Pentecost as God gave it through the heart of Jesus. Strive for this, contend for this. Teach the people to pray for this. For this alone will meet the necessity of the human heart and have the power to overcome the forces of darkness."

This vision and command from God stirred Lake to press even farther. For the next 11 years, he traveled throughout Oregon, California and Texas, duplicating his work and taking only one year off to rest.

By 1924, newspapers were calling Lake the "nationally known healing evangelist." He was reported to have established a chain of 40 churches and missions in the United States and Canada. And by now, his congregations had dubbed him "Dr. Lake"—and why not? In Spokane alone, 100,000 healings had been documented and recorded within just five years. That was backed up by a report out of Washington, D.C., that said: *Rev. Lake, through divine healing, has made Spokane the healthiest city in the world, according to United States statistics.*

Finally, in 1931, Lake made his last trip back to Spokane. He was 61, and had lived an intense life. Now his noted vitality was declining, and he no longer had the physical strength to match his spiritual vision.

Another sign of fatigue setting in was Lake's weakening eyesight. He was starting to go blind. So one day he decided to go for a walk, just he and God. As Lake walked around the block he prayed. He told the Lord about his vision and how it would be a shame for him to go blind after all the miracles he had seen. By the end of that walk, his vision had been restored—and remained with him for the rest of his life.

Lake still had his faith, and he still had his boldness.

Labor Day 1935 was a Sunday, and a hot one. Lake came home with his wife Florence from the Sunday school picnic very tired. And sometime that evening after supper he had a stroke. Two weeks later, on September 16, he met face to face, the Author and Finisher of the strong man's gospel that he had preached for more than 30 years.

John Graham Lake, at the age of 65, left behind a heritage of understanding God's healing power—and with it, the clear vision of even greater power:

"I can see...that there is coming from heaven a new manifestation of the Holy Spirit in power, and that new manifestations will be in sweetness, in love, in tenderness,...beyond anything your heart or mine ever saw. The very lightning of God will flash through men's souls."

Introduction

John G. Lake was forever a student of the Word. His Bible was either in hand or in reach, and he always kept pencil and paper handy. In fact, Lake studied the Word so much at night that it got to where his wife had to learn to sleep with a light on.

Though healing was a major thrust of his ministry, it wasn't the only topic that he knew anything about. Whatever teaching was necessary to build a good and balanced Christian life, Lake taught it. And when he taught—which was often six nights a week—he taught with a remarkable ability to build faith in the hearts of those who listened.

Frequently, Lake would get up in the early morning hours to record revelations he had received from the Holy Spirit. This was typically how he got most of his sermons...

Guidance

Oh, Soul, on the highway, from earth unto glory
Surrounded by mysteries, trials and fears;
Let the life of thy God, in thy life be resplendent;
For Jesus will guide thee; thou need'st never fear

For if thou wilt trust me, I'll lead thee and guide thee
Through the quicksands and deserts of life, all the way.
No harm shall befall thee; I only will teach thee
To walk in surrender with Me day by day.

For earth is a school to prepare thee for Glory;
The lessons here learned, you will always obey.
When eternity dawns, it will be only the morning
Of life with Me always, as life is today.

Therefore, be not impatient, as lessons thou'rt learning;
Each day will bring gladness and joy to thee here;
But heaven will reveal to thy soul, of the treasure
Which infinitude offers, through ages and years.

For thy God is the God of the earth and the heavens;
And thy soul is the soul that He died for to save;
And His blood is sufficient, His power is eternal
Therefore rest in thy God, both today and alway.

Given in the spirit in tongues with interpretation to
John G. Lake at Johannesburg, South Africa, 1908

1

Triune Salvation

This sermon was delivered in London, England by Rev. John G. Lake at a conference of Church of England ministry, presided over by Ingram, Bishop of London, who said, "It contains the spirit of primitive Christianity and reveals the distinctions between the Christian soul of the first and twentieth century, the spirit of Christ dominion, by which primitive Christianity attained its spiritual supremacy...It is one of the greatest sermons I have ever heard and I recommend its careful study by every priest."

"Mr. Lake had been invited to address us and traveled 7,000 miles to be here. A committee of the Church of England was sent to South Africa to investigate Mr. Lake, his work, his power, teaching and ministry and his presence here is the result of their satisfactory report."

Sermon delivered at London, England, and Washington, D.C. by Rev. John G. Lake.

Text: "I pray God your whole spirit and soul and body be preserved blameless [without defilement, corruption] unto the coming of our Lord Jesus Christ. Faithful is he that calleth you, who also will do it" [1 Thessalonians 5:23-24].

In the beginning of all things, even before the creation of man at all, there was a condition in which all things that then existed were obedient to God. Angels were obedient to the Lord. But there came a time when angels themselves rebelled against the government of God. In Isaiah, Satan is spoken of as *"Lucifer, son of the morning"* [Isaiah 14:12]. Again the Word says in substance concerning him, *Wast thou not pure and holy until pride was found in thine heart?*

Pride was the condition which, in the angel who was pure and holy, generated the desire to be separated from God, and to rebel against Him.

It was the same pride or desire to substitute his will for the will of God, which caused Adam to sin. From Adam humanity has derived the same instinctive desire to insist on its way instead of God's way; through the continued exercise of the human will and the world's way, the race had drifted into misty conceptions of the real will and the real way of God. This is particularly true in regard to the nature and substance of God.

It seems difficult to think of Him as a being and a substance. God is Spirit, but Spirit is a materiality. And God Himself is a materiality, a heavenly, not an earthly materiality. The forms of angels are a substance, otherwise they would not be discernible. It is not an earthly substance or material, but a heavenly one.

As we think of the substance of which heavenly beings are composed, and of which God Himself must necessarily be a composition, the mind settles on light and fire and spirit as a possibility.

Then the Word tells us that God breathed into Adam the breath of life, and man became a living soul. There came a time when God made man. The Word tells us: *He made man's body of the substance of the earth* [see Genesis 2:7]. He made man, the Word says, *"in his own image, in the image of God created he him"* [Genesis 1:27]; not just in the form that God was, but God breathed into him His own self, His own being...that heavenly materiality of which God consists. He injected or breathed Himself into the man, and the man then became a composition of that heavenly substance or materiality, and earth or the substance of earth.

Adam was the created Son of God. He was just like God. He was just as pure as God was pure. God fellowshiped with him. The Word of God tells us that God came down into the garden in the cool of the day, and walked with Adam, and talked with

Adam. There was perfect fellowship between God and Adam. He was a sinless man. He could look right into the face of God, and his eyes nor his spirit did not draw back. The purity of God did not startle him. He was just as pure as God was pure. That was the original man.

Man—being composed of God, of heaven, of a heavenly materiality, and his body of the earth, being a sovereign like God, being on an equality with God in sinlessness, God treating him on an equality and giving him dominion over the earth—was a reigning sovereign on the earth. Everything, all conditions, spiritual and physical, were subject to that God-man. The way of sin was this, that man chose to follow the inclinations of his earth-being, animal consciousness, or body instead of his God-man, God-being, or spirit. The result was that because of the suggestion of Satan there developed calls of the earth for the earthly. After a while he partook of things earthly and became earthly himself. Therefore the Fall of Man was his fall into himself. He fell into his own earthly self, out of his heavenly estate, and the separation was absolute and complete.

God had said, *"In the day that thou eatest thereof [sinnest], thou shalt die"* [Genesis 2:17]. That is, in the day thou sinnest, partaking of that which is earthy, the conditions of the earth being that of decay, the death process begins. So death reigneth from the time that sin came.

Sickness is incipient death. Death is the result of sin. There is no sickness in God. There never was, there never will be, there never can be. There was no sickness in man, in the God-man, until such time as he became the earth-man, until by the operation of will he sank into himself and became of the earth—earthy. Therefore, sin is the parent of sickness in that broad sense. Sickness is the result of sin. There could have been no sickness if there had been no sin.

Man, having fallen into that condition and being separated from God, needed a Redeemer. Redemption was a necessity because the Word says *"Ye must be born again"* [John 3:7]. God had to provide a means of getting man back into the original condition in which he had once been. One man cannot save another because one man is of the earth, earthy, even as another is, and man in the natural cannot save another. One cannot elevate another into a spiritual condition or put that one in a spiritual condition which is not in himself.

Thus it became necessary for God, in order to redeem the race, to provide a means of reuniting God and man. So Jesus was born, even as Adam had been made. He was begotten of God. He was born of God, but partook of the tendencies of the natural life and received his natural physical body through his mother, Mary. The Word of God speaks of the first Adam and the last Adam. They were both Adams. They both came to produce a race. The first Adam had fallen and sinned. Therefore the race that was produced through him was a race of sinful people with the same tendencies in their natures which were in his.

The last Adam, Jesus, had no sin. He had exactly the same privilege that the first Adam had. He could have sinned if he chose. Jesus was a man in this world just as every man is. *"...he took not on him the nature of angels: but he took on him the seed of Abraham"* (Hebrews 2:16). He did not take upon Him a heavenly condition. He took upon himself the natural condition of the human family...fallen human nature.

But Jesus Christ triumphed over that condition of fallen human nature and did not sin, though the Word of God emphasizes that *"...but was in all points tempted like as we are, yet without sin"* (Hebrews 4:15). The Word also says, *"Having been tempted, He is able to succor [or to save, or deliver] them that are tempted, having Himself been tempted even as we are tempted"* (Hebrews 2:18). This is what makes Him a sympathetic Savior and Christ.

The purpose of Jesus in the World was to show us the Father. So Jesus came and committed Himself publicly at His baptism at the Jordan before all the world in these words, *"unto all righteousness,"* to do the will of God. He willed not to obey his own natural human will, but to do the will of the Father, and to be wholly and solely and entirely obedient to the will of God. He declared, *"I came not to do mine own will, but the will of him that sent me"* [John 6:38].

When a Christian is born of God, and becomes a real Christian, he is made a Christ-man. If the world wants to see Jesus, it must look upon the Christian, who is the Christ-man, just as we who want to look upon the Father and understand Him, look upon the man Jesus, who was the embodiment of the Father. Everything that Jesus did was the will and the word of the Father. So everything the Christian does, if he is a real one, should be the will and word of Jesus Christ. The Christian commits himself as entirely to the will of Jesus, and becomes a Christ-man as Jesus committed Himself to the will of the Father, and became a God-man.

A low standard of Christianity is responsible for all the shame and sin and wickedness in the world. Many Christians think it is all right if they pattern after Jesus in a sort of way. They imitate Him and they do the things which He did; that is, they outwardly do them. They perform kind acts and they do other things which Jesus did. But the secret of Christianity is not in doing. The secret is in *being*. Real Christianity is in being a possessor of the nature of Jesus Christ. In other words, it is being Christ in character, Christ in demonstration, Christ in agency of transmission. When one gives himself to the Lord and becomes a child of God, a Christian, he is a Christ-man. All that he does and all that he says from that time on, should be the will and the words and the doings of Jesus—just as absolutely, just as entirely, as He spoke and did the will of the Father.

Jesus gave us the secret of how to live this kind of life. Jesus showed us that the only way to live this life was to commit oneself, as He did, to the will of God and not walk in his own ways at all, but walk in God's ways. So the one who is going to be a Christ-man in the best sense and let the world see Jesus in him, must walk in all the ways of Jesus, and follow Him. He must be a Christ-man, a Christian, or Christ-one.

Therefore, the things which possess the heart and which are unlike God fasten themselves because the inner being is not subject to the will of God. One of the reasons for this low standard of Christian living is the failure to recognize the Trinity of our own being. Man is triune...spirit and soul and body...just the same as God is triune, being Father and Son and Holy Ghost.

Salvation begins at the time when the spirit is surrendered to God, where the name is written in the Book of Life, and we receive the conscious knowledge of sins being forgiven. Then God witnesses to the spirit that our sins are blotted out. The Word, in Romans 8:16 says: *"The Spirit beareth witness with our spirit, that we are the children of God."* That is, the testimony of the Spirit of God to our spirit is that we are the children of God when we surrender our spirits to God.

People wonder why, after having given their hearts to God and after having received a witness of the spirit, they are troubled with evil desires and tempted in evil ways. The nature has three departments, and therefore, the surrender of the spirit to God is not all that He demands. God demands also the mind and the body.

The mind is the soul life; and it continues being of the earth—earthy—and doing earthy things until God does something to that mind, until we seek God for a new mind. It is similar to the change which occurs in the spirit; and the mind that formerly thought evil and that had wicked conceptions becomes as the mind of Christ.

The Church at large recognizes the salvation of the spirit. But they have not recognized the salvation of the mind from the power of sin, and that is why many church people will say there is no such thing as sanctification.

There are Christian bodies that believe in the power of God to sanctify the mind, even as the spirit is saved. John Wesley, in defining sanctification, says that it is: "Possessing the mind of Christ, and all the mind of Christ." An individual with all the mind of Christ cannot have a thought that is not a Christ thought, no more than a spirit fully surrendered to God could have evil within it.

In later years, as the revelation by the Spirit of God has gone on, man has begun to see that there is a deeper degree of salvation than these two. He is a triune being. As he needed salvation for the mind and spirit, so he has a body which needs to be transformed by God. The whole question of physical healing, the redemption of the body, the possible translation, the resurrection, are included there.

Christ is a Savior of the whole man; of spirit, of the soul, of the body. When Jesus, at the Jordan, committed Himself unto all righteousness to His Father, He committed His body just as He committed His mind and just as He committed His spirit. Christians have not been taught to commit their bodies to God, and therefore they feel justified in committing them to someone else or something else, rather than to God.

Therefore, it is clear that in a whole salvation it is just as offensive to God to commit the body to the control of man, as it would be to commit the spirit to man for salvation. Salvation for the spirit can only come through Jesus, through the blood of Christ, through receiving His Spirit. Salvation from natural thoughts and ways, and the operation of the natural mind, can only come through the natural mind being transformed into the mind of Christ. Salvation for the body is found in the same manner, by committing the body now and forever to God.

No one would think of sending to any other power than God for a remedy for the spirit. There is no spirit that one could go to, unless it is the spirit of the world or the spirit of the devil; and one goes not to either of these for the healing of the spirit or mind.

The real Christian is a separated man. He is separated forever unto God in all the departments of his life, and so his body and his soul and his spirit are forever committed to God. Therefore, from the day that he commits himself to God, his body is as absolutely in the hands of God as his spirit or his mind (soul). He can go to no other power for help or healing, except to God. This is what gives such tremendous force to such Scriptures as this: *"Cursed be the man that trusteth in man, and maketh flesh his arm, and whose heart departeth from the Lord"* [Jeremiah 17:5]. Second Chronicles 16 relates that Asa, the king of Israel, who in the thirty and ninth year of his reign became diseased in his feet, and in his disease he trusted not the Lord, but the physicians, and he died. Asa had been trusting God for many years by taking his little, insignificant army and delivering the great armies into his hand. But when he became diseased in his feet, he trusted not the Lord, but the physicians, and that was the offense of Asa against God.

The impression I wish to leave is this, that an hundredfold consecration to God takes the individual forever out of the hands of all but God. This absolute consecration to God, this triune salvation, is the real secret of the successful Christian life.

When one trusts any department of his being to man, he is weak in that respect, and that part of his being is not committed to God. When we trust our minds (souls) and our bodies to man, two parts are out of the hands of God, and there remains only our spirits in tune with heaven. It ought not to be so. The committing of the whole being to the will of God is the mind of God. Blessed be His Name.

Such a commitment of the being to God puts one in the place, where just as God supplies health to the spirit and health to the soul, he trusts God to supply health to his body. Divine healing is the removal by the power of God of the disease that has come upon the body, but the divine health is to live day by day and hour by hour in touch with God so that the life of God flows into the body, just as the life of God flows into the mind or flows into the spirit.

The Christian, the child of God, the Christ-man, who thus commits himself to God ought not to be a subject for healing. He is a subject of continuous, abiding health. And the secret of life in communion with God, the Spirit of God, is received into the being, into the soul, into the spirit.

The salvation of Jesus was a redemption of the whole man from all the power of sin, every whit...sin in the spirit, sin in the soul, sin in the body. If salvation or redemption is from the power of sin and every sin in our being, then the effects that sin produces in us must disappear and leave when the source is healed. Thus, instead of remaining sick, the Christian who commits his body to God becomes healed becomes at once, through faith, the recipient of the life of God in his body.

Jesus gave us an example of how perfectly the Spirit of God radiates not only from the spirit or from the mind, but from the body also. The transfiguration was a demonstration of the Spirit of God from within the man radiating out through his person, until the illumination radiated through his clothes, and his clothes became white and glistening, and his face shone as the light. It was the radiation of God through his flesh.

In a few instances God permitted me to see Christians thus illuminated in a measure. I am acquainted with a brother in Chicago, whose face is illuminated all the time; there is a radiation from it. His countenance is never seen in a condition of depression or as if the pores of his flesh are closed. There is an unmistakable something that marks him as one through whom the Spirit of God radiates.

God radiated through the purified personality of Jesus so that even his very clothes became white and glistening. Christians are Christ-men and stand in the stead of Jesus. The Word of God says to the Christian and the church: *Ye are His body* [see 1 Corinthians 12:27]. The accumulated company of those who know Jesus, who really have the God-life within, are the Body of Christ in the world, and through that Body of Christ all the ministry of Jesus is operative.

The nine gifts of the Holy Ghost are the divine equipment of God by which the Church, His Body, is forever to continue to do the works of Jesus. *"To one is given...the word of wisdom,...to another the gifts of healing, to another the working of miracles, to another prophecy,...to another the interpretation of tongues"* [1 Corinthians 12:8-10]. All these gifts Jesus exercised during His earthly ministry. The people who exercise these gifts create another practical Christ, the Church which is His Body, Christ being the head.

When this truth is seen, Christianity will be on a new-old basis. The illumination of God, the consciousness of our position in the world, the consciousness of our responsibility as the representatives of Christ, places upon us as Christ-men and Christ-women the burden of Christ for a lost world. Of necessity this lifts the heart and spirit into a new contact with God and the consciousness that if a son of God, if a Christ-man to the world, then one must be worthy of his Christ. The only way to be worthy is to be in the will of Jesus.

Men have mystified the gospel; they have philosophized the gospel. The gospel of Jesus is as simple as can be. As God lived in the body and operated through the man Jesus, so the man on the throne, Jesus, operates through His body, the church, in the world. Even as Jesus Himself was the representative of God the Father, so also the church is the representative of Christ. As Jesus yielded Himself unto all righteousness, so the Church should yield herself to do all the will of Christ.

"These signs shall follow them that believe" [Mark 16:17]...not the preacher, or the elder, or the priest, but the believer. The believer shall speak in new tongues, the believer shall lay hands on the sick and they shall recover. The believer is the Body of Christ in the world. The Word says; *There shall be Saviours in Zion* [see Obadiah 24]. As Jesus took us and lifted us up to the Father, and as He takes the Church and lifts it to the Father, and gave Himself to sanctify and cleanse it, so the Christian takes the world and lifts it up to the Christ, to the Lamb of God that taketh away the sin of the world.

The wonderful simplicity of the gospel of Jesus is itself a marvel. The wonder is that men have not understood always the whole process of salvation. How was it that men mystified it? Why is it that we have not lived a better life? Because our eyes were dim and we did not see and we did not realize that God left us here in this world to demonstrate Him, even as the Father left Jesus in the world to demonstrate the Father.

The man with Christ in him, the Holy Ghost, is greater than any other power in the world. All other natural and evil powers are less than God; even Satan himself is a lesser power. Man with God in him is greater than Satan. That is the reason that God says to the believer, he shall cast out devils. *"Greater is he that is in you, than he that is in the world"* [1 John 4:4]. The Christian, therefore, is a ruler; he is in the place of dominion, the place of authority, even as Jesus was. Jesus knowing that all power had been given unto Him, took a basin and a towel, and washed His disciples' feet. His power did not exalt Him. It made Him the humblest of all men. So the more a Christian possesses, the more of a servant he will be. God is the great servant of the world. The one who continually gives to men the necessity of the hour. Through His guidance and direction of the laws of the world, He provides for all the needs of mankind. He is the great servant of the world, the greatest of all servants.

Yea, Jesus, knowing that all power had been committed to Him, and as God gave the power to Jesus, so Jesus commits through the Holy Ghost, by His own Spirit, all power to man.

I tell you, beloved, it is not necessary for people to be dominated by evil, nor by evil spirits. Instead of being dominated, Christians should exercise dominion and control other forces. Even Satan has no power over them, only as they permit him to have. Jesus taught us to close the mind, to close the heart, to close the being against all that is evil; to live with an openness to God only, so that the sunlight of God shines in, the glory radiance of God shines in, but everything that is dark is shut out. Jesus said: *"Take heed how you hear"* [Luke 8:18], not what you hear. One cannot help what he hears, but he can take heed *how* he hears. When it is something offensive to the Spirit and the knowledge of God, shut the doors of the nature against it, and it will not touch you. The Christian lives as God in the world, dominating sin, evil, and sickness, bless God. I would to God, He would be lifted up until they would realize their privilege in Christ Jesus. Bless God, it is coming.

By the God within we cast out or expel from the being that which is not God-like. If you find within your heart a thought of sin or selfishness, by the exercise of the Spirit of God within you, you cast that thing out as unworthy of a child of God, and you put it away from you.

Beloved, so should we do with our bodies. So must we do when sickness or the suggestion of sickness is present with us. Cast it out as evil; it is not of God. Dominate it! Put it away! It is not honoring to Jesus Christ that sickness should possess us. We do not want disease. We want to be gods. Jesus said, *"I said ye are gods"* [John 10:34]. It is with the attitude of gods in the world that Jesus wants the Christian to live. Blessed be His Name!

Evil is real. The devil is real. He was a real angel. Pride changed his nature. God is real. The operation of God within the heart changes the nature until we are new men in Christ Jesus, new creatures in Christ Jesus. The power of God, the Holy Ghost, is the Spirit of dominion. It makes one a god. It makes one not subject to the forces of the world, or the flesh, or the devil. These are under the Christian's feet. John said: *"Beloved, now are we the sons of God"* [1 John 3:2].

Beloved, God wants us to come, to stay, and to live in that abiding place which is the Christian's estate. This is the heavenly place in Christ Jesus. This is the secret place of the most high. Bless God!

The Word of God gives us this key. It says: *"That wicked one toucheth him not"* [1 John 5:18]. When the Spirit of God radiated from the man Jesus, I wonder how close it was possible for the evil spirit to come to him? Do you not see that the Spirit of God is as destructive of evil as it is creative of good? It was impossible for the evil one to come near him, and I feel sure Satan talked to Jesus from a safe distance.

It is the same with the Christian. It is not only in his spirit that he needs to be rid of sin, not only in his soul that he is to be pure. It is God in the body that the individual needs for a well body. It is just God that he needs.

The complaint of the devil concerning Job was: *"Hast thou not made a hedge about him?"* [Job 1:10]. He was not able to get through that hedge to touch the man. Don't you know that the radiation of the Spirit of God around the Lord Jesus was His safeguard? The artists paint a halo around the head of Jesus. They might just as well put it about his hands, feet, and body, because the radiation of the Spirit of God is from all the being.

Now the Spirit of God radiates from the Christian's person because of the indwelling Holy Ghost and makes him impregnable to any touch or contact of evil forces. He is the subjective force himself. The Spirit of God radiates from him as long as his faith in God is active. *"Resist the devil, and he will flee from you"* [James 4:7].

"For this purpose the Son of God was manifested, that he might destroy the works of the devil" [1 John 3:8].

"Whatsoever is born of God overcometh the world... even our faith" [1 John 5:4].

"Who is he that overcometh the world, but he that believeth that Jesus is the Son of God?" [1 John 5:5].

The reason people become sick is the same reason that they become sinful. They surrender to the suggestion of the thing that is evil, and it takes possession of the heart.

Sickness is just the same. There is no difference. The suggestion of oppression is presented, and becoming frightened, the disease secures a foothold. "In the Name of Jesus Christ I refuse to have this thing."

For 15 years God has let me move among all manner of contagious diseases, and I have never taken one of them. The devil could not make me take them. I have prayed with smallpox patients when the pustules would burst under the touch of my hands. I have gone home to my wife and babies and never carried contagion to them. I was in the "secret place of the most High." Indeed contact with diphtheria, smallpox, leprosy, and even bubonic plague, and the whole range of diseases was in line of my daily work in connection with the work of the Apostolic Church of South Africa.

"Behold I give you power...over all the power of the enemy: and nothing shall by any means hurt you" [Luke 10:19]. So the prayer of the apostle comes to us with a fresh understanding. *"I pray God your whole spirit and soul and body be preserved blameless [without corruption, defilement] unto the coming of our Lord Jesus Christ. Faithful is he that calleth you, who also will do it"* [1 Thessalonians 5:23-24].

Consecration Prayer

My God and Father, in Jesus Name I come to Thee. Take me as I am. Make me what I ought to be, in spirit, in soul, in body. Give me Power to do right. If I have wronged any, to repent, to confess, to restore. No matter what it costs, wash me in the blood of Jesus that I may now become Thy child, and manifest Thee in a perfect spirit, a holy mind, a sickless body. Amen.

2

Christian Communion

I want to read a series of portions of Scriptures this morning, with this one general thought in view: *The presence of Christ.* Some of you may have read a little booklet by an old monk, whose name was Father Lawrence. It is called "Practicing the Presence of Christ."

One of the things the Christian world does not get hold of with a strong grip is the conscious presence of Christ with us *now.* Somehow there is an inclination in the Christian spirit to feel that Jesus, when He left the earth, returned to Glory, and in consequence is not present with us now.

I want to show you how wonderfully the Scriptures emphasize the fact of His presence with us now. When He was talking to the eleven, just prior to His Ascension (Matthew 28:19-20), after delivering to them the great commission, He said:
"Go ye therefore, and teach all nations, baptizing them in the name of the Father, and of the Son, and of the Holy Ghost." He ended the statement with these words: "And, lo, I am with you alway, even unto the end of the world."

It would naturally seem as if a separation had been contemplated because of His return to Glory, but no such separation is contemplated on the part of Christ. Christ promises His omnipotent presence with us always, Christ omnipresent everywhere—present in the soul, present in the world, present always unto the end of the age.

As Paul was going down the road to Damascus, when the presence of God's glory shone around him, he fell prostrate on the earth, and heard a voice speaking to him. When he demanded to know who it was, the voice replied, *"I am Jesus"* [Acts 9:5]. Jesus was present with him as a Savior to deliver him from his difficulties and his sins.

At a later time in Paul's career, he returned to Jerusalem, and was in danger of his life. While he prayed in the temple, he was overshadowed by the Spirit, and said, *"I was in a trance; And saw him saying unto me, Make haste, and get thee quickly out of Jerusalem: for they will not receive thy testimony concerning me"* [Acts 22:17-18]. Paul endeavors to argue with the Lord about it. That conversation has always been a blessing to my soul. It is so real. I have always been so glad that Paul answered back to the Lord, and the details of the conversation have been recorded.

Paul said, *"Lord, they know that I imprisoned and beat in every synagogue them that believed on Thee: And when the blood of thy martyr Stephen was shed, I also was standing by, and consenting unto his death, and kept the raiment of them that slew him."*

But the Lord replied, *"Depart: for I will send thee far hence unto the Gentiles"* [Acts 22:19-21].

Jesus is just as close to the Christian soul as He was to Paul. There is a beautiful verse that expresses that so sweetly, "Closer is He than breathing, and nearer than hands and feet."

Christ is the living presence, not only with us, but to the real Christian, He is in us, a perpetual joy, power and Glory in our life. When a soul reaches to the heights of God, it will only be because of the guiding and counseling and indwelling and in-filling of the Christ.

Blessed Jesus, Lord and God,
He who dwells within.
Blessed Jesus, He who came
To free our hearts from sin.
Give us now Thy presence in us
Sweetly verified by Thy Holy Word
Give us now Thy presence
That we too may call thee Lord.
Precious Jesus, Lord of Heaven,

Blessed Jesus, come and dwell,
Blessed Christ of all the Heaven,
Dearer to our heart—
Christ of God come in and dwell,
That within us we may be
Perfectly conscious of that indwelling,
And ever from sin set free.

Tongues and Interpretation

Many of us no doubt have been struck with the beautiful war story that has been going the rounds of the magazines for some months, called "The Comrade." It is the sense of comradeship that makes the Lord Jesus not only a Savior in the ordinary sense, but a Savior and Companion in all our ways and walks of life, filling the place in our soul that only a comrade can fill.

One of my exploring expeditions while in Africa, I met a man in Portuguese East Africa, who told me he had lived for eleven years with only natives as his associates. One evening as we came along, passing through the veld, I observed this little cabin, which indicated the presence of a European. So I started over, expecting to discover a man with some white blood in him at least. But I was overjoyed to find he was an intelligent English gentleman.

He had come to Africa in the early days with his wife and children. His sons had been killed in a native uprising. His wife had died of fever and only he was left. I said, "Why didn't you return to England?" He replied, "I did not have any desire to return. Many of my friends I used to know had died or gone to Australia, or with a new set of people. I concluded I would just settle down and spend the rest of my days here."

We sat all night and talked about the ordinary things that were going on in the world about us. It was the first time he had any outside news in several years. We sat fellowshiping during the night.

Before I went away in the morning I asked him what it was he missed more than anything else since he had been out there. He replied, "Mr. Lake, I guess one word will cover it. Comradeship. The lack of that real soul comradeship which makes life so dear to every man."

That is the place that Jesus purposes to occupy in the Christian life. That place of real comradeship, whereby through His grace and love He supplies to us that thing that we need so much to make this life the joyous, victorious life He purposed it to be. His presence with us, His guiding counsel, His transforming grace, His soul absorbing presence, which in the ultimate commands all the intensity of our nature, is for us. Paul expressed it so wonderfully in the words, *"Christ is all, and in all"* [Colossians 3:11].

Paul gives us a still different vision of the presence and power of Christ with us in the fourth chapter of Ephesians. This time it is as a transformer: *"Till we all come in the unity of the faith, and of the knowledge of the Son of God, unto a perfect man, unto the measure of the stature of the fulness of Christ"* [Ephesians 4:13].

This shows the ultimate purpose of Christ as Savior, of Christ as a companion, of Christ as the indweller. Christ's presence with us is not just as an outward companion, but an indwelling, divine force, revolutionizing our nature and making us like Him. Indeed, the final and ultimate purpose of the Christ is that the Christian shall be reproduced in His own likeness, within and without.

Paul again expressed the same thing in the first chapter of Colossians, the 22nd verse, where he says, *"To present you holy and unblameable and unreprovable in his sight."* That transformation is to be an inner transformation. It is a transformation of our life, of our nature into His nature, into His likeness.

Now the mechanical fades away in view of the living fact that Christ purposes to accomplish in us through the Spirit. How wonderful the patience, and marvelous the power that takes possession of the soul of man and accomplishes the will of God, in His absolute transformation into the real beautiful holiness of the character of Jesus.

Our heart staggers when we think of such a calling, when we think of such a nature, when we contemplate such a character. That is God's purpose for you and me.

In emphasizing this truth the apostle again puts it into a different form, He says, *"Until Christ be formed in you"* [Galatians 4:19]. Or until by the transforming operation of the Spirit of God we are remade, or transformed. Until our nature is transformed by the operation of the Spirit of God in our soul, then we are remade or transformed. Until our nature is transformed into the nature of our Lord and Savior Jesus Christ.

His was the perfect character. Consequently every other character that can be cojoined with Him in real heirship must be like God's Son. Jesus never can present that which is faulty or evil or weak to the Father. The transforming grace of God must take away, and does take away, sin from the soul of man. It gives him his strength instead of human weakness. It supplies the grace that makes him like the Lord Jesus Christ.

That is the mission of the Lord Jesus Christ. That is the marvel He has undertaken to accomplish, to transform the soul of man into the likeness and character of Himself, and then present mankind to the Father, *"Holy and unblameable and unreprovable in His sight"* [Colossians 1:22].

When Jesus stood before the disciples, just prior to His going out into the Garden, He delivered to them that wonderful address of the 14th, 15th, and 16th chapters of John. He climaxed it with that marvelous high priestly prayer of the 17th. He endeavored to bring them to understand His nature and power.

Knowing that all power had been given unto Him, He took a towel and a basin and proceeded to wash the disciples' feet. When He had finished He said, *"Know ye what I have done to you?"* [John 13:12]. In explanation He said, *"If I then, your Lord and Master, have washed your feet; ye also ought to wash one another's feet"* [John 13:14]. In assuming the attitude of a servant He had taught mankind what their relation as brother should be.

When we examine the human heart and endeavor to discover what it is that retards our progress, I believe we find that pride in the human soul perhaps is the greatest difficulty we have to overcome. Jesus taught us a wonderful humility, taking the place of a slave. So we are enjoined to thus treat and love one another.

His presence with us, His presence in us must produce, in our hearts the same conditions that were in His own. It must bring into our life the same humility that was in Him. It is one of the secrets of entrance into the grace of God.

> When the precious Christ enters into the unregenerated heart He becomes the very center of their being. He becomes the very acme of their ambition. That they might be like Him. He through true humility of His soul, left the things of His glorious Father's kingdom to come into

> this world of woe and sin; by which He was enabled to live the life of perfection in this earth and become the real Redeemer and Sympathizer of mankind.

Tongues and Interpretation

In the story of the comrade, the substance of it is practically that the comrade is ever present. In the course of the conversation with the comrade, it is observed that there are wounds in His hands, and He replies, "Yes, they are old wounds, but they have been giving me a good deal of trouble of late."

That is the vital sense of real comradeship that makes the Spirit of Jesus one with us, so that we realize and He realizes when the condition of our nature and mind affect Him.

For two days I have been under a tremendous burden, one of these spirit burdens that comes at times, when you cannot define them. I could not tell whence it came. But every little while I felt I wanted to sit down and cry. Presently during the day a friend came and unloaded the burden of her soul to me, and then I realized that I had been under the burden for that soul for two days. I had not known the trouble existed.

That is the character of comradeship, which is between the real Christian and the Christ. The Christian feels the burdens of the Christ and the Christ feels the burdens of the Christian and being united as one spirit, the interests of the Christ are the interests of the Christian, and the interests of the Christian are the interests of the Christ. That relationship is of the truest, deepest order. It is the relationship of spirit with Spirit.

When a young man, before I had entered into this life, indeed from my boyhood, there were times when my spirit would become overshadowed with the burden of another life, sometimes with the sorrows of another. I had one of these experiences when perhaps not more then ten or eleven years of age. On a particular Sunday, I arose with one of these burdens on my spirit, and I walked out into the fields. There was a high hill on my father's farm. The sun had not yet gotten over this hill. When I got to the top I looked down over the beautiful field. There was a lake, and I was thinking how beautiful it was and all the surroundings. In the midst of it tears commenced to run and I sat down on a stone and cried. After a while I got up and wondered why I was crying. Several days later we received a letter telling that dear old Grandfather had died. And then the old Grandmother had said, "Well, I do not want to live any more," and she died also. Around them was a group of sorrowing friends, and somehow my spirit contacted that sorrow.

One of the truest things in all my life, in my relationship with the Lord Jesus Christ, has been to feel that He was capable of knowing my sorrows, and yours. And that in the truest sense He thereby became our comrades.

In Isaiah there is a verse that wonderfully expresses that fact. *"In all their affliction he was afflicted, and the angel of his presence saved them: in his love and in his pity he redeemed them; and he bare them, and carried them all the days of old"* (Isaiah 63:9).

There is a union between the Christ and the Christian that is so deep, so pure, so sweet, so real, that the very conditions of the human spirit are transmitted to His, and the conditions of the Christ's Spirit are transmitted to ours. It is because of the continuous inflow of the Spirit of Christ in our heart that we appreciate or realize His power and triumph. It lifts man above his surroundings and causes him to triumph anywhere and everywhere.

The Christian life is designed by God to be a life of splendid, holy triumph. That triumph is produced in us through the continuous inflow and abiding presence of the Spirit of the triumphant Christ. He brings into our nature the triumph that He enjoys. Indeed the mature Christian, having entered into that consciousness of overcoming through the Spirit of Christ, is privileged to transmit that same overcoming power and spirit to other lives, in and through the power of the Spirit of God.

That is why the Christian who is joined with the Christ lives, moves and has his being in the same life, in the same Spirit that the Christ is and has, and is therefore the reproduction of the Lord Jesus Christ.

3

Ministry of the Spirit

November 24, 1916

One of the most difficult things to bring into the spirit of people is that the Spirit of God is a tangible substance, that it is the essence of God's own being.

We are composed of an earthly materiality, that is our bodies are largely a composition of water and earth. This may sound a little crude, but the actual composition of a human being is about sixteen buckets of water and one bucket full of earth. I am glad that there is one bucket full of good mud in us. Water, you know, is a composition of gasses, so you can see how much gas there is in mankind. But we are not all gas.

Now as to the composition of the personality of God, for God has a personality and a being and a substance. God is a Spirit and Spirit is a substance. That is the thing I am trying to emphasize. All heavenly things are of spiritual substance. The body of the angels is of some substance, not the same character of materiality as our own, for ours is an earthly materiality; but the composition of heavenly things is of a heavenly materiality. In other words, heavenly materiality is Spirit. The Word says, *"God is a Spirit"* [John 4:24]. He is a Spirit. Therefore, *"They that worship him must worship him in spirit"* [John 4:24].

You see, the spirit of man must contact and know the real Spirit of God, know God. We do not know God with our flesh, with our hands, nor with our brains. We know God with our spirit. The knowledge of God that our spirit attains may be conveyed and is conveyed to us through the medium of our mind, through the medium of our brains. The effect of God in our body comes through the medium of the spirit of man through the mind of man into the body of man.

There is a quickening by the Spirit of God so that a man's body, a man's soul or mind, and a man's spirit all alike become blessed, pervaded and filled with the presence of God Himself in us. The Word of God is wonderfully clear along these lines. For instance, the Word of God says that *"Thou wilt keep him in perfect peace, whose MIND is stayed on thee"* (Isaiah 26:3). Why? *"Because he trusteth in thee."* That is the rest that a Christian knows whose mind rests in God in real, perfect trust. *"Thou wilt keep him in perfect peace, whose mind is stayed on thee."*

The Word of God again says that our FLESH shall rejoice. Not our mind, but our very flesh shall rejoice. The presence of God is to be a living presence, not only in the spirit of man, nor in the mind of man alone, but also in the flesh of man, so that God is known in ALL departments of our life. We know God in our very flesh. We know God in our mind: we know God in our spirit. Bless His precious Name.

The medium by which God undertakes to bless the world is through the transmission of Himself. Now the Spirit of God is His own substance, the substance of His being, the very nature and quality of the very presence and being and nature of God. Consequently when we speak of the Spirit of God being transmitted to man and into man, we are not talking about an influence, either spiritual or mental. We are talking about the transmission of the living substance and being of God into your being and into mine. Not a mental effect, but a living substance, the living being and actual life transmitted, imparted, coming from God into your being, into my being. Bless God!

That is the secret of the abundant life of which Jesus spoke. Jesus said, *"I am come that they might have life, and that they might have it MORE ABUNDANTLY"* (John 10:10). The reason we have the more abundant life is because that by receiving God into our being, all the springs of our being are quickened by His living presence. Consequently, if we are living today and we receive God, we live life in a fuller measure, we live life with a greater energy because we become the recipients of the energy of the living God in addition to our normal energy, through the reception of His being, His nature, His life into ours.

The wonderful measure that the human being is capable of receiving God is demonstrated by some of the incidents in the Word of God. For instance, the most remarkable in the Scriptures is the Transfiguration of Jesus Himself, where, with Peter, James, and John, the Spirit of God came upon Him so powerfully that it radiated out through His being until His clothes became white and glistening and His face shown as the light.

Now one must be the recipient of the light, glory and power of God before he or she can manifest it. Jesus demonstrated these two facts: the marvelous capacity of the nature of man to receive God into his being, and the marvelous capacity of the nature of man to reveal God. In the glory shining through His clothes, in the glistening of the glory of God that made His face glorious and wonderful, He demonstrated man's capacity to reveal God.

The human being is God's marvelous, wonderful instrument, the most marvelous and wonderful of all the creation of God in its capacity to receive and reveal God. Paul received so much of God into his being that when men brought handkerchiefs and he took them in his hands, and when the women brought aprons and handed them to him, the handkerchiefs and aprons became so impregnated with that loving Spirit of God—that living substance of God's being—that when they were carried to one who was sick or possessed of devils, the Word says when they laid the handkerchiefs or aprons on the sick man, or on the insane man, the sick were healed and the devils were cast out.

You see, people have been so in the habit of putting Jesus in a class by Himself that they have failed to recognize that He has made provision for the same living Spirit of God that dwelt in His own life and of which He, Himself, was a living manifestation to inhabit your being and mine just as it inhabited the being of Jesus or Paul.

There is no more marvelous manifestation in the life of Jesus than that manifestation of healing through the Apostle Paul.

You remember the incident of the woman who touched the hem of Jesus' garment knowing how His whole being, His whole nature radiated that wondrous, blessed life of God of which He was Himself the living manifestation. She said with in herself, *"If I may touch but his clothes, I shall be whole"* [Mark 5:28]. So she succeeded, after much effort, to touch the hem of His garment, and as she touched the hem of His garment, there flowed into her body the quickening life stream, and she felt in her body that she was made whole of the plague.

And Jesus, being conscious that from Him something had flowed, said to Peter, *"Who touched me?"* [Luke 8:45].

Peter replied, "Why Master, you see the crowd, and do you say, who touched me?"

He said, *"SOMEBODY hath touched me: for I perceive that virtue is gone out of me"* [Luke 8:46].

If you will analyze that Greek word you will see it means the life or substance of His being, the quickening, living power of God, the very nature and being of God.

If I transmit to another the virtue of my life, I simply transmit a portion of my life to another, the life power that is in me, blessed be God. The life of God that flows through me is transmitted to another, and so it was with Jesus.

Now then, because of the fact that people brought to Paul handkerchiefs and aprons and they became impregnated with the Spirit of God, and the people were healed when they touched them, it is a demonstration in itself that any material substance can become impregnated with the same living Spirit of God.

In my church in South Africa we published a paper in ten thousand lots. We would have the publishers send them to the tabernacle, and we would lay them out in packages of one or two hundred all around the front of the platform, and at the evening service I would call certain ones of the congregation that I knew to be in contact with the living God to come and kneel around and lay their hands on those packages of papers; and we asked God not alone that the reading matter in the paper might be a blessing to the individual and that the message of Christ come through the words printed on the paper, but we asked God to make the very handkerchiefs became filled with the Spirit of God. And if I were in my tabernacle now I could show you thousands of letters in my files from all quarters of the world, from people telling me that when they received our paper, the Spirit came upon them and they were healed, or when they received the paper the joy of God came into their hearts, or they received the paper and were saved unto God.

One woman wrote from South America, who said, "I received your paper. When I received it into my hands my body began to vibrate so I could hardly sit on the chair, and I did not understand it. I laid the paper down, and after a while I took the paper up again, and as soon as I had it in my hands I shook again. I laid the paper down and took it in my hands a third time, and presently the Spirit of God came upon me so powerfully that I was baptized in the Holy Ghost."

Beloved, don't you see that this message and this quality of the Spirit contains the thing that confuses all the philosophers and all the practice of philosophy in the world? It shows the clearest distinction which characterizes the real religion of Jesus Christ and makes it distinct from all other religions and all other ministries.

The ministry of the Christian is the ministry of the SPIRIT. He not only ministers words to another but he ministers the Spirit of God. It is the Spirit of God that inhabits the words, that speaks to the spirit of another and reveals Christ in and through him.

In the old days when I was in Africa, I would walk into the native meetings when I did not understand the languages and would listen to the preacher preach for an hour, and I did not understand a word he said. But my soul was blessed by the presence of the Spirit of God.

As Bishop of the church, as I went from place to place holding conferences here and there among white and native people, in many of them, people would speak either in English or Dutch. But I was just as much blessed when a Dutchman spoke and I did not understand him as when an Englishman spoke. Why? Because the thing that blessed my soul was the living Spirit of God. Perhaps I had heard better words than his, perhaps clearer explanation of the Scriptures than he could give, but I was blessed by the presence of God. The thing that the individual was ministering to my soul was the living Spirit of God.

The ministry of the Christian is the ministry of the Spirit. If the Christian cannot minister the Spirit of God, in the true sense he is not a Christian. If he has not the Spirit to minister in the real high sense, he has nothing to minister. Other men have intellectuality, but the Christian is supposed to be the possessor of the Spirit. There should never be any misunderstanding along these lines in the minds of any.

A minister of Jesus Christ is as far removed above the realm of psychological influences as heaven is above the earth. Blessed be God. He ministers God Himself into the very spirits and souls and bodies of men. That is the reason that the Christian throws down the bars of his nature and he invites God to come in and take possession of his being. And the incoming of God into our body, into our soul, into our spirit accomplishes marvelous things in the nature of man.

A man came into my healing rooms one day, and said, "I am almost ashamed to call myself a man because I have simply indulged the animal of my nature so that I am more a beast than a man. You say, 'Why don't you quit such a life?' I have not the strength of my being to do so. Unless something takes place that will deliver me from this condition I do not know what I will do."

I tried to show him what the Gospel of Jesus Christ was. I tried to show him that through living in the animal state, thinking animal thoughts, surrounding himself with beastly suggestion, and contacting the spirit of beastiality everywhere that element had taken such a possession that it predominated in the nature. I said, "My son, the gospel means there shall be a transference of nature. Instead of this living hell that is present in your being, the living holy God should flow into your life and cast out the devil, dispossess the beast, and reign in your members."

We knelt to pray, and today he came back with tears in his eyes, and said, "Mr. Lake, I feel I can shake hands with you now. I am a beast no more. I am a man."

Yesterday a dear woman was present in our afternoon service. She had a tumor that for ten months the physicians believed to be an unborn child. She came with her nurse a few days ago to the healing rooms and told me her symptoms. The thing that fooled the physicians was that there was a movement that they considered similar to life movement, and the result was that during all these months they believed the woman would become a mother until the normal time had long passed. She was the first one to be prayed for after the Thursday afternoon service. Today she returned and said, "Mr. Lake, I want you to see me. I have my corsets on. I am perfectly normal. When I went to bed I was not aware that anything had taken place except that the choking had ceased and I felt comfortable. I was not aware of any diminution in my size. But when I awoke this morning I was perfectly normal."

I said, "How did the tumor disappear? Was it in the form of a fluid?" She said, "No, nothing came from my person."

Now I am going to ask you, "Where did a great tumor like that go?" What happened to it?

Voice from the audience: "Dematerialized."

Yes, the living Spirit of God absolutely dematerialized the tumor, and the process was accomplished in one night while the woman slept. That is one of God's methods of surgical operation, isn't it?

Beloved, the Spirit of God took possession of that dear soul's person. That tumor became filled with the Spirit of God, and the effect of the Spirit of God in that tumor was so mighty, so powerful, that the Spirit of God dissolved it.

That is the secret of the ministry of Jesus Christ. That is the secret of the ministry of Christianity. That is the reason that the real Christian who lives in union with the living God and possesses His Spirit has a ministry that no other man in all the world possesses. Why? He is full and experiences in his own soul the dissolving power of the Spirit of God that takes sin out of his life and makes him a free man in Christ Jesus. Blessed be His name Forever.

A few weeks ago a dear woman called me over the telephone and said, "I have a young friend who is a drunkard, and the habit has such power over him that he will go to any excess to obtain. Dry state or no dry state, he has to have it. He is an intelligent fellow. He wants to be free. We have invited him to my home for prayer, and he is here now. I want you to join me in prayer for him."

I said, "All right, but first you call one of your neighbors to join you in prayer for this man; then when you are ready, call me on the phone, and Brother Westwood, and Mrs. Peterson, and we will join you in prayer."

She called me in a little while, and we united our hearts in prayer for the young man, who was on the other side of the city. About twenty minutes afterward he arose from his knees and with tears in his eyes he took the woman by the hand and said, "I am a man of sense . I know when something has taken place within me...and the appetite has disappeared." That is the ministry of the Spirit, the ministry of God to man. Blessed be His Name.

Isn't it a marvelous, wonderful thing that God has ordained an arrangement whereby man becomes God's own co-partner and co-laborer in the ministry of the Spirit, *"the Church, which is His body"* [Ephesians 1:22-23]. Just as Jesus Christ was the human body through which the living Spirit was ministered to mankind, so God has arranged that the living Church, not the dead member, but the living Church, alive with the Spirit of the living God, should minister that quickening life to another and thereby become a co-partner, a co-laborer together with God. Blessed be His Name forever.

Men have mystified and philosophized the Gospel of Jesus, but the Gospel is as simple as can be.

Just as God lived and operated through the body of the man, Jesus, so Jesus, the Man on the throne, operated in and through the Christian, also through His Body, the Church, in the world. Just as Jesus was the representative of God the Father, so the *Church* is the representative of Christ.

And as Jesus yielded Himself unto ALL RIGHTEOUSNESS, so the Church should yield herself to do all the will of God.

The secret of Christianity is in BEING. It is in being a possessor of the nature of Jesus Christ. In other words, it is being Christ in character, Christ in demonstration, Christ in agency of transmission. When a person gives himself to the Lord and becomes a child of God, a Christian, he is a Christ man. All that he does and all that he says from that time forth should be the will and the words and the doing of Jesus, just as absolutely and entirely as He spoke and did the will of the Father.

4

The Power of Consecration to Principle

The great purpose of Jesus Christ's coming to the world was to establish the kingdom of God. The kingdom of God is universal, containing all moral intelligences, willingly subject to the will of God, both in heaven and on earth, both angels and men. The Kingdom of heaven is Christ's kingdom on the earth, which will eventually merge into the kingdom of God. We read of that merging period in 1 Corinthians 15, where it says:

> **Then cometh the end, when he shall have delivered up the kingdom to God, even the Father; when he shall have put down all rule and all authority and power...And when all things shall be subdued unto him, then shall the Son also himself be subject unto him that put all things under him, that God may be all in all.**

Now then, in order to establish a kingdom, there must be a basis upon which it is to be founded. When the Revolutionary fathers got together in '76 they laid down in The Declaration of Independence, the principles upon which American government was to be founded. They laid down as one of the first principles this one: "All men are born free and equal"—That every man, by his being born a man, is likewise born on an equality with all others. All men are born free and equal before the law; there is no special privilege.

Next, they considered this as the second principle: That man, because of his birth and his free agency, was entitled to "Life, liberty, and the pursuit of happiness."

Third: That government rests on the consent of the governed.

These were the underlying principles upon which the government was to rest. There was nothing little about them. They did not discuss the doctrines by which these principles were to be made effective, but they laid down the foundation principles upon which was built the greatest system of human government in the world's history.

Now Jesus likewise, when He came to found His kingdom, first enunciated the principles upon which His government was to rest. The eight Beatitudes, as they are given in His official declaration in His Sermon on the Mount, were the great principles upon which His government was to be founded.

A principle is not a dogma, or a doctrine. It is that underlying quality, that fundamental truth, upon which all other things are based, and the principles of the kingdom of heaven are those underlying qualities upon which the whole structure of the Christian life rests, and the principles upon which the real government of Jesus Christ will be founded and exercised. The eight Beatitudes are the principles of the kingdom, the Sermon on the Mount is the constitution, and the commandments of Jesus are its law or statutes.

First, the kingdom is established in the hearts of men. The principles of Jesus Christ are settled in our own spirit. We become citizens of the kingdom of heaven. The aggregate citizenship of the kingdom in this present age constitutes the real church, which is His Body. And throughout the Church Age the working of the body is to be apparent in demonstrating to the world the practicability and desirability of the kingdom of heaven, that all men may desire the rule of Jesus, in the salvation of men.

It is the purpose of Jesus to make the Church, which is His Body, His entire representative in the world. Just as Jesus came to express God the Father to mankind, and Jesus was necessary to God, in order that He might give an expression of Himself to the world, so the Church is necessary to Jesus Christ as an expression of Himself to the world.

Now the first principle that He laid down was this one: *"Blessed are the poor in spirit: for theirs is the kingdom of heaven"* [Matthew 5:3]. Usually we confound this with the other one, *"Blessed are the meek"* [Matthew 5:5]—and we have commonly thought of one who is poor in spirit as being a meek, quiet person, possessing the spirit of meekness. But it is much more than that. The thing Jesus urged upon men was to practice what He had done Himself.

Jesus was the King of Glory, yet He laid down all His glory. He came to earth, took upon Himself our condition. *"He took not on him the nature of angels; but he took on him the seed of Abraham"* (Hebrews 2:16). He took upon Himself the condition of mankind, that is, of human nature's liability to sin. Therefore, He was *"in all points tempted like as we are, yet without sin"* [Hebrews 4:15]. And because of the fact that He took upon Himself our nature, and understood the temptations that are common to man, He is *"able to succour them that are tempted"* (Hebrews 2:18). He understands. He is a sympathetic Christ. Bless God!

Now see! *"Blessed are the poor in spirit"* [Matthew 5:3]. Blessed is he who regards the interests of the kingdom of heaven as paramount to every other interest in the world, paramount to his own personal interest. Blessed is he whose interest in life, whose interest in the world is only used to extend the interest of the kingdom of heaven. Blessed is he who has lost his own identity as an individual and has become a citizen of the kingdom. Blessed is he who sees the kingdom of heaven as the ultimate, to be possessed. Blessed is he who forgets to hoard wealth for himself, but who uses all he has and all he is for the extension of the kingdom of heaven. It is putting the law of the love of God and of one another in practice.

So after Jesus had laid down the things that He possessed, then, bless God, He was able to say to us, as He had experienced it Himself, *"Blessed are the poor in spirit: for theirs is the kingdom of heaven"* [Matthew 5:3].

We commonly think as we read the Word of God that some of the teachings of Jesus were accidental, or were applied to a particular individual and to no one else. So we think of the rich young ruler who came to Jesus and said, *"Good Master, what shall I do to inherit eternal life?"* [Luke 18:18].

Jesus said, *"Thou knowest the commandments, Do not commit adultery, Do not kill, Do not steal, Do not bear false witness, Honour thy father and thy mother."*

The young man said: *"All these have I kept from my youth up."*

Then Jesus said to him, *"Yet lackest thou one thing: sell all that thou hast, and distribute unto the poor, and thou shalt have treasure in heaven: and come, follow me"* (Luke 18:20-22).

Don't you see, Jesus was applying to that young man that first principle of the kingdom. We have said that young man was covetous, and he loved his wealth, etc., and that was keeping him out of the kingdom of heaven. Not so. Jesus was applying one of the principles of the kingdom to that young man's life. He turned away sorrowful. He had not developed to the place where he could do that thing.

There is an apocryphal story that tells us that the rich young ruler was Barnabas. After the resurrection and the coming of the Holy Ghost, Barnabas received from heaven the thing Jesus had tried to impart to him. He forgot all about Barnabas, his own interest and his own desires, and he sold his great possessions and came with the others and laid them at the apostles' feet. *"Blessed are the poor in spirit: for theirs is the kingdom of heaven"* [Matthew 5:3]. So Jesus was able, after all, to get the real thing in the heart of Barnabas that He desired in the beginning.

The real miracle of the Holy Ghost at Pentecost was not the outward demonstration of tongues, etc.; but it produces such intense unselfishness in the hearts of all baptized, that they each sold their lands and estates, parted the money to every man as he had need. They were moved by God into one family. Their brother's interest was equal to their own. That was *"Blessed are the poor in spirit."*

The second principle of the kingdom is this: *"Blessed are they that mourn: for they shall be comforted"* [Matthew 5:4]. This figure is taken from the old prophets, who when the nation sinned, took upon themselves the responsibility of the nation. They put sackcloth on their body, and ashes on their head, and in mourning and tears went down before God for days and weeks, until the people turned to God. They became the intercessors between God and man, and in some instances in the Word, we read where God looked and wondered. He wondered that there was no intercessor. There were no mourners who took upon themselves the responsibility of the sins of the people, who dared to stand between man and God.

We see how wonderfully Moses stood between God and the people. When God said to him, after they had made the golden calf, *"Let me alone...that I may consume them: and I will make of thee a great nation."* (Exodus 32:10). Moses said, *Not so, Lord. What will the Egyptians say, what will be the effect upon Thy great Name? Will they not say that their God destroyed them?* [see Exodus 32:11-12]. God had said to Moses, *"I will make of thee a great nation;"* but Moses was big enough to turn aside the greatest honor that God could bestow upon a man...to become the father of a race. *"This people have sinned a great sin, and have made them gods of gold. Yet now, if thou wilt forgive their sin—; and if not, blot me, I pray thee, out of thy book"* (Exodus 32:31-32).

The prophet became the great intercessor. He took upon himself the burdens and sins of the people, and when he got down to confess he did not say, Oh! these people are so weak, and they do this and that.

But when he got down to pray he would say, "Lord God, WE are unworthy." He was ONE with his people. He was identified with them, as one with them. He was not putting any blame on them. He was big enough to take the whole blame, the entire responsibility, and go down before God, and lay the whole matter before God, until the blessed mercy of God was again given to the people.

"Blessed are the poor in spirit...Blessed are they that mourn." Blessed is the man who comprehends the purposes of God, who understands his responsibility and possibility, who by God-given mourning and crying, turns the people to God. With heart yearning for sinners, he becomes a mourner before God, and takes the responsibility of fallen men on his own life. He goes down in tears and repentance before God, until men turn to God and the mercy of God is shown to mankind.

In the day that God puts the spirit of mourning upon Pentecost, it will be the gladdest day that heaven has ever known. Blessed be His precious Name!

Do you know, it always jars me down in the depths of my spirit, when I hear people say hard things about churches and sects? That is not our place. Our place is as intercessors...as the one who is to stand between the living and the dead, as those whom God can trust and use to pray down the power and mercy and blessing of God.

First we see that the kingdom is based on principles. Principles are greater than doctrines. Principles are the foundation stones upon which all other things rest. Doctrines are the rules, the detail by which we endeavor to carry out things that the principles contain; but the principles are the great foundation stones upon which all things rest.

Absolute Consecration

Let us turn away from this until we see Jesus at the Jordan, consecrating Himself of His own life work, then we will understand how the Christian is to consecrate himself to carry out the principles.

The Word tells us that when Jesus began to be about thirty years of age, He came down to the River Jordan, where John was baptizing, and presented Himself for baptism. John looked in amazement on Him and said, *"I have need to be baptized of thee, and comest thou to me?"*

But Jesus said, *"Suffer it to be so now: for thus it becometh us to fulfill all righteousness"* (Matthew 3:14-15). Unto *"all righteousness."*

Listen! Hear the declaration to which Jesus Christ was baptized; it was His consecration unto *"all righteousness."* There was no further to go. It comprehends all there is of consecration and commitment unto the will of God, and all there is of good. Unto *"all righteousness."* Bless God!

So Jesus understandingly permitted Himself to be baptized of John unto *"all righteousness."* Now listen! You and I have also been baptized. But see! Immediately after He was baptized, something took place. First, the Spirit of God came upon Him as a dove, and abode upon Him. Then we read He was led by the Spirit, into the wilderness. It was the Holy Ghost.

In Leviticus 16, we see one of the beautiful figures, which will illustrate that to you. On the day of Atonement there were brought two goats. One, the priest laid his hands upon, put a towrope around its neck, then the Levite took the towrope and led it three days into the barren sands of the wilderness, and left it there to die. That is the picture of the LIFE-DEATH of Jesus Christ.

The Holy Ghost is God's Levite. He put the towrope on the neck of Jesus Christ, and led Him likewise three days—a year for a day, God's three days—into the wilderness. What for? To prove out, to test out, the real fact of His obedience unto God, and whether His consecration was going to stand. So the Spirit, the Holy Ghost, led Jesus into the wilderness.

Now I want you to see something. We are triune beings just as God Himself is triune. You will see the character of the consecration that Jesus made at the Jordan. God is TRIUNE. He is God the Father, God the Son, and God the Holy Ghost. Man is also TRIUNE. The Word says, *"I pray God YOUR whole SPIRIT and SOUL and BODY be preserved blameless unto the coming of our Lord Jesus Christ"* (1 Thessalonians 5:23).

So Jesus, when He went into the wilderness, encountered a peculiar temptation, a temptation peculiar to each separate department of His being. The Word of God says He fasted forty days and was an hungered. Satan comes to Him and says, *"If thou be the Son of God, command that these stones be made bread"* [Matthew 4:3]. But Jesus could not do it. If He had done that, He would have been exercising His own authority in His own behalf, and He had committed Himself unto *"All righteousness."* He only lived to express God, He only lived to express the Father. He said, *The words I speak, I speak not of myself. The work that I do I do not of myself* [see John 14:10]. All He said and all He did and all He was, was the expression of God the Father.

May the Lord give us an understanding of the utterness of what a real baptismal consecration ought to be. When an individual comes and commits himself to Christ once and for all and forever, he ceases to be, he ceases to live in his own behalf, to live for himself any longer, but becomes the utter expression of Jesus Christ to mankind.

So Satan had no power to tempt a man who had made a consecration like that. The hunger calls of Jesus' body, after He had fasted for forty days, were not enough to turn Him aside from the consecration He had made to God.

The second temptation was one peculiar to the MIND (soul). He was taken to a pinnacle of the temple, and Satan said, do something spectacular, cast yourself down; let the people see you are an unusual person, and that you can do unusual things, and they will give you their acclaim.

Jesus could not do that. There was nothing, bless God, in the mind of Jesus Christ, that could tempt Him to be disobedient to the consecration He had made to God, unto *"All righteousness."* So He turned the temptation aside.

The third temptation was one peculiar to the SPIRIT. By a supernatural power Jesus is permitted to see *"all the kingdoms of the world, and the glory of them,"* in a moment of time. Then Satan said unto Him, *"All these things will I give thee, if thou wilt fall down and worship me"* [Matthew 4:8-9]. But Jesus turned him aside. No crossless crowning for the Son of God, no bloodless glory for my Lord. He had come to express God to the world. He had come to demonstrate one thing to you and me. That is, that man relying on God can have the victory over sin and Satan. Bless God! That is the peculiar thing about the life of Jesus Christ, that makes Him dear to your heart and mine.

After going on the towrope of the Holy Ghost for three years as the first goat, though the sorrows and the trials and disappointments of life ever ministering and blessing, though the world cursed Him, He was able to come as the second goat and present Himself as the sinless, spotless sacrifice unto God at the cross.

If Jesus had fallen down anywhere along the line, if there had been a single instance where He had failed to express God to the world, He could never have been the Savior of the World. *"HE BECAME the author of eternal salvation"* [Hebrews 5:9]. He was honored of God in being permitted to die for mankind, having triumphed, having presented Himself the sinless, spotless sacrifice unto God. His blood flowed for all the race. Blessed be His Name!

We have seen two things. We have seen the principles of Jesus Christ. We have seen His consecration to carry out those principles. He consecrated Himself utterly unto the mind and will of God. But now we are going a step further.

Even Unto Death

We come to the last night of the Lord's life. He is with His disciples in the upper room. Here comes the final act, the consummation of all His life. There is a phase of this act I know the Lord has not made clear to many.

They sat around the table after they had eaten their supper; Jesus took bread, and brake it, saying, *"Take, eat: this is my body, which is broken for you"* [1 Corinthians 11:24], and yet He was there in the flesh. Now what did it mean? What was its significance?

This: By that act the Lord Jesus Christ pledged Himself before God, before the holy angels, before men, that He would not stop short of dying for the world. There was no limit. He was faithful *"even unto death."* Just as He had been faithful in life, and had lived each day the conscious life-death, dying to every desire of His mind and will and being, He is now going one step further. He is going to be faithful *"even unto death."*

So He said, *"Take, eat: this is my body, which is broken for you."* After supper likewise, He took the cup, when He had drunk, saying, *"my blood of the new testament"* [Mark 14:22-24].

Now you listen. From time immemorial mankind have been in the habit of pledging themselves in the cup. There is no date that mankind has of its origin. It is so ancient we do not know when the custom began, when men began to pledge themselves in the wine cup, but our Jesus sanctified the custom to God and His Church forever.

Jesus poured the wine into the cup, took it, and said, *"this is my blood of the new testament,"* and He drank that Himself. That was the pledge of the Lord Jesus Christ. Having laid down the principles of the gospel of the Son of God, having walked and lived and suffered for three years, now He was going to the very uttermost. There was no further to go. He said, *"this is my blood of the new testament,"* meaning He would give His life for the world.

That is not all. That was His pledge, but after He had drunk saying, *"Drink ye all of it"* [Matthew 26:27]. And when they took the cup, of which their Lord had drunk, they drank to that pledge. They were made partakers in the same pledge, and likewise pledged themselves, *"my blood of the new testament."* Bless God.

Christianity had character in it. Jesus Christ put character in it. Bless God! *"My blood of the new testament."* The other day I was going over the list of the apostles, as they are given by Hippolytus, one of the early writers, and he tells us that five of the twelve were crucified, just as Jesus was. Others died by the spear and sword, and three died natural deaths, after enduring tortures. So it meant for them just what it means for their Lord, *"my blood of the new testament."* We see the degree of faithfulness to which they pledged themselves that night.

We have loved and admired the spirit of the apostles. The Spirit of Jesus Christ was so intense in the early Christians, that millions of them gave their lives for the Son of God; multitudes of whom died the death of martyrs, and multitudes died in the war to exterminate Christianity. 30 Million! Think of that. It gives some meaning to the saying that "The blood of the martyrs was the seed of the Church."

How often have you and I taken the Lord's cup? Has it meant that to you and me, and does it mean that to you and me now? Beloved, I have no doubt that the sacred cup has touched many lips, perhaps the lips of most of you. If we have been understanding, comprehending Christians, we have realized it meant to us just what it did to the Lord—our everlasting pledge of faithfulness.

There is no place for sin in the Christian's life. There is no place for letting down in the Christian's life. There is no place for weakening in the Christian's life. Paul said, when they were having a hard time, *"Ye have not yet resisted unto blood, striving against sin"* (Hebrews 12:4). That was expected of them. They were expected to resist *"even unto death;"* so Paul says, *"Ye have not yet resisted unto blood."* In the Revelation, the Church in Smyrna is commanded, *"be thou faithful UNTO death, and I will give thee a crown of life"* (Revelation 2:10).

In this land, after our fathers had signed the old Declaration of Independence, they pledged, "Our lives, our fortunes, and our sacred honor," then they went out and gave themselves to eight years of war in order to make it good.

When people make a declaration on principles, it is going to cost them something, and it costs them something. After a while the men in the old Revolutionary Army got where they did not have shoes on their feet, but in the depth of winter they tied straw and rags on their feet. They had stood by principles, and the British tracked them by the bloodmarks on the snow.

So Jesus Christ, in enlisting an army, put them under a kindred pledge with Himself. He pledged Christians on the same plane with Himself. Just as far as the Lord went, they went *"even unto death."*

The real purpose of becoming a Christian is not to save yourself from hell, or be saved to go to heaven. It is to become a child of God, with the character of Jesus Christ, to stand before men, pledged unto the uttermost, *"even unto death,"* by refusing to sin, refusing to bow your head in shame, preferring to die rather than dishonor the Son of God.

If the character of Jesus Christ has entered into you and into me, then it has made us like Him in purpose. It has made us like Him in fact. Bless God! His Spirit is imparted to us. Bless God for that same unquenchable fidelity that characterized the Son of God.

"BE THOU FAITHFUL UNTO DEATH, AND I WILL GIVE THEE A CROWN OF LIFE" [Revelation 2:10].

Consecration Prayer

"My God and Father, In Jesus' Name I come to Thee. Take me as I am. Make me what I ought to be, in SPIRIT, in SOUL, in BODY. Give me power to do right, if I have wronged any, to CONFESS, to REPENT, to RESTORE, no matter what it costs. Wash me in the BLOOD of Jesus, that I may now become Thy CHILD, and manifest Thee, in a perfect SPIRIT, a holy MIND, a SICKLESS BODY, to the glory of God. Amen."

Successful Christian life rests on three essentials:

First: A knowledge of the teaching of the Lord and Savior Jesus Christ, Whose words are the final authority, the bar where every question must be brought for final decision. The words of every other must be measured, and their value determined by their statements of Jesus Christ. *"In him dwelleth all the fulness of the Godhead bodily"* [Colossians 2:9].

Second: Consecration to do all the will of God as declared by the Lord Jesus.

Third: Recognition of the Holy Spirit as revealer, guide, interpreter, teacher and empowerer. For without the presence of the Spirit of God in our hearts, our consecration would be valueless. We would not be able to live it and without a knowledge of the teaching of Jesus, our consecration would be nonintelligent.

5

The Strong Man's Way to God

Musicians talk of an ultimate note. That is a note you will not find on any keyboards. It is a peculiar note. A man sits down to tune a piano, or any fine instrument. He has no guide to the proper key, and yet he has a guide. That guide in the note that he has in his soul. And the nearer he can bring his instrument into harmony with that note in his soul, the nearer perfection he has attained.

There is an ultimate note in the heart of the Christian. It is the note of conscious victory through Jesus Christ. The nearer our life is tuned to that note of conscious victory, the greater the victory that will be evidenced in our life.

In my ministry in South Africa there was a young lady, one of the most beautiful souls I have ever known. She was baptized in the Spirit when perhaps only seventeen or eighteen years old. One of the remarkable developments in her after her baptism in the Spirit was that the Spirit of God would come powerfully upon her on occasions, and at such times she would sit down at the piano and translate the music her soul heard. Other times the Spirit would come upon her so powerfully that she would be caused to sing the heavenly music in some angelic language.

God gave her the gift of interpretation, so that quite frequently when the Spirit would come upon her, she would re-sing the song in English, or Dutch as the case might be. Her father and mother were both musicians. They soon learned that when the Spirit thus came upon her, they could record the music. The father would stand at one side and take the words of the song as she sang them, while the mother stood at the other side and recorded the music as she played the music on the instrument. In this way a great deal of the music was preserved.

Some years later Clara Butts, the great prima donna, came to Africa. She was singing at the Wanderers Hall in Johannesburg. One evening after the concert, while being entertained at the hotel, I was introduced to her. She said to me, "Mr. Lake, I have been very anxious to meet you, for I have heard that among your people is a remarkable woman who receives music in the Spirit, apparently of a different realm than ours."

I said, "Yes, that is a fact."

She inquired if it would be possible to meet her, and so a meeting was arranged.

One evening, we went to her hotel, and as we sat down, Clara Butts said to the young lady, "I wish you would sit down and play some of the music I have heard about." She did not understand that such music only came at such times as the Spirit came powerfully upon the woman. However, the young lady sat down at the piano.

I said to the company, "Let us bow our heads in prayer." As we did and waited, presently the Spirit of God descended upon her, and then there poured through her soul some of that wondrous, beautiful, heavenly music. I waited to note the affect on the company. When the song was finished, I looked especially at Clara Butts, who was weeping silently. She arose to her feet, and coming forward to the piano she reached out her hands, saying, "Young lady, that music belongs to a world that my soul knows little about. I pray every day of my life God may permit me to enter. In that realm is the ultimate which my soul sometimes hears, but which I have never been able to touch myself."

Beloved, in the Christian life, in the heart of God, there is an ultimate note. That note which is so fine and sweet and true and pure and good that it causes all our nature to respond to it, and rejoices the soul with a joy unspeakable.

All down through the ages some have touched God and heard that ultimate note. I believe that as David sat on the mountainside as a boy, caring for his father's sheep, God by the

Spirit taught him the power and blessing of that ultimate note. I believe at times that his soul ascended into God so that many of the Psalms of David are the real soul note of that blessed expression of heavenly music and heaven consciousness which came into the soul of the shepherd boy.

Mary, the Mother of Jesus, understood that note. I remember when I was a young man in a Methodist Bible Class, which I taught, we were discussing the subject of the Magnificat, that glorified expression which burst from the soul of Mary as she met Elizabeth, when the Spirit came upon her and revealed to her friend that she was to be the Mother of Jesus. In our worldly wisdom we decided, of course, that the Jewish woman of necessity must have been educated to compose that character of poetry spontaneously.

Many a day afterward as I saw the Spirit of God descend upon a soul, and the soul break forth into a song of God, the song of the angels, in a note so high and sweet and pure and clear as no human voice ever had produced perhaps without it, I understood the marvel that was taking place in the soul of Mary when she broke forth into the heavenly expression of that holy song. *"My soul doth magnify the Lord, And my spirit hath rejoiced in God my Savior"* [Luke 1:46-47], etc.

It was the Spirit of the Lord. Her spirit had ascended, bless God, into the heavenlies. Her spirit had touched heaven's note. Her spirit was receiving and reproducing the song of joy that she heard, possibly of the angels, or perhaps intuitively from the heart of God.

There is a Christianity that has that high note in it, bless God. Indeed, Christianity in itself, real Christianity, is in that high note of God, that thing of heaven, that is not of earth and is not natural. Bless God, it is more than natural. It is the note of heaven. It comes to the earth. It fills the soul of man. Man's soul rises into heaven to touch God, and in touching God receives that glorified expression and experience into his own soul, and it is reproduced in his own life and nature.

Beloved, there is a victory in God, the victory that characterizes the common walk of a high born Christian. It is the strong man's salvation. It is the salvation that comes from God because of the fact that the spirit of man touches the Spirit of God and receives that experience that we commonly speak of as the blessing of salvation from God.

But beloved, the soul that receives from God into his spirit that heavenly touch, knows, bless God, he does not have to be told by man, he knows by the Spirit of God that he has become the possessor of the consciousness of union with the Spirit of God which has enlightened his heart, filled his soul with holy joy, and caused his very being to radiate with God's glory and presence.

The hunger of my soul for many a long day has been that I might be able to so present that high true note of God, that the souls of men would rise up in God to that place of power, purity and strength where the presence and character and works of Christ are evidenced in and through them. There can be no distinction between the exercise of the real power of God as seen in Jesus and its reproduction in a Christian soul. There is a purity, the purity of heaven, so high, so holy, so pure, so sweet that it makes the life of the possessor radiant with the glory and praise of God.

During one of the periods of extreme necessity in our great work in South Africa, our finances became cut off for various reasons. I was anxious that there should be no letting down of the work we were then doing, and was trusting that it would not be necessary to withdraw our men, who had labored and suffered to get the work established on the frontier.

However, not being able to supply funds to those on the front, I deemed it the only wise thing to do to get them all together in a general conference, and decide what was to be our future action. By great sacrifice, a sacrifice too great for me to tell you of this afternoon, we succeeded in bringing in our missionaries from the front for a council. I told them the existing conditions and we sat down in the night time to decide what would be our future policy. After a time I was invited by a committee to leave the room for a minute or two. While I was in the vestry the brethren in the body of the tabernacle continued their conference and went on discussing the general question. When I returned they said to me, "Brother Lake, we have arrived at a decision." Old Father Van de Wall spoke for the company. He said, "We have reached this conclusion. There is to be no withdrawal of any man from any position. We feel that the time has come when your soul ought to be relieved of responsibility for us. We feel we have weighted your life long enough, but now by the grace of God we return to our stations to carry on our work. We live or die depending on God. If our wives die, they die, if our families die, they die, if we survive, we survive, but we are going back to our stations. This work will never be withdrawn. We have one request. Come and serve the communion of the Lord's supper to us once more while we stand together."

And as I took the cup they arose and stood in a large circle. I took the bread and passed it. It went from hand to hand around the circle. When it came time to pass the wine I took the cup in my hand, and with the usual statement that Jesus gave in the committal of Himself to God, *"My blood of the new testament"* [Mark 14:24]. I passed it on, and the next one, looking up to God, he said too, *"My blood of the new testament."* And so it passed from hand to hand clear around the circle.

Within a few months I was compelled to bury twelve out of that company. Every one of them might have lived if we could have supplied the ordinary essential things they ought to have received. But beloved, we had made our pledge to God. We had declared by the love of God in our souls, and because of what Christ had done for us, that we would be true to Him, and that in the Name of Christ His gospel should be spread abroad as far as it was in our power to do.

Men have said that the cross of Christ was not a heroic thing, but I want to tell you that the cross of Jesus Christ has put more heroism in the souls of men than any other event in human history. Men have lived, and rejoiced, and died believing in the living God, in the Christ of God Whose blood cleansed their hearts from sin, and who realized the real high spirit of His holy sacrifice, bless God. They manifested to mankind that same measure of sacrifice, and endured all that human beings could endure, and when endurance was no longer possible they passed on to be with God, leaving the world blessed through the evidence of a consecration deep and true and pure and good, like the Son of God Himself.

We see the note that was in the soul of Paul, and which characterized his message, when he made the splendid declaration which I read from Romans 1:16: *"For I am not ashamed of the gospel of Christ: for it is the power of God unto salvation to every one that believeth; to the Jews first, and also to the Greek."*

You see the note that touched the souls of men, the note that rang down through the centuries, and which rings in your heart and mine today. Christianity NEVER WAS DESIGNED BY GOD TO MAKE A LOT OF WEAKLINGS. It was designed to bring forth a race of men who were bold and strong and pure and good, blessed be God. The greatest and the strongest and the noblest is always the humblest.

The beautiful thing in the gospel is that it eliminates from the life of man that which is of himself and is natural and fleshly and earthly, bless God. It brings forth the beauteous things within the soul of man, the unselfishness, the life of purity, the peace, the strength and the power of the Son of God. How beautiful it is to have the privilege of looking into the face of one whose nature has been thus refined by the Spirit of the living God within. How beautiful it is when we look into the soul of one whom we realize God has purged by the blood of Christ until the very characteristics of the life and attitudes of the mind of Christ are manifest and evident in him to the glory of God.

Christianity is a strong man's gospel. Christianity, by the grace of God, is calculated to take the weak and fallen and erring and suffering and dying, and by applying the grace and power of God, through the soul of man, to the need of the individual, lift them up to the *"Lamb of God, which taketh away the sin of the world"* [John 1:29]. Blessed be God.

> "Down in the human heart,
> Crushed by the tempter,
> Feelings lie buried that grace can restore,
> Touched by a loving heart,
> Wakened by kindness,
> Chords that were broken
> Will vibrate once more."

I care not how crushed the soul, how beastialized the nature, I care not how sensual, if touched by the Spirit of the living God he will shed off that which is earthly and sensual, and give forth once again the pure note of the living God, heaven's high message, heaven's triumphant song, heaven's high note of living praise to the living God. Blessed be His Name.

God is endeavoring by His Spirit in these days to exalt the souls of men into that high place, that holy life, that heavenly state whereby men walk day by day, hour by hour in the heavenly consciousness of the presence of Christ in the heart of man all the time.

And the presence of Christ in the souls of men can only produce, first the purity that is in Him. For the *"wisdom that is from above is first pure"* [James 3:17], bless God. Purity is of God. Purity is of the nature of Christ. Purity is heaven's highborn instinct, filling the soul of man, making him in His nature like the Son of God. Upon that purified soul there comes from God that blessed measure of the Holy Spirit, not only purifying the nature, but empowering him by the Spirit so that the activities of God, the gift of His mind, the power of His Spirit is evident by the grace of God in that man's soul, in that man's life, lifting him by the grace of God into that place of holy and heavenly dominion in the consciousness of which Jesus lived and moved and accomplished the will of God always. Not the earth-consciousness, that holy consciousness, the consciousness of the living God, of His union with Him, which caused the Christ to walk as a Prince indeed. Bless God.

He was not bowed and overcome by conditions and circumstances about Him, but realized that the soul of man was a creative power, that it was within his soul, and common to his nature, and the nature of every other man, to protect, accumulate and possess, as sons of God; that through the creative faculty of His soul, the desires of his heart might be brought to pass. Blessed be His Name.

That is the reason God dared to talk as He did to Moses. That is the reason God dared to rebuke a man when he stopped to pray. That is the reason God said, *Why standest thou here and criest unto me? Lift up the rod that is in thy hand, and divide the waters* [see Exodus 14:15-16].

Beloved, your soul will never demonstrate the power of God in any appreciable degree until your soul conceives and understands the real vision of the Christ of God, whereby He knew that through His union with the living God His soul became the creative power through which He took possession of the power of God and applied it to the needs of His own soul, and the needs of other lives.

"I am the resurrection, and the life" [John 11:25], bless God. Lazarus was dead. The friends were weeping, but the Christ was there, bless God. Opening His soul to God in a cry of prayer the Spirit of God so moved within him that the consciousness of his high dominion in God so possessed Him, that He gave forth that wondrous command, *"Lazarus, come forth!"* [John 11:43]

and the dead obeyed the call, and the spirit that had gone on into the regions of the dead returned again, was joined to the body, and Lazarus was restored by the power of God. Blessed be His Holy Name.

When a boy, I received my religious training in a little Methodist class meeting. I wish there were some old time Methodist class meetings in these modern days—the kind that had the power of God, and the needs of men's souls were met in them. Where people could open their hearts and tell of their temptations and their trials and victories and receive council from one who guided the class.

In such a class meeting, and to such a class meeting, I owe a great deal of the development which God has brought forth in my life.

In one of these class meetings one day, as I sat listening to the testimonies, I observed that there was a kind of weakening trend. People were saying, "I am having such a hard time." "I am feeling the temptations of the world so much." etc. I was not able at the time to tell people what was the difficulty. I was only a young Christian. But when they got through I observed the old class leader, a gray headed man. He said something like this, "Brethren, the reason we are feeling the temptations so much, the reason there is a lack of sense of victory is because we are too far away from the Son of God. Our souls have descended. They are not in the high place where Christ is. Let our souls ascend, and when they ascend into the realm of the Christ, we will have a new note, it will be the note of victory."

Beloved, that is the difficulty with us all. We have come down out of the heavenlies into the natural, and we are trying to live a heavenly life in the natural state, overburdened by the weights and cares of the flesh and life all about us. Bless God, there is deliverance. There is victory. There is a place in God where the flesh no longer becomes a bondage. Where, by the grace of God, every sensuous state of the human nature is brought into subjection to the living God, where Christ reigns in and glorifies the very activities of a man's nature, making him sweet and pure and clean and good and true. Bless His Holy Name.

I call you today, beloved, by the grace of God, to that high life, to that holy walk, to that heavenly atmosphere, to that life in God where the grace and Spirit and power of God permeates your whole being. More, where not only your whole being is in subjection, but it flows from your nature as a holy stream of heavenly life to bless other souls everywhere by the grace of God.

There was a period in my life when God lifted my soul to a wondrous place of divine power. Indeed, I speak it with all conservatism when I say that I believe God gave me such an anointing of power as has seldom been manifested in modern life. That anointing remained with me for a period of eight months. One of the evidences of the power of God at that period was that God gave me such a consciousness of dominion to cast out evil spirits that the insane were brought from all quarters of the land, slobbering idiots. In many instances as I approached them, the Spirit of Christ would rise up in me in such dominion that when I got to them I could take hold of them, and looking into their face, would realize that God had given me power to cast it out. Hundreds of times the insane were healed instantly right on the spot.

I have been a student all my life. Not just a student of letters, but of the things of the soul. God helped me by His grace to take note of and analyze the conditions of my own soul. I noted that when that high consciousness of heavenly dominion rested upon my life, there was one thing that stood uppermost in all my consciousness. That was the vision of the triumphant Christ, the Son of God, as pictured by John in the first chapter of Revelation, where He stands forth in the mighty dignity of an overcomer, declaring, *"I am he that liveth, and was dead; and, behold, I am alive for evermore, Amen; and have the keys of hell and of death"* [Revelation 1:18].

Beloved, I want to tell you that the soul joined to Christ and who exercises the power of God, ascends into that high consciousness of heavenly dominion as it is in the heart of Jesus Christ today, for He is the overcomer, the only overcomer. But yet, when my soul is joined to His soul, when His Spirit flows like a heavenly stream through my spirit, when my whole nature is infilled and inspired by the life from God, I too, being joined with Him, become an overcomer, in deed and in truth. Glory be to God.

I am glad that God has permitted man, even at intervals, to rise into that place of high dominion in God, for it demonstrates the purpose of God. It demonstrates that He purposes we should not only rise into the high place at intervals, but that this should be the normal life of the Christian who is joined to God every day and all the time.

Christianity is not a thing to be apologized for. Christianity was the living conscious life and power of the living God, transmitted into the nature of man until, bless God, man's nature is transformed by the living touch, and the very spirit, soul and being is energized and filled by His life. Thus you become indeed, as Christ intended, a veritable christ.

That startles some people. But the ultimate of the gospel of Jesus Christ and the ultimate of the redemption of the Son of God is to reproduce and make every man—bound by sin and held by sensuousness and enslaved by the flesh—like Himself in deed and in truth, sons of God. Not sons of God on a lower order, but sons of God as Jesus is.

Paul declares, *"He gave some, apostles...some evangelists; and some pastors and some teachers."* What for? *"Till we ALL come...into the measure of the stature of the fulness of Christ"* [Ephesians 4:11-13]. Bless God. Not a limited life, but an unlimited life. The idea of Christ, the idea of God was that every man, through Jesus Christ, through being joined to Him by the Holy Spirit, should be transformed into Christ's perfect image. Glory be to God. Christ within and Christ without. Christ in your spirit, Christ in your soul and Christ in your body. Not only living His life, but performing His works by the grace of God. That is the gospel of the Son of God. That is the thing that Paul was not ashamed of. He said, *"For I am not ashamed of the gospel of Christ: for it is the power of God unto salvation to every one that believeth; to the Jew first, and also to the Greek"* [Romans 1:16].

If any man has a question within his soul of the reality of the Baptism of the Holy Spirit as it has been poured out upon the world in these last ten years, that question ought to be settled in your soul forever by one common test. That test is that it has raised the consciousness of Christianity to realize what real Christianity is.

If any one wants to analyze the development that has come into Christian consciousness during the last two hundred years, all they have to do is to begin and follow the preaching of the great evangelists who have moved the world. Think of Jonathan Edwards, who thundered the terrors of God and what hell was like until men grasped their seats and hung on to them, fearing they were falling into hell itself. Men were moved by FEAR to escape damnation. That was believed to be Christianity. Why any coward wanted to keep out of hell. He might not have had one idea in his soul of what was the real true earmark of Christianity.

After a while others went a step further, and you can note the ascending consciousness. They said, "No, saving yourself from hell and punishment is not the ideal of the gospel. The ideal is to get saved so as to go to heaven." And so men were saved in order to get to heaven when they died. I have always had a feeling in my soul of wanting to weep when I hear men pleading with others to become Christians so they will go up to heaven when they die. My God, is there no appeal outside of something absolutely selfish?

Beloved, don't you see that Christianity was unselfishness itself. It had no consideration for the selfish individual. The thing held up above everything else in the world, and the only ideal worthy of a Christian was that you and I and He Himself might demonstrate to mankind one holy, high beauteous thing, of which the world was deficient, and that was a knowledge of God. So Jesus said, *Unto all righteousness* [see Matthew 3:15] and He wrote it on the souls of men and branded it on their consciences, and stamped it on their hearts until the world began to realize the ideal that was in the soul of Jesus.

Unto all righteousness—becoming like Christ Himself, a demonstrator of the righteousness of the living God. That is Christianity, and that only is Christianity, for that was the consecration of the Christ Himself.

The test of the Spirit, and the only test of the Spirit that Jesus ever gave, is the ultimate and final test. He said, *"By their fruits ye shall know them"* [Matthew 7:20]. That is the absolute and final test. *"Do men gather grapes of thorns, or figs of thistles?"* [Matthew 7:16].

So I say to you, if you want to test whether this present outpouring of the Spirit of God is the real thing, the real pure Baptism of the Holy Ghost or not, test it by the fruits that it produces. If it is producing in the world, as we believe it is, a consciousness of God so high, so pure, so acceptable, so true, so good, so like Christ then it is the Holy Ghost Himself. Bless God. No other test is of any value whatever.

I want to tell you beloved that the ultimate test to your own of the value of a thing that you have in your heart is the common test that Jesus gave, *"By their fruits ye shall know them" "By their FRUITS ye shall know them. Do men gather grapes of thorns or figs of thistles?"*

Men tell us in these days that SIN is what you think it is. Well, it is not. Sin is what God thinks it is. You may think according to your own conscience, God thinks according to His. God thinks in accordance with the heavenly purity of His own nature. Man thinks in accordance with that degree of purity that his soul realizes. But the ultimate note is in God. The finality is in God.

When men rise up in their souls' aspirations to the place of God's thought, then bless God, the character of Jesus Christ will be evident in their lives, the sweetness of His nature, the Holiness of His character, the beauty of the crowning glory that not only overshadowed Him, but that radiated from Him. Blessed be God. And the real life of the real Christian is the inner life, the life of the soul.

"Out of the heart..." said Jesus, "proceed evil thoughts, adulteries, fornications" [Mark 7:21], etc. These are the things common to the flesh of man. Out of the soul of man, likewise, proceeds by the same common law, the beauty, virtue, peace, power and truth of Jesus, as the soul knows it.

So he whose soul is joined to Christ may now, today, this hour, shed forth as a benediction upon the world the glory and blessing and peace and power of God, even as Jesus shed it forth to all men to the praise of God.

Prayer

My God, we bless Thee for the ideal of the gospel of Christ which Thou hast established in the souls of men through the blessed Holy Ghost. God, we pray Thee this afternoon that if we have thought lightly of the Spirit of God, if we have had our eyes fixed on outward evidences instead of the inward life, we pray Thee to sweep it away from our souls.

May we this day, God, see indeed that the life of God, His inner life, the true life, God's holy life, His practical purpose, that from a race of sinful men, saved through the blood of Christ, cleansed by the power of God, cleansed in the inner soul, in every department of their nature, that the Christ-life is to be revealed, and the Lord Jesus through them is to shed forth His glory and life and benediction and peace and power upon the world. Blessed be Thy precious Name.

So my God, we open our nature to heaven today, asking that the Spirit of the living God will thus move in our own soul, that by

His grace we shall be so perfectly, truly cleansed of God that our nature will be sweet and pure and heavenly and true, so that we can receive from God indeed the blessed sweetness of His pure, holy, heavenly Spirit to reign in us, to rule in us, control us and guide us for ever more. In Jesus' Name. Amen.

6

As He Is, So Are We In This World

The mind of the world is fixed on the Redeemer. The Old Testament Scriptures, looking up to Christ, are particularly prolific in their description of His life, His sorrows, His sufferings, His death, His sacrifice. All these were qualities of the Redeemer. All these were endured and exercised by the Redeemer in order to obtain something. That something was REDEMPTION.

What redemption means is best seen by following the chain of Christ's life from the Crucifixion on—not back of the cross, this side of it. If you want to understand the Redeemer, see Him before the cross comes into view. That is, if you want to understand the Redeemer who obtained the redemption. But if you want to understand the redemption that He obtained, look on this side of Calvary.

The great majority of the Christian world is still weeping at the foot of the cross. The consciousness of man is fixed on the Christ who died, not on the Christ who lives. They are looking back to the Redeemer who was, not the Redeemer who is.

On this side of the cross we see all the marvel of opposites to what we see in the Christ on the other side of the cross. On the other side of the cross we see a man of sorrows and acquainted with griefs, bearing our sicknesses, carrying our sorrows. He had no where to lay His head. Poverty was one of His characteristics.

Nobody ever stops to think, or rarely so, that He bore His poverty, and what for? Answer: *"That through His poverty we might be made rich"* [2 Corinthians 8:9]. He bore our sorrows, what for? That we through His sorrows might be made glad. He bore our sufferings, for what? That we through His stripes might be healed. He gave His life a sacrifice for sins, for what? That we should know no sin. Then having completed the redemption, or purchased the redemption, the redemption becomes manifest on this side of Calvary.

I sometimes wish that I could turn the face of the believer the other way. You may observe that I very rarely turn the face of believers to the cross. The world looked to the cross until they passed it. But if they had never passed it, redemption would be no more of a reality than it was before. Redemption becomes a reality as we obtain the redemption. To obtain the fact that the Redeemer purchased is the purpose of the Christian life. On this side of the cross we see the victory, not the suffering, not the humility, and dejection, and rejection but the VICTORY.

We see the first glimmer of that victory when Jesus, who was crucified as a Redeemer, steps forth as the redeemed. The Redeemer, the first fruits of them that slept, BECAME the Redeemer of mankind, or the pattern of redemption. He was not the pattern of redemption back there on the other side of the cross. He BECAME the pattern of redemption. Paul puts it in such terse terms, *"He BECAME the author of eternal salvation"* [Hebrews 5:9]. Not "was manufactured the author of eternal salvation," not was born, but *"BECAME the author of eternal salvation."* Why? Because, having as the Redeemer entered into the redemption by Himself, *"the first fruits of them that slept"* [1 Corinthians 15:20]. The first Victor, the first example of victory, He became the manifestor, the demonstrator, the revealer, the embodiment of eternal salvation.

On this side of the cross is the victory of His resurrection, the marvel of all victories, the victory over death, by which He took death captive. A living man, Himself, He came forth the Conqueror of death itself, having put all things under His feet. What an ascent into triumph! What a change in His consciousness! What a distinction between the Redeemer and the redeemed! No longer subject to death, but triumphing over it. No longer subject to humiliation, but now becoming the exalted One, bless God.

For in the ascension we see the exaltation of Jesus, instead of the man of sorrows, acquainted with grief or sickness. We see the living, triumphant, exultant Son of God ascending to the throne of God, receiving from God the Father, what Jesus and the Father considered worthy of the suffering, and death and sacrifice and redemption of Jesus Christ. A reward so great that Jesus Himself considered it worth all His sufferings, all His buffetings, His Earth career, His humiliation, His sacrifice and death. All to obtain it, the GIFT OF THE HOLY SPIRIT (Acts 2:16-18).

On this side of the cross we see the distributing of His new life. Not the life that was on the other side, but the life that IS on this side—the life of triumph, the life of victory, the life of praise, the life of power, the life of glory, exultant, triumphant.

The other night as I lay in bed I was thinking and praying over some of the things that were passing through my mind concerning Jesus. The scripture of Revelation 1:18 came with new force to me, where Jesus, not as a humiliated Savior, but as a Kingly Conqueror, stands forth with the marvelous declaration that *"I am he that liveth, and was dead; and, behold, I am alive for evermore, Amen; and have the keys of hell and of death."*

It seems to me that in all the Word of God there is no such shout of triumph as that. Why, it seems to me as if the very heaven and the earth and all that in them rings with that exultant shout of a real Victor, *"I have the keys of hell and of death."* The enemies of man, taken captive by the Son of God, subject to His dictate. That is the Christ that speaks to my soul. That is the Christ on this side of Calvary. That is the Christ my soul worships.

I am going to tell you a strange thing. I am not much interested in the Christ on the other side of Calvary. Not half so much as I am in the Christ this side of Calvary. Bless God, I love the Redeemer, but I GLORY in His REDEMPTION.

The marvel of Christianity and the wonder of this scripture that I called your attention to is that it does not say that "as He WAS" back there, so are we to be in this world. Don't you see, that is where the world fell down, where the Christian life became submerged in a vale of tears and shadows and darkness and poverty and humiliation and suffering. All of which Christian mankind accepted joyfully, because they believed they were exemplifying Jesus Christ, and thinking they were glorifying Him. They still visioned NOT the Christ that IS, but the Christ that WAS. The Christ who bore and endured and suffered and died in order to obtain the privilege of the Christ who is, and to become the Christ who is.

Now if I could radically turn your minds tonight clear around from the vision of the Christ before the cross, to the vision of the Christ who IS, this fact would mean that your souls must ascend in consciousness and union with the overcoming Son of God. Not bowed and bound with the humiliated Savior, but joined in holy glory-triumph with the Son of God who obtained the victory and revealed it and distributes its power and glory to the souls of men.

"As HE IS," not as He was, John said, *"so are we in this world"* [1 John 4:17]. Not in the life to come. The glory is not for the life that is coming, but for the life that is now. The victory is not for the future. It is for the NOW. It is not for the good days bye and bye. It is for the NOW. Not for heaven to come, but for heaven on earth NOW.

Sin, sickness, death under His feet. Hell itself taken captive and obedient to His word. Every enemy of mankind throttled, bound, chained by the Son of God. Mankind joined with Him by the Holy Ghost in living triumph. Why, if I receive of the Spirit of Jesus Christ, of the Christ who IS, I receive the spirit of victory and power and might and dominion, of grace, of love, of power, blessed be God, of all the blessed estate of which Jesus Himself is now the conscious Master. All these things He gives to the Christian through imparting to him the Holy Ghost.

Holy Spirit Message

The Spirit of the Lord says within my soul that: The universal sound of praise in which angels and men, all creatures in the earth, the sea, and the sky, will eventually join, comes because the consciousness of the overcoming Christ has dawned upon them and possessed their soul.

Some of the final song, the song of the ages, that shout of victory, we find in the fifth of Revelation:

> **And I beheld, and I heard the voice of many angels round about the throne and the beasts and the elders; and the number of them was ten thousand times ten thousand, and thousands of thousands; Saying with a loud voice, Worthy is the Lamb that was slain to receive**

> **power, and riches, and wisdom, and strength, and honour, and glory, and blessing. And every creature which is in heaven, and on the earth, and under the earth, and such as are in the sea, and all that are in them, heard I saying, Blessing and honour, and glory and power, be unto Him that sitteth upon the throne, and unto the Lamb for ever and ever. And the four beasts said, Amen. And the four and twenty elders fell down and worshipped him that liveth for ever and ever [Revelation 5:11-14].**

Should I carry your soul tonight into the place of victory in God, I must carry it into the consciousness of Christ's overcoming life. All His healing virtue, His saving grace, His transforming spirit, all the angelic communion, the heavenly foretaste, the consciousness of the estate of the redeemed, the glory triumph of Jesus Christ is in the consciousness born from the resurrection and revealed in the Revelation, *"For as He is, so are we in this world"* [1 John 4:17].

Jesus in His earth life reached forth into that life and kingdom and triumph and exhibited in this world, in a measure, that victory and triumph that His soul knew and visioned. But when the cross came He entered actually into the life that His soul formerly visioned and knew through the Word of God and the consciousness of God within His heart. And so His ministry in the Spirit is a ministry in the ALL POWER, ALL CONSCIOUSNESS, ALL KNOWLEDGE, ALL GRACE, ALL VICTORY, ALL SALVATION. Bless God.

I would lift your soul tonight in the Spirit of God into that glow and glory of the triumphant life. Do you know that it is only as your mind settles back into the humiliation and the suffering and the weakness and the fear and doubting of the dispensation that is past, that you grow weak and sickly, and sinful? But as your soul looks forward and possesses in the present the glorious victory that Jesus acquired and exhibits and enjoys, does it rise out of its sorrows, out of its sins, into that glorious triumph of the Children of God?

It would not be pleasant to always have to live with babies and imbeciles, or a lot of half grown-up folks. I want you to sympathize with God. I want you to catch the vision of the ordinary

Christian conception. Think of God having to live forever and forever and ever in association with people who were not half big enough to comprehend His will. That is not God's purpose. Jesus Christ undertook the biggest contract that heaven or earth, or sea or sky ever knew. He undertook the redemption of mankind and their transformation by the Spirit of the living God into His own likeness and image and stature and understanding in the grace and power and fullness of His own nature. Jesus Christ is the associate of God, one with Him, and with every son of God. He has purposed that redeemed men, grown up in God, transformed into the very image and likeness and nature and fullness of Jesus Christ, becoming like the Son of God, shall be associates of God.

What did God create man for anyway? Answer: "The chief end of man is to glorify God and enjoy Him forever."

God's purpose in the creation of mankind was to develop an association on His own plane. Otherwise God would have been eternally living with babies or imbeciles. He would have been compelled forever to associate with those who were not able to understand or comprehend His nature or character or the marvel of His being or the wonder of His power.

The wonder of the redemption of Jesus Christ is revealed in the matchlessness of God's purpose to transform man into His very nature and image and fullness. Thereby men as sons of God become, bless God, the associates of Almighty God, on His own plane of life and understanding.

When my soul saw the vision of God Almighty's marvelous purpose, I felt like falling on my face afresh and crying out, "Worthy is the Lamb that was slain!" For *"as He is, so are we in this world."* All the glory and power that Jesus knows at the throne of God, all the wonders of His overcoming grace, all the marvel of the greatness of His power, is yours and mine to receive through faith in the Son of God, yours and mine to expect through the faith of the Son of God, yours and mine to possess and enjoy and reveal to the glory of God.

The Vision

Jesus Thou King! Glorious and eternal!
Mighty and loving! Powerful and Grand!
Who through the blackness and darkness infernal
Guideth and holdeth Thy child by the hand.

Pierced to Thy soul! Grieved in Thy Spirit!
Bleeding Thy feet are! Wounded Thy hand!
Sorrowing Christ, through the veil now uplifted
See I Thy beckoning with uplifted hand.

Hear I Thy voice as to me Thou now speakest!
See I Thy teardrops silently fall!
Know I the anguish Thy sorrowing Spirit
Feels as Thou drinkest this wormwood and gall.

What, Lord, the cause of Thy anguish of Spirit?
Why doth this suffering come to Thee now?
Crucified once, on the cross wast Thou lifted?
Have not the cruel thorns pierced Thy brow?

Have not the sins of mankind on Thee rested
Causing Thy soul in anguish to be torn?
Has not the bloodsweat from Thee been wrested?
Have not Thy saints for the crucified mourned?

Why is it that again now I see Thee
Bruised and bleeding, anguished and lone?
Why is the Spirit of Christ now within me
Witnessing thus of Thy sorrow again?

List, to the answer! Let all the world hear it!
Jesus is speaking! Let all hear His voice!
It is because of the sins of my people.
It is because you will not heed my voice.

Do ye not bite and devour one another?
Do ye not slay with your tongue and pen
Many of my precious daughters and mothers,
Young men and maidens, Even boys and old men?

Have ye ever stood in the fire where they're tested?
Have ye ever felt of the withering blast?
Know ye how long and how hard they've resisted
Fighting and struggling unto the last?

Why did ye not stretch your hand out to help them?
Why from thy soul did not sympathy flow?
Did not My Spirit with thee say, "Help them
out of their bondage, or darkness or woe"?

Thus am I crucified! Thus My soul anguished!
This is the cause of My sorrow and woe!
This is the reason that Satan has vanquished
Many who once were as pure as the snow!

Oh, let thy heart in yearning compassion,
Gentleness, meekness and tenderness mild,
Give of My grace to the soul swept with passion
Power to live at My feet as a child.

Then shall the gladness and brightness of heaven
Flood thine own spirit and cause thee to move
Among the crushed and the wounded and broken
Bringing them sunshine, gladness and love.

Then shall thy spirit in tune with the heavenlies,
Rapturous joys in the Spirit shall know.
Then shall the power of God rest upon thee.
Then in the fruits of the Spirit thou'lt grow.

Then shall the earth know the glory of heaven.
Then shall dominion over death and over hell
Reign in thine own soul, spread as the leaven
Causing angels and men My praises to swell.

Then shall the Christ over the earth be victorious!
Then shall the power of My gospel be known!
My kingdom shall come! Eternal and Glorious!
United! The heavens and the earth shall be one!

Given to John G. Lake Oct. 10, 1909
in tongues with interpretation.

7

Reign As Kings

I want to bring you a message that came to me today. I have been for years on the verge of this message, but never did I receive it until this morning. In Romans 5:17, in another translation there is a remarkable rendering: *"For if by the trespass of the one, death reigned as king through the one, much more shall they who receive the abundance of grace and the gift of righteousness reign as kings in the realm of life, through Jesus Christ."*

That means that the moment you accept Jesus Christ, God becomes your righteousness. That is the "gift of righteousness." Let me read it again: *"For if by the trespass of one, death reigned as king through the one, much more shall they who receive the abundance of grace and the gift of righteousness reign as kings in the realm of life through Jesus Christ."* It means every one of us that has been born again comes into a kingly and queenly state, and we are accepted by God to reign as kings and queens in the realm of life.

We have reigned as servants in the realm of spiritual death. We have passed out of death, Satan's realm, into the realm of life, into the realm of the supernatural, or the spiritual, or the heavenlies.

Here are some significant facts. Man was never made a slave. He was never made for slavery. He was made to reign as king under God. If you noticed, I showed you this, that kingly being that was created was created in the image and likeness of God, that he was created on terms of equality with God that he could stand in the presence of God without any consciousness of inferiority.

I quote you from the eighth Psalm in which this expression is used: *"What is man that thou are mindful of him? and the son of man, that thou visitest him? For thou hast made him a little lower than [God][1], and crownest him with glory and honour"* [Psalm 8:4-5].

What does it mean? It means that God has made us as near like Himself as it is possible for God to make a being. He made you in His image. He made you in His likeness. He made you the same class of being that He is Himself.

He made Adam with an intellect with such caliber that he was able to name every animal, every vegetable and every fruit, and give them names that would fit and describe their characteristics. When God could do that with man, then that man belonged to the realm of God.

Adam had such vitality in his body that even after he sinned and became mortal, he lived nearly a thousand years, 930 years before mortality got in its work and put him on his death bed. Methuselah lived 969 years. Life was so abundant, so tremendous in their minds and spirits that it conquered century after century.

Jesus said: *"I am come that they might have life, and that they might have it more abundantly"* (John 10:10). More abundantly! Jesus made the declaration: *"I am come that they might have life."* The thing that was forfeited in the garden was regained. God gave him dominion over the works of His hand. God made him His understudy, His king to rule over everything that had life. Man was master. Man lived in the realm of God. He lived on terms of equality with God. God was a faith God. All God had to do was to believe that the sun was, and the sun was. All God had to do was to believe that the planets would be, and they were. Man belonged to God's class of being—a faith man. And he lived in the creative realm of God.

Friends, if you believe what I am preaching, it is going to end your impotence and weakness, and you will swing out into a power such as you have never known in your life.

Man lost his place by high treason against God. He lost his dominion in The Fall. With The Fall went his dominion over spirit and soul. But universal man ever yearned for the return of his dominion.

Brother, do you hear me? Here is one of the most tremendous facts that we have to face: that never a single primitive people that has ever been found has not yearned for dominion. Not a single primitive people has been found that did not have a golden past where they had dominion, a golden future where dominion was going to be restored. That is the tradition of universal man.

Man has craved dominion. Man has shrunk from bondage. Man has rebelled against it. Man has yearned to gain the mastery again over physical loss, over mind loss, and over the loss of spirit. This long ago desire to gain the lost dominion is seen in his offerings, in his drinking blood, in his priesthood that he has appointed.

I want to enter this a little bit with you. Darwin foolishly said that the reason man drank blood was because the blood was salty and he craved salt. Friends, human blood was never desirable to any people. Why did they drink it? They drank it in order that they might be like God. They drank it that they might become eternal, immortal.

The desire of immortality of the physical body lies latent in the heart of universal man. And for that reason they drank it, believing if they drank it they would be like God. They took the animal or man, and they laid it upon the altar of their God or god. Then they said, "If we drink the blood of the man or animal, we drink the blood of God, and if we drink enough of it, we will be God."

How far is that removed from the communion table? Do you see the analogy? The communion table is practically unknown as yet to the majority of Christians.

Now the ancients believed this, and the people of Africa, and it caused them to become cannibals. It was not because they loved human blood, but they believed if they could eat the flesh and drink the blood that was given to their god, they would be like God. You will find that all through the legends and poetry of the old world.

Universal man feels the lost dominion can be regained. They have a conviction that it is going to be regained. And this faith of universal man, reaching Godward, finally challenged God to make it a possibility. He believes that union with God will give him this dominion. He hates defeat. He wants to conquer death. He dreams of immortality. He fears death and disease.

Let me recapitulate. This universal man has believed that somewhere God was going to give him this lost dominion. He believed that dominion would come through his union with God, if that union could be affected. Can you understand now? It was the universal knowledge and the universal need and the universal cry of man for union with deity that caused the incarnation.

Let me come a step closer. On the ground of what Jesus Christ did, the substitutionary sacrifice, God is able to redeem us from our sins. He is able to impart to us His very nature. He is able to give us eternal life, take us into His own family so that we can call Him "Father," not by adoption only, but by an actual birth of our spirit, so we come into actual relationship and union with God, and the age old cry of universal man has been fulfilled. Do you see? The new birth has brought us into vital union with Jesus Christ.

This thing I am teaching you about our union with God is not known in the great body of Christians. All they have is forgiveness of sin. There is no actual union with God. They do not know that the new birth is a real incarnation. They do not know that they are as much the sons and daughters of God Almighty as Jesus is. The great body of the Christian Church has no dominion, does not know it. They have the most befogged concept of what God has done and what God is to them, and what they are to God.

Another step. That incarnation that God has given through the new birth has bestowed upon us the lost authority of the Garden of Eden. And only here and there has a man known it, or preached it, or dared to assume it.

Let me break in here. J. Hudson Taylor, after his first visit to China, was walking in England and a voice said: "If you will walk with Me, we will evangelize Inland China." He looked and there was no one there. An unseen angel had spoken to him. Then his heart caught the vision and said, "Lord, we will do it." He was the founder of the great Inland China Mission.

Taylor was returning on a sailing vessel and they were going through the Yellow Sea. It was in the section where the seven winds come at eventide, but from a certain hour in the day until evening there is no wind. One afternoon the captain said to Mr. Taylor, "Take this." And he took the glasses and looked. He could see they were nearing land. The captain said, "The worst pirates in all this awful section of the ocean are there. Our vessel is in the clutches of the tide, and in three hours will strike the rocks and there is no hope of saving it."

J. Hudson said, "Are you a Christian?"

He said, "I am."

He said, "Are there any other Christians here?"

He said, "Yes, the cook and the carpenter and another man are Christians."

Taylor said, "Call them, and let's go and pray."

He called them and the five or six of them went to their respective places, and they had not been praying but a little while when he heard commands being given on board, and men rushing about. He came up, and he could see the wind breaking on the sea that had been so glassy. In a few minutes the wind had filled the sails, three hours before nature would have sent it.

In my own experience I have seen God many times set aside natural law. I told you one day about one miracle. We were putting on a roof on one of our buildings. A storm came up. The boys had unwisely torn off too many shingles for us to cover before the storm reached us. I saw that storm go around us and leave ten or fifteen acres where the rain did not fall for more than one-half hour, and the water flowed down the gutters past our buildings. Those boys worked and sang and shouted. When the last shingle was in place, the water fell on it, and we were drenched to the skin. I have seen God perform His prodigies in answer to believing prayer. What God does for one He can do for another.

This inferiority complex that makes men seek God and create religions and priesthoods is a relic of the Fall and comes because man is conscious that once somewhere he had power, he had dominion, and he galls under it like a mighty athlete that feels his strength leaving him until by and by he becomes helpless as a little child. Oh, the agony of the thing!

Every man has within him the entire history of every man. That cry of agony of the athlete, that cry of agony of the man that once had physical and mental health is the cry of universal man crying for the lost authority and dominion that he once enjoyed.

He seeks through rites a new birth, a recreation that does not come. How many lodges and secret societies have a rite, a symbol of the new birth. I cannot mention them, but you look back. You are initiated into such and such an organization, I can name four that have a new birth rite. It is latent in the universal man.

Every religion has some kind of recreation. Why? Every man has a consciousness (I am speaking of men who think) down in them. There is something that cries out against death, against sickness, against sorrow, against defeat, against failure. There is something that rebels against the bondage of fear and that cries for rebirth, a recreation that will give them dominion and mastery over the forces that have held them in bondage.

Our redemption is God's answer to this universal hunger. We saw God's hunger creating man; now you see man's hunger bringing God to recreate him. Can't you understand it, men, that the hunger in the heart of God drove Him, forced Him until He spoke a world into being for the home of His love project, man. It has driven Him to create universes to hold this world by the law of attraction and make it a safe place for man.

Then when man fell and lost his standing and became a slave and subject to Satan, this universal cry went up until the very heart of God bled for this broken human. Then He made provision whereby this man that He had created who had sinned and had "decreated" might come back into fellowship with Him of a higher, holier sort than he had lost at the beginning.

I want to take you through some scriptures. Go with me to Romans 5:17: *"For if by the trespass of one, death reigned as king through the one, much more shall they who receive the abundance of grace and the gift of righteousness reign as kings in the realm of life through Jesus Christ."* By the new birth you have passed out of Satan's dominion and Satan's power, and you have come over into God's dominion, and you have come over into the kingdom of the Son of His love.

You will pardon me, but I have this consciousness when I am preaching; there comes up a wave from the congregation of a kind of stultified unbelief. Do you know where it comes from? It comes from all the years you have sat under false teachers. You have been taught that to be humble you have got to say you are a sinner, you are no good, you don't amount to anything. You sing: "Weak and sickly, vile and full of sin I am." I do not like to preach one thing, and Charles Wesley another. If you are born again, you are a son of God. And for you to tear yourself out of your sonship, your relationship and the righteousness of God, and put yourself over in the reality of death, and tell God you are dirty and unclean, that His blood has not cleansed you, and His life has not been delivered to you, it is a monstrous thing. It is all right to sing that as an unregenerate, but it is not the experience of the sons and daughters of God.

Here is our position through Jesus Christ. God has become our righteousness. We have become His very sons and daughters, and you sing weakness, and you talk weakness and you pray weakness, and you sing unbelief, and you pray and talk it, and you go out and live it. You are like that good old woman. She said, "I do love that doctrine of falling from grace, and I practice it all the time." Another man said, "Brother, I believe in the dual nature. I believe that when I would do good, evil is always present with me, and I thank God that evil is always there."

You live it and you believe it, and God cannot do anything with you. You magnify failure and you deify failure until to the majority of you, the devil is bigger than God. And you are more afraid of the devil than you are of God. You have more reverence of the devil than you have for God. It is absolutely true. If any saint would dare to say "I am done with disease and sickness; I will never be sick again," ninety percent of you would say, "Keep your eyes on that person. He will be sick in a week. The devil sure will get him." You believe the devil is bigger than God. Your God is about one and a half inches high and the devil is one and a half feet high. What you need to do is to change gods and change gods quickly. There have been only a few folk that had a good-sized God.

You go over in Genesis and you see the size of God. It is full-sized photograph. You see Jesus Christ rising from the dead, and you have seen the God-sized photograph of redemption. We reign as kings in the realm of life. And what is the reaction in you? You say, "That is all right and I wish it were true in my case; I would like to reign as king." And you think this moment how you are whipped, and you think how you have been defeated, and how weak you are, and you will be defeated all the next week. You reckon on the strength of the devil and on your own sickness. You say, "If he had what I have he wouldn't talk like that." How can the power of God come through such a mess of unbelief? How can God get near? Ninety percent of those who have received the Spirit have made God a little bit of a side issue, a sort of court of last resort. When you get where the devil can do no more, you say, "God, catch me. The devil has finished his work." God is simply a life insurance company that pays the premium at death.

Turn with me to Ephesians 1:7: *"In whom we have redemption through his blood, the forgiveness of sins, according to the riches of his grace."* For months and months that scripture has been burning its way into my soul. *"In whom we have [our] redemption through His blood, the forgiveness of sins,"* and it is *"according to the riches of His grace."* It is illustrated in Israel coming out of Egypt with the Red Sea before them, with vast desert stretching its burning waste between them and their promised land. We do not have any such redemption in our religion. I'll tell you what we need. Have you been in Canada? Do you know when I went to Canada, there was one thing that struck me peculiarly. The signs would read, "John Brown, Limited." Everywhere I saw that sign. That is a Scotsman's caution. I was holding meetings in the old St. Andrews Church in Sidney. I asked them one night why they did not put their national symbol on their churches. They wondered what I meant. I said, "Every other business house is 'LTD'. Why don't you put it over the church?"

An old Scotsman said, "We don't have to. Everybody knows it." Limited? Sure it is limited. Limit God, limit ourselves, limit His grace, limit the Word. Sure, our God is a little bit of a god. Most of us could carry Him in our vest pocket, and it wouldn't bulge the pocket. Our God with the "LTD" on Him.

Brother, sister, that challenge comes to us today to let God loose. There are a few places where they have let God have His way, and how the blessings have come!

"In whom we have redemption."

Have you? If you have your redemption it means that to you Satan has been defeated. Jesus conquered the devil as a Jew before He died. Then He let the devil conquer Him on the cross and send Him down to the place of suffering with our burden and guilt upon Him. But after He satisfied the claims of justice, Jesus met the devil in his own throne room and He stripped him of his authority and dominion. And when He arose, He said: *"I am he that liveth, and was dead; and, behold, I am alive for evermore...and have the keys of hell and of death"* (Revelation 1:18).

He had gone into the throne room, taken Satan's badge of dominion and authority that Adam had given him in the Garden of Eden, and every man that accepts Jesus Christ was identified with Him when He did it. He did it for you. He did it for me. He died as our substitute and representative. When He put His heel on Satan's neck, He did it for you, and you were in Christ. And to you who believe Satan is conquered and Satan is defeated, Satan can holler and bellow as much as he wants to, but you withstand him in the faith of Jesus Christ.

I saw a picture this morning as I was reading an article. I saw a company of men walk out, and I saw all the disease and all the crimes and agonies; I saw cancers and tumors and tuberculosis: and I saw a company of men and women walk down in the midst of it, and I heard them say, "Here come the sons of God: here come the conquerors." And the sons of God said to disease, "In the name of Jesus, depart," and disease fled. It fled as it did before the Son of God. It obeyed because the Son of God sent them out and gave them His name as authority. I saw the company of men enter into the lost dominion. They put upon them the garments of their authority and dominion and walked out conquerors over death and hell and the grave. They were masters. They were rulers.

Then I saw another picture. I saw David in the old cave of Adullam. I saw men coming down that were broken and in distress and in debt, and men that were in awful physical conditions. And they gathered four hundred strong around David. And out of that crowd David developed and trained the most invincible army that was ever seen [see 1 Samuel 22].

Then my mind passed over a few years of struggle. And I saw from that company some mighty men come forth. I saw one man come forth and go forth and go where there were thousands and thousands of Philistines, men that were shoulders above him, men that wore shields. I saw that man go among those giants, and he slew hundreds of them. And I piled them up in my hundreds until I had piled eight hundred.

Every one of those mighty men of David were simple men of extraordinary ability. There was no mark to indicate that they were more than common Jews, 5'11", but they knocked down men 6'6" and 6'8". They conquered them because they were blood covenant men.

That is the type of the Church of Jesus Christ. As I said, "Where are God's mighty men today?" Then I saw a picture. David sat there a little way from the spring of Bethlehem, and the Philistines had got control of the water. David said, "Oh, that I had a drink." And those three men came forth.

He said, "Where are you going, boys?" They just waved him off, and those three men conquered the whole company of the Philistines, filled their pitchers with water, and set them down at David's feet.

I cried, "My God, my God, where are the mighty men of valor of today, the men that can assail the forces of Satan?" God says they are coming out of you: they are going to arrive. God has in training some men and women that are going to do exploits for Him. Will you not come up and live in your realm?

God help you, brother, this afternoon to throw your reason that has led you into all kinds of doubt and fear, to throw it to the wind and say, "God, here goes. We trust in your omnipotence to put it over."

[1]In Psalm 8:4-5 the word "angel" is from the Hebrew "Elohiym" and it is the name of God in the first five chapters of Genesis.

8

The Spirit of God

I want to read to you one of the best incidents in the Word of God. It is the story of Elijah upon Mount Carmel (1 Kings 18:17-40).

In every land, among every people, throughout all history, there have been occasions when a demonstration of the power of God was just as necessary to the world as it was in the days of Elijah. It is necessary now.

The people had turned away from God. They had forgotten that there was a God in Israel. They were trusting in other gods, just as the people are today. If I were to call you heathen, I suppose most people would be offended; but I want to say that there are no people with more gods than the average American. Men are bowing down to the god of medicine. Men are bowing down to the god of popularity. Men are bowing down to this god and that god. Men are as afraid of the opinion of their neighbors as any heathen ever was in any time in the world. There is practically no Christian, let alone an un-christian, who has the real stamina to stand forth and declare his absolute convictions concerning Jesus Christ, the Son of God. Much less have men the necessary stamina to declare their convictions as to Jesus Christ, the Savior of mankind. That is the reason that the modern Church has lost her touch with God and has gone into a sleep unto death, a sleep that can only end in spiritual death and the disintegration of the church as she stands. The only power that will revive the church in this land and the world is that which she will receive when she throws her heart open to God as the people of Israel did and says, "Lord God, we have sinned." The sin she needs to repent of is not the committing a lot of little acts which men call sin and that are the out-growth of what is in the heart, but the thing that mankind needs to repent of is this...that they have denied the power of God and that He is the Almighty Savior. God's call to the Christian churches today is to come forth from their hiding place, just as Elijah came forth, and meet the king. Declare the ground on which you meet the enemies of God, and meet them in the Name of Jesus Christ.

The Christian Church is absolutely, solely and entirely to blame for the whole existence of metaphysical associations which are covering the earth like a plague of lice. The Church is to blame, for if the Church of Jesus Christ for the last 50 or 100 years had declared to mankind in the power of the Spirit the Christ of NAZARETH as He is, there never would have come into existence the whole tribe of metaphysical societies.

The world today is being taken by the metaphysical associations to such an extent that they are bowing before the metaphysical laws and calling them God. That is human nature and not God. The time has come when the Christian Church has got to give a new demonstration to the world. If metaphysicians, through the operation of natural laws, can produce a certain character and degree of healing, then it is up to the Church of Jesus Christ and the minister of the Son of God to demonstrate that there is a power in the blood of Jesus Christ to save men and heal men unto the UTTERMOST—not half healed or half the people healed; but I pray and believe that God's time has come for God's challenge to mankind and the challenge of the Christian Church to the world is to come on, and if it is God, let the FIRE FALL.

There was no bluffing with the old Israel prophets. When the people came, they laid their sacrifices on the altar, and they did not put artificial fire under it. But instead, the soul went down before God. He lifted his heart to heaven, and when the fire came down and consumed the sacrifice, that was the evidence that the sacrifice was accepted.

The time has come when God wants the fire to fall; and if you, my beloved brother and sister, will pay God's price and make Christ's consecration of yourself to God, we will see God's fire fall. And it will not be destructive either, except that sin and selfishness and sickness will wither under that fire, while purity and life and holiness and character will stand forth purified and refined by the glory and the power of the God-fire that comes from heaven. God's fire is creative of righteousness as well as destructive of sin.

Some years ago when I opened my work in South Africa and the Lord had moved marvelously for about six months, a movement was put on foot to congregate a crowd of Indian Yogi (The Indian Yogi are a society of people who utterly give themselves up to a demonstration of metaphysical things), Brahman priests, Buddhist priests, Confucian priests, and all kinds of priests and hypnotists. After a time they said, "We would like to have a demonstration."

And I said, "Yes, I would like to have a demonstration also. Come on with your Yogi and your Buddhas and your Confucians and hypnotists. Let them show their God. Let them heal people if they can. Let it be in the public, and let it be done on the platform of my tabernacle or any other place large enough to accommodate the public. Then when you have finished, we will call on the Christian's God and see what He will do."

Well, they came to the tabernacle to make the demonstration. One man, Professor Henerson, a professional hypnotist, was put forward. He said he was there to demonstrate what he could do through hypnotism. He brought with him as his subject a woman from Germiston who had a locked hip, probably from rheumatics or hip disease.

After he had tried and tried privately for months and publicly before the people, then I said, "Stand Off." Calling one of the brethren to pray with me, I said, "In the Name of the Lord Jesus Christ I command this hip to become unlocked." Instantly she was healed and walked. I want to tell you more of what God did. That was as far as my faith reached, but God met me at that point. As I stood looking at her, I said to myself, "That is the way Jesus did it when He was on the earth, and that is the way Jesus does it yet." It was Jesus who did it.

Well, as I stood looking at her, suddenly something came upon my soul from heaven. It was the anointing of the Spirit of God. I understood then what the blessed old Book talked about when it spoke of the Spirit of the Lord coming upon Elijah, and the Spirit of the Lord coming upon Samson, etc. Samson, under the power of the Spirit, took the gates of Gaza and carried them off [Judges 16:3]. He took the jawbone of an ass and killed a thousand men with it [Judges 15:16]. These were the things by which God endeavored to teach the world what the Spirit of the Lord is. Well, as I stood there, the Spirit fell upon me, not like the gentle dew of heaven but in power until my spirit towered up in such strength I did not know how to control it. In my heart I cried out, "My God, what does it mean?" When all at once I discovered the Spirit going out in operation to the spirit of that hypnotist. I said, "Are you the man who has been hypnotizing this woman for two years and grafting her hard-earned money? In the Name of Jesus Christ you will never hypnotize anyone else." Grasping him by the coat front, I struck him on the shoulder with my other hand, saying, "In the Name of the Son of God come out of him." And it came out. That hypnotic demon was gone out of him. He never hypnotized again but earned an honest living.

God is not the God of the dead. He is the God of the living. And the desire in my soul is that in this city God Almighty may raise up an altar unto the living God, not unto a dead God. Mankind needs an altar to the LIVING God, to the God that hears prayer, to the God that answers prayer, and the God that answers by fire. The time has come when God's challenge has gone forth. God is saying, "If there is a Christian, let him pray. If there is a God, let Him answer." God will meet the soul every time you turn to Him and meet Him face to face.

In emphasizing this, the Lord Jesus Christ says to the world, *"When ye pray, believe that ye receive them, and ye shall have them"* [Mark 11:24]. That is what is the matter. Your blank check is not worth ten cents in your hands. Why? Because you do not believe God. Fill in your check, believe God, and it will come to pass.

The call of Elijah is the call of the present hour. If the Christ is the Christ, get your answer from Him. If Jesus is the Son of God with power on the earth to forgive sins, then as Jesus put it, *"[Rise up and walk], that ye may know that the Son of man hath power on earth to forgive sins"* [Mark 2:10].

Jesus Christ was reasonable enough to meet man's reasonings and inquiries. And the minister of God who is afraid to walk out and believe his God and trust his God for results is no Christian at all.

What does Christianity mean to the world? Is it a hope for the glory land away off in the future? Is that Christianity? Is it a hope that you are not going to fry in hell all the days of your life? No! Christianity is the demonstration of the righteousness of God to the world.

So, brethren, God has given us something to do. He has given us a demonstration to make. If we do not make it, then we have no more right to the claims that we make of being sons of God than the other people. If God be God, serve Him; if Baal, then serve him.

Christ's Dominion

Every student of the primitive church discerns at once a distinction between the soul of the primitive Christian and the soul of the modern Christian. It lies in the spirit of Christ's Dominion.

The Holy Spirit came into the primitive Christian soul to elevate his consciousness in Christ, to make him a master. He smote sin and it disappeared. He cast out devils (demons); a divine flash from his nature overpowered and cast out the demon. He laid his hands on the sick, and the mighty Spirit of Jesus Christ flamed into the body and the disease was annihilated. He was commanded to rebuke the devil, and the devil would flee from him. He was a reigning sovereign, not shrinking in fear, but overcoming by faith.

It is this spirit of DOMINION when restored to the Church of Christ, that will bring again the glory-triumph to the Church of God throughout the world, and lift her into the place, where, instead of being the obedient servant of the world, and the flesh, and the devil, she will become the divine instrument of salvation in healing the sick, in the casting out of devils (demons), and in the carrying out of the whole program of Jesus' ministry, as the early Church did.

9

Spiritual Hunger

My text tonight is: *"Blessed are they which do hunger and thirst after righteousness: for they shall be filled"* (Matthew 5:6).

Hunger is a mighty good thing. It is the greatest persuader I know of. It is a marvelous mover. Nations have learned that you can do most anything with a populace until they get hungry. But when they get hungry you want to watch out. There is a certain spirit of desperation that accompanies hunger.

I wish we all had it spiritually. I wish to God we were desperately hungry for God. Wouldn't it be glorious? Somebody would get filled before this meeting is over. It would be a strange thing, if we were all desperately hungry for God, if only one or two got filled in a service.

"Blessed are they which do hunger."

Righteousness is just the rightness of God. The rightness of God in your spirit, the rightness of God in your soul, the rightness of God in your body, the rightness of God in your affairs, in your home, in your business, everywhere.

God is an all-round God. His power operates from every side. The artists paint a halo around the head of Jesus to show that there is a radiation of glory from His person. They might just as well put it around His feet or any part of His person. It is the radiant glory of the indwelling God, radiating out through the personality. There is nothing more wonderful than the indwelling of God in the human life. The supremest marvel that God ever performed was when He took possession of those who are hungry.

"Blessed are they which do hunger."

I will guarantee to you that after the Crucifixion of Jesus there were 120 mighty hungry folks at Jerusalem. I do not believe if they had not been mightily hungry they would have gotten so gloriously filled. It was because they were hungry that they were filled.

We are sometimes inclined to think of God as mechanical; as though God set a date for this event or that to occur. But my opinion is that one of the works of the Holy Ghost is that of preparer. He comes and prepares the heart of men in advance by putting a strange hunger for that event that has been promised by God until it comes to pass.

The more I study history and prophecy the more I am convinced that when Jesus Christ was born into the world He was born in answer to a tremendous heart-cry on the part of the world. The world needed God desperately. They wanted a manifestation of God tremendously, and Jesus Christ as the Deliverer and Savior came in answer to their soul cry.

Daniel says that he was convinced by the study of the books of prophecy, especially that of Jeremiah, that the time had come when they ought to be delivered from their captivity in Babylon. The seventy years was fulfilled but there was no deliverance. So he diligently set his face to pray it into being. (Daniel 9)

Here is what I want you to get. If it was going to come to pass mechanically on a certain date, there would not have been any necessity for Daniel to get that awful hunger in his soul, so that he fasted and prayed in sackcloth and ashes, that the deliverance might come.

No sir, God's purposes come to pass when your heart and mine get the real God-cry and the real God-prayer comes into our spirit, and the real God-yearning gets hold of our nature. Something is going to happen then.

No difference what it may be your soul is coveting or desiring, *if it becomes in your life the supreme cry,* not the secondary matter, or the third, or the fourth, or fifth or tenth, but the FIRST thing, *the supreme desire of your soul;* the paramount issue, all the powers and energies of your spirit, of your soul, of your body are reaching out and crying to God for the answer, it is going to come, it is going to come, it is going to come.

I lived in a family where for thirty-two years they never were without an invalid in the home. Before I was twenty-four years of age we had buried four brothers and four sisters, and four other members of the family were dying, hopeless, helpless invalids. I set up my own home, married a beautiful woman. Our first son was born. It was only a short time until I saw that same devilish train of sickness that had followed my father's family had come into mine. My wife became an invalid, my son was a sickly child. Out of it all one thing developed in my nature, a cry for deliverance. I did not know any more about the subject of healing than an Indian*, notwithstanding I was a Methodist evangelist. But my heart was crying for deliverance; my soul had come to the place where I had vomited up dependence on man. My father had spent a fortune on the family, to no avail, as if there was no stoppage to the train of hell. And let me tell you, there IS NO HUMAN STOPPAGE because the thing is settled deep in the nature of man; too deep for any material remedy to get at it. It takes the Almighty God and the Holy Spirit and the Lord Jesus Christ to get down into the depth of man's nature and find the real difficulty that is there and destroy it.

My brother, I want to tell you, if you are a sinner tonight and away from God, and your heart is longing, and your spirit asking, and your soul crying for God's deliverance, he will be on hand to deliver. You will not have to cry very long until you see that the mountains are being moved, and the angel of deliverance will be there.

I finally got to that place where my supreme cry was for deliverance, tears were shed for deliverance for three years before the healing of God came to us. I could hear the groans and cries and sobs, and feel the wretchedness of our family's soul. My heart cried, my soul sobbed, my spirit wept tears. I wanted help, I did not know enough to call directly on God for it. Isn't it a strange thing that men do not have sense enough to have faith in God for all their needs; do not know enough to call directly on God for physical difficulties, as well as for spiritual ones? But I did not.

But, bless God, one thing matured in my heart, a real hunger. And the hunger of a man's soul must be satisfied, it MUST be satisfied. It is a law of God; that law of God is in the depth of the

Spirit. God will answer the heart that cries; God will answer the soul that asks. Christ Jesus comes to us with divine assurance and invites us when we are hungry to PRAY, to BELIEVE, to take from the Lord that which our soul covets and our heart asks for.

So one day the Lord of heaven came our way, and in a little while the cloud of darkness, that midnight of hell, that curse of death was lifted, and the light of God shone into our life and into our home, just the same as it existed in other men's lives and other men's homes. We learned the truth of Jesus and were able to apply the divine power of God. We were healed of the Lord.

"Blessed are they which do hunger."

Brethren, begin to pray to get hungry.

At this point I want to tell you a story. I was out on a snow-shoe trip at Sault Ste. Marie, Michigan where they used to have four and five feet of snow. I tramped for thirty miles on my snow shoes. I was tired and weary. I arrived home and found my wife had gone away to visit, so I went over to my sister's home. I found they were out also. I went into the house and began to look for something to eat. I was nearly starved. I found a great big sort of cake that looked like corn bread. It was still quite warm and it smelled good, I ate it all. I thought it was awful funny stuff, and it seemed to have lumps in it. I did not just understand the combination, and I was not much of a cook. About the time I had finished it my sister and her husband came in. She said, "My you must be awful tired and hungry."

I said, "I was, but I just found a corn cake and ate the whole thing."

She said, "My goodness, John, you did not eat that?"

I said, "What was it, Irene?"

"Why that was a kind of cow bread, we grind up cobs and all."

You see it depends on the character and degree of your hunger. Things taste mighty good to a hungry man.

If you wanted to confer a peculiar blessing on men at large, it would not be to give them pie, but to make them hungry, and then every thing that came their way would taste everlastingly good.

I love to tell this story because it is the story of a hungry man. A short time after I went to South Africa and God had begun to work very marvelously in the city of Johannesburg, a butcher who lived in the suburbs was advised by his physicians that he had developed such a tubercular state he might not live more than nine months. He wanted to make provision that his family would be cared for after he was gone, so he bought a farm and undertook to develop it that when he died his family would have a means of existence.

One day he received a letter from friends at Johannesburg telling of the coming of what they spoke of as "the American brethren", and of the wonderful things that were taking place. Of how So-and-So, a terrible drunkard had been converted; of his niece who had been an invalid in a wheel chair for five years had been healed of God; how one of his other relatives had been baptized in the Holy Ghost and was speaking in tongues; other friends and neighbors had been baptized and healed, of the powerful change that had come in the community, and all the marvels a vigorous work for God produces.

Dan Von Vuuren took the letter, crawled under an African thorn tree. He spread the letter out before God, and began to discuss it with the Lord. He said, "God in heaven, if You could come to Mr. So-and-so, a drunkard and deliver him from his sin and save his soul and put the joy of God in him; if You could come to this niece of mine, save her soul and heal her body and send her out to be a blessing instead of a weight and burden upon her friends; if You could come to So-and-so and they were baptized in the Holy Ghost and speak in tongues; Lord, if You can do these things at Johannesburg, You can do something for me too." And he knelt down, put his face to the ground, and cried to God that God would do something for him. And don't forget it, friends, I have a conviction that that morning Dan Von Vuuren was so stirred by the reading of that letter that his desire to be made whole got bigger than any thing else in his consciousness. His heart reached for God, and bless God, that morning his prayer went through to heaven and God came down into his life. In ten minutes he took all the breath he wanted; the pain was gone, the tuberculosis had disappeared, he was a whole man.

But that was not all. He not only received a great physical healing, but God had literally come in and taken possession of the man's life until he did not understand himself any more. In telling me he said, "Brother, a new prayer from heaven was born in my spirit. I had prayed for my wife's salvation for eighteen years, but I could never pray through. But that morning I prayed through. It was all done when I got to the house. She stood and looked at me for two minutes, until it dawned in her soul that I was gloriously healed of God. She never asked a question as to how it took place, but fell on her knees, threw her hands up to heaven, and said, 'Pray for me, Dan, for God's sake pray for me. I must find God today,' and God came to that soul."

He had eleven children, splendid young folks. The mother and he went to praying and inside of a week the whole household of thirteen had been baptized in the Holy Ghost. He went to his brother's farm, told the wonder of what God had done, prayed through and in a little while nineteen families were baptized in the Holy Ghost.

God so filled his life with His glory that one morning God said to him, "Go to Pretoria. I am going to send you to the different members of Parliament." He was admitted into the presence of Premier Louis Botha. Botha told me about it afterwards. He said, "Lake, I had known Von Vuuren from the time he was a boy. I had known him as a reckless, rollicking fellow. But that man came into my office and stood ten feet from my desk. I looked up, and before he commenced to speak I began to shake and rattle on my chair. I knelt down, I had to put my head under the desk and cry to God. Why he looked like God. He talked like God. He had the majesty of God. He was superhumanly wonderful." Then he went to the office of the Secretary of State, then to the Secretary of the Treasury. Almost the same thing took place in every instance. For eighteen days God kept him going from this one to that one; lawyers, judges and officials in the land, until every high official in the land knew there was a God and a Christ and a Savior, and a Baptism of the Holy Ghost, because Dan Von Vuuren had really hungered after God.

"Blessed are they which do hunger."

I was sitting here tonight before the meeting began reading an old sermon I preached to a men's club at Spokane, Washington eight years ago, entitled "The Calling of the Soul." [See Chapter 13.] In it I observed I recounted the story of the original people who came to the Parham School in 1909, and whom in answer to the cry of their soul God came and baptized them in the Holy Ghost. All the Apostolic Faith Churches, Missions, Assemblies of God, and other movements are the result.

I knew Brother Parham's wife and his sister-in-law, Lillian Thistleweight. She was the woman that brought the light of God for real sanctification to my heart. It was not her preaching or her words. I sat in Fred Bosworth's home one night before Fred thought of preaching the gospel. I listened to that woman telling of the Lord God and His love and sanctifying grace and power and what real holiness was. It was not her arguments or logic, it was herself, it was the divine holiness that came from her soul. It was the living Spirit of God that came out of the woman's life. I sat way back in the room, as far away as I could get. I was self satisfied, doing well in the world, prosperous with all the accompaniments that go with successful life. But that night my heart got so hungry that I fell on my knees, and those who were present will tell you yet that they had never heard anybody pray as I prayed. Bosworth said long afterward, "Lake, there is one instance that I shall always remember in your life. That was the night you prayed in my home until the rafters shook, until God came down, until the fire struck, until our souls melted, until God came in and sanctified our hearts." All the devils in hell and out of hell could not make me believe there is not a real sanctified experience in Jesus Christ; when God comes in and makes your heart pure and takes self out of your nature, and gives you divine triumph over sin and self, blessed be the Name of the Lord!

"Blessed are they which do hunger."

Beloved, pray to get hungry.

Coming back to Dan Von Vuuren. For several years before I left Africa he went up and down the land like a burning fire. Everywhere he went sinners were saved, sick were healed, men and women were baptized in the Holy Ghost, until he set the outlying districts on fire with the power of God—and he is going still.

Here is a point I want to bring to you. As I talked with Lillian Thistleweight, I observed the one supreme thing in that woman's soul was the consciousness of holiness. She said, "Brother, that is what we prayed for, that is what the baptism brought to us."

Later Brother Parham was preaching in Texas. A colored man* came into his meeting by the name of Seymour. In a hotel in Chicago he related his experience to Brother Tom and myself. I want you to see the hunger in that colored man's* soul. He said he was a waiter in a restaurant and preaching to a church of colored people.* He knew God as Savior, as the sanctifier. He knew the power of God to heal. But as he listened to Parham he became convinced of a bigger thing, the Baptism of the Holy Ghost. He went on to Los Angeles without receiving it, but he said he was determined to preach all of God he knew to the people. He said, "Brother, before I met Parham, such a hunger to have more of God was in my heart that I prayed for five hours a day for two and a half years. I got to Los Angeles, and when I got there the hunger was not less but more. I prayed, God, what can I do? And the Spirit said, pray more. But Lord, I am praying five hours a day now. I increased my hours of prayer to seven, and prayed on for a year and a half more. I prayed God to give me what Parham preached, the real Holy Ghost and fire with tongues and love and power of God like the apostles had." There are better things to be had in spiritual life but they must be sought out with faith and prayer. I want to tell you God Almighty had put such a hunger into that Negro's* heart that when the fire of God came it glorified him. I do not believe that any other man in modern times had a more wonderful deluge of God in his life than God gave to that dear fellow. Brother Seymore preached to my congregation, to ten thousand people, when the glory and power of God was upon his spirit, when men shook and trembled and cried to God. God was in him.

"Blessed are they which do hunger...for they shall be filled."

I wonder what we are hungering for? Have we a real divine hunger, something our soul is asking for? If you have God will answer, God will answer. By every law of the Spirit that men know, the answer is due to come. It will come! Bless God, it will come. It will come in more ways than you ever dreamed of. God is not confined to manifesting himself in tongues and interpretation alone. His life in man is rounded.

When I was a lad, I accompanied my father on a visit to the office of John A. McCall, the great insurance man. We were taken to McCall's office in his private elevator. It was the first time I had ever been in a great office building, and ridden on an elevator, and I remember holding my breath until the thing stopped. Then we stepped into his office, the most beautiful office I had ever beheld. The rugs were so thick I was afraid I would go through the floor when I stepped on them. His desk was a marvel, pure mahogany, and on the top of his desk, inlaid in mother of pearl, was his name, written in script. It was so magnificent that in my boyish soul I said, "I'm going to have an office just like this and a desk like that with my name on it when I am a man."

I did not know how much of an asking it was in my nature, and it seemed sometimes that it had drifted away, until I was in my thirtieth year. I was invited to come to Chicago to join an association of men who were establishing a Life Insurance Association. They said, "Lake, we want you to manage this Association." We dickered about the matter for three weeks until they came to my terms, and finally the president said, "Step into this office until we show you something. We have a surprise for you." And I stepped into an office just exactly the duplicate of John A. McCall's office, and there in the center was a desk of pure mahogany, and instead of the name of John A. McCall, it was John G. Lake, in mother of pearl. I had never spoken of that soul desire to a person in the world.

Friends, there is a something in the call of the soul that is creative. It brings things to pass. Don't you know that when the supreme desire of your heart goes out to God, that all the spiritual energy of your nature and the powers of God that come to you begin to concentrate and work along that certain line, and form and there comes by the unconscious creative exercise of faith into being that which your soul calls for. That is the creative action of faith, you and God together working out and evidencing the power of creative desire.

> Ye shall receive the desire of your heart if you come before Me in prayer and supplication, for I am a God that answers my children. Go ye forward in the battle for I shall be with you and fulfill the desire of your heart. Yea, pray that ye may become hungry.
>
> Call and I shall answer, for I am a God that hears. I shall answer your call. Come before Me; humble yourselves before My feet, and I shall answer your call.
>
> Be ye diligent before Me, and pray, yea, be ye in prayer and supplication, for ye are living in the last days, and my Spirit shall not always strive with men. But ye that humble yourselves before me will know I shall be your God, I shall strengthen you on the right hand and on the left, and ye shall understand and know that I am your living God.

Tongues and Interpretation
Mrs. James Wilson - Brother Myreen

When Moses stood at the Red Sea he tried to back out of that relationship God was establishing and tried to throw the responsibility back on God. He was overwhelmed. It was too marvelous, surely God must not have meant it, but God knew. When he began to recognize himself as an individual and God as another it was offensive to God. He thought he could back up and pray for God to do something for him the same as God used to do in the old relationship. He could not do it. When he got down to pray, in the mind of God the idea of Moses not backing water and getting out of that close place, that inner relationship, that divine symphony of Moses' soul and God's, it was offensive to Him. And God said, *"Wherefore criest thou unto me?"* [Exodus 14:15]. In other words, shut up your praying. Get up out of there.

*Kenneth Copeland Publications acknowledges that references to race and nationality considered acceptable in the Rev. Lake's day are offensive and not acceptable to today's reader. However, these references in no way reflect the attitude or policies of KCP. To fully understand Rev. Lake's heart toward other races, we recommend you read his biography located at the front of the book.

10

Christ Liveth in Me

That is the text, *"Christ liveth in me."* That is the revelation of this age. That is the discovery of the moment. That is the revolutionizing power of God in the earth. It is the factor that is changing the spirit of religion in the world and the character of Christian faith. It is divine vitalization.

The world is awakening to that marvelous truth, that Christ is not in the heavens only, nor in the atmosphere only, but Christ is IN YOU.

The world lived in darkness for thousands of years. There was just as much electricity in the world then as now. It is not that electricity has just come into being. It was always here. But men have discovered how to utilize it and bless themselves with it.

Christ's indwelling in the human heart is the mystery of mysteries. Paul gave it to the Gentiles as the supreme mystery of all the revelation of God and the finality of all wonder he knew. "Christ in you. Christ in YOU."

Christ has a purpose in you. Christ's purpose in YOU is to reveal Himself to you, through you, in you. We repeat over and over that familiar phrase, *"The church, Which is His body"* [Ephesians 1:22-23], but if we realized the truth of it and power of it, this world would be a different place. When the Christian church realizes that they are the tangible, living, pulsating body—flesh and bones and blood and brain of Jesus Christ—and that God is manifesting through each one every minute, and is endeavoring to accomplish His big will for the world through them, not through some other body, then Christian service and responsibility will be understood. Jesus Christ operates through you. He does not operate independently of you, He operates through you. Man and God become united. That is the divine secret of a real Christian life. It is the real union, the real conscious union of man and God. There is no substitute for that relationship. You can manufacture all the ordinances on earth, all the symbols there ever were until you become dazed and you lose yourself in the maze of them, and still you must still find God.

There is only one reality. That reality is God. The soul of man must contact God, and unless the spirit of man is truly joined to God, there is no such thing as real Christian manifestation. All the processes of preparation, but which a soul is prepared by God for such a manifestation, are only preliminary processes. The final end is that man may reveal God and that God may not only have a place of residence, but a right action in the body and spirit of man. Every Spirit-taught man in the world is aware of how gradually his own nature has become subjected to God and His will.

I was visiting with a gentleman who had a grouch on me. He said, "I wrote you a twenty-four page letter, and you have not received it. If you had, you would not be here."

I laughed. That man has been a Christian for thirty or forty years, always a devout man, and I have spoken of him frequently to my wife and my friends as one of the most consistent Christian men I ever knew. Yet every once in a while we see how the big human just rises up above the spirit and spoils the beauty and delight and wonder of the life that is revealing God.

God's effort and God's purpose in us is to bring all the conditions of our being into harmony with His will and His mind. God's purpose is not to make an automaton. We see a ventriloquist operating a little wooden dummy, and the wooden dummy's lips move and it looks as though it is talking. It is just moving because another power is moving it.

Now God has a higher purpose than making man an automaton. God's highest is to bring out all the qualities of God in your own soul, to bring out all the individuality that is in your life, not to submerge or destroy, but to change it, to energize it, to enlarge it, until all your individuality and personality and being are of the nature and substance and quality of God.

You notice among the most devout Christians how continuously their thought is limited to that place where they can be exercised or moved by God. But God's best is more than that. Receive the Spirit, then use the Spirit for God's glory.

While I was in Chicago, I met a couple of old friends who invited me to dinner. While at dinner the lady, who is a very frank woman, said: "Mr. Lake, I have known you so long and have had such close fellowship for so many years, I am able to speak very frankly."

I said, "Yes, absolutely."

"Well," she said, "there is something I miss about you. For lack of words I am going to put it in Paul's words, *'I bear in my body the marks of the Lord Jesus'* [Galatians 6:17]. You do not seem to have the marks of Jesus."

I said, "That depends whether or not it is the marks of mannerisms. If you are expecting that the personality that God gave me is going to be changed so that I am going to be another fellow and not myself, then you will miss it. If that is the kind of marks you are looking for you will not find them. But if you are expecting to observe a man's flesh and blood and bones and spirit and mind indwelt by God, then you will find them—not a machine, not an automaton, or an imitation, but a clear mind and a pure heart, a son of God in nature and essence."

What is all God's effort with the world but to bring out the real man in the image of Christ, that real man with the knowledge of God. That real man, reconstructed until his very substance is the substance of God. And when you stop to reason that to its proper conclusion, that is the only way that Jesus Christ Himself or God the eternal Father will have fellowship with man forever.

When one stops to analyze that fact, we see that God is trying to make us in all our nature and being and habits and thought, in all the structure of our life, just as beautiful and just as real and just as clear minded and just as strong as Jesus Himself. Then we understand what Christ's redemption means. It is the bringing out of Christ IN YOU, until Christ in you is the One manifest—manifest through your eyes just as God was manifest through the eyes of Jesus; manifest through your touch just as God was manifest through Jesus. It is not a power nor a life separate from yourself but two lives made one, two natures co-joined, two minds operating as one, Christ in YOU.

In the Chicago conference I sat with an old colored* lady one afternoon after meeting, and she told me of her woes and sicknesses—and they were many. After a time when she had grown somewhat still, I said, "Dear Mother, how long have you been a Christian?"

She replied, "Since I was a child."

Then I tried to show her that God expected a development of God and His nature and the working and action of God in her in transforming power through the agency of the Holy Spirit, and that there was a process of remaking and remolding that should change her nature and life, and dissolve the rheumatism and Bright's disease and all the other difficulties, just as truly as long ago sin dissolved out of her soul.

After the conversation had gone on to the proper point, I said, "Dear Sister, anybody can see that Christ dwells in your spirit." Her eyes were lovely, delightful. "Let your mind extend just a little bit. Let your thought comprehend that just as Jesus dwells in your spirit and also possesses your soul, in just exactly the same way He is possessing your blood and your kidneys and your old rheumatic bones, and that the very same thing will happen in your bones when you realize that truth as happened in your spirit when you were converted at the altar."

(She told me how she had prayed twenty-two days and nights until Christ was revealed in her soul as Savior. She seemed to want to wait twenty-two days and nights for God to manifest Himself in the rheumatic bones, and I was trying to get her away from it.) She said, "Brother, lay your hands on me and pray for me, and I will be healed."

I answered, "No, I want you to get well by realizing that right now that same Christ that dwells in your spirit and your soul is in your bones and in your blood and in your brain." Presently the old lady hopped to her feet and said, "My God, He is." She had it. Christ had been imprisoned in her soul and spirit, now He was permitted to manifest in her body.

Brother Tom Hezmalhalch came into a Negro* meeting in Los Angeles one day where they were talking about the Baptism of the Holy Ghost. He had picked up a paper and read of these peculiar meetings, and among other things that they spoke in tongues. That was new to him. He said, "If they do, and if it is real, that is an advance in the Spirit of God beyond what is common. I am going to get it." He went, and listened as the old black boy* taught. He was trying to develop the thought of conscious cleansing, and he used a beautiful text: "Now ye are clean through the Word which I have spoken unto you." That became very real to Tom, and after a while they were invited to come and kneel at the altar to seek God for the baptism of the Spirit.

Tom said unto me, "John, I got up and walked toward that old bench with the realization in my soul of the truth of the Word, and that the real cleansing and cleanser was in my heart. Now are ye clean through the Word which I have spoken unto you."

He knelt down and he prayed for a minute or two, his soul arose and his heart believed for the Baptism of the Holy Ghost. Then he arose and took one of the front seats. One of the workers said, "Brother, don't stop praying until you are baptized in the Holy Ghost."

Mr. Seymour said, "Just leave him alone. He has got it. You wait and see." A few days passed, and one day Tom said the Spirit began to surge through him, and a song of praise in tongues, angelic voice, broke through his lips.

An old preacher came into my office in Africa and said, "Brother Lake, there is something I want to talk to you about. There used to be a very remarkable manifestation in my life. It was the manifestation of tongues and interpretation. But I have not spoken for a year. I wish you would pray for me."

I said, "No, go over and lie down and get still and let God move in your life." I went on writing a letter. Presently I observed that something wanted to speak in me, and I turned my head just a little to see that the old man was speaking in tongues and I was getting the interpretation of it as I wrote the letter.

Don't you know Christians are stumbling every day over that fact. You are doubting and fearing and wondering if Christ is there. Beloved brother and sister give Him a chance to reveal Himself. He is there. Probably because of your lack of realization your soul is closed and He is not able to reveal Himself. You know God is never able in many to reveal Himself outside of the spirit or soul. The real secret of the ministry of healing is in permitting the grace of God in your heart to flow out through your hands and your nerves into the outer life. That is the real secret. And one of the greatest works God has to perform is to subject our flesh to God. Many Christians, the deepest Christians who really know

God in their spirits and enjoy communion with God, are compelled to wait until there is a process of spiritualization takes place in their bodies before God can reveal Himself through them. Do not imprison Christ in you. Let Him live, let Him manifest, let Him vent through you.

There is one great thing that the world is needling more than anything else, and I am convinced of it every day I live. Mankind has one supreme need, and that is the LOVE of God. The hearts of men are dying for lack of the love of God. I have a sister in Detroit. She came over to Milwaukee to visit us for two or three days at the convention there. As I watched her moving around, I said, "I would like to take her along and just have her love folks." She would not need to preach. You do not need to preach to folks. It is not the words you say that is going to bless them. They need something greater. It is the thing in your soul. They have got to receive it, then their soul will open and there will be a divine response. Give it to them, it is the love of God.

You have seen people who loved someone who would not respond. If there is any hard situation in God's earth, that is it, to really passionately love someone and find no response in them.

I had an English friend and was present at his marriage. Some years later he and his wife came to visit our home. He was the cold type of closed up Englishman, and his wife was the warm type. One day they started out for a walk, and I noticed the passionate yearning in her soul. If he would just say something that was tender, something that would gratify the craving of her nature for affection: but he seemed to go along absolutely unconscious of it. After a while they came back from their walk. I was sitting on the front steps. After the lady had gone into the house, I said, "Hibbs, you are a stiff. How is it possible that you can walk down the street with a woman like your wife and not realize that her heart is craving and crying for you to turn around and do something that shows you love her?"

He said, "Do you think that is the difficulty? I will go and do it now." And everything subsided while he proceeded to do it.

What is it men are seeking? What is it their hearts are asking for when they are seeking God? What is their soul crying for? Mankind is separated from God. It may not be mountains of sin between you and God at all. It may be that your nature is closed and unresponsive. My! When the real love touch of God is breathed into your soul, what a transformation takes place.

There is probably no more delightful thing on earth than to watch a soul praying to God, when the light of God comes on and the life of God fills the nature and that holy affection that we seek from others finds expression in Him.

That is what the Lord is asking from you; and if you want to gratify the heart of Jesus Christ, that is the only way in all the world to do it. You know the invitation is not "Give Me thine head." The invitation is, "My son, give Me thine heart." That is an affectionate relationship, a real love union in God. Think of the fineness of God's purpose. He expects that same marvelous spiritual union that is brought to pass between your soul and His own to be extended so that you embrace in that union every other soul around you.

Oh, that is what it means when it talks about being baptized in one spirit, submerged, buried, enveloped and enveloping in the one Spirit of God.

While I was in Milwaukee recently, I went out one morning with Rev. Fockler to make a call on a sick person. We stepped into one of the most distracted homes I have ever been in. A strange condition had developed in one of the daughters, and the household was distressed. They were the saddest group. They were German people. Fockler speaks German. Presently he began to talk to the household. I just sat back and watched. Presently I noticed the faces began to relax and the strain was gone. The girl was apparently insane. She came down the stairs, stood outside the door where she could not be seen except by me. He continued to converse with the family, and as their souls softened and their faith lifted, her eyes commenced to change. She was moved upon by the same Spirit until her nature responded, and in just a little while she stepped into the room. She had tormented that household. Nobody could get near her. She slipped up behind Fockler's chair, stood with her hands on the back of the chair. He understood and disregarded. After a little while she put the other hand on the other shoulder. And in fifteen or twenty minutes we left that home and there was just as much distinction between the attitude of those dear people when we came in and left as between heaven and hell. If hell has a characteristic, it is that of distraction. If heaven has a particular characteristic, it is the presence of God, the calm of God, the power of God, the love of God.

There were days when the Church could club men into obedience by preaching hell to them, but that day has long passed.

The world has outgrown it. And men are discovering there is only one way and that is the Jesus way. Jesus did not come with a club, but with the great loving heart of the Son of God. He was *"moved with compassion"* [Matthew 9:36, Matthew 14:14, Mark 1:41].

This morning I lay in bed and wrote a letter, an imaginary letter to a certain individual. I was getting ready so that when I came down I could dictate the sentences that would carve him right. One of the phrases was, "You great big calf, come out of it and be a man." As I lay there I got to thinking, *If Jesus was writing this letter, I wonder what He would write?* But somehow it would not frame. My soul was not in an attitude to produce such a letter. So I came down this morning and called Edna and commenced to dictate, and I was trying to dictate a letter in the Spirit of Jesus. Presently I woke up to the fact that I was putting the crimp into it like a lawyer. After she had written and laid it down for me to sign, I commenced to read it over. It was not what I wanted to write at all. The first two paragraphs had a touch of the right spirit but that was all. So I laid it aside. Then I went in and prayed a little while. After I had been praying for twenty minutes, the telephone rang. It was that fellow. He wanted me to come down to the Davenport Hotel. We had three of the best hours without being aware of the time.

We boast of our development in God, we speak glowingly of our spiritual experiences, but it is only once in a while that we find ourselves in the real love of God. The greater part of the time we are in ourselves rather than in Him. That evidences just one thing, that Christ has not yet secured that perfect control of our life, that subjection of our nature, that absorption of our individuality, so that He is able to impregnate it and maintain it in Himself. We recede, we draw back, we close up. We imprison our Lord.

The secret of a religious meeting is that it assists men's hearts to open. They become receptive, and the love of God finds vent in their nature for a little while and they go away saying, "Didn't we have a good time? Wasn't that a splendid meeting?"

I wonder if there is anything that could not be accomplished through that love of God. Paul says there is not. *"Charity [love] never faileth"* [1 Corinthians 13:8]. That is one infallible state. Try it on your wife, try it on your children, try it on your neighbors.

Ah, sometimes we need to get things over on to the bigger love, the greater heart. It is a good thing to detach your soul. Do not hold people. Do not bind people. Just cut them loose and let God love them. Don't you know we hold people with such a grip when we pray for them that they miss the blessing. Why, you have such a grip on your humanity that it is exercising itself and the spirit is being submerged. Let your soul relax and let the Spirit of God in you find vent. There is no substitute for the love of God. *"Christ in you"* [Colossians 1:27]. Oh, you have the capacity to love. All the action of the Spirit of God has its secret there.

I stood on one occasion by a dying woman who was suffering and writhing in awful agony. I had prayed again and again with no results. But this day something just happened inside of me. My soul broke clear down, and I saw that poor soul in a new light. Before, I knew it I reached out and gathered her in my arms and hugged her up to my soul, not my bosom. In a minute I knew the real thing had taken place. I laid her back down on the pillow. In five minutes she was well. God was waiting on men, until He could get to my soul the sense of that tenderness that was in the Son of God.

That is the reason that His Name is written in imperishable memory. And the Name of Jesus Christ is the most revered Name in earth or sea or sky. And I am eager to get in that category of folks who can manifest the real love of God all the time.

The real Christian is a SEPARATED man. He is separated forever unto God in ALL the departments of his life. So his BODY, so his SOUL and his SPIRIT are forever committed to God the Father. From the time he commits himself to God, his BODY is as absolutely in the hands of God as his spirit or his soul. He can go to no other power for help or healing.

An hundredfold consecration takes the individual forever out of the hands of all but God. "Ye are not your own."

*Kenneth Copeland Publications acknowledges that references to race and nationality considered acceptable in Rev. Lake's day are offensive and not acceptable to today's reader. However, these references in no way reflect the attitude or policies of KCP. To fully understand Rev. Lake's heart toward other races, we recommend you read his biography located at the front of the book.

11

A Trumpet Call

The 13th chapter of Acts tells us the story of the ordination and sending forth of the Apostle Paul, his ordination to the apostleship. Paul never writes of himself as an apostle until after the 13th chapter of Acts. He had been an evangelist and teacher for thirteen years when the 13th chapter of Acts was written, and the ordination took place that is recorded there. Men who have a real call are not afraid of apprenticeships.

There is a growing up in experience in the ministry. When Paul started out in the ministry he was definitely called of God and was assured of God through Ananias that it would not be an easy service but a terrific one: for God said to Ananias:

> **Arise, and go into the street which is called Straight, and inquire in the house of Judas for one called Saul, of Tarsus: for, behold, he prayeth...he is a chosen vessel unto me, to bear my name before the Gentiles, and kings, and the children of Israel: For I will show him how great things he must suffer for my name's sake (Acts 9:11, 15-16).**

That is what Jesus Christ, the crucified and glorified Son of God told Ananias to say to the Apostle Paul. He was not going to live in a holy ecstasy and wear a beautiful halo, and have a heavenly time and ride in a limousine. He was going to have a drastic time, a desperate struggle, a terrific experience. And no man in biblical history ever had more dreadful things to endure than the Apostle Paul. He gives a list in his letter to the Corinthians of the things he had endured.

> **Of the Jews five times received I forty stripes save one. Thrice was I beaten with rods, once was I stoned, thrice I suffered shipwreck, a night and a day I have been in the deep; In journeyings often, in perils of waters, in perils of robbers, in perils by mine own countrymen, in perils by the heathen, in perils in the city, in perils in the wilderness, in perils in the sea, in perils among false brethren; In weariness and painfulness, in watchings often, in hunger and thirst, in fastings often, in cold and nakedness (2 Corinthians 11:24-27).**

They stripped him of his clothing, and the executioner lashed him with an awful scourge, until bleeding and lacerated and broken, he fell helpless, and unconscious and insensible; then they doused him with a bucket of salt water to keep the maggots off, and threw him into a cell to recover. That was the price of apostleship. That was the price of the call of God and His service. But God said, *"bear my name before the Gentiles, and kings, and the children of Israel"* (Acts 9:15). He qualified as God's messenger.

Beloved, we have lost the character of consecration here manifested. God is trying to restore it in our day. He has not been able to make much progress with the average preacher on that line. "Mrs. So-and-So said so-and-so, and I am just not going to take it." That is the kind of preacher with another kind of call, not the heaven call, not the God call, not the death call if necessary. That is not the kind the Apostle Paul had.

Do you want to know why God poured out His Spirit in South Africa like He did nowhere else in the world? There was a reason. This example will illustrate. We had one hundred and twenty-five men out on the field at one time. We were a very young institution; were not known in the world. South Africa is seven thousand miles from any European country. It is ten thousand miles by way of England to the United States. Our finances got so low under the awful assault we were compelled to endure, that there came a time I could not even mail to these workers at the end of the month a ten dollar bill. It got so I could not send them $2. The situation was desperate. What was I to do? Under these circumstances I did not want to take the responsibility of leaving men and their families on the frontier without real knowledge of what the conditions were.

Some of us at headquarters sold our clothes in some cases, sold certain pieces of furniture out of the house, sold anything we could sell, to bring those hundred and twenty-five workers off the field for a conference.

One night in the progress of the conference I was invited by a committee to leave the room for a minute or two. The conference wanted to have a word by themselves. So I stepped out to a restaurant for a cup of coffee, and came back. When I came in I found they had rearranged the chairs in an oval, with a little table at one end, and on the table was the bread and the wine. Old Father Van de Wall, speaking for the company said, "Brother Lake, during your absence we have come to a conclusion; we have made our decision. We want you to serve the Lord's Supper. We are going back to our fields. We are going back if we have to walk back. We are going back if we have to starve. We are going back if our wives die. We are going back if our children die. We are going back if we die ourselves. We have but one request. If we die, we want you to come and bury us."

The next year I buried twelve men, 16 wives and 9 children. In my judgment not one of the twelve, if they had had a few of the things a white man needs to eat, but what might have lived. Friends, when you want to find out why the power of God came down from heaven in South Africa like it never came down before since the times of the apostles, there is your answer.

Jesus Christ put the spirit of martyrdom in the ministry. Jesus instituted His ministry with a pledge unto death. When He was with the disciples on the last night He took the cup, *"when He had supped, saying"* [1 Corinthians 11:25]. Beloved, the SAYING was the significant thing. It was Jesus Christ's pledge to the twelve who stood with Him, *"This cup is the new testament in my blood"* (1 Corinthians 11:25). Then He said, *"Drink ye all of it"* (Matthew 26:27).

Friends, those who were there and drank to that pledge of Jesus Christ, entered into the same covenant and purpose that He did. That is what all pledges mean. Men have pledged themselves in the wine cup from time immemorial. Generals have pledged their armies unto death. It has been a custom in the race. Jesus Christ sanctified it to the church forever, bless God.

"My blood of the new testament." "Drink ye all of it." Let us become one. Let us become one in our purpose to die for the world. Your blood and mine together. *"My blood of the New Testament."* It is my demand from you. It is your high privilege.

Dear friends, there is not an authentic history that can tell us whether any one of them died a natural death. We know that at least nine of them were martyrs, possibly all. Peter died on a cross. James was beheaded, for Thomas they did not even wait to make a cross...they nailed him to an olive tree. John was sentenced to be executed at Ephesus by putting him in a caldron of boiling oil. God delivered him, and his executioners refused to repeat the operation, and he was banished to the Isle of Patmos. John thought so little about it that he never even tells of the incident. He says, *"I...was in the isle that is called Patmos, for the word of God, and for the testimony of Jesus Christ"* [Revelation 1:9]. That was explanation enough. He had committed himself to Jesus Christ for life or death.

Friends, the group of missionaries that followed me went without food, and went without clothes, and once when one of my preachers was sunstruck, and had wandered away, I tracked him by the blood marks of his feet. Another time I was hunting for one of my missionaries, a young Englishman, 22 years of age. He had come from a line of Church of England preachers for five hundred years. When I arrived at the native village the old native chief said, "He is not here. He went over the mountains, and you know, mister, he is a white man and he has not learned to walk barefooted."

That is the kind of consecration that established Pentecost in South Africa. That is the reason we have a hundred thousand native Christians in South Africa. That is the reason we have 1,250 native preachers. That is the reason we have 350 white churches in South Africa. That is the reason that today we are the most rapidly growing church in South Africa.

I am not persuading you, dear friends, by holding out a hope that the way is going to be easy. I am calling you in the Name of

Jesus Christ, you dear ones who expect to be ordained to the gospel of Jesus Christ tonight, take the route that Jesus took, the route the apostles took, the route that the early church took, the victory route, whether by life or death. Historians declare, "The blood of the martyrs was the seed of the church." Beloved, that is what the difficulty is in our day...we have so little seed. The church needs more martyr blood.

If I were pledging men and women to the gospel of the Son of God, as I am endeavoring to do tonight, it would not be to have a nice church and harmonious surroundings, and a sweet do nothing time. I would invite them to be ready to die. That was the spirit of early Methodism. John Wesley established a heroic call. He demanded every preacher to be "ready to pray, ready to preach, ready to die." That is always the spirit of Christianity. When there is any other spirit that comes into the church, it is not the spirit of Christianity. It is a foreign spirit. It is a sissified substitute.

I lived on corn meal mush many a period with my family, and we did not growl, and I preached to thousands of people, not colored people*, but white people. When my missionaries were on the field existing on corn meal mush, I could not eat pie. My heart was joined to them. That is the reason we never had splits in our work in South Africa—one country where Pentecost never split. The split business began to develop years afterward, when pumpkin-pie-eating Pentecostal missionaries began infesting the country. Men who are ready to die for the Son of God do not split. They do not holler the first time they get the stomachache.

Bud Robinson tells a story of himself. He went to preach in the southern mountains. It was the first time in his life that no one invited him to go home and eat with them. So he slept on the floor, and the next night, and the next night. After five days and five nights had passed, and his stomach began to growl for food terribly, every once in a while he would stop and say, "Lay down, you brute!" and he went on with his sermon. That is what won. That is what will win every time. That is what we need today. We need men who are willing to get off the highway. When I started to preach the gospel I walked twenty miles on Sunday morning to my service and walked home twenty miles in the night when I got through. I did it for years for Jesus and souls.

In early Methodism an old local preacher would start Saturday and walk all night, and then walk all night Sunday night to get back to his work. It was the common custom. Peter Cartwright preached for sixty dollars per year, and baptized ten thousand converts.

Friends, we talk about consecration, and we preach about consecration, but that is the kind of consecration that my heart is asking for tonight. That is the kind of consecration that will get answers from heaven. That is the kind God will honor. That is the consecration to which I pledge Pentecost. I would strip Pentecost of its frills and folderols. Jesus Christ, through the Holy Ghost, calls us tonight not to an earthly mansion and a ten thousand dollar motor car, but to put our lives...body and soul and spirit...on the altar of service. All hail! Ye who are ready to die for Christ and this glorious Pentecostal gospel, we salute you. You are brothers with us and with your Lord.

*Kenneth Copeland Publications acknowledges that references to race and nationality considered acceptable in Rev. Lake's day are offensive and not acceptable to today's reader. However, these references in no way reflect the attitude or policies of KCP. To fully understand Rev. Lake's heart toward other races, we recommend you read his biography located at the front of the book.

12

The Calling of the Soul

If I were to choose a subject for the thought in my soul tonight, I would choose "The Calling of the Soul."

Someone has given us this little saying that has become prevalent among many people: "My own shall come to me." Jesus framed that thought in different words. He said: *"[He] that hungers and thirsts after righteousness shall be filled."* It is the same law. *"Blessed are they which do hunger and thirst after righteousness: for they shall be filled"* [Matthew 5:6].

RIGHTEOUSNESS is simply God's rightness. God's rightness in a man's soul; God's rightness in a man's spirit; God's rightness in a man's body. In order that man may be right or righteous, God imparts to man the power of His Spirit. That Spirit contains such marvelous and transforming grace that when received into the nature of man, the marvelous process of regeneration is set in motion and man becomes thereby a new creature in Christ Jesus.

The deepest call of our nature is the one that will find the speediest answer. People pray, something happens. If they pray again, something still deeper occurs within their nature, and they find a new prayer. The desire is obtained.

In my ministry in South Africa I had a preacher by the name of Von Vuuren. That name means "fire." Von Vuuren had been a butcher in the city of Johannesburg, and was given up to die of consumption. His physician said to him: "You have only one year to live." So he gave up his business and went down into the country to develop a farm, that his family might be able to support themselves.

After he left the city many were baptized in the Holy Spirit and healed, etc., and his friends wrote him a letter and said: "So-and-So, who was sick, has been healed; So-and-So, your niece, has been baptized in the Holy Spirit and is speaking in tongues by the power of God; So-and-So has been blessed of God," etc.

Von Vuuren took the letter and went out into the fields and got down under a thorn tree and spread the letter out before God. Then he began to pray: "God, if You can do these things for the people at Johannesburg, You can do something for me. I have been a Christian for eighteen years, and I have prayed and prayed for certain things which have not come to pass. God, if others can be baptized in the Holy Ghost, surely I can; if others' hearts are made pure by the power of God, the power that made theirs pure can make mine pure also; if others have been healed, then You can heal me."

As he thus gave himself to God, and opened his soul to heaven, suddenly the Spirit came upon him and he became the most transformed creature I ever knew.

God moved into the man. For eighteen days he walked as though overshadowed by the Spirit of God, God talking continuously to his soul, directing him to this one and that one, judges and lawyers, statesmen and physicians, rich and poor. When he would reach them, the Spirit of God would pour forth through his soul such messages of God that in many cases they fell down and wept.

This is the point of the story I wanted you to get. He said for eighteen years he had prayed for the real conversion and transformation of his wife, and it had not come to pass. But that morning after the Lord had baptized him in the Holy Ghost, a new prayer came into his heart. A new depth had been touched in the man's nature, and from that great inner depth flowed out to God a cry that had been going out from his soul for years. But that morning the cry of God touched the soul of his wife, and before he reached the house she had given her heart to God. In three months all his family—his wife, eleven children and himself, had been baptized in the Holy Spirit.

The desire of which Jesus spoke, (for when He spoke of desire, He spoke of this same call of the soul) was not the simple attitude of the outer man. Certainly it included it. Perhaps the desire in the beginning was simply that of the mind, but as the days and years passed, and the desirability of obtaining grew in the soul, it became a call of the deepest depth of the man's nature. And that is the character of desire that Jesus spoke of when He said: *"Blessed are they which do hunger and thirst after righteousness: for they shall be filled."*

The spiritual action that takes place within the nature of man, that strong desire for God, His ways, His love, His knowledge, His power, causes everything else, perhaps unconsciously to himself, to become secondary.

Politicians talk about a paramount issue. That is the issue that stands out by itself above all others, and is the greatest and largest and of most interest to the nation. It is the paramount issue.

The soul has its paramount issue, and when the desire of your heart is intensified so that it absorbs all your energies, then the time of its fulfillment is not far away. That is the desire that brings the answer. It is creative desire.

A woman testified in my hearing one day to this fact. She had been pronounced hopeless and was going blind. No human remedy could do her any good. Someone opened to her in a dim way the possibility of seeing through the power of God. She was not very well taught, but she said this: That every day of four years she gave up two and one-half hours absolutely to expressing the desire of her soul for real sight. Not only expressing it in words, but calling the power of God to her that would recreate in her the function of sight in her eyes and make her see. At the end of four or four and a half years she said: "My eyes are as well as they ever were."

That is the reward of persistence, of a desire toward God. Your nature may have sent out just as deep a cry to God as my nature has, and still is doing. Is the cry to God continuous? Gradually as the forces of life concentrate themselves in line with that strong desire, the Spirit of God is operating through your heart, is being directed by that desire and concentrated on a particular line, intensifying every day because of the continuous desire of the soul to possess. The effect of that concentration of the Spirit of God on that soul is that by the grace of God there is brought to your soul all the elements necessary to formulate and create and fulfill the desire of your heart, and one morning the soul awakens to discover that it has become the possessor of the desired object.

Jesus started men on the true foundation. Many simply desire health, others temporal blessings. Both are good and proper, but bless God, Jesus started the soul at the proper point, to first desire RIGHTEOUSNESS, the righteousness of God, to become a possessor of the kingdom. *"Seek ye first,"* said Jesus, *"the kingdom of God, and his righteousness; and all these things shall be added unto you"* [Matthew 6:33].

Jesus was bringing forth and establishing in the world a new character, a character that would endure forever, a soul quality that would never fail, a faith that knew no possibility of defeat. In establishing such a character Jesus saw that the character could only be established in the depth of a man's being, in the very spirit of his being. Then when once the soul was grounded in the paths of righteousness, then all the activities of the nature would be along righteous lines, and in harmony with the laws of God.

God has a call in His own Spirit. If we study our own spirit we will understand the nature of God. The call of the Spirit of God is the call of righteousness, the call of truth, the call of love, the call of power, the call of faith.

I met a young man on one occasion who seemed to me to be the most blessed man in some ways of all the men I had ever met. I observed he was surrounded by a circle of friends of men or women, the deepest and truest it had ever been my privilege to know. One day I said to him: "What is the secret of this circle of friends that you possess, and the manner in which you seem to bind them to you?"

He replied, "Lake, my friendships are the result of the call of the soul. My soul has called for truth and righteousness, for holiness, for grace, for strength, for soundness of mind, for the power of God, and the call has reached this one, and this one, and this one, and brought them to me."

Over in Topeka, Kansas, in the year 1900, one morning a man stepped off the train, walked up the street, and as he walked up a particular street he stopped in front of a large fine dwelling, and said to himself: "This is the house." A gentleman who happened to be out of sight around the building said: "What about the house?" and this story came out.

He said: "For years I have been praying to God for a certain work of God among Christians known as the Baptism of the Holy

Ghost. In my researches I have visited every body of Christian people in this country that I knew of that claimed to be possessors of the baptism, but as I visited and examined their experiences and compared it with the Word of God, I became convinced that none of them possessed the Baptism of the Holy Ghost as it is recorded and demonstrated in the New Testament."

He said one day as he prayed, the Spirit of the Lord said: "Go to Topeka, Kansas." As he prayed, he observed in the Spirit a certain house, and the Lord said, "I will give you that house, and in it the Baptism of the Holy Ghost will fall."

So he took the train and came to Topeka, walked down the street, and exclaimed as he passed by: "This is the house," and the voice around the corner replied: "What about it?"

When the man had heard his story, he told him he was the owner of the house; that it had been closed for years. He asked him what he wanted it for, and he replied that he was going to start a Christian school. The owner said: "Have you any money?"

He replied, "No."

He said, "All right, you can have the house without money."

About an hour later a little Quaker lady came down the street, hesitated and looked around and said, "This is the house, but there is no one living there." After a struggle with her soul she went up and rang the door bell and the first gentleman answered the bell and asked what she wanted.

She said: "I live over in the country at such a place. As I prayed, the Spirit told me to come here to this house."

He said, "Who are you?"

She replied, "Just an unknown Christian woman."

He said: "What have you been praying about?"

She said: "About the Baptism of the Holy Ghost."

Beloved, in three weeks eighteen persons were brought to that house. They formed a little company and began to pray. The company grew to thirty-six. On New Years night, 1900, the Spirit fell on that company, and the first one was baptized in the Holy Ghost, and in a few weeks practically the whole company had been baptized in the Holy Ghost. And from there it spread over the world.

Yesterday morning a woman came to my healing rooms, a stranger in the city. She said, "I have been praying for healing and asking God to show me where I could be healed. I heard of friends in Chicago who pray for the sick, and I visited them, but when I arrived, the Spirit said, 'Not here.'"

She said, "I bought a ticket and was about to take a train back home, but as I sat in the station I was approached by a little lady on crutches, and pitying her, I turned to speak a kind word to her. While conversing with her I saw she was a Christian of a deep nature rarely found. I told her my story."

She said, "Oh, I know where the Lord wants you to go. The Lord wants you to go to Spokane, Washington"—3,000 miles from Chicago. She asked her if she knew anybody in Spokane, and the lady replied, "Why yes, I know Mr. Lake, I used to nurse in his home years ago."

I prayed for her, and told her the thing to do was to come in for ministry every day until she was well. She said she would. This morning I received a call on the telephone, and she said, "I am not coming up to the healing rooms."

I said, "Oh, is that the kind of individual you are? The one that comes once and gets nothing."

"No," she said, "I came once and got something, and I do not need to come back. I am healed, and I am going home."

There is a call of faith in this church that is reaching away out, far out and in unaccountable ways. Away at the other end the Spirit of God is revealing truth to this soul and that soul, and they are moving into this life, and coming into unity with this church.

Is there a note of despair in your heart? Have you not obtained the thing your soul covets? Have you desired to be like that sinless, unselfish, sickless One? God will answer the call of your soul. You shall have your heart's desire. But before that call becomes answerable, it must be the paramount call of your being. It is when it becomes the paramount issue of the soul that the answer comes. Jesus knew. That is the reason He said, *"Blessed are they which do hunger and thirst after righteousness: for they shall be filled."* There is not a doubt about it. All the barriers of your nature will go down before the desire of the soul. All the obstacles that ever were will disappear before the desire of your soul. All the diseases that ever existed in your life will disappear before the desire of your soul, when that desire becomes the one great purpose and prayer of your heart.

I love to think of one great soul: he was not a great Christian, but he was a great soul. He was the son of a Church of England clergyman, and came to South Africa, thinking he might get his system back to a normal state of health. He came to the diamond mines at Kimberly and took a pick and shovel and worked with them long enough to understand diamonds. Indeed, he studied diamonds until he knew more about them than any other man in the world. Then he went to studying Africa, until one paramount desire grew up in his soul. He said, "I will plant the British flag across the continent." Eventually, this is what he did.

He told me that in the beginning his vision extended to the Vaal River, then to the Zambezi and then across the trackless desert. He also planned a railroad six thousand miles long. John Cecil Rhodes died before he could fully bring to pass the paramount issue of his soul. *"Blessed are they which do hunger and thirst after righteousness."* Oh, if I had one gift, or one desire that I would bestow on you, more than all others, I would bestow upon you the hunger for God.

"Blessed are they which do hunger." Hunger is the best thing that ever came into a man's life. Hunger is hard to endure. It is the call of the nature for something that you do not possess. The thing that will satisfy the demands of the nature and the hunger of a man's soul is the call of his nature for the Spirit of life that will generate in him the abundant love of God.

Years ago I was one of a family of which some member was an invalid in the house for thirty-two consecutive years. During that time we buried four brothers and four sisters. A call arose in my nature to God for something to stay that tide of sickness and death. *Materia medica* had utterly failed. One after another the tomb stones were raised. The call arose in my soul for something from God that would stem the tide and turn it backward.

Nothing else but healing could have come to my life, no other thing but the knowledge of it. God had to bring from the furthest ends of Australia the man who brought to my soul the message of God and the manifestation of His power that satisfied my heart. And healing by the power of God became a fact to me.

We live that our souls may grow. The development of the soul is the purpose of existence. God Almighty is trying to obtain some decent association for Himself. By His grace He is endeavoring to have us grow up in His knowledge and likeness to that stature where as sons of God we will comprehend something of His love, of His nature, of His power, of His purpose, and be big enough to give back to God what a son should give to a great Father—the reverence, the love, the affection that comes from the understanding of the nobleness and greatness of His purpose.

Great Britain produced two marvelous statesmen, a father and his son. They are known in history as the old Pitt and the young Pitt. The young Pitt was as great a statesman as his father. The son grew to that largeness where, catching the vision of his great father his soul arose to it, and he became his father's equal. As I walked through the House of Commons I came across the statues of the old and young Pitt. I have forgotten the inscription at the bottom of the elder Pitt's statue, but at the base of the son's statue were these words: "My father, the greatest man I ever knew." Do you see the call of his soul for his father's largeness, for his father's nobility, for his father's strength and influence?

"Blessed are they which do hunger." Bless God! What are we hungering for, a little bit of God, enough to take us through this old world where we will have the dry rot and be stunted and then squeeze into heaven? *"Blessed are they which do hunger"* for the nature and power and love and understanding of God. Why? They shall be filled.

Not long ago I stood before great audiences of the churchmen of the world. They said, "Through all your ministry there is one note. It is the call for power." They said, "Do you not think it would be better if the church was calling for holiness instead of power?"

And I replied, "She will never obtain the one without the other. There is something larger than holiness. It is the nature of God." The nature of God has many sides. From every angle that the soul approaches God, it reveals a new and different manifestation of Him: love, beauty, tenderness, healing, power, might, wisdom, etc.

So the Christian who hungers and hungers, bless God, and lifts his soul to God brings God down to meet his own cry. The spirit of man and the Spirit of God unite. The nature of God is reproduced in man as God purposed it should be. There are no sick folk in God. There is no sickness in His nature.

There is an incident in the life of Jesus that is so marvelous. Jesus Christ demanded His right to heal a woman who was bound by Satan with a spirit of infirmity, and he was not satisfied until it was accomplished. Devil and church and creed and preacher went down before the call of the Son of God to assert His right to deliver that soul from sin and sickness. *"Blessed are they which do hunger."*

13

Isaiah

The "Fear Nots" of Isaiah

A. Isaiah 41:10-14

"Fear Not" appears three times in this text.

Five reasons we should not fear:

1. God's presence with us, *"Fear thou not; for I am with thee."* His companionship under all circumstances and all places guarantees our safety.
2. God's relation to us as our God, *"Be not dismayed; for I am thy God."* He gives Himself to us. We have the use of His Name.
3. The strength He promises to give us, *"I will strengthen thee."* This is actual imparted strength to us.
4. His promise of help, *"Yea, I will help thee."* Not only does He give us actual strength but He adds His strength to us.
5. His upholding, *"Yea, I will uphold thee with the right hand of my righteousness."* This is more than strength, more than help. It is God undertaking the entire responsibility for our case.

B. Isaiah 43:1-7

Four reasons to "fear not"

1. *"I have redeemed thee, I have called thee by thy name; thou art mine."* The fact He has purchased us with the precious blood should be enough to guarantee every blessing we need. He will freely give us all things (Romans 8:32). After Calvary, anything. He says, *"Thou art mine."* We are His property. He will take care of His property.
2. He promises to go with us through the waters and the fires. In the dark hour we know His consolations. *"Thou hast known my soul in adversities"* (Psalm 31:7). The consolation of God far outweighs the pressure of our troubles.
3. Isaiah 43:3-4. There is a suggestion here of the infinite pains and trouble that God has had with us. He is not likely to fail us. Nothing can work against His will.
4. He promises spiritual fruit. The seed we sow may seem to perish, but we shall all come rejoicing bringing our sheaves with us.

C. Isaiah 44:1-5

1. He comforts His children with promises of great spiritual blessings. The Holy Spirit is the best antidote to our fears. When He comes in, all the interests of His good cause are safe and all fears are turned to thanksgiving and rejoicings.

D. Isaiah 51:12-13

1. This passage shows the sin of fear. It is an act of unbelief. It leads us to forget the Lord our Maker. It comes because people are problem conscious instead of power conscious.
2. Fear of the oppressor is foolishness. People are worried about things that never come to pass. What a waste of life to worry!

E. Isaiah 54:4-17

Four great reasons are given for "fear not"

1. His personal relation to His own. *"Thy Maker is thine husband..."* The husband cherishes his wife even at the cost of his life. The love of a true wife is stronger than death. God loves His children equally with His Son (John 17:23). We shall not be put to shame nor be confounded (Isaiah 54:4).

2. His covenant and oath. *"So have I sworn that I would not be wroth with thee, nor rebuke thee"* (54:9). Many Christians are under the law and they look to God as though they ever expected a frown or a blow. We should live in such perfect love that we could not imagine His failing us or forgetting us. Christ has died for us and God in His great love is striving to get us to forget that there ever was sin between His heart and ours.
3. He promises us His protecting care (54:17). There will be enemies. There will be temptations. He wants our spirit, soul and body to be preserved blameless unto His coming (1 Thessalonians 5:23). Preserved means to guard from loss or injury by keeping the eye upon. It corresponds with the declaration of Jesus in Luke 10:19, *"...nothing shall by any means hurt you."* It simply means God will protect us from all the sicknesses and crippling diseases of the devil. It does not include the category of suffering that Jesus suffered for righteousness' sake.
4. He promises us His own righteousness. Jesus is made unto us righteousness (1 Corinthians 1:30). We receive the gift of righteousness (Romans 5:17). Who shall lay anything to the charge of God's elect? It is God that justifieth (Romans 8:33-34). I have accepted God's gift of righteousness. Who can charge me with unrighteousness?

F. Considerations that will help rid us of fear, "The fear that torments."

1. The devil's fears are always falsehoods. His suggestions are always lies, and if lies, they cannot harm. If fear comes from Satan, then we can conclude there is nothing to fear.
2. Fear is dangerous. It turns into fact the things we fear. It creates evil just as faith creates good.
3. The remedy for fear is faith and love. *"Perfect love casteth out fear"* (1 John 4:17-18). *"Herein is our love made perfect, that we may have boldness in the day of judgment; because as he is, so are we in this world."* Love is made perfect because we dwell in Him Who is Love (1 John 4:16).

14

Reality

Hebrews 2. When I read this chapter there is a thrill that goes down through my soul, and I would to God that the real spiritual truths of it could forever be established in the minds of men.

I once listened to an imminent divine preaching from the text, "What is Man?" and when he got through I had a feeling that man was a kind of whipped cur with his tail between his legs, sneaking to throw himself into the lake, and saying, "Here goes nothing."

I said, "He has never caught the fire of the thing Jesus is endeavoring to teach through the apostle; that man was the crowning creation of God; that God endowed him with a nature and qualities that by the grace of God can express more of God than any other of God's creations; that God purposed by the Holy Spirit to make the salvation of Jesus Christ so real in the nature of man that *'He that sanctifieth [Jesus Christ] and they who are sanctified'* through His grace are both of one nature, of one substance, of one character, one in life, one in righteousness of His death, and one in the consequent dominion that came because of His resurrection and glory. *'For both he that sanctifieth and they who are sanctified are all of one: for which cause he is not ashamed to call them brethren"* (Hebrews 2:11).

Brethren of the Lord Jesus Christ: He the elder brother, we the younger members of the family of the same Father, begotten by the same Spirit, energized by the same divine life of God, qualified through the Holy Ghost to perform the same blessed ministry. *"He took not on him the nature of angels; but he took on him the seed of Abraham"* [Hebrews 2:16]. I wish I could write these things in your soul and brand them in your conscience.

Sermon

When the purpose of God in the salvation of man first dawned upon my soul, that is, when the greatness of it dawned upon my soul, for experimentally I knew God as Savior from sin, I knew the power of the Christ within my own heart to keep me above the power of temptation and to help me live a godly life, but when I say to you that when I knew the purpose of God and the greatness of His salvation, life became for me a grand new thing.

When by the study of His Word and the revelation of His Spirit it became a fact in my soul that God's purpose was no less in me than it was in the Lord Jesus, and is no less in you and I as younger brethren than it was in Jesus Christ, our elder brother, then bless God I saw the purpose that God had in mind for the human race. I saw the greatness of Jesus' desire. That desire that was so intense that it caused Him as King of Glory to lay down all that glory possessed for Him, and come to earth to be born as a man, to join hands with our humanity, and by His grace lift us in consciousness and life to the same level that He Himself enjoyed. Christ became a new factor in my soul. Such a vision of His purpose thrilled my being that I could understand then how it was that Jesus as He approached man and his needs began at the very bottom, called mankind to Him, and by His loving touch and the power of the Spirit through His word, destroyed the sickness and sin that bound them and set them free in both body and soul, lifted them into union and communion with Himself and God the Father. Yea, bless God, by the Holy Spirit indwelling the souls of men, Christ purposed to bestow on mankind the very conditions of His own life and being, and to give to man through the gifts of the Spirit and the Gift of the Spirit, the same blessed ministry to the world that He Himself had enjoyed and exercised.

The old song that we used to sing became new to my heart. Its melody runs through my soul:

"Salvation, O the joyful sound,
In a believer's ear,
It soothes our worries, heals our wounds
And drives away our fears."

And lots more, bless God. I could then understand what was in Charles Wesley's heart when he wrote his famous hymn, "Jesus Lover of My Soul," and penned its climax that marvelous verse:

"Thou, O Christ, art all I want,
More than all in Thee I find;
Raise the fallen, cheer the faint,
Heal the sick and lead the blind.
Just and holy is Thy name;
I am all unrighteousness,
Vile and full of sin I am,
Thou art full of truth and grace."

(This was not the last verse, but the third.)

The same thing was in the spirit of Isaiah when in the beautiful thirty-fifth chapter of Isaiah his exultant soul broke forth in the shout of praise: *"He will come and save you. Then the eyes of the blind shall be opened, and the ears of the deaf shall be unstopped. Then shall the lame man leap as an hart, and the tongue of the dumb sing"* [Isaiah 35:4-6].

I could understand then the thrill that must have moved David, when he sang the 103rd Psalm: *"Bless the Lord, O my soul, and forget not all His benefits: Who forgiveth all thine iniquities; Who healeth all thy diseases"* [Psalm 103:2-3].

The vision that has called forth the shouts of praise from the souls of men in all ages is the same vision that stirs your heart and mine today—the vision of the divine reality of the salvation of Jesus Christ, by which the greatness of God's purpose in Him revealed to mankind, by the Spirit of the Living One, transformed and lifted and unified with the living Christ through the Holy Ghost, so that all the parts and energies and functions of the nature of Jesus Christ are revealed through man, unto the salvation of the world. Bless God.

The vision of God's relation to man and man's relation to God is changing the character of Christianity from a groveling something, weeping and wailing its way in tears, to the kingly recognition of union and communion with the living Son of God. Yea, bless God, to the recognition of the real fact that the Word of God so vividly portrayed in the lesson I read. That *in the bringing of many sons into the world* (not one son in the world, but in the bringing of many sons into the world) *"it became him to make the captain of their salvation perfect through suffering"* [see Hebrews 2:10]. Blessed be God.

I am glad, bless God, that the Scriptures have dignified us with that marvelous title of *"sons of God"* [John 1:12]. I am glad there is such a relation as a *"Son of God,"* and that by His grace the cleansed soul, cleansed by the precious blood of Jesus Christ, filled and energized by His own Kingly Spirit, that He too by the grace of God has become God's king, God's gentleman in deed and in truth.

The Spirit of the Lord says within my soul, that the kingly nature of the Son of God is purposed to be revealed in the nature of every man, that Christ's kingliness may be prevalent in all the world and govern the heart of man, even as it governs the heart of those who know Him and have entered.

(A young man called up from the audience.)

I listened to this young man's testimony on Friday night with a thrill in my soul. I want him to tell you what God has done in him and for him.

Testimony

"I do not know whether I can tell it all or not. I am sure there is a good deal I cannot tell.

"When I was a lad of about 14 years old I was forced into the mines to work, and I worked a great deal in the water, which brought on rheumatism. I was crippled up for years in my younger days, and gradually grew worse. I could walk around, but you could hardly notice where I was afflicted. It was in the hips and back.

"A great many physicians said there was not relief for me. When I came down here to Spokane and was laboring on anything, I could not stoop down. When I would drop my pick or shovel, I would have to pick it up with my feet and reach for it with my hands.

"I came to this meeting last fall, and with one prayer by Dr. Lake I was healed in thirty minutes of rheumatism, which had been a constant torture to me for years.

"Later on I contracted tuberculosis, and was examined by the county physician Stutz, who advised me that the best thing to do was to go to Edgecliff. Also other physicians said I was very bad, and they did not think I could live more than six or eight months, unless I went out there right away.

"I took the same thing for it. I went to the healing rooms for prayer, also Brother Peterson prayed for me, and in three weeks I went to Dr. Stutz and he could not find a trace of it. I have gained 11 pounds, and I never felt better in my life."

That is a simple story isn't it? But that story is a revealer of the question that has probably caused more debate in Christian life than almost any other, and of which the world has little understanding: That is that the Spirit of God is a force that takes possession of the nature of man and works in man the will of God, and the will of God is ever to make man like Himself. Blessed be His precious Name.

It would be a strange Word indeed, and a strange salvation if Jesus was not able to produce from the whole race one man in His own image, in His own likeness and of His own character. We would think that salvation was weak, would we not?

If the world were nothing but cripples, as it largely is, soul cripples, physical cripples, mental cripples everywhere, then I want to know what kind of a conception the world has received of the divinity of Jesus Christ, of the Power of His salvation? Is there no hope, is there no way out of the difficulty, is there no force that can lift the soul of man into union with God, so that once again the life of God thrills in his members?

Our purpose, by the grace of God, is to reveal to the world what is the real truth and purpose and power of the salvation of the Lord Jesus Christ. My soul rejoices every time I see a man set free, for I say within my heart, "There is one more witness to the divine fact that the Christ of God is a living power, taking possession of the nature of man and transforming man's being into His own image."

The mere fact of our brother's deliverance from suffering and inability to help himself, and a possible premature death, is a very small matter in itself, in comparison with the wonder it reveals to us. The revelation of the power of God at the command of man, to be applied to the destruction of evil, whether spiritual or physical, mental or psychological, shows us Christ's purpose and desire to bring man by the grace of God once more into his heavenly estate, where he recognizes himself a son of God. Blessed be His Name.

Years ago I found myself like my brother, but worse crippled than he. When my legs drew out of shape and my body became distorted by the common curse of rheumatism, my pastor said, "Brother you are glorifying God," and my church said, "Brother, be patient and endure it. Let the sweetness of the Lord possess your soul." And I was good enough to believe it for a long time, until one day I discovered that it was not the will of God at all, but the will of the dirty crooked-legged devil that wanted to make me like himself. And then, bless God, everything was changed and I laid down everything and went to Chicago to the only place where I knew then that a man could get healed. I went to John Alexander Dowie's Divine Healing Home at 12th and Michigan Streets, and an old gray harried man came and laid his hands on me and the power of God went through my being and made my leg straight, and I went out and walked on the street like a Christian.

Do you know when my legs straightened out it taught me the beginning of one of the deepest lessons that ever came to my life. It taught me that God did not appreciate a man with crooked legs any more than He does with a crooked soul. I saw the abundant power of the gospel of salvation, and that it was placed at the disposal of man to remove the unchristlikeness of his life, and if there was unchristlikeness in the body, we could get rid of the curse by coming to God and being made whole. For there is just as much unchristlikeness in men's bodies as in men's souls. That which is in the inner life will also be revealed in the outer life. That which is a fact in the mental and psychological will become a fact in the physical also. And, bless God, that which is the divine fact of all facts, that the spirit of man and the Spirit of God are of one substance and one nature, and his mind and body take on the spiritual power imparted, until it too becomes Christlike. Blessed be His holy Name.

The Spirit of the Lord speaks within my soul and says: "Within the breast of every man is the divine image of God (living God), in whose image and likeness he was made, that sin is a perversion, and sickness an impostor, and the grace and power of God through the Holy Ghost delivers man from all bondage of darkness, and man in all his nature rises into union and communion with God and becomes one with Him the truest sense. One in the thoughts of God, one in the aspirations of God, one in the Spirit of

Jesus Christ as the Savior of man and man then gives himself a Savior also lifting man by the grace of God to the Lamb of God that taketh away the sin of the world." Blessed be His holy Name.

> "There's a wideness in God's mercy,
> Like the wideness of the sea:
> There's a kindness in His Justice,
> Which is more than liberty.
>
> But we make His love too narrow
> By false limits of our own,
> And we magnify His strictness
> With a zeal He will not own.
>
> There is welcome for the sinner,
> And more graces for the good;
> There is mercy with the Savior;
> There is healing in His blood.
>
> For the love of God is broader
> Than the measure of Man's mind
> And the heart of the Eternal
> Is most wonderfully kind.
>
> If our lives were but more simple,
> We should take Him at His word;
> And our lives would be all sunshine
> In the sweetness of our Lord."

So the divine realities remain. The reality of God a living power. The divine assistance, the heavenly nature known to every man who enters by the Spirit through the door, Christ Jesus, into a living experience. The man who doubts is the man on the outside. The man on the inside has not questions to settle that do not comprehend God, as that soul that has never been in contact with His life and power. But Christ invites mankind to enter with Him into the divine knowledge and heavenly union that makes the spirit of man and the Spirit of God to be one in deed and in truth. Bless God!

Man is the divinest reality that God has given in His great creation. Man in the image of God, man renewed by the life of

God, filled with the Holy Spirit, revealing and giving forth by the living Spirit, transformed even as himself has been transformed. Blessed be His Name.

God has made us in the truest and highest sense co-partners and co-laborers with our Lord and Savior Jesus Christ. He has not withheld one possibility that was manifested in Jesus from any man, but on the contrary invites mankind to come forth in the dignity and power of sons of God, and to that Christ and in Christ join in the mighty wonder of the salvation of the world over sin and sickness, and the power of death and darkness and hell. Bless God.

Salvation to my heart is Christ's glorious reality. Under a tree away back in Canada one night I knelt and poured out my heart to God and asked Him by His grace to take possession of my life and nature and make me a Christian man, and let me know the power of His salvation. And Christ was born in my soul. Such a joy of God possessed my heart that the leaves of the trees seemed to dance for months following, and the birds sang a new song and the angels of God witnessed of the glory of heaven in my own heart. Blessed be His name.

Salvation is a progressive condition. The difficulty with church has been that men were induced to confess their sins to Christ and acknowledge Him as a Savior and there they stopped, there they petrified, there they withered, there they died—dry rotted. I believe in these phases I have expressed the real thing that has taken place in 85 percent of professing Christians in the world. Oh, bless God, we never saw Christ's intention. That day away back there, when the glory light of God first shone into my soul, was a glorious day, the best I had ever known to that moment. But, beloved, it would be a sorrowful thing in my life if I was compelled to look back to that day as the best. No, bless God, there were better days than that. There were days when the Lord God took me into His confidence and revealed His nature and revealed His ministry. Yea, bless God, there came a day when God once more in His loving mercy endowed me with the Spirit of God, to be and perform the things that He had planted in my soul and had revealed in His own blessed Word and life.

I invite you to this life of divine reality. I invite you to enter into the Lord Jesus. I invite you to enter into His nature that you may know Him, for no man can say that Jesus is the Lord, but by the Holy Ghost. It is through the revelation of the Spirit of Christ in the soul of man that he is privileged to know Jesus as the Lord.

Blessed be God. We may know Him as an historic character, we may know Him as the ideal man, we may know Him as the Christ and Savior, but we do not know Him as the living God Who imparts His own nature and life and power to us, until we know Him as the Scripture says in the Holy Ghost. Bless God!

He who has lived and felt that religious life was a dream or a myth or an abstract something that was hard to lay your hands on, an intangible condition, has been mistaken. I bless God. In the bosom of the Living One is the divine realities of God, filling and thrilling the soul of Christ Himself, filling and thrilling the soul of every recipient of the life of the Lord Jesus.

And the Spirit of the Lord once more speaks within my heart and says that, "the joys of God and the glories of heaven and the understanding of angelic existence and being are only known to him who is privileged in consciousness to enter that life and realm. That God by His grace has purposed that man in his nature and consciousness shall live in union and communion with our Father God, and with the Lord Jesus Christ His Son, the innumerable company of angels and the presence of just men made perfect and we shall know the power and wonder of the blood of Jesus that speaketh better things than that of Abel."

And the Spirit of the Lord speaks yet again and says that as Jesus was the Prophet of all prophets, because of the completeness of the union of His nature with God, that man in turn becomes the prophet of prophets as his spirit assimilates with the Spirit of Him, the divine One; that man becomes the lover of all lovers, even as Jesus Christ was the lover of all men, thrilling men with the intensity of His affection in the union of spirit with Himself, binding them by the love of His nature as the bondslaves of Christ forever.

So the Christian draws to himself the love of men, not because he slavishly desires it, but because of the fact that he obeys

Christ's divine law: *"Give, and it shall be given unto you; good measure, pressed down, and shaken together, and running over, shall men give into your bosom"* [Luke 6:38]. Blessed be God.

And I want to tell you that this little church is one of the most loved of all churches in the world. I want to tell you that more hungry hearts are turned in longing toward this little company of people than to any other company of worshipers in the land. Why? They have heard that God is here and the longing nature of man to know God causes them to turn their hearts and their faces toward the source of heavenly blessing. Shall we give it to them, or will they turn away hungry and dissatisfied? Yea, I know your answer, for I know the answer of the Spirit, *"Give and it shall be given unto you."* Blessed be God. The greatest giver is the greatest receiver. He who gives most receives most. That is God's divine law. The reverse of God's law is always evidenced in the soul of man as selfishness. Always getting, always getting, until the nature contracts and the face distorts and the brain diminishes and the life that God gave to be abundant becomes an abomination, that men are compelled to endure.

15

Spiritualism

August 26, 1923

"*And Samuel said to Saul..." (1 Samuel 28:7-19).*

The old prophet appeared and proceeded to tell what was going to take place and what was going to happen to Saul and his sons in the battle to come... Now then we read a surprising thing. He had light in the promise of Christ's redemption. Where did he get it? The word says "sheol" or the regions of the dead. They were there without something. What was it? The deliverance of the Son of God.

The prophets prophesied concerning the deliverance the Son of God was to bring, and after Jesus Christ entered into the regions of death and liberated those who were held by its chains, those who had died in the hope of the promise, those who had died in the fullness of faith that the Redeemer was to come, He came and the actual deliverance from the power of death took place. *"He ascended up on high, he led captivity captive"* (Ephesians 4:8) and their place of residence was transferred from that place (sheol) governed by the power of death and the angel of death to wherever the Lord Jesus Christ went. They ascended up on high and their place of residence was changed. We do not know where those who went with Jesus stopped. You call it Paradise, but so far as Jesus is concerned, it is perfectly plain in the Word that He never stopped until He came to the throne of God.

You go through the Book and find where anyone was ever called down out of heaven, and you won't find it. Those who have their residence with the Lord Jesus Christ, from the day of His resurrection and onward, would have to be called down, not up.

Now one of the things we have lost out of our Protestant faith from the days of the Reformation onward has been the wonderful truth of the ministry of Jesus in the Spirit to the dead. Do you get it? The ministry of Jesus to the dead.

"For this cause was the gospel preached also to them that are dead" [1 Peter 4:6]. Oh, you mean dead in this world, and dead in sins? Not at all, because the rest of the verse explains, *"For this cause was the gospel preached also to them that are dead."* Why? *"That they might be judged according to men in the flesh"* (1 Peter 4:6). On the same grounds that men in the flesh were. They heard the words of Jesus, They received the words of Jesus, or they rejected the words of Jesus, just as men in the flesh do.

Well, what does it mean? You ask, "Are you preaching on the subject of a second chance?" No, brother, but I am calling attention to the state of the dead before Jesus came. They died in the *hope* of the promise. Jesus came and the promise was fulfilled. He fulfilled it on the cross of Calvary, and went into the regions of the dead and fulfilled it to them, and delivered them and took them out the power of death and transferred them to His kingdom. *"He led captivity captive, and gave gifts unto men"* (Ephesians 4:8).

With the above thoughts I have laid a kind of foundation. There is no such thing in the whole New Testament as a re-occurrence of those instances I have just read. No such a suggestion or its possibility in the New Testament. It belonged to a day and an age and a state that ceased to be when Jesus Christ the Lord and redeemer came.

> Oh, listen to the Word, the living Word of God that is coming forth. You shall live, you shall live throughout eternity; but deny the living Word and ye shall go down, ye shall go down into the pit. Believe the Word and ye shall live.

Tongues and Interpretation
Given to Fred Wilson

A number of years ago when I was a missionary in Africa I formed the acquaintance of W.T. Stead, who later was one of the victims of the Titanic. I came to London at his invitation and expense for a personal interview. He took me to his office and after he had become acquainted he introduced this fact. He maintained a spiritualistic bureau associated with his great work known as the Julia Bureau. Julia was a friend who had died, and he believed after she was dead he could contact the spirit of Julia. So eventually he published a book entitled, *Letters From Julia.* Later he changed the name to *After Death,* and these letters from Julia are published in this book.

Stead presented me with a copy of the book and requested that I should read it carefully. I did so and made notations of the various letters, and when I got a chance to talk to him I said: "Julia in a very cunning manner indeed avoids the deity and divinity of the Lord Jesus Christ. Now in order that you may see it, I went over the different letters where reference was made to the Lord Jesus Christ."

I said, "You listen, Stead, that cunningness is altogether out of harmony with the other statements in the other letters of this book." When it came to that subject of the divinity of Jesus the peculiar cunningness of wording was observable, even to the most ordinary mind, by which she carefully, studiously avoided any reference to the divinity or deity of Jesus Christ.

I said, "Stead, I am going to put you up against the Word on this matter: *'Every spirit that confesseth not that Jesus Christ is come in the flesh is not of God'* (1 John 4:3)." W.T. Stead was a big man and a great soul. He thought that he might convince me if I were at all reasonable.

Finally a meeting was arranged between Sir Oliver Lodge, Sir Arthur Conan Doyle, W.T. Stead, and myself. I want to say a word concerning these two great men. Both have been knighted by the King as Knights of the Realm because of their contributions to scientific knowledge.

When a knight is knighted he kneels before the King; the King touches him and says, "Rise, Sir Knight," etc. What I want you to see is that a man must have contributed something of unusual value to the Empire in order to be knighted. He must also be able to maintain his social status as a knight. Both men were great men, great as men speak of worldly greatness; great men intellectually; great men in the secrets of science.

After we had spent a whole night reviewing these varied things (experiences) that we considered vital, I said, "Gentlemen,

I want to tell you of one experience that I think goes further than any of these you have told me. My late wife died in South Africa. I buried her on Christmas Eve, 1908, at Johannesburg. The following sixth of May, which was the anniversary of her birthday, as I sat at the table I occupied an hour telling the family incidents of their mother, and trying to fix the memory of their mother in their young minds. The baby was only eighteen months old and the eldest only fourteen years when she died. Later I went to the post office, and a lady tapped me on the shoulder and said: 'When you are through with your business, come up to the office,' and handed me a card with the address. When I was through I strolled up to the office. I recognized her as one of the members of my audience. There were a couple of gentlemen in the room, one a Frenchman, Massalie, and another Frenchman.

"As we sat talking, I wondered why she had asked me to come up. I observed as I watched her she seemed to be distressed, and one side of her face was purple with erysipelas. I stepped over and asked her if it was because she was sick that she had asked me to come, and she said, 'Certainly.' I laid my hands on her and began to pray, and as I prayed I was conscious of the Spirit coming in power, and that purple disappeared as I watched it. The healing was so remarkable that the gentlemen were surprised.

"Massalie said, 'Mr. Lake what is that?'

"I said, 'Massalie, that is God.'

"He replied, 'Oh, everything is God. I lived among the East Indians and everything is God.'

"The phrase was offensive to my spirit and I said, 'Well, Brother, I do not want to discuss it.'

"He said, 'Well if it is God, I'll tell you how to prove it.' He said, 'I put over a bad business deal, was very angry and in a high temper one day. Instead of opening the door gently, I opened it with a push. A lady happened to be behind the door. It took her an awful blow on the side of the head, she became unconscious, and in a few days we discovered the skull was fractured. Not only that, but the optic nerve had been detached and the eye became blind.' He had spent quite a fortune on the woman, but nothing availed. The eye remained blind.

"He said, 'If that is God, you put your hands on her eye and pray sight back into that eye.'

"The Spirit was resting on my soul. I stepped over and began to pray. Instantly the Spirit came upon her until she was absolutely submerged in the Spirit. She remained in that condition a little while, and this strange thing took place. She arose from her chair, her eyes quite shut, and came in my direction. I got up and moved my chair. She walked right around and came to me. She slipped her fingers down, gave me a little chuck just like my late wife would have done, and said, 'Jack, my Jack, God is with you all the time. Go right on. But my baby, my Teddy, I am so lonesome for him, but you pray so hard, you pray so hard.'

"After Mrs. Lake died the little boy fell into a decline, and it required all the energy of my soul to keep that boy alive for months. Eventually he survived.

"After the incident had passed I asked her to write it. You get people to write things down so you can analyze them.

"Listen, it is not dragging spirits up, and it isn't dragging some spirits down. There is nothing about calling spirits down from God in the Word; only about calling them up out of the depths. The Apostle Paul says he was *'caught up to the third heaven'* (2 Corinthians 12:2). The attractive power is where the Lord Christ is. Jesus Christ is the attraction of the blood washed soul. If you are going to travel anywhere you will go His way.

All right, somewhere in my files I have that incident as she gave it to me. After a while she sat down and the Spirit came upon her. Presently she said it seemed as if she escaped out of herself and traveled so far and so fast. Presently she said, 'I observed I was being approached by a beautiful lady who was tall (and she gave a general description of her). She said her name was Jene. It is sympathy that brings me. I had a visual defect and the Lord healed me. You come with me, I will take you to Jesus, and He will heal you. She linked her arm in mine, and we traveled together. As we went along I observed the most wonderful landscape. Presently we came to a mountain, and while we stood there this lady repeated to her the entire 35th chapter of Isaiah: *'The wilderness and the solitary place shall be glad for them; and the desert shall rejoice, and blossom as the rose,* etc.'

"This dear woman did not know there was such a chapter in the Bible, until I told her it was the 35th chapter of Isaiah. Then they came to a broad stretch of water and on the opposite side were groups of angels, and Jesus stood in the midst of one of these groups. The lady took her to within a respectful distance and bowed her into the presence of Jesus. She said He looked on me sympathetically and said, 'Wherefore didst thou doubt? I am the Lord that healeth thee,' and He stooped down and took the waters of the river and bathed my eyes and bade me see.

"All this took place as we sat in the office. Presently her eyes opened and she became normal. Her employer asked her what had happened, and if she could see. She looked out across the street to the market square and proceeded to read the signs on the wall. Then he brought a book of ordinary type and she read that. He handed her a Persian Bible he had on his desk. It had very fine type. She opened the book and began to read."

Well that was the story I recited to W.T. Stead and the others as we five sat together that night in Stead's office. They said, "Mr. Lake that is the most wonderful thing we have ever heard. That is the best case of spiritualism we know of. If you will just give us the privilege of publishing that story."

I said, "Brethren, you have not seen the secret of that. Nobody came up to give that message, and nobody came down." And they opened their eyes.

That dear soul got through. She was a child of God and she started straight for the Lord. And so would you. The day that God sets your spirit free from this old temple, bless God, you will go straight to the Lord Jesus Christ.

Now let me review a moment. *Spiritualism* is trying to drag the dead up to you. CHRISTIANITY, bless God, is making the blood washed spirit free to go to the Lord. They are just as opposite as night and day.

Last Sunday night a lady came into this audience from upstairs for the first time and got under conviction and was saved and gave her heart to God. On Wednesday night she was sanctified by the precious blood of Jesus, and on Friday night she was baptized in the Holy Ghost. Last night I talked to her for a few moments. She said, "Oh, Brother, if I could just tell you the delights of my soul during these last thirty-six hours. If I could only explain how my spirit has found a freedom in God and how it seems to me my heart would rush to Him!"

Would it not? Where do you think it would go? Who occupies your mind? Who keeps your soul? Where is your treasure? In heaven, bless God! Well, you will go where your treasure is. You will go where the attraction is.

Don't confuse yourself with a lot of Old Testament scriptures concerning the dead. In the Old Testament you read *The dead know nothing at all* [see Ecclesiastes 9:5], but you never read it in the New Testament. Something happened to the dead when Jesus came. They changed their place of residence, and after that you begin to read *"To be absent from the body and to be present with the Lord"* [2 Corinthians 5:8].

Now I want to fix this in your mind. The blood washed always go there, and if you ever talk to anyone that is over there you will GO TO THEM. They are not going to leave the throne, but they will say, "Brother, come up here." That is the only way you will ever communicate with them.

In these days when this stuff is being proclaimed around the world by men like Lodge, Doyle and others who have been recognized as leaders of thought, naturally people are ready to listen.

But after a night with them in their office, I said, "Dear God it is absolutely impossible to make an unenlightened, unsaved soul to understand the difference between the Spirit of God and every other spirit. The Spirit of God is the attractive power that animates the Christian heart, and they do not want to listen to anything else. *"[My sheep] know My voice"* [see John 10:4].

Years afterward as I considered these things, and discussed them with a brother, he said, "Lake, you had a wonderful opportunity. Tell me, what was the effect in your own soul of that night that you spent with these men?"

I said, "Brother, I left there next morning with profound sympathy in my heart. I said as I walked away, 'Dear God, here are the greatest intellects in the world, but concerning the things of God and the light of the Spirit they are just as blind as though their eyes were sealed.'" And their eyes were sealed concerning the light of God.

Men come in the name of science. Naturally there is a certain reverence for knowledge, but don't you be fooled. Just because somebody comes along with the light of worldly knowledge, no matter how minute and wonderful it may seem, the knowledge he has is worldly; the knowledge you have is heavenly. The knowledge that his soul possesses is material; the knowledge that your soul possesses is divinely spiritual, bless God. It comes from the heart of the Son of God.

So when I came to Portland and Sir Oliver Lodge was announced to speak I did not take the train a day sooner in order to hear him. I would not take the trouble to go across the street if I could listen to every one of them, because they could not tell me anything that is vital. The vital things belong to the kingdom of God, to the knowledge of Jesus Christ. The vital things belong to the Holy Ghost.

It would take too long to tell of the thousands that have gone to spiritualism. I mean people honestly deceived. Just one instance. I had a little friend, Jude and his dear old wife. They were old fashioned Methodist people. They had one dear daughter who died at sixteen. I was absent most of the time in the city, but our home in the country joined theirs. Some friends said to me one night, "You know our old friend Jude whose daughter died? Some months past a spiritualistic medium came to South Bend and they began attending. They have gone wild over the thing. We did not know how to help them, and wondered if you cannot help them."

I went over and had a talk with them, and went with them. At the proper time this gentleman was supposed to be giving them a message from their daughter. After they got through I said, "I would like to talk to her," and I began to talk to this spirit. I said, "Are you Miss Jude? Where were you born? Where did you go to school?"

"The Willow Street School." Where did you attend church?

"The Willow Creek Methodist Church." The answers were perfectly correct. Finally I said, "I remember a night at the Willow Creek Methodist Church when a very wonderful thing happened to you. Do you remember what that was?" She did not know a thing about it. I said, "Your memory don't seem to be good. Don't you remember when a revival meeting was being conducted and you sat with Mrs. Lake and myself? When the altar service came I invited you to go and give your heart to the Lord, and you did, and the glory of God came into your soul?" She did not remember anything about that.

I said, "That is strange. Don't you remember on certain occasions you used to come to our home and we used to kneel and the glory and presence of God came on your soul?" She did not remember anything about that. I said, "You are not the spirit of Miss Jude. You are an old liar. In the Name of Jesus Christ you get out of here." And it got out. Beloved, do not be fooled by every voice you hear.

One other thing, Conan Doyle is greatly distressed about President Coolidge, and he thinks the proper thing to do is to immediately confer with the spirit of the late President Harding and be directed about the things of state, or he will make some blunder. This is the advice of one of the greatest scientists of all the world, a man who has been knighted by the King of England because of his knowledge of scientific methods. Strange council, a darkened soul. Bright mind filled with knowledge of this world, but a darkened soul without a knowledge of eternal things. Do you see the distinction?

The instance I told you of has been the practice of men whenever they have had opportunity to go into such matters. One of these days, the first time I hear somebody announcing that they are going to confer with President Harding, I am going to present myself. In case of a public man, his speeches are on record and they have been available to everybody. Here is an example. In Edinburgh I attended a seance where the medium was giving a wonderful message, supposedly from the spirit of the late W.E. Gladstone. I put in my pocket several copies of Gladstone's addresses. I had a stenographer take down the message, and I took the old addresses I had in my pocket and this one that had come through the medium and compared them.

I said, "It seems to me that something terrible has happened to W.E. Gladstone if he is the author of this message. The thing is not comparable with the things he uttered in this life. It looks to me as if dying has had an awful bad effect on him." They were very much surprised. Most mediums have gotten wise now. Comparison is a wonderful thing.

There is one source of knowledge; that is God. The sin of spiritualism is in this fact: God said to His ancient people Israel not to, *"Seek unto them that...peep, and that mutter"* [Isaiah 8:19]. This describes the conditions prevalent in any seance. What should they do? *"Should not a people seek unto their God?"* (Isaiah 8:19). This Word of God does not even give me the privilege of seeking guidance of angels, let alone the spirit of the dead, or the spirit of a living man either. It gives me one privilege. There is One Mind that knows all, that is the mind of God, and if I am His child, and if my heart is made pure by the blood of His Son, then I have a right to come into His presence and secure anything my heart may want.

I do not believe the world has ever begun to conceive of the treasures of the wisdom of the heart of God. Our conception of the possibility of receiving wisdom and knowledge from God is very limited. Here is an experience from my own life.

In the course of my preaching in Africa I observed I would begin to quote things from historical records that I had never heard. I could not understand it. After a while I became troubled about it and I must stop the practice. It was going on the record as a part of my sermon, and I felt if you quoted something historical you ought to be able to lay your hand on the record in order to be convinced. Then I observed there was difficulty when I checked these utterances.

Then I told my stenographer that when these unusual things would come, I would raise my finger and she was to put a special mark on these paragraphs. After a while I had quite a collection of them. When I came to the United States I had them with me. I was visiting in the office of Senator Chamberlain, talking with his secretary, Grant. As I sat talking with Grant, I showed him this list and told him my experience. He was a Holy Ghost baptized man. He said, "That is an easy matter. We have the most phenomenal man in the Congressional Library here. You give him a quotation from any book, and he will tell you where to find it." We sent the list in to him one evening and left it with him overnight. The next day when we returned he told us just where we could find each of these quotations.

Beloved who knows the facts? Some wondering mind somewhere? Some mind of a dead man? No sir, they were in the mind of God and the soul that enters into the mind of God can get them any time. But, Beloved, it is the blood of Jesus Christ that enters there. *"In [Him] are hid all the treasures of wisdom and knowledge"* [Colossians 2:3].

Oh God, some day may we become big enough to know God, to appreciate our Christ and our Savior and the wonder of His soul and the Christian privilege of entering there!

Portland Vision

In May, 1920, Rev. Lake moved to Portland, Oregon to start and oversee another Apostolic Church. During this time he had the following vision.

He could not sleep so he walked in the shadows of the tall trees in Mount Tabor Park.

"Through the park is a foot-path coming down through the trees that leads out to the street where we live, and in my vision I was seemingly out in the street, at the foot of this foot-path, and as I looked up in the park I was attracted by a quite brilliant light far up in the park. It was very slowly coming down the pathway to the street. I stood somewhat surprised, supposing it was some night man on some duty in the park, probably searching for something or somebody. As it approached I discovered that, instead, it was an angel presence, and the brilliance was an illumination surrounding him. He stood a few feet from me, and said to me, 'I have come to answer your prayers. Come with me.'"

Three wreaths: black, pink and white.

One dropped in San Francisco.

One in Honolulu. He said: "Through great suffering, through much tribulation, these have conquered."

China: A man, a European, was lying on the ground. Close by lay his wife. On one side of her a boy of about seven or eight and on the other side a girl of about ten or twelve. Turning to me the angel said, "These have given their all for the Lord and His Kingdom." He took a white wreath and as he held it in his hands tears fell upon the wreath and each tear turned into a diamond. It was covered by sparkling diamonds. He dropped the wreath and it lit by the head of the dead missionary.

Trans-Siberian Railway to Moscow and Petrograd. He explained the state of suffering of those under Soviet rule. Some scenes were so pitiable that my own soul was moved to tears. He said, "The Dragon, the great red dragon, the hater of Jesus, the enthroner of the human beast—he shall come to his end and none shall help."

He wanted to ask about Africa but was restrained by the demeanor of the angel. Only limited questions were permitted and some he did not consider worthy of an answer.

Johannesburg, South Africa: "The heart of Jesus was once gladdened here through the glory, the grace and the power of God manifested here. But human pride, formalism and lack of faith have brought disappointment to the heart of Him we love. But the glory will return, and the tried and true, those who have suffered and labored and prayed, will be rewarded. But all self-seekers shall be dethroned."

India: He could comprehend the soul struggle of certain elements. The angel said, "The present struggle is not a struggle to attain a knowledge of Jesus or to know His salvation. It is, rather, an endeavor to enthrone the heathen ideal of human efficiency."

Palestine: He was made conscious of the enmity between the Jews and the Arabs. The angel said, "The Kingdom must first be in the hearts of men."

Portland: Church at Portland: "To my amazement, on approaching the building, high in the atmosphere a half a mile or more, I discerned millions of demons, organized as a modern army. There were those who apparently acted as shock troops. They would charge with great ferocity, followed by a wave, and yet another wave, and yet another wave. After a little while I observed there operated a restraining influence that constituted a barrier through which they could not force themselves. With all the ingenuity of humans at war, this multitude of demons seemed to endeavor to break the barrier or to go further, but were utterly restrained. In amazement, I said to the angel, 'What does it mean?' He said to me, 'Such is the care of God for those that strive in unselfishness for His best.'"

He discerned the heart of the Angel was overburdened. In answer to this the Angel said, "Human selfishness and human pride have consumed and dissipated the very glory and heavenly power that God once gave from heaven to this movement as you have beheld tonight."

We were now at the foot of the pathway again. He took a step or two away, and in a sort of despair my heart cried out, "Angel, these are all struggling for want of an ideal. What constitutes real Pentecost? What ideal should be held before the minds of men as the will of God exhibited through a movement like this?"

During all this time I had carried my Bible in my hand. Reaching for the Bible, he opened to the Book of Acts, ran his finger down over the second page, that portion where the Spirit of God came down from heaven. Proceeding through the Book of Acts to its great outstanding revelations and phenomena, he said, "This is Pentecost as God gave it through the heart of Jesus. STRIVE FOR THIS. CONTEND FOR THIS. TEACH THE PEOPLE TO PRAY FOR THIS. For this, and this alone, will meet the necessity of the human heart, and this alone will have the power to overcome the forces of darkness."

When the Angel was departing he said, "Pray. Pray. Pray. Teach the people to pray. Prayer and prayer alone, much prayer, persistent prayer, is the door of entrance into the heart of God."

White wreath is God's best.
Pink second best.
Black for those who have failed in the fight.

16

Spiritual Dominion

The lesson that God seems to have put in my soul tonight is found in 2 Timothy, the 1st chapter. Do you know we do not read the Scriptures like people read a text book. Have you ever observed how a scientist reads his text book? He weighs every single word, and each word has a peculiar meaning. If we read the Word of God like that we would get the real vitality of what it says. I wonder if we have caught the force of this Scripture: *"Paul, an apostle of Jesus Christ by the will of God, according to the promise of LIFE which is IN Christ Jesus"* (verse 1). There is no life outside of Jesus Christ, no eternal life outside of Jesus Christ, by the declaration of Jesus Himself. John said: *"God hath given to us eternal life, and this life is in his Son. He that hath the Son hath life; and he that hath not the Son of God hath not life"* (1 John 5:11-12).

All the Scriptures are dear to my heart, and bring their peculiar ministry and lesson, but the words of Jesus are the supreme words of the Gospel. Jesus said: *"It is the spirit that quickeneth...the words that I speak unto you, they are spirit, and they are life"* (John 6:63). Do you know the difficulty in our day is that we have run away from *Jesus.* That is, the church at large has. The world is making a great struggle at the present hour, and we are in the midst of it ourselves, to get *back* to Jesus. We have run into false theology, we have run into "churchanity" and human interpretations, and a hundred other follies, but friends, it is a perfectly lovely and refreshing thing to get back to Jesus. Take the words of Jesus and let them become the Supreme Court of the Gospel to you.

I consider all the Word of God the Common Court of the Gospel, but the words of Jesus are the Supreme Court of the Gospel. If there is a question that is not clearly decided according to your vision in the Common Court of the Gospel, then refer it to the Supreme Court, which is the words of Jesus, and the words of Jesus will settle anything that is in your mind.

If our questions were settled by the words of Jesus, we would be out of all the confusion that the world is in at present. I do not see any other way for the world to come out of her present confusion unless it is to accept the words of Jesus as final authority, to accept Jesus as the divine finality where all questions are finally adjudicated, and stay by the words of Jesus.

Just as an example on that line, I suppose there is not any question in the Scripture that is more muddled and fuddled and slobbered over than the subject of water baptism, and we have a dozen forms of baptismal practice, emphasizing different phases of baptismal consecration. But, beloved, the words of Jesus would settle the whole controversy. Jesus' words settle both the spirit and mode of baptism forever. All the damnation that the Christian world has been in over that question is because we simply refused to take the words of Jesus and believe and obey them. I am such an enthusiast on the words of Jesus that if I was compelled to choose between the practice of the apostles and the words of Jesus, I would stand by the words of Jesus. It is the only method that has kept my soul from the confusion I see in other lives.

Coming back to our lesson, observe these words: *"According to the promise of life."* There is no promise of life outside of Jesus Christ. Jesus was the most emphatic teacher the world ever saw. He said: *"Ye must be born again"* [John 3:7]. There is no arbitration by which you can get around the matter. There is no possibility of avoiding that truth. You have got to come straight to it and meet it. *"According to the promise of life which is in Christ Jesus..."*

"When I call to remembrance the unfeigned faith that is in thee, which dwelt first in thy grandmother Lois, and thy mother Eunice; and I am persuaded that in thee also" [2 Timothy 1:5]. Timothy had two generations behind him of women of faith.

"Wherefore I put thee in remembrance that thou stir up the gift of God, which is in thee BY THE PUTTING ON OF MY HANDS" [2 Timothy 1:6].

Paul had some faith in the value of the putting on of his hands. It was not a mere form. I want to call your attention to the Word of God especially on this line. Paul's own convictions were that through the laying on of hands on this young man, an impartation of God to his life had been given. It was so real that even though Timothy was not aware of it and was not exercising the power of God thus bestowed, yet Paul's conviction was that the power of God was present. Why? Because he had laid his hands on him in the Name of the Lord Jesus Christ, and he believed the Spirit of the Lord Jesus Christ had been imparted to him: Therefore the gift of God was in him. Therefore, the faith to exercise that gift ought to be present, and he believed it was present because of the fact that the faith of God had already dwelt in his mother and grandmother, and he believed in him also.

Beloved, it takes faith to exercise your gift of God. There are just lots of people around everywhere who have gifts of God, and they are lying dormant in their lives, and there is no value for the kingdom of God through them because of the fact they have no faith in God to put the gift in exercise and get the benefit of it.

Probably Timothy was a timid fellow, and Paul is going to show him why he should be exercising this gift of God, which he believed to be in him.

There are so many preachers who are afraid of the devil. They have no idea of how big God is Who dwells in you. They have no idea of the power given to you because God dwells in you. They preach fear of the devil, fear of demons, and fear of this influence, and fear of that influence and fear of some other power. If the Holy Ghost has come down from heaven into your soul, common sense teaches us that He has made you the master thereby of every other power in the world. Otherwise the Word of God is a blank falsehood. For it declares: *"Greater is he that is in you, than he that is in the world"* (1 John 4:4). *"Behold, I give unto you power to tread on serpents and scorpions, and over all the power of the enemy: and nothing shall by any means hurt you"* (Luke 10:19). And if we had faith to believe that the *"greater than he"* is in us, bless God, we would be stepping out with boldness and majesty. The conscious supremacy of the Son of God would be manifest in our lives and instead of being subservient and bowed down and broken beneath the weight of sin and the powers of darkness around us, THEY would flee from us and keep out of our way. I believe before God there is not a devil that comes within a hundred feet of a real God-anointed Christian. That is the kind of vision God put in my soul.

When I went to South Africa years ago, I attended a great missionary conference a short time after I was there. It was a general conference of the Christian missions of the country. On account of our teaching the Baptism of the Holy Ghost and the power of God to heal, we were a peculiar feature in the conference. We were bringing a new message and they wanted to hear us, and get us sized up and classified.

Among the difficulties they discussed in that Conference was the tremendous influence of the native medicine men over the people. They call them witch doctors. They are a powerfully developed psychic type of man, and for generations and generations they have studied psychic things until they understood the practice of psychic laws. It is marvelous to see the psychic manifestations they bring to pass. I have seen shocking things take place at the hands of witch doctors, things that nobody would believe unless they beheld them.

On one occasion two men had become extremely jealous of each other, both native chiefs, and they lived sixty miles from each other. One time, as I was in the kraal of one of them, I heard them discussing this difficulty with the other chief and it was decided by the chief that the next Sunday morning he was going to set the other fellow on fire. I wanted to see this phenomenon and I got a horse and went across the country to be there on Sunday morning.

The chiefs go out and round up their cattle and herds, look over their flocks, etc. It is a sort of Sunday exercise. I rode along. We had not ridden for more than an hour when I observed this fellow was becoming very hot. Within half an hour he was absolutely purple. I knew somewhat of medicine; I would have said the man was likely to have a paralytic stroke from blood pressure. After a while he began to complain of terrible pain, and finally he became exhausted, got down and lay on the ground, and passed into a state of terrible exhaustion. I believe the man would have died. I had heard about these sort of things, but this was taking place under my own eyes. I saw that unless the man got deliverance he would die. When it got to that point, I said to the brethren, "It is time that we prayed." I stepped over and laid my hands on, and called on God to destroy that damning psychic power that was destroying the fellow, and God shattered it.

I talked to the Conference about this matter. I said, "It is a strange thing to me that in all the years of missions in this land, that your hands are tied on account of witch doctors. Why don't you go out and cast the devil out of these fellows, and get the people delivered from their power?"

They took a long breath and said, "Cast the devil out? He will cast the devil out of you!" The secret of our work, the reason God gave us one hundred thousand people, the reason we have twelve hundred native preachers in our work in Africa, is because of the fact we believed the promise of, *"Greater is he that is in you, than he that is in the world"* [1 John 4:4]. We not only went to seek them, but challenged them separately and united, and by the power of God delivered the people from their power, and when they were delivered the people appreciated their deliverance from the slavery in which they had been held through their superstitions, psychological, spirit control, and they are most terrible. *"God hath not given us the spirit of fear; but of power, and of love, and of a sound mind"* (2 Timothy 1:7).

Whenever I got in the presence of one of these fellows and wanted to cast out the devil, I always felt I wanted to get his eye. I search to get his eye. The eyes of a man are the windows of his soul. In teaching a class of children I asked them what the eyes were for. One little chap said, "Your eyes are for you to look out of." Do you get it? It is not a poetic expression, they are the windows through which you look out. It is wonderful the things you see when you look out. Sometimes you see fear, and the spirit of darkness, and you see the devil in the other life—marvelous things that you see with your inner eyes.

The world laughs at our Pentecostal people because they sometimes talk about seeing by the Spirit, and sometimes we talk about seeing psychically. We see all the time naturally, as you and I do now.

God anoints your soul. God anoints your life. God comes to dwell in your person. God comes to make you a master. That is the purpose of His indwelling in a Christian. The real child of God was to be a master over every other power of darkness in the world. It was to be subject TO HIM. He is to be God's representative in the world. The Holy Ghost in the Christian was to be as powerful as the Holy Ghost was in the Christ. Indeed, Jesus' words go to such an extreme that they declare that *"Greater works than these shall he do"* (John 14:12). It indicates that the mighty Holy Ghost from heaven in the life of the Christian was to be more powerful in you and in me after Jesus got to heaven and ministered Him to our souls than He was in Jesus.

Beloved, who has the faith to believe it? Who has faith to exercise it? We cannot exercise anything beyond what we believe to be possible. Listen: *"God hath not given us the spirit of fear."*

Fear of the devil is nonsense. Fear of demons is foolish. The Spirit of God anointing the Christian heart makes the soul impregnable to the powers of darkness. How I love to teach men that when the Lord Jesus Christ anoints your soul and baptizes you in the Holy Ghost, that the almightiness of the Eternal God, the Father, by the Spirit, and Jesus Christ combined has come into your soul.

One of the thirty-six articles of the Church of England says, "The Holy Ghost which proceedeth from the Father and the Son." There is no truer thing in all the world. Do you get it? "Which proceedeth from the Father and the Son." In the fourth and fifth chapters of Revelation you see the distinctive personalities of God the Father and Jesus Christ. God the Father occupies the Throne, and is holding the seven-sealed book in His hand. And Jesus Christ, the silent Lamb, without an attendant, not an angel to accompany Him, absolutely alone, in lonesomeness as the slain Lamb, presents Himself to the Father, and the Father hands Him the seven-sealed book, as He whose right it is to unseal and open the seals.

What I want to bring to you is that the Spirit of God, the divine master, the eternal power of God, the combined life and presence by the Spirit, of the Father and the Son, is given to you...not to leave you a weakling, and subject to all kinds of powers of darkness, but to make you a MASTER, to give you *dominion* in God over every devilish force that ever was.

"God hath not given us the spirit of fear, but of power, and of love, and of a sound mind" [2 Timothy 1:7]. The Spirit of Power is the Holy Ghost, bless God. And not only of power, but of LOVE and of a SOUND MIND. Not a craziness and insanity, but a sound mind, by which you can look in the face of the devil and laugh.

Once I was called to come and pray for a blacksmith at Johannesburg, South Africa. He was in delirium tremens. When I got to the house they had him locked in a room, and the windows barred.

The wife said, "Mr. Lake, you are not going into that room?"

I said, "Yes, I would like to."

"But, Brother, you do not understand. My sons are all more powerful than you are, and four of them tried to overpower him and could not do it. He nearly killed them."

I said, "Dear Sister, I have the secret of power that I believe matches this case. *'Greater is he that is in you, than he that is in the world'* [1 John 4:4]. Sister, you just give me the key, and go about your work, and do not be troubled."

I unlocked the door, slipped into the room, and turned the key again, and put the key in my pocket. The man was reclining in a crouch like a lion ready to spring. I never heard any lips blaspheme as his did. He cursed me by every expression I ever heard, and worse. He threatened me if I came near him he would tear me limb from limb and throw me out the window. He was as big as two of me. I never saw such an arm in my life.

I began to talk to him. I had the confidence that *"Greater is he that is in you, than he that is in the world."* I engaged him in conversation until the Holy Ghost in me got hold of that devil, or a legion, as the case might be. I approached the bed step by step, sometimes only three inches, and in a half hour I got up close enough where I could reach his hand. He was still reclining in a posture like a lion. I caught his hand and turned his wrists. I was not practicing any athletic tricks, but I unconsciously turned his wrists over, and as I did it brought my eyes down near his, and all at once I woke up; I could see the devil in that man begin to crawl. He was trying to get away. God Almighty can look out of your eyes, and every devil that was ever in hell could not look in the eyes of Jesus without crawling. The lightnings of God were there.

My spirit awoke, and I could see the devil was in terror and was crawling and trying to get back away from my eyes as far as he could. I looked up to heaven and called on God to cast that devil out, and lent Jesus Christ all the force of my nature, all the power of my spirit, all the power of my mind, and all the power of my body. God had me from the crown of my head to the soles of my feet. The lightnings of God went through me and the next thing I knew he collapsed in a heap and flopped down like a big fish. Then he turned out of the bed on his knees and began to weep and pray because he had become human again, and the devil was gone.

Dear hearts, don't you see in a moment that that character of education develops a certain confidence in God, and it makes your soul sick when you see Christian men and women sneak around, afraid of the devil, and teaching people the devil is going to jump on you and take possession of you. Not a bit of it! There never was a devil in the world that ever went through the blood of Jesus, if the individual was in Christ.

In the Jewish Bible, among the listings of the covenants, is the one that is known as the Threshold Covenant. That was the Covenant by which the Israelites went out of the land of Egypt when God told them to slay a lamb, and put the blood in the door posts and lintel. And the Jewish Bible adds they put the blood on the threshold. And a lot of people get the blood of Jesus on their head, but it seems to me they do not get it under their feet. The Word of God teaches us to get the blood under your feet, and on the right hand and on the left hand and over your head. That is your protection. There was no angel of death in the land of Egypt, or in hell, that could go through that blood unto that family. No Sir! He was absolutely barred.

Friends, do you believe it was the blood of the lamb that was barring the angel of death? Do you believe the red stains on the doors frightened him away? No sir, the blood signified to me that there is one that goes *through* the blood; that is the Holy Ghost. And, beloved, the Eternal God by the Spirit went through the blood to the inside, and stayed there and defended the house.

"Greater is he that is in you, than he that is in the world."

All these little insignificant devils that came along in this sickness or that sickness, or that temptation of sin have no power over you. Dear friends, from heaven there comes to your heart and mine that dominion of Jesus by which the God-anointed soul walks through them, through myriads of demons and they cannot touch you.

I was in Pretoria, South Africa, visiting with a friend and trying to keep out of the hot sun, to meditate and pray; and as I meditated and prayed, I seemed to be lifted up in the Spirit until I was a mile or more above the city and could see the city like you would from an airplane. When I got up there I made a discovery. There were myriads of spirits of darkness and myriads of spirits of light in the most awful conflict I ever saw. Naturally you think of a weapon when you see a fight. I thought, "If only I had a weapon I would get into that fight."

Presently, the Spirit of God got hold of me and when these demons came at me from all sides, I waded into them and began to knock them down. It continued until I had knocked so many down I had to climb over them to get at the rest.

When the vision lifted I prayed, "Dear Lord, what does it mean?" And the Spirit of the Lord said to me, "This contest that you have seen in the upper air will exist among your own people in six months. This lesson is to teach you that there is a dominion in Jesus Christ, and *'Greater is he that is in you, than he that is in the world.'*"

Friends, it is time you and I, as the blood-washed in Jesus, awake to our privilege whereby in the Name of the Lord we cease to sin and let no unholy condemnation remain upon our life any longer.

I do not know, but maybe I have come through a different school from what others have in the lines of the Spirit, but I am sure of one thing, that if Christianity was to leave me a weakling, to be oppressed by the power of darkness, I would seek something else because it would not meet the need. It is that which meets the need that gives you divine supremacy in Jesus Christ. Friends, when your heart is surcharged by that faith in God so that *"Greater is he that is in you, than he that is in the world,"* you will pray a new prayer.

Moses came to the Red Sea with impassable mountains on the right hand and impassable mountains on the left hand, the army of Pharaoh behind him, and the sea in front of him. If any man had a right to stop and pray, surely you might say that man had.

Over and over and over again, when we get to the real ditch, we try to jump the thing and put the responsibility back on God. Just watch God make a real man. When Moses got his prayer nicely started, God rebuked him and said, *"Wherefore criest thou unto me? speak unto the children of Israel, that they go forward: But lift THOU up thy rod, and stretch out thine hand over the sea, and DIVIDE it"* (Exodus 14:15-16).

I want you Pentecostal Christians to get this. God did not say, *"Moses, you stretch forth your hand, and I will divide the sea."* He said, *"Stretch forth thine hand over the sea, and DIVIDE it."* You have faith in me, YOU stretch forth your hand and divide the sea.

Jesus said practically the same thing to His disciples: *"When he had called unto him his twelve disciples, he GAVE them the power against unclean spirits, to cast them out, and to heal all manner of sickness and all manner of disease"* (Matthew 10:1 and Luke 9:1-6).

Beloved He gives it to you. What is the Holy Ghost? It is the gift of God Himself to you. The Holy Spirit is not simply given that you may be a channel, and always a channel. No Sir! But instead of that, the most magnificent thing the Word of God portrays is that Christ, indwelling in you by the Holy Ghost, is to make you a son of God like Jesus Christ, God anointed from heaven, with the recognized power of God in your spirit to command the will of God.

It may not be that all souls have grown to that place where such a life as that is evident, but surely if the Son of God by the Holy Ghost has been born in our heart, it is time we began to let Him have some degree of sway in our heart, and some degree of heavenly dominion of value, and some degree of the lightnings of Jesus Christ breaking forth from our spirit.

That is what the Word of God speaks to my soul tonight. That is why my spirit rejoices in this blessed Word. *"God hath not given us the spirit of fear; but of power, and of love, and of a sound mind."* The sanest man is the man who believes God and stands on His promises, and knows the secret of His power, receives the Holy Ghost and gives Him sway in his life, and goes out in the Name of the Lord Jesus to command the will of God and bring it to pass in the world.

At the end of the first three hundred years of the Christian era, there were millions of Christians. Christianity was an aggressive power. Christianity went into the heart of heathendom to undo their superstitions, to break down their psychological forces, to leave the consciousness of Jesus Christ in the heart, to heal the sick, to raise the dead. Oh, God in Heaven, bring our hearts back to it! Christianity was a conquering force.

But friends, there was a consecration secret in the life of the early church. It was this: If they could not conquer, they could die. Dear friends, you will never exercise very much of the dominion of the Son of God in your spirit until your heart is ready to say, if I cannot get the mastery, "I can die." The early Christians died, plenty of them. Millions of them. That is the reason people say the blood of the martyrs was the seed of the church. Bless God, they died for their faith.

Friends, you and I will never know or have the big ministry and the big victory until our souls have arrived at the place where we will die for our faith also. Lord God, help us. These days, if a man gets a stomachache, he is afraid he will die. Die if you have to die, but do not disgrace the cause of Christ and weaken in your faith and sell it to man or the devil. When that degree of consecration comes into your heart, when that degree of determination comes into your spirit, you will not have to die.

But I tell you, most of us will do our dying before we enter there. That is the life into which dead men enter. That is the resurrection life. You have to die to get it. You have to die to enter there. We die to our sin, we die to ourselves, we die to the opinions of men, and we die to the old world, we die to fear of spooks and demons and devils, and prove the truth of the text, *"Greater is he that is in you, than he that is in the world."* In My Name they shall cast out devils. Rebuke the devil and he will flee from you. We live in Jesus Christ. Blessed be His Name.

Ephesians 4:27
Ephesians 6:11
James 4:7
1 Corinthians 10:13
Matthew 17:20
Luke 10:19

17

Lake's Reply to Dr. Elwood Bulgin

"Lake's Book, *Lake's Reply to Bulgin,* is the clearest statement on the truth of divine healing ever written, a remarkable document."
Dr. Frank N. Riale, Field Secretary, Presbyterian Board of Education

This letter to Dr. Bulgin was printed in the leading daily newspaper in Spokane, Washington, 1920.

Spokane, Washington
February 28, 1920

Dr. Elwood Bulgin
Spokane, Washington

Dear Brother in Christ:

It was my privilege to be present at your meeting at the St. Paul Methodist Church at Spokane last Monday night and listen to your sermon. I was deeply impressed by the masterful manner in which you marshaled your facts, and the spirit in which they were presented to your great audience.

Your presentation of the deity of Jesus Christ, and the sharpness with which you brought the facts of the denial of the deity of Jesus by the Christian Scientists, were striking. The masterful handling of the whole subject commanded my admiration, and I believe the admiration of a great majority of your audience.

Men can speak with frankness to each other, particularly when their interests in the Kingdom of Jesus Christ are identical. You have lived, loved, and denied yourself, and suffered for the cause of the Kingdom of Christ in the earth. I, too, have loved and suffered for my fidelity to the vision of the redemption of Jesus Christ which God revealed to me.

For twenty-five years I have labored, as few men in the world have labored for so long a period, to bring before the world as far as I could the magnificent truths of the redemptive blood and life and power of the Son of God.

Your method and my methods have been different. You, in your forceful, philosophical manner, have undertaken to destroy faith in Christian Science through opposition, ridicule, and exposure of what you believe to be its fallacies. On the other hand, I have undertaken by specific revelation of the truth of Jesus Christ concerning the healing power of God and its availability for all men today, to show the world that there is no need for any man to leave any stable Christian body in order to secure the benefits of salvation and healing specifically declared by Jesus Christ Himself to be available for every man.

Jesus, in contrast with the ancient philosophers and reformers of the past and present, first gave Himself in consecration to God, body, soul and spirit, thereby establishing the pattern of consecration for all Christians forever. His baptism was the dedication and commitment of Himself *"unto all righteousness"* [see Matthew 3:14-15]. He undertook to reveal the righteousness of God. Note the nature of this revelation.

Having definitely committed Himself, His body, His soul, His spirit, to God forever, immediately there descended upon Him the witness to His hundredfold consecration. The Holy Ghost came from heaven as a dove and abode upon Him, as it ever will upon every man who will meet Almighty God with the same utterances of real consecration to God, of spirit and soul and body. This reveals the demand of God upon the Christian's person and conscience, and the answer of God from heaven to this fullness of consecration.

Being thus definitely equipped, He proceeded to the wilderness for testing by Satan to see if this consecration of body and soul and spirit would endure.

He overcame all the efforts of Satan to tempt Him in the specific departments of His life: first, the body; second, the soul; third, the spirit. He overcame through reliance on God and His word, and came forth in the power of the Spirit. He announced the constructive platform of His life and ministry, containing the following six planks.

"The Spirit of the Lord is upon me, because he hath anointed me."

First—*"To preach the gospel to the poor."*
Second—*"He hath sent me to heal the brokenhearted."*
Third—*"To preach deliverance to the captives, and"*
Fourth—*"Recovering of sight to the blind."*
Fifth—*"To set at liberty them that are bruised."*
Sixth—*"To preach the acceptable year of the Lord"*
[Luke 4:18-19].

God's acceptable year had come. No more waiting for the year of Jubilee and all its consequent blessings. God's never-ending Jubilee was at hand in Jesus Christ.

He then went throughout all Galilee *teaching* in their synagogues, and preaching the gospel of the Kingdom, and *healing* all manner of sickness and all manner of disease among the people, and so established *forever* the ideal of Christian ministry for the Church of God.

Then He empowered twelve men, and *sent them to preach the kingdom of God, and to heal the sick* [see Matthew 10:7-8]. Profiting by their experience, and advancing in faith and knowledge of the power of God, He *"appointed other seventy also"* [Luke 10:1].

But in sending forth the seventy He reversed the order of instruction. To the seventy He said: *Go your ways:... "and heal the sick that are therein, and say unto them, The kingdom of God is come nigh unto you"* [Luke 10:9]. And they returned rejoicing that even the devils were subject to them *"through thy name"* [Luke 10:17].

Then came His wonderful entrance into death, His redemption on the cross, His resurrection from the grave, His interviews with His disciples, His last commission in which, according to Mark, He established in the Church of Christ to be born through their preaching in all the world, the very same ministry of salvation and healing that He Himself during His earth life had practiced. That ministry contained the message of Jesus to all the world and the anointing with power from on High, just as He had received it at His baptism. Indeed He commanded them to wait in Jerusalem until *"Ye shall be baptized with the Holy Ghost, not many days hence"* [Acts 1:5].

He declared to them that certain signs should follow, saying: These signs shall follow them that believe. Every one, every Christian soul, was thus commissioned by Jesus to heal the sick and sinful from sickness and sin.

"In my name shall they—

First—*"Cast out devils."*
Second—*"They shall speak with new tongues."*
Third—*"They shall take up serpents."*
Fourth—*"And if they drink any deadly thing, it shall not hurt them."*
Fifth—*"They shall lay hands on the sick, and they shall recover"* [Mark 16:17-18].

The same Holy Spirit of God which flowed through Jesus Christ, the anointing that was upon Him and which flowed through His hands and into the sick, was an impartation of God so real that when the woman touched the hem of His garment, she was conscious of the instant effect of the healing in her body through it. "She felt in her body that she was healed of that plague," while Jesus Himself was likewise conscious of an outflow. He said: *"Somebody hath touched me: for I perceive that virtue is gone out of me"* [Luke 8:46].

Divine Healing is the particular phase of ministry in which the modern church does not measure up to the early church. This failure has been due to a lack of knowledge of the real nature and the real process of Christian healing. The above incident reveals the secret of what the power was, how the power operated, by what law it was transmitted from the disciple to the one who needed the blessing. The power was the Holy Ghost of God, both in Jesus Christ after His baptism in the Holy Ghost, and in the disciples after the baptism in the Holy Ghost came upon them on the day of Pentecost. It flowed through the hands of Jesus to the sick: it permeated the garments He wore. When the woman touched even the hem of His garment there was sufficient of the power of God there for her need.

The disciples healed the sick by the same method. Indeed, the Apostle Paul, realizing this law, permitted the people to bring to him handkerchiefs and aprons that they might touch his body, and when they were carried to the sick, the sick were healed through the power of God in the handkerchiefs, and the demons that inhabited their persons went out of them.

Herein is shown the secret of the early church, that which explains the whole miracle-working power of the apostles and the early church for four hundred years. The same is evident in branches of the modern church. Herein is revealed the secret that has been lost. That secret is the conscious, tangible, living, incoming, abiding, outflowing Spirit of God through the disciple of Christ who has entered into blood-washed relationship and baptism in the Holy Ghost.

This is the secret that the modern church from the days of the Reformation onward has failed to reveal. We have, however, retained a form of godliness, *but have denied the power thereof* [see 2 Timothy 3:5].

When Jesus laid His hands on people, the Holy Ghost was imparted to them in healing virtue. When the disciples and early Christians likewise laid their hands on the sick, the Holy Ghost was imparted through them to the needy one. Likewise the Holy Ghost was imparted to preachers *"for the work of the ministry"* [Ephesians 4:12], including healing. Primitive church history abounds in examples of healing in the same manner. Paul specifically enjoins Timothy to *Forget not the gift [power] that is in thee, that came through the laying on of my hands* [see 2 Timothy 1:6]. It was an impartation of the Holy Ghost to Timothy for the work of the Christian ministry.

In the whole range of church history we have retained the form, but have lost its power in a great degree. The Pope lays his hands on the head of the Cardinal, the Cardinal lays his hands on the head of the Bishop, the Bishop lays his hands on the head of the Priest, the Priest lays his hands on the head of the communicant when he receives him as a member of the church.

In the Protestant church in all her branches, the laying on of hands in ordination for the ministry is practiced. But in the early church it was not the laying on of hands alone, but through the laying on of hands the impartation of the definite living Spirit of the living God to the individual took place. Through its power in him he was constituted a real priest, a real elder, a real preacher with grace, healing power and faith anointed of God from on High.

God gave the blood of Jesus to the Christian Church. God gave the power of healing to the Christian Church in the Holy Ghost, and as long as they lived under the anointing of the Holy Ghost and exercised the faith of Jesus in their hearts, the healing power of God manifested and is still manifest where this condition exists. Christian Science exists because of the failure of the Christian Church to truly present Jesus Christ and His power through the Spirit and minister it to the world.

Robert C. Ingersoll assailed the Holy Scriptures, laughed at the Christian God, destroyed the faith of men, wrecked their hopes and left them stranded and abandoned amid the wreckage. Through this means he brought the just condemnation of the world upon himself. The world condemns him to this hour in that he destroyed the faith of men without supplying to their souls something to take its place, as he should have done, and as any man who is honorable and true must do.

You recommended divine healing in one breath and denied its potency in the next. You have attacked Christian Science, the followers of Dowie, and others and arraigned them at the bar and condemned them, without giving to men a tangible way by which the healing of God might be brought to them. Why do you not study and practice Jesus Christ's own way of healing and so make your ministry constructive? What are you going to do with the multitude of dying that the doctors cannot help? Leave them to die? The doctors have got through with them. And in many instances even though they are still prescribing for them and are perfectly aware of their inability to heal the sick ones and are candid and willing to say so, Dr. Bulgin, what have you got for these? What have you given to these?

If a man were walking down the street with a very poor set of crutches and a ruffian came along and kicked the crutches from under him and let him fall, every honest soul would rise in condemnation of the ruffian's act and demand reparation. You come to the dying, kick their hope from under them, and let them fall to the ground, and leave them there to die without bringing them the true healing power in the blood and Spirit of Jesus. It is not sufficient to say "I believe in Divine healing." If they are sick they must be healed.

This must not be construed as a defense of Christian Science. It is not given with that thought, not in that spirit. It is given rather in the hope that as an influential man in the Christian Church, you may see the weakness of your position and of the position of the church, and by the grace of God call the Church back again to faith in Jesus Christ, the Son of God, for healing for every man from every disease, as Jesus Christ intended it should be and as the scriptures definitely, positively teach, and make proper scriptural provision for a definite healing ministry.

In the hope of supplying this need of the Church, the Protestant ministers of the city of Los Angeles have agreed in formal resolution to begin the teaching and study and practice of healing. How has this come to pass, and why? They have been whipped into it by the success of Christian Science.

A recent issue of a New York daily paper announces that the pastors of New York have likewise undertaken to teach the people the power of God to heal. The Protestant Episcopal Church is endeavoring through the ministry of a layman of the Church of England from the old country, a Mr. Hickson, to educate their people in the truth of healing through the atonement of Jesus Christ, the Son of God, by the laying on of hands and the prayer of faith. In a few days the gentleman will appear at All Saints Cathedral, Spokane, for that purpose, and the sick will be invited to be ministered to in the Name of the Son of God and healed through His blood purchase.

The Church of England in England and also in Africa for ten years has been endeavoring to organize societies, not to teach their people Christian Science, psychic therapeutics, or mental healing, all of which belong to the realm of the natural, but to teach and demonstrate the pure power of God from Heaven by the Holy Ghost, purchased by the blood of Jesus Christ, to heal diseases.

Frank N. Riale, a secretary of the Presbyterian Board of Education of New York, with sixty-three universities and colleges under his control and supervision, is the author of a remarkable book, *The Sinless, Sickless, Deathless Life,* in which he recounts in a chapter entitled, "How the Light and the Fire Fell," the marvelous story of his own conversion. He was a minister of the gospel and a graduate of Harvard. He found his Lord at the hands of an Indian in Dakota. He tells of the light of God that came to his soul in sanctifying power through the ministry of a Salvation Army officer, Col. Brengle. He related his marvelous healing when a diseased and dying wreck through the reading of a religious tract on healing and his experience in seeing many healed of all manner of diseases by the power of God. You are a Presbyterian, my Brother. You need not go out of your own Church for the truth of God concerning healing.

The question before the Church, now that the break toward healing has come, and it has come, is who is prepared to teach and demonstrate the truth of God concerning healing? Will it be a fact that in the absence of knowledge of God by the ministry of the church for healing, will the church in her blindness and ignorance and helplessness be overwhelmed by Christian Science, New Thought and the thousand and one cults which teach psychological healing?

Where is the prophet of God who should come forward, teach and demonstrate the pure spiritual value and power of the Holy Ghost, secured for men because Jesus Christ, the Son of God, gave His blood to get it for them? Is it not time that such men as yourself arise in the dignity of Christ and throw off the shackles of formal religion and by the grace of God enter into the real life of living power through the Son of God in the Holy Ghost, and rescue the Church out of her present degradation, re-establishing forever Divine Healing on its true and scriptural basis, the atonement of Jesus Christ?

Twenty-five years ago the light concerning healing came to my soul, after four brothers and four sisters had died of diseases, and when four other members of the family were in a dying state, abandoned by the physicians as hopeless, and after my father had spent a fortune trying to obtain human help. One man of God who had the truth of God in his heart came to the rescue. All four sick ones were healed. I was an ardent Methodist. I loved my Church. My parents were members of an old Scotch Presbyterian Kirk. The Presbyterian Church had no light on the subject of healing; the Methodist Church had no light on the subject of healing. I received my light through a man who had been a minister of the Congregational Church. He knew God. He knew Christ the Lord. He knew the power of God to save, and the power of God to heal.

When I accepted this blessed truth and saw my family healed out of death, what was the attitude of the Church? Just what the attitude of all the leading churches has been. When I declared this truth before our conferences, she undertook to ostracize me: and from that day to this many of her ministry, who have prayed through to God and secured the blessing and power of God upon their soul to heal the sick, have been forced out of her ministry.

Dr. Bulgin, is it not time to quit attacking forms of faith, whether good or bad, and turn your attention and the attention of the church to the only thing that will deliver her out of her present wretchedness and inability to bless, and to bring her back again to Christ, to the foot of the cross, to the blood of Jesus, to the Holy Ghost from on High, to the power of God and the real faith including healing, "once delivered to the saints?" Through this healing ministry the Church at Spokane reports 100,000 healings by the power of God through five years of continuous daily efforts and the kindred blessed fact that the majority of those healed were saved from sin also.

The dying world is stretching out her hands for help. The Church on account of her laxness in this matter opens the doors for the existence of Christian Science and all the thousand and one worn out philosophies that follow in her train. Let the manhood of the Church arise, take the place of the prophet of God, call her back to the ministry of real salvation, a blessed salvation not alone for men after they are dead, or that will give them bliss in heaven when they die, but to a salvation that gives eternal life in Christ, health for the mind, and health for the body, and supplies likewise the power of God for the immediate need, for the need of the sick, for the need of the sinful, the wretched and dying and sin-cursed and disease smitten.

Let the Church return in the glory of God and the power of Christ to the original faith as clearly demonstrated in the New Testament, as perpetuated forever in the Church through the nine gifts of the Holy Spirit, demonstrating beyond controversy that as long as the Holy Spirit is in the Church, so long are the gifts of the Holy Spirit not only present but exercisable through faith. (See 1 Corinthians 12.)

"For to one is given by the Spirit"

First—*"The word of wisdom."*
Second—*"The word of knowledge."*
Third—*"Faith by the same Spirit."*
Fourth—*"The gifts of healing."*
Fifth—*"The working of miracles."*
Sixth—*"To another prophecy."*
Seventh—*"To another discerning of spirits."*
Eighth—*"To another divers kinds of tongues."*
Ninth—*"To another the interpretation of tongues."*

The unchanging order of government, spiritual enduement, and ministry of the gifts of the Spirit are further declared as follows: *"And God hath set some in the church, first apostles, secondarily prophets, thirdly teachers, after that miracles, then gifts of healings, helps, governments, diversities of tongues"* [1 Corinthians 12:28].

When the Church exercises these gifts, then she may condemn Christian Science, Dowieism, or New Thought; then she may condemn every other philosophical cult; then she may condemn Unitarianism, and everything else that you preach against, though she will not need to. Jesus never did. There were just as many strange philosophies in His day as in ours. The constructive righteousness of Christ, the presence of the living Son of God to save and heal, the revelation to the world of His divine power will stop the mouths of every "ism" and manifest one glorious, triumphant, all-embracing power of God through Jesus Christ, His Son, and its everlasting superiority. Neither will you be compelled as you are to glorify doctors, medicines, surgery, etc., when the greatest physicians on earth have deplored their inability to deliver the world from its curse of sickness. Then you cannot only teach the theory of the atonement of our Lord and Savior Jesus Christ, but demonstrate its reality and power to save both soul and body.

All the abstract criticism in the world is powerless to stop the drift from the churches to Christian Science so long as Christian Science heals the sick and the church does not. Men demand to be shown. When the authority of Jesus to forgive sins was challenged, He met the challenge with the healing of the palsied man, not with negations and criticisms. He said: *"Whether is it easier to say to the sick of the palsy, Thy sins be forgiven thee; or to say, Arise, and take up thy bed, and walk? But that ye may know... I say unto thee, Arise, and take up thy bed, and go thy way..."* (Mark 2: 9-11). He was too big for abstract criticism. So must the Christian and the Church become.

18

The Sabbath

October 6, 1912, Johannesburg, South Africa

During the Conference I was asked by the brethren to deliver a discourse on the subject of the Sabbath Day for the guidance of the workers.

It is not my purpose to deal with the subject in an argumentative manner, but rather in the form of a pronouncement of the position of the Church.

The Word of God is sufficiently clear. It has already defined the position for the Christian in the most emphatic way. The 2nd chapter of Colossians is perhaps as clear a portion of Scripture on this particular issue as any portion of the Word. It seems most difficult for Christians to understand and realize, in our entrance into Christ Jesus by the reception of the Spirit of God who abides within, our Christian experience has been moved into a different place from that in which we lived before.

I have tried at different times to define the operation of the Spirit of God in the different dispensations, that we may get a clear basis on which to rest. I will review this morning in a word.

The Patriarchal Dispensation

In the Patriarchal Dispensation God seems to have been approaching man from this standpoint, as if man was far removed from God, and as if God was endeavoring to reveal Himself to man.

Abraham perhaps furnishes the best example in the Word, and to him God appeared twice, twenty years apart. There was a lapse of twenty years, in which Abraham heard nothing from God. Then God spoke to him again. Now, that is the best revelation from God to man that is given us in the Patriarchal Dispensation. And it seems as if the position was, "God revealing Himself to man."

The Mosaic Dispensation

The Mosaic Dispensation was different. It was a fuller revelation. It did not destroy any of the revelation of God that the Patriarchs had known. So God was present with the Jewish people in the Pillar of Cloud and the Pillar of Fire, and the Shekinah over the Mercy Seat, an ever present God.

When the temple was built, the Lord abode in the Holy of Holies. In it there was no artificial light. The holy place was lit by candles, but in the Holy of Holies there was neither window nor door, nor artificial light of any kind. The presence of God illuminated the Holy of Holies, the continuous presence of God with man.

The Christian Dispensation

Patriarchal revelation was "God to man," and the Mosaic revelation was "God with man," but the Christian revelation was greater than all. Jesus said in His own words, *"He dwelleth with, and shall be IN you" [John 14:17]*. And the revelation of God to the Christian is *Christ within you* by the Holy Ghost, not "to" man nor "with" man but "in" man. Man becoming the embodiment of God.

It will be readily seen, then, that our conception and standard must be in accordance with the revelation that God gave to us, and the Christian cannot base his standard of life upon the Mosaic law in any way. Jesus lifted us up above that standard: as high as the heavens are above the earth.

When the Christian, then, endeavors to go back and live under Christ Jesus and the communion of the control of the law, he has descended from the standard of the Spirit of God abiding within, and has placed himself in the same position where the Mosaic people were.

PAUL'S WARNING: Over and over again Paul warns us about this thing, and to the Galatians particularly he gives this wonderful warning that *having begun in the Spirit they were now going to return to the flesh* [see Galatians 3:3]. And that is the danger with many Christians these days, that having begun in the Holy Ghost, they might return to obedience to commandments.

The Lord Jesus Raised the Standard for the Christian Dispensation

Then someone says: "What about the commandments?" We can see what Jesus says of them in the Sermon on the Mount (Matthew 5). Jesus said, *"It was said by them of old time, Thou shalt not kill"* [Matthew 5:21]. But Jesus lifted that standard miles above where Moses placed it and said, *"But I say unto you, That whosoever is angry with his brother without a cause shall be in danger of the judgment"* [Matthew 5:22]. That is to say, he is a murderer. (1 John 3:15).

Under the Mosaic law they had to commit an act in order to be guilty. Under the law of Christ the presence in the heart of the desire is sufficient to condemn. So in every instance the Lord raised the standard.

The commandment says, *"Thou shalt not commit adultery"* [Exodus 20:14]. Jesus says, *"That whosoever looketh on a woman to lust after her hath committed adultery with her already in his heart"* [Matthew 5:28]. Jesus took it out of the regime of commandments into the regime of the heart experience, and, *"as the heavens are higher than the earth, so are my ways higher than your ways, and my thoughts than your thoughts"* (Isaiah 55:9).

THE GREAT DEBATE: The greatest debate that has come through these fifty years, between those who contend for the observance of the Sabbath Day (the Seventh), and we who accept the Christian Sabbath, has ever been on that one point. Are we still bound by the law or has Christ made the Christian free from the force of the commandment? And it seems to me that the Word of God makes this clear as daylight, that the Word places our feet emphatically on this ground that to us, in the Holy Ghost, the law has become a dead thing. Indeed, it has been spoken of as blotted out (Colossians 2:14), even that which was written on stone (2 Corinthians 3:7-17).

The first chapter of Colossians deals with the history of the fact of the indwelling of Christ, and after establishing this fact Paul goes on to review the subject of our obedience to the law. Commencing with the 13th verse of the 2nd chapter, we have the declaration of the expulsion of the law:

> **And you, being dead in your sins and the uncircumcision of your flesh, hath he quickened together with him, having forgiven you all trespasses; Blotting out the handwriting of ordinances that was against us, which was contrary to us, and took it out of the way, nailing it to his cross; And having spoiled principalities and powers, he made a show of them openly, triumphing over them in it. Let no man therefore judge you in meat, or in drink, or in respect of an holyday, or of the new moon, or of the sabbath days: Which are a shadow of things to come; but the body is of Christ [Colossians 2:13-17].**

Thus far the interpretation is given of the destruction by Christ of the ordinances and laws that were contrary to us, by having established within us by the Holy Ghost of His own indwelling, He having been the Lord of the Sabbath, and we, as sons of God and joint heirs with Jesus Christ, will also enter into that place of dominion, where we, too, in Him, become lords also of the Sabbath and every other commandment. Blessed be God!

The New Covenant

The 16th verse: On Thursday last, among the questions that were asked, was this: "Do we advocate the partaking of a meal in connection with the Lord's Supper?" And in this thing once again we see the Christian's failure to separate between the Old and New Dispensations. For, when Jesus partook officially of the last Passover Supper that was ever given to mankind, and by that act forever closed the Jewish Dispensation, there was nothing further to do but make the sacrifice on the Cross: and the instant after the closing of that Supper the Lord instituted a new ceremony, the one we observe today, the communion of the Lord's Supper. No longer the Passover feast and Passover lamb, but the Christ of God, Who now pledges Himself to shed His own blood for the salvation of the world.

Between these two acts there is as great a distance as between East and West. The one was the mark and stamp of that which was old and ready to decay (Hebrews 8:13), and the other was the birth of mankind through the shedding of the blood of Jesus Christ.

And so, beloved, when the Christian undertakes that his life shall be governed by commandments, he is going back again into this old life, into the old realm, forgetting his state with Jesus Christ.

It does not mean we shall turn anarchists and that to us there is no law, but rather that we are now obedient unto the higher law by the Son of God.

The Sabbath Day

On the subject of the Sabbath itself: All the other Commandments are spoken of in the New Testament and reiterated, but the Sabbath Commandment not; and no doubt for this reason, that the prophecies all along had pointed to the Son of God, Who was Himself the fulfillment of the law. *"I came not to destroy [the law], but to fulfill it"* (Matthew 5:17). *"Wherefore the law was our schoolmaster to bring us unto Christ"* [Galatians 3:24]. When we got to Christ, beloved, we were beyond the sphere of the law. The law was a schoolmaster to bring us to Christ. Blessed be His Name.

So with the Sabbath. Christ Himself, the Eternal Rest into which the Christian enters not to abide on the Sabbath Day, but to abide always, every day, and forever. He is our Sabbath alone.

When we live in the Son of God we have come beyond the sphere of commandment, for the law was made for the unlawful and unholy, for murderers of fathers and mothers, for whoremongers, etc. (1 Timothy 1:9-10). Upon our statute books today there are no doubt a thousand laws that you and I know nothing about, and we care less. Why? They are of no interest to us. We hardly pay any attention to the law of murder, nor can we tell the details because of the fact that being sons of God we are living in love and are not interested in what the law says of murder. There is no murder in our hearts. Blessed be God! We have passed on.

And so the Christian who has entered into Christ Jesus and is abiding in Him and is a possessor of the Holy Ghost, has moved beyond the regime of the law and commandments. They are of no value to him. He lives in obedience to one law and one commandment, the Eleventh. This includes all the rest in one: *"That ye love one another, as I have loved you"* (John 15:12). Blessed be His Name.

An Apt Illustration

Henry Drummond, I believe it is, in his "Greatest Thing in the World," gives an illustration that is so fitting. He says that he visits at a friend's home. He finds that he and his wife have lived together in the most beautiful unity for many years. But a friend of his is still anxious that he shall be a strict observer of the law, and he sits down and writes a code of rules for the government of this man and wife who have always lived together in unity. He says, *"Thou shalt not kill her. Thou shalt not bear false witness against her. Thou shalt not steal from her"* and so on through the other commandments. He takes it up and laughs. Of what value is such a code to him? Has he not for all the years past been giving to his wife his heart's affection that makes it impossible for such things to enter his soul? And there is just that much difference between the Christian standard and the standard of the law. May God help us that we shall not take backward steps but realize our positions as sons of God. We shall live in Him and abide in the Holy Ghost and realize the freedom of sons, not the bondage of servants. Blessed be His Name. Nevertheless, to the man outside Christ the commandment still stands. As on our statute books today the law of murder applies to the man who commits murder, but the man in Christ has passed beyond that sphere. *"Let no man therefore judge you in meat, or drink, or in respect of an holyday, or of the new moon, or of the sabbath days: which are a shadow of things to come; but the body is of Christ"* [Colossians 2:16-17]. Blessed be His Name! Blessed be His Name!

Our High Christian Privilege

Now, we will never get the force of the 2nd chapter of Colossians where the Word portrays the exaltation of the Son of God, even to the sitting down at the right hand of the Father in the heavenly places far above all principality, and power, and might, and dominion, and every name that is named (Ephesians 1:19-23), and the second chapter of Ephesians portraying our lifting up out of the regime of death and sin into the same exaltation of the Son of God, until we realize our high privileges in Christ Jesus.

Indeed, I have this in my heart that the low state of Christian experience that is common among men is mostly accounted for by this one fact, that Christians have failed to grasp the exalted place into which Jesus Christ puts us when we have been made sons of God. May God write that deep in our soul, that we may not keep the Seventh Day (which was a shadow of good things to come, but the BODY IS OF CHRIST), not the commandments, but by holy Christian privilege keep one day sacred to God, and that without any commandment at all, but out of the gladness of the Christian heart. Blessed be His Name!

The First Day

But, beloved, have we not cause to rejoice that in Christianity there has been established a day of commemoration of His resurrection, and that altogether the Christian world unites in exalting the Son of God by keeping that day holy? We may not let down on our reverence for the first day of the week: but may we as Christians exalt the day, not by obedience to commandment, but, as Jesus Himself did, by making it a day when His life was given forth for the benefit of others; and I know God will bless us.

Now, I hope that forever this question is settled in our hearts. That, so far as our church is concerned, God has helped us to come together to recognize the fact that every man has the privilege to be led by the Spirit, not to observe all the law, but to be led by His Spirit.

The Sabbath

Psalm 118:22-24: *"The stone which the builders refused is become the head stone of the corner. This is the Lord's doing; it is marvelous in our eyes. This is the day which the Lord hath made; we will rejoice and be glad in it."*

When did the rejected stone become the head of the corner? When Jesus rose from the dead on that wonderful resurrection morning. This is one reason we worship on the day of His resurrection. It is the Sabbath of the New Covenant.

19

Have Christians A Right To Pray "If It Be Thy Will" Concerning Sickness?

I am going to read a familiar portion of the Word of God. It is the Lord's Prayer as recorded in the 11th chapter of Luke.

I purpose this afternoon to speak on this subject. "Have Christians a right to pray, 'If it be Thy will' concerning sickness?" Personally, I do not believe they have, and I am going to give you my reasons. Luke 11:1-4:

> **And it came to pass, that, as he was praying in a certain place, when he ceased, one of his disciples said unto him, Lord, teach us to pray, as John also taught his disciples. And he said unto them, When ye pray, say, Our Father which art in heaven, Hallowed be thy name. Thy kingdom come. Thy will be done, as in heaven, so in earth. Give us day by day our daily bread. And forgive us our sins; for we also forgive every one that is indebted to us. And lead us not into temptation; but deliver us from evil.**

Beloved, if there is one thing in the world I wish I could do for the people of Spokane, it would be to teach them to pray. Not teach them to say prayers, but teach them to pray. There is a mighty lot of difference between saying prayers and praying. *"The prayer of FAITH shall save the sick, and the Lord shall raise him up; and if he have committed sins, they shall be forgiven him"* (James 5:15).

The prayer of faith has power in it. The prayer of faith has trust in it. The prayer of faith has healing in it for soul and body. The disciples wanted to know how to pray real prayers, and Jesus said unto them, *"When ye pray, say, Our Father which art in heaven...Thy will be done"* [Luke 11:2].

Everybody stops there, and they resign their intelligence at that point to the unknown God. When you approach people and say to them, "You have missed the spirit of prayer," they look at you in amazement. But, beloved, it is a fact I want to show to you this afternoon as it is written in the Word of God. It does not say, "If it be thy will" and stop there. There is a comma there, not a period. The prayer is this, *"Thy will be done, as in heaven, so in earth"* [Luke 11:2]. That is a might different, is it not? Not "Thy will be done. Let the calamity come. Let my children be stricken with fever, or my son go to the insane asylum or my daughter go to the home of the feeble minded." That is not what Jesus was teaching the people to pray. Jesus was teaching the people to pray, *"Thy will be done on earth as it is in heaven."* Let the might of God be known. Let the power of God descend. Let God avert the calamity that is coming. Let it turn aside through faith in God. *"Thy will be done on earth* (here) *as it is in heaven."*

How is the will of God done in heaven? For a little time I want to direct your thoughts with mine heavenward. We step over there and we look all about the city. We note its beauty and grandeur. We see the Lamb of God. We do not observe a single drunken man on the golden streets; not a single man on crutches; not a woman smelling of sin.

A man came in the other day and was telling me what an ardent Christian he is. But after he left, I said, "Lift the windows and let the balance of the man out." Men ought to smell like they pray. We defile ourselves with many things.

A dear man came to me the other day in great distress. He said his eyes were going blind. The physician told him he had only a year of sight, perhaps less. As I endeavored to comfort him and turn his face toward God, I reverently put my hands on his eyes and asked God for Christ's sake to heal him, and as I did so the Spirit of God kept speaking to my soul and saying "Amaurosis."

I said, "What is amaurosis?" As soon as I could get to a dictionary, I looked up the word to see what it is. It is a disease of the eyes, caused by the use of nicotine. That was what was the matter with the man. The Spirit of the Lord was trying to tell me, but I was too dull; I did not understand. I do not know what the man's name is, but the other day God sent him back to my office. As we sat together I related the incident to him and said, "My brother, when you quit poisoning yourself, the probability is that you may not need any healing from God."

We defile ourselves in various ways; we go on defiling ourselves; and some people are able to stand the defilement a long time and throw it off. Others are not able to. It poisons their system and destroys their faculties. One man may drink whiskey and live to be an old man. Another may go to wreck in a few months or years. Some systems will throw off much; others will not.

Now, when we got to the beautiful City, we did not find any of these conditions and so we said, "Angel, what is the reason you do not have any sin up here?"

"Why the reason we do not have any sin here is because THE WILL OF GOD IS BEING DONE."

I have been used to looking for the sick, and if I see a man with a lame leg or a woman with a blind eye, I will see that a way down the street. I have mingled with the sick all my life. So I look around up there, and I do not see anybody on crutches or anybody that is lame, no cancers or consumption, or any sickness at all. So I say to my guide, "Angel, tell me what the reason is that you do not have any sickness up here."

The Angel replies, "THE WILL OF GOD IS BEING DONE HERE." No sin where the will of God is being done. No sickness where the will of God is being done.

Then I return to the earth, and I can pray that prayer with a new understanding. *"Thy will be done in me on earth as thy will is done in heaven."* Just as the will of God is done there, so let the will of God be done here. Let the will of God be done in me. *"Thy will be done, as in heaven, so in earth."*

But someone says, "Brother, do you not remember in Matthew 8 how a leper came to Jesus one day and said to Him, *"Lord, if thou wilt, thou canst make me clean?"* [Matthew 8:2].

The leper said, when he prayed, "If it be thy will," why should I not say that too? Well, he was ignorant of what the will of Christ was concerning sickness. Perhaps he had been up on the mountainside and had heard Jesus preach that wonderful sermon on the mount, for it was at its close that he came to Jesus and said, *"If thou wilt, thou canst make me clean."* He knew Christ's ability to heal but did not understand his willingness. Jesus' reply settled the question for the leper and it should settle the question for every other man for ever. Jesus said, *"I will; be thou clean"* [Acts 8:3]. If He ever had said anything else to any other man, there might be some reason for us to interject "If it be thy will" in our prayers when we ask God for something He has declared His will on. "If" always doubts. The prayer of faith has no "ifs" in it.

Suppose a drunken man kneels down at this platform and says, "I want to find God. I want to be a Christian." Every man and woman in this house who knows God would say, "Yes," right away. "Tell him to pray, to have faith in God, and God will deliver him."

Why do you do it? Simply because there is no question in your mind concerning God's will in saving a sinner from his sins. You know He is ready to do it when a sinner is ready to confess his sins. But you take another step over, and here is another poor fellow by his side with a lame leg, and he comes limping along and kneels down, or tries to, and right away a lot of folks say, "I wish he would send for a doctor," or else pray, "If it be thy will, make him well," forgetting *"who forgiveth all thine iniquities; who healeth all thy diseases"* [Psalm 103:3].

Instead of Christians taking the responsibility, they try to put the responsibility on God. Everything there is in the redemption of Jesus Christ is available for man when man will present his claim in faith and take it. There is no question in the mind of God concerning the salvation of a sinner. No more is there question concerning the healing of the sick one. It is in the atonement of Jesus Christ, bless God. His atonement was unto the uttermost; to the last need of man. The responsibility rests purely, solely and entirely on man. Jesus put it there. Jesus said, *"When ye pray, believe that ye receive them, and YE SHALL HAVE THEM"* [Mark 11:24]. No questions or "ifs" in the words of Jesus. If He ever spoke with emphasis on any question, it was on the subject of God's will and the result of faith in prayer. Indeed, He did not even speak them in ordinary words, but in the custom of the East. He said, *"Verily, verily."* Amen, amen—the same as if I would stand in an American court and say, "I swear I will tell the truth, the whole truth, and nothing but the truth, so help me God." So the Easterner raised his hand and said, "Amen, amen," or "Verily, verily"—"with the solemnity of an oath I say unto you." So Jesus said, *"When ye pray, believe that ye receive them, and ye shall have them."*

James, in expounding the subject, says concerning those that doubt, *"Let not that man think that he shall receive any thing of the Lord"* [James 1:7]. Why? Well, he says, a man that doubteth is like a wave of the sea, driven with the wind and tossed. There is no continuity in his prayer. There is no continuity in his faith. There is no continuity in his character. There is no concentration in God for the thing that he wants. He is like the waves of the sea, scattered and shattered, driven here and there by the wind because there is IF in it. *"Let not that man think he shall receive anything of the Lord."*

Now that leper did not know what the mind of Jesus was concerning sickness. Perhaps he had seen others healed of ordinary diseases, but leprosy was a terrible thing. It was incurable and contagious. The poor man was compelled as he went down the road to cry out, "Unclean! Unclean!" in order that people might run away from him.

In my work in South Africa, I saw dozens of them, hundreds of them, thousands of them. I have seen them with their fingers off of the first joint, at the second joint, with their thumbs off, or nose off, their teeth gone, the toes off, the body scaling off, and I have seen God heal them in every stage. On one occasion in our work, a company of healed lepers gathered on Christmas Eve and partook of the Lord's supper. Some had no fingers on their hands, and they had to take the cup between their wrists, but the Lord had been there and healed them. That was not under my ministry but under the ministry of a poor, black* fellow who five or six years before did not even wear pants. He wore a goat skin apron. But he came to Christ. He touched the living One. He received the power of God, and he manifests a greater measure of the real healing gift than I believe any man ever has in modern times. And if I were over there, I would kneel down and ask that black* man to put his hands on my head and ask God to let the same power of God come into my life that he has in his.

You have no more right to pray "If it be Thy will" concerning your sickness than the leper had. [Actually] not as much, because for two thousand years the Word of God has been declared and the Bible has been an open book. We ought to be intelligent beyond any other people in the world concerning the mind of God.

"But Brother," someone says, "you have surely forgotten that when Jesus was in the garden He prayed *'Oh my Father, if it be possible, let this cup pass from me: nevertheless not as I will, but as thou wilt'*" [Matthew 26:39]. No, I have not forgotten. You are not the Savior of the world, beloved. That was Jesus' prayer. No other man could ever pray that prayer but the Lord Jesus. But I want to show you, beloved, what caused Jesus to pray that prayer because a lot of folks have never understood it.

Jesus had gone into the garden to pray. The burden of His life was upon Him. He was about to depart. He had a message for the world. He had been compelled to commit it to a few men—ignorant men. I believe that He wondered, *Will they be able to present the vision? Will they see it as I have seen it? Will they be able to let the people have it as I have given it to them?* No doubt, these were some of the inquiries besides many more.

Do you know what the spirit of intercession is? Do you know what it means when a common man comes along, as Moses did, and takes upon himself the burden of the sin of the people and then goes down in tears and repentance unto God until the people are brought back in humility and repentance to His feet? When in anxiety for his race and people Moses said, *Lord, if you forgive not this people, blot my name out of thy book* [see Exodus 32:32]. He did not want any heaven where his people were not.

Think of it! Moses took upon himself that responsibility, and he said to God, *If you forgive not this people, blot my name out of thy book.* God heard Moses' prayer, bless God!

Paul, on one occasion, wrote practically the same words. *"I could wish that myself were accursed from Christ for my brethren, my kinsmen according to the flesh"* [Romans 9:3]. He felt the burden of his people. So Jesus in the garden felt the burden of the world, the accumulated sorrows of mankind, their burdens of sin, their burdens of sickness. And as He knelt to pray, His heart breaking under it, the great drops of sweat came out on His brow like blood falling to the ground. But the critics have said, "It was not blood."

Judge V.V. Barnes, in his great trial before Judge Landis, actually sweat blood until his handkerchief would be red with the blood that oozed through his pores. His wife said that for three months she was compelled to put napkins over his pillow. That is one of the biggest men God has ever let live in the world. His soul was big, and he saw the possibility of the hour for a great people and desired as far as he could to make that burden easy for them. He did not want the estate to go into the hands of a receiver. The interests of one hundred thousand people was in his hands, the accumulated properties of families who had no other resource. He was so large that the burden of his heart bore down on him so that he sweat blood and did so for three months. But people of these days say, "It looked like blood" and are so teaching their Sunday school scholars. The Lord have mercy on them! The blood came out and fell to the ground.

Jesus thought He was going to die right there in the garden, but He was too big to die there. He wanted to go to the cross. He wanted to see this thing finished on behalf of the race of man, and so He prayed, *"Oh my Father, if it be possible, let this cup pass from me: nevertheless not as I will, but as thou wilt"* [Matthew 26:39]. What was the cup? Was it the cup of suffering that was breaking Him down, that was draining the life blood out right then, and that would be His death instead of the cross? But He towered above that and prayed, *"Lord, if it be possible, let this cup pass from me. Nevertheless, not as I will, but as thou wilt."* Instantly the angels came and ministered to Him, and in the new strength He received, He went on to the cross and to His death as the Savior of mankind.

Beloved, I want to tell you that if there was a little sweating of blood and that kind of prayer, there would be less sickness and sin than there is. God is calling for a people who will take upon them that kind of burden and let the power of God work through them.

People look in amazement in these days when God answers prayer for a soul. A week ago last night my dear wife and I went down to pray for a soul on the Fort Wright line, a Mrs. McFarland. She is going to be here one of these days to give her testimony. Ten years ago a tree fell on her and broke her back. She became paralyzed, and for ten years she has been in a wheel chair, her limbs swollen, and her feet a great senseless lump that hangs down useless.

She says many preachers have visited her in these years, and they have told her to be reconciled to the will of God, to sit still and suffer longer. She said, "Oh, I would not mind not walking; if the pain would just stop for a little while, it would be so good." We lovingly laid our hands upon her and prayed. You say, "Did you pray, 'If it be thy will?'" No! You bet I did not, but I laid my hands on that dear soul and prayed, "You devil that has been tormenting this woman for ten years and causing the tears to flow, I rebuke you in the Name of the Son of God. And by the authority of the Son of God I cast you out." Something happened. Life began to flow into her being, and the pain left. In a little while she discovered that power was coming back into her body. She called me up the other day and said, "Oh, such a wonderful thing has taken place. This morning in bed I could get up on my hands and knees." Poor soul, she called in her neighbors and relatives because she could get on her hands and knees in bed.

Do you know you have painted Jesus Christ as a man without a soul? You have painted God to the world as a tyrant. On the other hand, He is reaching out His hands in love to stricken mankind desiring to lift them up. But He has put the responsibility of the whole matter on you and me. That question of the WILL OF GOD was everlastingly settled long ago—eternally settled—no question about the will of God.

The redemption of Jesus Christ was an uttermost redemption, to the last need of the human heart, bless God, for body, for soul, for spirit. He is a Christ and Savior even to the uttermost. Blessed be His Name. Who shall dare to raise a limit to the accomplishment of faith through Jesus Christ? I am glad the tendency is to take down the barriers and let all the faith of your heart go out to God for every man and for every condition of life, to let the love of God flow out of your soul to every hungry soul.

Instead of praying, "Lord, if it be thy will" when you kneel beside your sick friend, Jesus Christ has commanded you and every BELIEVER, lay YOUR hands on the sick. This is not my ministry nor my brethren's only. It is the ministry of every believer. And if your ministers do not believe it, God have mercy on them; and if your churches do not believe it, God have mercy on them.

In these days the churches are screaming and crying because Christian Science is swallowing up the world, and that it is false, etc. Why do the people go to Christian Science? Because they cannot get any truth where they are. Let the day come when the voices of men ring out and tell the people the truth about the Son of God Who is a redeemer even unto the uttermost for body and soul and spirit. He redeems back to God. Beloved, believe it and receive the blessing that will come into your own life. Amen.

*Kenneth Copeland Publications acknowledges that references to race and nationality considered acceptable in Rev. Lake's day are offensive and not acceptable to today's reader. However, these references in no way reflect the attitude or policies of KCP. To fully understand Rev. Lake's heart toward other races, we recommend you read his biography located at the front of the book.

20

The Habitation of God

God has been seeking a habitation a long time. God found a habitation in Jesus Christ, and He became the dwelling place of God. Christ's purpose for the world was that men, like Himself, should become the dwelling place of God. It was not purposed that Jesus Christ was to be a particular or special dwelling place of God. It was rather purposed that mankind should be just as much a holy and desirable dwelling place of God as Jesus Himself was. The purpose of the gospel of God was that through Jesus Christ His Son many sons would be begotten of God, should be begotten of Christ.

Christ's undertaking was to save mankind from their sins and transform them into sons of God like Himself. That is the purpose and work of our Lord and Savior Jesus Christ.

In 1 Corinthians 15 we read of the consummation of His purpose—that is, the finality, the conclusion of that purpose, when Jesus Himself having subjected all things unto Himself, is Himself also subjected unto the Father, that God may be all in all. There will not be a dissenting voice nor a rebellious heart. The will of God has been received and as a result of the will of God having been received there is no longer a necessity for a Savior, and Jesus Christ in His capacity of Savior of the world has been completed. His mission is completed.

We are so liable to feel in this great struggle we see about us, and the struggle we recognize in our nature, that there cannot possibly be a time of ultimate and final victory of the Lord Jesus Christ in the souls of men.

I want to encourage you, beloved. The Word of God portrays a time and conception of the purpose of Jesus Christ when the world, being redeemed unto Christ, no longer needs the redeeming merit of the Savior. So Jesus, having subjected all things unto Himself, is Himself also subjected unto the Father, that God may be all in all.

God is not all in all, and never will be all in all, until the will of God rules in the heart of every man, in the soul of every man, until the redemption of Jesus Christ in its great and ultimate purpose becomes a reality, a finality.

Paul Sees Christ's Purpose

I have always regarded the first and second chapters of Ephesians as two of the most remarkable in the entire Word of God. Perhaps no soul ever visioned the real purpose of God and portrayed it in words with more clearness than did Paul in these two chapters.

In the first chapter he begins by showing us that Jesus fulfilled the purpose of the Father. That as a reward for His consecration to the will of God, his death, Resurrection, Ascension and glorification, the power of God ruled in His nature, and in very truth He was the Son of God, to Whom was committed all power—principalities and powers, Paul says, being subject unto Him.

Then, in the second chapter he begins to make this truth applicable to our own hearts, and he undertakes to show us that just as Jesus Christ was dead and in the grave, so mankind, possessed and dominated by the powers of sin and selfishness, have become "dead in sin"—that is, senseless to the Spirit of God. And as Jesus was raised from the dead, so He has purposed to lift the veil or cloud, the obsession or possession of sin, and cleanse the nature of man and unify him with God.

When he reaches this climax he puts it in this terse form: *"For to make in himself of twain one new man, so making peace"* [Ephesians 2:15]. He shows that the ultimate and final peace that comes to the soul of man comes as the result of a divine union having taken place between Jesus Christ and the Christian soul, and there is no longer any worry or discussion over commandments or ordinances. The soul has risen above them. It has risen out of the region of commandments and laws, into a government of love. The soul joined to Christ in His divine affection, the spirit of man entering into Christ, the Spirit of Christ entering into man, causes such a transformation that the man becomes a new creature. All his impulses have changed, the ruling of his human nature ceases, and finally he is a son of God.

That is the wonder of the cleansing power and cross of Christ in the nature of man. The wonder is that Jesus purposed to make your heart and mine just as sweet and lovely and pure and holy as His own. That is the reason that He can accept the Christian as His bride. Who could imagine the Christ accepting Christians polluted, defiled, of a lower state of purity or holiness than Himself?

> The Spirit of the Lord says that thus is the wonder of the redemptive power of Jesus Christ revealed to man and in man. Such is the transforming grace that through Him, through His merit, through His love, through His Spirit, the soul of man—cleansed, purified, beautified, glorified—becomes like the soul of Jesus Himself, and man and Christ meet as equals in purity. Blessed be his Name.
>
> *Message in Tongues and Interpretation*

If you have felt, dear brother or sister, that you have been a sinner above all that dwelt in Jerusalem, as some did, be assured that the cleansing power of Jesus Christ is equal to your need, and the thoroughness and almightiness of His Spirit's working in you can make you a king and prince, lovely and beautiful, pure of heart and life, like unto Himself.

The triumph of the teacher is always in bringing his student to his own understanding, and even more than that, endeavoring to inspire within the student the possibility of going beyond himself in his search of knowledge and truth. Could we expect of Jesus a lesser purpose than that which we recognize in teachers everywhere? If Jesus is a redeemer, unto what is He to redeem us? What is the ideal, what is the standard to which Christ purposes to bring us? Is the standard less than that which He holds Himself? If so, it would be unworthy of the Son of God. He would not be giving to us the best of His soul.

Verily, the Word of God stands clear in one respect, that the blood of Jesus Christ, His Son, cleanseth us from all sin. Bless God. We become clean in our nature, thoroughly infilled by His grace, every atom and fiber of the spirit and the soul and the body of man made sweet and holy, like unto Jesus Himself. Bless God.

The Purpose of Cleansing

Now this marvelous cleansing by the Spirit and power of Jesus Christ is for a definite purpose; it is a definite preparation. When we make an elaborate preparation of any kind, it is that something may follow. So this preparation in holiness and righteousness and truth in the nature of man by Jesus Christ, the Word declares, is that there may be a fitting climax; the climax is THAT MAN MAY BECOME THE DWELLING OF GOD.

God demands a holy temple in which His holiness and through which His holiness may be revealed. Consequently it becomes a matter of necessity to the Lord Jesus Christ that if He is to reveal Himself in a hundredfold measure through the Church to the world, He must have the ability to cleanse the church and present her, as the Word portrays, *"[Without] spot, or wrinkle, or any such thing"* [Ephesians 5:27]. Blessed be the Lord. She must be pure as Jesus is pure, beautiful within, beautiful without. The scars and wrinkles must disappear. So Christ will receive the really Christ-cleansed church as His own virgin, the bride. Blessed be the Lord.

The Wonder of His Grace

The wonder of the grace of God is revealed in us, though we have sinned, though we have become polluted, though in our soul life we have practiced adultery with the spirit of the world until the nature of the world has entered into our nature and soiled it and made it unlike the nature of Jesus Christ. And the wonder of His grace is revealed in that He receives us, cleanses us, purifies us, saves us, and being thus redeemed and cleansed by the Spirit of Christ we stand sweet and lovely and holy in His presence, prepared to be His bride. One in which He can live, with whom He can fellowship, into whose nature He purposes now to come and abide.

The Apostles' Cleansing and Baptism

If you will study with care the life of the apostles you will observe that there was a process that took place in their lives so thorough and complete that Jesus said unto them, just prior to His departure, *"Now ye are clean through the word which I have spoken unto you"* [John 15:3].

They had arrived in soul cleansing at the place where, by the grace of God, they were prepared for the next experience and higher purpose of Jesus, which was that they might now receive the Holy Ghost. That is, that the Spirit of Jesus Christ might come from heaven to abide in them, and thus in very truth cause them to become the dwelling place of God.

The purpose of Christ was that not only the twelve, and the hundred and twenty upon whom the Holy Ghost came at Jerusalem, and the Church at Samaria, and the household of Cornelius should be cleansed and receive the Holy Spirit, but that every son of God should receive a like experience. (The Church at Samaria was different from the Church at Jerusalem, in that it was composed of the wandering heathen tribes, and it was different from the household of Cornelius, which were intelligent Romans. But they all, in common with all the race, became the habitation of God through the Spirit.)

In common with these, the Ephesian elders in Acts 19, who were advanced in righteousness and holiness and entrusted with the care of others as shepherds of the flock, likewise received the Spirit of the Lord.

In all these instances then, we see the purpose of God is not only to cleanse a man, but being cleansed to empower him, infill him, indwell him by His own blessed almighty Spirit. The Spirit of Christ present in a holy temple has appeared to reveal Himself through that person, just as He did through the Lord Jesus Christ.

If we study the manner by which the Spirit of God revealed Himself through Jesus, then we will have the pattern or example of how the Spirit of God reveals Himself through all believers all the time.

The Spirit of God spoke through him the word of love, the word that brought conviction, the word of power. Through His nature there flowed a subtle something that no religionist but Himself and His followers possessed—the living Spirit of the living God, the anointing of the Holy Ghost, bless God, the one characteristic that makes Christianity a distinctive religion forever. It can never be identified with any other. So long as Christianity is dependent on the presence of the Holy Ghost it will remain distinctively the one religion, that of divine power and saving grace.

Prayer

God, our heavenly Father, our hearts are asking that since the wondrous provision has been made, that we may seek, with all the earnestness that should characterize men and women, for this blessed almightiness, that the cleansing grace and power to be revealed in our own life. May this not be just a beautiful vision tonight, but, oh, Lord, may we receive Thee in this moment into our hearts as our Lord, our Savior, our Redeemer, that the Word of Christ may be accomplished in us, and that in very truth we may look into the face of Jesus, knowing that our souls are cleansed. Amen.

When a young man, I stood in an aisle of the Methodist Church and was introduced to a young lady. As I touched her hand the marvelous moving of our natures was revealed. Presently something from her soul, that subtle something that Christians know and recognize as spirit, her spirit passed to me, went through my person until presently I realized that my soul had rent itself in affection for that woman, and we never had looked into each other's eyes in an intimate way before. From me went that subtle something to her. The result was that we were just as much soul mates and lovers in the next ten minutes as we were in the next seventeen years and had raised a family.

She was a woman of fine sensitive qualities, and she told me later that she had been in the habit of searching a young man's spirit to know if he was pure; but, she said, "In your case, the strange thing was, that my spirit made no such search. I just knew it."

I want to tell you in that matter she was not wrong, for when I was a boy, though I was surrounded by as vile a set of men as have ever lived, I determined in my soul that one day I would look into a woman's soul and tell her that I was pure.

If you held the hand of Jesus tonight, do you suppose your spirit would be capable of searching His soul to know whether He was pure? No, instinctively something in that purer spirit would cause you to know that it was your Lord.

Then I want to ask you on the other hand, suppose the Spirit of Jesus searched our own, what would he discern? That is the question, that is the big question that men are compelled continually to ask of themselves. What would the Spirit of Jesus discern in you? What would the Spirit of Jesus discern in me?

Would the Spirit of Jesus be drawn to us, or would we repel Him because of unholiness?

The Word of God lays blessed and splendid emphasis in the fact we need the cleansing power of Jesus to make our spirit pure and sweet and lovely like His own. Then having cleansed us and sanctified us to Himself, then He Himself by the Spirit, the Holy Spirit, comes in to dwell in our nature and take up His eternal abiding and residence in us. This we welcome, bless God, the HABITATION OF GOD through the Spirit.

I sat one day on the platform of a great tabernacle in the presence of ten thousand persons who had collected to hear me preach. I had received a promise from God the night before for that occasion. The Spirit of the Lord had given in His own words an outline of the history of man's nature from the creation to the redemption and empowering by the Spirit of God. But the anointing from heaven that would make possible the presentation of such an ideal, and make it acceptable to the hearts of thousands who listened, had not yet come.

Presently from the soul of an old gentleman next to me, as I sat praying, I was conscious of the Spirit's falling about me until my nature was overcome by it. I had difficulty to maintain my seat, waiting for the preliminaries to be finished so that I could get a chance to deliver the message.

That man became the agency of divine transmission of the Spirit of God to me, just the same as Jesus Christ was the agency of divine transmission through which the Spirit of God was imparted to the people of His Day.

Such is the marvel of the nature of man united to the Lord Jesus Christ, when all the abundant fullness—the ABUNDANT FULLNESS of His holy nature—may come to you and me when our temple has been prepared to receive Him.

Beloved, if you have been getting along with an ounce of healing, bless your soul, if you have been getting along with a limited measure of blessing in your daily life, let me encourage you that the fountain will not be exhausted when your spirit is filled with the overflow.

The Spirit of God is like the bread that the disciples held in their hands; when it became filled with the Spirit of God it multiplied in their hands. When they broke off some there was more remaining than when they began. The Spirit of God is creative, generative, constructive, and the more you give the more you receive. There must be a great opening in the nature of man in order that he may be a large receiver, and the strangeness of it is that it depends upon whether you are large givers. Nothing like it in the world. It is a violation of every law of man, but it is the common law of the Spirit. Why? Because the Spirit, unlike other things, is creative. It grows, it magnifies in your soul, it multiplies as you distribute it to another.

So Jesus laid down a perpetual law: *"Give, and it shall be given unto you; good measure, pressed down, and shaken together, and running over, shall men give into your bosom"* [Luke 6:38].

In my experience of twenty-five years of healing ministry, I have known very few instances of a person being healed when they approached you with such words as these: "If I am healed, I will give the church so much" or "I will make a large donation." You see the reason is that the Spirit is not received at that place. We are just entering into a knowledge of the law of Jesus Christ: *"Give, and it shall be given unto you."* God tried through the Mosaic Law to demonstrate to mankind that the way of blessing was the way of giving. See old Isaac when he approached God, coming with his lamb or dove in his hand, or whatever the sacrifice was that he was about to offer on his behalf.

The Christian's Offering

But beloved, Christianity has a deeper revelation of the same truth. We come, not with a dove, nor a lamb, nor a he goat, nor a heifer. No, we come with our LIFE, we come with our nature, we come with our all offering it to the Lord. Not bargaining with Him, not endeavoring by a shrewd bargain to obtain the blessing. That is the reason many a soul loses its blessing. Quit it.

Very rarely have I known people to miss the blessing of God when they came openly, saying, "I desire to receive; I want to give." Their spirit, their nature has come into harmony with God's law, *"Give, and it shall be given unto you."* Don't you know that is the secret of all affection between man and man, between the sexes. Men are not always seeking for some one to love them; they are seeking for some one that they can love. When two souls are seeking for the one they can love, there is a union, and the world very gradually is learning that there are real marriages. There is a union of spirit so indissoluble that nothing on earth or in heaven will ever sunder them.

Christ is seeking for the soul that will receive His love, and the Christian, the real one, is seeking for the Christ Who will receive his love. Bless God. Both are practicing the unalterable law of God, *"Give, and it shall be given unto you."*

Frequently we observe that sympathy becomes the door through which affection enters lives. I once talked with a nurse, and I asked her what the hardest thing in a nurse's life was. She said, "If you remain a woman and do not become steeled in your nature and hardened in your affections, you will find it most difficult to keep from permitting your affections to follow your sympathy."

And over and over, as a law of life, a woman will nurse a man, and before she is through she will love him. Why? Because sympathy for him has opened the door of her nature, and unconsciously has flowed out in affection to him.

There is a thing that is dearer to God than anything else, and the only thing that is worthwhile. It is the same thing that is dearer to every man. That thing is the affection of your heart.

You can see your son rise to a place of eminence and respect in the world, and yet he will disappoint your soul. Why? Because the soul of the real father is seeking something besides that. He is seeking the affection of the son, and if he fails to receive it, all the rest is barren.

Christ is seeking the affection of mankind, the union of their spirit with His, for without their affection there can never be that deep union of the spirit between God and man that makes possible a richness of life, made glorious by His indwelling. That is why the love of God is held forth in the Word as the one supreme attraction to draw the soul of man in returned affection.

And you can give to your Lord your money and your property and your brain, and all the other things that are usually considered to be very excellent, but if you withhold your affections from Him and give them to another, the Word says you are an adulterer.

Prayer

Our Father, teach us to love thee, teach us dear Lord its value, teach us its power, teach us our spirit's need. My God, in the richness of Thy beautiful Spirit all the impoverished nature's need is supplied. In turn, if we can add to Thy joy by giving to Thee the affection of our heart, great God, who could withhold? Amen.

So long as religion exists you will never be able to separate real religion from emotions of the soul. The emotions will be an open door which the Spirit uses to gain access to your life. When you reduce religious life to a science, and take from it the warmth of Christ's affection, you have robbed it of its charm and its almighty power.

God in Man's Mind

When we become the habitation of God, God lives in the mind, God lives in the brain, what will be the result? What will we do and what will we say or think? What will be the tenderness of our emotions, of our soul, and what will be the depth of our feeling? What will be the growth of our capacity to love?

God in Man's Spirit

When God lives in a man's spirit, the spirit of man reaches out into the boundless, touching the almightiness of God, discerning His nature, appropriating His power, securing His almightiness.

God in a Man's Body

God living in a man's flesh, giving off a vibration of God life, God power: God indwelling his blood, God indwelling his hands, God indwelling his bones and marrow—a HABITATION OF GOD.

A real Christian woman will keep her heart clean and calm. A real Christian man will take a bath as often as he needs it, and a lot of other things. Otherwise he has a poor conception of the Son of God, who inhabits man. He will be beautiful within, beautiful without. You cannot retain the dirt and filth and rottenness and Jesus Christ at the same time.

But if there begins a mighty war in your nature, the Spirit of God striving with devils, and God overcomes, then you will understand the power and redemption of Jesus Christ.

I was present in a meeting in Los Angeles one time, when the Spirit fell on a man and he fell prostrate on the floor, and a group of friends gathered around. That man would fight like a mad dog until he would actually swear. In the next two or three minutes that spirit would be overpowered by the Spirit of God, and he would pray like a saint and cry for help. Again that evil spirit would come into evidence.

The brethren said, "Mr. Lake, why don't you cast the devil out?"

I replied, "There is someone else at that job."

So we sat until four in the morning. At two-thirty the evil spirit departed and the glory of God broke forth, and the worship of the soul when he recognized his Lord was wonderfully sacred. The man arose, transformed by the indwelling of the living God.

Beloved, I want to say that if any unholiness exists in the nature, it is not there by the consent of the Spirit of God. If unholiness exists in your life it is because your soul is giving consent to it, and you are retaining it. Let it go. Cast it out, and let God have His way in your life.

Prayer

God my Father, as we kneel tonight, some may feel and do feel the Spirit of God coming in to overpower and cast out every unholy thing. Lord God we are glad that Thou hast made this divine provision for our deliverance. We would be Thine. We would be Thine alone. We would be Thine forever and forever. It is not that we may get to heaven when we die. We put away that littleness and that selfishness from our souls. And it is not, Lord God, that we may escape from punishment, for God we have put away that devilish littleness.

We would be Thine because it is worthy of a son of God to be like his Lord. We would be Thine because we have desired to join our hands and hearts in the biggest thing the world ever knew—the REDEMPTION OF THE RACE TO GOD FOREVER.

My Father God, with such a vision, we look to Thee, asking that by Thy grace Thou wilt cleanse our hearts and make us indeed the dwelling place of God. Amen.

The triumph of the Gospel is enough to make any man the wildest kind of an enthusiastic optimist. The unifying of the nature of man and God is the crowning achievement of Jesus Christ. The reason for the cross was thus revealed. Man in God and God in man one and indissoluble—one mind—one purpose—one power—one glory.

21

Incarnation

One of the outreachings of the natural, universal man is to be in union with God. Christianity brings us into union with God.

Here is a point in this great truth that is utterly ignored: the ministry of Jesus at the right hand of the Majesty on High. Some of you are critical Bible students, and if you have been critically studying the book of Romans you know the great argument closes with the redemption argument, and have said like me, "It is not all there."

Now the book of Romans from the third through the eighth chapters is the great redemption program, and covers exactly three days and three nights. The nailing of Jesus on the cross, His resurrection from the grave. I said, "Lord, where is the rest of it?"

Like a flash of lightning I saw it was in Hebrews. The center around which Hebrews revolves is Jesus' ministry at the right hand of the Father. We see Jesus taking the blood and carrying it into the Holy of Holies, and pouring it out on the mercy seat. Only in the book of Hebrews is He called the great High Priest. That is His great ministry. He sat down. A man sat down. He had to be incarnate so a man could sit down at the right hand. He is sitting there as a Mediator between God and man. He has a new ministry. He is there as the intercessor. He is there as the Lord. He is there as the Head of the Church.

A man. He simply had to become man for that reason. I want you to understand that He is perfectly man. He is perfectly God, seated there at the right hand of the Majesty on High. And that man can be touched with the feeling of our infirmity. He is our representative at the throne of the highest authority in the universe. He is there as our substitute and representative.

My little girl said to me one day: "Papa, I don't like this number work."

I said, "Why don't you like mathematics?"

She said, "Papa, what is the use of it?"

I said, "Dear, you are going to see it all the time."

She said, "I never use it."

I said, "Suppose you had eight apples, and I told you to give three to your chum. If you did not know anything about mathematics how could you tell how many three were?"

By and by she said, "Papa, it is some good, isn't it?" And she had courage to go on.

You have the theory of redemption, but you don't know how to put it into practice. Every time I go over these great teachings I get one step nearer the goal. So I am going over them again and again, not only for your sake, but for mine too. My privileges and place in Christ become more real. The tremendous possibilities of the divine life are almost within grasp. Sometimes when the Word is unfolding itself to me it seems to me if I would close my eyes I could plunge into it.

Christ is at once the spotless descent of God into men, and the sinless ascent of man into God.

He was God coming down into man, and He did no violence to His Godhead when He united to man, but He is God. Being glorified as He took on man, He did no injury to man, but He magnified man by taking man on. It is God incarnate. It is God living on earth.

Turn to John 14:8-9: *"Philip saith unto Him, Lord, show us the Father, and it sufficeth us. Jesus saith unto him, Have I been so long time with you, and dost thou not know me, Philip, he that hath seen me hath seen the Father; how sayest thou, Show us the Father?"*

Of course, I can understand that Philip's eyes were not open yet. But after the day of Pentecost then his eyes were open.

I want you to hear what Jesus said about Himself. God was in Christ, wasn't He? An incarnation. God is in you, an incarnation, if you are born again. You are incarnate. God is in you. God was in Christ, reconciling the world unto Himself. God is in you. He has committed unto us the word of reconciliation (2 Corinthians 5:19). As God was in Christ, so God is in you (John 14:23, 17:23; 1 John 4:15-16). God is in you in two ways. Jesus is in you by imparting His nature (2 Peter 1:4). Second in the person of the Holy Spirit (John 14:16-17). He is imparted to you, so you are an incarnation.

The first time I saw it I stood before a mirror, and I said, "Is it possible that inside of that suit of clothes there dwells a man in whom God dwells?" God has not only come in the person of the Holy Spirit, but He has imparted to me His own nature, so that God's nature has come in and dispossessed me of another nature, and imparted to me His own nature (2 Peter 1:4). And after He did that, then He said, "I will live in you" (2 Corinthians 6:16). And He has come in. Oh, the miracle of the thing! The life of God is in me, the Spirit is in me. We are members of the Body of Christ (1 Corinthians 6:17; Ephesians 5:30). That is an incarnation.

If you could hear this every morning, and then about noon time, and then at evening time and again before you went to bed, after a while it would seep into you.

A young man said to me: "There is one lesson on identification that thrilled me through and through. I laid your manuscript down and went about my daily business, but my mind kept coming back to it." He said, "I am going to read it over with all those scriptures every day." And I wanted him to tell me why. He said, "I am going to do it for this reason. It is not mine yet. It is not a part of me." He said, "I remember when I took up Latin. I studied it for two years before Latin became mine. So I could translate English into Latin and Latin into English..." He said, "Now I know about this incarnation. I know about this indwelling of God. I know my legal rights, but it is not mine yet in a practical way so I can use it. The devil has me at a disadvantage still, but I will stand before the devil just as Jesus stood before the devil yet."

That young man has the same life as Jesus had. He has the same Holy Spirit as Jesus had. Friends, you are a son of God. You are a partaker of the divine nature. That is incarnation. Plus that, you have the Holy Spirit dwelling in you. You have the nature of God in you. You are His child. You have the Name of Jesus.

After a little bit this truth will get hold of us, and after a little while it will master us. He says this is yours. All He wants of you is to go and act normal.

Do you know what miracles are? Miracles that Jesus performed were God coming down out of His realm, the faith realm, down into the human realm, the reason realm, and doing things that were normal up there, but abnormal down here.

When this thing I am telling you, when the new birth fact becomes a reality to me, having received the nature of God, and when I reach the place quietly that "Greater is He that is in you (me) than he that is in the World", I will get this eternal life of God clear, and this indwelling presence of God, and the Name of Jesus, it puts me on a par with God. He says, "All things are possible to God" (Matthew 19:26; Luke 1:37). "All things are possible to the believer" (Mark 9:23; Matthew 17:20). The believer has the right to use the Name of Jesus.

If I could teach that to little children they would get it off the bat. Reason runs contrary to fact. Faith does not come out of reason. Both come out of your spirit. That is the reason that faith and reason do not work together. They are jealous of each other. Reason is always jealous of faith. Reason is butting in on it all the time.

When you and I learn the three centers of our being, the spirit center, the soul center and the body center, we will have gone a long way.

You have eternal life, haven't you? You have become a new creation (2 Corinthians 5:17). You are His son, you are God's child. You are a life child. You are not just an adopted child; you are a blood child. You are a life child. You could be adopted. That would be legal. But you are His real, honest to goodness, child (Ephesians 5:30).

You know you have His nature. You know that is a fact. You do not have to believe that you are born again. You do not have to believe that the Bible is true, and that you are born again. You know that. You do not have to believe that you have eternal life. That is a fact. You know that. You do not have to believe that the Holy Spirit has come in. He is there.

This is the process of elimination. You do not have to believe you are a child. You do not have to believe you have received eternal life. You do not have to believe you are an incarnation. You have the Holy Spirit. Then all things are possible to them that believe. You are a believer because you are a son. You are a child. You have received eternal life. You have the Holy Spirit and the Name of Jesus. That means you are in the thing. To be a full-fledged believer then all these things are possible to you. You do not have to try to believe it.

You are in the family of God. You have a right to the use of the Name of Jesus, just like a pass belongs to you when you work for the railroad. You are part of a definite system. You are in the family of God. You have a right to the Name of Jesus. That is the pass. It carries you up into the Holy of Holies.

Now another thing, beloved. You do not have to try to believe the Word, do you? That would be an awful thing for me to have to try to believe my own Father. How would I feel if I were to write to my little boy, and say, "Son, I am going to send you $5.00." And then he would go to his mother and say, "I want you to help me believe that Papa will send me $5.00. I want you to stand with me in faith that I will believe that Papa will send me the $5.00."

Do you know I would get a telegram from her if he would talk like that. She would say, "John, you better pray for that boy. Something has gone wrong with his head." There must be something wrong with us when we try to believe what He says. Let's stop all that baby business. In the Name of Jesus Christ don't ever magnify the devil by letting him know you do not believe that Book. Don't you ever lower the standard. Don't you weaken it. It is God's Book. Of course you believe it. His people for ages and ages have believed it, and it has never failed.

This is what we have done. We have sung unbelief. We have talked unbelief until we have robbed ourselves of our strength and Him of His glory. Are you an incarnation? If you are you are in the family and He is yours and you are in Christ.

Now let us take the next step up. Now you walk in the realm of faith. We walk by faith, not by sight. Sight means reason. You walk by faith, not by reason. You are a faith walker. That puts you absolutely in the class with the Lord.

Now Jesus was a faith worker. The Father was a faith worker before Him. Our Heavenly Father has done everything He has done by faith. When He wanted the earth, He said, "Let there be." *"Through faith we understand that the worlds were framed by the word of God, so that things which are seen were not made of things which do appear"* (Hebrews 11:3).

All He had to say was, "Let it be." He said, "I want you to come into being." And Orion and Pleiades came into being. He said to the place where the North Star was, "Let it be", and it was.

You are following in the footsteps of a God that says to the things that are not, and they become, and who says to the things that are and they stop being.

Sometimes I tell the story of a woman who had a cancer in her mouth. Dr. Dowie put his finger on it and began to feel of it, and by and by faith said something to that cancer, and then Dr. Dowie took the cancer out of her mouth and put it in a bottle.

What was that? Could reason do that? Oh, no, no. Reason would say, "You have to have that cut out." Faith says, "It is dead, and after it is dead I will pull it out." Dowie acted in Jesus' stead. I am to walk in Jesus' footsteps, and Jesus is my example in faith.

I had a sister, Maggie Otto, who had cancer of the breast. She had been operated on five times at Detroit, Michigan by Dr. Carstens, and finally turned away to die with five cancers. We took her on a stretcher to Dr. Dowie. He was conducting a healing meeting. She was writhing in pain on a cot. The old doctor laid his Bible down, stepped down and prayed for her, and she was utterly healed. A few days afterward I got to examining the breast and discovered the cancer was black as your boot. One morning I put my finger in and touched the cancer and I saw it was detached from the body. I had the other case of Ethel Post in my mind, I began to twist that thing and it came out, roots and all. Some roots were an eighth of an inch in diameter, some were a sixteenth of an inch, some were as fine as thread, some were as fine as a silken hair. We put that cancer in alcohol and it was in Dr. Carsten's hospital for years.

That puts a man in God's class. Can you see what the incarnation means? It is not something to reason and talk about. It is life. I do not want you to try to believe that. You ARE that. I want you to go over it in your mind until you can say it. Just like my little daughter did with her mathematics.

In my school work I said to the teachers, "We must teach geometry." There was a debate on.

They said, "What has geometry to do with the Holy Spirit and teaching the Word?" But I made my case. They said, "I do not believe God brought me here to teach geometry, but to teach the Bible."

I looked over and said to one woman, "Will you teach geometry? I do not want you to teach geometry like you did in school, but I want you to teach it as a spiritual duty, a part of your daily life." I could see her eyes open. She began to teach geometry, and the other teachers had to fight to keep the interest in their classes up to hers. Geometry was in everything. It became a living part of their lives. She learned how to teach it as God would teach it.

Friends, you have the theory of this thing. Now in the Name of the Lord Jesus Christ you have seen the reality of it. You go out and let this reality govern your life.

A fellow in California and his boy were working in the garden about two years ago. They had to dig up a stone, and in digging out the stone they discovered a pocket of gold nuggets, something like six or eight thousand dollars worth. The father said, "Let's not say anything. Maybe this was buried here." They dug around a little more, and the boy found about two thousand more, and they found they had a gold field, a limited one.

There is none of you folks here but have a gold field. First you have the nature and life of God. Second you have the great, mighty Holy Spirit. Third, you are the son of God. Do you need any more capital to begin to do business?

What are you? A child of God. You are in the family. You do not have to try to do that. You have the nature of God. You do not have to try to have that. You have the use of the Name of Jesus. You have the authority in heaven and earth in the Name of Jesus, and in the commission (see Mark 16; Luke 10:19).

You do not have to try to exercise authority. "Whatsoever is bound on earth is bound in heaven." You do not have to believe anything when you use the Name. "In my Name you shall do it..." You have the use of the Name of Jesus.

You have a lot. You have all the authority there is in heaven. All you have to do is to go and practice it. You have the Holy Spirit in you. You do not have to believe anything. He is in you. He is speaking to you, "Let me have charge of things now."

The meaning of the word incarnate, as a verb: 1. To embody in flesh; cause to assume a living form. 2. To give or endow with shape or form; actualize; as a doctrine incarnated in institutions. 3. To embody in a living being; as, the warrior incarnates the spirit of battle.

Incarnate, adjective: 1. Invest with flesh. 2. Hence embodied in flesh; personified, in such cases as a fiend incarnate, the adjective is nearly synonymous with arrant, unmitigated. 3. Flesh-colored; roseate.

Incarnation, noun: 1. The act of becoming incarnate; especially the assumption of the human nature by Jesus Christ as the second person of the Trinity. 2. That which is personified by, or embodied in or as in human form; personification; embodiment of a quality, idea, principle, etc., specifically an avatar. 3. The process of healing in a wound.

Some additional scriptures: John 15:5; Galatians 2:20; 2 Corinthians 13:5, 3:16-18, 6:16; Galatians 4:19: *"Until Christ be formed in you anew";* Ephesians 3:19: *"Filled with all the fulness of God";* Ephesians 4:6.

The triumph of the gospel is enough to make any man the wildest kind of an enthusiastic optimist. The unifying of the nature of man and God is the crowning achievement of Jesus Christ. The reason for the cross was thus revealed. Man in God and God in man one and indissoluble, one mind, one purpose, one effort, one power and one glory.

22

The Second Crowning

April 16, 1916

Reading: Revelation 5

"Oh, God, upon our souls we call the blessing of the Holy Spirit today to quicken every instinct of our being that by Thy grace we may comprehend the power of Thy Word and the might of Thy Spirit. And we pray that the Spirit of the Lord Jesus Christ may be present in every heart that we may realize, oh God, not only the elevation and crowning of our Lord and Savior, but our own elevation and crowning with Him as sons of God."

Somehow the minds of men the world over have ever been concentrated around the cross of Christ. One of the strangest things to me in all Christian life has been the manner in which the souls of men cling to the cross of Calvary. And I have sometimes felt that is one of the great reasons why there has been so little progress made in the higher Christian life.

While we revere the cross of Calvary, while the soul of man will ever love to think of Him who gave His life for us, yet I believe the triumph of the Christ began at the cross and ends only WHEN THE RACE, LIKE HIMSELF, HAS RECEIVED FROM GOD THE FATHER, THROUGH HIM, THE GRACE, POWER AND GLORY OF GOD THAT MAKES THEM SONS OF GOD LIKE HIMSELF.

It is a long way between the cross of Calvary and the throne of God, but that is the way that Jesus traveled, and that is the course for every other soul of man. Bless God. I am glad that God is never hurried. He has plenty of time. A few years makes much difference in this life, but God has plenty of time for the elevation of the soul, for the perfect tuition of every heart, until that heart comes into such complete and perfect unison that the nature of man is absolutely changed into the nature of Christ.

The triumph of Jesus, as we see it outlined in the Scriptures I have just read, has always been one of the splendid inspirations to my own soul. It seems to me if we had not been permitted to have that foreview of that final triumph of the Son of God, there might have been the conception in the minds of many that, after all, the life and death of our Lord Jesus Christ was not the perfect triumph that it ought to have been. It seems, therefore, that no one can have the highest appreciation of the real Christian life and the consciousness that real Christianity brings, unless they see the triumph of the Christ.

Yea, more. It is only as we become possessors of that consciousness ourselves and as the knowledge of His triumph grows in our own souls and takes possession of our hearts, that we are able to comprehend what Christianity really is.

If we stop to think that one-half of the great Christian world is still carrying a little crucifix representing a dead Christ, we will realize how the mind of man is yet chained to the cross of Calvary, to a dead Christ, to a tomb, not empty; but the tomb that contains the One they love.

Beloved, that is not Christianity. Christianity, bless God, is the ringing triumph that began on the morning of the Resurrection and ends when the race of man has come to the understanding, knowledge and consciousness of God Himself.

Christianity is not a dreary outlook. Christianity is the ringing, splendid triumph of the mind of God. Christianity is the blessed victory that the individual feels in his own heart of the consciousness of the presence and power of God within the soul, which makes man the master now, and gives him the consciousness of mastery over the powers of sickness and death. Yes, bless God, the greater consciousness by which the soul of man comprehends the life eternal because the forces of darkness and sin and death have been conquered in his own heart through the presence and power of the Lord Jesus Christ in him. Bless God.

I have always wondered how a Christian could be anything less than an optimist. It is a sad thing when you hear Christians with a groan in them. When I meet the groaner, I say in my heart, "God, move the man on into the place where he comprehends what Christianity is."

The Christian with a groan in him never moved the world except to groans. In a divine healing meeting some months ago, as I was teaching I tried to develop the thought that as a man thinketh in his heart, so is he; and I was endeavoring to show the people that the spirit of victory in Christ Jesus in one's heart not only affected the attitude of one's mind, but likewise his soul. In fact, through the nervous system, man's mental attitudes are transmitted clear through his body.

The attitude of our soul has much to do with, not only our mental states and our spiritual life, but likewise our physical health. Indeed, it seems to me that as the spirit of man is tuned with God, all the outgrowth of his life will be in harmony with his spirit. The attitude of his mind will be in accordance, and the condition of his body will be a revelation of the attitude of his mind. That is the reason I have always endeavored in my preaching to bring before the mind of man the consciousness of triumph, the consciousness of victory, the power of mastery. It seems to me there is a great deal of superficial endeavor in the world to pump oneself up to a certain state of consciousness, which is similar to a man taking himself by the bootstraps and trying to lift himself over the fence.

Beloved, the secret of Christianity is the secret of the Christ possessing the heart of man; man being yielded to Him so that His victory, His consciousness, and His power possess your spirit and mind. Then, bless God, we are kings...not because we say we are kings, but because we know we are kings, and because we feel we are kings by the grace of God and His inworking power.

We speak of mastery, not because we are endeavoring to lift our consciousness into the place where we can possibly conceive of mastery, but because the spirit of mastery is born within the heart. The real Christian is a royal fighter. He is the one who loves to enter into the contest with his whole soul and take the situation captive for the Lord Jesus Christ.

They tell a story of an old time English Officer. He was a very important individual, and it would never do for him to speak out his commands so they could be understood. He had a raw Irishman whom he was endeavoring to break in. They were engaged in a sham battle. Presently the officer let a certain kind of roar, and the Irishman broke from the ranks toward the supposed enemy, and grabbing a man by the neck, brought him with him. The officer said, "Hold on. What are you doing?"

"Well," he said, "I did not know what you said, but it felt as if you wanted me to go for him, and I did."

When the Lord Jesus Christ is born indeed in the soul of man, when by the grace and power of the Son of God, you and I yield ourselves to God until our nature becomes the possessor of that spirit that is in Christ, then, bless God, we begin to realize the spirit of mastery that Jesus possessed when He said: *"I am he that liveth, and was dead; and, behold, I am alive for evermore, Amen; and have the keys of hell and of death"* [Revelation 1:18].

That is the reason I do not spend much time in talking about the devil. The Lord took care of him, bless God! He has the keys of hell and of death, and He has mastered that individual and that condition once and for all. If you and I had as much faith to believe it as we have to believe that the Lord Jesus Christ is our Savior, we would have mighty little trouble with the devil or his power while we walk through this old world. It is not worthwhile talking about a man after he is wiped out.

It is a hard thing for the Christian mind to conceive that the power of evil is really a vanquished power. When I think of examples of Christian triumph, my mind very frequently reverts to a minister I have spoken to you about many times. He was a great soul. The consciousness of Christ's dominion seemed to dwell in the man's heart intensely.

I was with him on one occasion when he was called to a dying man down in the slums. It was late at night. It was always interesting to me to watch the sparkle of his eye and to note here and there the splendid flash of his spirit. We were walking through the streets, and I said to him, "Do you know anything about this man's condition?"

"Well," he replied, "the messenger told me the man was in a state of great suffering and likely to die. But he is not going to die."

I said, "Amen."

You see, there was the ring of conscious mastery in his soul that made it possible for such a splendid burst of confidence to come forth from his spirit. I said to myself that night, "There is not going to be much difficulty tonight. The fellow has the victory in his soul in advance." When we finally knelt by the man's side, and he put his hands on him and called on the mighty God to deliver the man, I felt the flash of his spirit, and I knew before I arose from my knees that the man was healed: and he was.

Beloved, you and I have bowed our heads before a vanquished enemy. We have failed through lack of faith to comprehend that the Christ is the Master. But he who dares by the grace of God to look into the face of the Lord Jesus Christ knows within his own soul the divine mastery that the Christ of God is exercising now.

The power of God through which men are blessed is not an individual matter that belongs to you or to me. It is the conscious presence of the living, risen Son of God dwelling in our heart by the Holy Ghost, which causes you and I to know that the power of God is equal to every emergency and is great enough for the deliverance of every soul from every oppression.

There are times when it seems to me it is not fitting even to pray. There is a life of praise: Once while in conversation with Dr. Myland, the pastor of the Christian and Missionary Alliance Church of Columbus, Ohio, I happened to mention the fact that I had not prayed concerning a certain personal matter. Turning to me he said, "I have not prayed for myself for four years." That sounded very strange to me at that time. I did not understand. He said, "No, I passed beyond the place of praying, Brother, into the place where I was ready to accept what the Lord Jesus Christ has wrought and to receive the power of His Spirit in my life so that the thing that He has wrought for me should become evident through me." And that man had walked for four years in that conscious victory.

And the Spirit of the Lord says within my soul that he who trusteth in the living God shall never be confounded. Yea, according to the Word of God, he shall mount up on wings as eagles. He shall run and not be weary, he shall walk and not faint.

Bless God, there is a place of strength, of security, of victory, a life of triumph.

An hour of consternation came to the prophet John as the mighty God unfolded to him that which was to occur in the future. A book appears, a marvelous book, sealed with seven seals. An angel with a trumpet voice proceeds to utter a proclamation, *"Who is worthy to open the book, and to loose the seals thereof?"* [Revelation 5:2].

And mankind stood dumbfounded. No man in heaven nor on earth was able to loose the seals or to open the book. And it seemed to the prophet as if a great disappointment was at hand. He says, *"I wept much"* [Revelation 5:4].

But presently the angel guide said to him, *"Weep not: behold, the LION OF THE TRIBE OF JUDAH, the Root of David, hath prevailed to open the book"* [Revelation 5:5].

John says, *"I looked and beheld as it were a Lamb"* [see Revelation 5:6]. Blessed be God. The real overcomer does not always evidence his overcoming power with much noise. In this case His overcoming was in the consciousness that was in His heart. He was as a lamb; gentle, sweet, loving, tender and true.

But the consciousness of power was IN the Christ. When others stand dumbfounded, when others stand baffled, the Christ appears. He takes the book, opens the seals and discusses its contents. Beloved, the triumph of the Christ of God is not the triumph of loud shouting. It is the triumph of what you know in your own soul. The victory of the Christ and the victory of a soul is in the knowledge of the relationship between your soul and the soul of the Christ.

He, into whose heart there comes the Spirit of the living God, has within himself the consciousness of One Who has overcome and Who is set down at the right hand of God, triumphant over every power of sickness and death and hell. Beloved, the triumph of the Gospel is enough to make any man the wildest kind of an enthusiastic optimist.

It is said of Napoleon Bonapart that when he was First Counsel of France, he proceeded to proclaim himself Emperor of France. And one day one of the statesmen came and asked him, "By what authority do you dare to proclaim yourself Emperor of France?"

He replied: "By the divine right of ability to govern." The consciousness of power was in the soul of the man. He knew in his own soul that he qualified to govern.

The Christian has the consciousness of that character of soul. Within the soul of the real Christian there is born the consciousness of capacity to govern. And the first place to apply it is in his own life. For no man ever successfully governed another life until he was first able to govern himself. *"[Greater] is he that ruleth his [own] spirit than he that taketh a city"* [Proverbs 16:32]. The poise of the father of a household will be revealed in the mind of every child of his family. The attitude of the mother's mind will be evidenced in everyone of the household.

A dear brother came to me recently and said, "I do not know what is the trouble. I have worked so hard, and I am not able to accomplish the thing I am trying to do."

I replied: "My friend, the difficulty is in your own soul. You have not attained the mastery of that condition in your own heart. The same condition of confusion that is in your soul is being evidenced in the souls of others about you. It is transmitted from you to them."

How often have you and I walked into the presence of a man whose calmness gave instant strength? How often in life when the minds of men were driven to confusion, we have seen a single soul maintain his poise in God and become a balancing power in society. History records that at the death of Lincoln, when the news of his assassination became known in New York, the city was almost on the point of breaking into a mob. Three men lay dead on the streets when James A. Garfield appeared on the verandah of one of the hotels. Raising his hands, he spoke these simple words which brought a calm to the whole mob and the whole city and was transferred all over the nation. "God is our King, and the government at Washington still lives." The storm was over, as when Jesus spoke the marvelous words, *"Peace, be still"* [Mark 4:39]. There flowed over the nation the calm of poise in God.

It is said at the time of the great Chicago fire that the day following two hundred men committed suicide in that city. The old Chicago Tribune came out with a big red letter headline: "Any coward can commit suicide, but it takes a MAN to live under these conditions." And the whole thing stopped. There were no more suicides. That wave of cowardice was broken up. The consciousness of one great soul who had the poise of God within his heart was able by the grace of God to transmit it to other lives.

The success of your life as a child of God will be in exact accordance with the consciousness of the Christ and the power of God that is in your heart. The old prophet arrested the great wave of human despair that was sweeping over the nation on one occasion with these magnetic words, "Underneath are the everlasting arms." Bless God. The nation was not going to pieces. The world was not going to ruin, for underneath were the everlasting arms in which the souls of men could rest down with confidence, and God brought the victory.

When the souls of men learn to rest in confidence upon the living God, peace will possess this world that will be like unto the Kingdom of God...heaven on earth.

Most of our difficulties are the difficulties that we anticipate or fear are coming tomorrow. How many people are worrying about the things of today? But the world is in consternation concerning tomorrow, or the next day, or the next day. Jesus said, *"Sufficient unto the day is the evil thereof"* [Matthew 6:34]. Do not worry about tomorrow. Rest down in God. The mighty arms of the living God will be underneath tomorrow, just as they are today.

The Spirit of God says within my heart that the Kingdom of Christ, for which every child of God looks, is characterized by the peace of God possessing the souls of men, so that worry and care cease to be because we trust in His arms.

If I could bring to you today one blessing greater than another, it would be the consciousness of trust in God. *Be not afraid, neither be thou dismayed: for the Lord thy God is with thee whithersoever thou goest* [see Joshua 1:9].

A little woman came into the healing rooms recently weeping so that I could hardly talk to her. She said, "I am the mother of three children. I am afraid I am going to die. The doctor said so-and-so; there is no hope for me. I must leave my husband and my children."

I said, "The doctor is a liar." And that woman is sitting in the audience today a well woman. Beloved, she might have been dead. We might have been celebrating another funeral. But confidence in the living God brought the confidence of power over the thing that was crushing the life out of that soul, and it went by the grace of God. No case is too hopeless.

Last evening in the healing rooms, just at six o'clock, I was visited by a woman whom I met four or five months ago in the Deaconess Hospital. The dear lady had been given up to die. She had been examined by X-ray, and a large cancer in the stomach was discovered. They told her there was nothing to be done for her. So the dear husband sent for me to speak a kindly word to his supposedly dying wife.

I did not understand what I had been sent for and when I got to the dear soul I supposed I had been called to pray the prayer of faith for healing. I said, "Dear Mother, you do not have to die."

"But," she said, "the doctor says so. The X-ray shows such a sized cancer. I guess, Brother, I will have to die."

And I said, "It is a lie. You do not have to die." For two or three months we battled against that condition in the woman's soul. The Spirit of God would come upon her every time we prayed. Her pains would disappear, she would go to sleep, etc., but she was not really healed. That went on week after week and month after month until I was almost worn out before her soul arose to take victory. But last night she walked into the healing rooms. She told me that she weighed only seventy-five pounds when I met her and that now she weighs one hundred twenty pounds. She went to the hospital this week and had the same physician X-ray her. When they saw the picture they said, "There must be some mistake." And they got the original and examined it. They could not understand it.

She said, "Doctor, I found a new Physician, the Great Physician, the Christ of God, and I do not care about your plates. I know the cancer is gone." But the plates showed it was gone. The woman has gone back home a happy woman. But, Beloved, the victory only came when the consciousness of the power of the living Christ took possession of the woman's heart. Blessed be God.

Not a dead Jesus, but a living Christ! Not a sepulcher with a dead man in it, but the glorious, risen, present Christ in your heart and mine. The Christ lives, bless God, not only at the right hand of God, but the Christ lives in your soul and mine. The victory that He attained is evidenced not alone by the declaration: *"I am he that liveth, and was dead; and, behold, I am alive for evermore"* [Revelation 1:18]; but the victory He attains through you and me now. That was His peculiar victory; but the victory of the Christ that gives the Son of God its gladness now is the consciousness that the Christ lives and the Christ reigns and that by the power of God, sin, darkness and death and hell become obedient to the Christian through the Christ that is in him.

Testimony of Mrs. Peterson

"I was healed when dying. I was in a state of death forty minutes. My womb and ovaries had been removed in an operation; and at my healing God restored them, and I am a normal woman."

I want to give some of you folks a conception of what a battle for a life means. This soul kept up the fight for her life until her forces weakened and she lapsed into unconsciousness. The last thing she said to Brother Westwood was, "I can fight no more. You have got to do it for me or I will die."

And God Almighty healed her through and through, and she stands before the world today a marvel of the power of God because she refused to be beaten. This is a miracle, not a healing only. The work of God in her was creative. To one is given by the Spirit the gift of Healing, to another the working of miracles.

The conception of the Lord Jesus Christ that we are battling against in these days is that which the poet has framed in these beautiful words, (and I say this with all reverence):

"Gentle Jesus, meek and mild, look upon a little child."

In that child thought of Jesus there is no conception of the triumphant Son of God, who entered into death and took the victory, who established eternal life in the souls of men. Bless God for the Christ who dared to enter into the very jaws of death and to grapple with the enemy that no man had ever dared to tackle, and came forth the victor. He took him captive, and broke his power and bound him in chains, and declared liberty to a world that was crushed and bound by the consciousness of the power of death.

As the coming of the Christ approaches, that coming which I believe a multitude of Christian hearts are looking for in these days, the flash and flame and consciousness of the Master Son of God takes possession of their hearts and minds, and in the Name of Jesus men are rising up everywhere, who refuse to be bound by sin and sickness and death.

That is the reason that John saw in his vision of the Revelation, a day of triumph, when all that were in the earth and the sea and under the sea, when heaven, Earth and hell united to send forth a shout of triumph that will ring through the eternities, because the Christ of God had become the acknowledged Master, Ruler, Prince and King of the race.

If the blessed Spirit of God keeps on revealing the mighty power of the living Christ in the souls of men, we will have to have a new hymn book. We will have to have a new class of poets in the world. It will come, too, as sure as you are born. They used to sing dreary old hymns in the little Scotch church when I was a boy, and I remember one particular hymn:

Hark! From the tomb a doleful sound.
Mine ear, attend the cry.
Ye living men come view the ground
Where you must shortly lie. Ah.

Afterward I learned that "ah" was Amen, but I did not know it then.

Oh, bless God for the revelation of the living Christ in the souls of men that lifts the consciousness of men from the place of defeat into the place of power, the exultant, present mighty power of the living God.

One Sunday afternoon a tall Englishman walked into my church in Johannesburg, South Africa. He was six feet two and a half inches high and twenty-six inches across the shoulders. A top of red hair made him as conspicuous as a lion. He walked up the aisle and took a seat quite near the front. My old preaching partner was endeavoring to explain the mighty power of the living Christ as best he could, and this man sat listening. Presently he arose, saying: "Old Man, if the things you are talking about are all right, I am your candidate."

He said, "I used to be a Christian. I came from Port St. Mary's, Isle of Man, and I was a Christian boy. I came to Africa and lived the usual African life, and the result is that for three years I have been unable to do anything, and my physicians say I am incurable. If you mean what you are talking about, tell me what to do."

My old partner said, "John, what shall we do?"

I said, "Call him up; we will pray for him right now."

We stepped off the platform, put our hands on William T. Dugan, and instantly, as a flash of lightning blasting a tree or rock, the power of God went through the man's being, and the Lord Jesus Christ made him well.

A few days afterward he came down to my house in the middle of the day, and said: "Lake, I want you to show me how to get a clean heart." I took the Word of God and went through it with him to show him the mighty cleansing, sanctifying power of the living God in a man's heart. Before he left he knelt by a chair and consecrated his life to God. Raising his hands to heaven he said, "Lord God, I receive into my life the sanctifying power of God to dissolve every condition in my nature that is adverse to the living God." And bless God, he received it from heaven, just as he received his healing.

Three months passed. One day he called and said, "Lake, I have had a call from God." I knew it was. There was no mistaking it. The wonder of it was in his soul. He went down into the country where a great epidemic of fever was on. Some weeks afterward I began to receive word that people were being healed. Hundreds of them. Bless God. So one day I concluded I would go down and join in the same work a couple of hundred miles from where he was. Somehow the news traveled that I was at Potgietersrust, and he came there.

The next afternoon we were called to the home of a man who said his wife was sick with diabetes. We prayed for the wife and several other persons who were present. Then the man stepped out into the kitchen and said, "Would you pray for a woman like this?" When I looked at her I saw she had club feet. The right foot was on an angle of forty-five degrees, and the left one at right angles.

Dugan replied, "Yes. Pray for anybody." He said to her, "Sit down," and taking the club foot in his hands he said, "In the Name of Jesus Christ become natural." And I want to tell you, that man is in the glory presence of God today. I am going to stand there some day with him. Before I had a chance to take a second breath that foot commenced to move, and the next instant that foot was straight.

Then he took the other foot up, saying: "In the Name of Jesus Christ become natural." Beloved, it was not only the voice of the man, or the confidence of his soul, but the mighty divine life of Jesus Christ flashed through him, and it melted that foot into softness, and it instantly became normal by the power of God.

Beloved, we have not begun to touch the fringes of the knowledge of the power of God. However, I want to encourage your hearts. I know your soul and my soul are hungering after the living God. I am glad we can say, what perhaps has never been said in the Christian world from the days of the apostles to the present time, that since the opening of this work in Spokane, about sixteen months ago, ten thousand people have been healed by the power of God.

Is Jesus dead? No, bless God. Is He alive in glory? Is He alive in your heart? Bless God, that is the place to crown the Christ. That is the place, in your soul and in my soul.

We are just beginning to grow up. The old prophets were so big in their soul, so gigantic in their spirit life that when a poor soul sinned, or the whole nation sinned, the prophet removed his clothes, shaved his head, and put sackcloth on his body and ashes on his head, and went before God. He said, "Lord God, I have sinned. We have sinned." And he poured out his soul before God until the nation returned in repentance and love to the feet of the Holy God. I trust one day we will grow up big enough in God that we can do things like that.

Some three or four years ago, when one of the marvelous anointings of the Holy Ghost was on my life, a man came into my healing room one day to tell me how he was in a dying state, and hopeless. As I put my hands on him and prayed I was conscious of the Spirit of God going through him like a stream of light, and presently he jumped up vibrating under the power of God until his teeth rattled. When his surprise was over, I said to him: "Brother, how about your pain?" That was the first he had thought about it.

He said, "My pain is gone."

I said, "Did you feel the power of God?"

He said, "It went through me like buck shot."

Beloved, one of the sorrows of my soul is this, that though we rejoice in the fact God is healing a multitude of people, even in this city, and now they are coming to this city from all quarters of the land, yet so many of them have not been healed at all, and they should have been healed. Some have had to come to the healing rooms twenty times instead of once. But, bless God, there is a day coming when the power of God will come upon your soul and mine mightily, so it will be like it was with Christ. They will not have to come back a second time. At the touch of Jesus the mighty power of God flashed through their life until the disease in them was gone forever. Blessed be His precious Name. I do not want to give you an idea that there are not people who are instantly healed. There are lots of them, but not all.

Mr. Greenfield Comes on the Platform

Mr. Greenfield was in the hands of physicians for tuberculosis of the kidneys. He was compelled to leave his work. He was just a poor man, and it meant that he should become dependent on his family instead of being the support of the house. When he came to the healing rooms he talked this over a little. He said, "The doctors say I must die."

I said, "Greenfield, don't you believe it. There is a God in heaven." After I laid my hands on him and prayed, I said

"Greenfield, go back to your work." Bless God, he did, and he does not look much like a man dying of tuberculosis now.

Oh, Hallelujah: There is a living Christ. There is a triumphant Son of God. There is a living Spirit of the living God, Who will flow through the soul of a man just as He flowed through the soul of Jesus. The trouble is with the soul of man. The trouble I am having is, with the soul of this man. And the prayer of my life every day and hour is, "Mighty God, purify the soul of this man like the soul of Jesus was pure, and give my soul the consciousness of faith in God like the soul of Jesus possessed." Then, Beloved, you and I can say in deed and in truth, we are the Sons of God, blessed be His Name.

23

The Platform of Jesus

There has always been a passage in the Declaration of Independence that has rung very deeply in my spirit. It was the thought of the Revolutionary Fathers in giving an explanation and reason to the world for undertaking to set up a new government among the families of nations. They said something like this: out of due respect for mankind they felt it necessary to give a reason for such an act.

As we invite this company of people together in this section of the country, I feel that a due word of loving explanation may be helpful.

I have been in this particular manner of ministry for many years. I believe Brother Fogwill and I began in this ministry some 16 or 17 years ago, or there about. Of course, we had been Christian ministers before that, but at that period God enlarged our vision of Himself and His purposes.

Personally, I received my ministry in the gospel of healing through John Alexander Dowie, a man whom I have loved with all my soul. And though in his later life he became broken in mind and committed many foolish things, so that discredit for a time was brought upon his work, I knew him from the beginning until the day of his death. I have gone to his grave since I have returned to this land, and as I have thought over that wonderful life, I have prayed in the silence of the nighttime, "Lord God endue me with the Spirit of God in the measure that you did that life."

I have always regarded it as a privilege in my life and as a unique thing, that after his death I was invited to preach in his pulpit, and I preached there for several months. I remember as I stood on the platform, above my head was a great crown possibly eight feet in diameter. It was made from boots with iron stirrups on them, thick soles, and all that character of thing that had come from people who had been healed of short limbs. Can you wonder, as I stood in that place, and looked around those walls, and saw plaster of Paris casts fastened on the walls, some of which had come off my own friends who had been healed, iron braces that cripples had worn, cots on which the dying had been brought, one of them Anna Hicks. That cot was fastened to one of the walls above the gallery. And I thought of the day when she was carried in practically dead, and that old man prayed for her and she was healed. And the company of her students who had lovingly escorted her to the station at Berea, Kentucky said to me, "We carried her as if we would if she had been dead, as pall bearers, and we received her back as from the dead."

Her friends cabled her and telegraphed her from all over the earth, and she gladly told the story, the wonderful story, almost the same character of story that our Brother Zienke told you this morning, of the love of God, of the tenderness of the Christ that mankind has not known, of Jesus the Healer still.

Beloved, there is a deep passionate yearning in my soul, that above all else, this congregation may set forth to the praise of God such a character of righteousness in God, such a purity of holiness from God, that this people may not only be recognized in this city, but throughout the world, as a people among whom God dwells.

Beginning this work, as I do at this time, I want to say that I do not come as a novice to this time of my life. God has permitted me in the years that are past to assist in the establishment of two great works of God, each of them on a new plane in God. I trust, blessed be His Name, that in calling together once again the people of God, that it shall be to establish a work on a new plane. Indeed, a higher one than our souls have ever known, where the radiant purity of the holiness of God shall be shed forth into the whole world. And I believe that is God's purpose.

Jesus, Himself, stood at Nazareth on an almost similar occasion. He had been raised in one of the country towns. He had disappeared from His community, gone down to the Jordan, and had been baptized of John. The Holy Ghost had come upon Him, and He had returned to His own hometown, to the synagogue where He had worshiped as a boy.

One thing I have always praised God for is that when God put me into public ministry, He made me start in the very town, in the very community, next door to the very house where I had been raised. When a man fights out the battles of life in his own community, in his own home town, among his friends and neighbors, and receives love and confidence from them, I always feel he has received a good preparation for the next step in life. Jesus knew the place for a man to begin to serve God when He had said to the demoniac of Gadara, who was delivered, *"Go home to thy friends, and tell them how great things the Lord hath done for thee"* (Mark 5:19).

If your wife does not know you are a Christian, nobody else will be likely to. If your husband does not know you are a Christian, it is a poor testimony. It is the woman that is with you, who eats with you, and sleeps with you, that will know whether you are a child of God or not. It is the man who lives in the same house with you, and the people in your community, who will know best how much of the life of God radiates from your own soul.

So Jesus stood in His own home town of Nazareth, and read this wonderful text that I am going to read this morning. It is known, or ought to be, as the platform of Jesus Christ. *"The Spirit of the Lord is upon me, because he hath anointed me to preach the gospel to the poor"* [Luke 4:18].

THE POOR. (Jesus Christ has an anti-poverty program.) That is the first duty of every child of God and every Church of God that ever came into existence. And the Church that fails in that duty to mankind has failed in the first principle, and has denied the first principle of the platform of the Son of God.

My heart has never gone out in sympathy to a body of Christian people, who became a little clique, and represent a certain select number of society. My conception of the real Church of God is one where rich and poor, bless God, alike feel at home. Where there are no barriers, and no boundaries, but where soul flows out to soul, and in the larger life, man knows only man and God. Blessed be His precious Name. *"The Spirit of the Lord is upon me, because he hath anointed me to preach the gospel to the poor"* [Luke 4:18].

The ministry of the things of God must ever be without money and without price. My soul could never descend to the place where charges are made for the services of the minister of the gospel of Christ. Never, bless God!

It is our privilege to make possible a ministry to the people without money and without price, bless God. The magnanimity of the Lord Jesus Christ has stood out as a blessed and wonderful feature in all His ministry. I have sometimes wondered how many people really knew how the Lord existed during His own earth life. The Word of God gives us one little hint, in these words: *"Joanna the wife of Chuza Herod's steward, and Susanna, and many others, which ministered unto him of their substance"* [Luke 8:3]. That was how the Son of God was able to minister without money and without price to mankind. We today have that privilege too. It is ours. I have faith in God that this Church will demonstrate Christ's ministry to the poor.

For ten years God has privileged me to preach the gospel without salary, without collections. I never asked a man for a cent in my life, and I have lived, bless God, and been able to minister every day. God has met me every time, and I believe He will meet every other man and woman who will likewise put their trust in God and go forward.

The second plank in the platform of the Gospel of Jesus Christ is this: *"To heal the brokenhearted"* [Luke 4:18].

There are lots of them. I tell you since I have been in Spokane the Lord has let me into the homes of the rich and poor, and it is not in the poor districts that you find all the brokenhearted by any means. *"He hath sent me to heal the brokenhearted."* That is the ministry of this body. If there is a brokenhearted soul in your locality, you are the one, who in the Name of Jesus Christ, has the privilege of ministering in the things of God to that soul, brokenhearted because of sin, brokenhearted sometimes by sickness, brokenhearted because of the conditions around them that they seem unable to control.

When I see the living God in His tender mercy touch one and another and make them whole, whether in spirit, in soul, or in body, I rejoice equally in either case, for what God does is always good and worthy of praise. I regard the healing of a man's body to be just as sacred as the healing of his soul. There is no distinction. Jesus made none. He provided a perfect salvation for mankind—all that man needed for spirit, soul or body.

So this ministry, bless God, will be a healing ministry. This church will be a healing church. This will be a church to which you can invite your friends who are ill, and bring them here, and help them. I trust after a time we will be able to bring the people in great numbers, the sick who are on cots and stretchers and crutches, that the Lord Jesus through this church and its ministry may make them well.

It is my purpose that a number of brethren, who have had this same burden on their hearts for many years as I have had it, may come together in this city as a headquarters, and that from this city we may extend this ministry throughout the land. I have particularly invited my old preaching partner, Brother Cyrus B. Fockler, of Milwaukee, my dear, precious brother, Archibald Fairley, of Zion City, a prophet of God and one of the anointed of the Lord, Brother (Rev.) Bert Rice of Chicago, my dear Brother (Rev.) Charles W. Westwood, of Portland, Oregon, and Reverend Fogwell to assist me in this ministry. Brother Westwood visited with me a few days, and is now going on to Chicago to make the necessary arrangements.

This is the outline so far as God has made it clear. This is to be a healing church. Everyone who has been called to this ministry and those who will be called in the future will minister to body and soul and spirit through the Lord Jesus Christ.

The third plank in the platform of Jesus Christ is this: *"To preach deliverance to the captives"* [Luke 4:18].

How many there are! One day, not long ago, I received a telephone call from a lady in one of the missions saying that she had a man there who was a terrible drunkard. Every once in a while he would get delirium tremors. He saw devils: he was haunted by them.

The lady said, "We cannot do anything for him. We thought perhaps you could help him."

He came up to see me. He sat down to tell me about himself. Right away I could discern that he was a soul who from his very birth had been gifted with spiritual sight. But instead of associating in the spirit with angels, with God, with Christ, all his spiritual association was with devils, demons, horrors, until that, to escape from that condition, he had become a drunk in his youth. In order to have relaxation for a time, he had paralyzed himself with drink, and that was his difficulty.

I said to him, "My son, kneel down. We are going to pray to God." And I prayed that God would bind every last demon and lift his soul into union with God, and fill him with the Holy Ghost, so he might associate with the angels of God and become a new man in Christ, and have fellowship with the Holy Spirit.

In a few days he returned and said, "Oh, brother, it is all so new, so different. As I walk along the street there are no more demons, no more devils; but as I came up to the church today an angel, so beautiful, so sweet, so pure, walked by my side. And, Brother, there He is now, and He has wounds on His hands and on His feet."

But my eyes were dim; I could not see Him. I presume they were like the eyes of the servant of Elisha. *"To preach deliverance to the captives"* [Luke 4:18] from all kinds of powers, earthly and sensual. It is the privilege of the real Church to bring deliverance to the captives of sin, of disease, of death and hell, not only proclaim the message of deliverance, but also exercise the power of God to set them free.

The fourth plank: *"Recovering of sight to the blind"* [Luke 4:18]. Among the blessed healings of the past few weeks, is one dear soul, who is not yet completely healed, a blind woman, whose eyes have gradually opened day by day from the first morning of prayer, and who will be present with us in the near future, as Brother Zienke was this morning, to praise God for her deliverance.

"Recovering of sight to the blind." But there are many blind hearts, blind minds, blind souls, just as well as blind eyes, who do not see the beauty and power of the things of Christ. And to them we bring today the message of our Christ, *"Recovering of sight to the blind."*

I pray above every other thing this church will be a church that will know God so intimately that when men come in contact with any one of us, they will feel that they have met one who is able to reveal the Lord Jesus Christ to them. I believe it will be so.

The fifth plank: *"To set at liberty them that are bruised"* [Luke 4:18]. There are the bleeding ones, the bruised ones, those who have been hid away, and those whose life has been made a burden. May I tell you this incident?

The last night I preached in my tabernacle in Johannesburg, they brought a young man for whom life had gone so very hard.

He had lost hope and gone into despair so that he tried to blot himself out by committing suicide. He shot himself in the mouth, and the bullet came out the back of the head, strangely without killing him. This left him with a violent pain in the base of the brain, that caused him to suffer untold agony, and his neck was rigid.

This night the greatest part of the congregation was composed of Cornish miners, whom I have regarded as the hardest men I have ever met in South Africa. They lived a very hard, terrible life. They dissipated terribly.

This man came up on the platform to be prayed for, and I wanted the sympathy of the people. So I made a plea in some such words as these, "Here is a poor fellow with whom life has gone so hard that he tried to blot himself out, and in his endeavor to do so, he shot himself, with the result that he is in the condition you see him in now." Presently, I began to observe that up from the audience there came a wave of loving sympathy. I said, "If you never prayed in your life, if you never prayed for yourself, bow your head and pray tonight, and ask God to deliver your fellow man."

I put my hands on him and prayed, and the power of God came down upon him and instantly the joints became loose, the neck pliable, the pain gone. Looking up into my face, he said, "Who did that?"

I said, "That was the Lord Jesus Christ." And dropping on his knees before me, he said, "Brother, show me how to find that Christ, I want to know Him."

Down in the audience that night was one of the most cultured gentlemen it has ever been my privilege to know. He raised in his seat and reverently raising his hands, he said, "My Lord and my God." He had not been a Christian, but he saw a new vision of the love of God for man that night.

Away back in the audience, another soul was touched. He was a different type of man. He came from a different environment. He raised up and slapped himself on the hip, and shouted, "Bully for Jesus!" It came out of the depth of his soul.

Beloved, it is my conviction that the purity of Jesus Christ and the radiant holiness and the power of God will manifest Christ alike to the cultured and the uncultured, for both hearts are hungry when they see the living Christ.

The sixth plank of the platform: *"To preach the acceptable year of the Lord"* [Luke 4:19].

Not next year, not in five years, not when you die, but a present salvation, a present healing for spirit, soul and body. Blessed be His Name. All you need, bless God, is to bring your whole being into perfect harmony with the living God, so that the Spirit of God radiates through your spirit, radiates through your mind, and radiates likewise through your body. Blessed be His Name.

Among the most precious privileges that is given to the real church is to be in fact, not in word alone, the Body of Christ. The Word of God speaks of *"the church, which is His body"* [Ephesians 1:22-23]. And as God, the Father, manifested Himself through that one beautiful, holy, purified body of Jesus Christ in such a perfect manner, when men looked upon Him they did not see the man Jesus, but they saw God. Then He ascended and sent the Holy Spirit to the Church, to you and to me. What for? That the new Body should come forth, and the church, the real church, united to God and filled with the Holy Ghost, should manifest God, again to mankind through this Body. That Church is made up of all that are written in the Lamb's Book of Life.

When God wants to heal a man, the healing does not fall down from heaven, but it does come through the medium of the child of God. Therefore, God has given us the exalted privilege of being co-laborers together with God. And among our high privileges is to radiate, to give forth from the love passion of our souls the courage and strength to help other souls to come to God. And the business of the Church is to be a savior, or saviors, for the Word of God says, *"And saviours shall come up on Mount Zion"* [Obadiah 21]. These are those in such union with God that they are able to lift mankind up to the "Lamb of God" which taketh away the sin of the world.

What Must I Do To Be Saved?

Probably the most simple way is to pray, "Father, forgive all my sins. I take Thy Son, Jesus Christ, to be my personal Savior. I invite You to come and live in my heart."

"Will God hear me?" you may ask. God has commanded *"all men everywhere to repent"* (Acts 17:30). Certainly He will hear and accept you, for you are obeying His own command. Jesus said in John 6:37 that he that comes to Him He *"will in no wise cast out."* It is God's will that *"all should come to repentance"* (2 Peter 3:9). *"He is able also to save them to the uttermost that come unto God by Him,"* [that is by Jesus Christ] (Hebrews 7:25). What happens to your sins and iniquities? *"And their sins and iniquities will I remember no more"* (Hebrews 10:17). What love God is willing to bestow on us! *"For God so loved the world [you] that he gave his only begotten Son"* for you and for me (John 3:16). Why not bow and repeat from your heart that simple prayer this very moment. It will revolutionize your life and give you that more abundant life and the peace of God that passeth understanding. God bless you.

24

Compassion

I wonder if you ever settled in your own mind what is the greatest blessing, or revelation of the Spirit or power of God. I believe the greatest thing is that Jesus showed the world how to exercise compassion for one another. The law of Moses, that preceded Jesus, was exacting in its demands, as all law is. That is the nature of law. And Jesus undertook to reveal the Father-heart to the world. The greatest movement in the soul of God Himself was that movement of compassion for a needy world, which was so great, that the Word says, that *"God so loved the world, that he gave his only begotten Son, that whosoever believeth in him should not perish, but have everlasting life"* [John 3:16].

We are inclined to think, sometimes, that God is careless about the world. Not so. *"For God so loved the world, that he gave his only begotten Son, that whosoever believeth in him should not perish, but have everlasting life. For God sent not his Son into the world to condemn the world; but that the world through him might be saved."*

When the multitude had followed Jesus into the wilderness, He was moved with compassion for them, for they were like sheep without a shepherd. The disciples said, *"Send them away"* [Mark 6:36].

Jesus understood men's humanity. He understood the fact that they were hungry; and the heart of the Christ was moved with compassion for them. He said: "No, get them to sit down. All there is in the company is 5,000 people, besides women and children. You get them to sit down."

When they were seated, He took the five loaves and the two fishes, blessed them, brake, and gave to His disciples to give to the multitude. Jesus taught the world to have compassion. Men have loved to have compassion on the lovable, and on the beautiful, but Jesus taught the world to have compassion on the unholy, the sinful, and the ignorant.

One day they brought to Him a sinful woman, and they said: "According to our law, she should be stoned." According to the law there was nothing else for her; but the compassion of Jesus covered that soul, and He said *"Go, and sin no more"* [John 8:11].

Someone told me this incident: A lady who lives in the country, a widow who had one daughter, was laboring for small wages; her great ambition was to be able to educate her daughter. She had toiled, and worked, and invested the money in Liberty Bonds to hold for the education of her daughter. Recently she came down from one of the country towns to Spokane to make a few purchases for the daughter that would be necessary for the girl's new life and school. She stood at one of the counters of the Crescent Store; she turned her back for a moment, and presently discovered that the little treasure was gone. The savings of a whole life, the struggles of a mother's heart! The endeavor to gratify the one big love of her soul, in the education of her daughter. In spite of the assistance of the officials of the store, she was unable to find any trace of it. At last she sat down and wept bitterly. A lady, the widow of a banker, who saw her, told her to come up on the balcony with her, and sit down. Another lady joined them, and the lady who first saw her said: "Now come, we are going to believe that God will move the soul of the person who took that little treasure, until his soul sees that thing like this mother sees it."

Men are learning, blessed be God. And they sat down together, to pray for that soul. The mother returned to the country, and in the mail following her came a letter, with the little treasure, and a little note, saying: "I couldn't keep it; forgive me, and may God forgive me."

Compassion reaches further than law; further than demands of judges. Compassion reaches to the heart of life, to the secret of our being. The compassion of Jesus was the divine secret that made Him lovable. Religious people are exacting; good people are exacting; but good folks have to learn to exercise compassion just like others do.

We remember the incident with the disciples and the Samaritans. The Samaritans did not want Jesus and His disciples to come. They said: "We have heard strange stories: how this thing happened, and how that thing happened. How a great amount of swine were drowned, etc." They heard about the pigs, but they probably had never heard how the widow's son was raised from the dead, how the water had been turned into wine, etc. The disciples loved their Lord; they were exercising His power, they were ministering to the sick, they were endeavoring to alleviate the sufferings of the world; but still that sense of insult was so overpowering, that they said: *"Lord, wilt thou that we command fire to come down from heaven, and consume them?"* [Luke 9:54].

My, how the big thing in your soul gets hurt; and how easy it is for us to feel the righteousness of the issue, rather than the compassion of the Son of God. There is no limit to the compassion of Jesus.

Two blind men were crying by the wayside, calling on the Lord to have mercy on them. And He stopped, and asked what they wanted. They answered: *"Lord, that our eyes may be opened"* [Matthew 20:33]. And He healed them. And if you want the real explanation for His saving men out of their sins and sicknesses, it is in the love of His soul: that Divine compassion of God, and His desire to help men out of their sorrows and difficulties, and back to God.

Jesus' example on the cross is set forever and ever as the very acme and the very soul of the compassion of God, through Christ. After they had pierced His hands, and pierced His feet, with His last breath He prayed to God, *"Father, forgive them; for they know not what they do"* [Luke 23:34]. When a man is able to look upon his own murderers, and speak such words as these, surely it shows, that he speaks beyond that which the human heart is capable of giving, and is speaking only that which the soul of God can give.

How long should we endure? How long should we endure the misunderstandings of friends without rebuff? If we consider these things, surely we see the secret of the life that He endured all the way. And unto the very end, and also in the very end, He was blessed by God. His triumph was there. The ignorant crucify you, and trample over the loveliest things of your soul, like they bruised the soul of Jesus. The triumph is there.

In the Divine fullness of the heart of God in Christ, is the revelation of a Divine conception, that alone endures, even unto death, and through which the nature and love of God is revealed to a dying world. When Jesus was trying to give us balance in the life of God, He gave us, once more, a beautiful parable, the parable of the Good Samaritan:

> **...A certain man went down from Jerusalem to Jericho, and fell among thieves, which stripped him of his raiment, and wounded him, and departed, leaving him half dead. And by chance there came down a certain priest that way: [and one should have expected compassion of a priest] and when he saw him, he passed by on the other side. And likewise a Levite [the holy man of the people]...came and looked on him, and passed by on the other side. But a certain Samaritan, [the dog in the mind of the Jew]...and when he saw him, he had compassion on him, And went to him, and bound up his wounds, pouring in oil and wine, and set him on his own beast, and brought him to an inn, and took care of him. And on the morrow when he departed, he took out two pence, and gave them to the host, and said unto him, Take care of him; and whatsoever thou spendest more, when I come again, I will repay thee (Luke 10:30-35).**

He did not do the best thing, but he did the best thing he knew, and Christ commended it. How often you have had the loveliest things of your soul trampled upon? Not by some drunken person, but probably by the one nearest to your heart; probably by the one who ought to have understood more than any other.

And do you not see the manner in which we wound the soul of Jesus continuously, through our lack of holy compassion? There is something a man has never divined, and probably that a man never will be able to divine: that subtle something in the nature that can be touched and moved by Divine compassion. It takes down the bars of our life, and lets the Divine love of God flow through our soul.

How often you and I have stood or knelt by the side of the dying and disease smitten, and have waited and prayed, ineffectively, until, within our own heart, something melted, something dissolved, and something richer than tears came from our soul, and by the grace of God, we saw the answer to our prayers before our eyes.

There is such a thing in the world as stigmata: that is contemplating something so much that it actually becomes a fact in your own being. It is well explained by telling an incident from the life of St. Francis, who had contemplated the Cross of Christ with such intensity, and it so moved him, that he said to his followers: "When I am dead, open my body, and you will find the impress of the Cross of Christ on my heart." And sure enough, after his death, when they opened his body, there was the impress of the Cross of Christ on his heart. There is an inner life; an in working of God.

The compassion of Jesus was illustrated when He broke up a funeral procession one day as He passed along in that little city of Nain. He [the deceased] was named by these tender terms: the only son of his mother, and she was a widow. When Jesus looked on that procession, something broke loose in His soul, He stepped up to the bier, being moved with compassion, and said: *"Young man, I say unto thee, Arise"* [Luke 7:14].

The sorrows of others moved the soul of Jesus, and touched His heart. Lazarus, His friend, died, and four days later the Lord went there; and hearing that He was approaching the village, one sister came to meet Him; and she said to Him: *"Lord, if thou hadst been here, my brother had not died"* [John 11:21].

The other sister poured out her heart to Him in a similar manner. Eventually, He stood by the grave of His friend. *"And Jesus wept."*

Something terrific was moving in His soul. He said: *"Father, I thank thee that thou hast heard me."* Then *"He cried with a loud voice, Lazarus, come forth"* [Luke 11:41-43]. And he that was dead came forth.

Once in South Africa, we were praying for a sick lady, for a time without result. Then I said: "I will take my sister and go and pray for her." We prayed again, and there was no victory. A day or two afterwards, we were down in the city, in one of the large department stores. As we stood there, the Spirit of the Lord said to me: "Go to her now." I said to my sister: "As soon as you are through, we will go over and pray for that sick lady."

We went and I watched her writhe in pain and agony until I put my arms about her, and cuddled her head close to my heart. And then, presently, something broke loose in my soul: and then in one moment, (I hadn't even started to pray) she was lifted out of her agony and suffering. A Divine flood moved her, and I knew she was healed. Then I laid her down on the bed, and took my sister's arm and we went away praising God.

And yet one more incident; and I want to give you this for your own help and blessing. I knew a man in South Africa, who was an ardent Methodist. He had ten sons, all Methodist (local) preachers, and three daughters, three beautiful daughters, holy women, a wonderful family, one of the most wonderful families I have ever known. The old gentleman had been stricken with disease, and the agony of his suffering was so great, that there seemed to be only one way—and that was to drug him into insensibility.

As the years passed, he became a morphine fiend. He told me that he smoked 24 cigars, drank two quarts of whiskey, and used a tremendous quantity of morphine every day. Think of it.

So the old man, until he was 73 years old, was drugged into senselessness most of the time. I prayed for him unceasingly for 16 hours without result. William Duggin, one of my ministers, hearing of the situation, came to my assistance; and I remember how he stood over him and prayed for him in the power of God. Somehow there was no answer.

I watched that man in convulsions, until his daughters begged me just to let them give him morphine, and let him die senseless, rather than to see him suffer longer. And I said, "No. I have had your pledge and his, too, that life or death, we were going to fight this battle through."

Presently, as I stood there, and was watching the awful convulsions, particularly in his old bare feet that were sticking out at the bottom of the bed, this came to my mind: *"Himself took our infirmities"* [Matthew 8:17]. And I reached out and got hold of them, and held them as in a grip of iron; and that thing that is too deep for any form of expression that we know broke forth in my soul and in a single moment I saw him lie still, healed of God.

Many a day after that I have walked with him over three vast estates, on which there were 50,000 orange trees and 50,000 lemon trees, and the old man told me of his love for God, and of the richness of His presence, and I had my reward, blessed be God.

If this Church ever succeeds in doing that big thing, that great thing, that unspeakable thing that God purposes that we should do, it can only be when we enter into that Divine compassion of the Son of God.

25

Adventures in God

Incidents From the Ministry of Dr. John G. Lake

Introductory:

Among the pioneers, and probably the big pioneers, who brought the ministry of healing back into the church were Alexander Dowie, A.B. Simpson, A.J. Gordon, and Dr. John G. Lake. Dr. Lake was in the healing ministry ten years before he received the Baptism in the Holy Spirit. He was in the healing ministry before the outpouring of the Holy Spirit at the beginning of this century. What men of his generation had to say about John Graham Lake:

"Lake is the embodiment of the spirit of primitive Christianity."

W.T. Stead, the greatest editor of the century[1]

"'Lake's Reply to Bulgin' is the clearest statement of the truth of divine healing ever written, a remarkable human document."

Dr. Frank N. Riale, field secretary of the Presbyterian Board of Education

"John Graham Lake has a ministry more like Jesus Christ than any man I know."

Rev. A.C. Grier in "Truth Magazine"

"Dr. Lake's teachings will eventually be accepted by the entire world."

Mahatma Gandhi,
outstanding spiritual leader of India
Assassinated June 30, 1948[2]

"...his message has swept Africa. He has done more toward South Africa's future peace than any man."

Cecil Rhodes, the empire builder

"Dr. John Graham Lake's healing ministry is one of the most remarkable the world has ever seen."

Dr. William T. Gentry,
author of "Materia Medica," a work in 27 volumes

"The man reveals more of God than any other man in Africa."

Rev. Andrew Murray, D.D.

"The triumph of the gospel is enough to make any man the wildest kind of an enthusiastic optimist. The unifying of the nature of God and man is the crowning achievement of Jesus Christ. The reason for the cross was thus revealed, man in God and God in man, one spirit, one purpose, one effort, one power and one glory."

Dr. John G. Lake

[1] William T. Stead was a British newspaper editor. He went down with the Titanic. His relationship to Dr. Lake is revealed in the sermon, "Spiritualism."

[2] Gandhi, full name Mohandas Karamchand Gandhi, became acquainted with Rev. Lake in South Africa. Gandhi was in South Africa on law business. After giving up his law practice he became the leader of India's millions. He was a tireless worker for India's independence by non-violent methods.

How I Came to Devote My Life to the Ministry of Healing

No one can understand the tremendous hold the revelation of Jesus as a present day healer took on my life, and what it meant to me, unless they first understood my environment.

I was one of sixteen children. Our parents were strong, vigorous, healthy people. My mother died at the age of seventy-five, and my father still lives, and is seventy-seven.

Before my knowledge and experience of the Lord as our healer, we buried eight members of the family. A strange train of sicknesses, resulting in death, had followed the family. For thirty-two years some member of the family was an invalid. The home was never without the shadow of sickness during all this long period. When I think back over my boyhood and young manhood, there comes to my mind remembrance like a nightmare of sickness, doctors, nurses, hospitals, hearses, funerals, and a grief-stricken father, struggling to forget the sorrows of the past, in order to assist the living members of the family who needed their love and care.

At the time Christ was revealed to us as our healer, my brother, who had been an invalid for twenty-two years, and upon whom father had spent a fortune for unavailing medical assistance, was dying. He bled incessantly from his kidneys. He was kept alive through the assimilation of blood creating foods, which created blood almost as fast as it flowed from his person. I have never known any other man to suffer so extremely and so long as he did.

A sister, thirty-four years of age, was then dying of five cancers in her left breast, having been operated on five times at Harpers Hospital, Detroit, Michigan, by Dr. Karstens, a German surgeon of repute, and was turned away to die. There was a large core cancer, and after the operation four other heads developed—five in all.

Another sister lay dying of an issue of blood. Gradually day by day her life blood flowed away, until she was in the very throes of death.

I had married and established my own home. Very soon after our marriage the same train of conditions that had followed my father's family seemed to appear in mine. My wife became an invalid from a heart disease and tuberculosis. She would lose her heart action and lapse into unconsciousness. Sometimes I would find her lying unconscious on the floor, having been suddenly stricken, sometimes in her bed. Stronger and stronger stimulants became necessary in order to revive the action of her heart. Finally we were using nitroglycerine tablets in a final heroic effort to stimulate heart action. After these heart spells she would remain in a semi-paralytic state for weeks. It was the result of overstimulation, so the physicians said.

But in the midst of the deepest darkness, when baffled physicians stood back and acknowledged their inability to help, when the cloud of darkness and death again hovered over the family, suddenly the message of one godly minister, great and good enough to proclaim the whole truth of God, brought the light of God to our souls.

We took our brother who was dying to a Healing Home in Chicago. Prayer was offered for him with the laying on of hands, and he received an instant healing. He arose from his dying cot and walked four miles. He returned to his home and took a partnership in our father's business, a well man.

Great joy and a marvelous hope sprang up in our hearts. A real manifestation of the healing power of God was before us. Quickly we arranged to take our sister with five cancers to the same Healing Home. We carried her on a stretcher. She was taken into the healing meeting. Within her soul she said, "Others may be healed because they are so good. They may be healed because of their goodness, but I fear healing is not for me." It seemed more than her soul could grasp. Rev. Dowie laid down his Bible, stepped down, and prayed for her. She was utterly healed. A few days later the cancer was black as your boot. One morning I put my finger in and touched the cancer and saw it was detached from the body. I began to twist that thing and it came out, roots and all. Some roots were an eighth of an inch in diameter, some were a sixteenth of an inch, some were as fine as thread, some were as fine as a silken hair. We put that cancer in alcohol and it was in Dr. Karsten's hospital for years. The mutilated breast began to grow and became a perfect breast again.

How our hearts thrilled! Words cannot tell this story. A new faith sprang up within us. If God could heal our dying brother, and our dying sister, and cause cancers to disappear, He could heal anything or anybody.

Our sister with the issue of blood began to look to God for her healing. She and her husband were devout Christians, but though they prayed, for a time prayer seemed unanswered. One night I received a phone call saying that if I wished to see her in life, I must come to her bedside at once. On arriving I found that death was already upon her. She had passed into unconsciousness. The body was cold. No pulsation was discernible. Our parents knelt by her bed weeping. Her husband knelt at the foot of the bed in sorrow. Her baby lay in his crib.

A great cry to God, such as had never come from my soul before, went up to God. She must not die. She could not die. I would not have it. Had not Christ died for her? Had not God's healing power been manifested for the others, and should she not likewise be healed?

No words of mine can convey to another soul the cry that was in my heart. A flame of hatred for death and sickness that the Spirit of God had stirred within me arose. The very wrath of God seemed to possess my soul. I discovered this fact—that there are times when your spirit lays hold on the spirit of another and he or she cannot get away from you. Somehow I felt my spirit lay hold of the spirit of my sister. I prayed, "Dear Lord, she just cannot go." I walked up and down for some time. My spirit was crying for somebody with faith in God that I could call on to help me. As I walked up and down my sister's room, I could think of but one man who had faith on this line. That was Alexander Dowie, six hundred miles away. I went to the phone and called Western Union and told them I wanted to get a telegram through to Mr. Dowie and an answer back as quickly as possible. I received this answer back: "Hold on to God. I am praying. She will live."

It was the strength of his faith that came over the wire that caused the lightnings of my soul to begin to flash, I prayed, "This thing of hell cannot be; it will not be. In the Name of Jesus Christ I abolish death and sickness, and she shall live."

And as I finished my praying, I turned my eyes toward the bed and I saw her eyelids blink. But I was so wrought up I said, "Maybe I have deceived myself."

Presently I observed her husband get up and tiptoe to her head, and I knew he had seen it. I said, "What is it Peter?"

He replied, "I thought I saw her eyelids move" and just then they moved. She was healed.

My wife, who had been dying slowly for years and suffering untold agonies, was also healed. But, oh, ere God's power came upon her I realized as I never had before the character of consecration God was asking, and that a Christian should give to God. Day by day death stole over her, until the final hours had come. A brother minister was present. He went and stood by her bedside, and returning to me with tears in his eyes said, "Be reconciled to let your wife die." I thought of my babies. I thought of her whom I loved as my own soul, and a flame burned in my heart. I felt as if God had been insulted by such a suggestion, yet I had many things to learn.

In the midst of my soul storm I returned to my home, picked up my Bible from the mantel piece, and threw it on the table. And if ever God caused a man's Bible to open to a message that his soul needed, surely He did then for me. The book opened at the tenth chapter of Acts, and my eyes fell on the thirty-eighth verse which reads, *"God anointed Jesus of Nazareth with the Holy Spirit and with power: Who went about doing good, and healing all that were oppressed of the devil; for God was with Him."*

Like a flash from the blue these words pierced my heart, *"Oppressed of the devil!"* Then God was not the author of sickness, and the people whom Jesus healed had not been made sick by God! Hastily taking a reference to another portion of the Word, I read again from the words of Jesus in Luke 12:16, *"Ought not this woman...whom SATAN HATH BOUND, lo, these eighteen years, be loosed from this bond?"* Once again, Jesus attributed sickness to the devil. What a faith sprang up in my heart, and what a flame of intelligence concerning the Word of God and the ministry of Jesus went over my soul. I saw as never before why Jesus healed the sick. He was doing the will of His Father, and in doing His Father's will, was destroying the works of the devil (Hebrews 2:14). (See also 1 John 3:8.)

I said in my soul, "This work of the devil, this destruction of my wife's life, in the Name of Jesus Christ shall cease, for Christ died and *Himself took our infirmities and bear our sicknesses"* (Matthew 8:17).

We decided on 9:30 a.m. as an hour when prayer would be offered for her recovery. I telephoned and telegraphed friends to join me in prayer at that hour. At 9:30 I knelt at her dying bed, and called on the living God. The power of God came upon her, thrilling her from head to feet. Her paralysis was gone, her heart became normal, her cough ceased, her breathing was regular, and her temperature normal. The power of God was flowing through her person seemingly like the blood flows through the veins. As I prayed I heard a sound from her lips. Not the sound of weakness as formerly, but now a strong, clear voice, and she cried out, "Praise God, I am healed." With that she caught the bed clothing, threw them back from her, and in a moment was out on the floor.

We all met at Christmas time. For the first time in many years the Lake family sat down to a Christmas dinner without a sick person in the family.

What a day! Will I ever forget it! When the power of God thrilled our souls, and the joy of God possessed our hearts because of my wife's recovery. The news spread throughout the city and state and nation. The newspapers discussed it. Our home became a center of inquiry. People traveled great distances to see her and to talk with her. She was flooded with letters of inquiry.

A new light had dawned in our souls. Our church had diligently taught us that the days of miracles were passed. Believing thus, eight members of the family had been permitted to die. But now, with the light of truth flashing in our hearts, we saw that that was a lie. A lie invented no doubt by the devil, and diligently heralded as truth by the church, thus robbing mankind of their rightful inheritance through the blood of Jesus.

People came to our home. They said, "Since God has healed you, surely He will heal us. Pray for us." We were forced into it. God answered, and many were healed. Many years have passed since then, but no day has gone by in which God has not answered prayer. People have been healed, not by ones and twos, nor hundreds, or even by thousands, but by tens of thousands. For I have devoted my life, day and night, to this ministry.

In due time God called me to South Africa, where I witnessed such a manifestation of the healing power of God as perhaps has not been seen since the days of the apostles. Christian men were baptized in the Holy Ghost, and went forth in the mighty power of God, proclaiming the Name of Jesus. They laid hands on the sick and they were healed. Sinners, witnessing these evidences of the power of God, cried out in gladness, and gave themselves to the service of God. It was like it was in the days of Jesus, "There was great joy in the city" and that nation.

Finally, God brought me to Spokane, where we have ministered to two hundred to five hundred sick per week. The city is filled with the praises of God because of the blessed manifestations of

God's healing power everywhere. People have come from one to five thousand miles for healing. Some have written letters, others have telegraphed, and some have cabled from half way around the world, for prayer and God has graciously answered. Ministers and churches throughout the land have seen that, though the church has taught that the days of miracles only belonged to the times of the apostles. That statement was a falsehood. The healing power of God is as available to the honest soul today as it was in the days of Christ on the earth. "The gifts and callings of God are without repentance" (Romans 11:29). Jesus is the healer still.

(An article similar to this [How I Came to Devote My Life to the Ministry of Healing] appeared in the *Spokesman Review* of Spokane March 3, 1918.)

How God Sent Me to Africa

I planned to go to Africa as a boy. I looked forward to it through my young manhood.

One day I went out to help a chore boy pull a cross-cut saw. We were cutting down an oak tree, and as I did the Spirit of God spoke to me and said, "Go to Indianapolis. Prepare for a winter campaign. Get a large hall, and in the spring you will go to Africa." And it all came to pass.

It is power. Power manifests in many ways. There is the power of FAITH which draws to you what seems to be impossible. One day after I had gone to Indianapolis, Indiana and had been preaching for some time, my old preaching partner said, "John, if we are going to Africa in the spring it is time we were praying for the money."

I replied, "Tom, I have been praying ever since New Years and have not heard from heaven or anybody else."

He said, "Never mind, John, how much will it take?"

I replied, "Two thousand dollars."

He said, "Come on, John, we are going to pray."

So we knelt down by Tom's bed and prayed. I heard him saying, "Jesus, you told me you would send that money in four days?" After awhile he slapped me on the back, saying, "Don't pray any more, John. Jesus told me He would have the money and it would be here in four days."

Four days later he came back from the post office with a letter containing four five hundred dollar drafts. The letter read, "I was standing in the bank at Monrovia, California and something said to me, 'Send Tom Hezmalhaltz two thousand dollars.' It is yours, Tom, for whatever purpose God has shown you."

We went out and bought our tickets. I had a little money. Tom had bought the tickets, but when you are traveling with a wife and seven children there are a lot of expenses besides tickets. We followed this practice. We never told what our needs were, but we did tell the Lord. So finally all the little money I had was gone.

When I paid the expressman I had $1.50 left. As the train pulled out of Indianapolis my secretary threw in a $2 bill; then I had $3.50. There was a lady in our party traveling with us as far as Detroit. I needed $10 to buy her a ticket to northern Michigan. As we rode along I said to Mrs. Lake, "Jen, I need $10 to buy Winnie a ticket." So we prayed. We came on into Detroit at 8 o'clock. As the train pulled into the station my brother and married sister were there to meet us, and among them was a younger brother, Jim. Jim was a student at the university. Jim took me by the arm and we walked to the other end of the station. Then he said, "Jack, I hope you will not be mad about it, but I would like to give you this." He gave me a $10 bill. I thanked him for it, and went and bought Winnie her ticket.

I still had the $3.50 left. We took ship at New Brunswick. So I bought some canned beef, canned beans, etc., and still had about $1.50 left. When we finally boarded the ship I had $1.25 left. I gave fifty cents to the table steward and fifty cents to the bedroom steward, and I still had 25 cents left when we reached England. We were five days in Liverpool, and as we had through tickets it entitled us to hotel expenses.

I arrived with my party in South Africa about May 15, 1908. Before I could go ashore, it was necessary for me to put up $125 with the Immigration Department. I had not a cent. As I stood in the line of people who were making these payments, awaiting my chance to explain to the immigration officer my dilemma, suddenly a man tapped me on my shoulder. He called me out of the line, handed me a traveler's check for $200 and said to me, "I feel led to give this to help your work."

On the arrival at Johannesburg, I and my family had nowhere to go. We were absolutely strangers in the country and had no friends or acquaintances there. As we arrived in Johannesburg a lady came up looking for an American missionary with seven children.

She said, "Oh, you are the family. The Lord has sent me to meet you, and I want to give you a home." At three o'clock that same day we were in a furnished cottage. God had provided us a home.

And that is how we got to Africa.

Jesus never intended Christians to be an imitation. They were to be bone of His bone, and blood of His blood, and flesh of His flesh, and soul of His soul, and spirit of His spirit. And thus He comes to us Son of God, Savior and Redeemer forever, and we are made one with Him, both in purpose and being. Ephesians 5:30 and 1 Corinthians 6:17.

I was in the home of DeValeras, in Krugersdorp, South Africa one day, when a man came in who had traveled all over the country with a sunstroke, which had affected his mind. He had developed a great cancer. He had been following us from place to place, trying to catch up with me. He came into the house and proved to be a friend of the family. In a little while a 6-year-old child, who had been sitting near me, went across the room, climbed on the man's knees, put her hands on the cancer on his face and prayed. I saw the cancer wither and disappear, so that in one-half hour the thing had disappeared. The wound was there, but it healed in a few days. When the child laid her hands on the top of his head, he arose, saying, "Oh! the fire that has been in my brain has gone out." His mind was normal.

POWER BELONGETH UNTO GOD. The simplest soul can touch God and live in the very presence of God and in His power.

One evening in my tabernacle, a young girl about 16 or 18, by the name of Hilda Daniels, suddenly became overpowered by the Spirit of God. She arose and stood on the platform beside me. I recognized at once that the Lord had given the girl a message. So I simply stopped preaching and waited. The Spirit of God came upon her and she began to chant in some language that I did not know. She made gestures like a Mohammedan priest would when chanting prayers. Away back in the house I observed a young East Indian, whom I knew. He became enraptured, and commenced to walk gradually up the aisle. No one disturbed him, and he proceeded up the aisle until he got to the front. He stood looking into the girl's face with intense amazement.

When her message had ceased, I said to him, "What is it?"

And he answered, "Oh, she speak my language."

I said, "What does she say?" And he came up on the platform and stood beside me and gave the gist of her message. "She tell me that salvation comes from God. That in order to save men Jesus Christ, who was God, became man. That one man cannot save another. That Mohammed was a man like other men, and had no power to save a man from his sins. But Jesus was God, and He had power to impart His Spirit to me, and make me like God."

While preaching in a church in South Africa, an American lady, whose son lived in the state of Iowa, was present in a week night service. Before the service began she called me into the vestry and told me that she had just received a letter from her daughter-in-law, stating her husband, a college professor, had apparently passed into a decline. He appeared to be tubercular. He had to give up his position. He was in a condition of great weakness and he was nearing death.

I returned to the audience room, and as we were about to pray I stepped to the end of the platform and asked the lady to hand me the letter. Taking it in my hands I knelt to pray, I invited all present to join me in faith for the man's deliverance. My spirit seemed to ascend in God and I was lost to all consciousness of my environment. Presently I stood in the home of the young man in Iowa, about ten thousand miles from Johannesburg. The man sat by a hard coal heater, with a little boy of about two years on his lap. I observed him critically and remarked to myself, "Though your face is hard and shows no evidence of soul development or spiritual life, yet your affection for your son is a redeeming quality." His wife sat on the opposite side of the table reading a magazine. Observing her I remarked to myself, "When he got you he got a Tartar."

I stood behind his chair and laying my hands on his head silently prayed God to impart to him His healing virtue and make the man well, that he might bless the world and that his mother's heart might be comforted.

In this case there was no knowledge of my return, beyond that in a moment I became aware that I was kneeling on my church platform, had been uttering audible prayer, and that the Spirit of God was resting deeply upon the people.

Some six weeks later word was received that the young man was again quite well. His recovery began on a certain date, corresponding exactly with the date on which prayer was offered.

In 1912 I was Pastor of the Apostolic Tabernacle, Johannesburg, South Africa. The ministry of healing through faith in Jesus Christ, the Son of God, was one of the cardinal teachings of our organization. The sick were brought from all parts of the land. Thousands were healed through the prayer of faith and the laying on of the hands of those who believed. Our church was then enjoying a great period of spiritual blessing and power. Various remarkable manifestations of the Spirit commonly occurred.

At a Sunday service, before public prayer was offered, a member of the congregation arose and requested that the audience join in prayer on behalf of a cousin in Wales, (seven thousand miles across the sea from Johannesburg) that she might be healed. He stated that the woman was violently insane, and the inmate of an asylum in Wales.

I knelt on the platform to pray. An unusual degree of the spirit of prayer came upon my soul, causing me to pray with fervor and power. The spirit of prayer fell on the audience at the same time. The people ordinarily sat in their seats and bowed their heads while prayer was being offered. On this occasion some hundred or more in different parts of the house knelt to pray with me. I was uttering the audible prayer. They were praying silently. A great consciousness of the presence of God took possession of me. My spirit rose in a great consciousness of spiritual dominion. I felt for the moment as though I were anointed to cast out demons. My inner or spiritual eyes were opened. I could see in the spirit, and observed that there was a shaft of seeming light accompanied by moving power coming from many of those who were praying. As the prayer continued these shafts of light increased in number. Each of them reached my own soul, each brought an increasing impulse of spiritual power, until I seemed nigh overcome by it. While this was going on I was uttering the words of prayer with great force and consciousness of spiritual power.

Presently I seemed out of the body, and to my surprise observed that I was rapidly passing over the city of Kimberly, three hundred miles from Johannesburg. The next consciousness was the city of Cape Town, on the sea coast, one thousand miles away. The next consciousness was the island of St. Helena where Napoleon was banished. Then the Cape Verde Lighthouse on the coast of Spain came into view. By this time it seemed as if I was passing through the atmosphere, observing everything, but moving with great lightning-like rapidity. I remember the passage along the coast of France across the Bay of Biscay, then into Wales. I had never been in Wales. It was new country to me. As I passed swiftly over the country, I said, "These are like the hills of Wyoming along the North Dakota border."

Presently a village appeared, nestled in a deep valley among the hills. Next, a public building that I recognized instinctively as the asylum. On the door I observed an old fashioned sixteenth century knocker. Its workmanship attracted my attention, and this thought flashed through my spirit, "That undoubtedly was made by one of the old smiths who manufactured armor."

I was inside the institution without waiting for the doors to open, and present at the side of a cot on which lay a woman. Her wrists were strapped to the sides of the cot, also her ankles. Another strap passed over her legs above the knees, and a second over her breasts. These were to hold her down. She was wagging her head and muttering incoherently. I laid my hands upon her head, and with great intensity commanded in the Name of Jesus Christ, the Son of God, that the demon spirit possessing her be cast out, and that she might be healed by the power of God. In a moment or two I observed a change coming over her countenance. It softened and a look of intelligence appeared. Presently her eyes opened and she smiled up in my face, and I knew she was healed.

I had no consciousness of return whatever. Instantly I was aware that I was still kneeling in prayer, and was conscious of all the surrounding environment of my church and service.

Three weeks passed, when my friend who had presented the request for prayer came to me with a letter from one of his relatives, stating that an unusual thing had occurred. Their cousin, who had been confined for seven years in an asylum in Wales, suddenly became well. They had no explanation to offer. The doctors said it was one of those unaccountable things that sometimes happen. She was perfectly well and had returned to her friends.

Nearby a city in South Africa in which I was ministering were hills with out-croppings of rocks—like a series of cliffs, one above the other. I used to go up these to be alone and get some rest. One day I observed a lady bring a young child and set him on one of the shelves above a small cliff. She left him some water and food. It seemed a dangerous thing to do as the child might fall and hurt himself. However, I observed that the child was crippled and could not move around. I went over and laid my hands on the child and prayed. Immediately he bounded off down the hill to catch his mother. Not caring to meet anyone I moved around the hill out of sight.

A HOLY MIND cannot repeat a vile thing, let alone be the creator of a vile suggestion. It is an unholy mind that is capable of such an act. I say with Paul, "Mark such a person." He may talk, but he does not know God. He does not comprehend the power of salvation, and is not the possessor of the Holy Spirit.

Jesus Christ is at once the law and life of God.

During my ministry in South Africa I came across a bachelor who hated everything that was Christian. He had a reputation for cussing preachers off his place. One day I found out that he had not been seen for a while. So I decided to pay him a visit. Immediately I was warned as to what kind of reception I could expect. I went anyway. I entered his home and observed he was a very sick man. Before he could say a thing I tossed my hat down, and prayed that God would heal him. I left. A few days later he came to church. He was a changed man.

When I lived in Africa, one of our departments was the native work. I bless God for the privilege of witnessing the marvels of God among the native* people. I believe we had the privilege that has never been accorded any other white man in the world in modern times. On Christmas Eve 1912, in Basutoland, the Lord's prayer was administered to seventy-five healed lepers. They were healed under the ministry of a black* fellow whose sole raiment when we first met him was a goat skin apron. It was a beautiful thing to sit with this man in the service.

THE LIFE OF THE CHRISTIAN, without the indwelling power of the Spirit in the heart, is a weariness to the flesh. It is an obedience to commandments and an endeavor to walk according to a pattern which you have no power to follow. The Christian life that is lived by the impulse of the Spirit of Christ within your soul, becomes a joy, a power, and a glory.

A few months ago I was absent from the city of Spokane. When I returned Mrs. Lake was not at home. It was just about time to leave for my afternoon service. Just then someone came in and said, "Your secretary, Mrs. Graham, is in the throes of death, and your wife is with her." So I hurried down to the place. When I got there the wife of one of my ministers met me at the door and said, "You are too late; she has gone." And as I stepped in I met the minister coming out of the room. He said, "She has not breathed for a long time." But as I looked on that woman, and thought how God Almighty three years before had raised that woman out of death, after her womb and ovaries and tubes had been removed in operations, and God Almighty had given them back to her, after which she married and conceived; how my heart flamed. I took that woman up off that pillow, and called on God for the lightnings of heaven to blast the power of death and deliver her. I commanded her to come back and stay. She came back after not breathing for 23 minutes.

When you and I are lost in the Son of God, and the fires of Jesus burn in our hearts, like they did in Him, our words will be the words of spirit and of life, and there will be no death in them.

A boy of twelve years, suffering from tuberculosis of the spine, so extreme that he was compelled to wear a steel jacket both day and night, was brought to the healing rooms for prayer. In less than ten days his condition was so improved that he discarded the jacket entirely. His shoulders straightened. The vertebrae remained fixed. He returned to his home at Rosalia, praising God that He had proven in our own city in March, 1919, Jesus Christ is still the healer.

A Mrs. McDonald was brought to the healing rooms so emaciated by tuberculosis that she weighed only seventy pounds. Her condition improved so rapidly that she put on flesh at the rate of one pound per day. This afternoon she attended our divine healing meeting, and gave public testimony to her healing. An hour later she called on the telephone, exclaiming, "I am so happy I just had to tell somebody. I have walked all the way home, kindled a fire in two stoves, and am preparing supper, a thing I have not been able to do for over a year."

In my assembly in Spokane is a dear little woman who was blind for nine years. She had little teaching along the line of faith in God. She sat one day with her group of six children to discover that her dirty brute of a husband had abandoned her and his children. He had left them to starve. A debased human being is capable of doing what no beast will do, for a beast will care for its own. You can imagine what that little heart was like. She was crushed, broken, bruised, and bleeding. She gathered her children around her, and began to pray. They were sitting on their front porch. Presently one of them got up and said, "Oh! Mama, there is a man coming up the path and he looks like Jesus. And, oh, Mama, there is blood on His hands and blood on His feet!" The children were frightened and ran around the house. After a while the biggest one looked around the corner, and said, "Why, Mama, He is laying His hands on your eyes!" Just then her eyes were opened. THAT IS DIVINE POWER.

One day a lady came to the healing rooms in the old Rookery Building in Spokane. She could not raise her arm up. She said that she had an open sore on her side. She could get no help from the physicians. She told me that she had no faith in doctors, no faith in man, no faith in Jesus Christ, no faith in God. Could I help her? I prayed for her three times with no results. After praying the third time I said to God, "God her soul is closed. Open her soul that she might receive."

She went to bed that night. The next morning as she was putting up her hair, she suddenly discovered that she was using her bad arm and had it up to her head. She felt her side and the open sore was gone. She immediately got on the telephone and told us about it. I said, "Sister, you come down here, there are people who are waiting to hear your testimony."

Though this lady professed no faith in God, yet her coming and asking and being willing to submit to prayer was an act of faith.

I found God as a boy. For years and years, fifty of them almost, I have been walking in the light of God, understanding fellowship with God, listening to the voice of God. As I was coming up one of the highways, a voice said to me, "Pull on to the left side of the road and stop." That voice is so common that I never even spoke of it to my wife. The left side is the wrong side of the road, and you are breaking the traffic law. I have listened to that voice so long, and for so many years that I have learned in most cases to obey the voice of God. "My sheep [know] My voice" [John 10:3, 27].

The thought I am trying to bring you dear friends is the value of knowing the Lord, what communion with God means.

Salvation is not just something that God gives that is going to bless you after you die. It is having the presence of the Lord now. God has promised the Christian the guidance and direction of the Holy Spirit.

Very well, I pulled on to the left side of the road and ran my wheels close to the ditch and stopped. Presently I heard the grinding of a great truck coming around the curve. Instead of coming normally, it was coming down the left-hand side of the road at an angle of 45 degrees. The thing had gotten out of control, and was covering the whole road. If I had been on my side of the road it would have side-swiped me and pushed me over a hundred foot bank. I was on the other side and the great thing just went by me. A little ways, about 50 or 100 feet, it struck a rough spot in the road and righted itself. The driver got the truck under control and went on.

Listen, men in this Word of God were guided by the voice of God. God talked to them. That is the inner thing or real Christian experience. That is the reason that men seek by the grace of God to enter into the real heart of God, into the real soul of Jesus Christ, into the place where He lives within you, where His voice speaks to and in your heart.

One time I was in Seymore's meeting in Los Angeles. There was a man who insisted on getting up and talking every little while. Some people have a mania for talking. Mr. Seymore endured it for a long time. Presently the fellow got up again, and the old man stuck his finger out and said, "In the Name of Jesus Christ sit down." He did not sit down. He fell down and his friends carried him out.

That is only one of the living facts of what Christianity is. The divine power of Jesus Christ by the Holy Spirit, filling a man's soul and body, flashing through his nature like a holy flame, accomplishing the will of God.

There is a baptism that belongs to Jesus. It is in His supreme control. No other angel nor man can bestow it. It comes from Him alone. "He it is who baptiseth with the Holy Spirit." So the individual who wants the Holy Spirit must come into definite, conscious contact with Jesus Christ Himself.

One day I sat in Los Angeles, talking to old father Seymore. I told him of an incident in the life of Elias Letwaba, one of our native preachers in South Africa. I went to his home, and his wife told me that he had gone to pray for a little baby who had been hurt. So we went over, and I got down on my knees and crawled into the native hut. I saw he was kneeling in a corner. I said, "Letwaba, it is me. What is the matter with the child?"

He told me that the mother had the child in a blanket, as natives carry their children, and it fell out and he thought it had hurt its neck. I examined it and saw its neck was broken. I said to Letwaba, "Why, Letwaba, the baby's neck is broken." It would turn from side to side like the neck of a doll.

I did not have faith for a broken neck, but poor old Letwaba did not know the difference. He discerned the spirit of doubt in my soul. I said to myself, "I am not going to interfere with his faith. He will just feel the doubt generated by all the old traditional things I ever learned, so I will go out." I went and sat in another hut and kept on praying. I lay down at 1 a.m. At three Letwaba came in.

I said, "Well, Letwaba, how about the baby?" He looked at me so lovingly and sweetly and said, "Why, brother, the baby is all well." I said, "The baby is well! Letwaba, take me to the baby at once." So we went to the baby, and I took the little black* thing on my arm, and I came out praying, "Lord, take every cursed thing out of my soul that keeps me from believing the Lord Jesus Christ." And Mr. Seymore shouted, "Praise God, brother, that is not healing, it is life."

In a party of our Brother Saunders, is a native man, Edward Lion, who a few years ago didn't even wear clothes. He was illiterate and knew nothing of our conception of scholarship. God anointed that man with the faith of God and measure of the Holy Ghost so intense that on one occasion when a multitude of sick folks had been brought and collected in a valley, the power of God came upon him and he went upon the mountain side, stretched out his hands over the sick below, and poured out his heart to God. In a minute hundreds of them were healed. Healing power fell upon them. There is no such instance recorded in the New Testament. Jesus promised that the last days should be marked by greater works than He Himself had wrought.

The Christian, the child of God, the Christ-man, who has committed his body as well as his soul to God, ought not to be a subject for healing. He should be a subject of continuous, abiding HEALTH, because he or she is filled with the life of God.

> Christ is at once the spotless descent of God into man, and the sinless ascent of man into God, and the Holy Spirit is the Agent by whom this is accomplished.

Tongues and Interpretation
South Africa, June 1910

Consecration of John Lake

One day, when a young man, I needed healing from heaven. There was nobody to pray for me. I was not even a Christian in the best sense of being a Christian. I was a member of a Methodist Church. I had seen God heal one dear soul who was dear to me.

As I sat alone one day I said, "Lord, I am finished with the doctor and the devil. I am finished with the world and the flesh, and from today I lean on the arm of God. I committed myself to God Almighty right there and then, though there was no sign of healing or anything else, except my consecration to Him, the disease that had struck my life and almost killed me for nearly nine years, was gone. It was chronic constipation. I would take three ounces of castor oil at a single dose three times a week.

The place of strength and the place of victory is the place of consecration to God. It is when a man shuts his teeth and says, "I go this way with God," that victory is going to come. There is no man that lives who can define the operations of faith in a man's heart. But there is one thing for sure, that when we cut ourselves off from every other help, we never find the Lord Jesus Christ to fail. If there is any failure, it is our failure, not God's.

Over in Indiana some years ago was a farmer who used to be a friend of Brother Fockler and myself. His son had been in South America. He had a dreadful case of typhoid fever, and no proper nursing. The result was that he developed a great fever sore, ten inches in diameter. The whole abdomen became grown up with proud flesh; one layer on top of another layer until there were five layers. The nurse had to lift up those layers and wash it with an antiseptic to keep the maggots out of it.

When he exposed the body for me to pray for him I was shocked. I had never seen anything like it before. As I went to pray for him I spread my fingers out wide, and put my hand right on that cursed growth of proud flesh. I prayed God in the Name of Jesus Christ to blast the curse of hell, and burn it up by the power of God. Then I took the train and came back to Chicago.

The next day I received a telegram saying, "Lake, the most unusual thing has happened. An hour after you left the whole print of your hand was burned into the growth a quarter of an inch deep."

You talk about the voltage from heaven, and the power of God! Why there is lightning in the soul of Jesus. The lightnings of Jesus heals men by its flash; sin dissolves, disease flees when the power of God approaches.

Yet we are quibbling and wondering if Jesus Christ is big enough for our needs. Let's take the bars down. Let God come into your life. And in the Name of Jesus your heart will not be satisfied with an empty Pentecost, but your soul will claim the light of God, the lightnings of Jesus to flood your life.

Before I went to Africa, almost a year, one night as I prayed I was overshadowed by the Spirit of the Lord. The Lord showed me various places in which I would labor for five years, and by the illumination that would appear in the heavens, I knew the extent of the work in each place. That night as I knelt on the floor, I was present in a church in Johannesburg, South Africa. I walked in at the front door of the church and walked to the front, and into the vestry. I looked around the place and took note of everything there, furniture and all. This occurred in my own home in this country.

In less than one year I was in that church, and pastor of that church. God did the whole thing, and I had nothing to do with it. God showed me by the illumination all over the land the marvelous extent and character of the work that He was going to do. I had faith to believe that the thing God showed me would come to pass, and I have lived to see it through.

I have a brother, a splendid fellow, a finely educated man, a professor. I returned from Africa some years ago, and we were visiting together. As we sat visiting my sister, who was present, he said, "John, I have some old neighbors over here. They are old German people. They are having a very hard time. The old man died, and one of the sisters died. This thing happened and that thing, and finally the son, who is a ship builder, fell one day and was carried to the hospital. They say his leg has to be amputated. Gangrene has set in. The physicians have amputated the toe and a piece of the foot. And now they say the leg has to be amputated. The old mother has been sitting in a wheel chair, a rheumatic cripple, for two and a half years and cannot move."

My brother and I had been having somewhat of a discussion over this thing. He said, "Jack, don't you think these things are all psychological?"

I answered, "Not much."

He said, "I think it is. Don't you think it is a demonstration of the power of the mind over matter?"

And I said, "No, if that was all it is, you could give just as good a demonstration as I could."

After a while my sister said, "I have been across the street and made arrangements for you to come and pray for these people."

I said, "All right, Jim, come along."

I said to the old lady, "Mother, how long have you been here?"

She replied, "I have been here two and a half years. It is awfully hard. Not just hard to sit here all the time, but I suffer night and day. There has been no moment of relaxation from acute suffering in these two and a half years."

As I listened to her, the flame of God came into my soul, and I said, "You rheumatic devil, in the Name of Jesus Christ I will blot you out, if it is the last thing I ever do in the world." I laid my hands on her. I looked to heaven and called on God to cast that devil out and set her free.

I said to her, "Mother, in the Name of Jesus Christ get out and walk." She arose and walked.

My brother said, "My, it beats the devil."

I replied, "That's the intention."

We went into the room where the son was, whose leg was to be amputated. I sat for a few minutes and told of the power of God. I said, "We have come to you with a message of Jesus Christ, and we have not just come with the message, but with the power of God." And laying my hands on the limb, I said, "In the Name of the living God they shall never amputate this limb." It was healed.

I was gone for three to six months, and then once again stopped at my sister's house. The young lady called and said, "You must come across the street and see my mother and brother. They are so well." I called, and found the old mother very happy. She said, "Oh, Jake, he is not at home. Why he is so well he went down to the saloon and danced all night."

I waited to see Jake. I tried to tell him something about the living God that he had felt in his body, and Who wanted to take possession of his soul and reveal the nature of Jesus Christ in him.

Five years passed and I returned again to the United States, and was stopping at my sister's home. She said, "Do you remember some people that you prayed for across the road? Here is Jake now coming from his work."

We sat on the porch and talked and I said, "Well, Jake, how is it?"

"Oh," he said, "I do not understand it all, but something has been going on and on. It is in me. First I could not go to the dance, and next I could not drink beer, and next my tobacco did not taste good, and then a joy came into my heart, and then I found it was Jesus."

BORN OF GOD, the nature of man brought into union with God by the Holy Spirit.

Story of William Bernard, Canadian Artilleryman

as told by John de Witt

I met William Bernard, or "Billy" as his friends call him, some three years ago. We became warm friends. He walked with his hand drawn over his side. One day he told me the reason for it.

"When I was a child of about three and a half years, I was dropped by my nurse, and suffered curvature of the spine. It affected my whole life. When other children played their rough games, I could not take part. I grew up with a longing for athletics but was shut out. I went to several of the best doctors in London, but no hope of a cure was given. Then I came to America and interviewed other physicians, but though they did their best I still remain the same."

My sympathy went out to Bernard. One day I suggested that he go with me to Rev. John Lake. He laughed and said, "I have no faith." But I kept urging him, so he consented. I introduced him to Mr. Lake and he immediately said, "I have no faith." I remember how Mr. Lake looked up in his face, and threw his head back, and laughingly said, "But I have enough faith for both of us."

Mr. Lake prayed with him, and then turned him over to his assistant, the Rev. Mr. Westwood, who probably ministered to him six times. Then, one day Bernard said to me, "I have always longed to give my service to my country. I believe I am well and I am going to test it. I will go over to the Canadian Recruiting Office and see if I can get in."

Bernard did so, and was passed by two physicians as absolutely perfect.

The healing work in Spokane involved about 2,000 letters a month. This gives an idea of the magnitude of the correspondence.

A cablegram from Pretoria, South Africa requested prayer for a

Mrs. Devillus. She was sick with cancer. Her case was hopeless. Rev. Lake wrote her a letter and prayed for her. A letter was received saying that she was totally healed upon receiving Rev. Lake's letter.

An anointed handkerchief was sent to Sweden. It was for a little girl with a hip disease. A return letter testified that upon application of the handkerchief she was totally healed. Distance is no barrier to God.

In one of the services in South Africa I preached on repentance. A powerful anointing of the Spirit was present. A small man arose from the back and came forward. When about ten feet from the altar, *the Spirit of the Lord struck him* and he fell flat on his face. *One man after another came up and was struck down until there was a pile of fifteen men.* I was troubled for I was afraid the little fellow on the bottom would smother.

I had never witnessed such a situation before. I tried to get some of the men off so I could get to the little fellow. Then the Lord spoke to my soul, "If God has slain these can you not trust Him to keep them from smothering?" I replied, "Excuse me, Lord."

My interpreter was disturbed. I assured her, "The Lord is doing this. We will wait and see what the Holy Ghost does and learn how He does it. You remember *"He made known His ways unto Moses, His acts unto the children of Israel"* [Psalm 103:7]. We have seen His acts, strange ones, perhaps we can now learn His ways.

In about fifteen minutes one of the prostrate men began to confess his sin at the top of his voice. He arose with the light of God in his face. This continued until all of them were up and returned to their seats. The last to arise was the little fellow. He confessed his sin and the light of God shone on his face. He sat down. When God is moving let Him have His way, all will be well and to His glory.

When preaching at Bloomfontein, O.F.S., a man by the name of Johnson, an epileptic for twelve years, attended the meetings. He took from twelve to fifteen seizures a day.

After the service a group of us were in an attitude of prayer and communion with God, preparatory to going out for an open air meeting.

Someone turned and asked this young man if he would not like to be a Christian. He said, "Well I guess not. I would do the same things tomorrow I have done today if I were." Like a flash out of the blue the Spirit of God fell upon him and he fell prostrate upon the floor, and remained there until ten o'clock the next morning.

Before morning, that fellow, who had been having about fifteen seizures a day was not only saved, but healed and went forth at ten o'clock baptized in the Holy Ghost.

One day our minister of Bloomfontein was going out to conduct a meeting for Basuto natives. He could not speak Basuto enough to preach to them directly, so when he wanted to preach, it was necessary to have an interpreter. Johnson was with him. The interpreter did not arrive, but when the time for the meeting came, the power of God came upon Johnson, and to the amazement of all he stood up and spoke forth the Word to those native people in the purest Basuto.

One evening as I was preaching the Spirit of the Lord descended upon a man in the front row. It was Dr. E. H. Cantel, a minister from London, England.

He remained in a sitting posture, but began rising from the chair: gradually he came down on the chair: and again gradually he began to rise, somewhat higher, then gradually he came down. This was repeated three times.

Was it a reversal of the law of gravitation? I think not. My own conception is that his soul became so united with the Spirit of God that the attractive power of God was so intense it drew him up.

One day I stood at the railway station in Logansport, Indiana waiting for my train, and observed a group of Italian men, apparently laborers, sitting on a bench. They were going out somewhere to work.

As I walked up and down the platform I said, "Oh God, how much I would like to be able to talk to these men about the living Christ and His power to save." The Spirit said, *"You can."*

I stepped over to them and as I approached them I observed myself commencing to speak in some foreign language. I addressed one of the group and he instantly answered me in Italian. I asked where he was from, and he replied, "Naples." For fifteen minutes God let me tell of the truths of Christ and the power of God to that group of laborers in Italian, a language of which I had no knowledge.

That was a little flash, a gleam, but one day, bless God, there will come from heaven a shower that will so anoint the souls of men that they will speak in every language man speaks in by the power of God. *"For this gospel of the kingdom must first be preached to all nations"* [see Matthew 24:14].

While in Africa the Church of England sent a delegation of three men to Johannesburg, who remained there a whole year to make a report back to England concerning the work in South Africa. The result was that they called a great conference of Church of England preachers, and I was sent for to come and preach to that conference. It resulted in the establishment in the Church of England of healing societies. We have recently been blessed in this land with one of their healers, Mr. Hicks, who is holding meetings in the varied Episcopal Churches all around the land. I have just come from Portland, where they blocked the streets for ten blocks around the church with automobiles carrying the sick to his meetings.

Mr. Clark Mitchell

Forest Grove, Oregon—March 26, 1922

Mr. Mitchell was in a logging accident ten years ago, in which his left side was severely injured, the knee was crushed, and the left shoulder was also crushed. For ten years he has been a great sufferer. The knee developed a tumor so large it filled his pant leg. He tells me that during this time there were occasions when he would be able to walk with great suffering, perhaps a single block, and then other periods when he was compelled to be confined to his home and his chair.

Three weeks ago Thursday, about 2 p.m. I was passing down Pacific Avenue, and as I passed along, his daughter, Mrs. Crowe, waved to me. Mrs. Crowe is Mr. Mitchell's daughter and they live in the same home. I was on my way to the Free Methodist Church to my meeting, and was hurrying when the lady waved me over.

She had seen me coming, and said to her father, "I see Mr. Lake and I am going to call him in."

Mr. Mitchell replied, "No, don't do it. I do not take any stock in that kind of stuff." However, I knew nothing of these circumstances, and would have paid no attention if I had. I am Scotch.

When I went into the house I said, "Mr. Mitchell, I have no time to talk to you." I threw off my overcoat and hat, and knelt to pray. He indicated it was his knee. I laid my hands on his knee, and began to pray. As I did I was conscious that he was healed. I said, "Mr. Mitchell, stick out your leg." He did. I said, "Get up and walk." He did.

As he walked he kept saying, "I don't understand. I don't understand. I don't understand." He came back and sat down, still saying, "I don't understand."

As he sat in his chair I told him of the healing of Mr. Charles Lousignont, and of the fact that he had a hip where the bones would grind.

Mr. Mitchell said, "That is like my shoulder." That was the first time I knew he had a bad shoulder. I called his daughter again, and we prayed for the shoulder. Then I said, "Put up your arm, Brother." He put his arm up. I asked him if it was perfectly free, and he replied, "Perfectly free."

The next day he spaded up his entire garden, and the next day he went to work for a plasterer, and he has been working ever since.

"Mr. Mitchell, are these statements true?"

"Yes, Sir."

One thing I forgot. I asked, "What is it you do not understand, Brother?"

"Why" he said, "I cannot understand God healing me. I am not a Christian."

I said, "Is it possible you have not yet given your heart to God?"

He said, "It is."

Then Brother, in the Name of the Lord let us do it now." And the dear daughter herself and another lady knelt with us and all three yielded their hearts to the Lord Jesus Christ.

At 8:30 p.m. that tumor that had been there for ten years had totally disappeared. He came to the printing office the next morning, presented himself and said to the editor, "Mr. Scott, I am the man the Lord has healed." And the newspaper wrote up a statement of the man's healing.

The day of miracles had not passed three weeks ago.

Dominion

Now I want to teach you something of the inner things of healing that people are not aware of. *There is a conscious dominion that Jesus Christ gives to the Christian soul.* It was that thing in the soul of Peter when he met the lame man at the Beautiful Gate. Instead of praying for the man's healing, he said to the lame man, *"In the name of Jesus Christ of Nazareth rise up and walk"* [Acts 3:6]. No prayer about it, no intercession. *He exercised the dominion that was in his soul. The divine flash of the power of God from his soul went forth,* and the man instantly arose, and went with them into the temple, *"walking, and leaping, and praising God"* [Acts 3:8].

Those who minister to the sick are aware of what takes place sometimes, though the individual is not aware of any healing himself. There is a dominion in the soul of the real man of God that is in touch with heaven, and when the real thing takes place, and he is saved or healed from disease, you know what it is. We pray until we are satisfied in our souls that the work is complete.

In the same building where we had our healing rooms was an X-ray outfit. They asked us to let them take pictures of some of our prospects for healing. It was a unique opportunity. Among those we sent to them was a man with tuberculosis. *Each time he was ministered to in prayer they would take a picture or X-ray.* You could see the progress of the healing. Each picture showed less and less of the disease until there was no more evidence of it. He was completely well. There was no charge for this service. The X-ray people just wanted to see what it was all about. *We always prayed for a person until we were satisfied that the healing was complete.* There was no dependence on the arm of man.

Mr. W.A. Fay

Mr. Fay suffered with cancer of the stomach. *Mr. Fay has perhaps been ministered to thirty times.* I think for the first ten days there was no evidence of healing whatever, or subsiding of the suffering. After that there was a gradual subsiding of the suffering. After a while the color began to return to his face, and he began to put on flesh. Now he can eat anything and everything and as much as he can get of it. And that is not all, beloved, he has found the Lord and Savior Jesus Christ while the process was going on, and he says that is the big part of it.

I guess the Lord knows how to open doors in people's hearts. A good many Christians overlook the fact that Jesus Christ made the ministry of healing just as broad as He could make it. To the seventy He said, *"Into whatsoever city ye enter, and they receive you...heal the sick that are therein, and say unto them, The kingdom of God is come nigh unto you"* [Luke 10:8-9]. Go heal them first, do you get that? Go heal them first, brother; go heal them first, sister. Then say to them, *"The kingdom of God is come nigh unto you."*

I lived near a man who was sick unto death. Some came to him and told him that he must be baptized or he would die and go to hell. I always said that was a kind of a system of coercion, and Jesus Christ never used it. He was too much of a gentleman. He never took advantage of a man when he was down, to grind his soul and try to influence him to be a Christian. If he was a sick man, Jesus went and healed him by the power of God. And when that man was healed the natural response of his loving soul led him to Christ.

Thatcher, Oregon

February 1, 1922

I wonder if you have ever paid attention to the different occasions in reading the scriptures when the VOICE OF GOD is mentioned. You know the thing that makes the Bible the Bible is the fact that somebody had an interview with God. Somebody heard from heaven before there was any Bible. Then the conversation or the incident was recorded, and these became the

Word of God. Now the Word of God is indestructible because it was a real voice, because it was a real experience, because God really did or said something and the record thereof is true.

If you wanted to prove, like you do in mathematics, concerning the Bible and its inspiration it is very simple. Every child is taught to prove whether his sum is correct or not. And if you have doubts and questions and fears concerning the Bible and its inspiration, we know that if one soul ever heard from heaven another soul may. If ever one soul had an interview with God, another soul may. If any man ever knew his sins were forgiven at any period another man may know his sins are forgiven now. If there ever was a man or woman healed by the power of God at any time, then men and women can be healed again. And the only thing necessary is to return again in soul experience to that same place of intimacy with God where the original individual met God. Now is that clear?

That is the way you prove the Word of God. That is the reason that Christians love the Word of God. That is the reason that the Word of God becomes the thing that men live by and that men will die by. The Word of God becomes a present living reality to them—not just a theory.

In my church in South Africa, we published a paper in ten thousand lots. We would have the publishers send them to the tabernacle, and we would lay them out in packages of one or two hundred all around the front of the platform, and at the evening service I would call certain ones of the congregation that I knew to be in contact with the living God to come and kneel around and lay their hands on those packages of papers, and we asked God not alone that the reading matter in the paper might be a blessing to the individual and that the message of Christ should come through the words printed on the paper, but we asked God to make the very substance of the paper itself become filled with the Spirit of God, just like the handkerchiefs became filled with the Spirit of God. And if I was in my tabernacle now I could show you thousands of letters in my files from all quarters of the world, from people telling me that when they received our paper, the Spirit came upon them and they were healed, or when they received the paper the joy of God came into their hearts, or they received the paper and were saved unto God.

One woman wrote from South America, who said, "I received your paper. When I received it into my hands my body began to vibrate so I could hardly sit on the chair, and I did not understand it. I laid the paper down, and after a while I took the paper up again and as soon as I had it in my hands I shook again. I laid it down and took it in my hands a third time, and presently the Spirit of God came upon me so powerfully that I was baptized in the Holy Ghost."

Beloved, don't you see that this message and this quality of the Spirit contains the thing that confuses all the philosophers, and all practice of philosophy in the world? It shows the clearest distinction which characterizes the real religion of Jesus Christ, and makes it distinct from all other religions and all other ministries.

The ministry of the Christian is the ministry of the SPIRIT. He not only ministers words to another, but he ministers the Spirit of God. It is the Spirit of God that inhabits the words, that speaks to the spirit of another and reveals Christ in and through him.

Miss Koch

Spokane, Washington—January 23, 1916

Here is a woman I term a victim of surgery, operated on twenty-six times and left to die. She was an invalid for 13 years, visited and ministered to by different physicians for six years. I know this audience will pardon me this afternoon if I speak with great plainness. In order to let you know what God has done in this woman's life, I will have to speak plainly.

In one operation an incision was made connecting the rectum and the vagina. Now think of this condition. That wound refused to heal, and three times she was opened and that wound sewed up, but without avail. They said she was tubercular and no doubt she was.

One day this dear soul called Brother Westwood to minister to her. We commenced to pray the prayer of faith on her behalf, and right away the wounds on her body began to heal, until all the outer wounds were healed. If you were close enough you could see the scars all down her throat and neck, where some of these operations have taken place.

Now I want you to see the power of God. When she discovered that the rectal incision had not healed, it became a matter of special prayer. Presently her bowels ceased to operate entirely, and she had no movement for twenty-eight days. Think of it! If such a thing occurs in your lives for three or four days you think you are going to die. If you would wait for nature to do her work, you would be perfectly normal.

God's Surgery

Note the purpose of God. During that 28 days her rectum became perfectly still. There was no action whatever. The result was that the wound healed up. She went up on the south side of the city to do some dress making, and while working she became unconscious, caused by the gas pressing up on her heart and lungs. A physician was called, and in his examination discovered that the incision was perfectly healed, but during the long time that the lower end of the rectum had not been used, it had adhered, and now according to the doctor, she could never have another movement of the bowels until she was operated on. They were about to carry her off to the hospital when she became conscious, and she said, "No more operations for me, not if I die. I have committed my body, my soul, and my spirit to God." So they brought her home.

Twenty-seven days had passed without a movement. She came down to the tabernacle to drill the children for their Christmas entertainment. On her way back, she fainted on the street, and was carried to the emergency hospital. They examined her there, and corroborated the statement of the other physician. They were in the act of taking her to St. Luke's when she became conscious, and said, "No sir! No more operations for me if I die." When they asked her what she wanted to do, she told them she was coming out to my home. She was being entertained there for a few days. That was on Saturday, November 27th.

On Sunday afternoon, November 28th, she was sitting in the audience, and as prayer was being offered she said it seemed to her as though a hand was laid upon her body (abdomen) and another on her head, and a voice said, "You are healed." She left the audience room, and became perfectly normal, and has remained a normal woman ever since.

Beloved, people who oppose this ministry and do not understand it will say, "That is all right. We know God does do such things as that on special occasions, but they are special cases. You know Paul had a thorn in the flesh, and he prayed three times that it might be healed, and the Lord said, 'Paul, *My grace is sufficient for [you]* [2 Corinthians 12:9].' and he was not healed" Who said so? Who gave you the interpretation? Did you have the voice of God, or are you repeating the old fable that has come down through theology for one hundred years?

Do you not see, beloved, it is just one of the many tricks the old theological dodgers use to get away from the responsibility of praying the prayer of faith that saves the sick. My! The church has had a time trying to dodge this issue of healing. They come up to Paul's thorn in the flesh. Who knows what it was. He says, "I wrote this large letter with my own hand," and they interpret that to read that he had bad eyes. Who said so? On another occasion the people said they loved him so they would pluck out their eyes for him. I believe they would have cut off their leg, or their right arm if it would do him any good, but none of these things argue for a moment that there was anything wrong with his leg or his arm, or his eyes.

Paul prayed three times. The first and second time he was not conscious of the answer. He prayed again, bless God, and this time God met his faith and said to him, *"Paul, My grace is sufficient for you."* Apply it, Paul. Dive in Paul and take all you want of the grace of God. It will fix your thorn in the flesh, and everything else that is troubling you.

1909

In company with a group of Church of England people who had been appointed as a committee to visit all the institutions of repute along healing lines in Europe, we went to Lourdes, France. There we visited a Catholic institution where they heal by the waters of Lourdes and where they maintain a board of 200 physicians whose business it was to examine all candidates and report on them. At Lourdes we also visited the greatest hypnotic institution for healing in the world. This institution sent its representatives to demonstrate their method before the Catholic board of 200 physicians, and hearing of our committee, invited us to come before this body and give demonstrations along our lines. I agreed to take part, if I were given the final demonstration. The committee selected five candidates, people pronounced absolutely incurable. The hypnotists tried their several methods without success. I then had the five candidates placed in chairs in a row upon the platform, in view of this large audience of physicians and scientists, I prayed over each one of them separately, at the same time laying my hands upon them. Three were instantly healed, a fourth recovered in a few days and one died.

In 1901, I joined the Dowie Institution and moved to Zion City with the object of becoming a student and teacher of Divine Healing. I remained there until 1904.

I was made manager of Dowie's Building Department. During that year we put through our office business amounting to $100,000 per month, or $1,200,000 a year. We issued 1200 building contracts. This was the year that Dowie made his trip to New York City, taking with him 3,000 people from Zion City in ten trains. We had a road choir of 1200 selected voices and a road processional of 100 church officers. Dowie rented the Madison Square Garden which holds about 20,000 and the New York Police said that some nights they turned away as many as 100,000 people and that the streets were congested for four blocks away.

In South Africa, one Saturday night the church was packed. All available standing room was occupied with men standing shoulder to shoulder. The majority of those who were standing were men from the Tattersal Racing Club. Most of them were Jews. They included horsemen of all classes, bookies, jockeys, stablemen, race track gamblers, etc.

I was preaching on the subject of the power of God, and in a strong spirit was endeavoring to demonstrate that Jesus Christ was the same yesterday, today and forever. That His power was as great as it ever was, and that the only necessary qualification for touching God for anything was faith in Him. The audience was greatly moved.

At this point I observed a gentleman with two ladies endeavoring to squeeze through the crowds who were standing in the aisles. I asked the crowd to separate if possible and permit the ladies to come through, and tried to arrange sitting space for them on the steps of the platform. As they approached, I observed that one of the ladies held her arms perfectly stiff and did not move them at all. By instinct I knew at once that she was a rheumatic cripple. As she approached me, I said, "What is the reason you do not move your arms?"

She said, "My shoulders are set from rheumatics."

I said, "How long have they been like that?"

She replied, "Ten years."

I inquired if she had been treated by physicians. She replied, "I have been discharged from three hospitals as incurable."

I said, "What hospitals?"

She answered, "Kimberly, Johannesburg and Pretoria."

Then addressing the gentleman who accompanied her, I said, "Do you know this lady?"

He said, "Yes, she is my sister-in-law."

I said, "Do you know her story to be correct?"

He said, "Absolutely."

I asked her what she had come for. She replied, "In the hope that the Lord would heal me."

I inquired, "Do you wish me to pray for you for healing?"

She said, "Yes."

Then addressing the noisy crowd in the aisles and around the doors, I said, "You men never saw Jesus heal a person in your life. You do not know anything about this matter. You have never witnessed an exhibition of the power of God, and therefore should be considerate enough to keep still, confess your ignorance of such matters, and learn. This is what I want. Select two of your company, let them come and examine this woman, and see if her arms are stiff, as she states."

I waited for them to make their selection, and they put forward two men. I have forgotten the name of one of the men at this time, but the name of the other was Mr. Mulluck, a barber, a very intelligent gentleman. His shop was in the Market Building. I afterward learned he was an American.

They examined the lady critically, and found her arms as she had said, quite immovable. Addressing them I said, "Have you finished your examination, and are you satisfied her condition is as stated?"

They said, "We are."

"Then," I said, "stand back, for I am going to pray for this woman, that the Lord will heal her." Placing my hands on her shoulders I commanded in the Name of Jesus Christ the Son of God that this rheumatic devil that bound the woman be cast out, and in Christ's Name commanded it to go, rebuking it with all the energy of my soul. The power of God flashed through me like a burning fire, until the perspiration burst from the woman's face. Then taking her by the hands I said, "In the Name of Jesus Christ put your arms up." The right arm went up. Then I said, "In the Name of Jesus put the other arm up too." She instantly obeyed. Her arms had become free.

As I moved the arm, making the shoulder to rotate, I observed that there was a grinding sound in the joint, and addressing the men who had examined her, I said, "You have never heard a dry joint in your life. Come and put your ear to this woman's back, while I make her arm move." As they did so, I moved the arm, and the shoulder joints would grind. The oil had not yet returned to the joints.

In the woman's delight, she threw up her hands and praised God, and started for the door. The crowd parted for her, and she disappeared, and I did not see her again for some months.

*Kenneth Copeland Publications acknowledges that references to race and nationality considered acceptable in Rev. Lake's day are offensive and not acceptable to today's reader. However, these references in no way reflect the attitude or policies of KCP. To fully understand Rev. Lake's heart toward other races, we recommend you read his biography located at the front of the book.

A dream come true—Lake, the young apostle to Africa. As a boy, he dreamed of going there. At age 38, he stepped onto the soil of South Africa with the fire of God pumping through his veins. By the time he left, the nation was not the same.

Counting the cost—John and Jennie Lake seated with their three sons and two daughters, sometime around 1900—they later had two more sons. By age 30, Lake had become a wealthy businessman in Chicago and was even reported to have been a millionaire. But in 1907, the Lakes decided to dispose of their wealth and bring souls "to the feet of Jesus." (*Photo courtesy of the Assemblies of God Archives.*)

Revival—Lake seated (right) with Azusa Street revival leader William J. Seymour, outside the Azusa Street Mission in Los Angeles, Calif.—possibly sometime between 1906 and 1909. (Standing from left to right): Mr. Adams, healing evangelist F.F. Bosworth and British preacher Thomas Hezmalhalch who accompanied Lake to South Africa. (*Photo courtesy of the Assemblies of God Archives.*)

Students of healing—Lake (right) standing with Cyrus B. Fockler, pastor of the Milwaukee Gospel Tabernacle. Their association traces back to Zion, Ill., where Lake moved to study and teach divine healing under the ministry of John Dowie from 1901 to 1904.

Divine Healer Ask
DOCTOR'S
VESTIGATION

ke promises demonstratio
healing at meeting tonig
s God heal the sick?
ight this question will
ed for many Spokane pe
the claims of Dr. John C
d of the Church Elect, wh
a series of divine healing
ing meetings in a group o
sh and Chelan, are true.
p.m. the first healing
the series will start. All
Spokane have been invit-
end and be prayed for
Lake.

ES DOCTORS TOO

issued a special invita-
doctors of the city and
them permission to
applicant for healing
ter we pray for them,"
ay. "We have reserved
for those wishing to
healings."

transportation of a
ve been completed by
ton Water Power

able to handle sev-
ersons if necessary,"
on, traffic manager
W.W.P. Company today. "I
will watch closely and if extra cars
are needed they will be on hand,"
he declared. Cleveland, Northwest
Boulevard and Hollywood cars go to
the Divine healing tents.

CAN'T ESTIMATE CROWD

"There is no way of estimating
in advance the size of the crowd,"
said Lake this morning. "We hav

New beginnings—Lake with his wife Florence, around 1920. Lake's first wife died in South Africa. In 1913 he returned to America and married Florence Switzer of Milwaukee, and eventually they had five children. Florence was the reason why so many of Lake's sermons were recorded and preserved— she happened to be an excellent stenographer.

"Modern

Spokane minist
cure by faith a
check up on his

Are the days of m
see? The lame walk?
Can John G. La
series of evangelisti
prove to Spokane t
faith?
Is Lake right
the same today
nationally kno
Lake who
has a chain
and Canad
nationally
applicant
a

Tent Meetings—Lake standing with his crusade team outside their tent (above), and seated inside (below). In the summer of 1924, a local newspaper ran a four-week series of daily articles on Lake's tent meetings. During that time, the paper received 500 requests for new subscriptions, and later gave credit for that sharp increase to the feature on Lake's ministry.

Dressed in God's Presence—Lake in one of his fine suits of clothes which he was known for wearing. As he got dressed each day, Lake made a habit of walking over to his mirror, pointing to it as if to another person and saying: "God lives in that man in that suit of clothes. And where that suit of clothes goes, God goes."

The Healing Rooms—Lake seated (center) with some of his "healing technicians"—as he called them—outside the Divine Healing Institute he founded in Spokane, Wash. The office space Lake rented in this old building became known around the world as "the Healing Rooms," where at least 100,000 supernatural healings were eventually documented.

Hopeless?—A boy who was healed at the Healing Rooms. In Spokane, as many as 200 sick people a day came to the Healing Rooms. Most of the cases had been declared hopeless by physicians.

"PRAISE GOD I CAN WALK!"

Shrill screams follow girls cry at Lake healing tent; another woman loses consciousness under stress of violent prayer; Grandma says girl made to hear wasn't deaf.
"Oh, praise God—I can walk—
alk!" ...eams followed the
...hundred dif-
...dred

World's healthiest city—Lake (right) shaking hands with the mayor of Spokane, sometime between 1915 and 1920. According to U.S. government statistics, Spokane had become the healthiest city in the world—thanks to Lake's healing ministry.

Dr. Lake—Lake in his advertising car, around 1931. His congregation in Spokane had dubbed him *Doctor* as an honorary title due to his powerful healing ministry. The title stuck and much of the world knew him as Dr. Lake.
(*Photo courtesy of the Assemblies of God Archives.*)

HEALED BY
PARADE TOWN

50 auto carry 250 persons healed by Lake's prayers

Thousands of Spokane persons witnessed the unique parade of "healed" persons from the "Church Elect," when they rode thru downtown streets in automobiles Saturday

The Lightning of God—Lake, just weeks before his third and final stroke. He left this life with a vision that greater manifestations of power—the very lightning of God—would flash through men's souls.

THE CHRISTMAS ANGEL

The Healing of a Leper

A TRUE STORY
By REV. JOHN G. LAKE

It was the Christmas season in the mountains of Basotoland, South Africa. Everything seemed extremely unchristmaslike to an American. Instead of snow and skating, green Christmas trees with their brilliant lightings, the thousand gifts of love, the splendid turkeys and Christmas puddings, and all that goes to make an American Christmas, the boiling sun and the hot winds from the desert search every nook and corner. Santa Claus himself, instead of appearing with bells and reindeer, fur coat and whiskers, comes with a loose red robe, and rides a camel.

On the Eastern hemisphere, the seasons are reversed. Instead of Christmas coming in winter, it comes in the midst of the summer season. Indeed, everything is different. Even the skies, which have always seemed to us to be a fixture, have changed. The great bear has disappeared, the North Star, which to every Westerner, is the traveler's guide, cannot be seen here. On the opposite side of the earth new stars appear. Instead of the North Star is the Southern Cross, possibly the most loved of all the starry groups.

A native hut, in general form like a round bee hive, is seen in the distance. The frame work is made of poles stood on end about three feet apart. Between these poles native women weave the small branches of trees, inside and out, as you would weave a basket. It is then plastered with mud, and made smooth. The roof is of thatch, composed of long grasses, found in the marshes a hundred miles away. They are cut by the women and carried in bundles on the heads of the children to the site of the hut.

The floors of these huts are made of ant heaps, beaten until they are almost like cement. Then as top dressing for the floors soft cow manure is spread about an inch thick. When dry it is like a brown paper. Every week the native girls give the floors a light dressing of fresh manure to fill in the cracks and indentations, which keeps the floor perfectly smooth. For brooms a bunch of long grass is tied with strings.

In place of a soft mattress a mat of rushes lies on the floor, and for a pillow a stick of wood two inches thick stands on legs about six inches from the floor. No windows of any kind in these huts. Inside it is semi-darkness. The only light admitted is through the low door, when it is permitted to be open. There is no chimney or exit for the smoke. A fire of dry cow manure is made in the middle of the floor and the place is densely filled with smoke.

When inside of the hut one stands on their feet until the upper part of the hut is so filled with smoke that you breathe it in such quantities that you feel the need of relief. You try sitting down, and gradually the smoke comes down to you. Eventually you lie on the floor, and when you have learned the ways of natives thoroughly and want to sleep, you turn your face toward the floor, as the smoke is lighter at the bottom.

In one corner of the hut a young man lies suffering. We tell him of the glad Christmas season, of the Christ who was born. As the Babe of Bethlehem, of the host of angels who sang at His birth, of the shepherds and the wise men. We tell him that He is the Redeemer of the world, that He came to take away the sorrows and sickness of man. And suddenly rising on his elbow he inquires, "Will He take away Basuto sickness?" (Leprosy) We tell him that our Christ is a Savior from both sin and sickness and is able to heal all disease.

A year has flown. It is Christmas again. This time we are traveling in a Boer wagon, almost as large as an American freight car. Sixteen oxen draw the wagon over the mountains. The wagon is fitted with great brakes to keep it from running on top of the oxen as they descend the mountains.

It is evening time. A great shouting of the native drivers and a mighty cracking of their long whips indicates that they are endeavoring to stop the team. Then the Boer farmer (a Dutchman), who is the owner of the wagon, shouts "Outspan," meaning unhitch, and the native men proceed to loose the oxen and turn them out for pasture. The other natives prepare supper on a fire built on the ground under the wagon.

We are just preparing to spread our blankets and lie down for the night when across the veld, a mile away, another wagon is seen to be approaching. When it comes close, one of the natives in the party accompanying the wagon, salutes us, and asks if he may talk with the white man. We all sit together on the ground while he tells us at great length that his brother, a sick man, is in the wagon, also his aged mother. That many moons ago a white man had come to their hut and talked to the sick brother of one, Jesus, who loved men, who died for them, who saves them from their sin and heals them of sicknesses. He said pathetically, "We are seeking for Him, that my brother may be healed."

The native told us that four days before, in the night time, an angel came to his brother in the hut as he slept, and taking him by the shoulder awoke him, saying to him, "Come with me." The sick man replied that he was too weak, that he could not walk. Then the angel took him by the arm and permitted him to lean upon him, led him out of the hut and down the road a short distance to where two roads divided. Pointing down the road leading to the right the angel said, "Take your oxen and wagon and go three days on this road; cross the great river into the Orange Free State, and on the third evening, when the sun is set, you will find some white men camping by a wagon. They are missionaries. They will pray for you and you will be healed of your sickness."

In the morning, the young man, believing it to be a dream, told his aged mother, who related it to the brother. The old mother was not inclined to pay much attention, saying simply, "My son has dreamed." But the younger brother said: "The white people are having a Christmas, and I have heard that at Christmas angels come to the earth to help the poor and the sick. Perhaps it is the Christmas angel that has come to my brother. We had better obey the words of the angel."

So the oxen were found and hitched to the wagon; a pile of grasses was put in the bottom and the sick man laid upon them and for three days they laboriously traveled over the mountains, looking for the fulfillment of the angel's words.

We were greatly impressed by the simplicity and sincerity of the native's statement, and at 11 o'clock at night, when he had finished relating to us in true native fashion his story, we accompanied him to the wagon where the sick man lay. Looking into the beautiful heavens and realizing that possibly at that very hour, under the same beautiful skies of Palestine the Christ had been born, and the shepherds had listened to the joy notes of the angel host, when "Peace on earth, good will to men," had come as the message of God to the sorrowing world.

We reverently obeyed the word of Christ, laid our hands upon the sick man, praying that the power of God should come upon him and heal him of his terrible disease and enlighten his spirit with a knowledge of God and His love. His face changed; a glory light began to appear in his soul, the peace of God was in him, the virtue of Jesus flowed through him and his pains were gone. He fell asleep. Christmas morning he bid us good-bye, saying, "I am going home again to tell all my people of your Jesus and of how He healed me, and of your Christmas angel, and of the power of your wonderful God, who has made me well." While we proceeded on our journey rejoicing that the Christmas angel ever leads the way to the healing Christ.

26

The Offense of the Cross

"*And I, brethren, if I yet preach circumcision, why do I yet suffer persecution? then is the offense of the cross ceased*" (Galatians 5:11).

"Offense"—the stumbling block of the cross. This word calls for careful consideration. After writing to the Galatians, Paul calls attention to the *"offense of the cross."* He suggests that those who read his letter would understand what he was saying. The "offense of the cross" was expected. As it was absent there was something wrong.

And remember brethren, *"if I preach circumcision....then hath the [stumbling block] of the cross ceased."*

We sing: "In the cross of Christ I glory, Towering o'er the wrecks of time, All the light of sacred story, Gathers round that head sublime." We have almost with astonishment, and even with a tendency toward reluctance, come to a phrase like this, "The stumbling block of the cross," or "the offense of the cross." And in meditation I ask you to consider with me the word, the arresting, challenge of that word "offense" or "stumbling block." It is very interesting to see how the great translators have attempted to get over to us the import of the word.

Wycliff's translation employed the word that is now obsolete in our language. He rendered it the "sclaunger" of the cross. That was two words merged. We have divided them into "slander" and "scandal." Cranmer translated it "Slaumger." The Geneva council translated it "Slander." The Roman Catholic translated it "Scandal." The *King James* translated it "Offense." The *English* and *American Revised Standard* versions put it "Stumbling Block." They were all trying to interpret the word. I am daring to submit for your consideration the Revised Version, as exactly expressing the word: "Scandalon—Stumbling block."

Listen: Something in the way—in the way of progress. Suddenly you trip and stumble and fall. That is the word. I am not quarreling with the word "offense."

What does this mean, *"the stumbling block of the cross"?* It is something that men stumble over intellectually; stumble over emotionally. It is a stigma attached to the cross.

The cross was well known throughout the Roman world. The Romans had taken it over from the Venetians for capital punishment. But even in that world it never produced anything in the sense of scandal or upheaval. It was the symbol of *justice.* It was the symbol of punishment for breaking the law. It was the poetic result of wrong doing, against righteousness and justice. Men were not scandalized by the cross.

Then what is Paul talking about? It is the cross of Christ. Yes, but why should it be a scandal? It was the cross of Christ as presented to the world. What was being presented to the world that would make it a scandal? What were those early ministers and preachers declaring about the cross of the Nazarene?

What were they declaring? They were declaring that the cross was the very center of religion, the secret of government, and the inspiration of culture. That was what characterized the scandal. Jews from Jerusalem were moving out over all the world. Wherever they went they were telling that the cross of the Nazarene is the center of religion. It is the secret of authority and government. It is the inspiration of true culture to human life. Men laughed. They stumbled over it. They were against it emotionally, morally and intellectually.

We can see that there is the same sense in the minds of men today. The cross is still spelling to men a scandal. Men are still intellectually tripped by it. They still revolt against it. The cross is still bearing a stigma.

You and I are called to represent that cross in word and life, and if we fail to do it, we are failing in loyalty to our Lord and Master.

Will you come patiently with me to the historic scene? Yes, I would remind you of the well known fact that while Pilate had the superscription written over Jesus, *"THIS IS JESUS THE KING OF THE JEWS"* [Matthew 27:37], that the wording of the superscription was not the significant thing. The significant thing was that he had put it in Hebrew, Latin and Greek. The purpose was that no stranger near the cross should fail to read it. The three languages of the world powers were there.

Now look at the cross. First look at it from the soul of the Jew. Then look at it from the mind of the Roman. Lastly look at it from the person of a Greek.

Now supposing you could put yourself back of the scene, and could see it as a Jew, and was aware of the fact that its witnesses were telling that it was the secret of religion. The Jew looking at that cross, what did he see? Disgrace! To the Jew the cross was the place of moral disgrace. *"Cursed is every one that hangeth on a tree"* [Galatians 3:13]. Criminals; cursed.

Then for the Jew to be told that the cross was the CENTER of religious life, the secret, and the only secret of righteousness for an individual and the world, don't you see intellectually how he stumbled over it; that the cross of the crucified malefactor is the secret of righteousness? PREPOSTEROUS!

Then imagine you are a Roman and look at the cross from that standpoint. In the time that our Lord was born into this world and exercised His ministry and went to that same cross, was the only period in human history where a great power had mastered the known world. It had been attempted and never succeeded. It was the period known a *Pax Romana,* Roman peace. While I agree that "war is hell," I declare that, that period was worse. Man or woman, boy or girl did not own his or her own soul under the rule of Rome. Her proconsuls were everywhere; her soldiers were everywhere. An example is shown by Pilate, the Roman governor, he had mingled the blood of the Galileans with the Jewish sacrifices.

A Roman comes and looks at the crucified Nazarene, and the Roman is told that is the throne of an imperial power and imperial empire. That is the King; that is the One and the only One Who ever will subdue humanity so that His rule will be universal. I can hear the laughter of Rome at the very suggestion. The Roman suggestion of the cross is that the man there is not in disgrace, but that the man is DEFEATED, not a question of morality to them. They had their laws and jurisprudence, but were not bothered with morality.

Notice this, that at that moment on the throne in Rome was a man that was known notoriously. The Roman believed that power was all that was necessary. And that Galilean, whether He had done anything that was wrong or not, being on the cross could He be a King? If the Jew says "preposterous," the Roman says, "ridiculous."

Why do the Romans object? Naturally we see why. A defeated man be king! They had a false philosophy of government. The philosophy of force. If you have plundered a man so that he dare not do what he wants to do, you have conquered. Rome did not care if in my inner heart I was in revolt; if they bludgeoned me and I had to do what they said, "That is victory." Yes the whole scheme of government is that; we have not escaped it yet. We still think we can compel a man to be moral. You can restrain him, but that doesn't change his heart.

There He was on the cross. What do I see there? The weakness of God! Paul says it is stronger than men. You look at the cross and there is one supreme thing manifested. It is the exhaustion of human power. Man attempting to govern has done all he can. He can do no more. He has taken the criminal and put Him on a cross. He has executed Him. All the armies of Rome can do no more. In a few moments that malefactor will have left the world. Is that all? They have done their utmost; they are powerless.

Jesus said, *"Fear not him that killeth the body, and after that"* [see Luke 12:4]—that laughter of the man that thinks he is done for when he kills the body. He faces a rude awakening.

Now for a moment do not be a Jew or a Roman, but a Greek. I am not thinking of the chattering Greek merchant. I am thinking of some chance traveler from Athens. He looked at that cross. If he had looked once, he would never have looked again. A mutilated man was disgusting to the Greek. Greek idealism was looking for the perfection of personality, and there was no room for mutilation in their thought.

It is not a question whether this is the result of morality. A broken and mutilated man, the Greek with his esthetic culture turned from it. He would not have looked twice.

Then there passes through the Greek cities, one after another, men who proclaim that that broken, mutilated man on Judea's cross is the inspiration of culture, and of all that is refined and beautiful in life. The Greek intellect stumbled over it.

Emotionally the Greek revolted against it. If the Jew said "preposterous," and the Roman "ridiculous," the Greek said "absurd!" Wherever the Gospel was preached the scandal of the cross became known, the offense of the cross was created.

Why were these things so? What is the real meaning in the Jew's objection of the cross that is the center of religion? And to the Romans when they were told it was the secret of government? And to the Greeks when they were told it was the inspiration of culture?

Take the Jew. Why was the Jew scandalized by the cross? Because he had an inadequate sense of sin, and was ignorant of the God of his fathers. In the presence of that cross when told it was the center of religion he objected, because he only saw there the moral delinquency. It was not the curse of the King, but the man who put Him there. *He was made sin* [see 2 Corinthians 5:21]. That is the sinner's place, and they did not see it; and men still do not see that is the only place for sin and that God cannot deliver a man except his sin is put there. The route of religion is the cursing and canceling of sin. Unless sin is cursed and canceled there is no approach to God.

A man tells me he is disgusted at the cross, and that it is the religion of the shambles, that man has never had an adequate sense of sin. A man tells me that he does not go to church; he goes to the country to worship. Worship God through nature, while sin is in the heart? Nonsense. Earth is crammed with God, and every bush ablaze with Him, but only he who sees takes off his shoes. You cannot worship God while there is still sin in your soul. There on that bitter cross, the God of eternity and the God of Moses was dealing with sin, so it would be blighted, blasted, cursed, canceled, and the way open! And when He cried, *"It is finished!"* [John 19:30], the veil of the temple was rent in twain, and there was a way to the heart of God opened for humanity [see Matthew 27:50-51]. They did not see it. Men were ignorant of God. God is holy, yet so full of infinite love that He would bow and bend and stoop, and when sin must be cursed, gathering the curse into His own being and bearing our sins in His own being on the tree, brought deliverance. The cross in religion which is blind and ignorant of God is still made a scandal and a stumbling block.

Why do the Romans object? A defeated man, dying on a cross, a King. Whoever had heard of such a thing. To the

Romans, the Man on the cross had no power as He would soon die and it would be all over.

I repeat what Jesus said, *"Fear not them which kill the body, but are not able to kill the soul"* (Matthew 10:28). After that, then what? His resurrection from the dead. He is God's King. He is going to rule over this world. The secret of His rule is love. His subjects will serve Him because they love Him. He will not bludgeon a man into submission and call it victory while that man in his heart is still in rebellion. Men are afraid of God because of wrong concepts. Let a man meet God in Jesus and he will love God.

To the man with the ideal of bludgeoning power we point to the power of the resurrection. Don't look at the cross and stop there. Look beyond and see the mighty Christ at the right hand of the Father. Listen to the greatest declaration and cry of victory in the history of the world. *"I am the first and the last: I am he that liveth, and was dead; and, behold, I am alive for evermore, Amen; and have the keys of hell and of death"* (Revelation 1:17-18).

Why did the Greek revolt at the sight of a mutilated man? The soul of Greek idealism was expressed in the observance of the Olympic Games. It was the perfect person, the perfect personality, the perfect body with its smooth flowing muscles. The sculpture of ancient Greece displayed this high idealism. Their statues are marvels of perfection that express a high ideal of physical beauty. It is no wonder the Greek would not take a second look at the mutilated Man on the cross.

To the man who is looking for physical perfection we would say, Look at the cross and what it stands for, then look beyond. What will he see? What will the Greek see? He will see one *"...clothed with a garment down to the foot, and girt about the paps with a golden girdle. His head and his hairs were white like wool, as white as snow; and his eyes were as a flame of fire; And his feet like unto fine brass, as if they burned in a furnace..."* (Revelation 1:13-15). His transfiguration was a foretaste of His beauty. *"...His face did shine as the sun, and his raiment was white as the light"* (Matthew 17:2). Our body shall be like His glorious body (Philippians 3:21).

To the Jew, to the Greek, to the Roman and their counterparts today we point you to the cross, and point out what it means, and then take you beyond into the glories that are there and are yet to come to us.

"But we preach Christ crucified, unto the Jews a stumbling block, and unto the Greeks foolishness; But unto them which are called, both Jews and Greeks, Christ the power of God, and the wisdom of God" (1 Corinthians 1:23-24).

Christ, the power of God, can change your life. He can make a new creature out of you. Old things will pass away and all things will become new (2 Corinthians 5:17). Old things are passed away. That is the power of the cross. All things are become new. That is the power of being raised in newness of life in Him (Romans 6:4).

There is the power of His resurrection yet ahead for the physical body (Philippians 3:21). We are to be presented perfect in Christ Jesus, perfect in spirit, perfect in soul, and perfect in body (Colossians 1:28 and 1 Thessalonians 5:23).

James and Peter

Acts 12

Herod killed James with the sword. With the same intent he arrested Peter and put him in jail. In answer to prayer, God delivered Peter. This incident is used to show that God will deliver some but not others. Some God will heal but not others. What does deliverance or non-deliverance from martyrdom have to do with deliverance from disease? They are two vastly different areas of activity. There is no relationship between them. Jesus said that men would kill you (Matthew 24:9 and John 16:2). He never said disease would kill you. He healed all that came to Him. Martyrdom is partaking of Christ's sufferings. Disease and sickness were not in the category of Christ's sufferings.

Allow God to rid your life of sin and sickness, for they are the inner cankers that destroy life.

27

The Ministry of Healing and Miracles

Divine Healing Is Scientific

Atonement through the grace of God is scientific in its application. Jesus used many methods of healing the sick. All were scientific. Science is the discovery of how God does things.

Jesus laid His hands upon the sick in obedience to the law of contact and transmission. Contact of His hands with the sick one permitted the Spirit of God in Him to flow into the sick person.

The sick woman who touched His clothes found that the Spirit emanated from His person. She touched the *"hem of his garment"* [Matthew 9:20] and the Spirit flashed into her. She was made whole. This is a scientific process.

Paul, knowing this law, laid his hands upon handkerchiefs and aprons. The Bible says that when they were laid upon the sick they were healed, and the demons went out of those possessed. Materialists have said this was superstition. It is entirely scientific.

The Spirit of God emanating from Paul transformed the handkerchiefs into "storage batteries" of Holy Spirit power. When they were laid upon the sick they surcharged the body, and healing was the result. (Read Acts 19:12.)

This demonstrates, firstly: The Spirit of God is a tangible substance, a heavenly materiality. Secondly: It is capable of being stored in the substance of cloth as demonstrated in the garments of Jesus or the handkerchiefs of Paul. Thirdly: It will transmit power from the handkerchiefs to the sick person. Fourthly: Its action in the sick man was so powerful, the disease departed. The demonized were also delivered. Fifthly: Both the sick and insane were delivered and healed by this method.

Men received Jesus Christ into their hearts as one receives a lover. It is an affectionate relationship. Men obey Him because they have received Him affectionately. He has become their soul lover.

His love and power in them redeems them from the sin and sickness, and eventually, we are promised in His Word, He will redeem us from death also. Redemption from sin, sickness and death constitutes man's deliverance from bondage to Satan and his kingdom, and establishes the kingdom of Heaven.

The Power of the Name

Jesus called His twelve disciples and commanded upon them power and authority to cast out devils and heal disease (Luke 9). He superseded this by declaring: *"If ye shall ask ANY THING in my name, I will do it"* (John 14:14).

The first was a limited "power of attorney." The second was unlimited. This unlimited "power of attorney" was authorized before His crucifixion. It was to become effective when the Holy Ghost came (Luke 24:49 and Acts 1:8).

On the day of Pentecost this "power of attorney" was made fully operative. The Spirit came. First, legally; they had His Word. Then, vitally; He sent His Spirit.

Peter and John instantly grasped the significance of the Name. Passing into the temple they met a beggar-cripple. He was 40 years old and had been crippled from birth. Peter commanded: *"In the name of Jesus Christ of Nazareth rise up and walk"* [Acts 3:6]. Heaven's lightning struck the man. He leaped to his feet, whole.

A multitude rushed up. They demanded, *"By what power, or by what name, have ye done this?"*

Peter and John replied, *By the Name of Jesus Christ of Nazareth, whom ye crucified, whom God raised from the dead* [see Acts 3:11-16 and Acts 4:7-10].

Matchless Name! The secret of power was in it. When they used the Name, power struck. The dynamite of heaven exploded.

Peter and John were hustled to jail. The church prayed for them in "the Name." They were released. They went to church.

The entire church prayed that signs and wonders might be done. How did they pray? In "the Name." They used it legally. The vital response was instantaneous. The place was shaken as by an earthquake. Tremendous Name!

Jesus commanded: *"Go ye into all the world"* [Mark 16:15]. What for? To proclaim that Name. To use that Name. To baptize believers. How? In the Name (His authority: what He commanded). Amazing Name! In it was concentrated the combined authority resident in the Father, the Son and the Holy Ghost. Almighty Name!

The apostles used the Name. It worked. The deacons at Samaria used the Name. The fire flashed. Believers everywhere, forever, were commanded to use it. The Name detonated around the world.

More Bibles are sold today than any other 100 books. Why? The Name is in it. It is finality—at the Name of Jesus every knee shall bow and every tongue confess!

Prayer in this Name gets answers. The Moravians prayed. The greatest revival till that time hit the world.

The grace and love of God in the soul opens the nature to God. Then they asked of the blind man, *"What sayest thou of Him?"* [John 9:17].

He replied, *"He is a prophet"* [John 9:17].

Later Jesus found him and said to him, *"Dost thou believe on the Son of God?"* [John 9:35].

The man asked, *"Who is he, Lord, that I might believe on him?"* [John 9:36].

Jesus answered, *"It is he that talketh with thee"* [John 9:37].

The struggle of the centuries has been to free the soul from narrow interpretations. Jesus has sometimes been made to appear as a little bigot, sometimes as an impostor. The world is still waiting to see Him as He is, Jesus the magnificent, Jesus the giant, Jesus the compassionate, Jesus the dynamic, the wonder of the centuries.

Take the shackles off God. Let Him have a chance to bless mankind without limitations.

As a missionary I have seen the healing of thousands of heathen. Thus was Christ's love and compassion for a lost world revealed.

And thus the writer was assisted into the larger vision of a world Redeemer Whose hand and heart are extended to God's big world, and every man, saint and sinner, is invited to behold and love Him.

In one of the letters received from readers, this question is asked: "Why are not all persons healed instantly—as Jesus healed?"

The writer of this letter is mistaken in thinking that Jesus always healed instantly. A case in point is the healing of the ten lepers: *"as they went, they were cleansed"* [Luke 17:14]. The healing virtue was administered. The healing process became evident later.

Again: Jesus laid His hands on a blind man, then inquired, *"What do you see?"*

The man replied, *"I see men as trees, walking."* His sight was still imperfect. Then Jesus laid His hands on him the second time—*"and he saw every man clearly"* [see Mark 8:23-25].

Healing is by degree based on two conditions: first, the degree of healing virtue administered; second, the degree of faith that gives action and power to the virtue administered. *"The word preached did not profit them, not being mixed with faith in them that heard it"* (Hebrews 4:2).

The miracles of Jesus have been the battle ground of the centuries. Men have devoted their lives in an endeavor to break down faith in miracles. More believe in miracles today than ever before.

Pseudo-science declares miracles impossible. Yet the biggest men in the scientific world are believers in the supernatural and know that miracles are the discovery, the utilization of which the material scientist knows nothing.

The miracle realm is a man's natural realm. He is by creation the companion of the miracle-working God. Sin dethroned man from the miracle-working realm, but through grace he is coming into his own.

It has been hard for us to grasp the principles of this life of faith. In the beginning, man's spirit was the dominant force in the world. When he sinned, his mind became dominant. Sin dethroned the spirit and crowned the intellect. But grace is restoring the spirit to its place of dominion. When man comes to realize this, he will live in the realm of the supernatural without effort.

No longer will faith be a struggle, but a normal living in the realm of God. The spiritual realm places man where communion with God is a normal experience.

Miracles are then his native breath. No one knows to what extent the mind and the spirit can be developed.

We have been slow to come to a realization that man is a spirit and his spirit nature is his basic nature. We have sought to educate him along educational lines, utterly ignoring the spiritual, so man has become a self-centered, self-seeking being.

Man has lost his sense of relationship and responsibility toward God and man. This makes him lawless. We cannot ignore the spiritual side of man without magnifying the intellectual and the physical. To do this without the restraint of the spirit is to unleash sin and give it dominance over the whole man.

There must be a culture and development of the spiritual nature to a point where it can enjoy fellowship with the Father God. It is above the mind, as God is above nature.

Man's intellect is ever conscious of supernatural forces that he cannot understand. He senses the spirit realm and longs for its freedom and creative power, but cannot enter until changed from self and sin—the spirit enthroned and in action rather than the intellect, spirit above BOTH MIND AND MATTER.

The Life of God, the Spirit of God, the nature of God are sufficient for every need of man.

In the highest sense of the word, he is real Christian whose *body, soul* and *spirit* alike are filled with the Life of God.

Healing in any department of the nature, whether spirit, soul or body, is but a means to an end. The object of healing is health, abiding health of body, soul and spirit. The healing of the spirit unites the spirit of man to God forever. The healing of the soul corrects psychic disorder and brings the soul processes into harmony with the mind of God. And the healing of the body completes the union of man with God when the Holy Spirit possesses all.

28

Remarkable Manifestations of the Spirit

While ministering at Johannesburg, South Africa, I received an invitation to preach in the city of Pretoria, Transvaal. Consequently a series of meetings was arranged for. It was my first visit to Pretoria, and the congregation to whom I ministered were strangers to me. I was entertained at the home of a member on Hamilton Street. I arrived about three o'clock in the afternoon. About 4:30 a gentleman called and inquired if an American stranger was at her house. She replied, "Yes. Rev. Lake has just arrived this afternoon from Johannesburg." She told him I was an American and had recently come to Africa. He asked for an interview.

In the course of this interview he told me that he had been Secretary to Dr. Leyds, and acting Secretary of State for the old Transvaal Government under Paul Kruger, the last Dutch President of the Transvaal Republic. He told me that when the Boer War closed, because of what he considered faithfulness to the cause he had represented, he refused to sign the Agreement recognizing the authority of the British, and in consequence had been blacklisted as an incorrigible.

This prevented him from obtaining employment. His family had been sent to Europe during the war, and he had no money to bring them back. His property and money had all gone in the cause of the Boers, and he was impoverished. He did not have proper clothes to wear, nor sometimes food to eat. He said that notwithstanding these conditions his soul was consumed with the problems of state, and the desire to alleviate the condition of the Boer people and see the people restored to happiness. And in the agony of his soul he had been in the habit of going into one of the mountains for prayer. After several months of this practice, one day the Lord revealed to him that a great deliverance was coming; that a man would arrive in Pretoria from America on a certain date and could be found at 75 Hamilton Street at 4:30 p.m.

He said, "This is the date, and I have come in response to the direction of the Spirit, as I received it." He welcomed me as a messenger of the Lord, and proceeded to give me the details of the revelation as he had received it. His revelation included political changes that were to transpire, a religious revolution that would grow out of my own work, and many events of national importance, which became historic facts during the next few years.

He further gave detail in prophecy of the European war, and Britain's part in it. This was in August, 1908.

It was only after I had witnessed event after event come to pass that I became deeply impressed with the real significance of his revelation. He told me that the present meeting I was about to conduct in Pretoria would be marked with extraordinary manifestations of the Spirit. That these manifestations of the Spirit would eventuate in a profound impress of the majesty and power of God upon the minds of the people of South Africa, and in later years would create a stimulus of faith in God throughout the world.

Our meeting began at a church on Kerk Street, Pretoria on Thursday night. At the close of the first service the Spirit of God was deeply manifest upon the people. On Friday afternoon when we assembled, the Spirit of God proceeded to work mightily in the people. Many came to God and confessed their sins. Others who already were Christians sought God with profound earnestness for the real sanctifying power of God in their lives. Some were baptized in the Holy Spirit, their baptism in the Spirit being marked by speaking in tongues under the power of the Spirit, and interpretations of these messages by the spirit; also blessed healings of greatly diseased people.

The meetings practically ran without cessation from then until the following Wednesday at 3:00 a.m. Each service marked a decided increase in the presence and power of God.

On Saturday night the church was packed. All available standing room was occupied with men standing shoulder to shoulder. The majority of those who were standing were men from the Tattersall Racing Club. Most of them were Jews. They included horsemen of all classes, bookies, jockeys, stablemen, race track gamblers, etc.

I was preaching on the subject of the power of God, and in a strong spirit was endeavoring to demonstrate that Jesus Christ was the same yesterday, today and forever, that His power was as great as it ever was and that the only necessary qualification for touching God for anything was faith in Him. The audience was greatly moved.

At this point I observed a gentleman with two ladies endeavoring to squeeze through the crowds who were standing in the aisles. I asked the crowd to separate if possible and permit the ladies to come through, and tried to arrange sitting space for them on the steps of the platform. As they approached, I observed that one of the ladies held her arms perfectly stiff and did not move them at all. By instinct I knew at once that she was a rheumatic cripple. As she approached me, I said, "What is the reason you do not move your arms?"

She replied, "My shoulders are set from rheumatics."

I said, "How long have they been like that?"

She replied, "Ten years."

I inquired if she had been treated by physicians.

She replied, "I have been discharged from three hospitals as incurable."

I said, "What hospitals?"

She answered, "Kimberly, Johannesburg and Pretoria."

Then I addressed the gentleman who accompanied her, and said, "Do you know this lady?"

He said, "Yes. She is my sister-in-law."

I said, "Do you know her story to be correct?"

He said, "Absolutely."

I asked her what she had come for.

She replied, "In the hope that the Lord would heal me."

I inquired, "Do you wish me to pray for you for healing?"

She said, "Yes."

Then addressing the noisy crowd of men in the aisles and around the doors, I said, "You men never saw Jesus heal a person in your life. You do not know anything about this matter.

You have never witnessed an exhibition of the power of God, and therefore should be considerate enough to keep still, confess your ignorance of such matters, and learn. This is what I want. Select two of your company, let them come and examine this woman, and see if her arms are stiff, as she states." I waited for them to make their selection, and they put forward two men. I have forgotten the name of one of the men at this time, but the name of the other was Mr. Mulluck, a barber, a very intelligent gentleman. His shop was in the Market Building. I afterward learned he was an American.

They examined the lady critically, and found her arms as she had said, quite immovable. Addressing them I said, "Have you finished your examination, and are you satisfied her condition is as stated?"

They said, "We are."

"Then," I said, "stand back, for I am going to pray for this woman, that the Lord will heal her." Placing my hands on her shoulders I commanded in the Name of Jesus Christ the Son of God that this rheumatic devil that bound the woman be cast out, and in Christ's Name commanded it to go, rebuking it with all the energy of my soul. The power of God flashed through me like a burning fire, until the perspiration burst from the woman's face. Then taking her by the hands I said, "In the Name of Jesus Christ put your arms up." The right arm went up. Then I said, "In the Name of Jesus put the other arm up too." She instantly obeyed. Her arms had become free.

As I moved the arm, making the shoulder rotate, I observed that there was a grinding sound in the joint, and addressing the men who had examined her, I said, "You have never heard a dry joint in your life. Come and put your ear to this woman's back, while I make her arm move." As they did so, I moved the arm, and the shoulder joints would grind. The oil had not yet returned to the joints.

In the woman's delight, she threw up her hands and praised God, and started for the door. The crowd parted for her, and she disappeared, and I did not meet her again for some months.

Another lady arose and came forward, saying "I wish you would pray for me." I asked her what was the matter, but she did not reply. I bowed my head, saying, "Jesus, show me what is the matter with this woman." Instantly the Spirit moved my hand down her body from the throat to the stomach, and I prayed for her. She thanked me and sat down. Later I learned that her name was Mrs. Vlyate and that she had had a cancer of the stomach. I said to her, "When you came for prayer, why did you not tell me what was the matter with you?"

She said, "I was doubtful whether you were real. I thought, the Lord will show him, and I will not have to tell him what is the matter with me." She was perfectly healed. I visited with her and enjoyed the association of the family during the years that followed.

At a later time her son, a man of 20 or thereabout, was healed of total deafness in one ear, a result of an ear drum having been absolutely destroyed in an operation. His healing was instantaneous.

Jabber

On Sunday morning as the service progressed, a gentleman of prominence, who was an employee of the government, came into the meeting. Mr. Jabber, a man of great stature. As he walked into the church, the Spirit of the Lord fell upon him while walking up the aisle, and he fell prostrate on the floor. Several sons were present in the audience, and Mrs. Jabber was conducting the choir.

The mother, daughter and sons gathered from their places in the audience and reverently knelt in a semi-circle about him, while the audience remained in quiet prayer. The Spirit of the Lord dealt marvelously with him, revealing his sins, and Christ unto salvation.

Presently the Spirit fell upon one of the sons, who fell prostrate by the side of the Father; then upon another and another, until the whole family lay prostrate under the power of God. When the Spirit of the Lord had lifted somewhat from them, these sons confessed their disobedience to their parents and to God. And the whole family knelt with their arms around one another, melted by the tenderness of the presence and power of God. Confession and repentance on the part of each to the other and to God made the household of one soul.

Words are a poor medium to describe such an event as this. It would have to be seen to be realized. The tenderness and conscious presence of God, the melting power of His mighty Spirit, could only be understood by one who had looked on. No words can tell the story.

Notwithstanding these mighty manifestations of the Spirit, I was anxious that the real working out of the Spirit of God that would remove all character of denominational prejudices, and those elements in man's nature that keep him from loving and serving God with the broadness in the beauty and grace of holy charity, should be utterly removed from the people's hearts.

Jabber Girl

As I was preaching during the afternoon, the Spirit fell on a young lady, Miss Jabber, a cousin of the family aforementioned. She fell from her chair prostrate on the floor where she remained for a considerable time. The young gentleman who accompanied her, and who reverently knelt beside her when she became prostrate, was attracted by her desire to speak to him. She said to him, "Send Mr. Lake to me."

I ceased preaching and went to her. I asked her what it was she wanted.

She said, "Jesus came and talked to me and told me to tell Mr. Lake not to be discouraged tonight."

About 4:00 p.m. I left the service and went home to rest. I had been on my feet so long without rest or sleep that it seemed as if I could continue no further. I laid down to sleep, saying, "Wake me at 7:30 for the evening service." I fell into a sound sleep and when it came 7:30 the family reasoned that I was so exhausted that it would be a shame to wake me, and that they would endeavor to get through the evening service without my aid.

However, I awoke at 8:00 and hastened to the church. When I arrived I found that in view of my absence the church service was being conducted in their former formal manner, instead of the open character of services we had been having. An air of formality pervaded the house. The choir, consisting of about thirty members, was in their place, including the organist, pianist and director.

The choir gallery was arranged with raised steps, so that each row of singers sat above the other. The choir chairs were fastened together in sections, but were not fastened to the floor.

When I came into the meeting the pastor who was in charge invited me to preach in his stead. As I preached my spirit was annoyed by the extreme air of formality that pervaded the meeting, and in my soul I kept praying, "God, do something with this choir. Do something to break up the formality of this service, so there may be freedom of the spirit, that sinner's hearts may be melted, and the power of God may descend upon the meeting, and the baptism of the Spirit fall." (Rather a long prayer to pray while preaching.) The Lord suddenly spoke within me, saying, "Go on with your service. I will take care of the choir."

The anointing of the Spirit came powerfully upon me, and I spoke with great liberty in the Lord, and was soon lost in the spirit so that I forgot altogether about the choir, and the formality of the service entirely disappeared. I preached until ten o'clock, when I stepped from the platform and knelt on the floor of the church to pray. An unusual spirit of prayer came upon me. The burden of which was so intense that it caused me to pray out my soul to God in a more than ordinary manner. As I prayed the Spirit continued to deepen upon me, until I was unable to speak in English any longer, and the Spirit caused me to pray in tongues. At such times the Spirit of the Lord would give me the interpretation of the prayer in English, which would immediately follow the prayer in tongues.

I was lost in prayer, but was conscious of a considerable noise. I did not raise my head or open my eyes until the burden of prayer was lifted from my soul. When I looked up, to my amazement the audience was standing, and at the back of the house many were standing on the seats, and all looking toward the choir gallery.

As I turned toward the choir I saw that the Spirit of the Lord had fallen upon the choir, and almost every one of them lay prostrate under the power of the Spirit.

When they fell from their seats they pushed the chairs on the row in front of them forward, so that the front legs of the chairs dropped over the edge of the narrow platform. The whole row would turn upside down on top of those who had fallen in the row in front.

The deacons of the church came and gathered the chairs off of the prostrate ones as quickly as possible. The unbelievers in the house were startled and frightened at this manifestation, so that they arose and rushed out of the door. I instructed the doorkeeper to turn the key in the door and not permit any one to come in. The awe of God overshadowed the house. I felt it was not time for unbelievers to be present. God wanted to deal with the church.

I went and sat down in the audience. We remained perfectly quiet in prayer for some time. Then one after another of the prostrate ones began to pray and confess their waywardness and sin to God. There seemed to be but one passion in their soul, to tell out to God the burden of their unbelief, of their sin, of their backslidings, and to call on God for forgiveness and restoration and power to overcome. As a soul would thus confess out and pray through into the presence of God, the Spirit of the Lord would raise from them, and they would be permitted to arise. As they did so they were in a perfectly normal state of mind, excepting that the awe of God's presence and power was mightily realized by each.

Many sat and wept. Others sang for joy. Many were baptized in the Holy Spirit. One young man, among the tenor singers, lay on the lower platform. Close to him was his sweetheart, a young lady who was a member of the church. Like the others, he was pouring out the confession of his life to God and to her, and telling of his peculiar sins which were many and vile. Husbands were confessing to wives and wives to husbands, children to their parents, sweethearts to sweethearts, and all to God.

The pianist, Mr. Braun, lay beside the piano stool for possibly an hour helpless and speechless, the Spirit of God working in him. I was moved by the Spirit of God to go to him and pray. As I knelt beside him my hands involuntarily moved to his breast, and laying my hands on his breast I prayed. I did not know why I did so. I just obeyed the guidance of the Spirit. As I prayed, I was conscious of the Spirit of God flowing through me to him. I returned to my seat, and in about half an hour he began to pray out his heart to God. When he had finished, he motioned me to come to him. When I reached him he said, "Send my wife to me." I went to the back of the house where his wife sat weeping, and brought her to him. She knelt beside him. He put his arms about her and confessed that for three years he had been living in adultery. They wept together for hours. God worked so mightily in them that at three or four in the morning they returned to their home praising God together.

The next day at ten o'clock he called on me to tell me that the Lord had baptized both him and his wife in the Holy Spirit, and that when they were baptized the Spirit of God came upon both and caused them to speak in tongues and praise God in a spirit of prophecy. His soul was aglow.

He said, "When you prayed for me last night, why did you put your hands on my breast?"

I replied, "I do not know. I simply obeyed the impulse of the Spirit."

He asked, "Did you know I was sick, and needed healing?"

I said, "No. I did not know it."

"Well," he said, "I want to show you something." Opening his clothing he showed me a cancer on the breast, saying, "Three years ago when I went into adultery this cancer appeared on my body within a few days. I have endeavored to hide it from every one. Even my wife did not know of its existence, no one but my physician. But look at it now. See how the power of God has withered it." It had turned brown as if burned by a fire, and in a few days it utterly disappeared.

Among other things, the Spirit of the Lord directed Mr. Braun to make restitution to parties with whom he had had dishonest dealings at different times. One that I especially remember was this. He was employed by the government as a civil engineer on a monthly salary. He had been in the practice at intervals of filling out a report saying that he was sick and unable to attend to his duties, and would be gone for some days. He was compelled to confess to his superiors that this was not a fact, and that he used this time in recreation.

The thoroughness with which God dealt with each and all of these was very remarkable. Lives were cleansed to the very inmost, every sin, both outward and secret. The Spirit of God had taken possession and natures were changed into the likeness and nature of Jesus Christ.

These meetings were the beginning of a mighty work of God at Pretoria, which continues to this day.

Descent of the Spirit Upon Jabber Family in Their Home

I accompanied the Jabber family to their home at 75 Hamilton Street, Pretoria, when we left the meeting on Monday morning at 4:00 a.m. A meal was prepared, and we sat down around a large dining room table, Mr. Jabber at one end of the table and Mrs. Jabber at the other end. As I gave thanks to God for the meal the Spirit descended upon Mrs. Jabber and she broke forth in angelic song in tongues, and we listened in rapture to a song of most exceeding sweetness and power. Mrs. Jabber was a trained singer, but under this anointing of the Spirit she had a new voice of peculiar richness and depth. It surely was the song of the angels and heaven itself had descended into her soul as she sang. Our hearts were melted as it were into water.

Then the Spirit fell on Mr. Jabber and he was baptized in the Holy Ghost as he sat at the table, and the Spirit found vent through him in a volume of tongues of high praise and glorified exaltation of the Lord Jesus Christ who had saved him from his sins, sanctified his heart, and now consciously baptized him in the Holy Ghost.

Mrs. Jabber, under the power of the Spirit, arose as if to come to him, at the same instant he arose to go to her. They met in the middle of the floor. She was still singing the angelic song, and together they knelt on the floor. The rest of the family and myself arose from the table and reverently knelt around them. The song continued. The power of God fell on us until it seemed as if we were enveloped in glory, or had been translated into the heavenlies.

The neighbors who had attended the meeting, and had not yet retired, heard the singing and in amazement came to the house. The news spread around the neighborhood. The house was filled with wondering people. The Spirit of God fell on one and another, who were consciously baptized in the Spirit, and as they were baptized in the Spirit each in turn broke into the song of joy in other tongues.

As the Sister's song continued, her brother, who had been a very wicked man, a black sheep of the family, and who had been out all night, came in. As he stood looking at the glorified face of his sister, and listened to the angelic song, the Spirit of God so smote him that he fell on his knees, threw up his hands, and confessed his sins, some of which it would not be wise to record. He called on God for pardon and salvation, and after a time arose praising God.

I cannot describe the glory of that moment. As the sun arose over the mountains and its mellow rays fell upon the sight, it seemed as if we were no longer in this world, but had been elevated into the very presence of the holy angels, and the King of Glory, the joy of God so enraptured our hearts that the only thing we could do was to praise God.

I remember walking out under the orange trees, my soul flooded with the wonder, the glory and the magnificence of the revelation of God's Spirit falling again upon my own, as it did on the day of Pentecost, hearing with my own ears the shouts of joy, the glorified praises of our Redeemer in the languages of the Spirit, as the wondering multitude undoubtedly heard on the day of Pentecost.

Eight years have passed since then, but the glory of that hour remains in my spirit still.

On the Congregation Monday Night

On Monday night the church was again packed to the doors. All available standing room was taken. The news had spread throughout the city. Many had come out of mere curiosity. A great company of the rougher elements of the city filled the standing space around the door. They were crowded shoulder to shoulder.

I was in the act of preaching when suddenly the Spirit of God fell on the thickest of the group near the door, and a dozen men fell across one another in a heap under the power. Their friends were so amazed that they rushed from the church. Others caught their friends by the arms and literally dragged them out of the church. Some they even carried to the club rooms across the street, and in their ignorance tried to revive them by pouring whiskey down their throats. Many were saved and baptized in the Spirit that night. The meeting broke up some time about daylight.

29

Science of Healing

Chicago, 1920

"*In* him *was life; and the* life *was the light of men*" (John 1:4).

There is a difference between Christianity and philosophy. (I presume some folks are inquiring why it is that there is always that key note in my addresses.)

God gave me the privilege of living in the heart of philosophic South Africa, where we have one million five hundred thousand who are ministered to by Buddhist, Confucianist and Brahman priests. Every imaginable cult has its representatives there. I was amazed to discover that the whites were gradually assimilating the philosophy of the East, just as we Westerners are assimilating the philosophy of the East, and have been doing so for a long time.

When you take the philosophies, Christian Science, New Thought and Unity today and examine them, you discover they are the same old philosophies of India, Egypt and China from time immemorial.

The difference between philosophy and religion, particularly the religion of Jesus Christ, is in the words I quoted from the Scriptures, "*In* him *was life; and the life was the light of men.*" Philosophy is light. It is the best light the individual possessed who framed the philosophy. But it is not a LIFE GIVER.

But from the soul of Jesus there breathed a holy, living life of God, that comes into the nature of man, quickens him by its power, and by the grace of God he has the life of Jesus in him, eternal life.

Many of the ancient philosophies have a marvelous light. One of the Indian philosophies, Bhagavad, was written five hundred years before Isaiah. In it they predicted the coming of a Son of God, a Redeemer, who was to come and redeem mankind.

Buddha presented his philosophy five hundred years before Jesus. Pythagoras wrote four thousand years before Jesus Christ. In each one of them you will find many of the teachings of Jesus. The teachings of Jesus were not unique in that they were all new. They were new because they contained something that none of the rest possessed. It was the divine content in the word of Jesus Christ that gave His teachings their distinguishing feature from the other philosophies. That content (element) is the LIFE of God. *"In him was LIFE; and the LIFE was the light of men."*

Beloved, the real Christian, and the real Christian Church undertakes to bring to mankind the real life of the Lord Jesus, knowing that when the LIFE of Jesus comes, the light of civilization and Christianity will follow, but the LIFE is the first thing.

As men traveled from God, and as the world traveled from God, men naturally fell into their own consciousness and soul states, and proceeded in the common way of the world to endeavor to bless the world through LIGHT. But LIGHT never saved a world. Light will never save the world. There must be a divine content from on high that comes to the soul to enrich it and to empower it, to illuminate it and to glorify it, and more to deify it. For God's purpose through Jesus Christ is to outward appearance and habits of life, but in nature and substance and content, in spirit and soul and body, LIKE THE SON OF GOD.

Jesus never intended Christians to be an imitation. They were to be bone of His bone, and blood of His blood, and flesh of His flesh, and soul of His soul, and spirit of His Spirit. And thus He becomes the Son of God, a Savior and Redeemer forever.

In my youth I took a course in medicine. I never practiced medicine, for I abandoned the whole subject a few months before the time of my graduation, when it came to the place where diagnosis became the general subject for examination. It was then that I discovered that the whole subject of diagnosis was very largely a matter of guesswork, and it so remains.

Consequently throughout my life there has remained in me somewhat of the spirit of investigation. It has never been easy to accept things readily, until my soul stepped out inch by inch and proved them for myself.

When I approached the matter of the baptism, I did so with great care, but I approached it as a hungry soul; my heart was hungry for God. And one day the Spirit of the Lord came upon me, God flooded my life and baptized me in His Holy Spirit. And then began in my heart a new and powerful working of God, which has gone on for fifteen years, until Christ has become to my soul a divine reality.

Having had former acknowledgment as a medical student, it is still my privilege to attend a medical clinic, which I frequently do. I submitted myself at one time to a series of experiments. It was not sufficient to know that God did things, I had to know HOW God accomplished these things.

So when I returned from Africa at one time I visited at the Johns Hopkins institution, and submitted myself for this series of experiments.

First, they attached to my head an instrument to record the vibrations of the brain. This instrument had an indicator that would mark according to the vibrations of the mind. I began by repeating soothing things, like the twenty-third Psalm; then I repeated the thirty-seventh Psalm and then the thirty-fifth chapter of Isaiah, then the ninety-first Psalm; then Paul's address before Agrippa. Then I went into secular literature, and I repeated the *Charge of the Light Brigade,* Poe's *Raven,* with a prayer in my heart that somehow God would connect my soul with the Holy Ghost. My difficulty was that while this was going on I could not keep the Spirit from coming upon me, and when I got through with Poe's *Raven,* they said: "You are a phenomenon. You have a wider mental range than any human being we have ever seen." But it was this, that the Spirit of God kept coming upon me in degree, so I could feel the moving of the Spirit within me.

But I prayed in my heart, "Lord God, if you will only let the Spirit of God come like the lightnings of God upon my soul for two seconds, I know something is going to happen that these men never saw before."

So I closed the last lines. All at once the Spirit of God struck me in a burst of praise and tongues, and the old indicator on the instrument went to the end of the rod, and I haven't the least idea how much farther it would have gone if there had been an indicator to record it. The instructors said, "We have never seen anything like it." I replied, "Brethren, it is the Holy Ghost."

Now, in order to get the force of what I want to tell you into this next experiment, something of the process of digestion, I want to explain the assimilating power of your nature, your capacity to assimilate God and take the life of God into your being, and keep it in your being. I am not talking to you about what I believe. I am talking about what I KNOW.

For twenty-five years God has kept me so that sickness, nor the devil, were able to touch me, from the day that I saw in the ninety-first Psalm a man's privilege of entering into God, not only for healing, but HEALTH, and having God and the life of God in every fiber of his being.

Scientists tell us that in a single inch of a man's skin there are one million five hundred thousand (1,500,000) cells. They have almost doubled that statement now. But be that as it may, I want you to see that the whole structure of man's life is one wonderful cellular structure. Your body, your brain, your bone is just one great cellular structure.

In the process of digestion it is something like this. The food we eat is reduced to vegetable lymph before it is absorbed by the body. But no scientist in the world has ever been able to satisfactorily explain what it is that changes the lymph and makes it LIFE. Something happens when it is in the body that changes it to life.

I want to tell you what grew up in my soul, and how I proved the fact. I could feel sometimes in the attitude of prayer just as you have felt hundreds of times, the impulse of the Spirit moving down through your brain and your person to the end of your fingers...just little impulses of God's presence in your life. And I have said, "If there was an instrument powerful enough, I believe men could see the action of the brain cells, and see what took place."

Here is the secret of digestion. When, from the spirit of man and through the spirit of man there is being imparted to every cell of your body waves of light, waves of life, it is the movement of your spirit. Spirit impulses passing from the cortex cells of the brain to the very end of your fingers and toes, to every cell of your body. And when they touch that vegetable lymph it is transformed into LIFE. That is common transmutation.

In the material world you can dissolve zinc and attach a wire, and transmit it to the other end of the wire. They dissolve that zinc, and the battery at the one end, and transmit the zinc to the other end of the wire, where it is deposited. How is it done? There is a process of transmutation. That is what it is called. There is change from one form to another.

My brother, you listen to me, if that is not true in the spiritual world, there is no such thing as divine LIFE. There is no such thing as salvation through the Son of God. For that which is soulish must be transformed by the Spirit of God in us, until it becomes spiritual, until it is of God.

Jesus sat with His disciples and ate with them, both bread and fish. He went to the mount and ascended before them to glory. What happened to the fish and bread that He ate? I tell you there is a transmutation. That which is natural becomes spiritual. That which was natural is changed by the power of God into the life of God, into the nature of God, into the substance of God, into the glory of God.

So when I returned to this country this time, I submitted myself for this experiment. They attached to my head a powerful instrument that could take some kind of picture one after another, in order to see if possible what the action of the brain cells would be. Then I repeated things that were soothing and calculated to reduce the action of the cortex cells to their lowest possible action. Then I went on into the scriptures to the better and richer things, until I came to the first chapter of John, and as I began to recite that, and the fires of God began to burn in my heart. Presently once again the Spirit of God came upon me, and the man who was at my back touched me. It was a signal to keep that poise until one after another could look through the instrument. And finally when I let go, and the Spirit subsided, they said, "Why man, we cannot understand this thing; but the cortex cells extend so that we can hardly imagine it possible to a human brain."

Oh, I'll tell you, when you pray, something is happening to you. It is not a myth. It is the action of God. It is scientific that the Almighty God comes into the soul, takes possession of the brain, lives in the cortex cells, and when you will or wish, either consciously or unconsciously, the fire of God, the power of God, that life of God, that nature of God, throbs through your nerves, down through your person into every cell of your being, into every million five hundred thousand cells in every square inch of your skin, and they are alive with God.

Men have treated the Gospel of Jesus Christ as though it were a sentiment and foolishness. Men who posed as being wise, have scorned the simple things that were taking place every day. But I want to tell you that no dear old mother ever knelt before the Throne of God, and raised her heart to heaven without demonstrating the finest process of the wireless of God that ever was produced.

In these days they are now able to transmit by wireless from six to seven thousand miles...and even 12,000 miles recently (1920). Once again they have been able to demonstrate that in one-tenth of a second they can transmit the first section of thought twelve thousand miles. Think of it! There is practically no such thing as time.

Beloved, the very instant your soul moves with your heart cries, that yearning of your soul, it registers in the soul of Jesus Christ, and the answer comes back.

I said to them, "Gentlemen, I want to see one more thing. You go down in your hospital and bring a man who has inflammation in the bone." So they brought up a man with inflammation in his bone. I said, "You take your instrument, and attach it to that fellow's leg, but you leave enough space to get my hand on his leg; you can have it attached on both sides."

So when the thing was all ready, I put my hand on that man's shin, and I prayed just like Mother Etter prays. No strange prayer, but the cry of my heart to God, I said, "God kill the devilish business by the power of God, let it live in him, let it move in him."

Then I said, "Gentlemen, what is taking place?"

They replied, "Every cell responds." All there is to it, is that the life of God comes back into the part that is afflicted, and right away the blood flows in, and the work is done.

My soul has grown tired long ago of men treating the whole subject of Christianity as though it were child's play. We have our physical sciences, we have our psychological sciences, the action of the mind, taught in the great schools of the land, but there is something greater. One of these days there is going to be a new chair. It will be the chair of pneumatology...the science of spirit, by which men will undertake to discover the laws of God. And by the grace of God, men shall know that God is alive, and the living Spirit of God is no dream.

In my Healing Rooms at Spokane there came one day a dear woman whose name is Lamphear. She is the wife of a merchant in the city. She had fallen down stairs, causing a prolapse of the bowels and stomach. She had been an invalid for eleven years. On top of that she had become tubercular. On top of that the poor thing developed inflammatory rheumatism, until she was terribly deformed. She was going to die. The doctors said there was nothing they could do for her. They advised that she be taken to Hot Lake, Oregon, and perhaps that would do her some good. So they put her in hot baths there and she suffered just as much as ever. So they thought they would try superheated baths. They put her in water hotter than any human being had ever been in before. The result was that instead of having any healing effect, the left leg developed an abnormal growth, and it became three inches shorter than the other leg. It is a simple condition of sarcoma. The foot became an inch longer. She came away from the institution worse than when she went. She got as far as Portland. Her parents were living at The Dalles. She wanted to see her parents before she died. Her husband carried her in his arms onto the ship. As he did so, a Pentecostal missionary stopped up and said, "Dear woman, we understand now why God told us to take this boat. The Lord told us last night to take the eight o'clock boat for The Dalles." He had called up on the telephone and found the fare was $1.80, and as that was all the money they had, they went without their breakfast so as to be able to take the boat.

As she lay crying with her suffering, they said, "When we get to The Dalles, we will pray for you." (They were timid folks.) Eventually they reached The Dalles and went to a hotel. The two knelt to pray for her. She says as they prayed and put their hands on her knees, their hands became illuminated until they looked like the hands of Jesus, their faces looked like the face of Jesus, and she was afraid. But something happened. The pain went out of her.

Strangely, she retained the tuberculosis and the struggle for breath. The leg remained the same length. When she examined herself, she was surprised that it was not shorter. She said, "Pray again that the Lord may make it the same length as the other," but the poor missionary was staggered. He said, "Dear Sister, the pain is gone. You be satisfied and give praise to God."

So she went on three and a half years coughing her lungs out and with her leg longer than the other. One day she came to the

Healing Rooms and was ministered to by Mr. Westwood, and she felt wonderfully relieved. She said, "Mr. Westwood, I can breathe clear down into my stomach."

He said, "What makes you limp?"

She answered, "There is a big lump on the inside of my knee."

He said, "I'll pray for that."

"But," she said, "the man told me I should be satisfied if the pain was gone."

Mr. Westwood said, "He had not grown up in God yet." He put his hands on that lump and prayed, and God Almighty dissolved that lump of bone, and that leg grew at the rate of one inch a day, and she wears shoes like anyone else.

There is a difference between healing and miracle. Healing is the restoration of diseased tissue, but miracle is a creative action of the Spirit of God in a man's life. And the salvation of a soul is a divine miracle of God. Every time Christ speaks the word LIFE to a man's heart there is a divine creative miracle of God in him, and he is a new man in Christ Jesus.

One day I sat in Los Angeles talking to old Father Seymour. I told him an incident in my life of Elias Letwaba, one of our native preachers, who lived in the native country. I came to his home, and his wife said, "He is not home. A little baby is hurt, and he is over praying for it."

So we went over and got down on our knees and crawled into the native hut. I saw he was kneeling in a corner by the dying child. I said, "Letwaba, it is me. What is the matter with the child?" He told me that it hurt its neck. I examined it and saw that the baby's neck was broken, and I said to Letwaba, "Why, Letwaba, the baby's neck is broken." I did not have faith for a broken neck, but the poor old Letwaba did not know the difference, and I saw he did not understand; but he discerned the spirit of doubt in my soul.

I said to myself, "I am not going to interfere with his faith. He will just feel the doubt and all the old traditional things I ever learned, so I will go out," and I did. I went and sat in another hut and kept on praying. I went to bed at one o'clock; at three o'clock Letwaba came in.

I said, "Well, Letwaba, how about the baby?" He looked at me lovingly and sweetly and said, "Why, Brother, the baby is all well." I said, "The baby is well! Take me to the baby at once." I went to the baby and took the little black* thing on my arm, and

I came out and prayed, "Lord, take every cursed thing out of my soul that keeps me from believing the Lord Jesus Christ."

In my meeting in Spokane is a dear man who came from Texas. He told us he was dying of pellagra. He came to Sister Etter's meeting at Dallas. Apparently on the train he died, and they laid his body in the station house, covered him with some gunny sacks, but discovered in the morning he was still alive. So they carried him to Mother Etter's meeting, and she came down off the platform and prayed for him. That man is living, and has been preaching the gospel for seven years at Spokane.

Why, there is more science in the Son of God in five minutes than the ignorant old world ever knew. *"In Him was LIFE, and the LIFE was the light of men."* The LIFE of God is that which the mind of men, and the keenest of them, never knew, and never discovered. *"The world by wisdom knew not God"* [1 Corinthians 1:21]. They could not discern His death nor understand the marvels of His life, until the Lord Jesus came and lived and died and entered into Hades and destroyed the powers of darkness and liberated the souls of men, liberated them from the chains of darkness and came forth into the world to speak God's Word and reveal God's power and show God's nature. And by the grace of God, man has been privileged to enter into the nature of Jesus, and the fires of God burn in his soul like they burned in the soul of Jesus.

The scientific world has been startled by one of the English scientists who has come forward with a formula for transmitting the grosser metals into gold. It did not work. Years ago this knowledge was known to the world, but somehow it disappeared from the world. Recently men again have attempted to change lead, silver and iron, transmuting them into gold.

Beloved, that is the thing that Jesus Christ has been doing all the time. It is as old as Christianity, is as old as the Son of God. He has been coming to the hearts of men, taking the old base conditions of the nature, injecting His life into them, injecting His power into the nature, and in the mighty action of the Holy Ghost they have been changed into the pure gold of God.

If there never was another blessing that came to the world through Pentecost but this one, all the price that men could pay would be as nothing for it. For I want to tell you there has been more real divine researching by the Holy Ghost into the nature of God and the nature of men in these last fifteen years than there ever was in the whole world. When anyone comes to me with the statement that there is nothing in the Holy Ghost but a psychological manifestation, I say, "Brother, Sister, come with me and see the gems of God and the beautiful gold that has come out of the dross and the dirty lives, and then you will know."

In my assembly at Spokane is a dear little woman who was totally blind for nine years. She had little teaching along the line of faith in God. She sat one day with her group of six children to discover that the dirty brute of a husband had abandoned her. A debased human being is capable of things that no beast will do, for a beast will care for its own. You can imagine what that little heart was like. She was broken and bruised and bleeding. She gathered her children around her and began to pray. They were sitting on their front porch.

Presently the little one got up and said, "Oh, Mama, there is a man coming up the path, and he looks like Jesus. Oh, Mama, there is blood on His hands and blood on His feet!" And the children were frightened and ran around the corner of the house. After a while the biggest one looked around the corner and said, "Why, Mama, He is laying His hands on your eyes!" And just then her blind eyes opened.

And Beloved, if we could have seen the reason, we would have seen that there were some Christians at Zion Gate or some other place who were praying the power of God on a hungry world, and Jesus Christ in His search, rushed into her life and sent her forth to praise God and teach the Gospel of Jesus.

I would not have missed my life in Africa for anything. It put me up against some of the real problems. I sat upon the Mount of Sources one night, and I counted eleven hundred native villages within the range of my eyes. I could see the color of the grass on the mountains sixty miles away. I could see the mountains one hundred and fifty miles away. Then I began to figure, and I said, "Within the range of my eyes there lives at least ten million native people. They never heard the Name of Jesus. In the whole land there are at least one hundred million people, perhaps two hundred million. They are being born every day at a tremendous rate. Do you know there are more heathen born every day than are Christianized in fifty years? When are we going to catch up by our present method of building schools and teaching them to read? Never! I tell you it will never come that way. It has got to come from heaven by the power of God, by an outpouring of the Holy Ghost."

That is the reason that in my heart I rejoice in the blessed promise. *"In the last days, saith God, I will pour out of my Spirit upon all flesh"* (Acts 2:17). And every last one of the two hundred million poor black* people [in Africa] are going to hear and know of the Lord Jesus Christ.

And beloved, I would rather have a place in the kingdom of God to pray that thing into existence, and to pray the power of God upon them, than anything else in the world.

I began to pray. I said, "Has God no interest in these people; and if He has an interest, why is not something done for them? What is the matter with God?" My heart was breaking under the burden of it. I said, "God, there is an explanation somewhere. What is it, Lord? Tell me about this thing."

After a while the Spirit said, *"The Church, which is His Body"* [Ephesians 1:22-23], and I knew that was God's answer. I said, "Yes, the Church should have sent missionaries and built schools and done this and that."

But the Spirit kept on saying, *"The Church, which is His Body." "The Church, which is His Body."* And I sat and listened to that voice repeat that sentence for a half-hour. I said, "My God, my soul begins to see. The Church is the generating power of God in the world; the Church has been negligent in one thing. She has not prayed the power of God out of heaven."

Then I saw that which has become a conviction in my soul from that day. There never was a soul born to God in the whole earth at any time until some soul in the world got hold of the living Spirit of God and generated that Spirit in saving grace and creative virtue until it took possession of a soul, no difference if it was a million miles away.

When I try to induce men to forget their little squabbles and little differences and go on praying, it is because my soul feels the burden of it. Mother Etter has been like a marshal for fifty years. The sick have been healed, people have been converted and blessed. But beloved, when I heard of Brother Brooks shutting himself up night and day to pray the power of God on a world, I said "That is where she gets her fire; and that is from where it comes to my soul; that is from where it comes to every other soul."

Look how beautifully this hall is lighted. Do you know the world lived in darkness for five thousand years and they had no way of lighting a place except by torches. But there was just as much electricity five thousand years ago as there is today. Somebody found how to handle it, discovered the laws that governed it. To this day, there is not a man who can tell us what electricity is, or what its substance is. We know we can control it this way and guide it that way, and make it do this and that, but what it is nobody can tell us. But down somewhere on the river there is a thing called a dynamo, and it draws the electricity out of the air, and transmits it over the wires, and these days they are even sending it wireless.

Do you know what prayer is? It is not begging God for this and that. The first thing we have to do is to get you beggars to quit begging until a little faith moves in your souls. PRAYER is God's divine dynamo. The spirit of man is God's divine dynamo. When you go to pray, that spirit of yours gets into motion...not ten thousand revolutions or one hundred thousand thousand. The voltage of heaven comes to your heart, and it flows from your hands, it burns into the souls of men, and God Almighty moves on their behalf.

Over in Indiana some years ago was a farmer who used to be a friend of Brother Fockler and myself. His son had been in South America, had a dreadful case of typhoid fever, had no proper nursing, and the result was a great fever sore developed until it was seven inches in diameter. The whole abdomen became grown up with proud flesh, one layer on top of another layer, until there were five layers. The nurse would lift up those layers and wash them with an antiseptic to keep the maggots out of it. When he exposed the body for me to pray for him, I had never seen anything like that before. I was shocked. As I went to pray for him, I spread my fingers out over that sore. I prayed, "God, in the name of Jesus Christ, blast this curse of hell and burn it up by the power of God." Then I took the train and came back. The next day I received a telegram saying, "Lake, the most unusual thing has happened. An hour after you left the whole print of your hand was burned into that thing a quarter of an inch deep, and it is there yet."

You talk about the voltage of heaven and the power of God. Why, there is lightning in the soul of Jesus. The lightnings of Jesus heal men by its touch, sin dissolves, disease flees when the power of God approaches.

And yet we are quibbling and wondering if Jesus Christ is big enough for our needs. Let's take the bars down. Let God come into your life. And in the Name of Jesus your heart will not be satisfied with an empty Pentecost, but the light of God and the lightnings of Jesus will flood your life. Amen.

*Kenneth Copeland Publications acknowledges that references to race and nationality considered acceptable in Rev. Lake's day are offensive and not acceptable to today's reader. However, these references in no way reflect the attitude or policies of KCP. To fully understand Rev. Lake's heart toward other races, we recommend you read his biography located at the front of the book.

Lake and Divine Healing Investigated

On June 15 we were waited upon at our Healing Rooms by a committee of the Better Business Bureau of the city of Spokane, whose duty in part it is to investigate the truthfulness of all public announcements appearing in the city papers. For some time previous to this we had been publishing some of the wonderful testimonies of healing by the power of God that had taken place in the daily course of our ministry at the Divine Healing Institute.

Among the testimonies that had appeared was the wonderful testimony of Mrs. John A. Graham, nee Peterson, whose healing astonished the medical world. Testimony of Reverend Joseph Osborne, left to die of Bright's disease at the Deaconess Hospital, analysis showing 15 per cent albumen; Reverend Charles B. LeDoux, healed when in very death from pneumonia; Mrs. Mary Mero, Mrs. Lena Lakey, Grover Risdon, Baby Agnes Young, Mrs. Mary Matheny, of Portland, Oregon, who was healed of 40 cancers and others.

These testimonies were so astounding that complaints reached the Better Business Bureau to the effect that the testimonies must certainly be untrue. The Better Business Bureau promptly undertook an investigation and the call at our Healing Rooms was for that purpose.

In the presence of the committee, as they waited, we called 18 persons, whose testimonies had appeared in the public print, who in turn gave testimony as to their own condition and the wonder of their healing by the power of God in the Name of the Lord Jesus Christ, under this ministry. After 18 had been examined we presented them with names of many healed persons in the city, desiring them to go personally to these persons and investigate for themselves whether these things were so.

Realizing the amount of labor necessary for a proper investigation, I suggested to the committee that on Sunday, June 23, at 3 o'clock in the afternoon, at our public service, we would present 100 cases of healed persons for their investigation and invited them to form a committee composed of physicians, lawyers, judges, educators and business men who should render a verdict.

In the days lapsing between the interview at the Healing Rooms and Sunday, June 23, the committee continued their investigation, interviewing persons whose names we had furnished them. On Friday, June 21, before our great Sunday meeting, we received a letter from the committee, assuring us that they had no desire in any way to interfere with the good which we were doing, and gently let themselves down so that their appearance at the Sunday meeting would not be necessary. Two members of the committee saw us privately and said that the committee was astounded. They said, "we soon found out, upon investigation, you did not tell half of it."

One of the committee was visiting at Davenport, Washington, where the firm had a branch store. As he looked around the store he found printed announcements advertising a meeting which we were about to conduct at Davenport. He made inquiry from the manager as to why these announcements were being made through their store and the manager replied as follows:

"The whole countryside around Davenport is aflame with surprise at the marvelous healing of a girl in this community, well known to me, and, I believe, well known to yourself, Miss Louise Reinboldt, daughter of Mr. Jake Reinboldt. About three and a half years ago Miss Reinboldt and her sister were operated on for what the doctors thought was appendicitis. The one girl died as the result of the operation. Louise came out of it unable to speak excepting in the merest whisper that only her nearest friends could understand. She was taken to throat specialists, who pronounced her case absolutely incurable. Recently she was taken to Spokane to Mr. Lake's Healing Rooms and ministered to for twenty-six days. On the twenty-sixth day she startled her mother and family and, in fact, the whole countryside, by calling her mother on the long distance telephone and announcing to her in plain words the fact that she was healed.

"While preparing for her daily visit to the Healing Rooms one morning she suddenly discovered herself whistling, and said to herself, 'If I can whistle I can speak also,' and so discovered the paralyzed condition of her throat was truly healed."

Other members of the committee reported similar remarkable healings and not being desirous of becoming a public laughing stock they hastily wrote as above quoted.

Mr. Lake, however, announced that there would be no change in the program, but that the meeting as announced would take place and if the Better Business Bureau would not take their place he would appeal to the public for a verdict. The meeting took place at the Masonic Temple before a large audience, estimated by the police to number one thousand. Hundreds being compelled to stand throughout the entire service and hundreds were refused admittance.

After a brief statement by Dr. Lake on the reasons for the meeting and of the desire to glorify God by permitting the city and the world to know that Jesus Christ has never changed, that prayer was answerable today as it ever was, and the days of miracles had not passed, but were forever possible through the exercise of faith in God, the following testimonies were given:

Reverend R. Armstrong, a Methodist minister, of N2819 Columbus Avenue, healed of sarcoma, growing out of the left shoulder three times as large as a man's head, was healed in answer to prayer.

Reverend Thomas B. O'Reilly of 430 Rookery Building, testified to being healed of fits so violent that when stricken with them it required seven policemen to overpower and confine him in the hospital, of his instantaneous healing and perfect restoration to health through the prayer of faith.

Baby Agnes Young, N169 Post Street, healed of extreme malnutrition. Patient at the Deaconess Hospital for nine months, from the time of birth until her healing. She weighed six and a half pounds at birth and at the age of nine months only four and a half pounds. One evening when one of the ministers from Reverend Lake's Healing Rooms was called to minister to her, she was found in a state of coma and the nurse, supposing her to be dead, had removed her to the dead-room. He took the supposedly dead child in his arms, praying the prayer of faith, removed her from the hospital and placed her in the hands of a Christian woman for nursing. In six weeks she was perfectly well and strong. The father and mother arose to corroborate the testimony. They are both members of Dr. Lake's church.

Mrs. Chittenden, pastor of the Church of the Truth at Coeur D'Alene, Idaho, testified to her healing of cancers of the breast, one breast having been removed in an operation and the other breast becoming likewise affected with cancer. She was healed of the Lord in answer to prayer.

Mrs. Everetts, 1911 Boone Avenue, testified to her healing of varicose veins. She had suffered from them for 38 years. The veins were enlarged until they were the size of goose eggs in spots. Under the right there was a sack of blood so large that the knee was made stiff. She had exhausted every medical method. After being ministered to at the Healing Rooms for a short period, she was entirely well and the veins are perfectly clear.

Mrs. Constance Hoag, Puyallup, Washington, broke her knee cap. A section of the bone protruded through the flesh. She wrote requesting that the ministers of the Healing Rooms lay their hands upon a handkerchief in faith and prayer and send it to her, in accordance with Acts 19:12. This was done. She applied the handkerchief to the knee and in 15 minutes the pain had gone, and in an hour the bone had returned to place. A few days later she visited Spokane—well.

Mrs. Walker, Granby Court, was an invalid at the Deaconess Hospital from internal cancer; after an exploratory operation was pronounced incurable by the doctors. She also had a severe case of neuritis. Her suffering was unspeakable. She testified to her healing and of her restoration to perfect health, the cancer having passed from her body in seven sections. Since then many have been healed through her prayer and faith.

Mrs. John A. Graham, nee Peterson, E369 Hartson, a nurse and hospital matron, was operated on for fibroid tumor. The generative organs were removed, and at a later date was operated on a second time for gallstones. The operation not being a success, she was eventually left to die and when in the throes of death and unconscious she was healed by the power of God in answer to prayer of one of the ministers called from the Healing

Rooms. The organs that had been removed in the operation regrew in the body and she became a normal woman.

Mr. Asa Hill, a farmer from Palouse, Washington, testified that he had been a rheumatic cripple for 15 years and was instantly healed at a meeting conducted by Mr. Lake, through prayer with the laying on of hands. The meeting was held at a theater at Moscow, Idaho.

Mrs. Wolverton was injured in a Great Northern railroad wreck and was awarded large damages by the court. (See court record.) Physicians testified her injuries to be such that motherhood was impossible. After her marriage the physicians' testimony was confirmed. She was healed in answer to prayer and gave birth to a son, and since has given birth to twins.

Miss Jennie Walsh, S116 Fiske Street, had a disease of the gall bladder, which became filled with pus. Her physicians insisted on an immediate operation to save her life. Mr. Lake and Dr. Penn laid their hands upon her in prayer at 11 o'clock p.m. Ten minutes afterward her pain ceased, the pus emptied from the bladder naturally and she was entirely healed.

Mrs. Lamphear, 115 1/2 Sprague Avenue, was an invalid for 11 years, suffering from prolapsus of the stomach, bowels and uterus, also from tuberculosis and rheumatism. Her husband carried her from place to place in his arms. After 11 years of terrible suffering, upon the advice of her physicians who were unable to assist her, she was sent to Hot Lake, Oregon, for bath treatments. Ordinary baths had no effect on her and the superintendent testified that they had finally placed her in superheated baths, hotter than they had ever put any human being in before. Through this treatment an abnormal growth was started in the left leg and foot. Her leg became three inches shorter than the other and her foot one inch longer. A bone as large as an orange grew on the knee. She received an instant healing of rheumatism. After several other events and prayer, she came to the Healing Rooms and was ministered to by Mr. Westwood. He put his hands on that lump and prayed, and God dissolved that lump of bone, the leg grew at the rate of an inch a day, the foot also shortened to its normal length and the bone growth on the knee totally disappeared. Her tuberculosis was healed and she is praising God for His goodness.

Mrs. Ben Eastman, nee Koch, 1115 First Avenue, pronounced incurable from the tubercular glands by 73 physicians. She was operated on 26 times and remained in the same dying condition.

Later she was taken to the Osteopathic Institute in Los Angeles, California, was a patient there for three and a half years. Her father testified that his daughter's illness cost him three houses in the city of Davenport, a valuable wheat ranch of 160 acres, 147 carloads of wood and all the money he had. She is now healed of the Lord and since then has become the happy wife of Mr. Ben Eastman.

Mrs. Carter of S714 Sherman Street, wife of Policeman Carter, was examined by seven physicians who pronounced her to be suffering from a fibroid tumor, estimated to weigh 15 pounds. She was ministered to at the Healing Rooms at 4:30 in the afternoon and at 11 o'clock the next day returned to the Healing Rooms perfectly healed and wearing her corsets. The enormous tumor having dematerialized.

Mrs. O.D. Stutsman, Hansen Apartments, testified to having been an invalid for 13 years. On one occasion she lay in the Sacred Heart Hospital with a 20-pound weight attached to her foot for 32 days, while suffering from inflammatory rheumatism. Her suffering was so intense that she begged her husband to take her home, preferring to remain a cripple rather than endure such suffering. The Reverend Lake was called to minister to her at her home. As prayer was offered the power of the Spirit of God came upon her. Five minutes after his hands were laid upon her she arose from her bed perfectly healed.

Mr. John Dewitt of Granby Court, testified on behalf of Frederick Barnard, 32 years of age, who was injured in his babyhood from a fall from a baby cab, causing curvature of the spine. As he grew to boyhood and manhood he was never able to take part in the sports common to boyhood and manhood. When the great war came on he would stand around the recruiting offices, longing and covetously watching the men who enlisted for the war. One day he expressed to Mr. Dewitt the sorrow of his soul that he was not able to enlist also. Mr. Dewitt told him of Mr. Lake's Healing Rooms and invited him to come and be ministered to. The curvature of his spine straightened and his height increased one inch. He applied for enlistment in the Canadian army and was accepted by the army physician as first class and sent abroad.

God in Surgery

Mrs. O. Gilbertson, N4115 Helena Street, testified that through disease her hip came out of joint, and the limb would turn like the leg of a doll, showing that it was entirely out of the socket. Her home is about five miles distant from the Healing Rooms. Reverend Lake and his co-workers engaged in prayer for her at the Healing Rooms and as prayer was offered the power of God came upon her, resetting the joint.

The following remarks were made by the Reverend Lake as the testimony was given: "Do you hear it, you folks who worship a dead Christ? You doctors, hear it? You preachers who lie to the people and say the days of miracles are past, do you hear it? You doubters, hear it? God set the woman's hip. Because faith in God applied the blessed power of God to her life and limb."

Now comes one of the most remarkable cases in history. The Risdon family stand holding their six-year-old son on their shoulders. This boy was born with a closed head. In consequence, as he increased in years, the skull was forced upward like the roof of a house, the forehead and the back of the head also being forced out in similar manner, giving the head the appearance of the hull of a yacht upside down. The pressure on the brain caused the right side to become paralyzed and the child was dumb. Physicians said that nothing could be done for him until he was 12 years old, and then the entire top of the head would have to be removed, the sides of the skull expanded and the entire head covered with a silver plate. Under Divine Healing ministration in answer to prayer the bones softened, the head expanded, the skull was reduced to its normal size, the paralysis disappeared, the dumbness was gone. He speaks like other children and now attends the public school.

Remarks by Reverend Lake: "I want you to see that in the Spirit of God there is a science far beyond physical or psychological science and the man or woman who enters into the spirit relation with God and exercises His power is most scientific; that the power of God in this instance was sufficient to soften the bones of the head, expand the skull and bring the head down to normal when the child was four and a half years old. Something that no medicine could do and no surgical operation could accomplish without endangering the life of the child. The doctors plainly stated the chances of recovering were one in a thousand."

Casting Out of Demons and Healing of Insane

Mrs. Lena Lakey, W116 Riverside Avenue, testified of having suffered with violent insanity. She was a cook at a lumber camp. She told of the men at the camp endeavoring to overpower her and tie her in the bed; of her tearing the bed to pieces and breaking her arms free; of how she struck one man with the side of the bed, rendering him unconscious. Another was in the hospital three weeks recovering from injuries. She escaped into the woods in a drenching rain. Eventually falling exhausted in a copse of trees, where she lay unconscious for six hours until a searching party found her. She was brought to Spokane in an auto by six men and was tied with ropes. Before taking her to the court to be committed to the insane asylum they decided to take her to the Healing Rooms. Reverend Lake and Reverend Fogwill laid their hands on her in prayer and the demons were cast out and she was instantly healed. An abscess in her side, from which she had suffered for 15 years, totally disappeared in 24 hours, and a rheumatic bone deposit between the joints of the fingers and toes, so extensive that it forced the joints apart, was gone in 48 hours. She was made every whit whole.

Mrs. Holder gave testimony of healing by the power of God in answer to prayer, having been healed from insanity while an inmate of the Medical Lake Insane Asylum in answer to the prayers of Mr. Lake and his assistants.

Other Incurables

Mr. and Mrs. Harry Lotz stand holding their baby in their arms. The baby developed pus in the kidneys and was pronounced incurable by several physicians. The child was brought to the Healing Rooms. Reverend Lake laid his hands upon the child in prayer and it was instantly healed.

Mr. Allen, pastor of the Pentecostal mission, was dying of pellagra. He was carried unconscious from the train. The men thought him to be dead and put him in the baggage room. He was instantly healed through the laying on of hands and prayer. His case is a matter of record by the government pellagra investigation commission.

Mrs. Ben Long, 1971 Atlantic Street, testified to being instantly healed of paralysis of the left side. She was brought to the Healing Rooms and ministered to by Dr. Lake, and when 10 feet from the Healing Room door she found that she had been made whole. Discovering that she was well, she returned to the waiting room and showed herself to Mr. Lake and offered praise to God for her healing.

Mrs. John Dewitt, Granby Court, gave testimony to having been healed of neuritis after years of suffering. Later she was healed when in a state of apparent death following two strokes. A group of friends was present and witnessed her instant healing as Reverend Lake prayed.

Mrs. Mary Mero, lady-in-waiting at the Healing Rooms, who resides at W717 Nora Avenue, broke her ankle when a child. In endeavoring to favor the broken ankle the other ankle became diseased and for fifty years she had suffered violently. She was instantly healed after she was ministered to at the Healing Rooms. She was also healed of ulcers of the stomach after twenty years of suffering.

Mrs. Miles Pearsons, E2815 Illinois Avenue, suffered a broken ankle a year ago. It was not properly set and remained inflamed and swollen as though the leg would burst. She was healed in answer to prayer two weeks ago.

Mrs. Thomas Olsen, Rowan Street, healed when dying of internal cancer. For ten days she had neither touched food nor drink. A group of Christian friends gathered about her and prayed. As prayer was offered Jesus appeared to her, standing in front of her, reaching out His hand appealingly. She endeavored to rise from her wheelchair and grasp the hands of her Lord and as she did so thrills of Divine life flashed through her body and she was healed. Two days later she vomited the entire cancer, body and roots.

Mrs. Richards, Sandpoint, Idaho, testified that she had been healed when dying of paralysis on one side and tumors. After prayer the tumors loosened and passed from the body.

Mrs. Allen of Waverly, rising in audience with a friend who corroborated her testimony, was dying from internal cancers. She was brought to Spokane by Mr. Ramey, a hardware merchant of Waverly. She was perfectly healed and is now earning her living as a saleslady.

Mrs. Kellum, nee Slater, Bovill, Idaho, testified to having been blind nine years. As prayers were offered a vision of Jesus laying his hands upon her eyes appeared to her and she was instantly healed.

Addressing the audience, Mr. Lake said: "All persons who have been healed by the power of God and who desire to add their testimony to these who have already been given, stand." Two hundred and sixty-seven persons arose. While they stood Mr. Lake said: "Gentlemen of the committee and audience, you see these witnesses, you have heard the testimonies. Gentlemen of the committee and audience, has this been a fair presentation?" (Shouts of "Yes, Yes," from all parts of the house.) "Did God heal these people?" (Cries of "Yes, Yes.") "Is divine healing a fact?" (Replies from audience, "It surely is.") "Gentlemen of the committee and audience, are you entirely satisfied?" (Replies from the audience, "Indeed we are.")

The service then closed with the following prayer of consecration spoken clause by clause by the Reverend Lake and repeated by the audience:

In Jesus' Name I come to Thee. Take me as I am. Make me what I ought to be, in Spirit, Soul, in Body. Give me Power to do right, if I have wronged any. To repent, to confess, to restore. No matter what it costs, wash me in the blood of Jesus, that I may now become Thy child, and manifest Thee, in a Perfect Spirit, a Holy Mind, a Sickless Body. Amen.

30

Results of Believing Prayer

February 7, 1923

Healed Insanity

A woman, holding the infant baby of Mrs. Lloyd McLaughlin, was asked to stand.

Mr. Lake: This baby is just one month old. When the baby was born the mother was given twilight sleep, which resulted in insanity, as it so often does. This church has been praying for the dear woman. On Monday a group of our people went aside to particularly pray for this dear woman. I called them on the phone about five o'clock and asked one of the sisters, "What is the answer from heaven?"

She replied, "Well, brother, we have the answer. Our hearts have the victory, and we know the woman is healed."

Yesterday morning the woman awoke healed, Praise the Lord.

Child Helpless and Dumb Healed

There was another case I wanted to present at this time, but the mother is delayed. This dear mother comes from Grangerville, Idaho. Her baby was injured in the birth, due to the child being delivered by instruments. The principle object of instruments these days is the $25 extra that is charged. God has had babies born for five thousand years without any of their accursed use. This little one had the usual thing that takes place in such cases; an injury so terrible that the child was never able to walk or speak. Apparently it was a partial detachment of the spinal cord from the brain. The mother testifies the baby has begun to walk and talk now.

Paralysis in Process of Healing

A dear young business man of the city, who has been paralyzed from the neck down for six years, is walking now.

Healed When Totally Paralyzed

Some of you will remember Mr. Kelly who was totally paralyzed from the shoulders down. Himself, his wife and their new baby were present in the meeting last night, and he testified to his perfect healing.

Mrs. Raymond

We have inquiries regarding Mrs. Raymond, who was dying of tuberculosis. Day before yesterday she was out for three and half hours for the first time. Her mother says she is healed. She was delivered from very death.

Another Deliverance

We have a dear mother in Wooster, Massachusetts. Four years ago her son broke down and went out of his mind. We ministered to him, and the Lord healed him. Recently, almost the same thing has taken place with the daughter. Here is the telegram asking us to pray for her. The daughter is greatly recovered since we prayed for her, but the mother says she still suffers from bad dreams, fear of fire, and fear of death. (Rev. Thompson was asked to present this case to the Lord.)

Scripture Reading With Comments

Numbers 12

"And Miriam and Aaron spake against Moses because of the Ethiopian woman whom he had married....And the Lord heard it" [verses 1-2].

A great many people lose the blessing that they might have had, by sticking their nose into other people's affairs. The Lord has been trying from the very beginning to get folks to learn this truth. This is one of the most severe lessons in the Word of God on the disadvantage of sticking your nose into other people's affairs. The Lord somehow succeeds in looking after most people who put their confidence in Him, and regulating them fairly well. You like to be governed by the Spirit of the Lord Himself, and so do I, so we must accord the same privilege to the other party.

"Now the man Moses was very meek, above all the men which were upon the face of the earth" (verse 3).

No other man in all history had so many reasons to get puffed up, if he had been puffable. The little fellow puffs up—the big fellow puffs down. No man ever listened to such words as the Lord spake to Moses. No one was ever dignified by the same commission that God gave to Moses. When God called Moses to His service and sent him to Egypt, He spoke these most startling words to him, *"Thou shalt be [as] God"* [see Exodus 4:16]. He was endowed with all the authority of God, and was sent with the commission to deliver His people from the hands of Pharaoh. His word became the Word of God, his action became the action of God. *"Now the man Moses was very meek, above all the men which were upon the face of the earth"* [verse 3].

Aaron was the brother and Miriam the sister of Moses. When Moses was called at the burning bush, he began to make excuses because of his slowness of speech, and God gave him his brother Aaron, saying, *"He shall be thy spokesman unto the people"* [Exodus 4:16].

"Behold, Miriam became leprous, white as snow: And Aaron looked upon Miriam, and, behold, she was leprous" (verse 10).

Some time ago I was called to minister to a leper in the state of Montana, ex-Senator Willets, who had been in confinement several years. It was the first time since leaving Africa that I had a chance to examine a leper with care. So I went with him to his rooms and had him strip. The leprosy was as white as snow. His fingers were dead and swollen three times the normal size. When he would put wood in the fire he would burn his fingers and would not know it. His feet were in the same condition. He wrote me afterward that the first evidence of healing he noticed was in his toes. The color and feeling returned.

> **The cloud departed from off the tabernacle; and, behold, Miriam became leprous, white as snow: and Aaron looked upon Miriam, and, behold, she was leprous. And Aaron said unto Moses, Alas, my Lord I beseech thee, lay not the sin upon us, wherein we have done foolishly,...and Moses cried unto the Lord, saying, Heal her now, O God, I beseech thee [verses 10-13].**

Moses' prayer is characteristic of so many of the prayers of the Bible. It is brief. It contains only eight words: *"Heal her now, O God, I beseech thee."* But with Aaron's wholehearted confession, the heart of Moses was moved even as the heart of God.

Lecture on Prayer

I want to talk to you a little about this subject of prayer. It seems to me that this prayer of Moses is a wonderful example of that remarkable teaching of Jesus on the subject of FAITH in the eleventh chapter of Mark. After the cursing of the fig tree, Jesus utilized the instance to give voice to His marvelous teaching of faith in God.

He said, *"Verily, verily."* When an Oriental used the words "Verily, verily," he raised his hand, and it gave it the solemnity of an oath. *"[With the solemnity of an oath] I say unto you...What things soever ye desire, when ye pray, BELIEVE that ye RECEIVE them, and ye shall have them"* (Mark 11:23-24). The Revised Version gives greater force to it. *"[When ye pray] believe that you HAVE received."* When? Why, bless your soul, *"When you pray."*

Healing of Appendicitis

Mrs. Ferguson, will you kindly stand? (Woman stands.) A week ago Saturday Brother Wiggins, Brother Doogan, Mrs. Lake and I were just leaving the Healing Rooms on our way to Forest Grove, Oregon, when a gentleman came in and told us of this woman's suffering and begged us to come. We went, knelt by her bedside, laid hands on the woman, and in one minute the Lord delivered her. I put my fingers into her side, holding the appendix between my fingers, to demonstrate the perfectness of the healing. Observing how the Lord had touched her body, she said, "Brother, I want to give my heart to God." So we called in her sons, and the other man, a cousin, and our sister gave herself to the Lord. Last Sunday she became a member of the church, and today is present to give public thanks to God for her salvation and healing.

"When ye pray, believe that ye receive, and ye shall have," or *"believe that ye HAVE received."* You have it: that is what it means. We used to have a little Englishman in our evangelistic party who would say to the people when they were praying, "Now let us stop praying for five minutes and BELIEVE God, and see what will happen." It is perfectly amazing the wonderful things that will happen when people believe God.

The Soul Cry of a Brother

There is an attitude of faith, an opening of the soul to God, a divine laying hold in the Spirit. I can imagine the soul cry in the prayer of Moses under these circumstances. Miriam, his own sister, now smitten and leprous, white as snow—what were the feelings of his heart? I sometimes have thought that there is no circumstance in my own life that ever called out so much faith in God and determination of soul to see God's will done as in the healing of a sister. One of my sisters and I had been chums from our childhood. She was a little older than I. The vision of the Christ as the Healer had just opened to my soul.

She was dying of an issue of blood. My mother called me one night and said, "John, if you want to see your sister alive, you must come at once." When I arrived my mother said, "You are too late, she is gone." I stepped to her bedside and laid my hand on her forehead; it was cold and dead. I slipped my hand down over her heart, and the heart had ceased to beat. I picked up a small mirror and held it over her mouth, but there was no discoloration. The breath was gone. I stood there stunned. Her husband knelt at the foot of the bed weeping—her baby asleep in a crib on the opposite side of the room. My old father and mother knelt sobbing at the side of the bed. They had seen eight of their children die; she apparently was the ninth. My soul was in a storm.

Just a few weeks before, my wife was healed when she almost died. Just a few weeks before, my brother had been healed after having been invalid for twenty-two years. A short time before, my older sister with five cancers in the breast, who had been operated on five times, and turned away to die, was healed. As I looked at my sister I said, "God, this is not the will of God, and I cannot accept it. It is the will of the devil and darkness. He that hath the power of death, that is the devil."

I discovered this fact, that there are times when your spirit lays hold of the spirit of another, and they just cannot get away from you. Somehow I just felt my spirit lay hold of the spirit of that woman. And I prayed, "Dear Lord, she just cannot go." I walked up and down for some time. My spirit was crying out for somebody with faith in God that I could call on to help me. That was twenty-five years ago when the individual who trusted God for healing was almost insane in the mind of the church and the world. Bless God, it is different now. That is the advantage of having people who trust God, and walk out on God's lines, come together, and stay together, put their hands and hearts together, and carry one another's load, and form a nucleus in society which has some force for God. I have no confidence or faith in these little efforts that people run after here and there. Most of them go up in vapor. If you want something done for God and humanity put your hearts and your hands together and your souls together. Organize your efforts.

That baby's mother (referring to the baby in the audience) would not have been healed, except that a little nucleus determined to pray until the woman was healed, and they stayed in prayer all day Monday. At five o'clock they had the victory. It took them all day. I wish we had spirituality and faith enough to look through the mists and see what was taking place all that day long, until the powers of darkness were dispelled, and the healing came.

As I walked up and down my sister's room, I could think of but one man that had faith on this line. That was John Alexander Dowie six hundred miles away. I went to the phone and called the Western Union, and told them I wanted to get a telegram through to Mr. Dowie, and an answer back as quickly as possible. I sent this wire: "My sister has apparently died, but my spirit will not let her go. I believe if you will pray, God will heal her." I received this answer back: "Hold on to God. I am praying. She will live."

Oh, God, I have said a thousand times, what would it have meant if instead of that telegram of faith I had received one from a weakling preacher who might have said: "I am afraid you are on the wrong track," or "Brother, you are excited," or "The days of miracles are past."

It was the strength of his faith that came over the wire that caused the lightnings of my soul to begin to flash, and while I stood there at the telephone and listened, the very lightnings of God began to flash in my spirit I prayed, "This thing of hell cannot be, and it will not be. In the Name of Jesus Christ I abolish death and sickness, and she shall live."

And as I finished praying, I turned my eyes toward the bed, and I saw her eyelid blink. But I was so wrought up I said, "Maybe I deceived myself." So I stood a little while at the telephone, and the lightnings of God's Spirit were still flashing from my soul. Presently I observed her husband get up and tip-toe to her head, and I knew he had seen it.

I said, "What is it, Peter?" He replied, "I thought I saw her eyelids move." And just then they moved again. Five days later she came to Father's home and the Lake family sat down to Christmas dinner, the first time in their lives when they were all well.

Persistent Prayer Sometimes Necessary

Beloved, it is not our long prayers, but believing God that gets the answer. However, I want to help somebody who finds persistent prayer a necessity, as we all do sometimes. We have not the least idea, Paul says, of the powers of darkness we are praying against. *"For we wrestle not against flesh and blood, but against principalities, against powers, against the rulers of the darkness of this world, against spiritual wickedness in high places*" (Ephesians 6:12). And sometimes you have to lay hold of God, and stay before God, and stay through the blackness and through the darkness and through the night of it, until the faith of God penetrates, bless God, and the work is done.

Daniel's Experience

Do you remember the experience of Daniel, one of the finest in the Book? He had to hear from heaven. He fasted and prayed for twenty-one days. On the twenty-first day an angel came to him right out of heaven, and the angel said, *"Daniel, a man greatly beloved...from the first day...thy prayer was heard."* Not the last time you prayed, but the very first.

> **O Daniel, a man greatly beloved, understand the words that I speak unto thee, and stand upright: for unto thee am I now sent...Fear not, Daniel: for from the first day that thou didst set thine heart to understand, and to chasten thyself before thy God, thy words were heard, and I am come for thy words. But the prince of the kingdom of Persia withstood me one and twenty days: but, lo, Michael, one of the chief princes, came to help me; and I remained there with the kings of Persia. Now I am come to make thee understand what shall befall thy people in the latter days (Daniel 10:11-14).**

Michael is spoken of again as the warrior angel. He made way against the devil and cast him out of heaven. Get the circumstance. Daniel had prayed, and God heard his prayer and answered it by sending an angel messenger, but the messenger himself was held up on the way by some other power of darkness, until reinforcements came, and God dispatched "Michael" one of the chief angels to his help. I wonder what was necessary to be accomplished in the minds of those interested, before God could answer that prayer?

You are praying for somebody, you are praying for your friend, or your brother, or your son, or your daughter who needs your love and faith. Beloved, have you faith in God to stay and pray until the Spirit has a chance to work out the problem? That is the issue. Keep right down to it. Do not let go. It is the will of God, you have a right to an answer.

There is a ministry of intercession that comes from heaven. Oh, it is prayer by the Spirit of God. It is entering into the prayer spirit of the Holy Ghost. He prays, He prays for you, He prays for me, *"with groanings that cannot be uttered"* [Romans 8:26]. Our spirit in union with His, we enter into oneness of faith, reaching out into the ether of God, and the love of His Spirit, and taking that power of God and fashioning the power of God into the soul's desire. A lot of folks stop when half through. You hold on to God and pray through.

Then there are times like the one when my sister was restored, when the faith and power of God comes like the lightning flash, and to Moses when he prayed: *"Heal her now, O God, I beseech thee,"* and the healing is instant.

There are times when it is only your humanity that prays. You know these times yourself, when your soul does not enter into your prayer, much less your spirit. There are times when your soul prays. People these days do not even have much conception of the realm of the SOUL, or psychic. Then there is a prayer in the Spirit, that deeper quality of your life, deeper than the psychic or soul. Oh, bless God, there is still a prayer where the spirit of man and the Spirit of God unite and become one.

No one can imagine as Moses prayed that day how his soul must have been stirred. Here is his own sister, the woman who had stood by the river side when he was a babe, had put him in a basket, hid him in the bulrushes and watched over his welfare. Don't you think she was interested in him? Sometimes I have sympathized with Miriam. She had a sisterly and motherly affection for Moses. She wanted to keep him straight. She was afraid he had made a great mistake in his marriage.

Say beloved, you are a father probably, or you are a mother, or a sister or brother, and you have laid hold so tight on the other one that you are afraid to leave them in the hands of God. That is one of the hardest things folks have to learn, to just take their hands off the other and let God have them. There is no record that God had any quarrel with Moses about his wife.

The Experience of Stephen Merritt

Stephen Merritt was a godly old undertaker in the City of New York. His dear old wife and himself had lived a godly life. They had raised one son, and if there was ever a reprobate it was that son, Charley. Charley would get into some disreputable affair, and the police would come and say, "Charley has done so and so. It will take so much money to get him out of the difficulty."

The next week another would come along with something else, and so it went on and on. And the two old gray heads were praying and pouring out their tears for that boy's salvation. Stephen Merritt had a habit of receiving people into his office and helping them. John G. Wooley was one that he helped. He handed Wooley five dollars and said, "You meet me at such and such a camp ground." Wooley was a drunkard. He had not been accustomed to being trusted with money, and he met the old man there and found God.

One day as he sat in his office he was praying about his son, and the floor was wet with his tears, when he heard the voice of God saying, "How long have you been trying to save Charley?" So many of us are "trying to save Charley," and we have gotten in the way of the Lord. He replied: "Lord, a long time." The Lord said, "Now if you are through, I will undertake." The old man considered, and it worked out in his soul this way.

The police came and said, "Charley did so and so."

He asked, "Who is Charley?"

"Why he is your son."

"No, I have no son, Charley." That day as he knelt there he said, "Lord, he is not my son any more. I give him over to you until he is saved." So he told the police, "No, I have no son." They looked at him and shook their heads. Then they sent another officer. But it was no use to go to him any more. It looked as if the old man had gone crazy.

About nine months passed, and one day an officer came and said: "Charley has jumped off the Brooklyn Bridge and finished." He wanted the old man to have the river dragged to obtain the body. But he said, "Oh, no, I have no son, Charley. Drag the river if you want to." So they dragged the river, but the body they found was not Charley's. Three months more passed, and one day a clerk said, "There is one of your friends in the office." And when he came in it was Charley. He was beautifully dressed, clean faced, everything indicating the light of God, and when the old father came in the son fell at his feet, kissed them, and asked his forgiveness. He said in explanation, "Three months ago I was saved in a mission, but I did not want to come and see you until I came as a man."

The Human Clutch

Not only is it so in your prayers for others, but in your prayers for yourself, some of you are holding to your sickness, or difficulty, with such a clutch, and are so everlastingly conscious of it, that God cannot get it out of your hands. You are in the very place spiritually where old Stephen Merritt was. He was so determined to save his boy that he was just doing it himself, and God was not getting a chance.

Open your hands, let go of the old difficulty. I was praying for a woman who had appendicitis, and as I prayed I saw she was holding on to it mentally so hard I had to do something. So I told one of the craziest stories I ever told, and finally she burst out laughing in spite of the pain, and when she got through the pain was gone. She just opened her clutch.

Maybe you are holding on to sin with that same clutch. Maybe you are holding on to disobedience to God with that same clutch. Maybe it is your sickness. If there is something that is keeping you from being blessed, let clear go and let your hands and heart open.

When I was a boy I used to visit the Soo Locks at Sault Ste. Marie, Michigan, where my home was. One day a sailor was up in the masts, he lost his balance and shot over the ship into the water. Another sailor stood on the railing of the ship and watched him. He went down and came up, and went down and came up again, and everything was in foam around him. Still the fellow stood there. Then the chap went down the third time, limp, and just as he was disappearing he shot down into the water and came up with him. A couple of gentlemen were standing by, one remarked, "That fellow has taken men out of the water before." He just waited until the kick was all out of him. Otherwise both might have drowned.

A lot of us have to thresh and struggle and fight until the kick is all out of us before we are ready to let God take us. As a young fellow I was as proud as Lucifer—every Lake I ever knew was. Robert Burns wrote, with his diamond on the window of a Highland Inn, "There's nothing here but Highland pride, Highland pride and poverty." It did not make any difference how poor they were.

The hardest thing I had to do was to make my surrender to God. I heard Riley tell the other night of having been a dope fiend, and gambler, and of how God saved him. I never knew anything about that kind of life. Never touched whiskey in my life, never used tobacco, never committed an unholy act in the moral sense, but that proud heart of mine had to struggle like a drowning man until I was ready to say, "Lord, you save me." The final consummation came when I knelt behind an old elm tree and poured out my heart to God, and made my surrender to Him. The light of heaven broke into my soul, and I arose from my knees a son of God, and I knew it.

Let God have you. Quit sweating, quit wrestling. About the most difficult class in the world to get healed is Christian Scientists. Why? Because they are working at it so hard. They have been reading so many lessons and concentrating their mind on healing, until almost exhausted. You have to lead them away from it all to that place where, "It is not TRY but TRUST." That is the secret of Christ's healing; that is the secret of Christ's salvation. It is trusting Him for it, and believing HIM when He says he will do it, and the mind relaxes and the soul comes to rest.

There is a wonderful help in disarming people. I read a story of the healing of Sam Leake. He had become a most notorious drunkard. He bought whiskey and buried it until he filled his whole lot with buried whiskey. It was a mania.

Everybody who tried to help him would say, "Leake, just make one promise, that you will not drink any more." Finally he went to a woman who was wiser than the others. Before he went out of the room she said, "I want you to promise one thing."

He said, "I will promise you anything, except that I will not drink whiskey. I'm nearly crazy for a drink now."

She said, "I want you to promise that every time you feel like taking a drink of whiskey you will do so."

"Sure I will." Do you get the secret of that? She disarmed him right away. The thing he was clutching all the time was the fear that someone was going to make him promise not to drink whiskey. One morning when he awoke he discovered that the cursed appetite was gone.

Say, dear hearts, let go! Open your clutch! Let God take you. Let God have you, whether it is for your spirit, whether it is for your soul, whether it is for you body. No matter what, just let go. "It is not TRY, but TRUST." God bless you.

The nearer the soul is to God, the less its perturbations; as the point nearest the center of a circle is subject to the least motion.

For he that is entered into his rest, he also hath ceased from his own works, as God did from His.

"Let us labour therefore to enter into that rest..." (Hebrews 4:11). Have you entered that rest?

31

The Power of Divine Healing

My soul used to be able to enjoy as much lightness in the Lord Jesus as anybody, but various processes of life reduced my capacity to enjoy jingle, and God brought me down into the solids of life. No man could live in the environment in which a large portion of my life has been spent, without realizing that unless men can contact the living God in REAL POWER, power out of the ordinary, power sufficient for tremendous needs and unusual occasions, he could not live.

Man Could Not Live!

In South Africa some years ago, in a single night a fever epidemic struck the country for three hundred and fifty miles. As I rode through a section of that country I found men dead in their beds beside their wives, children dead in their beds alongside the living, whole families stricken, dying and some dead. In one single month one-fourth of the entire population of that district, both white and black, died. We had to organize an army to dig graves, and an army of men to make caskets. We could not buy wood enough in that section of the country to make caskets, so we buried them in a blanket, or without a blanket, when it was necessary to save the blankets for a better purpose.

I had a man in my company who perhaps some of you know. God had appointed that man to pray, as I have never found anybody else anointed to pray. For days he remained under a thorn tree, and when I passed that way in the morning I would hear his voice in prayer, and when I returned in the evening I would hear his voice in prayer. Many times I got a prepared meal and carried it to him, and aroused him long enough to get him to eat it. I would say, "Brother, how is it? Are you getting through?" He would reply, "Not yet." But one day he said, "Mr. Lake, I feel today that if I had just a little help in my faith that my spirit would go through into God." And I went on my knees beside him, joined my heart with his, and voiced my prayer to God.

As we prayed the Spirit of the Lord overshadowed our souls, and presently I found myself, not kneeling under the tree, but moving gradually away from the tree some fifty or one hundred feet. My eyes gradually opened, and I witnessed such a scene as I had never witnessed before—a multitude of demons, like a flock of sheep. The Spirit had come upon him also, and he rushed ahead of me, cursing that army of demons, and they were driven back to hell, or to the place from whence they came. Beloved, the next morning when we awoke that epidemic of fever was gone. THAT IS THE POWER OF DIVINE HEALING. God destroying Satan.

Now when you consider that I have been a man of some scientific training, you can understand what an introduction into a life where everything was made new and of a different order meant. Instead of being on the hard, natural plane of materialistic life and knowledge, suddenly introduced into the Spirit you can realize what a revolution was brought to pass in my soul, and how gradually discovery after discovery revealed the wonder of God and the mighty action of God through the souls of men. There is a little keynote in one of Paul's Epistles that gives the real key to successful prayer. In successful prayer there is a divine action, a divine interaction, an interaction just as real as any chemical interaction in any experiment in the world. You bring two opposite chemicals together, and you realize a little flash or flame, an explosion. There has been an interaction. Your chemicals have undergone a change. They are no longer the same properties they were before. For instance, oxygen and hydrogen united is water. So it is in the spiritual realm.

Paul said in giving us this key: *"The word...did not profit them, not being mixed with faith"* [Hebrews 4:2]. There is a quality and content in the soul of man, a necessary quality. That quality is the POWER OF THE SPIRIT. And when faith and Spirit come together there is an interaction. There is a movement of God. There is a manifestation of the Spirit. There is a divine explosion! FAITH AND GOD UNITED IS DIVINE HEALING.

When I was a boy a neighbor employed a chemist. They were trying to manufacture a new explosive of some kind. A section of the barn was being used for the experiments. Johnnie [John Lake himself] was strictly reminded that he had no business around the barn, but like many Johnnies his curiosity was aroused. One day when they had gone to town he discovered that the door was not thoroughly locked. Just a little picking and prying and it opened and Johnnie was inside. There were some packages on the bench and some liquid on the floor. Presently Johnnie bungled, a package fell into a bucket of liquid, and that is the last Johnnie remembered. When he came to himself he was some fifty or seventy feet away, and they told me I was carried there by a section of the wall. It just went off. That package in the liquid interacted.

We look at the wonderful powers in nature and marvel. A group of scientists not long ago compressed such a quantity of nitrogen in a solid block thirteen inches square, that they declared if it could be placed in the heart of the city of Chicago, and permitted to explode, it would wreck the city. One can imagine somewhat of the terrific energy stored up in that little block of nitrogen thirteen inches square, but when you come to think of the marvel of the nature of God, the dynamic of His being, how staggering His almightiness becomes. The world's conception of religion is that it is a matter of sentiment, for in the minds of most men religion is just sentiment to them. It is not a thing of power, and they do not understand the properties of the soul of God, nor the quality of His life, nor how it is that God moves in the nature of men to change their heart, to dissolve the sin out of their soul, to cleanse them by His life and power, to heal their body, and reveal His light and life in them.

I believe the very beautiful thing we call SALVATION, and the holy statement of Jesus Christ, *"Ye must be born again"* [John 3:7] is itself a scientific fact, and declaration of God's divine purpose and intent, based on the law of being. We are inclined to think that God just desires, and our hearts are changed. But I want to tell you, beloved, that there is a process in a man's soul that admits God into his life. Your heart opens because it is touched by the love of God, and into the heart, into the nature of man, there comes the divine essence of the living Spirit, and bless God, it has an action in him. *Sin* dissolves from his *nature* and from the mind of man. The Spirit of God takes possession of the cells of his brain, and his thoughts are changed by its action. There is a new realization of divine holiness. By the grace of God he discovers himself SANCTIFIED in deed and in truth, because Christ in truth dwells there.

Beloved, Jesus Christ had His eye and His soul fixed on that one dynamic power of God, the HOLY GHOST. And His holy life, His death, His resurrection, His ascension to glory were all necessary in the process of soul development to arrive at the throne of God where He could receive from the Father the gift of the Holy Ghost, and have the privilege of ministering to your soul and mine.

So in my heart there has grown a wondrous reverence for the mighty Son of God, who saw beyond the ken [Scottish for *to know*] of man, who visioned in the distance, who sought in His soul for the key to the mighty powers of the nature of God, who determined for our relief and for our benefit and salvation to leave the throne of God, come to earth, be born as a man, take upon Him the nature of man (not the nature of angels). He looked to God as men do, overcame by His power through reliance on His Word, and so believing, so advancing step by step in the nature of God and the likeness of God, one day He stood forth, the Eternal Sacrifice before the throne of God, and received the eternal reward of His fidelity—the Holy Ghost. In life, Jesus the man was in the LIKENESS of God. In resurrection, the NATURE of God. In glorification, the SUBSTANCE of God, and thus *"became the author of eternal salvation"* [Hebrews 5:9].

And the man or the woman who does not understand the Holy Ghost, and its magnificence and the wonder of its power, must turn his heart again heavenward and see the price that Jesus paid in order to secure it for you and me, *in order to give it to the world that was in sin, sickness and death,* to lift it out of darkness. I love that blessed old hymn, "Ye Must Be Born Again." Can we not sing it?

A ruler once came to Jesus by night,
To ask Him the way of salvation and light;
The Master made answer in words true and plain;
"Ye must be born again!"

Chorus:

"Ye must be born again!
Ye must be born again!
I verily, verily say unto thee,
Ye must be born again!"

Ye children of men, attend to the word
So solemnly uttered by Jesus the Lord;
And let not this message to you be in vain;
"Ye must be born again!"

O ye who would enter this glorious rest,
And sing with the ransomed the son of the blest;
The life everlasting if ye would obtain,
"Ye must be born again!"

A dear one in heaven thy heart yearns to see,
At the beautiful gate may be waiting for thee;
Then list to the note of this solemn refrain:
"Ye must be born again!"

There is a process of divine TRANSMUTATION. But beloved, by the power of God's Spirit in a man's heart, that process is going on every single day of your life, sister, where God takes that which is natural, that which is earthly, touches it by His divine power, moves upon it by His heavenly nature, and in the Name of Jesus Christ you come forth no longer self and selfish, but now TRANSFORMED, changed, by the power of Christ, into the nature of the Son of God, into the likeness of the Lord, into His character and nature and understanding and knowledge. Blessed be the God and Father of our Lord and Savior Jesus Christ!

"[To us is given] exceeding great and precious promises, that BY THESE ye might be partakers of the divine nature" [2 Peter 1:4]. And being a partaker, in consequence *"[Escape] the corruption that is in the world through lust"* [2 Peter 1:4].

Bless God, His divine purpose is not to whitewash the soul, but to change the character, transmute the life by the grace of God, make the man a christ and king, a deliverer and savior, in common with the Lord Jesus Christ, his elder brother. If I am a brother of the Lord, then I am bone of His bone, and flesh of His flesh; and substance of His substance, like my elder brother. The source of life is the same source of life that is in Him. The same purpose that is revealed in Him is His high purpose for you and for me.

Men have little understanding of the quality of faith, or what it accomplishes because of the fact that they are not aware of the process by which that work is done. FAITH has the quality and power, with the Spirit of God, to do what a match does to power. It is the touch of God. It is the touch of FAITH through us that ignites the Spirit and produces the divine action that takes place in the soul, when sin is rebuked and cast out, when sickness is destroyed and dissolved from the life, the nature set free, and man rejoices as a son of God, saved in spirit, soul and body.

One day there came to my healing rooms a little boy that we know on the streets as a newsboy, just one of the little ragged chaps. A lady had observed the little fellow on the street in an epileptic fit, afterwards took him by the hand and led him into the healing rooms. We talked to the little chap about the Lord, prayed for him, and told him to return again. The Lord healed him. He was a manly little urchin, and one day he said: "Mr. Lake, I haven't any money to reward you with now, but you are not going to lose any money on me." We smiled and were glad to see the spirit of the little chap, and he went his way. About two weeks later, in the midst of a great meeting, he strutted in, marched up and laid five silver dollars on the table, and marched out again.

Then he got up against his first real problem of living his new life in his business. Every boy has a corner. He can sell papers on his own corner and it is up to him to keep all other boys away. He had given his heart to the Lord. One day he came around with a long face. He said, "It's all off."

"Well, my boy, what's the trouble?"

"They were going to rush my corner, until I could not stand it, and I cleaned up the whole bunch." The little chap was getting his first introduction into the real problem of being a Christian in this old world, under a competitive system, the outgrowth of human selfishness devised by the devil.

One day a gentleman came along and wanted to buy a paper. His arm was disabled, and he could not get his purse. He said to the boy, "I have put my purse in the wrong pocket. Put your hand in and get it for me."

The boy said, "What is the matter with your arm?"

He replied, "I have what is called neuritis. My arm is paralyzed."

The little chap said, "Well, if the doctors can't do you any good, I'll tell you where you can get it fixed up. There are some men up in the Rookery Building that pray, and folks get well."

The man said: "How do you know?"

He replied: "I used to take fits, and fall on the street, and they would carry me off to the police station. I was like that for four years, but I don't take fits any more. If you want me to, I will take you up there."

So he brought him up. He was the head of a great lumber concern; his name was Rose. He sat down and told me how he was moved by the child's simple words, but he had no more idea of how God could heal a man or save man from sin than one of the Indians. So we began to tell of the Lord Jesus and His power to save, and continued to minister to him each day. Three weeks afterward he returned again to the medical clinic, where two hundred and seventy-five physicians had declared four weeks before that they could do nothing for him. They reexamined him, and found him perfectly well, healed by the power of God. THAT IS THE POWER OF DIVINE HEALING.

I went to the medical association and got a copy of the lecture that was given by Dr. Semple on the seriousness of the disease, and the utter impossibility of medicine ever to help him, or change his condition. In so far as they were concerned, he was a cripple. The nerves were dead, atrophied. It would require a miracle, they said, to reproduce the original life and restore power in the tissue of the arm. But the miracle took place, because there is a Fountain of Life, the Life of God, available for every man. Bless His Name! THAT IS THE POWER OF DIVINE HEALING.

When the LIFE of Jesus comes in, the dearth of your soul ends. When the Spirit of God comes in, your DEAD nerves come alive. God by the Spirit takes possession of the blood, and the brain, and the bone. He dwells in the very cellular structure of your whole being. His quickening LIFE regenerates you, and generates LIFE in you, and by the Christ of God you come forth, not a dead, senseless lobster, but a living man, a LIVING Christian.

Let me tell you a story to illustrate this point. They say a man died, and he appeared at the Beautiful Gate, and said to Peter: "I am from Philadelphia. I subscribe to the *Ladies' Home Journal.* I have a bed of mint in the back yard, but I never drink intoxicants."

Peter replied, "Go on to heaven and stay dead." He was dead already. Some folks think, you know, that because they are not committing this sin and that sin that they are dutiful, beautiful children of God. But, beloved, there is an awful lot more to Christianity than delivering a man's soul from the power of sin.

Professor Riddell tells this story: "I was walking along the Sea Beach and I encountered a lobster. I said, 'Lobster, did you ever chew tobacco?'

"Never!"

"Lobster, did you ever stay out nights?"

"Never!"

"Say, Lobster, shake hands. We are both lobsters."

Oh, there is a negative thing, and that negative thing in religious life is what is killing the real *power* of God. That negative thing, when we are all the time NOT DOING this and that and something else. It is a religion of DON'T do this, and DON'T DO THAT. My God! When Christ comes into the soul and into the spirit, it is all changed. Instead of deadness, there is LIFE in God. Instead of inaction, there is POWER by the Spirit of God. The Christian is a MAN, not a lobster.

"Down in the human heart,
Crushed by the tempter,
Feelings lie buried
That grace can restore.
Touched by a loving heart,
Wakened by kindness,
Chords that were broken
Will vibrate once more."

Oh, the grace of God is the lovely thing, the grace of God is the powerful thing. The grace of God is the life and Spirit of the Lord and Savior Jesus Christ. And ministered to the soul, breathed into the heart, transmitted to the life, MAN becomes like Christ, because the Christ of God is moving in the heart of him, generating and regenerating, and man comes forth a finished product by the hands of his Lord, saved from sin, healed of disease, kept by the indwelling Christ, who is the power of God.

I am looking to God for some real finished products these days, real men grown up in the Lord Jesus Christ, established, in the splendid solidarity of His holy nature and divine character, beautified by His holy glory, enriched by his divine nature—LIKE THE SON OF GOD.

So, my brother, my sister, I want to bring your heart this afternoon into this blessed confidence, this holy truth, this divine reality. If religious life has been a sort of sentiment, let me tell you beyond it there is the power of God, the moving, dynamic, burning force of LIFE in Christ Jesus, waiting to come into your heart, to revitalize your thought and change your spirit, and indwell the very flesh and bone and blood of you and make you a new man, and a new woman in the Lord Jesus. Say, beloved, that is the POWER OF DIVINE HEALING.

On one occasion I was entertaining myself by examining some typhoid bacteria, as they developed in dirty water. A neighbor woman came one morning and was anxious for me to show her one of her hairs under the microscope. I told her I had the microscope set, and was waiting for the development of the bacteria, and would be obliged if she would come back another day when my experiment was over. Instead of paying attention to what I said, she returned the next day with the same request. Again I explained to her, but the next morning she was back again, and finally the fourth morning I was annoyed and thought I would just take one of her hairs, let her see it anyway and not disturb the microscope. So I pulled it through under the microscope, and let her look. Presently she jumped up and hurried away and never even said, "Thank you."

When I came home that evening, Mrs. Lake said: "What did you do to Mrs. B___?"

I said, "I really do not know. Why?"

She said, "Well, she has been on the back porch all day, and the servant has been drenching her hair with kerosene." Why, she saw more crawling things than she ever saw before. She saw the bacteria and believed the crawling beasts were attached to her hair. Her hair and head were perfectly clean. The presence of the beasts she saw was explained in another way.

I want to bring home the truth of God. In the minds and lives of many religion is simply an illusion. There is no divine reality in it. But, beloved, real religion is God's divine reality, for it is the heart of God and the life of Christ. And when it comes into the soul of man it generates the same divine reality and heavenly power in him, and man becomes God's new creature.

In my younger days, when I first touched the ministry of healing, and as yet had developed a very small portion of faith in God, a young lady who lived nine miles in the country had a tubercular limb. Her physicians had tried to build her up in strength so they could amputate the limb, but on the final examination the disease was found to have made such progress that the amputation would not save her life. One day we received a request to join in prayer for her the next morning at nine, and to invite all the people who know God and had faith in Him, to unite with us. So I telegraphed all around the country to those I knew.

The physician told me that the knee had become so decayed that he could put his finger through the joint. Her suffering was more than ordinary. It required three men to hold her in bed the night before she was healed.

But in the morning she desired to be left alone for the last half hour before prayer. She lay with her eyes closed and her body still, and after a while she said, "I opened my eyes and saw it was just exactly the time for the people to pray for me." She said in her soul, "It is time for the people to pray for me. It is the time I ought to be healed." And letting her faith reach out to God, she said, "In the Name of Jesus Christ it is the time I AM healed." And she made a motion toward the side of the bed, and landed out on the floor, perfectly whole. She rushed downstairs two steps at a time. Her sister-in-law had a tub of water on the floor. She stuck her diseased limb into it, and the entire mass of rotten flesh of the leg disappeared in the tub, and there was a new leg, as new as a newly born baby, both flesh and bone. That is the POWER OF DIVINE HEALING.

I traveled down to Chicago and met old John Alexander Dowie, and I told him. He said, "Do you know the facts in this case?"

I said, "I do."

He said, "I want to see the woman." And he handed me one hundred dollars, and I wired for her to come. Beloved, even in that man's life he had never realized the creative power of God. He had seen wonderful healings, but here was the creative action of God making muscle and bone and flesh by God's power instantly.

Beloved, may every one of these holy demonstrations work out in your life, as they worked out in mine, a divine consciousness that God by the Spirit never comes to a man's life to whitewash him over or smooth him over or clean him up, but God comes to him to make him NEW and give him a new heart, and a new mind, and a new spirit, new blood, and new bone, and new flesh, and to send him out with a new song in his mouth, and a new shout of praise in his heart and a new realization of holiness—a truly REDEEMED man.

> Thou God eternal, Who lifts the soul of man from degradation and shame and sin, and exalts him in Jesus Christ, and lifts him by God's grace into His presence and power, we pray thee this day that thy action in our heart will purify our souls forever, and illuminate our natures in God, and fill us by Thy Divine Spirit, and send us forth among men—not whitewashed, but WASHED WHITE with God's power and God's grace.

Tongues and Interpretation

Dr. John G. Lake 1920

First commit your body and soul and spirit in entire, hundredfold consecration to God forever. Do not be satisfied with sins forgiven. Press on, press in, let God have you and fill you, until consciously He dwells, lives, abides in every cell of your blood, of your bone and your brain, until your soul (psychic) (mind), indwelt by Him, thinks His thoughts, speaks His word, until your spirit assimilates God, and God's Spirit assimilates you, until your humanity and His divinity are merged into His eternal Deity. Thus BODY, SOUL and SPIRIT are God's forever and forever. Amen. THAT is the POWER OF DIVINE HEALING. *Behold I give you power...over all the power of the enemy: and nothing shall by any means hurt you* (Luke 10:19).

The Truth About Divine Healing

This is a series of articles that appeared in the newspaper "Sacramento Union," Sacramento, California, July and August, 1927.

Article 1

Does God heal the sick in answer to prayer? What is the truth about divine healing?

Millions throughout the world are asking these questions today. Thousands in the Sacramento district are asking them.

Unfortunately the truths about divine healing have been greatly obscured by acts of sensationalism on the part of those who felt called upon to bring divine healing to the public.

It is the purpose of this series of articles, 24, to place the subject of divine healing before the reading public simply and plainly. It is my hope that I can do something to tear away the veil of supposition, superstition and misunderstanding from this subject, and present it in a way that all can understand.

Can God heal the sick?

Does God heal the sick?

Does God heal sinner as well as saint?

How does God heal the sick?

What must one do to be healed?

These and many other questions will be answered in these articles. Those who would learn the mighty simple truths regarding divine healing, as taught by evangelists who believe that God heals today just as He did 2,000 years ago, will do well to read these articles from first to last.

Some of these articles may prove startling to those who have not been taught along these lines. However, every statement will be backed by evidence. Every instance of healing cited will be of persons whose testimonies can readily be verified.

Article 2

Does God Heal?

Does God heal?

This is an age-old question.

The miracles of Jesus have been the battle ground of the centuries.

Millions declare that God does heal the sick. Millions scorn the assertion.

"Go into all the world, and proclaim the Gospel," said Jesus. *"And these signs shall follow them that believe; In my name shall they cast out devils; they shall speak with new tongues...they shall lay hands on the sick, and they shall recover"* (Mark 16:17-18).

The Bible says that Jesus Christ is the same yesterday, today and forever (Hebrews 13:8). If His gospel was true then, it is true now.

His disciples healed the sick then (Luke 10). His disciples should heal the sick now. The power of healing was bestowed on the Christians in Jerusalem 2,000 years ago. This power is still available. Healings are just as certain in Sacramento today as they were in Judea then.

It is said that many of those who would bring the joyful message of salvation and healing to the public have obscured the vision and darkened the simple sweet truths with a blare of trumpets, and the din of sensationalism. The public has listened, pondered and in many cases turned away disgusted.

However, truth is unalterable. God does heal today. Christ healed all that came to Him 2,000 years ago. He is still willing to heal all who come asking.

He is the same yesterday, today and forever.

Article 3

Does God Heal Sinner As Well As Saint?

To this question the World Bible Truth Crusaders answer, "Yes." The Bible says, "He healed all that came unto Him" (Luke 9:11; Matthew 12:15; Acts 10:38).

That they came to Jesus was enough. They were not asked if they belonged to this church or that. They were not asked what form of worship they subscribed to. They came unto Him—that satisfied Jesus.

When they possessed faith he hastened to commend it. He never told anyone that it was God's will they were sick. He never told anyone they were being "perfected" in character through sickness.

He commanded His 12 disciples to heal the sick (Luke 9:1-16). He commanded the "70" to first heal the sick, and then to say: *"The Kingdom of God is come nigh unto you"* (Luke 10:9).

The World Bible Crusaders, of which I am the president, teach that all may be healed—that all may find salvation. The Crusaders invite you to bring the halt, the sick, the lame and the blind. It makes no difference what they may be—Protestant, Catholic or Jew.

The Crusaders believe that the cause of Christianity had been hurt by petty limitations established by those who have failed to see the magnificent scope of the ministry of Jesus.

Jesus is still willing and able to heal all that come.

Article 4

Is Healing By Process or Instantaneous?

God does not always heal instantaneously.

Jesus' miracles of healing were not always instantaneous.

Healing takes place by process as well as instantly. Recall when Jesus prayed for the blind man, and asked: "What do you see?" The blind man answered, *"I see men as trees, walking."* Then Jesus ministered to him the second time, and he saw clearly (Mark 8:22-26).

Let us reason.

A tubercular person is consumed of the disease. Healing may come at once, or it may come over a period of time. The returning weight and fullness of health is the evidence that the healing is real.

Jesus in cursing the fig tree, did not kill it instantly. It "dried up from the roots." The death stroke dealt the tree by Jesus was effectual and complete. He struck the root. The leaves withered by process (Matthew 21:19).

At one time I was a rheumatic cripple. When healing came to me on a wave of divine power, my pains departed gradually. I was well in five days. This is healing by process.

Later I was stricken with blindness and was healed instantly when Mrs. Robert Brown, of Glad Tidings Mission, of New York, prayed for me.

There we have the two forms of healing. In one the disease is stricken at the roots and its evidences in the body wither by process, for the source of its being has been destroyed.

In the instantaneous healings the disease was expelled from the body by the divine power, root and branch, and the sick one becomes whole on the spot.

Under my ministry healings of both types are constantly taking place. In some cases 30 days pass from the time of prayer until the last evidence of disease has vanished. However, I believe instantaneous healings are in the majority.

Article 5

Does God Always Heal?

In Him there is no darkness at all. Can darkness come out of light? Can sickness come out of health? Is death born of life?

The issue resolves itself into: "Of what is the redemption of Jesus Christ constituted? What existing powers does He promise to destroy?"

First sin. When Christ's redemption is completed sin is gone. Through sin death entered into the world. Death entered through sin (Romans 5:12).

Sickness is incipient death—death in process.

"He healed all that were oppressed of the devil" (Acts 10:38). In Luke 13 Jesus demanded His right to heal the woman bowed together with the spirit of infirmity 18 years as follows: "Ought not this woman whom Satan hath bound these 18 years be healed?" And overriding traditions of the Jews He healed her then and there.

"The last enemy that shall be destroyed is death" (1 Corinthians 15:26). "For this cause was the Son of God manifested that He might destroy the works of the devil" (1 John 3:8).

Sin, sickness and death are doomed—doomed to death by the decree of Christ Jesus. Sin, sickness and death are the triumvirate of the devil; the triple curse.

Heaven is the absence of this triple curse—heaven is sinlessness, sicklessness and deathlessness. This is the ultimate of Christ's redemption.

Jesus anticipated the world's need. He commanded His power for the use of mankind, and invites us to help ourselves to His eternal quality and become thereby Sons of God.

Article 6

The Love of Jesus Healed Sick

Take the shackles off God.

Jesus did not heal the sick in order to coax them to be Christians. He healed because it was His nature to heal. The multitude surrounded him. His love gushed forth like an electric billow. *"There went virtue out of Him, and healed them all"* (Luke 6:19).

Some modern evangelists have degraded divine healing by making it a teaser to bring those desirous of healing under the sway of their ministry. Jesus healed both saint and sinner—to the dismay of his apostles, who had not yet grown to the soul-stature of Jesus.

They reported to Jesus: *"We saw one casting out devils in thy name...and we forbad him, because he followeth not us."* Jesus replied, "Forbid him not, for no man can do a miracle in My Name and speak lightly of Me" (Mark 9:38-39).

He met a man at the pool of Bethesda, a paralytic. This man did not ask for healing. Jesus went to him and said: *"Wilt thou be made whole?"* Here Jesus is asking for the privilege of healing the sufferer. He healed him. His love compelled it.

Next day Jesus met the healed man in the temple and said: *"Behold, thou art made whole: sin no more, lest a worse thing come unto thee"* (John 5:1-14).

Jesus' action is a perpetual rebuke to the priestcraft who endeavor to use the possibility of the individual's healing as a means to force him into the Church.

The outgushing of His love for the world burst all bounds, and four times he healed multitudes. But some say: "This was Jesus. No apostle had such an experience."

When Peter went down the street as the evening shadows fell; when his shadow reached across the street, "They brought the sick, that his shadow might overshadow them" (Acts 5:15). The clear inference is that they were healed (see Acts 5:16).

James, writing to the 12 tribes scattered abroad—not the little group of Jews constituting the kingdom of the Jews, but the whole body of the nation of Israel scattered throughout the world, both the ten-tribed kingdom and the two-tribed kingdom—shouts: *"Is any sick among you, let him call for the elders of the church, and let them pray over him"* Not prepare him for death, but that he might be healed. *"If he have committed sins, they shall be forgiven him"* (James 5:14-16).

Healing was the evidence of God's forgiveness—heaven's testimony that their sins were remembered no more.

Take the shackles off God. Enlarge our theologies to Christ's standard, and the world will love and worship Him forever.

Article 7

Jesus Created Miracles in Succoring Ill

(Continued From Yesterday)

Jesus not only healed the sick but performed a creative miracle on the man born blind (John 9).

Being born blind, it is self-evident the eyes were not a finished creation. Otherwise he would have seen.

The narrative reveals that the man did not know who Jesus was. Jesus did not make Himself known until after the miracle had been performed. Let us analyze the incident.

Jesus discovers the man born blind (verse 1). He spat on the ground and made clay of the spittle. Why? Because Jesus was a fundamentalist. The story of creation in Genesis says that "God made man of the dust of the ground." Jesus in finishing the creation of the eyes adopted the same method. He stooped down, took up some dust, spat on it, and put it on the blind man. That is not healing. That is a work of creation.

In 2 Corinthians 12, it is said that in distributing the gifts of the Spirit to the members of the Church, one was given the "gifts of healing" to another the "working of miracles." Healing is the renewal of the body from diseased conditions. A miracle is in the creative order.

The case of the blind man was an exercise of creative authority, not the restoration of diseased tissue. The man was made whole.

The grouchers made their kick. The Pharisees examined the man and asked, "Who healed you?" He answered, "I know not." Then they asked, "What do you think of him?" He replied, "He is a prophet."

Later Jesus found him and said to him, *"Dost thou believe on the Son of God?"* The man replied, "Who is He, Lord, that I might believe on Him?" Jesus answered, "I that speak unto thee am He."

The struggle of the centuries has been to free the soul of man from narrow interpretations. Jesus has sometimes been made to appear as a little bigot, sometimes as an impostor. The world is still waiting to see Him as He is. Jesus the magnificent, Jesus the spiritual giant, Jesus the compassionate, Jesus the dynamic—the wonder of the centuries.

Take the shackles off God.

Let Him have a chance to bless mankind without ecclesiastical limitations.

As a missionary, I have witnessed the healing of thousands of Africans. Thus was Christ's love and compassion for a lost world revealed.

And thus the writer was assisted into the larger vision of a world-redeemer whose hand and heart are extended to God's big world, and every man, saint and sinner, is invited to behold and love Him.

Article 8

Are Jesus' Healings Instant?

(Continued From Yesterday)

In one of the letters received from readers this question is asked, "Why are not all persons healed instantly—as Jesus healed?"

The writer of this letter is mistaken in thinking that Jesus always healed instantly. A case in point is the healing of the ten lepers: "as they went they were cleansed." The healing virtue was administered. The healing process became evident later.

Again, Jesus laid His hands on a blind man, then inquired: "What do you see?" The man replied, "I see men as trees walking." His sight was still imperfect. Then Jesus laid His hands on him the second time—"and He saw clearly."

Healing is by degree, based on two conditions. First, the degree of healing virtue administered. Second, the degree of faith that gives action and power to the virtue administered. *"The word preached did not profit them, not being mixed with faith"* (Hebrews 4:2).

It is clearly evident to students of divine healing that sometimes the Spirit of God is ministered to the sick person to a degree that he is manifestly supercharged with the Spirit. Just as a person holds a galvanic battery until the system is charged with electric force, yet no real and final healing takes place until something occurs that releases the faith of the individual; a flash of divine power is observed, a veritable explosion had taken place in the sick person, and the disease is destroyed.

The tangibility of the Spirit of God is the scientific secret of healing.

A diseased woman followed Jesus in a crowd. She knew the law of the Spirit, and had observed that it flowed from the person of Jesus and healed the sick. She was convinced it must also be present in His clothing. So she reasoned: "If I could but touch the hem of His garment I would be made whole." She did so. She was healed of a 12 year sickness that had baffled physicians and left her in poverty (Matthew 9:20).

Jesus was aware that someone had been healed. He turned to ask who it was. Peter said: "See how the multitude is thronging and jostling you." But Jesus answered: "Some one has touched me for I perceive that virtue has gone out of me." Jesus was aware of the outflow (Mark 5:25-34).

The woman was aware of the reception. The healing was a fact. Here faith and the power of God were apparent.

It was a veritable chemical reaction. Healing always is.

I believe the reason people do not see the possibilities of divine healing is that they are not aware of its scientific aspects.

The grace and love of God in the soul opens the nature to God. The Spirit of God resounds as the sunlight and banishes darkness.

Article 9

Jesus Used Science to Heal Afflicted

Mrs. John W. Goudy, of Chico, writes: "How can you speak of divine healing as scientific if healing is through the atonement of Jesus Christ?" How can the matter of atonement and grace be considered scientific?

Atonement through the grace of God is scientific in its application. Jesus used many methods of healing the sick. All were scientific. Science is the discovery of how God does things.

Jesus laid His hands upon the sick in obedience to the law of contact and transmission. Contact of His hands with the sick one permitted the Spirit of God in Him to flow into the sick man.

The sick woman who touched the hem of His garment found that the Spirit emanated from His person. She touched the "hem of His garment" and the Spirit flashed into her. She was made whole. This was a scientific process.

Paul, knowing this law, laid his hands upon handkerchiefs and aprons. The Bible says that when they were laid upon the sick they were healed, and the demons went out of those possessed. Materialists have said this was superstition. It is entirely scientific.

The Spirit of God emanating from Paul transformed the handkerchiefs into "storage batteries" of Holy Spirit power. When they were laid upon the sick they surcharged the body, and healing was the result. (Read Acts 19:12.)

This demonstrates, firstly: The Spirit of God is a tangible substance, heavenly materiality. Secondly: It is capable of being stored in the substance of a handkerchief, as demonstrated in the garments of Jesus, or in the handkerchiefs of Paul. Thirdly: It will transmit power from handkerchiefs to the sick person. Fourthly: Its action in the sick man was so powerful the disease departed. The demonized also were relieved. Fifthly: Both the sick and insane were healed by this method.

While the scientific mind always asks "How and why?" it is not necessary for the soul desiring Christ's touch or blessing to have any knowledge of the scientific process by which healing or salvation is accomplished.

Jesus said: "He that receiveth Me." Men receive Jesus Christ into the heart, as one receives a lover. It is an affectionate relationship. Men obey Him "Because they love Him." They obey Him because they have received Him affectionately...He has become their soul's lover.

His love and power in them redeems them from sin and sickness, and eventually, we are promised in His Word, He will redeem us from death also. Redemption from sin, sickness and death constitutes man's deliverance from bondage to Satan and his kingdom, and establishes the Kingdom of heaven.

Article 10

Jesus Healed Ill by Word

Yesterday we discussed Jesus healing by the laying on of hands. Today we will examine into Jesus healing by the word of command, and other methods.

"They brought to him a man sick of the palsy, lying on a bed: and Jesus seeing their faith," the faith of those who brought the man as well as that of the man himself, *"said... Son, be of good cheer; thy sins be forgiven thee"* (Matthew 9:2-3).

The scribes said: *"This man (Jesus) blasphemeth."* Jesus met this opposition by saying: "Is it not as easy to say, Thy sins be forgiven thee; as to say, Arise and walk? But that ye may know that the Son of Man hath power...to forgive sins, I command, Arise and walk."

The man arose and walked. No hands were laid on this man. There was no external ministry of any kind. Jesus exercised His authority over disease. He commanded. The man was healed.

They brought a man dumb, possessed of a devil. When the devil was cast out the dumb spake. The people wondered. This also is His exercise of spiritual authority (Matthew 9:32). When Jesus commanded the power of God entered and ejected the demon.

At Capernaum a centurion came saying: "my servant lieth at home sick of the palsy, grievously tormented." Jesus said: "I will come and heal him." The centurion answered: "Not so. Speak the word only. It is enough." And Jesus said, "Go home. It is done." The record shows the servant was healed (Matthew 8:5-13).

Many have laughed at the idea of men being healed long distances from the one who ministers in Jesus' Name. But here is a clear case, and the God anointed may still command God's power (Matthew 3:15). To the needy distance is no barrier.

I now present mass healing. Four times it is recorded in the Gospels that "He healed multitudes." "There went out a virtue from Him and He healed them all." There was no personal touch.

This was a divine outflow, an outgoing of healing power. It flamed out of Jesus, and all were healed.

God is not confined to methods. Heaven bows to the soul with faith anywhere, under any circumstances. "Whosoever will, let him take of the water of life freely."

Again Jesus said, "If two of you agree on Earth as touching anything they shall ask, it shall be done for them." "Ask and ye shall receive," said Jesus (Matthew 18:19; 7:7-8).

The Apostle James gave command that elders of the church should pray for the sick and anoint them with oil. Olive oil is the symbol of the healing spirit. This is a command; "Pray for the sick that they may be healed" (James 5:14-16).

Where? Anywhere.

When? Forever. As long as Jesus Christ reigns in Heaven. As long as men on Earth have faith in Him.

The voice of Jesus still is heard saying: "Whatsoever ye shall ask in My Name, that will I do" (John 14:13). "Ask, seek, knock, find Jesus." "All things are possible to God," and all things are possible to him that believeth (Matthew 17:20).

Article 11

The Truth About Divine Healing

Divine healing through prayer is as old as the race of man. The first book of the Bible, Genesis, records the healing of the wives of a heathen king in response to the prayer of Abraham.

The second book of the Bible, Exodus, gives us the terms of a distinctive covenant between the nation of Israel and Jehovah Rophi, i.e.—"The Lord thy Healer."

In this covenant God not only agreed to heal the people when sick, but not to permit the sicknesses of Egypt to touch them. Its terms are: *"If thou wilt diligently hearken to the voice of the Lord thy God, and wilt do that which is right in his sight, and wilt give ear to his commandments and keep all his statutes"*—on this condition Jehovah agrees,—*"I will put (permit) none of these diseases upon thee which I have brought upon the Egyptians: for I am the Lord, that healeth thee"* (Exodus 15:26).

Under this covenant the nation, 12-tribed, lived without doctors or medicine for 450 years, until the nation of Israel had an army of 1,100,000, and Judah an army of 500,000. Figuring on the same basis as the number of Americans in the army during the World War, this would give Israel a combined population of between 25 and 30 million.

King David gives the most extraordinary report that history records. David says: *"There was not one feeble person among their tribes"* (Psalm 105:37).

Such historic data should go far to convince the world of our day that an absolute trust in God is not only a safe policy, but a most scientific guarantee of national health.

In this connection we must examine Israel's constitution as it was made the basis of national health. Its basic principles were the ten commandments. It contained a law in which Jehovah held perpetual title to the land. Thirdly: A credit and mortgage statute. Fourthly: Distribution of surplus wealth statute. Fifthly: The most extraordinary labor law ever written. Sixthly: An absolutely equitable tax law by which every citizen paid one-tenth of his increase.

For keeping this constitution Jehovah guaranteed the nation against wars, pestilence, poverty, destructive droughts, labor disputes, and lastly; "I will take sickness away from the midst of thee" (Deuteronomy 28).

The broad scope of divine healing in Israel is the basis of all faith in God for healing, and was the foundation of the ministry of Jesus Christ, Israel's redeemer and the world's Savior.

Article 12

The Truth About Divine Healing

(continued)

Israel had been kept free of disease for 450 years through divine healing. Outside of Israel there was no divine healing. No other religion in the world possessed healing power. There is not a single instance of this power in India, Egypt, China nor Africa.

The Hebrews alone from Abraham onward exhibited the power of healing at this time. Later, knowledge of Israel's God and His power to heal disease spread through the nations of the world.

The prophets of Israel were marvelous men of God. At their word empires rose and fell. Life and death obeyed their will. Earth and sky answered their call. Before their eyes future history marched with events of the present. No men of any other nation equaled them. No Biblothoan of any other nation compared with their Holy Scriptures.

Christ came as God's gift to Israel, and Israel only. To Judah, the remnant of Israel, He came. Despite all that has been written and imagined of miracles in His childhood, there is not a particle of evidence that He performed any miracles until, at Cana of Galilee, He turned water into wine. The Bible states this miracle was the beginning of miracles by Jesus.

Jesus performed no public ministry until He was 30. The law of Moses forbade it. So we read that when Jesus was about 30 He came to John the Baptist, and was baptized.

His baptism was His dedication of Himself to the Heavenly Father. He dedicated body, soul and spirit. To John He said: "into all righteousness."

He was dedicating Himself to God to reveal the righteousness of God. Jesus' dedication was wholly unselfish.

But His dedication in itself was not sufficient to qualify Him to reveal God. His humanity must be submerged in the Holy Spirit.

As He was baptized in Jordan, this took place.

Now he must be tested. He was led of the Holy Spirit into the wilderness to be tempted by Satan. This was to find if His dedication was a fact, or if He would fall under the 40-day test.

Three temptations were applied. Firstly, a psychological temptation to His mind, love of acclaim. Secondly, a spiritual temptation applied to His spirit, that He might by a simple acknowledgment of Satan "secure all the kingdoms of the world." When He conquered, the natural result took place in Himself: "He came forth in the power of the Spirit."

Article 13

The Truth About Divine Healing

(continued)

Jesus was tempted 40 days. Three temptations were presented. Firstly, physical hunger; secondly, psychological—the love of acclaim; thirdly, spiritual—Satan offered Him all the kingdoms of the world for the acknowledgement of his superiority. Jesus rebuked Satan and drove him from His presence.

Having overcome, the consciousness of inherent power was radiant in Him. "He returned in the power of the Spirit" (Luke 4).

Jesus now makes the next advance. He proclaims His platform. Returning to Nazareth, He boldly declares: "The Spirit of the Lord is upon me. (1) He has anointed Me to preach the gospel to the poor; (2) He hath sent Me to heal the broken-hearted, (3) to proclaim liberty to the captive, (4) recovering of sight to the blind; (5) to set at liberty them that are bruised, (6) to preach the acceptable year of the Lord."

No more waiting for the release of the year of Jubilee. Jesus Christ the Eternal Jubilee was at hand to save and heal.

Jesus' ministry of healing and the marvelous faith in God He exhibited in miracle working form were no accident. Miracles must be His breath, for 800 years before His birth the prophet Isaiah had proclaimed: *"He will come and save you. Then the eyes of the blind shall be opened, and the ears of the deaf shall be unstopped. Then shall the lame man leap as an hart, and the tongue of the dumb sing"* (Isaiah 35:4-6).

So to the Savior of the world He must be forever the miracle worker of the ages; the death destroyer; the finality of the revelation of the majesty, power and mercy of God.

Jesus! The very Name was a miracle. The angel announced it.

Jesus' birth was a miracle.

His wisdom was a miracle.

His life was a miracle.

His teachings were miraculous.

He lived and walked in the realm of the miraculous. He made miracles common. His death was a miracle.

His resurrection was a miracle.

His appearances after death were miraculous. His ascension was a staggering miracle.

His pouring out of the Spirit on the day of Pentecost was the outstanding miracle. It was the one event in which His whole Saviorhood climaxed. Out of Heaven was given to His followers the Spirit of the Eternal, to do in them all it had done in Him. Sin, sickness and death were doomed.

He came as a roaring tempest, as tongues of fire crowning "the 120" as the living Eternal Spirit entering into them. He proclaimed His triumphant entry into man through speaking in languages they knew not.

His deity had lifted them into His realm, transfigured, transformed, transmuted.

Article 14

The Truth About Divine Healing

Jesus having announced His platform, proceeded to demonstrate its practicability. In Matthew 4:23 we read: *"Jesus went about all Galilee, teaching in their synagogues, and preaching the gospel of the kingdom, and healing all manner of sickness and all manner of disease among the people."*

First, teaching; second, preaching; third, healing the sick. The eternal pattern of real Christian ministry. The multitudes overwhelmed him. He then appointed the 12 apostles, commissioned and empowered them to do as He had done.

Luke 9:1-2 says: *"Then he called his twelve disciples together, and gave them power and authority over all devils, and to cure diseases. And he sent them to preach the kingdom of God, and heal the sick."*

Soon they, too, were thronged by the multitudes, and Jesus was compelled to make a more extensive provision. This He did by the calling and sending forth of the 70.

Luke 10 says: *"The Lord appointed other seventy also, and sent them two by two...into every city...whither he himself would come."* They were the advance guard, the heralds of His coming.

In commissioning the 70, He reversed the order, and commanded, "Go into the cities roundabout and heal the sick that are therein, and say, The kingdom of God is come nigh to you."

To the 12 He had said: "Preach and heal." To the 70 He said: "Heal the sick and then preach."

One day the disciples came to Jesus and reported: "We saw one casting out devils in Thy Name, and we forbade him, because he followed not us." Jesus said, "Forbid him not." This man was not regular. He was an independent.

This now made 84 who were healing the sick during the earth-life of Jesus: Jesus, the 12, the 70, and the man who "followed not us." There is no Scriptural evidence of any others being authorized to heal until after the resurrection.

His death, his resurrection and His ministry for 40 days in Galilee after He rose from the dead followed.

And now Jesus breaks all barriers to the ministry of healing by making healing power and healing ministry the right of every believer on Him.

The hour of His ascension is at hand. He issues His final instructions. It is His last word on Earth. *"Go ye into all the world, and preach the gospel to every creature...And these signs shall follow them that believe; In my name shall they cast out devils; they shall speak with new tongues;"* and lastly, *"...they shall lay hands on the sick, and they shall recover"* (Mark 16:16-18). And so healing was made a universal blessing forever.

Finally, lest this wondrous power should be lost, it was included as one of the gifts of the Spirit.

In 1 Corinthians 12:8-12, we find enumerated the gifts of the Spirit. Heaven's inducements that "the church His body" should be qualified and empowered forever to carry on all the ministry of Jesus, and thus be a perpetual presence and power for salvation from sin and sickness.

"To one is given by the Spirit the word of wisdom; to another the word of knowledge...to another faith...to another the gifts of healing...to another the working of miracles; to another prophecy; to another discerning of spirits; to another divers kinds of tongues; to another the interpretation of tongues."

And lest we be negligent, we are reminded that Jesus Christ is the same yesterday, today and forever.

Article 15

The Truth About Divine Healing

In order to be fully informed on the question of divine healing, let us study this question as part of the fully rounded development and life of Jesus.

In beginning His revelation of the life of God for and in man, Jesus chose the Order of Nature as the realm of His first demonstration. (1) Jesus turned the water into wine. (2) He stilled the waves. (3) He walked on water. These revelations of power over nature each surpassed the other.

Then Jesus astounded His followers by turning to the creative life of God. He fed the multitude by an act of creative power when he created fish and bread to feed 5,000.

This shows the distinction between healing and miracle. Miracles are creative. Healing is a restoration of what has been.

Jesus now advances into a new sphere, the Order of Sickness. Here He meets the mind of the other that must be conformed to His. (1) Jesus heals Peter's wife's mother. This is first degree healing. (2) Jesus meets the blind man and heals him. This is second degree healing. (3) The lepers are healed. Healing in the third degree.

Again Jesus enters the creative realm and creates eyes in a man born blind. Blindness from birth is evidence of an unfinished creation of the eyes. The creative process was not complete. Jesus stooped, took dust from the road, spat upon it and put it on the man's eyes. In so doing He finished a work of creation—the man saw.

Now Jesus again advances. This time He chooses the Order of Death. (1) He raised the daughter of Jairus, dead a few minutes. This is the first degree. (2) Jesus meets a funeral procession coming out of the city of Nain. He commands the young man to live, "and he sat up." This man was dead many hours. This is the second degree. (3) His friend Lazarus is dead four days. His body is in a state of decomposition. Jesus commands Lazarus to come forth. He that was dead arose. This was the third degree.

Now Jesus again steps into the creative realm and announces His coming death. He declares of life: *"I have power to lay it down, and I have power to take it again"* (John 10:18).

Through this chain of successive abandonments to God we discover the soul-steps of Jesus. Every step was taken with reliance on the Word of God as the all-sufficient guide.

Jesus took the promises of God in the Scriptures, and permitted them to work out in His own soul. Therefore His promises to us are not made on His own speculation, but because of His soul's discovery of the Mind of God. But He did not let it rest there. He took each discovered promise and worked it out.

He discovered the promise of supply and fed the multitude. He discovered healing power and made the blind to see and the deaf to hear, the lame to walk. He discovered the promise of "man the master," when anointed of God, and He stilled the waves, and turned the water into wine, of life ever present and He raised Lazarus and the widow's son, of life everlasting and He rose from the dead.

He gave His promises as discovered and demonstrated truth and tells us these things shall be ours, as we are lifted by the Spirit into the God realm, the Christ conscious realm.

But it is the one real thing among the myriads of life's illusions, and contains in itself man's future hope, and his transcendent glory. Herein is the true dominion of man.

Article 16

The Truth About Divine Healing

We have followed Jesus through the continued ascents of His earthly career. Jesus has developed in faith and knowledge and in "favor with God and man" at every step. If we were to stop at this point and refuse to follow Him to the throne of the universe we would miss the whole purpose of His life. Divine healing and every other outflow of His holy soul would be beggared and perverted if we failed here.

Christianity is not a mere philosophy. It is more. It is very much more. Christianity is not simply obedience to beautiful commandments. Christianity is not only the acceptance of glorious promises.

Christianity is a divine content. Christianity is a heavenly dynamite. Christianity is the ultimate of all consciousness of God. Christianity is wholly supernatural. Christianity comes down from Heaven from the innermost heart of the glorified Christ. Christianity is in the innermost and uttermost of man declaring: *"I am he that liveth, and was dead; and, behold, I am alive for evermore, Amen; and have the keys of hell and of death"* (Revelation 1:18). Christianity is the spotless descent of God into man, and the sinless ascent of man into God. The Holy Spirit is the agent by whom it is accomplished.

The significance of Jesus' death was not in His sacrifice only, but also in His achievement in the regions of death. He took death captive. He liberated those who, in death, awaited His coming and deliverance. Jesus took them in triumph from the control of the angel of death and transferred them to His own glory.

David prophesied: "He ascended upon high. He led captivity captive. He gave gifts unto men, even unto the rebellious also, that they might know the mercy of the Lord" (Psalm 68:18).

Peter declared: *"He went and preached unto the spirits in prison...when once the longsuffering of God waited in the days of Noah, while the Ark was a-preparing."* And lest we fail to comprehend the source of His ministry in death Peter says again: *"For this cause was the gospel preached also to them that are dead, that they might be judged according to men in the flesh, but live according to God in the Spirit"* (1 Peter 3:20; 4:6).

It was this marvelous experience of Jesus in death ministry that produced in His soul the glory-power of the resurrection. Not only His personal triumph over death but the release of those held in death's chains.

Article 17

The Truth About Divine Healing
(continued)

In all the universe there was none with such triumph in His spirit as Jesus possessed when death's bars were broken. When He with power heretofore unknown, commanded His followers, saying: *"All power is given unto me in heaven and in earth"* (Matthew 28:18).

Glorifying in this amazing ascent in consciousness, He instantly found the "eleven" and breathed on them, and saith unto them, "Receive ye the Holy Ghost." This was Jesus' endeavor to lift them into the same soul triumph that He enjoyed.

The ascension was a further advance in triumphant consciousness, climaxed by His presentation of Himself at the throne of God, where Peter says He *"received from the Father the promise of the Holy Ghost"* (Acts 2:33). This was Jesus' divine equipment as World Savior. From then on He was empowered to administer the transcendent glory-power to all who would receive—divine healing, saving power, the empowering of the Christian soul from on high is the pouring forth of the Holy Spirit by Jesus Christ, High Priest of heaven.

That we might realize the uttermost of ultimate transcendence of the soul of Jesus in glory, hear Him declare anew; *"I am he that liveth, and was dead; and behold, I am alive for evermore, Amen; and have the keys of hell and of death."*

Who would not rejoice to place himself in the hands of such a Savior and physician? Answering forever the world's questions: "Is He able to heal? Does He ever heal? Does He always heal?" To all we boldly say—"Yes. He is Jesus triumphant, eternal, omnipotent."

Article 18

The Truth About Divine Healing

The transcendent miracle of all history had happened. Jerusalem was throbbing with its power. Men from every nation had congregated there. The Holy Spirit had come. Jesus had been crucified.

The world thought it had heard the last of Him. He had healed the sick, raised the dead, cast out demons from the insane, delivered epileptics, opened the eyes of the blind, filled the nation of Israel with the joy of it.

Jerusalem had become a world-center for travelers. The scholarship of the world was represented. All had heard that the ministry of Jesus was not only philosophic but powerful.

Now He was crucified and a shock went through the soul of the world. Why destroy one who had brought such light and blessing? A soul tremor ran through the city. Something extraordinary was taking place at the temple. A miracle of surpassing wonder had occurred. Fire had fallen from heaven on the followers of Jesus. A cyclone had swept the meeting house.

Galilean fishermen and tax gatherers, the mother of Jesus, and others noted for saintliness had been filled with power from on high. Stranger than these, Galileans were addressing the great multitude in its native tongues. Something had come out from heaven. It possessed "the hundred and twenty" who had watched in the upper room.

A shout arose. The multitude cried: "Explain this phenomenon. What is it? How hear we every man speaking in his own language. Are not all these speakers Galileans?"

Peter made a sign for silence: "This is that which was spoken by the prophet Joel," he said. "I will pour out my Spirit. Your sons and daughters shall become prophets. Your young men shall see visions. Your old men shall dream dreams. My Spirit will come upon your servants, both men and women, they shall become prophets also."

"Jesus whom ye crucified hath poured out this wonder. It came upon us from heaven. We are filled with God. All that He did we shall do. His ministry is now perpetual. He hath reproduced Himself in us. We have divine assurance. We speak with authority. He now lives in us."

This is the soul secret of Christianity, the point of departure from any other religion; power from on high. Jesus said: "It is best for you that I go away. If I do I will send the Holy Spirit upon you" (John 16:7).

All is now fulfilled. He had come. Real Christianity was now visible. It could be seen as well as felt. It was the birthday of the Spirit. It was currents of power, divine magnetism, heavenly virtue, God in man, miracles perpetuated forever; wisdom, knowledge, faith, healing, miracles, prophecy, discerning of spirits, tongues, interpretation of tongues. Christ in you, the hope of glory.

Article 19

The Truth About Divine Healing

Jesus called His 12 disciples and commanded upon them power and authority to cast out devils and heal disease (Luke 9). He superseded this by declaring: "If ye ask ANYTHING in My Name it shall be done" (John 16:23).

The first was a "limited power of attorney." The second unlimited. This unlimited "power of attorney" was authorized before His crucifixion. It was to become effective when the Holy Ghost came.

On the day of Pentecost this "power of attorney" was made fully operative. The Spirit came. First, legally, they had His Word. Then, vitally, He sent His Spirit.

Peter and John instantly grasped the significance of the Name. Passing into the temple they met a beggar-cripple. He was 40 years old and was crippled from birth. Peter commanded: *"In the name of Jesus Christ of Nazareth, rise up and walk."* Heaven's lightning struck the man. He leapt to his feet—whole.

A multitude rushed up. They demanded: "In what name, by what power, have ye done this?" Peter and John replied "In the Name of Jesus Christ of Nazareth, whom ye slew, whom God raised up" (Acts 3:6-15).

Matchless Name! The secret of power was in it. When they used the Name the power struck. The dynamite of Heaven exploded.

Peter and John were hustled off to jail. The Church prayed for them "in the Name." They were released. They went to the church. The entire church prayed that signs and wonders might be done. How did they pray? In "the Name." They used it legally. The vital response was instantaneous. The place was shaken as by an earthquake. Tremendous Name!

Jesus commanded: "Go into all the world." What for? To proclaim the Name. To use the Name. To baptize believers. How? In the Name. Amazing Name. In it was concentrated the combined authority resident in the Father, the Son and the Holy Ghost. Almighty Name.

The apostles used the Name. It worked. The deacons at Samaria used the Name. The fire flashed. Believers everywhere, forever, were commanded to use it. The Name detonated around the world.

More Bibles are sold today than any 100 books. Why? The Name is in it. It's finality—at the Name of Jesus every knee shall bow and every tongue confess!

Prayer in this Name gets answers. The Moravians prayed. The greatest revival till that time hit the world. Finney prayed. America rocked with the power. Hudson Taylor prayed. China's Inland Mission was born. Evans Roberts prayed seven years. The Welsh revival resulted.

An old Negro*, Seymore of Azusa, prayed for five hours a day for three and a half years. He prayed seven hours a day for one and a half more years. Heaven's fire fell over the world, and the most extensive revival of real religion in this century resulted.

Article 20

The Truth About Divine Healing

(continued)

Who has authority to pray for the sick? Is this holy ministry only given to the few? Is it a ministry to all Christians or to the clergy only?

Jesus said: "If ye shall ask anything in my Name I will do it, Ask, it shall be given; seek, ye shall find; knock, it shall be opened. These signs shall follow them that believe, in my Name they (the believers) cast out demons. They shall speak with new tongues...They shall lay hands on the sick and they shall recover."

The apostles were commanded to go into all the world—to MAKE BELIEVERS in every section. The signs were to follow the BELIEVERS, not the apostles only.

This was heaven's characteristic. It was the trademark of the Christ on HIS goods. It was the brand, the stamp burned into the soul of the BELIEVER with heavenly fire.

Baptism in the Spirit of Jesus was Christ reproducing Himself in the BELIEVER. To what extent was this reproduction to be a fact? We contend that Jesus taught that the BELIEVER was empowered by the Spirit's incoming and indwelling so that he was Christ's ambassador on earth (2 Corinthians 5:20).

Then he must perform Christ's most holy ministries to sinful and sick just as Jesus Himself would do.

If this is true then the believer is a priest in every respect.

The believer must then perform Christ's priestly ministry.

The believer then is expected to heal the sick. Jesus said: "He should lay his hands on the sick and heal them." They were not to die, they were to recover. They were healed through the believer by the power supplied from heaven by Jesus Christ to the believer.

We desire to ask should the believer-priest also forgive sins or pronounce absolution to the penitent seeker after God. We believe he should. We are sure that it is the privilege of the modern Church to see this tremendous truth and privilege that was purposed by the Lord to be the glory of Christianity.

Jesus said the believer should cast out devils. He believes he should. He does it. The devil is ejected from further possession.

How did he do it? By the exercise of the bestowed power as Christ's believer-priest. He exercises spiritual authority over the devil in the candidate and frees him from control.

In this he has performed the Christ function. The sick likewise are healed through the believer-priest. In this also he performs another Christ ministry. Then how about sin? Why does not the believer-priest by the same spiritual power and authority destroy the consciousness of sin in the soul and pronounce absolution for sins that are past.

We are asking these questions in order to discover what the believer's ministry as Christ's representative is.

We are not alone in our faith that the believer should perform the full ministry of Christ.

"I am a priest."—*Browning.*

"The early Church lost its power when it lost sight of its high priestly office."—*Bishop Brent.*

"The church needs to realize in new ways the inherent priesthood of Christian believers."—*Lambeth Conference of Anglican Bishops, 1906.*

"The authority to pronounce absolution and remission of sins that are past and fulfill the aspirations of the soul for the future, I believe to be spiritual and not ecclesiastical and traditional, and to belong equally to everyone who has received such absolution and remission, and such gifts of the spiritual life."—*Lyman Abbot.*

"The experience of the free Church confirms what we should expect from study of the New Testament and modern psychology that the priesthood of all believers rest on sounder evidence than the priesthood of some believers."—*Rev. Dr. Grover, of Cambridge.*

"With the Quaker it is not that there is no clergy, BUT THAT THERE IS NO LAITY, for we are all priests unto the Highest."—*John H. Graham in "The Faith of the Quaker."*

"I am ever in the presence not only of a Great Power or a Great Lawgiver, but a Great Healer."—*Lyman Abbot.*

Therefore every believer on Jesus Christ is authorized by the Lord to do as He has done, assured of Christ's assistance.

"Greater things than these shall ye do because I go unto the Father," said Jesus. "The Lord working with them by signs following. Lo, I am with you always even unto the end of the world" (John 14:12; Mark 16:20; Matthew 28:20).

Article 21

The Truth About Divine Healing

The miracles of Jesus have been the battle ground of the centuries. Men have devoted their lives in an effort to break down faith in miracles. More believe in miracles today than ever before.

Psuedo-science declares miracles impossible. Yet the biggest men in the scientific world are believers in the supernatural and know that miracles are the discovery, utilization and application of spiritual laws and powers of which the material scientist knows nothing.

The miracle realm is man's natural realm. He is by creation the companion of the miracle working God. Sin dethroned man from the miracle working realm, but through grace he is coming into his own.

It has been hard for us to grasp the principles of this life of faith. In the beginning man's spirit was the dominant force in the world; when he sinned his mind became dominant; sin dethroned the spirit and crowned the intellect. But grace is restoring the spirit to its place of dominion, and when man comes to realize this, he will live in the realm of the supernatural without effort.

No longer will faith be a struggle, but a normal living in the realm of God. The spiritual realm places men where communion with God is a normal experience.

Miracles are then his native breath. No one knows to what extent the mind and the spirit can be developed.

This is not the power of mind over matter, but the power of the spirit over both mind and matter. If the body is kept in fine fettle there is almost no limitation to man's development.

We have been slow to come to a realization that man is a spirit and that his spirit nature is his basic nature. We have sought to educate him along educational lines, utterly ignoring the spiritual, so man has become a self-centered, self-seeking being.

Man has lost his sense of relationship and responsibility toward God and man. This makes him lawless. We cannot ignore the spiritual side of man without magnifying the intellectual and physical; to do this without the restraint of the spirit is to unleash sin, and give it dominance over the whole man.

There must be a culture and envelopment of the spiritual nature to a point where it can enjoy fellowship with the Father-God. It is above mind as God is above nature.

Man's intellect is ever conscious of supernatural forces that he cannot understand.

He senses the spirit-realm and longs for its freedom and creative power but cannot enter until changed from self and sin; the spirit enthroned and in action rather than the intellect—spirit above BOTH MIND AND MATTER.

Article 22

The Truth About Divine Healing

Dr. Chapman said just before his passing: "I believe the gift of healing is a far greater divine attainment than the gift of the evangelist." No wonder Professor A.B. Bruce said in his "Miraculous Elements of the Gospel" cures should be as common as conversion, and that Christ's healing miracles are signs that disease does not belong to the true order of nature and are but a prophesy that the true order must be restored to us."

There is no question but what there is a universal longing for such a faith for the healing and quickening of our mortal bodies as this. Professor Bruce well expressed it in his Union Seminary lectures which have been a power ever since their utterance.

"What missionary would not be glad to be endowed with power to heal diseases, conferred by Jesus Christ on his disciples when He sent them on their Galilean mission. I know the feeling well. I spent part of my apprenticeship as a preacher as a missionary in a once prosperous but now decaying village in the west of Scotland, filled with an impoverished and exceptionally disease-stricken population. There daily I saw sights which awakened at once intense sympathy and involuntary loathing."

"There were cases of cancer, strange and demoniac-like forms of insanity, children in arms 20 years old, with the face of a full grown person and a body not larger than an infant's. I returned home offtimes sick at heart and unable to take food."

"What would I have not given to have had for an hour the charisma of the Galilean evangelists! And how gladly would I have gone that day not to speak the accustomed words about a Father in heaven ever ready to receive His prodigal children, but to put an end to pain, raise the dying, and to restore to soundness shattered reason. Or had I found some day, on visiting the suffering that they had been healed, according to their report, in answer to the prayer of some saintly friend, I should have been too thankful to have been at all skeptical. I should have seen how He Himself took our infirmities and bare our sicknesses, and we were to represent God whose supreme purpose is, as Jesus so clearly showed, to forgive all our sins and heal all our diseases..."

The place of the gift of healing in the great message of Jesus' full and complete salvation has been voiced in prophetic foregleams all through the Christian centuries as truly as the coming Messiah by the mouth of the prophets before the appearance of Jesus.

During recent years it has broken forth in many quarters with most unusual power. As far back as 1884, Rev. R.E. Stanton, D.D., a leading Presbyterian clergyman, who at one time was moderator of the General Assembly of the Presbyterian Church, wrote in a little volume entitled "Gospel Parallelisms" these remarkable words:

"It is my aim to show that the Atonement of Christ lays the foundation equally for deliverance from sin and deliverance from disease; that complete provision has been made for both; that in the exercise of faith under the conditions prescribed, we have the same reason to believe that the body may be delivered from sickness as we have that the soul may be delivered from sin; in short, that both branches of the deliverance stand on the same ground, and that it is necessary to include both in any true conception of what the gospel offers to mankind."

The atoning sacrifice of Christ covers the physical as well as the spiritual needs of the race."

Article 23

The Truth About Divine Healing

1. Healing by God, through faith and prayer, was practiced by the patriarchs. "Abraham prayed unto God, and God healed Abimelech, and his wife, and his maidservants, and they bare children" (Genesis 20:17).

2. God made a covenant of healing with the children of Israel. A covenant is an indissoluble agreement, and can never be annulled.

   God tested the nation at the waters of Marah and made a covenant with them, known as the Covenant of Jehovah-Rophi (The Lord, Thy Healer).

   a. "If thou wilt diligently hearken to the voice of the Lord thy God,

b. And wilt do that which is right in His sight,
c. And give ear to His commandments,
d. And keep His statutes,

I will put none of these diseases upon thee, which I have brought upon the Egyptians. For I am the Lord that healeth thee" (Exodus 15:26).

3. David rejoiced in the knowledge of this covenant: *"Bless the Lord, O my soul: and all that is within me, bless his holy name. Bless the Lord, O my soul, and forget not all his benefits: Who forgiveth all thine iniquities; who healeth all thy diseases"* (Psalm 103:1-3).
4. Isaiah proclaimed it. *"Then the eyes of the blind shall be opened, and the ears of the deaf shall be unstopped. Then shall the lame man leap as an hart, and the tongue of the dumb sing"* (Isaiah 35:5-6).
5. Jesus made healing one of the planks of His platform.

   a. *"The Spirit of the Lord is upon me, because he hath anointed me to preach the gospel to the poor.*
   b. *He hath sent Me to heal the broken hearted,*
   c. *To preach deliverance to the captives,*
   d. *And recovering of sight to the blind,*
   e. *To set at liberty them that are bruised,*
   f. *To preach the acceptable year of the lord"* (Luke 4:18).

6. Jesus ministered healing to the sick. "And Jesus went about all Galilee, teaching in their synagogues, and preaching the gospel of the kingdom, and healing all manner of sickness and all manner of disease among the people" (Matthew 4:23).
7. Healing is in the atonement of Christ. See Matthew 8:1-7, especially verse 17.

   a. Healing of the leper, Matthew 8:1-4.
   b. Healing of the centurion's servant, Matthew 8:5-13.
   c. Healing of Peter's wife's mother, Matthew 8:14-15.
   d. Healing of the multitude, Matthew 8:16.
   e. His reason for these healings, verse 17: "That it might be fulfilled which was spoken by Isaiah the prophet, saying, Himself took our infirmities and bare our sicknesses."

8. Jesus bestowed the power to heal upon His disciples. "Then He called His twelve disciples together and gave them power and authority over all devils and to cure diseases. And He sent them to preach the Kingdom of God, and to heal the sick...and they departed, and went through the towns preaching the gospel, and healing everywhere" (Luke 9:1-3, 6).

9. He likewise bestowed power to heal upon the seventy. "And after these things the Lord appointed other seventy also, and sent them two and two before His face into every city and place whither He Himself would come...Heal the sick that are therein, and say unto them, the kingdom of God is come nigh unto you" (Luke 10:1-9).

Article 24

The Truth About Divine Healing

(continued)

10. He said unto them, "Go ye into all the world, and preach the gospel to every creature. He that believeth and is baptized shall be saved; but he that believeth not shall be damned. And these signs shall follow them that believe: In My Name they shall cast out devils; they shall speak with new tongues; they shall take up serpents; and if they drink any deadly thing it shall not hurt them; they shall lay hands on the sick, and they shall recover" (Mark 16:15-18).

11. And lest healing should be lost to the Church, He perpetuated it forever as one of the nine gifts of the Spirit. "To one is given by the Spirit the word of wisdom; to another the word of knowledge by the same Spirit; to another faith by the same Spirit; to another the gifts of healing by the same Spirit; to another the working of miracles; to another prophecy; to another discerning of spirits; to another divers kinds of tongues; to another interpretation of tongues" (1 Corinthians 12:8-10).

12. The Church was commanded to practice it. "Is any among you afflicted? Let him pray. Is any merry? Let him sing psalms. Is any sick among you? Let him call for the elders of the church, and let them pray over him, anointing him with oil in the name of the Lord; and the prayer of faith shall save the sick, and the Lord shall raise him up; and if he have committed sins, they shall be forgiven him. Confess your faults one to another, and pray one for another, that ye may be healed. The effectual fervent prayer of a righteous man availeth much" (James 5:13-16).

13. The unchangeableness of God's eternal purpose is thereby demonstrated. "Jesus Christ the same yesterday, and today and forever" (Hebrews 13:8). "I am the Lord, I change not" (Malachi 3:6).

God always was the healer. He is the Healer still, and will ever remain the healer. Healing is for you. Jesus healed "All that came to Him." He never turned anyone away. He never said: "It is not God's will to heal you," or that it was better for the individual to remain sick, or that they were being perfected in character through the sickness. He healed them all, thereby demonstrating forever God's unchangeable will concerning sickness and healing.

Have you need of healing? Pray to God in the Name of Jesus Christ to remove the disease. Command it to leave you, as you would sin. Assert your divine authority and refuse to have it. Jesus purchased your freedom from sickness as He purchased your freedom from sin.

"His own self bare our sins in His own body on the tree, that we, being dead to sins, should live unto righteousness; by whose stripes ye were healed" (1 Peter 2:24).

Therefore, mankind has a right to health, as he has a right to deliverance from sin. If you do not have it, it is because you are being cheated out of your inheritance. It belongs to you. In the Name of Jesus Christ go after it and get it.

If your faith is weak, call for those who believe, and to whom the prayer of faith and the ministry of healing has been committed.

Psalm 91; Isaiah 35; Matthew 8 and 9; Mark 16; Luke 11; John 9; Acts 3, 4, 8, 9, 10 and 26; 1 Corinthians 12 and 13

All that Jesus was to the world He purposed that the Church of Christ should be. First, He blessed the world through His own physical personality. Second, He established a physical body composed of many members, joined in one by the Spirit of God.

When He established the second Body, the Church, He never intended that it should be of lesser authority or of lesser power than the first. It was His real purpose that the second Body, the Church, should exercise and fully accomplish all that the first had done.

Dr. Lake, February 18, 1917

32

Sin in the Flesh

I want to bring you tonight a message taken from Romans 8:3. I will read you the first verse:

> **There is therefore now no condemnation to them which are in Christ Jesus, who walk not after the flesh, but after the Spirit. For the law of the Spirit of life in Christ Jesus hath made me free from the law of sin and death. For what the law could not do, in that it was weak through the flesh, God sending his own Son in the likeness of sinful flesh, *and for sin*, condemned sin in the flesh [Romans 8:1-3].**

For a long time I wondered what these two expressions meant—sin in the flesh—in the second verse. *"For the law of the Spirit of life in Christ Jesus hath made me free from the law of sin and death."* And then what it meant about that God condemned sin in the flesh.

In the first place, we know that the physical body does not commit sin (1 Corinthians 6:18-20). It may be the instrument or weapon that does the thing, but there is no sin in the physical body itself. Sin lies in the will. If you choose to sin, then you can make your body do it. Now according to the law there isn't any sin except it is performed by a physical act. You can think murder as much as you are a mind to—you are not a murderer in the sight of the law because you thought it. If you speak murder, that lays you liable; but the law recognizes nothing that has not been translated into conduct, into an act.

Now there isn't any sin in your physical body, there is nothing wrong with your body. Your body is all right. It is you, the hidden man of the heart, that makes the body do things that are unseemly and are wrong (Matthew 15:16-20). Then what does He mean by sin in the flesh? For a long time that bothered me. I think I have found a key to it in the 11th verse of this chapter, because it is all one argument. *"But if the Spirit of him that raised up Jesus from the dead dwell in you, he that raised up Christ from the dead shall also quicken your mortal bodies by his Spirit that dwelleth in you."*

He is not talking about the resurrection. He is talking about giving life, healing life, to our physical bodies. Our physical bodies don't need life unless they are sick, do they? That is the conclusion of the argument of Romans 8:1-11—that is a progressive single argument. What is he talking about? He is talking about disease and sickness and the sin that is in the flesh is in the sin of a broken law in your body.

Now sin is breaking the law, some kind of law, and sin in the body is breaking a law of the body. Disease then is dis-ease isn't it? Make it two words: disease, broken law, wrecked ease, ease that has been destroyed. Ease is health. Dis-ease is sickness. There are three kinds of sickness—sickness in the body, sickness in the soul, and sickness in the spirit. The basic sickness is spirit sickness. I venture this: that if you could be healed in your spirit, every last one of you would be well in your bodies. But the whole problem is cleaning a man up in his spirit. Let me change it to business.

If you can become a successful salesman in the spirit, you will put your bodies over. Do you know the place you are whipped first is not in your mind, but in your body. You say, "Oh, my body is so tired." Your body is tired the moment that the spirit is discouraged. Your body breaks down under it. As long as your spirit is triumphant you are a victor and go right on. A man is defeated only when he is defeated in his spirit. Let a man lose courage—and courage is not a product of the intellect. When he loses courage he is whipped, and the only way to put the man on his feet again is to renew a right spirit within him. That isn't the Holy Spirit; it is to renew the spirit that has been defeated and conquered, whipped.

Healing then is in three planes, isn't it? Spirit healing, soul healing, body healing. Basically, the sick person that is sick in body has been sick in spirit quite a little while likely, and after a while it has gotten down into the soul, and passed through that into the body.

I cannot tell you, brethren, what this truth I am telling you now has meant to my life. I now can trace every physical change in my body to a spiritual condition. My body responds to my spirit.

Now beloved, I want to give you something that is of infinite value. Just to illustrate it—I was called to a home to see a man 82 or 83 years of age day before yesterday. He has been sick now two years. He had blood poisoning in his teeth and it went through his whole body, and when a man is past 80 it is bad you know. I went into his presence with a well spirit, a conquering spirit. Now I didn't think of this when I went there. When I went back today I saw the effect. I was there with a triumphant, victorious spirit. His spirit caught the contagion from me. He was whipped. He had sat there in that chair until he was whipped, just defeated. Well, I sat down by his side and began to open the Scriptures, and something in me—this is perfectly Scriptural—out from your inner life, that is, your spirit, that is the inner being—shall flow rivers of living water. Out from my spirit went into his spirit healing for his spirit. I didn't see it because he is a Scotsman, very reticent, didn't respond much; but I knew in me that it had gone into him. I knew that. I talked to him a little while and opened the Word, and then prayed for him and left.

This afternoon his beautiful, lovely, motherly wife, a woman along in years, called me up and said, "He wants to see you again. He is going to come down to the hotel to see you, because he don't think it is right to ask you to come away up here."

Think of that, will you! I said, no, I will go up. When I went into his presence this afternoon I carried into his presence—I discovered it in myself immediately after I left the house that I had carried into his presence— health in my own mind, in my spirit. I had carried a dominating, victorious spirit, and that man responded to it. Do you know what happened in his body? While I sat there and prayed for him, his spirit had become adjusted. The spirit in me received its health from the Lord and I communicated something to his spirit and his spirit made contact. Just as you press the button and turn on light, you contact with God's Spirit, and when it did, healing came down into his body. Why he changed his whole outward demeanor, changed everything about him.

I have been defeated, and I am full of defeat, and that corroding defeat has come down over me and I have lost out; I have broken connection. Did you ever see a battery in an auto corroded with something, and it had eaten off the wires, and the starter didn't move. What is the matter? Something corroded there. You should have kept that clean.

Corroding cares come and get in around your spirit life, and it just covers you and breaks your connection with the Lord. This is true. The real first healing is the healing of your spirit, getting your spirit adjusted to the Lord. The spirit is the part that contacts the Lord. If the spirit is out of harmony and out of condition, and is sort of broken down, you can't get faith for healing, can you? No, you must become adjusted to the Lord.

I said to a young man a little while ago—he was in a desperate condition, required a first-class miracle to touch his life at all. I sat by his side and I said, "If you will accept Jesus Christ as your Savior and confess Him as your Lord, and you receive eternal life, you are healed."

He said, "What do you mean?"

I said, "Just the moment you are born again you are healed." I have never been afraid to promise that to any unsaved person. Why I didn't know that for years. Now I can tell you—the simplest thing in the world—the moment you are born again, eternal life comes into your spirit. That spirit then can come into the closest relationship with the Father, the great Healer, and the life of God then pours down into his spirit, and soul, into his body, and he is immediately touched and made whole.

You cannot get healing for the body, as far as you are personally concerned—somebody else's faith may, but until your spirit is right you cannot get healing for your body. May I call your attention to another thing? Faith is a product of your spirit, not of your intellect. Your intellect does not produce faith. Your knowledge may give you ground for faith, but faith is resident in your spirit.

Joy is something in your spirit. Happiness is something connected with your surroundings. You are happy because of your surroundings. You are joyful because you are in right relation with the Father. Now faith, love, joy, hope, all spring from your spirit being, the hidden man of the heart. All are products of your spiritual life. The reason people do not have rich beautiful faith is because their spirit is denied the privilege of communion and fellowship with the Father. You understand me? You don't read your Bible; you don't pore over it; you don't live in it; you don't spend any time in fellowship with the Father. Consequently your spirit is depleted and weakened. Faith springs out of it, and the faith that grows out of it is a sickly plant. On the other hand, your spirit life is fortified and built up and enriched by communion with the Father and by reading His Word. And your spirit becomes strong and vigorous—there issues from it a faith that is triumphant and creative. I venture to say this: that the men and women who are weak in faith, that once were mighty in faith, are so because they have stopped feeding on the Word of God, and stopped close intimate fellowship with the Father.

Let me say to you with all frankness, brother, that you cannot lose your faith until you have broken your fellowship. Just as long as your fellowship is rich and your spiritual life is as flood tide, faith is triumphant. I have followed that in my own life. For years I did not understand the law that governs it. I see it now. You see here is the thing that is mightily important—that the spirit life in man is kept healthy and vigorous, and it is kept healthy and vigorous by three exercises. There are more ways, but three in particular.

One is feeding on the Word. Second, is a CONTINUAL PUBLIC CONFESSION of what you are and what Jesus is to you. I am not talking of sin: I mean confession of your faith in Christ, of what Christ is to you, of His fullness, His completeness, and His redemption. And the third thing is COMMUNION WITH HIM. Feeding on the Word, confession, and communion. Three simple things, aren't they? And yet they are the things that produce great spiritual life. You do not have it without them.

There are three planes of healing: spiritual, mental, and physical. Now just for a bit I want to call your attention to another very important fact—the relation of your body to your spiritual life. Paul said in 1 Corinthians 9 that he kept his body under, lest haply after he preached to others, he himself would be laid aside—not lost, but laid aside, no longer usable. Why? Because his body had gained the ascendancy over his spiritual life. If you become a glutton, and just live to gratify your appetite by eating and drinking, you will lose out spiritually. But if you will keep your appetite under control and your body under like Paul says he did, your spirit will have a chance to evidence itself.

Now let me state it again. You may be a great spiritual athlete, you may have been a great spiritual athlete, but somewhere you have stopped feeding on the Word. The Word lost its taste and flavor for you. You say, "How can it be?" It is.

I know of preacher after preacher that had great power at one time, but they have lost all joy in the Scripture. How do I know? Well, I know by the way they act. When a man loves a woman, he wants her with him, doesn't he? He doesn't care to go off and spend evenings alone. And when a man loves his Bible you will find the Bible with him, in his arms, somewhere. He has gotten hold of the thing. He is holding it.

When I find a man along in years and his hair is growing gray, I find he loves his Bible. I know that man is fresh in his spirit life. One of the mightiest men I ever fellowshipped with in my life in prayer, when he and I would be together in prayer, sometimes I would open my eyes and look at him, and he would be on his knees with his Bible kissing it. Didn't want anyone to see him. Thought my eyes were closed. He was holding it just as a man holds his wife in his arms and kisses and embraces her, kisses and loves her.

Whenever I reach a place where I lose my appetite for the Book, and rather talk with people than read the Bible, or rather read books about the Bible than to read the Bible, then I know I am backslidden in my spirit.

You can trace the downfall of every spiritual giant that I have ever known in my life to these three things. One of the greatest men this country ever produced—I heard him when that Book was in his hand, when he preached like this, he drove me to my knees—every time I would hear him I would go out and get alone and pray if I could possibly do it. He just battered me and hammered me and drove me into my hole, so to speak; or else he filled me and thrilled me and lifted me. I saw him 20 years later, when his name was on the lips of every man, and I heard him preach, and I noticed that he quoted a good many Scriptures, but he never picked up his Bible; and I noticed he had a theory and philosophy of redemption instead of the old time simple exposition of the Word. And I saw that man whose name was known in every part of the world, with something like 60 churches back of him, in a building that seated 3500, and the building was not half full. He had the greatest gospel soloist that this country has ever produced, but the meeting was as dry and dead as any formal service imaginable. They utterly failed. I said to the singer, who left that field and came with me for a campaign or two. I said, "Charley, what is the matter with him?"

"Well," he says, "I do not know, but he is no more like the man he used to be than anything in the world." There had no sin come into that man's life; his life was just as clean as it had ever been. But here is how it had come; somehow or other he had broken in his spiritual life with the food of the Spirit—the Bible. And the second thing, he used to have the most marvelous prayer life—he didn't have it anymore. And the third thing—in that whole sermon I didn't hear one personal confession. Because he was preaching in a place where personal confession was taboo, people criticized it. If you said anything about yourself and your own experience, the ministers right off the first thing would say, "He is bragging about his own life, isn't he?"

Brother, you will brag about your own life if you have power with God, and you can't help this bragging; you have something to brag about. You really have. You walk in the fulness of the life and fellowship of your spirit with His Spirit, and you have something to talk about, haven't you? Fresh new experiences are coming into you all the time. You are walking in the realm of miracles. I knew that man when he walked in the creative realm of faith. I knew him when he moved down into the purely intellectual realm.

Healing is basically a spiritual thing. The power that heals the sick comes down from God through your spirit, out through your hands into that man or woman. And if you are having the right kind of spiritual fellowship, you will have power with God, and there is no escaping it. But listen, brother, you can't get a powerful current of divine life from a little impoverished wire, can you? And you can't get it when the wire where it connects with you is corroded with world cares. Now we call in the electrician and say to him, "I want you to wire my spirit up with God. I want fresh equipment all the way through." Hallelujah.

You say, I will tell you what I want. I want to be able to stand about 10,000 volts. I want to be wired up to God so that the fullness of His power can pour down through me, through my soul, and out through my hands and voice to the people.

How does that come to you? Simplest thing in the world. Your spirit interlocks with His Spirit without any foreign substance intervening. One day my Reo car stopped right in traffic. A young lady sat with Mrs. Lake and she said, "Let me try it." She worked the accelerator and it wouldn't work.

She said, "Wait a moment." I jumped out of the car and I raised the hood. She said, "I can tell you where it is." She just opened up the distributor, and she said, "One of those points has got a fleck of dirt on it," She brushed it off with her handkerchief and put it on again. The car started right off. That point of the distributor had some little dust, something under it, some little corroding some way that just broke the current, and it was a delicate little thing, it didn't take much.

It doesn't take much to break the connection of your spirit and His. God is a Spirit. You are a spirit. And something breaks the connection and the power no longer flows through. You say you want me to pray for you and I pray for you.

There is no power. What is the matter? Something has broken the connection. The power comes down through the one who prays, but it can't get through your spirit and touch you. Or, there may be something in my spirit, and His Spirit wants to communicate with your spirit, but is hindered by something in my spirit. But suppose you and I are both right in our spirits. You will get your healing as sure as God sits on His throne. *"But if the Spirit of him that raised up Jesus from the dead dwell in you, he that raised up Christ from the dead"* [Romans 8:11] shall send healing through your spirit into your mortal flesh as sure as God is on His throne.

The second thing that must be done continually is, after you have fed on the Word, and your spirit is open to the truth of confession, you can't bottle God up. You can't lock Him up. It has been God's method throughout all the ages to speak to people through those that are in right relation with Himself, and when you are in right relation with Him, the most normal and natural thing is, that He will use you to communicate Himself to others, and so you act as the medium through which He is to pour His message, by song or by testimony or by prayer or by some other means; but you are His medium, you are His testifier, you are His spokesman, you are His instrument through which He is going to work. Beautiful, isn't it?

Now you see what keeps you in perfect communion, because you have to continually get new messages all the time from Him, so you live in perfect fellowship with Him, feeding on His Word, and telling out the things He does for you. And no Christian is safe that hasn't a NOW experience with the Lord, because sickness can come on you and you have no power to throw it off. You have your NOW experience in your spirit, and you are continually in contact, and the spiritual power is coming down and going back and forth continually. Things are coming down and things are going up—from Him to you and you to Him—down through your spirit. You have a beautiful picture: angels ascending and descending. It is the thoughts of God coming down and your thoughts going back. He feeding on you, and you feeding on Him.

Now the relation of your body to your spiritual life is almost an unexplored tableland of possibilities. In Romans 6:12, Paul says, *"Let not sin therefore reign as God in your mortal [death-doomed] body."* Let not sin reign. What is sin? What is sin? It is disease. It is dis-ease. He is not talking about sin, because if there is any sin in you it is not in your body. If there is any sin, it is in your spirit or in your soul, isn't it? It is somewhere active in your thinking processes. But he says, *"Let not sin reign as God in that [death-doomed] body."* Sin is a broken physical law in your body: that is sickness.

I have a boil, and that boil gains the dominion and runs my body, my mind and my spirit, and all I do is to nurse that miserable, throbbing, aching enemy that is in there raising the devil. That is sin in my flesh, and sin has been condemned in the flesh. God condemned the thing, and now sin has broken out in there. What is rheumatism? Sin in the flesh. And sin shall not have dominion over you in your body, for you are no longer under the law, but under grace, when your body has become the temple of God. Know ye not your body has become a member of Christ? Shall a member of Christ be made the member of a harlot? That does not necessarily mean a woman who is a harlot as we commonly use the word. It may be money, it may be gluttony, it may be a thousand things; but I have taken my body away from the Lord and the Lord's use, and I have committed it to some other use that should not be. *"Let not sin reign in your mortal body [as king]." Hallelujah. "Neither [present] ye your members as [weapons] of unrighteousness"* [Romans 6:12-13]. You turn your body over to be used by doctors to make money out of, and surgeons chop you up for a splendid fee.

A woman said to me recently, "My daughter has determined that she will have an operation."

I said, "What is the matter with her?"

"The doctor doesn't know, but he thinks he ought to explore in there."

Did you ever hear of it? And so he is going to cut her open and send a Livingston in there to explore. Great, isn't it? Then the daughter will go after she is all wrecked and ruined and when she can't get any healing, then she will turn to the Lord. Then she will expect to get her healing without asking the Lord's forgiveness for turning her body over to some man for examination and experimentation. *"Know ye not that your body is the temple of God?"* [1 Corinthians 6:19]. Shall I take the temple of God, then, and turn it over to idols and to demons?

That body of yours is God's holy house, God's holy dwelling place. Why, it is the most sacred thing on earth. Now, the temple that God designed and gave to Israel in the wilderness contained the Holy of Holies, the inner place, didn't it? And in that temple that Solomon was permitted to build for God was the Holy of Holies, for the Shekinah Presence dwelt there. The Shekinah Presence now dwells in your body.

Can you imagine, brethren, here a beautiful church which cost half a million dollars? Everything is in perfect harmony. Wonderful carpets and rugs, wonderful furniture, wonderful decorations and the most up-to-date lighting scheme. Everything is perfectly beautiful and artistic. It is just a dream of architectural beauty. They dedicate it to the Lord and go home. They dedicate it on Saturday. Sunday they are going to hold their first service in it, and when they open the door they make the most awful discovery—a horrible stench rushes out to meet them. What has happened? I will tell you. A sacrilegious man opened the door last night and drove a herd of hogs into the sanctuary, and the hogs have been staying in the beautiful edifice during the night.

That is just what we do with these bodies of ours. We have dedicated them to God; and then we let a flock of unclean thoughts come in, and we let disease come in and settle in our bodies until these precious bodies that belong to God are filled with the children of these unclean things. Tuberculosis is the child of a thought; it is the product of a mental and spiritual condition. That is true, that when we are in right communion and fellowship with the Lord, there is not power enough in all hell to put disease upon your little finger.

And we have permitted that flock of that dirty, devilish herd of swine to come into our bodies and fill them with disease.

Now beloved, let us go into the thing a little bit further. The real healing of your life begins in your spirit, doesn't it? Hebrews 7:25: *"Wherefore he is able also to save [heal] them to the uttermost that come unto God by him, seeing he ever liveth to make intercession for them."*

Now brethren, if God is able to heal to the uttermost, then there are no healings that are impossible, are there? Absolutely none. It doesn't make any difference how sick you are, there is healing for you if you are in contact with the Healer. I don't care how beautiful your chandeliers are, I don't care how beautiful your fixtures are, if outside there, there is one of the fuses blown out, you won't get any light. And the fuse that lets the light of God into you is your spirit, and if that thing is diseased and weak and sickly, you can't get much of a current through it, can you?

A man had a vision. He saw a strange sight. He saw a piece of desert land and sickly flowers and trees growing in it. And he awakened and the picture persisted in following him. The next night he had the same picture come before him again, and it persisted for three nights, and then he said, "Lord, what is this?"

And a voice answered, "Don't you know what it is?"

And he said, "No, Lord, I don't know that I do." He sat looking carefully at it again, and he could see it, oh, so vividly. He said, "Lord, that is me, myself." And he said, "That desert is myself." And he said, "I can see that faith and love and peace and joy that should grow there, are those weak sickly plants."

The Lord said, "What would you do if your garden was like that?"

He said, "I'd hoe it and cultivate it and irrigate it." And the Lord left him to think it over.

Now if your faith is weak and sickly, it is because your spiritual connection with the Lord is faulty. Maybe there is a fuse blown. Maybe a switch is out. But there it is. Now there must be a right adjustment of the soul to the body and of soul and body and spirit. Now I am a threefold being, if I want to put it that way. To get the highest results my spirit must be dominant. My soul must be subservient to my spirit. My body must be under the control of my soul. Then when my body and soul and spirit are in rapport, when they are in perfect fellowship with each other, they can bring forth real results, can't they?

"Know ye not that your body is the temple of God?" (1 Corinthians 6:19-20). Now when that comes to pass, then there comes two spirits. There are two spirits in your body now, there was one before. It was a renewed spirit, then the great mighty Holy Spirit came in. Now you have two spirits in your body, and one soul.

Now the Holy Spirit wants to dominate your spirit, and He wants through your spirit to communicate the unveilings of the Father through the Word to your intellect and bring your intellect and your affections up into perfect harmony with His will, and you yield yourself to Him, and you pore over the Book and take it as your own. You read it, you feed upon it, you eat it—more necessary than your daily food. *"Man shall not live by bread alone, but by every word"* [Matthew 4:4]—and you pore over the Word and you meditate on it, and you get at the heart of the thing, and your spiritual nature grows and develops until it dominates your intellect. But you just read intellectual things, read novels, and cheap stories, and your sickly intellect will absolutely dominate your whole life and break your communion with the Lord and leave your spirit life in darkness.

The way to health is back again to where we belong, isn't it? I venture this: that it is possible to rebuild your spiritual life, as you can rebuild a broken body. I have told you how many of the great athletes grow strong. One of them I met years ago was given up to die of tuberculosis. Another of the great athletes, one of the great wrestlers was given over to die of tuberculosis at 18. He became one of the outstanding wrestlers in America. What a man can do in his physical body he can do in his spirit, can be done with his intellect. There is absolutely no reason why our spiritual life should not be up to 100 percent efficiency.

I wish I was keen enough in my spiritual nature, I'd have a blackboard put behind us and I'd have some one come that understood art work. I would look over the audience, and I'd take each one of them, and I'd say to the artist, draw that man's spirit and let me show his spiritual condition, and you would see your spirit up there. If it was a weak, sickly, puny thing, you would see it. Do you know, some folks, if you could see them when they come in the meeting, their spirits are on a stretcher, emaciated, tubercular, no flesh on it, just a skinny, horrible looking, living corpse, and a great big husky body, but the spirit is a shrinking, feeble, emaciated thing, and you come up and say, "What is the matter with me? I don't seem to have any joy with the Lord."

Well, a tubercular spirit will have no special joy. "I know I have spiritual discernment." Imagine! I say, "Brother, you have spiritual tuberculosis. Your spirit is emaciated. I don't know whether it will survive the night."

Another comes to me and says, "What is the matter with me?" I look at him carefully for a moment. "Do you want me to diagnose it?"

"Yes sir."

"You have cancer. Yes sir, it is on your spirit, it is laying siege to the jugular vein of your spirit, and I don't think it will be but a little while before it will finish your spiritual life. It will kill you out right."

Another man says, "I will tell you what ails me." He said, "I will illustrate it. My little boy used to take his money to buy his lunch at the school. Instead of buying lunch, he bought candy and cheap soda water to drink, and he ate pie and cake and ate candy until by and by they found out." The man said, "I found out he would not eat meat, and he wouldn't eat vegetables, and we thought there was something desperately wrong with him, and there was. So we just put a spy on his track and we found out he was buying candy and eating it." Aha.

Now if your spirit has reached the place where it has no appetite for the things of God, you have been playing hooky. You have been feeding on things that you ought not to eat, and you have compelled your poor spirit to feed on trash and cheap scandal and cheap talk and useless talk, wise cracking and everything, and you have never given your spirit any real healthy food for a long time, and the poor thing is dying of hunger.

Do you understand me now? You can't get your healing until you get your spiritual healing. If you get your healing, you will get through the doctor's faith, don't you see? And you will lose it again. But if you get it through your own spirit being in perfect fellowship with the Lord, and somebody praying for you likely, or you praying for yourself, or else nobody praying for you, you will be able to keep it.

The doctor told of an experience he had down in Texas where a whole congregation had come, practically all of them for healing, and he said, "You just sit here and listen to me preach, and I won't pray for you at all." He said the largest percentage of that congregation was perfectly healed in just a little while. They came every 30 days. At the end of 30 days there was only about 7 percent of the whole congregation that was not healed. All they did was get spiritually healed, and when you get spiritually healed, the chances are a hundred to one you will be healed physically. And I want to tell you this—I don't want to hurt your feelings, God bless you, but brother, do you know I have discovered this—there are quite a number of folks that come to be prayed for, and they are healed over and over again. The healing you want is not physical but spiritual. You get right, and get adjusted so you are feeding on the Word, and so you are giving public testimony, and you will be well or in a condition to get well.

33

Sanctification

Reading Lesson: 1 Thessalonians 5

Beloved, the thought that is in my spirit tonight is the truth from the words we have just read, the sanctification of spirit and soul and body. Paul says, *"I pray God your whole spirit and soul and body be preserved blameless unto the coming of our Lord Jesus Christ. Faithful is he that calleth you, who also will do it"* [verses 23-24].

Most of us in our reading of the Scriptures have this difficulty, and it is a perfectly natural one, of recognizing body and soul only. And man is generally spoken of as a duality of body and soul. However, the scriptures do not recognize man as a dual being, but a triune being, like Himself.

Therefore, the Apostle says: *"I pray God your whole spirit and soul and body be preserved blameless unto the coming of our Lord Jesus Christ."*

One difficulty we have in the study of this subject is that in the common translation of our English Bible there is very little distinction made between soul and spirit. It is one of the most difficult things in the world to express the common truths we teach in another language. Paul coined seventeen distinct words in his letter to the Ephesians to express the fine distinctions of soul and spirit.

Paul declares in the book of Hebrews the possibility of divisibility of soul and spirit. He says: *"For the word of God is quick, and powerful, and sharper than any twoedged sword, piercing even to the dividing asunder of soul and spirit, and of the joints and marrow, and is a discerner of the thoughts and intents of the heart"* (Hebrews 4:12).

Beloved, the spirit of man is a great unknown realm in the lives of most men. My judgment is that the spirit lies dormant in most men until quickened by the living Spirit of God and until fertilized by the real Spirit of Jesus Christ. But when touched by the Spirit of God, a quickening takes place. The spirit of man comes into activity and begins to operate within him. It not only discerns things in this life, like the spirit of another, or in another, but it reaches way beyond this present life, and becomes that medium by which we touch God himself and by which we know and comprehend heavenly things.

In my judgment, the spirit of man is the most amazing instrument of God that there is in all the world. We have this declaration in the book of Job concerning man's spirit: *"There is a spirit in man: and the inspiration of the Almighty giveth them understanding"* [Job 32:8].

When a soul comes to God and surrenders his life to Him, we say he is converted, and by that we mean changed, born again of God, so that the common things which were evident in his life as a fleshly being fell away and were gone, and the spiritual life appeared in him, and in the truest sense he began his walk as a child of God.

I believe a real conversion is the awakening of the spirit of man to the consciousness of the Fatherhood of God through Jesus Christ. In order to be aware of that consciousness of union with God, it is necessary that everything be removed that hides that consciousness and dims the knowledge of God.

Sin is that peculiar thing in the life of man which dims the consciousness of man so he cannot comprehend God. When sin is removed the veil over the soul of man is gone and the spirit of man looks into the face of God and recognizes that God is his Father through the Lord Jesus Christ. Bless God, the spirit of man ascending into union with God brings into our soul the consciousness that God is over all and in all.

The SOUL of man is that intermediate quality between body and spirit. The soul, in other words, comprehends all the action of our mental powers, the natural mind. The soul of man is that which reaches out and takes possession of the knowledge that the spirit has attained and expresses that knowledge through the outer man. The soul of man is the governing power in the constitution of man.

I feel in my heart that one of the things we need to learn very much is this, that the soul of man, not the spirit, has a marvelous power.

If I were to endeavor to define in terms I feel the people would understand, I would speak of the action of the soul of man as that which is commonly spoken of by students as the subconsciousness. As you read the writings of psychic authors, you will observe the actions and powers they define are not the powers of the spirit in union with God but the actions of the soul of man. The soul of man is the real ego. When the Word of God speaks of the salvation of the SOUL, it speaks in truly scientific language. For unless the soul, the mind of man, is redeemed from his own self into the Spirit of God, that man is, in my judgment, still an unredeemed man.

Sanctification is calculated to apply to the needs of all our nature, first of the spirit, second of the soul, third of the body. Over and over again I have repeated those blessed words of John Wesley in his definition of sanctification. He said: "Sanctification is possessing the mind of Christ, and all the mind of Christ."

The ultimate of entire sanctification would comprehend all the mind of Christ. Christians are usually very weak in this department of their nature. Perhaps less pains have been taken by Christians to develop their mind in God than almost anything else.

We pay attention particularly to one thing only, the spirit; and we do not comprehend the fact that God purposed that the things God's Spirit brings to us shall be applied in a practical manner to the needs of our present life.

I was absolutely shocked the other day beyond anything I think my spirit ever received. A dear lady who professes not only to live a holy life but to possess the real Baptism of the Holy Ghost, and who discusses the subject a great deal, was guilty of saying one of the vilest things I ever heard concerning another. I said in my own soul, that individual has not even discerned the outer fringes of what sanctification by the Spirit of God means. I do not believe there is even an evidence of sanctification in that life. Certainly a mind that could repeat such a damning thing gives no evidence whatever but of a very superficial knowledge of God, very superficial indeed.

It shows us this thing, that people are placing their dependence in the fact that in their spirit they know God, that they have been saved from sin, and are going to heaven when they die, but they are living like the devil in this present life, talking like the devil. It is an abomination. It spells a tremendous degree of ignorance. It shows that that individual does not comprehend the first principles of the breadth of salvation as Jesus taught it to the world—a holy mind, a sanctified spirit.

Beloved, I tell you with all candor, a holy mind cannot repeat a vile thing, let alone be the creator of the vile suggestion. It is an unholy mind that is capable of such an act. And I say with Paul, mark such a person. Put your finger on him. Just note it. He can talk, but he does not know God. He does not comprehend the power of His salvation.

But bless God, here is the hope, here is the strength, here is the power of the gospel of Jesus Christ, that the power of God unto salvation, applied to the mind of man, sanctifies the soul of man and makes the mind of man like the mind of Christ.

Who could imagine from the lips of Jesus an unholy suggestion that would jar the spirit of another? The mind could not conceive of such a thing. Never could the mind conceive ought from God but the outflow of a holy life, quickening his mind, infilling it with love and purity and peace and power.

Beloved, in our home, in our life, in our office, wherever we are, we leave the impress of our thoughts there. If our thoughts are pure and holy like Christ, people will walk into that atmosphere and instantly discover it.

Prayer

God I pray that the power of God will come upon the Christian people, that they may feel, oh God, the necessity of submitting the wicked, accursed, vile mind of man to the living God to be purged and cleansed and remolded, that it may become in deed and in truth the mind of Christ.

If there is any particular place in our lives where as a rule Christians are weak, it is in the consecration of their minds. Christians seem to feel as if they were not to exercise any control over the mind, and so it seems to run at random, just like the mind of the world.

Real Christianity is marked by the pureness, by the holiness of the thoughts of man, and if Christianity, the kind you have, does not produce in your mind real holiness, real purity, real sweetness, real truth, then it is a poor brand. Change it right away.

Beloved, there is relief from such; there is a way of salvation. It is in the submission of that mind to the Lord Jesus to be remolded by the Holy Spirit so that that mind becomes the pure channel of a holy nature.

Beloved, surely we who profess to know the living God, who profess to live in union with Him, ought to present to the world that attitude of mind, that pureness of mind, that holiness of mind which needs no recommendation. The people know it, they feel it, they smell it. They know it is the mind of Christ. I love that definition of John Wesley's which says, "possessing the mind of Christ, and ALL the mind of Christ."

Prayer

Oh, God, I ask Thee that Thou wilt help me and the soul of this people to submit our minds to God so that they may be remolded in love and sweetness and purity and holiness, so that in the Name of Jesus they are the minds of Christ.

Beloved, we are going a step further—the effect of a pure mind on the body of man and in the flesh of man. Do you know that the sins of vileness in men's lives originate in the mind? A man's life will be of the character of his thought. If he thinks evil, he will be evil. If he thinks holy, he will be holy. His outward life will be as the inner impulse is. Jesus said:

> **From within, out of the heart of men, proceed evil thoughts, adulteries, fornications, murders, Thefts, covetousness, wickedness, deceit, lasciviousness, an**

> **evil eye, blasphemy, pride, foolishness: All these evil things come from within, and defile the man (Mark 7:21-23).**

They were troubled because Jesus and the disciples were eating and drinking from dishes which were not ceremonially cleansed. Jesus was trying to teach the great lesson of the deep and inner life. He said, *"Out of the heart...[cometh] evil thoughts..."* [Mark 7:21]. That which goeth into the mouth cannot defile a man, etc.

Beloved, our minds need to be stayed in Christ, kept by the power of God, infilled with the Holy Spirit of Christ, so that we reflect His beauty, we show forth His love, we manifest His sweetness and evidence His power.

Long ago I learned this splendid lesson. One night I was in a strange city and was sick. I wanted somebody to pray for me. A person was present, and they suggested that they would pray. I knelt by a chair on the floor and they put their hands on me, and I arose from that chair with one of the most tremendous passions in my nature, one of the most terrible conditions of sensuousness in me. It was days before I felt that I got back again where I was pure and holy in the sight of God. I did not understand it at the time, but afterward that individual came to me with the confession of the character of his life, and I understood then. I received the condition of that nature, and in my receptive attitude I received of the vileness of that person in my nature. It seemed my soul was soiled for days in consequence.

That taught me, beloved, to be careful who laid their hands on me. After that, I waited until the Spirit of the living God indicated in my soul that the person who offered to perform such a ministry was pure.

Isn't it marvelous, beautiful, wonderful to realize that mankind can receive into their nature and being the power and Spirit of the living Christ which contains the purging power to drive forth from the being every particle of evil, every sensuous thing in the thought and nature, so that the man becomes what Jesus was. That is what the blood of Jesus Christ is calculated to do. That is what the Spirit of Christ is purposed to do in the soul of a man—the cleansing of a nature from the power and dominion of sin.

Beloved, the inflow of Holy life into our body MUST PRODUCE holiness in the body, just as it does in the soul. We cannot even think beautiful thoughts, we cannot think holy thoughts, without them leaving their impression in our nature, in our very flesh.

That same divine power in us dissolves disease, restores diseased tissues. Our flesh is purged by the divine power being transmitted from our spirit, through our soul, into our body.

I have always loved to think of the holy flesh of Jesus, not just His beautiful mind, not just the pure Spirit, but is it not blessed and sweet to contemplate the flesh cleansed and purified until His very body—His hands, His feet, His person—were just as pure by the Spirit of God as His pure soul and His pure Spirit were.

That is why Jesus was the wonderful channel He was. The Spirit of God would flow through Him just as freely, just as fully, just as powerfully as it was possible for it to flow through a holy, purified personality.

I like to contemplate the Lord Jesus on the Mount of Transfiguration and think of the radiant glory that came through His flesh, not just the illumination of His spirit, but the holy glory emanating through His flesh until He became white and glistening, until His clothes were white and His face shown as the light. It is that radiant purity of God that my soul covets. It is that radiant power, evidenced in the pureness of my spirit, my mind, my very flesh that I long for.

So Beloved, we see that when something impure, of the character of disease, appears on your flesh and mine, and we feel we are being soiled by an unholy touch, in the Name of Jesus our spirit reaches up and rebukes that devilish condition, and by the Spirit of the living God we stand, believing that the Holy Spirit of God will flow through the spirit, flow through the soul, through the flesh and remedy and heal that difficulty that is in the person.

An old Baptist brother was in to see me about his wife. As I sat reasoning with him, I said, "Brother, I would just as soon have my brother commit a sin as to have sickness in his person. One is the evidence of an impure mind, the other is the evidence of an impure body. And the salvation of Jesus was intended to make him pure in spirit, in soul and body." *"I pray God your whole spirit and soul and body be preserved blameless unto the coming of our Lord Jesus Christ. Faithful is he that calleth you, who also will do it"* [1 Thessalonians 5:23-24].

There is a stream of life that God permits to flow from your nature and mine to all men everywhere. That blessed stream will be either sweet and pure as the stream that flows from the throne of God, or it will be soiled and foul, according to the condition of our nature. The value of the precious blood of Jesus Christ to you and me is that through it that life stream that flows from us may be made holy—that same holy living life stream that causes the tree of life to bloom.

Of all the pictures that the Word of God contains, the one described in the 22nd chapter of Revelation is the most beautiful: *"He showed me a pure river of water of life, clear as crystal, proceeding out of the throne of God and of the Lamb..."* (verses 1 to 21).

Beloved, if your life has not been satisfactory, if you have not recognized the holy character that Christ expects from a real Christian, then this call of the Spirit comes to your soul. *"The Spirit and the bride say come"* [verse 17]. Come up, come into the real life, the high life, the life hid with Christ in God.

"[I will be within thee] a well of water springing up into everlasting life" [John 4:14].

34

The Believer

There is only one thing I could preach on today, and that is: *"Go ye into all the world, and preach the gospel to every creature. He that believeth...."* He that BELIEVETH. He that believeth, bless God. The believer is the big fellow. *"He that believeth,"* Jesus said, *"He that believeth and is baptized shall be saved"* (Mark 16:15-16).

Don't you know Jesus Christ was the most drastic teacher this world ever saw. Jesus Christ demanded that every other dispensation and revelation of the true God be set aside in favor of the one pure existent demonstration and manifestation of Jesus Christ. That is the reason the Jew is seeking God for salvation through Jesus Christ, though he had the first and the greatest revelation, until Jesus came. Christianity is the most drastic thing in its demands on the human conscience that the world has ever known. No other teacher in all the world like the Son of God places such demands on the life. Listen, dear hearts, *"Go ye into all the world."*

The Lord began His preparation of the group to whom He said these wonderful words with the closest intimacy. My, He called them one at a time out of the course of the world into attachment with Himself; lived with them, ate with them, slept with them, worked with them, taught them and prayed with them for three years. Bless God, He took them to the bedside of the dying, took them out in the streets among the sick, the lame, the halt and blind, and healed them, and said, *"Go out likewise." "He that believeth."*

They came into the ranks of Jesus as believers, as believers in Him. Their abandonment of all that had gone before the divine superiority of Jesus Christ and His revelation was complete. They came to the Lord with open hearts and open minds and open souls to understand and know the way of God and receive the light of heaven into their hearts, and become divinely equipped by His eternal power.

Oh, the believer has a marvelous place. *"He that believeth!"* Sound it out dear ones. *"He that believeth."* Christianity is the most extraordinary democracy that the world ever knew. Jesus Christ laid its ground work and its strength and its soul and spirit of the life in the believer. *"He that believeth."* A personal relationship and union with Jesus Christ in heaven, bless God. My, how it sweeps out class distinction, and it wipes away everything and lets the believer stand in the first place of relationship with God.

How struck I was with our Brother Wilson's testimony the other night. He said he had studied Christian Science for five years. He said when he first got the light of Christian Science he thought it was the most beautiful and wonderful thing in the world. After a while he began to discover it was nice sounding phrases, beautiful words, but lacking in the divine secret, the secret of the eternal power of Jesus Christ through the blood of the Son of God, and he abandoned it.

Oh my, lots of that in the world. Before Jesus Christ came, Christian Science in a hundred forms was old and gray whiskered and outcast, and in the dump heap. Buddhism, Confucianism, Zoroastrianism, and all the rest of the long line of human philosophies had to go to the dump heap when Jesus Christ, the Son of God, revealed the Lord from heaven. No place, no contact, separation was the word of Jesus. Let them go; dump them for the divine superiority of Jesus Christ by the Holy Ghost in the human heart.

"He that believeth."
"He that believeth."

Christianity is not based on the mere statement of these words or mere belief in them. If it was it would be a philosophy equal to the others, possibly superior in its demands on the conscience, but it would be placed on the philosophic demonstration the same as the other philosophies are. No sir! That is not Christianity. The secret of Christianity is that Jesus Christ based it on an acceptance of Himself. Jesus Christ said, "Receive Me, receive Me. *He that receiveth Me*" [Matthew 10:40]. Not, he that receiveth My words alone, but he that receiveth Me.

"He that receiveth."
"He that receiveth Me."

Receive Him. That is what constitutes you a believer, when you receive the Lord into your heart—not when you receive some particular teaching or a partial statement of His word—but when you receive Him, the Lord, the Christ, the Redeemer into your heart.

"He that believeth."
"He that believeth Me."

Christianity is the most extraordinary revelation. It so far surpassed everything else in the form of religion in the known earth that there is no comparison whatever.

I have just written a letter to say that I am accepting an invitation to preach at the International New Thought Convention next July for five days. I am going to preach to them about the Son of God. In conference with one or two hundred of them, their national leaders a couple of years ago said, "Lake, we absolutely challenge you to show where the gospel of Jesus Christ or the teachings of Jesus are superior to the teachings of the philosophers."

I said, "Dear brethren, it is not the statements on the demands of the conscience that is it. The secret of Christianity is that Jesus gave HIMSELF to the BELIEVER, THAT Jesus Christ comes not to the believer's heart, that He comes to dwell within his soul, that He comes to anoint his spirit from heaven, that He comes to take possession of his heart and life, to live in him, move in him, act in him, speak in him, pray in him, and all the other activities of the Christian soul."

Did you ever see Buddha come into anybody? Ten thousands have accepted his philosophy, but he never came from heaven to dwell in any man's heart or life. Confucius never came to dwell in any man's heart yet. Zoroaster, in all the marvel of his wondrous teachings, never came from heaven to dwell in the human soul. When he died, he died, and the grave covered him, and there was not a thing left but the books that he wrote as a guide for others.

Ah, Christianity began where philosophies left off. I always feel sorry for the individual who only sees Christianity as a human code or a moral law, even though it was given by Jesus Christ Himself. Oh, that is not Christianity. This moral code that Jesus gave must be made a possibility in your soul, in your life by the Christ who came to dwell in your heart.

"He that believeth."

He has entered into an exalted place, into an amazing relationship. Christianity is absolutely distinguished among all the religions of the world in that it provides for the resurrection of the body, and that Jesus Christ Himself was made the "first fruits" of the resurrection. He came forth in a glorified body, in a glorified life, in glorified power, in glorified being to dwell by the Spirit in the heart of every other man in the world. Bless God.

Think of the royal, regnant, glorified Son of God of heaven, at the eternal Throne, coming into my heart, into your heart, believer! To dwell in your life, Bless God. Oh, say, I wish the blessed Lord would uncover our eyes to the divine majesty of the believer's relationship.

"He that believeth."

Why, Jesus had such an exalted concept of the relationship of the believer to the Eternal Christ by the throne that He ordained him with Himself. Hear it! He ordained him with Himself. I am telling you that Jesus Christ said that the BELIEVER had authority from heaven to say to the lame man, "Arise and walk."

Heaven conferred something on the souls of men when He made it possible for the risen Lord by the Spirit to come into your heart and mine. Oh, how the joy bells of heaven ought to be breaking loose in our soul, and the fires of heaven ought to shine forth from us because the Christ came into our hearts. Blessed be His Name.

Jesus of Nazareth did His work in the world, shed his tears over mankind, labored in the Spirit for their salvation, died on the cross and shed His blood. But Jesus my Lord, bless God came forth out of the tomb, a living, glorified, regnant sovereign of earth and heaven, with all power and authority within His hand. Hallelujah! Jesus of Nazareth was my Lord in the days of His humiliation, but Jesus the Christ at the Eternal Throne is the divine manifestation of the overcoming of God. The ultimate of all perfection, the final manifestation of all that is God-like. Hallelujah.

If I could not leave another thing in this service in your hearts, I would like to leave this one text in your soul, branded in your soul, stamped on your conscience, burned into your heart that Jesus Christ as is presented in Revelation, the first chapter, which I love to call the Twentieth Century Christ, is not Jesus in tears in Galilee, or on the Mt. of Olives weeping over Jerusalem; but the resurrected, glorified, masterful finality in God stands out and says, *"I am He."* Let the world look, let the universe behold, let the devil see, let the kingdoms of darkness take notice, *"I am He that liveth, and was dead; and, behold, I am alive for evermore, Amen; and have the keys of hell and of death"* (Revelation 1:18).

Would it not sound strange if you heard Buddha say that? You do not catch anything like that in his writings. He never gave a revelation like that. It took the Christ to get that.

A famous author of a new religion presented himself to Talleyrand and told him of an amazing religion he had evolved, and wanted to know the best means to quickly present it and fix it upon the minds of the people. Talleyrand told him to come back in three days, and he would give him an answer.

In three days he came back, and Talleyrand received him. The gentleman said, "Have you got my answer?"

He said, "Yes, it is this. You be crucified, lay in the grave for three days, come forth in resurrection, ascend to heaven as the glorified Son of God, and the whole world will receive you."

Beloved that is what makes Christianity the superior of every other religion. And listen, dear hearts, when Jesus Christ, that glorified Son at the eternal Throne, who speaks words that none other in all the universe of God ever spake, when he said, *"I am He that liveth, and was dead; and, behold, I am alive for evermore, Amen; and have the keys of hell and of death."* It is He Who by the Spirit deigns to come into the heart of the believer.

Oh, glory to God, if you have not appreciated the Baptisms of the Holy Ghost, look up to heaven and see the glorified One who purposes to come into your life and possess it.

Suppose I could get inside of Mrs. Lake. Can you imagine such a thing? She would be 190 pounds heavier than she is now. She would have a voice like a pirate, and all the other characteristics of me. She would be me. Do you see it?

Oh, listen, there is a divine secret in Christ's salvation. It is Christ in fact in you by the Holy Ghost, dwelling in you, speaking in you, living in you, blazing in you, flashing from you, bless God.

I lay half the night writing a letter to a brother. I have done that three times, and each time I have torn them up. I said, "They are not worthy. They have not sufficient of heaven's finality. I am going to wait until God gives the real light that boy needs. He has never seen Christ at the throne and the glorified, regnant Jesus in heaven that comes into a man's life."

Our eyes become clouded and our soul dimmed with the earthy things that we see around us, and it is only once in a while that our spirit rises above it into the light of heaven that we see the glorified Son of God.

To His feet I call you. To His heart I ask you to join your soul, and without that you will never know the abundance of His salvation.

Romans 10:9-10: *"That if thou shalt confess with thy mouth the Lord Jesus, and shalt believe in thine heart that God hath raised Him form the dead, thou shalt be saved. For with the heart man believeth unto righteousness; and with the mouth confession is made unto salvation."*

35

Moses Rebuked

Moses had his interview with the Lord at the burning bush, and God had definitely commanded him to go to Pharaoh in Egypt and demand the deliverance of the children of Israel. God gave him the signet of His presence with him—his shepherd rod. All the miracles that followed that demand had taken place, and the children of Israel were finally given permission by the king to leave.

They started toward the Red Sea when the king's heart drew back, and I presume he felt he had done an unwise thing. He was losing the services of two and a half, and probably four, million slaves. In his effort to recall what he had done, he started after them with an army. In the meantime Moses had gotten down to the Red Sea. On the right and on the left were impassable mountains, and Pharaoh and his armies behind him.

The situation from a natural point of view was desperate, and if there was ever a time when a man was seemingly justified in calling on God in prayer, it was then. But I want to show you tonight one of the things I regard as hindrance in our life for God. Most of us do just exactly what Moses did. When the test comes we stop and cry, and as a second thing we stop and pray and put ourselves in a position where we become amenable to exactly the same rebuke that came upon Moses.

Moses started to pray. It is not recorded how long he prayed, or what he said, but instead of God being pleased, He was grieved, and said to Moses: *"WHY STANDEST THOU HERE, AND CRIEST UNTO ME? SPEAK TO THE CHILDREN OF ISRAEL THAT THEY GO FORWARD."* I will turn to the Scripture and read the exact words:

> **The Lord said unto Moses, *Wherefore criest thou unto me?* speak the children of Israel, that they go forward: *But lift thou up thy rod, and stretch out thine hand* over the sea, and *divide it:* and the children of Israel shall go on dry ground through the midst of the sea (Exodus 14:15-16).**

God did not even say, you stretch out your hand, and I will divide the sea. But God said to Moses: *"Stretch out* thine *hand over the sea, and divide it."* It was not an act for God to perform, but it was an act for Moses to believe for. The responsibility was not with God, it was with Moses. A weak Christianity is ever inclined to whine in prayer, while God waits for the believer to command it.

In my judgment, that is the place of extreme weakness in Christian character. I feel that very frequently prayer is made a refuge to dodge the action of faith. And just exactly as Moses came down there and began to pray instead of honoring God's Word to him by the use of his rod, so many times our prayer becomes offensive to God, because instead of praying as Moses did, God demands us to stretch forth *our hand,* exercise our rod of faith and divide the waters.

In many respects it seems to me this is the most powerful lesson that the Word of God contains on the subject of prayer and faith. Just stop for a moment and think of God throwing the responsibility of making a passage through the sea on Moses. God would not take it. It was for Moses to believe God and act. God commands: *"Lift thou up thy rod, and stretch out thine hand,"* not my hand. He was to lift the rod that God had given to him—the signet of God's presence with him, and to be used by the hand of Moses.

In the consideration of the whole subject of an Apostolic Church, do you not see the principle in it? [It's the] principle of acceptance of responsibility from God.

I want to call your attention now to the New Testament on that line. In the ninth chapter of Luke we have Jesus commanding the twelve disciples: *"Then He called his twelve disciples together, and gave them power and authority over all devils, and to cure diseases. And he sent them to preach the kingdom of God, and to heal the sick"* [Luke 9:1-2].

Moses stood before God, and God gave him the commission to go down to Egypt. Then as an evidence of His presence, He said: *What is it you have in your hands?* [see Exodus 4:2].

Moses answered: *"A rod."*

He said: *Throw it down,* and as Moses obeyed it became a serpent. Then He said: *Take it up,* and it was changed to a rod again. This is one of the instances of taking up serpents. God said: Keep it. It is the signet of my presence with you, and it was so with Moses [see Exodus 4:1-5].

But you see Moses had forgotten, as he stood by the Red Sea, that God had given him a sign of His Presence with him... circumstances overpowered him and he commenced to pray, and that prayer was an offense to God.

Just as God had done with Moses, so Jesus called the twelve to Him, and *gave them* power and authority over all devils, and to cure diseases, and that was their rod. He sent them to preach the Kingdom of God and heal the sick. Suppose they came to the sick, and they commenced to pray and say: "Jesus, you heal this man." They would be in just exactly the same position Moses was when he got down to the Red Sea and prayed, "Lord God, you divide these waters." The two cases are absolutely parallel. God demands the action of the believer's faith in God. YOU stretch out YOUR hand and divide the waters.

God has likewise given to every man the measure (rod) of faith, and it is for man, as the servant of God, to use the rod that God has given him. In these days there is an attitude of mind that I do not know hardly how to define. It is a mock humility. Rather, it is a false humility. It is a humility that is always hiding behind the Lord, and is excusing its own lack of faith by throwing the responsibility over on the Lord. The Word of God, in speaking of this same matter concerning the disciples, says: *"They departed, and went through the towns, preaching the gospel, and healing every where"* [Luke 9:6].

Over and over again throughout the New Testament, the Word of God says, *"They healed them," "The disciples healed them,"* etc. You see they had received something from God. They were as conscious of it as Moses was conscious he had received a rod from the Lord. It was theirs to use. It was theirs to use for all purposes. Peter used the conscious rod of God to heal the man at the beautiful gate. He did not pray. He did not ask God to heal the man, but he commanded him: *"In the name of Jesus Christ of Nazareth rise up and walk"* [Acts 3:6]. And the man obeyed. That was not intercession. It was a command. It was the faith in Peter's soul that brought the result.

Peter used the rod. The rod in this case was the rod of faith. In whose hands was it? In the hands of Peter and John together, and they used that rod of faith. The word was spoken through Peter. The command was given through him. Unquestionably John's soul was in it just as much as Peter's was. By faith in His Name, by the faith of the disciples, the power of God was made active, and the lame man was healed.

Beloved, the lesson in my soul is this. There is a place of victory, and a place of defeat, but there is a hair-breadth line there. It is the place of *faith in action,* to believe the thing God says, and to do the thing that He commands, accepting as the servant of God the responsibility God lays upon you. Not interceding as Moses did, but as in Peter's case, through the faith that was in his soul, he commanded the power of God on the man. Suppose Peter had prayed, "Oh, Lord, you come and heal this man." It would have been his own acknowledgment of lack of faith to do what Jesus told the disciple to do—heal the sick.

In the story of Saul, in 1 Samuel 10, among other things the prophet Samuel says to him: *"The spirit of the Lord will come upon thee, and thou shalt prophesy with them, and shalt be turned into another man. And let it be, when these signs are come unto thee, that thou do AS OCCASION SERVE THEE; for God is with thee"* (1 Samuel 10:6-7).

The lesson I know God wants us to see tonight is this: that He endues a man or woman with the authority of God to accomplish the will of God. The power of God is bestowed upon the man. It is not the man that accomplishes the matter. It is the stretching forth of the hand; the dividing of the waters must be in response to the faith of the man. The man is the instrument. *"Thou do as occasion serve thee; for God is with thee."* That is, you simply go on about your business, and the power of God is present with you to accomplish the desire of your heart.

Returning to the case of Peter, Peter used the faith of God that was in his soul to restore a man who was born lame, and he was instantly restored.

In the case of Ananias and Sapphira, we see Peter using the same power, by the spoken word, not to restore a man's limbs, but to bring judgment on a liar. When Ananias lied, the Spirit of God fell on him and he died as an example of sin. His wife likewise died. *"Behold, the feet of them which have buried thy husband are at the door, and shall carry thee out"* [Acts 5:9].

Man is a servant of God. Man is an instrument through which God works. The danger line is always around this, that weak men have taken to themselves the glory that belonged to God, and they have said, "We did it." They did not do it. God did it, but the man believed God that it would be done.

How closely we are made co-workers with the Lord, *"co-laborers together with Him"* [see 1 Corinthians 3:9]. It is God's divine purpose to accomplish His will in the world through men. God placed a profound respect upon the Body, *"the church, Which is his body"* [Ephesians 1:22-23].I want to show you that.

In the tenth chapter of Acts we have that remarkable response to the prayers of Cornelius when an angel came to him and said: *"Cornelius...Thy prayers and thine alms are come up for a memorial before God. And now send men to Joppa, and call for one Simon, whose surname is Peter...he shall tell thee what thou oughtest to do"* [Acts 10:3-6].

The angel came from heaven. He was a direct messenger of God. Yet the angel did not tell Cornelius the way of salvation. Why did the angel instruct Cornelius to send for Peter? Because Peter was a part of the Body of Christ, and God ordained that the power of God, with the ministry of Christ, shall be manifest through the Body. Not through angels, but through the Body, *"the church, Which is his body"* [Ephesians 1:22-23].

It is, therefore, the duty of the Body to use the Spirit of God to accomplish the divine will of God, the purpose of God. With what strength then, with what a consciousness of the dignity of service, Christians ought to go forth! With what a conscious realization that God has bestowed upon you the authority, and not only the authority but the enduement of the Spirit to cause you to believe God and exercise the faith for the will of God to be accomplished. Is it any wonder that David said; *"What is man, that thou art mindful of him? and the son of man, that thou visitest him? For thou hast made him a little lower than the angels, and hast crowned him with glory and honour. Thou madest him to have dominion over the works of thy hands; thou hast put all things under his feet"* [Psalm 8:4-6]. Man and God working together, co-laborers, co-workers. Blessed be God.

36

Behold, I Give You Power

Matthew 8:1-2: *"When He was come down from the mountain, great multitudes followed Him. And, behold, there came a leper and worshipped Him, saying, Lord, if thou wilt, thou canst make me clean."*

That man knew that Jesus had the power to heal him, but he did not know it was God's will, and that Jesus had committed Himself to the healing of mankind. If he had known he would have said, "Lord, heal me."

It is always God's will to heal. Our faith may fail. My faith failed to the extent that unless someone else had gone under my life and prayed for me, I would have died. But God was just as willing to heal me as He could be. It was my faith that broke down. God is willing, just as willing to heal as He is to save. HEALING IS A PART OF SALVATION. It is not separate from salvation. Healing was purchased by the blood of Jesus. This Book always connects salvation and healing. David said: *"Bless the Lord, O my soul, and forget not all his benefits: Who* forgiveth *all thine iniquities; who* healeth *all thy diseases"* (Psalms 103:2-3).

There never has been a man in the world who was converted, and was sick at the same time, who might not have been healed if he had believed God for it. But he was not instructed in faith to believe God for healing.

Suppose two men came to the altar. One is sick and lame; the other is a sinner. Suppose they knelt at the altar together. The sinner says, "I want to find the Lord." Everyone in the house will immediately lend the love of their heart and the faith of their soul to help him touch God. But the lame fellow says, "I have a lame leg" or "My spine is injured. I want healing." Instead of everybody lending their love and faith in the same way to that man, everybody puts up a question mark.

That comes because of the fact we are instructed on the Word of God concerning the salvation of the soul, but our education concerning sickness and His desire and willingness to heal have been neglected. We have gone to the eighth or the tenth grade or the university on the subject of salvation, but on the subject of healing we are in the ABC class.

"Jesus put forth His hand, and touched him, saying, I will; be thou clean" (Matthew 8:3). Did He ever say anything in the world but "I will," or did He ever say, "I cannot heal you because it is not the will of God," or "I cannot heal you because you are being purified by this sickness," or "I cannot heal you because you are glorifying God in this sickness?" There is no such instance in the Book.

On the other hand we are told He healed ALL that came to Him. Never a soul ever applied to God for salvation or healing that Jesus did not save and heal! Did you ever think what calamity it might have been if a man had come to Jesus once and said, "Lord, save me," and the Lord had said, "No I cannot save you." Every man forever more would have a question mark as to whether or not God would save him. There would not be a universal confidence as there is today.

Suppose Jesus had ever said to a sick man, "No, I cannot heal you." You would have the same doubt about healing. The world would have settled back and said, "Well, it may be God's will to heal that man or that woman, but I do not know whether or not it is His will to heal me."

Jesus Christ did not leave us in doubt about God's will, but when the Church lost her faith in God, she began to teach the people that maybe it was not God's will to heal them. So the Church introduced the phrase, "If it be Thy will" concerning healing. But Jesus healed all that came to Him (Matthew 4:23; Luke 9:6; Luke 9:11).

Notice what it says in Isaiah 35, *"He will come and SAVE you. THEN THE EYES OF THE BLIND SHALL BE OPENED, AND THE*

EARS OF THE DEAF SHALL BE UNSTOPPED. Then shall the LAME MAN LEAP AS AN HART, and the TONGUE OF THE DUMB SING." Salvation and healing connected!

"That it might be fulfilled which was spoken by Esaias the prophet, saying, Himself took our infirmities and BARE OUR SICKNESSES" (Matthew 8:17). And lest we might be unmindful of that great fact that He *"bare our sicknesses and carried our sorrows,"* Peter emphasizes it by saying, *"Who his own self bare our sins in his own body on the tree, that we, being dead to sins, should live unto righteousness: by whose stripes ye were healed"* (1 Peter 2:24). Not "by whose stripes ye are healed," but *"by whose stripes ye were healed."*

The only thing that is necessary is to BELIEVE GOD. God's mind never needs to act for a man's SALVATION. He gave the Lord and Savior Jesus Christ to die for you. God cannot go any further in expressing His will in His desire to save man. The only thing that is necessary is to believe God. There is salvation by blood. There is salvation by power that actually comes of God into a man's life. The blood provided the power. Without the blood there would have been no power. Without the sacrifice there would have never been any glory. Salvation by blood, salvation by power.

The Church in general is very clear in her faith on the subject of salvation through the sacrifice of the Lord and Savior Jesus Christ. The Christian world in general, regardless of their personal state of salvation, has a general faith and belief of the Lord and Savior Jesus Christ for the salvation of the world. But they are ever in doubt and very inexperienced on the power of God.

> **When He was come down from the mountain, great multitudes followed him. And, behold, there came a leper and worshipped him, saying, Lord, if thou wilt, thou canst make me clean. And Jesus put forth his hand, and touched him, saying, I will; be thou clean. And immediately his leprosy was cleansed. And Jesus saith unto him, See thou tell no man; but go thy way, show thyself to the priest, and offer the gift that Moses commanded, for a testimony unto them (Matthew 8:1-4).**

Did you ever stop to think that they have no medical remedy for the real things that kill folks? Typhoid fever: Fill the patient with a tankful of medicine and he will go right on for twenty-one days.

In 1913, I was in Chicago in a big meeting when I received a telegram from the hospital in Detroit, saying, "Your son, Otto, is sick with typhoid fever. If you want to see him, come." I rushed for a train, and when I arrived I found him in a ward. I told the man in charge I would like a private room for him so I could get a chance to pray for him. Well, God smote that thing in five minutes. I stayed with him for a couple of days until he was up and walking around. He went along for four or five weeks, and one day, to my surprise, I got another telegram telling me he had a relapse of typhoid. So I went back again. This time there was no sunburst of God like the first time. Everything was as cold as steel, and my, I was so conscious of the power of the devil. I could not pray audibly, but I sat down by his bed and shut my teeth, and I said in my soul, "Now, Mr. Devil, go to it. You kill him if you can." And I sat there five days and nights. He did not get healing the second time instantly. It was healing by process because of the fact my soul took hold on God. I sat with my teeth shut, and I never left his bedside until it was done.

You may be healed like a sunburst of God today, and tomorrow. The next week or the next month when you want healing, you may have to take it on the slow process. The action of God is not always the same because the conditions are not always the same.

In the life of Jesus, people were instantly healed. I believe Jesus has such a supreme measure of the Spirit that when He put His hands on a man, he was filled and submerged in the Holy Ghost, and the diseases withered out and vanished.

But, beloved, you and I use the measure of the Spirit that we possess. [You can, as a member of His body, possess the Spirit in the same measure as He. God does not expect us to fulfill John 14:12 with less equipment than Jesus had. *W. H. Reidt]* And if we haven't got as much of God as Jesus had then you pray for a man today, and you get a certain measure of healing, but he is not entirely well. The only thing to do is to pray for him tomorrow, and let him get some more, and keep on until he is well.

That is where people blunder. They will pray for a day or two, and then they quit. You pray and keep on day by day and minister to your sick until they are well. One of the things that has discredited healing is that evangelists will hold meetings, and hundreds of sick will come and be prayed for. In a great meeting like that you get a chance to pray once and do not see them again. You pray for ten people, and as a rule you will find that one or two or three are absolutely healed, but the others are only half healed, or quarter healed, or have only a little touch of healing.

It is just the same with salvation. You bring ten to the altar. One is saved and is clear in his soul. Another may come for a week, and another for a month before he is clear in his soul. The difference is not with God. The difference is inside the man. His consciousness has not opened up to God. Every law of the Spirit that applies to salvation applies to healing likewise.

> **And when Jesus was entered into Capernaum, there came unto Him a centurion, beseeching Him, And saying, Lord, my servant lieth at home sick of the palsy, grievously tormented. And Jesus saith unto him, I will come and heal him. The centurion answered and said, Lord, I am not worthy that thou shouldest come under my roof: but speak the word only, and my servant shall be healed (Matthew 8:5-8).**

Here is healing at a distance. That centurion understood divine authority, and the same divine authority is vested in the Christian, for Jesus is the pattern Christian. *"For I am a man under authority, having soldiers under me: and I say to this man, Go, and he goeth; and to another, Come, and he cometh; and to my servant, Do this, and he doeth it"* (verse 9).

The same divine authority that was vested in Jesus is vested BY JESUS in every Christian soul. Jesus made provision for the Church of Jesus Christ to go on forever and do the same as He did, and to keep on doing them forever. That is what is the matter with the Church. The Church has lost faith in that truth. The result is they went on believing He could save them from sin, but the other great range of Christian life was left to the doctors and the devil or anything else. And the Church will never be a real Church, in the real power of the living God again, until she comes back again to the original standard where Jesus was.

Jesus said, *"Behold, I give you authority."* What authority? *"Against unclean spirits, to cast them out, and to heal all manner of sickness and all manner of disease"* (Matthew 10:1). Jesus has vested that authority in you.

You say, "Well, Lord, we understand the authority that is in your Word, but we haven't the *power*."

But Jesus said, *"Ye shall receive power, after that the Holy Ghost is come upon you"* (Acts 1:8).

Now the Holy Ghost is come upon every Christian in a measure. It is a question of degree. There are degrees of the measure of the Spirit of God in men's lives. The BAPTISM OF THE HOLY SPIRIT is a greater measure of the Spirit of God, but every man has a degree of the Holy Spirit in his life. *You* have. It is the Spirit in your life that gives you faith in God, that makes you a blessing to other people. It is the Holy Spirit that is *outbreathed* in your soul that touches another soul and moves them for God. Begin right where you are and let God take you along the Christian life as far as you like.

"When Jesus heard it, he marvelled, and said to them that followed, Verily I say unto you, I have not found so great faith, no, not in Israel" (Matthew 8:10).

Jesus always commended faith when He met it. Jesus did not always meet faith. All the people who came to Jesus did not possess that order of faith. They had faith that IF THEY GOT TO JESUS they would be healed. But here is a man who says, *"Speak the word only, and my servant shall be healed."*

Then you remember the case of the man at the Pool of Bethesda. He did not even ask to be healed. As he lay there, Jesus walked up to him and said, *"Wilt thou be made whole?"* He saw this poor chap who had been lying there for thirty-eight years, and Jesus did not wait for him to ask Him to heal. Jesus said, *"Wilt thou be made whole?"* [John 5:6] and the poor fellow went on to say that when the water was troubled he had no one to put him in, but while he was waiting another stepped in ahead of him. But Jesus saith unto him, *"Rise, take up thy bed, and walk"* [John 5:8]. He was made whole. Afterward Jesus met him and said, *"Behold, thou art made whole: sin no more, lest a worse thing come unto thee"* (John 5:14).

In the records of the Lake and Graham family away back, tuberculosis was never known to them until it appeared in my sister. My sister accompanied me to Africa, and she became so ill that when I got to Cape Town we had to wait until her strength returned. God healed her.

Regarding people being healed at a distance, we receive telegrams from all over the world. Distance is no barrier to God. The United States has just finished the building of the greatest wireless station in the world. They send messages that register almost instantly ten thousand miles. When the machine is touched here, it registers ten thousand miles away. Well, all right, when your HEART strikes God in faith, it will register there wherever that individual is just that quick. All the discoveries of later years such as telegraph, telephone, wireless and that sort of thing, are just the common laws that Christians have practiced all their lives.

Nobody ever knelt down and prayed, but that the instant they touched God, their soul registered in Jesus Christ in Glory, and the answer came back to the soul. Christians have that experience every day. The wise world has begun to observe that these laws are applicable in the natural realm. I asked Marconi once how he got his first idea for the wireless. He replied that he got it from watching an exhibition of telepathy in a cheap theater.

The prayer of the heart reaches God. Jesus replied to the leper, *"I will; be thou clean."* The next was the centurion's servant. The centurion said, "You do not need to come to my house. You SPEAK THE WORD ONLY, and my servant shall be healed." And in the soul of Jesus, He said, *"Be healed."* Distance is no barrier to God. Distance makes no difference. The Spirit of God in you will go as far as your love reaches. LOVE is the medium that conveys the Spirit of God to another soul anywhere on God's earth.

This is what takes place as you pray. The Spirit of God comes upon you and bathes your soul, and a shaft of it reaches out and touches that soul over there. If you had an instrument that was fine enough to photograph spirit, you would discover this is done.

Is it not a marvelous thing that God has chosen us to be co-laborers with Him, and He takes us into partnership to do all that He is doing? Jesus Christ at the throne of God desires the blessing of you and me, and out of His holy heart the Spirit comes, and the soul is filled, and we cannot tell how or why.

I have known thousands of people to be healed who have never seen my face. They send a request for prayer, we pray, and never hear anything more about them sometimes, unless a friend or a neighbor or someone comes and tells us about them. Sometimes someone sends in a request for them. They will tell you they do not know what happened. They just got well. But you know why. That is the wonderful power in the Christian life, and that is the wonderful cooperation that the Lord Jesus has arranged between His own soul and the soul of the Christian. That is *"the Church, which is His body"* [Ephesians 1:22-23].

37

Holiness Unto the Lord

Tongues and Interpretation, Rev. John G. Lake
Spokane, Washington, March 6, 1916

Holiness is the character of God. The very substance of His being and essence of His nature is purity. The purpose of God in the salvation of mankind is to produce in man a kindred holiness, a radiant purity like unto that of God Himself.

If God were unable to produce in him such a purity, then His purpose in man would be a failure, and the object of the sacrifice of Jesus Christ would be a miscarriage instead of a triumph.

The triumph of Jesus Christ was attained through His willingness to be led by the Spirit of God. The triumph of the Christian can be attained only in a similar manner. Even though God has baptized a soul with the Holy Spirit, there yet remains, as with Jesus, the present necessity of walking in humility, and permitting the Spirit of God to be his absolute guide.

The unveiling of consciousness, of the desire of the flesh, of the sensuality of the nature and the thought of man, the revelation of adverse tendencies, is part of God's purpose and is necessary for growth in God. How can the nature of man be changed except that the nature first be revealed? So there arises in the heart the desire and prayer for the Spirit of God to eject, crucify, and destroy every tendency of opposition to the Holy Spirit. Think not that thou shalt attain the highest in God, until within thine own soul a heavenly longing to be like Him, Who gave His life for us, possesses thine heart.

Think not to come within the court of God with stain upon thy garments. Think not that heaven can smile upon a nature fouled through evil contact. Think not that Christ can dwell in temples seared by flames of hate. No! The heart of man must first be purged by holy fire and washed from every stain by cleansing blood. Know ye that he whose nature is akin to God's must ever feel the purging power of Christ within?

He who would understand the ways of God must trust the Spirit's power to guide and keep. He who would tread the paths where angels tread himself must realize seraphic purity. Such is the nature of God. Such the working of the Spirit's power. Such the attainment of him who overcomes. In him the joy and power of God shall be. Through him the healing streams of life shall flow. To him heaven's gates are opened wide. In him the Kingdom is revealed.

Fear not to place thy hand within the nail-pierced palm. Fear not to trust His guidance. The way He trod is marked by bleeding feet and wet with many tears. He leadeth thee aright and heaven's splendor soon shall open to thy spirit, and thou shalt know that all triumphant souls, those that have overcome indeed, have found their entrance by this path into the realms of light.

38

The Resurrection

Sermon 2

Christianity through Jesus Christ stepped into the arena of world religions as a challenger. The Son of God, just as the ancient athlete did, threw down His gauntlet on the ground and challenged the religions of the world to take it up. Heaven's challenge still stands. Sophisticated religions, uncertainties, philosophic illusions and delusions have claimed the world's interest, but heaven's challenge stands just as vigorously today as it ever did. So long as the blessed Word of God lives in the world, so long shall that challenge endure. Other religions were old, long-whiskered and gray-haired when Jesus Christ entered the arena. Christianity was a babe among the ancient religions. Zoroaster had lived, taught his "purification by fire" and worshipped the sun, the fire god. Zoroaster could conceive only one possibility of purifying the human soul, a process of fire cleansing. There could be no other. That was the conclusion of the ancient world.

Buddha followed about 500 B.C., but with no better hope than Zoroaster. His ideal was oblivion, personality lost, individuality gone, merged into the great whole, without distinctive consciousness, vacuity.

Mohammed came at a later period, about 550 years after Jesus Christ. His heaven was a harem, the possibility of everlasting sensuality. Then in modern days Mormonism followed with its "spiritual marriages" and dream of eternal polygamy, all abominable to the Spirit of the Son of God and as unlike Christianity as anything could be.

Into the muck and the mess and the darkness came the Son of God with the glory of holiness, with divine righteousness, with heavenly purity, with angelic estate, never ceasing consciousness, perpetuated individuality, life forevermore, resurrection from the dead, man's enjoyment of God eternally, yourself a son of God, like the Son of God, Himself, in His likeness immortalized.

Heaven stood aghast, earth stood aghast, and hell stood aghast when Jesus Christ stepped into the arena. Could He accomplish the thing He talked about? Was there power in heaven or on earth to revolutionize the nature of man, change the darkness, take away sin and obliterate the night from his soul? Could the personality of man be preserved? Were Christians going to die just like others die? Did He truly possess eternal life? Could He impart it to others? Was Jesus Christ a boaster or a Savior?

Christianity did not come to the world to apologize for its existence or to beg a place to live. It came as heaven's champion: it has the champion soul. *"It shall bruise thy head, and thou shalt bruise his heel"* (Genesis 3:15). That champion consciousness is in the soul of the Christian. Being born of God, he is champion of the Son of God and a demonstrator of His salvation. He is the champion of God. He cannot be anything else. *"As he is, so are we in this world"* [1 John 4:17].

In our day we have almost come to the place where the world is being taught to believe that the message of Christianity is morality—be decent, don't act like a pig, keep the beast under control. That is about the message of modern Christianity. Jesus Christ never wasted His time establishing mere morality. Jesus Christ, the Son of God, declared IMMORTALITY to be the goal of Christianity, its attainment, the purpose of God for you and me. *"I will raise him up at the last day"* [John 6:40], said Jesus. *"I will give [him] eternal life"* [John 10:28]. *"The dead in Christ shall rise first"* [1 Thessalonians 4:16].

No religion in the world except Christianity ever suggested resurrection its declared intent. Who in the world was ever bold enough to suggest a resurrection? What dying creature could? It was only the Son of God Himself, out of heaven, with the knowledge of immortality and eternal life that would dare to suggest such a climax for mankind. If there were no other evidence of Jesus Christ's' eternality but that, it would be sufficient. *"Who only hath immortality"* [1 Timothy 6:16]. *"In Him was LIFE; and the LIFE was the light of men"* [John 1:4]. *"[He that] liveth and believeth in me shall never die"* [John 11:26]. *"Destroy this temple...and in three days I will raise it up"* [Mark 14:58]. Marvelous Redeemer!

Christianity stands today absolutely unique. No other religion of earth has our hope, or our consciousness, or our power. I fear sometimes that we moderns somehow have lost the spirit of original Christianity. We have lost the smash of it. We have lost the charge of it. We have lost the overcoming of it. We are begging the devil for a place in the world, apologizing for our faith in God, trying to conform our religion to the mind of the world.

Salvation is the transforming power of God. Jesus Christ looked upon the world which was saturated with sin, shaped in iniquity, and said that the task was not too great for Him. The biggest contract in this universe was undertaken back in the eternal ages when one time, in the council of the Godhead, Jesus Christ, the responsible Creator, became the responsible Savior and settled the sin question by offering Himself as the Savior of the world. He wrought our redemption. *"He...that believeth on him that sent me, hath everlasting life"* (John 5:24).

His dying on the cross was the first incident in connection with our redemption, but it was not the conclusive incident. If Jesus had died on the cross and the process of salvation had ceased then, there would not be a redeemed sinner today.

David was sitting on the mountainside one afternoon watching his sheep, and his spirit traveled out into the regions of God. He began to observe, as a seer does, the things that were taking place; and he broke out shouting, *"Thou hast ascended on high, thou hast led captivity captive: thou hast received gifts for men; yea, for the rebellious also, that the Lord God might dwell among them"* (Psalm 68:18). *"Lift up your heads, oh, ye gates, and be ye lifted up ye everlasting doors, the King of Glory is coming in"* (F.F.V., Psalm 24:7). That is the Christ of God; that is His salvation!

This was a battle of worlds. It was not a battle of earthly religions. It was the battle of every power of light and darkness in heaven and earth. Jesus Christ, the champion of righteousness and salvation, had to make good or, like the philosophers, pass into oblivion at the grave. Instead of being the life giver, He would have been just the propounder of another philosophy.

The resurrection morning came. Jesus, discussing His life had said, *"I have power to lay it down, and I have power to take it again"* (John 10:18). He took it at His will. He commanded life! He lived and death became a captive. Jesus Christ, the Son of God, was victor—none like Him in all the universe. He came out of the battle with the *"keys of hell and of death"* (Revelation 1:18). No other soul in heaven or on earth ever had such an experience. None other had ever challenged death: no other had ever taken death and hell captive. Jesus Christ stood unique in earth, in hell, in heaven.

When Jesus came forth in the resurrection, something breathed and throbbed and pulsed in Him that had never breathed or throbbed or pulsed before. It was the new *eternal* life. He used a new vocabulary—the ordinary language was not big enough. He said, *"All power is given unto me in heaven and in earth"* [Matthew 28:18]. Who else in the universe had ever experienced such a thing? None but the Son of God. *"ALL POWER"* language is Christian vocabulary only. Christianity came from the heart of the Glorified. Christianity is a heavenly triumph. Christianity is one hundred percent supernatural—God possessing man.

Just as God breathed the breath of life into Adam, so Jesus Christ breathed upon His disciples. If He could breathe into them this heaven-born life, they would be heaven-born like Himself. If He could breathe this consciousness of triumph into them, they would become triumphant also. If they could take the deathless life of Christ, they would become deathless likewise. *"He breathed on them, and saith unto them, Receive ye the Holy Ghost"* (John 20:22). In Peter's Pentecostal sermon he gives a revelation that no other writer gives us. Peter's broken heart was penetrative. He saw into the glory. He saw Jesus ascending to the throne of God. He saw the Almighty God receive Him at the throne. He observed what took place. He said, *"Having received of the Father the promise of the Holy Ghost, he hath shed forth this, which ye now see and hear"* [Acts 2:33]. He saw Him get the eternal saving marvel for universal distribution to all mankind.

Right then Jesus became the world's Savior, the Savior of all mankind. He now possessed the saving grace, the Holy Spirit. God had fulfilled His promise. It completed His saviorhood. It made Him heaven's High Priest. He had qualified as High Priest of things eternal. It was His right now to pour out the Holy Spirit on the world. He came to the balcony of glory and poured out the Holy Spirit on every hungry heart that was ready to receive. They were baptized in the Holy Spirit. So may you be.

The Secret of Power

Luke 24:49, Acts 1:8

He is risen, He is risen! Hear the cry
Ringing through the land, and sea and sky.
'Tis the shout of victory, triumph is proclaimed,
Heralds of God announce it, Deaths disdained.

Shout the tidings! Shout the tidings! Raise the cry.
Christ's victorious, Christ's victorious cannot die,
For the bars of death He sundered, Satan sees that
he has blundered,
As the shouts of angels thundered, "He is alive!"

Catch the shout, ye earth-born mortals, let it roll,
Till it echoes o'er the mountains from the center to the poles
That the Christ of earth and Glory death has conquered.
Tell the story, He's the Victor! He's the Victor!
So am I.

For this reason that my ransom He has paid,
I've accepted His atonement, on Him laid,
He, the Lamb of God that suffered all for me,
Bore my sins, my griefs, my sickness on the tree.

I am risen, I am risen from the grave,
Of my sins, my griefs, my sickness, and the waves
Of the resurrection life, and holy power.
Thrill by being with His new life every hour.

Now the lightnings of God's Spirit burn my soul,
Flames of His divine compassion o'er me roll,
Lightning power of God's own Spirit strikes the power of hell.
God in man, Oh Glory! Glory! All the story tell.

I have proved Him, I have proved Him. It is true,
Christ's dominion yet remaineth, 'tis for you,
Let the fires of holy passion sweep your soul. Let

the Christ who death has conquered take control.
He will use you, He will use you. Zion yet has Saviors still,
Christ the Conqueror only waiteth for the action of your will.

Given in tongues by the Holy Ghost to John G. Lake
at 2 a.m. June 18, 1910. Cookhouse C.C. South Africa

39

Christian Consciousness

Chicago, Illinois July 16, 1920

There is a wonderful single word that expresses what God is trying to develop in us. The word is CONSCIOUSNESS. I love it. It is an amazing word. Consciousness means, *THAT WHICH THE SOUL KNOWS.* Not that which you believe, or that which you have an existent faith for, or that which you hope, but that which the soul has proven which the soul *knows,* upon which the soul rests, the thing, bless God, which has become concrete in your life.

Consequently God's purpose, and the purpose of real religion, is to create in the nature of man a consciousness of God. And that church which will succeed in creating the high test degree of consciousness of God in the soul of men, will live longest in the world. And the only mode of possibility of perpetuating a church in the world forever is to bring into the souls of the people the full measure of the consciousness of God that Jesus Christ enjoys.

It is a good thing, not only to be good, but to know WHY you are good. It is not only a good thing to be an American, but to know WHY you are an American. It is a good thing, not only to be a Christian, but to know WHY you are a CHRISTIAN, and to know why CHRISTIAN CONSCIOUSNESS is superior to every other known consciousness.

And I want to declare that Christianity stands superior to every other form of religion under the heavens and in the whole earth; that no other religion under the heavens has the same consciousness of God or the same means of producing a consciousness of God that Christianity possesses.

In 1893 in this city, was the great Chicago World's Fair. Among the features of the fair was a Congress on Religions. All the religions of the world were invited to send their representatives, and present their peculiar religion for the good of all. Many regarded it as a great calamity that the varied forms of Eastern philosophy should thus be introduced into this country. I never felt that way. I have always felt that if Christianity could not demonstrate her superiority over every other religion, then Christianity has not the place and power that Jesus Christ said Christianity had in the world.

But the result of that Congress of Religions was that Christianity was so poorly presented, that the Indian philosophers ran away with the whole thing, and in the minds of thousands who listened, it left a belief that their knowledge of God, and God's laws, and the laws of life, were greater than the Christian possessed.

And fellow Christians, there began in my soul a prayer that Almighty God would reveal in my soul what the real secret of real Christianity is, in order that in this world Christians might become kings and priests, and demonstrate the superiority of the religion of the Son of God beyond that of every other in the whole earth.

In later years I went to South Africa. It was at a time of peculiar interest in South African history, just following the Boer War. The great industry there is mining. One-fourth of the gold of the world comes from Johannesburg and vicinity. The diamonds of the world come from South Africa, and the United States is the greatest diamond market of the world.

When the Boer War came on, the native* people became so frightened over war between white men, that after the war was over and settled, they could not coax them back to open the mines. The result was that in order to get the industries established again, they had to send to China and get two hundred thousand (200,000) Chinese, and put them to work to open the shops and mines, and all the other industries. These Chinese came in real colonies. Some were Confucianists, some were

Buddhists, some were Brahmans, some represented this form, and some that form of philosophy. They brought their priests, and their priests ministered unto them.

At the same time there were in South Africa one and a half million East Indians. These represented all the cults of India. They made complaint that they were not being properly cared for, and the British government sent to India and imported a great company of Buddhist priests, and Brahman priests, and Yogi priests, and all the rest of them, and they came to South Africa to assist their own people.

I had a Jewish friend, Rabbi Hertz, who became famous as a great rabbi, and because of his influence for the British during the war. There was also a Roman Catholic priest, Father Bryant, a wonderful man. I listened to Dr. Hertz give a series of lectures on the Psalms of David, which I regard as the finest of that character I had ever heard.

One day he said, "Did it ever occur to you what an amazing Congress of Religions we could have in this country? It would put the one in Chicago in 1893 in the shade."

I said, "I have thought of it, but do not have sufficient acquaintance among these other men to undertake it, but would gladly give a helping hand." So it was eventually brought to pass.

We gathered once a week. They sat on the floor all night, Eastern fashion, a priest with his interpreter, and we gave the individual a whole night if he wanted it, or two nights if he wanted it, or as long as he wanted, to tell out the very secret of his soul, to show the very best he could, the very depth of his peculiar religion, and the consciousness of God it produced. It was not the details of his religion we sought, but the soul of it, and the consciousness it possessed. We listened to the Indian Buddhist priest one night, and the Chinese Buddhist priest the next night, the Indian Confucianist priest one night, and a Chinese Confucianist priest the next night, the Indian Brahman priest one night, and a Chinese Brahman priest the next night, and it went on. Eventually it came to the night that Dr. Hertz, the Jewish rabbi, was to give the secret of the Jewish religion, and to tell out the whole of God that the Jewish religion revealed, and the consciousness of God that was produced by the Mosaic and the prophetic teachings.

Did you ever stop to think that in all religious history, the Jewish prophets knew more of God than all the philosophers of

Earth combined? They superseded all others of the ancients in knowledge of God, His ways and power. They gave to their day and generation such a revelation of God as the world had never known. Stop and think of the wonders of God that the Old Testament revealed. Think of the marvels, that it seems would stagger the very soul of modern Christianity.

When the Israelites were traveling over the deserts, God arrested the processes of decay in their very shoes and clothing, and they wore them continually for forty years [see Deuteronomy 8:4]. Think of the marvel of it, the arrest of the process of decay! And then someone wonders if it is possible to arrest the process of decay in a man's life. Yes, it is, bless God! Jesus Christ arrested the process of death by the power of God, through the introduction of the life and the Spirit of life in Jesus Christ, giving man eternal life.

Think again of the old prophet who, when they had lost the ax in the water and came to him in their distress, takes a stick and holds it in his hands. What for? Until that stick became magnetized by the Spirit and power of God. And when he threw it in the water, the ax arose and came to the stick [see 2 Kings 6:4-7].

Think again of the prophet, when he was called to the dying boy. He said to his servant, *"take this staff,"* the staff that he carried, *"go ahead of me, lay it on the child"* [see 2 Kings 4:29]. What for? Because he carried that staff next to his God-anointed hands until the staff itself became impregnated with the life and power of God.

So the servant went ahead, and there was enough of God in that staff to keep the life there, and the spirit there, until he [the prophet] arrived and called the child to life by the power of God.

Later they were burying a man, and in their haste they opened the grave of Elisha, and when the dead man touched his old God-filled bones, he became alive [see 2 Kings 13:21]. There was enough of God in the old bones to quicken him to life again. Bless God.

You say, "Well, how can Christianity demonstrate anything further than that?" When I listened to Dr. Hertz, my heart asked, "Dear God, when I get my turn to reveal what Christianity is, what am I going to say that is going to reveal Christianity as superior to Jewish dispensation, and the consciousness of God that it produced in the souls of the prophets?"

From eight o'clock at night until four-thirty, Dr. Hertz poured out his soul in a wondrous stream of God revelation, such as my soul had never heard. In the morning as I started for home I prayed, "God, in the Name of Jesus, when it comes next Thursday night, and it is my turn to show forth Jesus Christ, what am I going to say to surmount the revelation of God that he gave?"

I had searched Christian literature for it. I had searched the libraries of the world. I could not find it in the writings of the old Christian fathers. I searched the Word of God for it. I saw flashes of it, but somehow it would not frame in my soul. I decided there was only one way. I gave myself to fasting and prayer and waiting on God. And one day in the quiet GOD TOLD ME THAT SECRET.

And from that day my heart rested in the new vision of Jesus Christ, and a new revelation of the real divinity of Christianity came to my heart.

So it came my turn and I sat down and reviewed for hours with care, step by step, the consciousness that the philosophers and priests had shown as belonging to their respective religions, and finally the wonderful consciousness that Dr. Hertz had shown as belonging to the Mosaic dispensation.

Oh, bless God, there is a secret in Jesus Christ. CHRISTIANITY IS ALL SUPERNATURAL, every bit of it. The philosophies are natural. The Mosaic dispensation and its revelation was supernatural, but its revelation did not have the high degree of overcoming consciousness that belongs to Christianity. Yet you can go around the world, and you will not find one in a hundred thousand that can tell what the real secret of Christianity is, which makes it superior to all the religions.

You say, "It is the Holy Ghost." Well, the prophets had the Holy Ghost. There is no more marvelous record given than the Old Testament records. When Moses wanted mechanics and workmen for the new tabernacle, the Lord called a man by name and said: *"I have filled him with the spirit of God, in wisdom, and in understanding, and in knowledge, and in all manner of workmanship, To devise cunning works, to work in gold, and in silver, and in brass, And in cutting of stones, to set them, and in carving of timber, to work in all manner of workmanship"* [Exodus 31:3-5]. That is the way they learned their trade.

Later they were making preparations for the building of Solomon's temple. That temple is one of the seven wonders of the world. Did you ever stop to think of where the plans came from, or how they got them? Old David tells us that God gave him the plans of the temple in writing: *while the Spirit of God was upon me in writing [1 Chronicles 28:19]*, and he wrote the details of it. He put these details down with such accuracy that they prepared the temple in the mountains, and when they came to put it together, there was no sound of a hammer. Every piece fit to piece. Wonderful movings of God! Wonderful presence of God! Talk about the glory of God. Why, when Moses came down from the mountain, his face shone or radiated with the glory of God so intensely the people were afraid of him, and he was compelled to wear a veil until the anointing had somewhat left his soul.

But, beloved, Christianity is more than that. Paul declares that the glory of Moses' face was superseded. I said a moment ago, Christianity is not a natural religion. It has nothing natural in it. IT IS SUPERNATURAL from the top to the bottom, from the center to the circumference, within and without. It comes right from heaven, every bit of it. It is the divine outflow of the holy soul of the crucified, risen, glorified Son of God.

Why does God come down from heaven into the hearts of men, into the natures of men, into the bodies of men, into the souls of men, into the spirits of men? God's purpose in man is to transform him into the nature of God. Jesus said, *"I said, YE ARE GODS"* (John 10:34).

The philosophers came to the grave and died. They had no further revelation to give. They had left their tenets, and they exist to this day. I have studied the great EASTERN philosophies. I have searched them from cover to cover. I have read them for years as diligently as I have read my Bible. I have read them to see what their consciousness was. The secret of salvation is NOT in them.

But in my Bible is seen that the Son of God saves men from their sins, and changes them by His power in their nature, so that they become like Him. And that is the purpose of Jesus, to take a man and make a christ out of him. To take a sinner and wash him pure and white and clean, and then come into his life and anoint him with His Spirit, speak through him, live in him, change the substance of his spirit, change the substance of his body; until his body and his blood and his bones and flesh and his soul and his spirit, are the body, and blood and bones and soul and spirit of the Son of God (Ephesians 5:30 and 1 Corinthians 6:17).

Oh, Jesus was crucified. Jesus was crucified after there grew in the soul of Jesus the divine consciousness that He could go into the grave, and through faith in God, accept the Word of God, and believe that He would raise him from the dead. Jesus went into the grave with a divine boldness, not simply as a martyr. He was God's PRINCE, God's KING, God's SAVIOR. He went into the grave God's CONQUEROR. He was after something. He went after the power of DEATH, and He got it, and He took it captive, and He came forth from the grave. He had death and hell by the throat, and the key in His hands. He was Conqueror!

No more bowing before the accursed power that had been generated through sin. It was a captive. No more fear of hell! Do you hear it? No more fear of hell after Jesus Christ came out of the grave. He had death and hell by the throat, and the key in His hands. He was Conqueror!

When He came forth from the grave, He came forth bringing that wonderful spirit of heavenly triumph that was begotten in the soul of Jesus because He had not failed. He had gone and done it. No longer a hope; no longer a faith; now a knowledge—God's consciousness in His heart. It was done!

Oh, yes, bless God, I am coming back to that word with which I started. Do you know the secret of religion is in its consciousness? The secret of Christianity is in the consciousness it produces in your soul. And Christianity produces a higher consciousness than any other religion in the world; no other religion in the world, or other revelation of the true God equals it. It is the highest and holiest. It comes breathing and throbbing and burning right out of the heart of the glorified Son of God. It comes breathing and beating and throbbing into your nature and mind, bless God.

So that is the reason I love the religion of the Lord and Savior Jesus Christ. It is the reason the Cross of Calvary is a sacred place. That is the reason that the conquest of the Son of God in the Regions of Death makes a man's heart throb.

That is the reason He gathered His disciples together, and as if He could not wait, He said, Let me breathe it into you. Go forth in its power. *"All power is given unto me in heaven and in earth. Go ye therefore"* [Matthew 28:18-19]. These signs shall follow. Cast out devils, speak with new tongues, heal the sick. Amen.

In those early centuries of Christianity, Christianity did not go into the world apologizing. It went to slay the powers of darkness and undo the works of the devil, and it lived in holy triumph.

Healing Consciousness

I am going into the history of the Old Testament. It is surprising how ignorant people are of the Word of God. God made a covenant of healing with the children of Israel after they crossed the Red Sea, and they lived under that covenant four hundred and fifty years, unbroken, and there never was an Israelite for four hundred and fifty years, so far as the record goes, except Asa, who ever took one dose of medicine. One backslider went back on God and called the physicians like the heathen did, but the people trusted God, and God alone for four hundred and fifty years, or until Solomon got into polygamy. He went down into Egypt and married Egyptian wives, who brought their heathen physicians with them. And eventually the whole nation had fallen from grace, and gone back again and were taking pills and medicine and dope, just like some Pentecostal heathen do.

Do you want to get on God's territory? Cut it out. It belongs to the devil and the heathen, and the great big unbelieving world.

When you see those holy flashes of heavenly flame once in a while in a person's life, as we observe in our Sister Etter, when someone is healed, it is because her consciousness and Christ are *one*. She is fused into God. I saw a dying, strangling woman healed in thirty seconds, as Mrs. Etter cast out the demon. The flame of God, the fire of His Spirit, ten seconds of connection with the Almighty Christ at the Throne of God, that is the secret of it.

Oh, I would like to get you in touch with the Son of God for five minutes. I would like to see the streams of God's lightning come down for ten minutes! I wonder what would take place.

A few months ago I was absent from the city of Spokane, and when I returned we discovered Mrs. Lake was not at home. It was just time to leave for my afternoon service. Just then someone came in and said, "Your secretary, Mrs. Graham, is in the throes of death, and your wife is with her." So I hurried down to the place. When I got there the wife of one of my ministers met me at the door and said, "You are too late; she has gone." And as I stepped in I met the minister coming out of the room. He said, "She has not breathed for a long time."

But as I looked down at that woman, and thought of how God Almighty, three years before, had raised her out of death, after her womb and ovaries and tubes had been removed in operations, and God Almighty had given them back to her, after which she had married and conceived, my heart flamed. I took that woman up off that pillow, and called on God for the lightnings of heaven to blast the power of death and deliver her, and I commanded her to come back and stay, and she came back, after not breathing for twenty-three minutes.

We have not yet learned to keep in touch with the powers of God. Once in a while our soul rises, and we see the flame of God accomplish this wonder and that, but beloved, Jesus Christ lived in the presence of God every hour of the day and night. Never a word proceeded from the mouth of Jesus Christ, but what was God's Word. *"The words that I speak unto you, they are spirit, and they are life"* (John 6:63).

When you and I are lost in the Son of God, and the fires of Jesus burn in our hearts, like they did in Him, our words will be the words of life and of the spirit, and there will be no death in them. But, beloved, we are on the way.

I have read church history because my heart was searching for the truth of God. I have witnessed with my own eyes the most amazing manifestations of psychological power. I knew an East Indian Yogi who volunteered to be buried for three days, and he came up out of that grave well and whole. I saw them put a man in a cataleptic state, and place a stone fifteen inches square on his body, put his feet on one chair and his head on another, and strike that stone with a twenty-five pound sledge, seven times, until it broke in two.

I watched these things, and I said, "These are only on the psychological plane. Beyond that is the spirit plane and the amazing wonder of the Holy Spirit of God, and if God got hold of my spirit for ten minutes, He could do something ten thousand times greater than that."

Why Jesus was the triumphant One. Did you ever stop to think of Jesus at the throne of God? I like to think of the twentieth century Christ, not the Jesus that lived in the world two thousand years ago, not the humiliated Jesus, not Jesus dying on the cross for my sin, but the glorified, exalted Son of God at the throne of God, Who stands declaring, *"I am he that liveth, and was dead; and behold, I am alive for evermore, Amen; and have the keys of hell and of death"* (Revelation 1:18). Blessed be God.

And that is the Christ that breathes His power into your soul and mine, and that is the consciousness that is breathed from heaven in the Holy Ghost when it comes to your heart. Amen.

God purposed that the Christian Church should be the embodiment of the living, blessed Son of God—Christ living not in one temple, Jesus, but in multitudes of temples—the bodies of those yielded to God in holy consecration, God's real church, not in name only but in power. Many members, one in Spirit, one divine structure of divine faith and substance. Man transformed, transfigured, and transmuted into the nature, the glory, and the substance of Christ.

"That Evil One Toucheth Him Not"

When the Spirit of God radiated from the man Jesus, how close do you suppose it was possible for the evil spirit to come to Him? I believe it was impossible for the evil one to come to Him. The Spirit of God is as destructive of evil as it is creative of good. I am sure that Satan talked to Jesus from a safe distance.

The real Christian is a SEPARATED man. He is separated forever unto God in ALL the departments of his life. So his *body* and his *soul* and his *spirit* are forever committed to the Father. From the time he commits himself to God, his BODY is as absolutely in the hands of God as his spirit or his soul. He can go to no other power for help or healing.

A hundredfold consecration takes the individual forever out of the hands of all but God.

*Kenneth Copeland Publications acknowledges that references to race and nationality considered acceptable in Rev. Lake's day are offensive and not acceptable to today's reader. However, these references in no way reflect the attitude or policies of KCP. To fully understand Rev. Lake's heart toward other races, we recommend you read his biography located at the front of the book.

40

Development of Christian Consciousness

I want to talk to you tonight about my Lord. I want you to get acquainted with Him. Some know Him in one way or another. None of us have reached the place where we have it all. But, bless God, we are on the way. When I was a boy I thought the sole aim and object of the gospel was to keep from going to hell. A good many other folks observe Christianity from that point of view yet. After a while evangelists changed the idea somewhat. They began to teach that the object of being a Christian was not to keep from going to hell, but to go to heaven.

Then I began reasoning. I said, "One is just as selfish as the other." The one gets saved to keep from going to hell and the other gets saved to get to heaven. Both are wholly selfish and neither one is the real purpose of Jesus.

Jesus gave one final reason for men being Christians, and strangely very few people have ever discovered even from the Word of God what that real purpose is.

But one day Jesus came along by the River Jordan, when John was baptizing and asked for the privilege of being baptized. John was startled. He said, *"I have need to be baptized of thee, and comest thou to me?"*

Jesus said, *"Suffer it to be so now"*, and then He gave the real reason. In the *King James Version* it says, *"for thus it becometh us to fulfill all righteousness"* [Matthew 3:14-15]. But in one of the liberal translations it reads: *"UNTO ALL RIGHTEOUSNESS."*

Jesus was going to be baptized as His commitment of His body and His soul and His spirit to God forever, in order that from thenceforth He might MANIFEST THE RIGHTEOUSNESS OF GOD.

To MANIFEST THE RIGHTEOUSNESS OF GOD is the real reason for a man's desiring to be a Christian, not to go to heaven when he dies, or to keep out of hell, but to REVEAL THE RIGHTEOUSNESS OF GOD IN THIS WORLD. And then heaven and all our rewards will be the natural result of having lived in unity with God and having revealed His righteousness in this world.

God has a wonderful purpose. God's Christian is the most magnificent specimen in all the universe of God. God's ideal for a Christian surpasses everything else in the whole world. Varied churches and varied religious institutions have their peculiar idea of what a Christian is. One of their ideals seems to be that the individual must be able to whoop and hop around, and all that sort of thing. But Jesus never did it. He was too big for that. He had outgrown it. We had our ideals of religious meetings. Not one of them is like the meetings Jesus conducted, at least only in a slight way. Then we have our ideals of what constitutes a real message. MY! If you will read the words of Jesus over again, you will discover that few of our messages are like the message of the Lord. His messages were an uncovering of the soul of man, an uncovering of the nature of God, so man could discern Him, and when they discerned Him they loved Him. The message of Jesus was constructive not destructive, positive righteousness, not negative obedience.

Jesus gave a new name to God that no one had ever given Him before. The prophets were intimate with God, and the Old Testament is one marvelous revelation of intimacy with God. They knew Him as a great Governor, as a great Controller, as the One who guided the affairs of the universe, but Jesus knew Him as "Our Father." He introduced into Bible vocabulary a new name to express God to me.

I am going to talk to you along a line that perhaps may seem new. First, I want to place before you God's ideal of a Christian, then by His grace I am going to undertake an unfolding, step by step, how men arrive at that stature of Christ.

God's ideal of a Christian is not a man who is ready to go to heaven, nor a man who lives a good life in this world, nor a man who has victory over sin, nor victory over disease. It includes all these things, but it is ten thousand times more than that.

> **And he gave some, apostles; and some, prophets; and some, evangelists; and some, pastors and teachers; For the perfecting of the saints, for the work of the ministry, for the edifying of the body of Christ: Till we all come in the unity of the faith, and of the knowledge of the Son of God, unto a perfect man, unto the measure of the stature of the fulness of Christ (Ephesians 4:11-13).**

And that is the IDEAL of my heart. That somehow in God's divine grace, by the wonderful processes of His Spirit, He is going to help me to grow out of babyhood and infancy into the stature of Jesus Christ. And that is God's ideal for the Christian.

You say, "But brother, I was saved from my sins? Don't you know I was sanctified?"

Why surely, Jesus was. Don't you know Jesus was baptized in the Holy Ghost, but He went so far beyond that it reveals these were but the beginnings by which a Son of God was born and came into being. His development was beyond all that, and went beyond all our known Christian experiences.

I want to speak now of the growth of the knowledge of God that took place in Jesus Christ. This will sound strange to some of you. But you say, "Jesus Himself was God." Surely He was: He was likewise man. *"For verily he took not on him the nature of angels; but he took on him the seed of Abraham"* (Hebrews 2:16). *"[He] was in all points tempted like as we are, yet without sin"* [Hebrews 4:15].

He came to our level. He demonstrated in the beginning that man could be an overcomer over the powers of darkness through reliance on God and His Word.

His demonstration began, first, in the order of nature, where He met no mind but His own. He changed the water into wine—by the action of His own will. He stilled the sea by the Word of His command. He walked on the water. Each one of them an ascent over the other, each one of them revealing that in the soul of Jesus Himself there was an ever ascending scale in God.

Then the next thing in the life of Jesus, He began His ministry of healing. When He undertook His ministry of healing, He had another MIND to meet—the mind of the individual who needed the blessing: *"And Jesus went about all Galilee, teaching in their synagogues, and preaching the gospel of the kingdom, and healing all manner of sickness and all manner of disease among the people"* (Matthew 4:23).

Then Jesus entered a new realm. If you study the healing that took place under His ministry you will observe that, first, it was the healing of disease; next, the healing of the blind; lastly, the healing of the lepers and the creation of eyes in the man born blind—a gradual continuous assent.

And now there developed in the soul of Jesus a holy dawning of the power of God, even over death, and in His demonstration over the power of death there are three degrees, like the other.

The daughter of Jairus was dead for a FEW MINUTES. While the father was interceding, the servants came saying, *"Thy daughter is dead"* [Luke 8:49]. Jesus went instantly to her bedside and she arose to life.

The son of the widow of Nain was dead for several hours and they were carrying him out for burial, when Jesus touched the bier and he arose [see Luke 7:14].

Lazarus was dead for four days, and the testimony of his sisters was, *"by this time he stinketh"* [John 11:39].

First instance, death in the first degree, next, dead a few minutes: in the second degree, dead a few hours; and in the third degree, dead four days, *"by this time he stinketh."*

My, there is a wonderful revelation in connection with the raising of Lazarus that is not given in the story as it appears in the New Testament. I want to quote from the New Testament Apocrypha, from the book of Nicodemus. It will explain a whole lot to you.

Before I give this story I want to call your attention to one other thing because it concludes the thought I had in mind: that there are degrees in the experience of Jesus by which He took one step after another in every single realm, until He eventually manifested God's divine perfection. There was the Crucifixion, followed by the Resurrection, and climaxed by the Ascension. Each one of them a degree in the power of God beyond the other.

If Jesus had died on the cross, gone into the grave and been resurrected from the grave only, there would still be no such thing as a real salvation in the world. But because Jesus died on the cross, entered into death, arose from the grave, AND ASCENDED to the throne of God, and finally received from the Father the gift of the Holy Ghost with authority to minister it to mankind, there is in existence a divine salvation, sufficient to satisfy the nature of every man.

The Story of Lazarus

In the story that I wanted to bring to you is this marvelous incident. Just prior to the crucifixion of Jesus, Satan appeared in the regions of Death, and said to Beelzebub, the keeper of the Regions of Death, that he might now prepare to receive Jesus Christ, because he (Satan) had brought to pass such a combination of circumstances that Jesus was to be crucified. Beelzebub replied, "But, Satan, is not this Jesus of Nazareth, Who in His divine nature was so strong that He came here and took from our midst Lazarus when he was here, and we could not hold him?"

Satan said: "Yes, He is the one."

Beelzebub said, "But if in His divine nature He was so strong He came and took Lazarus from our hands, and we could not hold him, how can we hold Him Himself?" That was the problem.

Now I am going back. What is the real secret of the Resurrection? That Jesus arose from the dead? NO! Lots of men had risen from the dead. Away back in the Old Testament they opened a grave to bury a man, and when he touched the bones of Elisha there was enough of the spirit of God in the old dry bones to give him life, and he arose. But he brought no revelation of God and manifested no particular power of God in the world.

The son of the widow of Nain was truly dead, and was raised to life, but he brought no revelation from the dead. Lazarus was dead four days, and restored again. But so far as the record goes, Lazarus knew no more after his resurrection than he did before.

At the crucifixion of Jesus Himself, many that were dead arose and appeared in the city.

It was not in the mere fact, then, that they arose from the dead, or that Jesus arose from the dead that gives the secret of the Resurrection. I want you to see what it is.

All the way along in the life of Jesus there is a growth in consciousness of God. Step by step Jesus Christ discerned God and His purpose for man, and God's purpose for man, and God's purpose for Himself. Step by step Jesus revealed the power of God in the new light that had dawned upon His soul. Until finally, after He had manifested His power in these three degrees of death, ending in the resurrection of Lazarus, after he had been dead four days, He began to talk to His disciples about a new problem, and a new possibility. He began to open the fact that He Himself was to be crucified. In fact, that it was in the prophecies that He should be, and in the determined councils of the Godhead.

I want you to distinguish between Christianity and philosophy, for in these days the world is filled with philosophical religions, and everything psychological is used to impress the world that it is religious. And Christians ought to know what it is that makes the distinction between Christianity and philosophy, and what makes Jesus distinct from the philosophers and why it is that Christianity has a power that philosophy has not.

Some of the philosophies were old and gray whiskered and ready to die when Jesus was born. Bhagavad-Gita was written eight hundred years before Isaiah. Buddha lived hundreds of years before Jesus and taught most of the things Jesus taught. Confucianism was old. Brahmanism was old. Most of the ancient philosophies were old when Jesus came to the world. The philosophers wrote their tenets, left them, came to the grave and died, and their revelation ceased. There was nothing remaining but the tenets they had written.

Buddha wrote his tenets, came to the grave: Confucius wrote his tenets, came to the grave: Brahma wrote his tenets, came to the grave: the Zend-Avestas were written and their authors came to the grave. They all died and there was no further revelation. They ended all.

Not so with the Son of God. Not so with the Lord Jesus. Why CHRISTIANITY began where philosophy left off. The crucifixion of Jesus was but the entrance into the greatest of His divine revelations. Jesus not only rose from the dead, but also He determined in His own soul to take captive that power that had been captivating men and subjecting them to death's control. So Jesus entered into the grave.

The early church was much more conversant with this phase of the Lord's victory than we are. The literature of the early church fathers are full of the wonder of what took place in the life and ministry of Jesus, after He was in the grave. Peter gives us just two little flashes. He says, *"he went and preached unto the spirits in prison; Which sometime were disobedient, when once the longsuffering of God waited in the days of Noah, while the ark was a-preparing"* (1 Peter 3:19-20). Next, *"For for this cause was the gospel preached also to them that are dead."* What for? *"that they might be judged according to men in the flesh"* (1 Peter 4:6).

He carried His word of testimony and power to the very dead; those that were dead before the flood, and those who died between the flood and Himself. There are two classes—the spirits that were in prison from the days of Noah, and He went also and preached to them that are dead, that they might be judged according to men in the flesh. Remember that Jesus preached to the dead. The dead of His day had the prophets to listen to, and receive and believe their teachings, or reject them, just as you and I have. The purpose of His preaching was *"that they might be judged according to men in the flesh."*

Next: In the Soul of Jesus there grew that wonderful consciousness, that having liberated them from death's power, there was a step further yet to go. He must take captive the power that was binding their souls. So He entered into death and His ministry and victory in the Regions of Death were the result. And one day He came forth from the dead, a living man once more as He was before He died.

Over and over again, John tells us that He did this and He performed that work, and He wrought that marvel and that in order that we might believe; in order that He might reveal to the satisfaction of the souls of those who were trying to believe, that there was a foundation, and a reason, and a substantial ground on which your confidence in Christ could rest.

So He came forth from the dead with the consciousness of God, and His power, and His ability to command God's power and utilize it, that no other in all the earth or sea or heaven ever had. No philosopher ever had it, or has ever known anything of it. But when JESUS came forth from the dead, He came forth speaking a word that had never been spoken in the world before. He said *"All power is given unto me in heaven and in earth"* [Matthew 28:18]. Blessed be the name of God! He had proved it, faith had become fact, vision was now consciousness.

All the triumph of Jesus in the regions of death had wrought in His soul the wonder of God. No other life ever had it. No other soul ever got the flame of it; no other nature ever felt the burning of it. Bless God.

And He was so anxious to lift His followers into it that the very first thing He did after His reappearance among them, was to

BREATHE on them. He said Let me give it to you. Let me breathe it into your life. *"Receive ye the Holy Ghost"* (John 20:22). Let me put it into your hearts, burn it into your soul, establish it into your nature. His victory over death had wrought the marvel.

But, beloved, that is not all of CHRISTIANITY. Christianity is MORE THAN THAT. That is not the consciousness of Christianity. The consciousness of Christianity is greater than that. It was holier than that, more powerful than resurrection consciousness. When Jesus came forth from the dead He was able to declare, *"All power is given unto me in heaven and in earth. GO YE, therefore."*

Oh, then there were some wonderful days, forty wonderful days in which Jesus took the disciples, who had been in His own school for three and a half years, through a new course. In these days we would call it a post-graduate course. So they went out into the mountains of Galilee, all by themselves, for a post-graduate course with the risen Lord. And He taught them of the all-power of God. He taught them of power over Death and the divine fact that the dominion of the risen Christ is for every soul. David describing it said, *"Thou hast led captivity captive."* Not only that, but beyond it. *"Thou hast received gifts for men"* [Psalm 68:18].

So one day there came the Ascension. He took them out on the Mt. of Olives, and as He blessed them, He rose out of their sight to glory. Then there is one of those wonderful divine flashes in the Word of God that just illuminates a whole life.

Peter was preaching on the day of Pentecost. The power of God had fallen upon the people. The people demanded an explanation. *"What meaneth this?"* [Acts 2:12]. Peter replied: *"this is that which was spoken by the prophet Joel"* [Acts 2:16]. Then he goes on and teaches them concerning Christ; takes them from His crucifixion, through His resurrection, His ascension, up to the throne of God: and when he gets the people at the throne of God and their minds fixed there, He gave them the final explanation. Jesus having arrived at the throne of God, an interview between God the Father and Jesus Christ takes place, and God gave to Jesus the gift of the Holy Ghost, and the explanation was *"he hath shed forth this, which ye now see and hear"* [Acts 2:33].

Say, beloved, the Holy Ghost is born out of the heart of the Father God Himself, ministered through the soul of Jesus Christ, the High Priest of God, into your heart and mind. It is intended to lift our hearts and lift our lives out of the mud, and keep us there forever.

So the real CHRISTIAN ought to be the kingliest man in the whole earth, the princeliest man in the whole earth. As kingly and princely and lovely and holy as the Son of God. As big as Jesus, with the power of Jesus and the love of Jesus.

My, when the limitations of our life are taken down once in a while, a little flame, a little touch of that heavenly consciousness breaks through, and we wonder at it, and are amazed at what takes place.

One day the wife of a policeman, Mrs. Carter, of Spokane, Washington, was pronounced by her physicians to be in a condition of pregnancy. Natures time came and went; no child was born. So they gathered to council again and re-examined the woman, and this time made the discovery that it was a fibroid tumor. The tumor continued to grow until the fourteenth month had passed, and the physicians estimated that it would weigh fifteen pounds.

One day she came to the healing rooms at 4 p.m. with her nurse, was ministered to, returned home, and in the morning at 10 a.m. when she awoke there was neither part nor particle of the curse left; no blood, no pus, no evidence whatsoever. That thing of hell was totally dematerialized by the power of God. The woman is one of our ministering staff, and recently assisted us in the work at Portland, Oregon.

These little touches that seem to break through the darkness of our soul here and there, reveal to us the almightiness of the power of God in Jesus at the throne.

Beloved, Jesus had a purpose from the first day. That purpose was to secure, to ultimately secure on behalf of mankind, the gift of the Holy Ghost, and minister it to the world. That is the reason Jesus said, *"greater works than these shall he do; because I go unto my Father"* (John 14:12). Jesus knew that if He could receive that gift of the Holy Ghost, that promise of our Father God, and minister it to the world, a world of new men would arise.

Some years ago a Roman Catholic priest in this city said: "Christ was born that other christs might be born." God's intention was not that Jesus Christ was to be a lonely Son of God forever, but that Jesus Christ, ministering the Holy Spirit of God to the sons of men, shall see of the travail of his soul, and shall be satisfied, in that they too are raised to His own likeness and stature and glory and power and understanding, and they too become son of God.

So my heart has not been satisfied at all that I have been saved, not because the Lord has baptized me in the Holy Ghost, nor because God has used me in His ministry. Not at all.

I have had a vision before my soul that fascinates my heart night and day. The pure, radiant, wondrous Son of God, Jesus Christ, who purposes by His grace to keep me in His hands and in His heart, and you in His hands and in His heart, until by the grace of God you come forth in the holy likeness and the heavenly power and the magnificence and glory and wonder of His understanding, a Son of God indeed and in truth.

I am going to put a proposition to you. When I lived in Africa, one of our departments was the native* work, and I bless God for the marvels He let me witness among the native* people. I believe we had privileges that have never been accorded any other man in the world in modern times. On Christmas Eve, 1912, in Basutoland [currently Lesotho], the Lord's supper was administered to seventy-five healed lepers. They were healed under a black* fellow whose sole raiment when we first knew him was a goat skin apron. But the mere fact of the wonder of Christ's healing touched his own soul and changed his nature and life.

Oh, Beloved, it is one thing to redeem you and me from sin. It was a marvelous thing to see these men redeemed from ignorance and sin, and exalted in God. Consequently if he is going to develop a son of God out of you and me, the first thing necessary is to cleanse our hearts from sin, and the next is to give us His own Spirit and teach us of Himself, and reveal His love and power in us. And when that is accomplished, by the amazing processes of His continuous revelation in the soul, He lifts us into the place of light and life of love and power.

It was a beautiful thing for the brethren to sit with a man under whose ministry seventy-five lepers had been healed, some were without a nose, some without fingers, some without toes, and some without ears.

But I am going to tell you another leper story. A man by the name of Young was quarantined in the state of Nebraska until about seven weeks ago. We got into correspondence with him through Senator Willet, another leper. On my return trip I am going to stop and pray for Senator Willet. This man, Young, got in touch with us through Willet. He was Roman Catholic. God told him he was going to move in behalf of his deliverance. A few days after, the officers came and said, "You have been sending and receiving letters, contrary to instructions."

He said, "Yes, I have been corresponding with people who pray the prayer of faith, that I shall not die like a dog or pig."

They asked to see the letters, and in a few days after, came back and said: "If you think you can get healed, we will turn you loose on your pledge that you will go directly to Spokane to these people who heal."

So he started for Spokane with their pledge that they would furnish him with the necessary funds. The day before I left Spokane, I sat down with that man and he dictated the story of his healing by the power of God. He is now on the road to Key West to join his wife and children.

My Lord is not dead, but I'll tell you, dear hearts, we have been satisfied to live in Christ our babyhood and perpetuate our babyhood, and go on shouting like a lot of babies, instead of by the grace of God entering into the secrets of the heart of Jesus Christ and claiming from heaven the divine flames of God upon our souls. When that takes place, then we will stand amazed at the action of God in our own and other's lives.

Have you ever gone into the great hospitals of the land? Have you realized the amazing machinery of healing in the nation necessary to keep people well, and make them well when they are sick? My God, there is no end to it. Look at the sick on the right hand and on the left hand. Mighty God, the time has come when instead of being in our infancy, we ought to be in the stature of Jesus Christ and the power of God, and the life of Christ will be exhibited to consume the powers of hell in the world, and take the world captive for Jesus Christ. And one day, bless God, we will put the crown on the head of the Son of God and proclaim Him, King of kings and Lord of lords, forever and ever..

*Kenneth Copeland Publications acknowledges that references to race and nationality considered acceptable in Rev. Lake's day are offensive and not acceptable to today's reader. However, these references in no way reflect the attitude or policies of KCP. To fully understand Rev. Lake's heart toward other races, we recommend you read his biography located at the front of the book.

41

Discernment

I Corinthians 12:8-12

My first great interest in Africa was stimulated when I was a child through reading of Livingston's travels and explorations, and of Stanley finding Livingston in the heart of Africa, and still more by reading of Stanley's trip across the Continent and down the Congo.

As the years of my boyhood passed, I became conscious of a certain operation of my spirit, which I shall endeavor to describe.

In my sleep, and sometimes during my waking hours, it seemed to me as if I were present in Africa instead of America. At such times I would note the geography of the country, the peculiarities of the landscape, the characteristics of the various tribes of native people. I became deeply sympathetic with effort of the Boers as I watched them endeavoring to establish their republics.

As I reached manhood these excursions in the spirit became more intelligent to me. On one occasion, while in the attitude of prayer, I approached South Africa from the Indian Ocean, and traveled through Zululand over into the mountains of Basutoland. I noted the distinctions of the tribal characteristics as I passed through these states, also the Orange Free State and the Transvaal from Basutoland to Johannesburg.

This excursion, projection of spirit consciousness, or whatever it may be termed, occurred during hours of communion with God in prayer.

While meditating and praying while on the sea on my way to Africa, I would become suddenly conscious of the political conditions of South Africa. I would feel the struggles of the various political elements in their contest for supremacy. Then again I would realize the condition of the country financially, and still again see the religious aspects of the nation. I saw the predominating thought that bound the Boer people as a nation to the Dutch church and the struggles of the civilized native people to attain a religious independence.

While in the spirit I comprehended not only present fact, but also my consciousness would project itself into the future so that I saw the train of national events that are yet to take place; also the West coast of Africa when they had become great commercial seaports with lines of railways extending up into the Transvaal.

Much of this vision I have seen fulfilled at this writing, namely the uniting of the South African states into a national union (Natal, Orange Free State, Cape Colony and The Transvaal), the great religious upheaval, the settlement of political and financial problems, etc. I saw the conquest of German Southwest Africa by the British, including some of the battle scenes of the present war there. [World War I].

No one could realize, unless they had been associated with me in the work in Africa, how thoroughly this knowledge of the conditions in Africa was made to me. This was not the result of reading, for I had read practically nothing of Africa since my childhood.

In traveling through the country after my arrival, there was nothing new. I had seen it all in advance, and could recollect times and circumstances when in my visions of Africa I had visited one city or another.

This knowledge of affairs was of inestimable value to me when I actually stood on the ground. Business men and statesmen alike frequently expressed surprise at the intimate knowledge I possessed of conditions in the land, little realizing how this knowledge had come to me.

This spiritual consciousness of conditions, or gift of knowledge, continued with me throughout my first years as President of the Apostolic Church of South Africa.

It was my custom to dictate my letters in the morning before going to my office, or out among the sick, for the duties of the day. At such times, if I wanted to write a letter, for instance to Cape Town, Peitermaritzburg, Pretoria, or some other place, I would bow my head in quiet before God for a few moments. While in this attitude there would be born in my consciousness of the conditions of the Assembly or district, or town, as the case might be. I could see the difficulties the brethren were having there, if any, and hundreds of times have written revealing to them an inside knowledge of the conditions among them that they were sure no one knew about.

In the conduct of our native work, this feature was so marked that after a time, an adage grew up among the natives, "You cannot fool Brother Lake, God shows him." Many, many times when the natives would come and present perhaps only one side of a matter, I would be able to tell them the whole truth concerning the difficulty.

On one occasion a man from Robertson made charges against a brother who was one of the elders in the work there. When he got through I said to him, "Brother, let us bow our heads in prayer." Instantly I seemed to be in Robertson. I observed the assembly, saw the various brethren there, noted their piety and devotion to God, I saw that the condition was almost the reverse as it had been presented. The man, himself, was the troublemaker.

On another occasion a woman came to me several times requesting prayer for her deliverance from drunkenness. I urged upon her the necessity for repentance unto God, confession of her sins, etc. She assured me many times that she has done all of this.

One day she came while I was resting on the cot. My wife brought her into the room. She knelt weeping by the cot. As usual she asked me to pray for deliverance. I said to her, "What about the two hundred and fifty pounds sterling worth of jewelry that you stole from such and such a home?" She threw up her hands with an exclamation of despair, supposing that I would deliver her to the police, or tell the party from whom she had stolen it. I calmed her by assurance that as a minister of Christ no one should know from me concerning the matter. I regarded the knowledge as sacred before God because God had revealed it to me in order to assist her out of her difficulty. She was delivered from her drunkenness, and remained a sober woman, working earnestly in the vineyard of the Lord.

Some days afterward, a woman came to me, saying, "I have heard that So-and-So (naming the lady of whom I have spoken) has been converted, and I know if she has she must have confessed to you that she stole jewelry from my home." I explained to her that even if such a confession had been made, as a minister of Jesus Christ I could not reveal it and would not reveal it.

As we conversed I told her I believed God had sent her in order that we might discuss together the forgiveness of God. I showed her that God expected us to forgive, even as we are forgiven. Indeed, that we are commanded to forgive. The Spirit gave me such consciousness of the forgiveness of God that as I presented it to her it seemed to flow in liquid love from my soul. She broke down and wept, asking me to pray for her that God would deliver her from her own sins, and establish in her a knowledge and consciousness of His presence and life. She left saying, "Tell So-and-So that as far as the jewelry is concerned, I shall never mention it again. There will be no prosecution, and by the grace of God I forgive her."

My wife possessed the spirit of discernment in a more marked degree than I did, especially concerning difficulties in peoples lives, particularly regarding those seeking healing. She had the power to reveal the reason they were not blessed of God.

It was my custom in receiving the sick in my office to let them stand in a line, and I would pray for them, laying hands on each as they passed me. Some would not receive healing, and their suffering would continue. Some would receive healing in part, and some were instantly healed. I would pass those who received no healing into the adjoining room, and when I had finished praying for the multitude, I would bring my wife into the room where these unhealed ones were. She would go close to one, and would say, in substance, "Your difficulty is that at such-and-such a time you committed such-and-such a sin which has not been repented of and confessed." To another perhaps it would be, "God wants you to make restitution for such-and-such an act that you committed at such-and-such a time." To another, "The pride of your heart and the love of the world have not been laid on the altar of Christ."

Upon hearing the inner things of their hearts revealed, many would bow at once and confess their sins to God. We would pray for them again, and the Lord would heal them. Some would go away unrepentant. Some would go through the motions of repentance, but it was not of the heart, and they would not be healed. Thus we were taught to value highly the gift of God of which Paul speaks in 1 Corinthians 12:10, *"to another discerning of spirits."*

The Spirit of God is like the bread that the disciples held in their hands. When they broke it and distributed it to the multitudes there was more remaining than when they began. The Spirit of God is CREATIVE, GENERATIVE, CONSTRUCTIVE, and the more you give the more you receive. Jesus laid down a perpetual law when He said: *"Give and it shall be given unto you"* [Luke 6:38].

42

The Resurrection

Sermon 1

The resurrection of Jesus Christ is the greatest event in the human history, without any doubt. I believe that every sane man, every man who is accustomed to think through on the great problems of life, wants to believe that Jesus rose from the dead. I cannot believe that any man who is accustomed to weigh evidence can be happy as a skeptic.

The resurrection of Jesus Christ furnishes a solution of the human problem. By the human problem I mean man's being here. We may say what we will, the fact that man IS is tremendous. His ultimate end, the reason for his being, reaches up and grips our minds and holds us in deadly embrace. And if Jesus is not the Son of God, then there is no solution of the human problem. It is an enigma.

If Jesus rose from the dead, then the human problem is solved. We understand it. It solves the sin problem and that is the paramount problem. The universal man is conscious of the guilt of sin. I know by the altars that are built that cover the earth, by its universal priesthood. Thirty million priests in India. Why? Because India, with the rest of mankind, is conscious of guilt. Man's consciousness of guilt has made him formulate religions.

These are weighty matters I am bringing you tonight, gentlemen. These are the great basic problems of life. This is the solution of the sin problem. No religion among the religions of the world has ever offered a solution for the sin problem. Jesus Christ alone has brought the solution.

There is another problem that Jesus answers. Universal man has craved union with God. He has not only wanted to get rid of the sin problem and the sin burden and the sin guilt, but also he wanted to be able to partake of the life and nature of God.

Man became a blood drinker. We call them cannibals. He became a blood drinker because he believed that if he would drink the blood of the victim who lay on his altar, he would partake of the God-nature and never die. You can see the Lord's table behind that, can't you?

The outreachings of man after God are among the saddest of all the facts of human life. Man is God-hungry. Jesus is the solution of that problem. Through Jesus Christ we become partakers of the divine nature.

If Jesus arose from the dead, then redemption is a fact. If Jesus arose from the dead, man can go to heaven. At first that may not seem much to you. But you know, men, whether you have thought it through or not, the universal man believes in the life beyond the grave. Human religion has never had an adequate conception or hope.

What do I mean by human religion? The religions of India: Hinduism, Brahmanism, Buddhism. All are human religions. Christian Science is a human religion purely based upon philosophy. The very first step is to destroy the personal God, the conviction and concept of a personal God. I want to say with all candor that I believe that the men and women who have written against Christian Science, New Thought and Unity have made the greatest mistake that was ever made in the world of apologetics. They have ridiculed it, but they have missed the crux of the matter.

Christian Science is built upon atheism. The communism of Russia has been atheistic. Christian Science as a religion is atheistic. The very first step is the destruction of the personal God. God is a person. They destroy that utterly, and when they destroy that, aren't they atheists? If some man would write a book proving that Christian Science is atheism, it would destroy Christian Science in a great measure.

I am going to carry you through some facts that I want you to study with me tonight. If you are going to have a bona fide resurrection, it is necessary that you have an absolute death. You cannot have a genuine resurrection without genuine death. I remember that Mr. Anderson, who was a disciple of Mr. Ingersol, wrote a book, and that I found it one day on the desk in one of my student's rooms. In it Mr. Anderson made this assertion, that Jesus did not die, that He was in a state of coma. I want to refute it.

Turn to the nineteenth chapter of John. First, the Jewish Sanhedrin accepted the verdict of the Roman government that Jesus was dead. The Roman government pronounced Jesus dead. The Jewish Sanhedrin that had caused the death of Jesus accepted the verdict of the Roman government. But I want to give you something else.

John 19:31, Jesus is on the cross:

> **The Jews therefore, because it was the preparation, that the bodies should not remain upon the cross on the sabbath day, (for that Sabbath day was an high day,) besought Pilate that their legs might be broken, and that they might be taken away.**

It was customary when they wanted death to come quickly to a crucified man that they would break his legs. That jar upon the nervous system would act upon the heart so that they would die suddenly.

> **Then came the soldiers, and brake the legs of the first, and of the other which was crucified with him. But when they came to Jesus, and saw that he was dead already, they brake not his legs: But one of the soldiers with a spear pierced his side, and forthwith came there out blood and water [John 19:32-34].**

Let us get the picture clearly. Jesus is hanging on that cross. He has been there on the cross since early in the morning. It is now almost sunset. The Roman soldiers come, and the two men who were crucified with Jesus are not dead. They are hanging there moaning, and the soldiers break their legs. Death comes mercifully. One of the soldiers comes to Jesus, and his head is hanging forward. The body is cold and stiffened, and the soldier stands there and looks up at Him and then takes his spear and pierces the left side, not the right side that all the artists paint. Then he lifts on it. That spear head that is 4 to 6 inches wide, sharp as a razor, penetrates the side of Jesus; it goes up into the body, pierces the sack that holds the heart, and the miracle happens. Water flows out, and from that wide wound, 4 to 6 inches across, rolls great clots of coagulated blood. What happened? Jesus died of a ruptured heart. That last cry was the death agony cry. His heart had ruptured, and when it ruptured the blood came pouring in from every part of the body to the heart and filled it; and as the body began to grow cold, this blood gathered there separated. The red corpuscles came to the top. The white serum settled to the bottom, and then when that soldier pierced the body and reached the heart sack, the water poured out first, and that is what John saw—then the blood.

Jesus was dead. His heart had been ruptured. The prophesy of Psalm 22 had been fulfilled. It was written a thousand years before Jesus died, and it is the most graphic picture ever written. I want you to note now, that Jesus was dead.

Read the last part of this chapter beginning with verse 38:

> **And after this Joseph of Arimathaea, being a disciple of Jesus, but secretly for fear of the Jews, besought Pilate that he might take away the body of Jesus: and Pilate gave him leave. He came therefore, and took the body of Jesus. And there came also Nicodemus, which at the first came to Jesus by night, and brought a mixture of myrrh and aloes, about an hundred pound weight. Then took they the body of Jesus, and wound it in linen clothes with the spices, as the manner of the Jews is to bury [John 19:38-40].**

What was the custom of the Jews? The wealthy Jews followed the processes that they had learned in Egypt. And all of the wealthier Jews had slaves that had learned the art of embalming the human body. It was not the total process.

So they took the body of Jesus from the cross. Joseph of Arimathaea was wealthy. Nicodemus was wealthy. And they washed that precious body. Then they took the linen cloth and they tore it up into strips one and a half to two inches wide, and they took this sticky substance, a hundred pounds weight, and they smeared that cloth as you would a salve. Then they took a toe and wrapped it. Then the foot, then the leg, then the fingers and hands and arms. Then the body was wrapped round until they used one hundred pounds of that sticky substance. And they used linen cloth enough to use one hundred pounds. Jesus weighed likely 200 pounds before His crucifixion. He must have been a perfect man, six feet, broad of shoulders, deep chest. He was God's crown of creation—the Master man, and He stood a king and peer among men.

If He weighed 200 hundred pounds, He must have shrunk twenty pounds at the crucifixion: He would be one hundred and eighty pounds plus one hundred pounds. Jesus' body would weigh two hundred and eighty to three hundred pounds. The body was hermetically sealed. Across the chest it must have been three inches thick, perhaps more. One hundred pounds smeared like that over the body would be over an inch thick.

The entire body was covered except the face. That was left for loving hands to embalm, and the women came down to finish the embalming. If Jesus had not died of a ruptured heart, and had not died of the spear thrust, after the body had been covered as I have indicated by that substance, hermetically sealed, so no air could get to it, He would not have lived four hours. I want you to know that Jesus was dead. Rome pronounced Him dead. The Sanhedrin pronounced Him dead. The spear had found a ruptured heart. Blood and water had flowed out of it. He is now hermetically sealed and put in a tomb, and that tomb is as dry as it is around Los Angeles in the summertime. And that body put in that place, it would only take a little while until the grave clothes would harden. You know that cloth would shrink more or less and tighten on the body.

Jesus is dead in Joseph's tomb, and His body is hermetically sealed, and just that little place around the face is uncovered.

Turn with me now to the twentieth chapter of John. Do you know anything about the value of narrative evidence before a jury or judge? Suppose a man has been killed down here on the street in a brawl, and the trial has come. Here is the value of narrative evidence. The trial goes on, and finally a little newsboy goes on the witness stand. He is fearless in the presence of the judge. He knew the judge. He knew the lawyers. He had sold them papers. He stands there unabashed in the presence of the judge, and presently the prosecuting attorney says, "Tell us what you saw."

And in the vernacular of the street he begins to tell. He says, "I saw that guy over there and the man that was killed quarreling.

Mickey and I were shooting craps, and we heard the scrap and we saw that fellow there, Judge. I saw him pull out a knife and stab and then run."

What do they do with that kind of evidence? That is narrative evidence. The boy describes it exactly as he saw it. The judge sits and listens, the jury sits and listens, and the court draws out of that child the whole picture. You cannot bring any kind of rebuttal. That boy's story has been the evidence. The boy saw it. That settles it; he saw it.

Here is narrative evidence. Here is the type of evidence that has been overlooked by people trying to prove the deity of Jesus.

> **The first day of the week cometh Mary Magdalene early, when it was yet dark, unto the sepulchre, and seeth the stone taken away from the sepulchre. Then she runneth, and cometh to Simon Peter, and to the other disciple, whom Jesus loved, and saith unto them, They have taken away the Lord out of the sepulchre, and we know not where they have laid Him. Peter therefore went forth, and that other disciple, and came to the sepulchre. So they ran both together: and the other disciple did outrun Peter, and came first to the sepulchre. And he stooping down, and looking in, saw the linen clothes lying; yet went he not in. Then cometh Simon Peter following him, and went into the sepulchre, and seeth the linen clothes lie, And the napkin, that was about his head, not lying with the linen clothes, but wrapped together in a place by itself. Then went in also that other disciple, which came first to the sepulchre, and he saw, and believed (John 20:1-8).**

Now what was it John saw that made him believe in the resurrection? *"For as yet they knew not the scripture, that he must rise again from the dead"* [John 20:9]. Not one of the disciples believed that Jesus was going to rise from the dead. And after He arose from the dead they doubted it, and Jesus upbraided them for their unbelief.

Now what was it that made John believe? Let us go back and look at the story. Mary and the other women came down to finish the embalming of Jesus. Three days had gone by, and before the face lost its beauty to them, they were going to cover it like the rest of the body. A napkin had been lying on the face. But when Mary arrived she found someone had been there and opened the sepulchre. She did not stop to look in. Filled with anger and indignation, for to the Jew the dead are sacred, she starts back to the city to tell Peter and John. Down through the city she runs, burst into the room where they were, and says, *"They have taken away [the body] of the Lord...and [I] know not where they have laid Him"* [John 20:2].

Then Peter, who had gone through hell for three days and three nights because he had denied Jesus in the face of the Sanhedrin said, "John, let's go."

Peter is large and heavy of body, and they run and John outruns him, and he comes to the sepulchre hewn out, and a big stone had been rolled against it and sealed, but the stone is away now. And John drops on his knees and looks in. John has in him that refinement that you can feel through his writings.

But when Peter comes, he is a coarser type. He ducks his head and goes into the sepulchre. Then John reverently follows him. John SAW something that made him believe. When God revealed this thing to me, He revealed it to a skeptic. I had been preaching for years, but in my secret heart I had questions about the resurrection of Jesus.

Come now, we will step inside the sepulchre. If John, when he went in, had seen that someone had come and ripped down that thing, he would not have believed. If John had seen that some wild animal had torn those grave clothes to shreds, would he have believed? No! Well, had John gone in and seen the grave clothes intact, and that Jesus had come out of that cocoon without destroying the rest of it, what would John have done? What would you have done? You would have believed.

I want to tell you what I did when I saw that empty cocoon, and I saw that the broad shoulders of Jesus had come out of that aperture for His face, that had hardened like a board. I slipped off my chair on to my knees, and I said what Thomas said, "My Lord and my God!" I knew Jesus had risen from the dead. I submit this to you. This is perfectly in harmony with the Jewish custom of burying. It is within reason.

Josephus tells us there were more than a million visitors in Jerusalem. It was one of the cycle years when the Jews came from all over the world to make their sacrifices. Outside the city booths were built. Jews who were commercial travelers had come to their old home in Jerusalem. There was one thing that filled the very air—the story of Jesus. Thousands, ten thousands, had gone out and had seen the dead body of Jesus hanging on the cross. He was crucified early in the morning, and the city was shaken to the foundation. Everybody was talking about it.

And when Peter and John came down over the hillside to the cemetery where Jesus was buried, what do you think they did? What do you think impulsive, warmhearted Peter did? Did he keep it quiet? Peter rushing down to the first man he met, what do you suppose he said? What do you suppose John said? I know what I would say; I know what you would say. "He is risen." You would not have to say "Jesus is risen."

In an hour's time the whole city of Jerusalem was stirred to its foundations. It stirred under the impulse of the new miracle. What did they do? Do you suppose they stood and talked, or do you think they made a rush for the sepulchre? You can see them going. If it had been in Portland, a hundred thousand people would have visited it that day. A hundred thousand Jews visited that hillside and smote their breast and tore their hair, and they went back to tell it. All that day the empty cocoon preached and told the story that Jesus had risen from the dead. It went on day after day and week after week until forty-nine days, less three. For forty-six days the clothes on the hillside preached, and countless thousands of men were stirred and shaken to the foundation.

And then after that forty days, John says, "I saw Him!" Peter says, "I saw Him," and 500 men followed Him to Olivet and saw Him ascend. What do you suppose the 500 men told the multitude of visitors? There was no other subject talked about. That goes without arguing.

Then fifty days later another staggering thing happened. Early in the morning they heard the rushing, mighty wind, like a thousand airplanes over the town. God had planned the drama.

One hundred and twenty men and women in that great square filled with people, and they heard those men and women speaking in tongues and glorifying God, telling of the resurrection of Jesus. Every man and woman hears in his own language. Every man hears the first message of Jesus in his own tongue and from the lips of Galilean fishermen. Some laugh, but others were serious. It was the climax that for fifty days had rocked Jerusalem and staggered the Jewish nation.

Peter stands forth. In the presence of whom? The Sanhedrin, the Senate, and the elders of Israel. Who is Peter? He is a humble fisherman. He is an untutored man. He has the same reverence for the high priest that the Roman Catholics have for the Pope. The Sanhedrin was sacred to him. He bowed before them. He feared them. The high priest was sacred to him.

Yet, Peter stands out there in the presence of the Sanhedrin, and he indicts first the Roman Governor as having murdered the Son of God. Second, he indicts the Sanhedrin, then the Senate and priesthood as murderers of the Son of God. His indictment is the most severe, the most amazing ever uttered.

Peter speaks only about 25 or 30 minutes, not longer than that, and what happens? Three thousand Jews broke with Judaism and accepted Jesus Christ of Nazareth as the Son of God and were baptized.

Where did he preach that sermon? Within the very shadow of that cross, within ten or twelve minutes of where Jesus hung stark naked one day crowned with thorns as an outcast. And three thousand Jews broke with Judaism. And every Jew who accepted Jesus Christ indicted the Sanhedrin, the Senate and the Roman government with the murder of Jesus.

That was the most dramatic thing that ever happened in history. There is nothing like it. Why say, if that thing was not true, all Ananias or Caiaphas had to do was to stop it, raise his hand and say, "Gentlemen, we know where the body of Jesus is. It has never raised." But Caiaphas never raised his voice. Caiaphas knew Jesus had risen from the dead. The Sanhedrin could have wiped out the whole thing in one day, but they dared not move, until finally two thousand more Jews accepted Christ Jesus. In the next two or three days five thousand and a large company of the priesthood swung into line.

They had Peter and John arrested because they healed a man. I want to read to you from Acts 4:8-11:

> **Ye rulers of the people, and elders of Israel, If we this day be examined of the good deed done to the impotent man, by what means he is made whole; Be it known unto you all, and to all the people of Israel, that by the name of Jesus Christ of Nazareth, whom ye crucified, whom God raised from the dead, even by him doth this man stand here before you whole.**

> **This is the stone which was set at nought of you builders, which is become the head of the corner.**

If we have been arrested and locked up for healing a tramp, a beggar, an outcast, for a good deed, be it known unto you and to all the people of Israel, that in the Name of Jesus Christ of Nazareth, whom YE crucified, whom God raised from the dead, even in Him doth this man stand here before you whole.

That is the most masculine piece of frenzy ever used in the world. *"Neither is there salvation in any other: for there is none other name under heaven given among men, whereby we must be saved"* (Acts 4:12).

And when they heard it, they could say nothing against it; and they sent them out, and said:

> **That indeed a notable miracle hath been done by them is manifest to all them that dwell in Jerusalem; and we cannot deny it. But that it spread no further among the people, let us straitly threaten them, that they speak henceforth to no man in THIS NAME (Acts 4:16-18).**

You can preach anything you want to, but don't preach in THE NAME. The Name has dynamite in it. The Name will raise the dead, heal the sick, cast out devils. The Name: It is Jesus again on earth.

What are you going to do with that kind of evidence? Did Jesus rise from the dead? Before Jesus died He said something that would forever brand Him as an impostor. He said, after I am gone I am going to give you legal right to the use of My Name. And *"Whatsoever ye shall ask in my name, that will I do"* (John 14:13).

No other human being ever dared to talk like that. When a man was dead, he was dead. But here was a man that was going to do bigger things after He died than when He was alive, and He was going to give us the legal right to use His Name. "Just whisper my Name, and whatsoever you say, it will be done." That was the most staggering thing that was ever said. That brands Jesus as the very Son of God or as an impostor.

What happened? Did His Name have power after He was dead? Jesus is the Son of God. I think I have made my case, haven't I?

I believe, gentlemen, that this thing is only a little fragment out of the body of truth. I believe that if it were given to the world, 90 percent of our skepticism would cease to be.

I want to make a few deductions. What are the implications if Jesus Christ rose from the dead? What then? Here are three things. We know He is the Son of God. We know that *"He died for our sins according to the Scriptures;...and was raised again for our justification"* [see 1 Corinthians 15:3 and Romans 4:25]. We know that every man who accepts Jesus Christ, God redeems that man, and we know that Romans 3:26 is true, *"...that He might be just, and the justifier of him which believeth in Jesus."*

God automatically, when you confess Jesus and accept Him as your Lord, becomes your righteousness. And the moment that God becomes your righteousness, that moment your standing is like the standing of the Son of God.

For years I hunted for this thing I have given you tonight. That sense of unfitness and unworthiness (or as they call it in psychology, that inferiority complex) swamped me. But when I saw that God became my righteousness, I said, "I want you to know, Satan, that you have lost your case." I know what I am now. *Him that knew no sin he made to be sin for us; that we might become the righteousness of God in Him* (see 2 Corinthians 5:21).

You, by the new birth, have become the righteousness of God, and God has become your righteousness. God could not make it any stronger than that.

I say to you reverently, friends, that if you have accepted Jesus Christ and are born again, you are standing in the presence of the great eternal Father God as Jesus is. You have just as much right to step into the presence of God Almighty as Jesus has. Don't you see what that means? It means that Satan cannot stand before you any more than he can stand before Jesus. Not only that, Jesus gave you the legal right to use His Name. And the first thing He tells you to do is to cast out demons. The first thing He told the twelve to do was to cast out demons. When He sent the seventy out, He told them to cast out demons. When He gave the Great Commission He said, *They that believe shall cast out demons* [see Mark 16:17]. This is the first thing. Why?

The devil is the opposer, and as long as the devil reigns over the sinner, the sinner cannot do anything. It is your business to break the power. Can't you see sickness is called *sin in the flesh,* and God has *"condemned sin in the flesh: That the righteousness of the law might be fulfilled in us, who walk not after the flesh, but after the Spirit"* [Romans 8:3-4].

Your sickness has been condemned, indicted, and found guilty before the high court of God. And it has no more right in your body than I have a right to be in some other man's house or store that is locked up. And if I am found there, I will be arrested. And that disease has no right in your body, and you have no right to leave it there, to sympathize with it, or to harbor it, or to console it. You are consoling the enemy of God that is under indictment and condemnation. It is a serious thing I am bringing, gentlemen. Jesus Christ has absolutely redeemed you, for He rose from the dead, and disease has no right in your body and no power to stay there if you take sides with Jesus. You have a right to your healing, to redemption, to victory. You have a right to prayer. You have a right to your Father's fellowship.

43

The Baptism of the Holy Ghost

February 23, 1921

Sermon 1

The Baptism of the Holy Ghost is the greatest event in Christian history. Greater than the Crucifixion, of greater import than the Resurrection, greater than the Ascension, greater than the glorification. It was the end and finality of Crucifixion and Resurrection, Ascension and glorification.

If Jesus Christ had been crucified, and there had been no resurrection, His death would have been without avail, in so far as the salvation of mankind is concerned. Or if He had risen from the grave in resurrection, and failed to reach the throne of God, and receive from the Father the Gift of the Holy Ghost, the purpose for which He died, and for which He arose, would have been missed.

It is because there was no failure. It is because Jesus went to the ultimate, to the very Throne and heart of God, and secured right out of the heavenly treasury of the Eternal Soul, the Almighty Spirit, and poured it forth upon the world in divine baptism that we are here tonight.

Birthday of Christianity

The day of Pentecost was the birthday of Christianity. Christianity never existed until the Holy Ghost came from heaven. The ministry of Jesus in the world was His own divine preparation of the world for His ultimate and final ministry. His ultimate and final ministry was to be BY THE SPIRIT.

The ministry of Jesus during His earth life was localized by His humanity. Localized again in that His message was only given to Israel. But the descent of the Holy Ghost brought to the souls of men a UNIVERSAL ministry of Jesus to every man, right from the heart of God. Heavenly contact with the eternal God in power, set their nature all aflame for God and with God, exalted their natures into God, and made the recipient GOD-LIKE. Man became God-like!

Holy Ground

There is no subject in all the Word of God that seems to me should be approached with so much holy reverence, as the subject of the Baptism of the Holy Ghost. Beloved, my heart bleeds every day of my life when I hear the flippancy with which Christians discuss the Baptism of the Holy Ghost.

When Moses entered into the presence of God at the burning bush, God said, *"Put off thy shoes from off thy feet; for the place whereon thou standest is holy ground"* [Exodus 3:5]. How much more so when the individual comes into the presence of God, looking for the Baptism of the Holy Ghost, and remembers that in order to obtain this gift, Jesus Christ lived in the world, bled on the cross, entered into the darkness of death and hell and the grave, grappled with and strangled that accursed power, came forth again, and finally ascended to heaven in order to secure it for you and me. If there is anything under heaven that ought to command our reverence, our Holy reverence, our reverence beyond anything else in the world, it surely is the subject of the Baptism of the Holy Ghost.

My! Sometimes my soul is jarred when I hear people flippantly say: "Have you got your baptism?" Supposing that Jesus was on the cross, and we were privileged tonight to look into His face at this hour, I wonder what the feeling of our soul would be? Supposing we were to follow tonight behind the weeping company that bore His dead body and laid it in the tomb, what would our feelings be? Supposing we were to meet Him in the garden, as Mary did, in the glory of His resurrection or supposing that God in His goodness would let us look into that scene of scenes at the Throne of God, when the heavens lifted up their gates, and the Lord of Glory came in. Oh, if we could, beloved, we would have a better comprehension of the Baptism of the Holy Ghost.

I love that dear old word "Ghost." The Anglo-Saxon is "Ghost" a spiritual guest, heavenly visitor, spiritual presence, the Angel One. And that Angel One that comes to you and me, comes right out of the heart of the Eternal God, breathed through the soul of Jesus Christ! When it came upon a man originally, as it did upon the hundred and twenty at Jerusalem, no one went around saying: "Brother, have you got your baptism?" They were walking with their shoes off, with uncovered heads and uncovered hearts before the Eternal God!

I believe that the first essential in a real Holy Ghost church and a real Holy Ghost work, is to begin to surround the Baptism of the Holy Ghost with that due reverence of God with which an experience so sacred, and that cost such an awful price, should be surrounded.

A Lesson on Reverence

I sat one day on a kopje in South Africa, in company with a lady, Mrs. Dockrell, a beautiful woman of God, baptized in the Holy Ghost. As we sat together on the rocks, meditating and praying, the rest of the company being a little distance away, I observed the Spirit falling upon her powerfully, until she was submerged in the Spirit. Then she began to deliver a message, first in tongues, later giving the interpretation in English, and I listened to the most wonderful lecture on the subject of "REVERENCE" I have ever heard in all my life.

Afterward I said to her: "Tell me what you can about the experience through which you have just passed." She had never been in Europe. But she said, "I was carried by the Spirit somewhere in Europe. I approached a great cathedral." And she went on to describe its architecture. She said: "As I approached the door, I was greeted by an English priest, who led me down the aisle to the altar, and I knelt. A white cloud began to settle down, and presently out of the cloud came the face and form of Jesus Christ. The priest was standing in the rostrum, and began to speak, but I could see by the action of the Spirit that the words he spoke were simply words that were being spoken by the Lord." It has always been one of the sorrows of my life that I did not have a stenographer, who could have taken that wonderful message on reverence for the works of God.

I have been reading one of the most beautiful books I have ever read. It is written by an English lady, Mrs. Parker, a missionary to India and describes the life and teaching and mission of one, Sadhu Sundar Singh, an Indian Sadhu. A Sadhu is a HOLY MAN, who renounces the world absolutely, utterly, never marries, never takes part in any of the affairs of the world, separates himself to religious life, practices meditation on God and the spiritual life. Sundar Singh, when he found the Lord Jesus Christ, conceived the idea of becoming a Christian Sadhu. They walked from place to place. They wore no shoes, they sleep on the ground, but their life is utterly abandoned to God.

One of the statements of Mrs. Parker, who wrote of Sundar Singh, was to this effect: "As you approach his presence, an awe comes over the soul. It seems as if you are again in the presence of the original Nazarene." Let us approach the Holy of Holies with a similar awe. Let us be reverential in the presence of the glorified One.

The Baptism of the Holy Ghost is peculiar to the Lord Jesus Christ. *"I indeed,"* said John, *"baptize you with water unto repentance: but HE...shall baptize you with the Holy Ghost and with fire: Whose fan is in his hand, and he will thoroughly purge his floor, and gather his wheat into the garner; but he will burn up the chaff with unquenchable fire"* [Matthew 3:11-12]. Jesus Christ, the Glorified, must lay His hands on you and on me and bestow upon us all His own nature, the outflow of God, the substance of His soul, the quality of His mind, the very being of God Himself. *"Know ye not that your body is the temple of the Holy Ghost, which is in you?* [1 Corinthians 6:19]." A temple of God, a house of God in which God lives!

A Habitation of God

Sometimes I have tried to get it clear before my soul that God LIVES IN ME. I have tried to note the incoming influence and power of that pure, sweet, living Spirit of the Eternal God. I have tried to realize His presence in my spirit, in my soul, in my hands, in my feet, in my person and being—a habitation of God, a habitation of God! God equipping the soul to minister Himself, God, to the world. God equipping the soul of man that he may live forever in harmony of mind with God. God furnishing to the soul of man the POWER of His personality, by which man is made as God. For all the God-like qualities of your heart is due to the fact that God by the Spirit dwells in you. What is it that you look for in another? It is God. You look into the eyes of another to see God. If you fail to see God in the other life, your heart is troubled. You were looking for God.

I am not interested in the form or the figure or the name of an individual. I am interested in seeing God. Is God there? Is God in that man? Is God in that woman? Is it God that speaks? Is it God that moves? Are you seeing God?

You May Have God

The Baptism of the Holy Ghost was the incoming of God in personality, in order that the man, through this force, might be moved by God. God lives in him, God speaks through him, God is the impulse of his soul, God has his dwelling place in him.

YOU may have God. That is the wonder of the Baptism of the Holy Ghost. It is not a work of grace, it is God possessing you. Oh, your heart may have been as sinful as the heart of man ever was sinful. But Christ comes to your soul. That spirit of darkness that possessed you goes, and in its stead, a new Spirit comes in, the Spirit of Christ. YOU have become a new creature, a saved man, a God-filled man.

A Transformation

Sin manifests itself in three ways, in thought, in acts, in nature. Salvation is a complete transformation. God takes possession of man, changes his thoughts, and in consequence his acts change, his nature is new. A Christian is not a reformed man. A Christian is a man renewed, remade by the Spirit of God. A Christian is a man indwelt by God—the house of God, the tabernacle of the Most High! Man, indwelt by God, becomes the hands, and the heart, and the feet, and the mind of Jesus Christ. God descends into man, man ascends into God! That is the purpose and power of the Baptism in the Holy Ghost. A soul is saved. How does Jesus reach them? Through your hands, through your heart, through your faith. When God baptizes you in the Holy Ghost, He gives you the biggest gift that heaven or earth ever possessed. He gives you Himself! He joins you by the one Spirit to Himself forever.

The Requirement

The requirement is a surrendered heart, a surrendered mind, a surrendered life. From the day that a man becomes a child of God, baptized in the Holy Ghost, it was God's intention through Jesus Christ that that man should be a revelation of Jesus, not of himself any more. From that time on the Christian should be a revelation of Jesus.

If you were looking to know whether a man was baptized in the Holy Ghost or not, what would you look for? You would look for God in him. You would look for a revelation of the personality of God. God moving in him, God speaking in him, God speaking through him, God using his hands, God using his feet, a mind in harmony with God, a soul in touch with heaven, a spirit united and unified with and in Jesus Christ!

God's Great Purpose Not Comprehended

It is not in my heart to discourage any man, or to make you disbelieve for one minute in the trueness of your own baptism in the Holy Ghost. I believe that God by the Spirit has baptized many in the Holy Ghost. Hundreds and hundreds of people have been baptized in the Holy Ghost during the life of this Church in the last six years. But beloved, we have not comprehended the greatness of God's intent. Not that we have not received the Spirit, but our lives have not been sufficiently surrendered to God. We must keep on ascending right to the throne, right into the heart of God, right into the soul of the Glorified.

The Holy Ghost Not A Gift of Power But of God Himself

The common teaching that my heart these days is endeavoring to combat is that God comes to present the individual with a gift of power, and the individual is then supposed to go out and manifest some certain characteristic of power. No! God comes to present you with HIMSELF. *"Ye shall receive power, after that the Holy Ghost is come upon you"* [Acts 1:8].

Jesus went to heaven in order that the very treasury of the heart of the eternal God might be unlocked for your benefit, and that out of the very soul of the eternal God, the streams of His life and nature would possess you from the crown of your head to the soles of your feet, and that there would be just as much of the eternal God in your toe nails and in your brain as each are capable of containing. In other words, from the very soles of your feet to the last hair on the top of your head, every cell of your being, would be a residence of the Spirit of the living God. Man is made alive by God and with God, by the Spirit. And in the truest sense man is the dwelling place of God, the house of God, the tabernacle of the Most High.

Listen! *"The words that I speak...I speak not of myself: but the Father that DWELLETH in Me"* [John 14:10], *"but the Father that dwelleth IN ME."* Where did the Eternal Father dwell in Jesus Christ? Why in every part of His being, within and without—in the spirit of Him, in the soul of Him, in the brain of Him, in the body of Him, in the blood of Him, in the bones of Him! Every single, solitary cell of His structure was the dwelling place of God, *of God,* OF GOD.

When you look for God you do not look on the surface. You look within. When you discern a man to see whether God is in him, you look into the spirit of him, into the soul of him, into the depth of him, and there you see God.

How trifling are the controversies that surround the Baptism of the Holy Ghost. Men are debating such trifling issues. For instance, does a man speak in tongues, or does he not? Do not think for a moment that I am discounting the value of tongues. I am not. But beloved, I will tell you what my heart is straining for. Down there at Jerusalem they not only spoke in tongues, but they spoke the languages of the NATIONS. If it was possible for old Peter and old Paul, or for the Jewish nation, then it is possible to every last one. Not to speak in tongues alone, as we ordinarily understand that phase, but to speak because God dwells in you and speaks to whomsoever He will in whatever language He desires. And if our present experience in tongues is not satisfying, God bless you, go on into languages, as God meant that you should. Dear ones, I feel the need of that, and I feel it away down in my heart to a depth that hurts. I lived in South Africa for a number of years, where it is commonly said that there are a hundred thousand tribes of native people. Every last one of the hundred thousand speaks a different dialect. These tribes number sometimes as low as ten thousand people and sometimes as high as hundreds of thousands even millions of people.

Supposing we were going to undertake to evangelize Africa rapidly. It would be necessary to have a hundred thousand different missionaries, and have them all at one time, master one particular language, for there are a hundred thousand of them. No sir! I believe before high heaven that when the Spirit of the Eternal God is poured out upon all flesh, that out of the real Christian body will arise a hundred thousand men and women in Africa that will speak in the language of every separate tribe by the power of God.

The unknown tongue of the Spirit was to teach you of God, to be a faith builder in your soul, to take you out into God's big practical endeavor to save the world. And that is the reason, dear ones, that I bring this issue to your soul tonight. In the matter of the Baptism of the Holy Ghost we are in a state of the merest infancy of understanding, the merest infancy of divine control, the merest infancy in ability to assimilate our environment, including languages.

When we go to a school we see classes arranged for every grade. I was talking to a young school teacher, who teaches out in the country in a little public school. I said: "How many children have you in your school?"

She said: "Eight grades." Fifteen scholars divided into eight grades.

The Christian church is God's big school. What student in the eighth grade would think of saying to the child learning its ABC's, "You haven't anything. Why don't you have the eighth grade understanding?" Well in due time he will have it. That is the reason the student does not say it. It is because he knows the child will have it. One day that boy will understand just the same as he does. A weak Christianity always wants to drop to the imperfect, and adjust itself to the popular mind. But a real Christianity ever seeks to be made perfect in God, both in character and gifts.

My Personal Experience

Dear ones, I want to repeat to you tonight a little of my own personal history on the subject of the Baptism of the Spirit, for I know it will clarify your soul.

My Conversion

I knelt under a tree when about sixteen years of age, in repentance and prayer, and God came into my soul. I was saved from my sins, and from that day I knew Jesus Christ as a living Savior. There never was a single moment of question about the reality of His incoming into my life as a Savior, for He saved me from my sins. My friends said, "You are baptized in the Holy Ghost."

Sanctified

Sometime later, I think when I was yet under twenty, or thereabout, I met a Christian farmer, Melvin Pratt, who sat down on his plow handles and taught me the subject of sanctification, and

God let me enter into that experience. My friends said: "Now surely you are baptized in the Holy Ghost." Later in my life I came under the ministry of George B. Watson, of the Christian & Missionary Alliance, who taught with more clearness and better distinction between the Baptism of the Holy Ghost and sanctification, and I entered into a richer life and a better experience. A beautiful anointing of the Spirit was upon my life.

Ministry of Healing

Then the ministry of Healing was opened to me, and I ministered for ten years in the power of God. Hundreds and hundreds of people were healed by the power of God during this ten years, and I could feel the conscious flow of the Holy Spirit through my soul and my hands.

But at the end of that ten years I believe I was the hungriest man for God that ever lived. There was such a hunger for God that as I left my offices in Chicago and walked down the street, my soul would break out, and I would cry, "Oh God!" I have had people stop and look at me in wonder. It was the yearning passion of my soul, asking for God in a greater measure than I then knew. But my friends would say: "Mr. Lake, you have a beautiful baptism in the Holy Ghost." Yes, it was nice as far as it went, but it was not answering the cry of my heart. I was growing up into a larger understanding of God and my own soul's need. My soul was demanding a greater entrance into God, His love, presence and power.

My Baptism in the Holy Ghost

And then one day an old man strolled into my office, sat down, and in the next half hour he revealed more of the knowledge of God to my soul than I had ever known before. And when he passed out I said: "God bless that old gray head. That man knows more of God than any man I ever met. By the grace of God, if that is what the Baptism of the Holy Ghost with tongues does, I am going to possess it." Oh, the wonder of God that was then revealed to my heart!

I went into fasting and prayer and waiting on God for nine months. And one day the glory of God in a new manifestation and a new incoming came to my life. And when the phenomena had passed, and the glory of it remained in my soul, I found that my life began to manifest in the varied range of the gifts of the Spirit. And I spoke in tongues by the power of God, and God flowed through me with a new force. Healings were of a more powerful order. Oh, God lived in me, God manifested in me, God spoke through me. My spirit was deified, and I had a new comprehension of God's will, new discernment of spirit, new revelation of God in me. For nine months everything that I looked at framed itself into poetic verse. I could not look at the trees without it framing itself into a glory poem of praise. I preached to audiences of thousands night after night and day after day. People came from all over the world to study me. They could not understand. Everything I said was a stream of poetry. It rolled from my soul in that form. My spirit had become a fountain of poetic truth.

Then a new wonder was manifested. My nature became so sensitized that I could lay my hands on any man or woman and tell what organ was diseased, and to what extent, and all about it. I tested it. I went to hospitals where physicians could not diagnose a case, touched a patient and instantly I knew the organ that was diseased, its extent and condition and location. And one day it passed away. A child gets to playing with a toy, and his joy is so wonderful he sometimes forgets to eat.

Oh say, don't you remember when you were first baptized in the Holy Ghost, and you first spoke in tongues, how you bubbled and babbled, it was so wonderful, so amazing? We just wanted to be babies and go on bubbling and exhilarating. And now we are wondering what is the matter. The effervescence seems to have passed away. My! It is a good thing that it did. God is letting your soul down, beloved, into the bedrock—right down where your mind is not occupied any more with the manifestation of God. God is trying to get your mind occupied with HIMSELF. God has come into you, now He is drawing you into Himself.

Will you speak in tongues when you are baptized in the Holy Ghost? Yes, you will, but you will do an awful lot more than that, bless God. An awful lot more than that! You will speak with the soul of Jesus Christ. You will feel with the heart of the Son of God. Your heart will beat with a heavenly desire to bless the world, because it is the pulse of Jesus that is throbbing in your soul. And I do not believe there will be a bit of inclination in your heart to turn around another child of God and say: "You are not in my class. I am baptized with the Holy Ghost." That is as foreign to the Spirit of the Son of God as night is from day.

Beloved, if you are baptized in the Holy Ghost, there will be a tenderness in your soul so deep that you will never crush the aspiration of another by a single suggestion, but your soul will throb and beat and pulse in love, and your heart will be under that one to lift it up to God and push it out as far into the glory as your faith can send it.

I want to talk with the utmost frankness, and say to you that tongues have been to me the making of my ministry. It is that peculiar communication with God when God reveals to my soul the truth I utter to you day by day in my ministry. But that time of communication, with me, is mostly in the night. Many a time I climb out of bed, take my pencil and pad and jot down the beautiful things of God, the wonderful things of God, that He talks out in my spirit and reveals to my heart.

Many Christians do not understand the significance of tongues, any more than the other man understands the experience of your soul when you are saved from sin. It has taken place in you. It is in your heart, it is in your mind, it is in your being. The man who tries to make you doubt the reality of your touch with God when He saved you out of your sin is foolish. It is established IN you. The old Methodists could not explain the experience, but they said: "It is better felt than told." They knew it by internal knowledge. So it is in a real Baptism of the Holy Ghost. So it is in prophecy. So it is in healing. So it is in tongues. Do not throw away what you have. Go on to perfection.

The Language of the Spirit

The spirit of man has a voice. Do you get that? The spirit of man has a voice. The action of God in your spirit causes your spirit to speak by its voice. In order to make it intelligent to your understanding, it has to be repeated in the language that your brain knows. Why? Because there is a language common to the spirit of man, and it is not English, and it is not German, and it is not French, and it is not Italian, or any other of the languages of Earth. It is a language of the spirit of man. And, oh, what a joy it was when that pent-up, bursting, struggling spirit of yours found it's voice and "spake in tongues."

Many a time I have talked to others in the Spirit, by the Spirit, through the medium of tongues, and knew everything that was said to me, but I did not know it with this ear. It was not the soul of their words. It was that undefinable something that made it intelligent. Spirit speaks to spirit, just as mouth speaks to mouth, or as man speaks to man. Your spirit speaks to God. God is Spirit. He answers back. Bless God. And I believe with all my heart that is what Paul had in mind when he talked about the "unknown" tongue. The unknown tongue, that medium of internal revelation of God to you. The common language of the spirit of man, by which God communicates with your spirit.

Internal Revelation Made Intelligent by Interpretation

But if you want to make that medium of internal revelation of God intelligent to other folks, then it must be translated into the language that they know. That is the reason the apostle says: *"Let him that speaketh in an unknown tongue pray that he may interpret"* [1 Corinthians 14:13], that the church may receive edifying. Paul says: *"In the church I had rather speak five words with my understanding, that by my voice I might teach others also, than ten thousand words in an unknown tongue"* [1 Corinthians 14:19]. Your revelation from God is given to you in tongues, but you give it forth in the language the people understand.

Beloved, settle it. It is one of the divine mediums and methods of communication between your spirit and God's. And as long as you live, when you talk about TONGUES, speak with reverence, for it is God. When you talk about healing, speak with reverence, for it is God. When you talk about prophecy, remember it is God.

An Illustration

A German woman came to the healing rooms one day and a brother prayed for her. She had been a school teacher, but had to give up her profession because of her eye sight. She came back some weeks later, after having been alone for three weeks. She had never been in a religious service in her life where they speak in tongues, and had not knowledge of the Scriptures on that line. She came back to me with a volume of written material that God had given her. When she had been prayed for to receive healing, the Spirit of God came upon her and she was baptized in the Holy Ghost. And now God had commenced to reveal Himself to her, teach her of His Word, and of His will, until she filled a volume with written material of her conversations with God. She communed with God in tongues, her spirit speaking to God, but when she came to me I receive it in English.

The man that sits along side of you cannot understand that. He never talked to God. He does not understand anything about getting up in the middle of the night to write down what God has said to him. Well, he needs something else to convince him that there is a God. Tongues are for a sign, NOT to them that believe, but to them that believe not. But prophecy, the outspeaking for God is for all. Therefore, Paul does not want them to crush a man who is speaking in tongues, but to keep their hands off and stand back. Leave him alone with God. Let him travel away out in His love and power, and come back with messages in his soul.

But he must not monopolize the time of hundreds of people in the church with a private communication of God to his soul. But when he has completed his interview with God, he gives forth his knowledge as interpretation or prophecy.

There have been so many controversies over the various gifts of the Spirit as they appeared one after another. Twenty-five or thirty years ago when we began in the ministry of healing [this was preached in 192l], we had to fight to keep from being submerged by our opposing brethren in Jesus Christ, who thought you were insane because you suggested that the Lord Jesus Christ could still heal. In the state of Michigan, I had to go into the courts to keep some of my friends out of the insane asylum, because they believed God could heal without taking pills or some other material stuff. (To popularize healing, some have compromised on the use of medicines, but the real Christian still trusts God alone.)

It was because they did not understand the eternal and invisible nature of God. They had no idea God could be ministered through a man's hands and soul, fill a sick man's body, take possession of and make him whole. The world has had to learn this. It is a science far in advance of so-called material or physical science.

Then that marvelous wave of God came over the country from 1900 to 1906, when hundreds of thousands of people were baptized in the Holy Ghost and spoke in tongues. But listen! Old John Alexander Dowie, riding on the wave of that wonderful manifestation of healing power, wanted to build a church and stamp it with healing only, and his church practically did that, and died. Other churches branded theirs with holiness only, and died. Others with an anointing of the Holy Ghost, called "baptism", and they died in power also. Later on we wanted to build a great structure and stamp it with tongues. After a while the tongues got dry. Somehow the glory and the glow had gone out of them. They became rattly and did not sound right. What was the matter? Nothing wrong with the experience. God had not departed from the life, but was hidden from our view. We were absorbed in phenomena of God, and not in God Himself. Now we must go on. Now beloved, I can see as my spirit discerns the future and reaches out to touch the heart of mankind, and the desire of God, that there is coming from heaven a new manifestation of the Holy Ghost in power, and that new manifestation will be in sweetness, in love, in tenderness, in the power of the Spirit beyond anything your heart or mine ever saw. The very lightning of God will flash through men's souls. The sons of God will meet the sons of darkness and prevail. Jesus Christ will destroy anti-Christ.

A Deluge of the Spirit

In 1908, I preached at Pretoria, South Africa, when one night God came over my life in such power, in such streams of liquid glory and power, that it flowed consciously off my hands like streams of electricity. I would point my finger at a man, and that stream would strike him. When a man interrupted the meeting, I would point my finger at him and say: "Sit down!" He fell as if struck, and lay for three hours. When he became normal they asked him what happened, and he said, "Something struck me that went straight through me. I thought I was shot."

At two o'clock in the morning I ministered to sixty-five sick who were present, and the streams of God that were pouring through my hands were so powerful the people would fall as though they were hit. I was troubled because they fell with such violence. And the Spirit said: "You do not need to put your hands on them. Keep your hands a distance away." And when I held my hands a foot from their heads they would crumple and fall in a heap on the floor. They were healed almost every one.

That was the outward manifestation. That was what the people saw. But beloved, something transpired in my heart that made my soul like the soul of Jesus Christ. On, there was such a tenderness, a new-born tenderness of God, that was so wonderful that my heart reached out and cried and wept over men in sin. I could gather them in my arms and love them, and Jesus Christ flowed out of me and delivered them. Drunkards were saved and healed as they stood transfixed looking at me.

During that period men would walk down the isle, and when they came within ten feet of me, I have seen them fall prostrate, one on top of the other. A preacher who had sinned, as he looked at me, fell prostrate, was saved, baptized in the Holy Ghost, and stirred the nation with his message of love.

In eighteen months God raised up one hundred white churches in the land. That hundred churches was born in my tabernacle at Johannesburg. The multitude of those who composed that hundred churches were healed or baptized in the Holy Ghost under my own eyes, as I preached or prayed.

I continued in the ministry of healing until I saw hundreds of thousands healed. At last I became tired. I went on healing people day after day, as though I were a machine. And all the time my heart kept asking: "Oh, God, let me know yourself better. I want you, my heart wants YOU, God." Seeing men saved and healed and baptized in the Holy Ghost did not satisfy my growing soul. It was crying for a greater consciousness of God, the withinness of me was yearning for Christ's own life and love. After a while my soul reached the place where I said: "If I cannot get God into my soul to satisfy the soul of me, all the rest of this is empty." I had lost interest in it, but if I put my hands on the sick they continued to be healed by the power of God.

I will never forget Spokane, Washington for during the first six months I was there God satisfied the cry of my heart, and God came in and my mind opened and my spirit understood afresh, and I was able to tell of God, and talk out the heart of me like I never had been able to before. God reached a new depth in my spirit, and revealed new possibilities in God. So beloved, you pray through. Pray through for this church, pray through for this work. Oh, God will come! God will come with more tongues than you have ever heard. God will come with more power than your eyes ever beheld. God will come with waves of heavenly love and sweetness, and blessed be God, your heart will be satisfied in Him.

Will a man speak in tongues when he is baptized in the Holy Ghost? Yes, he will, and he will heal the sick when he is baptized, and he will glorify God out of the spirit of him, with praises more delightful and heavenly than you ever heard. And he will have a majestic bearing. He will look like the Lord Jesus Christ, and he will be like Him. Blessed be God.

The greatest manifestation of the Holy Ghost baptized life ever given to the world, was not in the preaching of the apostles, it was not in the wonderful manifestations of God that took place at their hands, it was in the unselfishness manifested by the church. Think of it! Three thousand Holy Ghost baptized Christians in Jerusalem from the day of Pentecost onward who loved their neighbor's children as much as their own, who were so anxious for fear their brethren did not have enough to eat, that they sold their estates, and brought the money and laid it at the apostle's feet, and said: "Distribute it, carry the glow and the fire and the wonder of this divine salvation to the whole world." That showed what God had wrought in their hearts. Oh, I wish we could arrive at that place where this church was baptized in that degree of unselfishness.

That would be a greater manifestation than healing, greater than conversion, greater than baptism in the Holy Ghost, greater than tongues. It would be a manifestation of the LOVE of 1 Corinthians 13, that so many preach about, and do not possess. When a man sells his all for God, and distributes it for the kingdom's good, it will speak louder of love than the evangelists who harp about love, and oppose tongues and the other gifts of the spirit.

That was the same Holy Ghost that came upon them and caused them to speak in tongues. No more grabbing for themselves. No more bantering for the biggest possible salary, no more juggling to put themselves and their friends in the most influential positions. All the old characteristics were gone. They were truly saved. Why their heart was like the heart of Jesus, their soul was like the soul of God, they loved as God loved, they loved the world, they loved sinners so that they gave their all to save them.

Do you want Him? You can have Him. Oh, He will come and fill your soul. Oh, the Holy Ghost will take possession of your life. He will reveal the wonder of heaven and the glory of God, and the richness and purity of His holiness, and make you sweet and God-like forever.

> Thou art not far away, Oh, God, our souls tonight are enveloped in the eternal God. We feel Thee round about us. We feel Thy precious loving arm, and the beating of Thy heart, and the pulsing of Thy heavenly soul, and we are asking Thee, my God, that the truth of

the Eternal shall be breathed into us forever until all our nature is submerged in God, buried up in God, infilled with God, revealing God.

Prayer in Tongues and Interpretation

The Baptism of the Holy Ghost

And some of the things it has produced in my life.

Sermon 2

The Baptism of the Holy Ghost was of such importance in the mind of the Lord Jesus Christ that He commanded His disciples to tarry in Jerusalem *"until ye be endued with power from on high"* (Luke 24:49). And they steadfastly carried out what the Lord had commanded, waiting on God in a continuous prayer meeting in the upper room for ten days until the promise of the Father was fulfilled, and that Baptism had fallen of which John the Baptist spoke of in Matthew 3:11, saying: *"I indeed baptize you with water unto repentance: but He that cometh after me is mightier than I, whose shoes I am not worthy to bear: he shall baptize you with the Holy Ghost, and with fire."*

In order to obtain from Heaven the Spirit of Jesus, (the Holy Ghost), it is first necessary that the individual shall know that his sins are blotted out, that the blood of Jesus Christ has sanctified his heart and cleansed him from the sinful nature, or Adamic nature, the inherent nature of sin (Ephesians 2:1-3).

Personally I knew that my sins had been blotted out, but it was only two months prior to my Baptism in the Holy Ghost that I learned by the Word of God and experienced in my life the sanctifying power of God subduing the soul and cleansing the nature from sin. This inward life cleansing was to me the crowning work of God in my life at that period. I shall never cease to praise God that He revealed to me the depth by the Holy Ghost, the power of the blood of Jesus.

Many inquire what is the reason that when your heart is sanctified and the conscious knowledge of your cleansing has taken place that you are not instantly baptized with the Holy Ghost. From my own experience and the experience of others it is readily seen that, not withstanding that the heart is cleansed from sin, it is still necessary in many instances for the dear Lord to further spiritualize the personality until the individual has become receptive to receive within his person the Holy Ghost. The forces of our personality must be subdued unto God. This we commonly speak of as spiritualizing. In many instances even though the heart is really pure, yet the individual has not at once received the Baptism of the Holy Ghost, and in some instances has given up in despair and turned back to his first works, believing that there must still be sin in his heart, thus discrediting what God has already done within him through the blood of Jesus. No, it is not always that the heart is still impure. It is not because you are not thoroughly sanctified. It is only God waiting and working to bring you to the place and to sufficiently spiritualize your personality that you may receive into your being the Holy Ghost.

The Baptism of the Holy Ghost is not an influence, nor yet a good feeling, nor sweet sensations, though it may include all of these. The Baptism of the Holy Ghost is the incoming into the personality of Him, the Holy Ghost, which is the (mind and animal life), yea, of your flesh. He possesses the being. The flesh is caused to quake sometimes because of the presence of the Spirit of God in the flesh. Daniel quaked with great quaking when the Spirit of the Lord came upon him (Daniel 10:1-13).

Beloved reader, do you realize that it is the Spirit of Jesus Who is seeking admittance into your heart and life? Do you realize that it is the Spirit of Jesus within the spirit, soul and body of the baptized believer Who moves him in ways sometimes strange, but Who accomplishes the wondrous work of God within the life. That is why every baptized believer praises God for what has taken place in him.

While yet a justified man, even without an experience of sanctification, the Lord committed to me in a measure the ministry of healing in as much that many were healed and, in some instances, real miracles of healing took place. Yet I did not know God as my sanctifier. Ten years later, after sanctification had become a fact in my life, a great and wonderful yearning to be baptized in the Holy Ghost and fire came into my heart. After seeking God persistently, almost night and day for two months, the Lord baptized me in the Holy Ghost causing me to speak in tongues and magnify God. I had looked for and prayed and coveted the real power of God for the ministry of healing and believed God that when I was baptized in the Holy Ghost that His presence in me through the Spirit would do for the sick the things my heart desired, and which they needed. Instantly upon being baptized in the Spirit I expected to see the sick healed in a greater degree and in larger numbers than I had before known, and, for a time, I seemed to be disappointed.

How little we know of our own relationship to God! How little I knew of my own relationship to Him; for, day by day, for six months following my Baptism in the Holy Ghost the Lord revealed to me many things in my life where repentance, confession and restitution were necessary, and yet I had repented unto God long ago. Oh! the deep cleansing, the deep revelations of one's own heart by the Holy Ghost. It was indeed as John the Baptist said, *"Whose fan is in his hand, and he will thoroughly purge his floor, and gather his wheat into the garner; but he will burn up the chaff with unquenchable fire"* [Matthew 3:12].

First, then, I will say the Baptism in the Holy Ghost meant to me a heart searching as I had never before known, with no rest, until in every instance the blood was consciously applied, and my life set free from the particular thing that God had revealed. As I say, this process continued for six months after my Baptism in the Holy Ghost.

Second, a love for mankind such as I had never comprehended took possession of my life. Yea, a soul yearning to see men saved, so deep, at times heart rending, until in anguish of soul I was compelled to abandon my business and turn all my attention to bringing men to the feet of Jesus. While this process was going on in my heart, during a period of months, sometimes persons would come into my office to transact business and even instances where there were great profits to be had for a few minutes of persistent application to business, the Spirit of Love in me so yearned over souls that I could not even see the profits to be had. Under its sway money lost its value to me, and in many instances I found myself utterly unable to talk business to the individual until first I had poured out the love passion of my soul and endeavored to show him Jesus as his then present Savior. In not just a few instances these business engagements ended in the individual yielding himself to God.

That love passion for men's souls has sometimes been overshadowed by the weight of care since then, but only for a moment. Again, when occasion demanded it, that mighty love flame absorbing one's whole being and life would flame forth until, under the anointing of the Holy Ghost on many occasions, sinners would fall in my arms and yield their hearts to God.

Others have sought for evidences of the Pentecostal experience being the real Baptism of the Holy Ghost. Some have criticized and said, "It is not a delusion?" In all the scale of evidences presented to my soul and taken from my experience, this experience of the divine love, the burning love and holy compassion of Jesus Christ filling one's bosom until no sacrifice is too great to win a soul for Christ, demonstrates to me more than any other one thing that this is indeed none other than the Spirit of Jesus.

Such love is not human! Such love is only divine! Such love is only Jesus Himself, who gave His life for others.

Again, the development of power: First, after the mighty love, came the renewed, energized power for healing the sick. Oh! what blessed things God has given on this line! What glorious resurrections of the practically dead! Such restorations of the lame and the halt and the blind! Such abundance of peace! Verily, *"Himself took our infirmities, and bare our sicknesses!"* [Matthew 8:17].

Then came as never before the power to preach the Word of God in demonstration of the Spirit. Oh! the burning fiery messages! Oh, the tender, tender, loving messages! Oh, the deep revelations of wondrous truth by the Holy Ghost! Preaching once, twice, sometimes three times a day, practically continuously during these four years and four months. Oh, the thousands God has permitted us to lead to the feet of Jesus, and the tens of thousands to whom He has permitted us to preach the Word!

Then came the strong, forceful exercise of dominion over devils, to cast them out. Since that time many insane and demon possessed, spirits of insanity, all sorts of unclean demons, have been cast out in the mighty Name of Jesus through the power of the precious blood. Saints have been led into deeper life in God. Many, many have been baptized in the Holy Ghost and fire. My own ministry was multiplied a hundredfold in the very lives of others to whom God committed this same ministry. Yea, verily the Baptism in the Holy Ghost is to be desired with the whole heart.

Brother, Sister, when we stand before the bar of God and are asked why we have not fulfilled in our life all the mind of Christ and all His desire in the salvation of the world, how will be our excuses if they are weighed against the salvation of imperishable souls. How terrible it will be for us to say we neglected, we put off, we failed to seek for the endowment that cometh from on high, the Baptism of the Holy Ghost.

Again, ere we close, may we say that it was only after the Lord had baptized us in the Holy Ghost that we really learned how to pray. When He prayed through us, when the soul cries born of the Holy Ghost rolled out of your being and up to the throne of God, the answer came back—His prayer, His heart yearning, His cry. May God put it in every heart that we may indeed see the answer to our Lord's prayer, *"Thy kingdom come. Thy will be done in earth, as it is in Heaven"* [Matthew 6:10].

But someone will say, "How about tongues? We understood that you taught that tongues were the evidence of the Baptism in the Holy Ghost?" So they are. Tongues are a sign to them that believe not (1 Corinthians 14:22). While I personally praise God for the wonderful and blessed truths of His Word by the Spirit, revelations in doctrine, in prophecy, in poems by the Holy Ghost in tongues with interpretation that He has given me, yet, above all the external evidences, that which God accomplishes in your own lives, demonstrating to your own consciousness the operations of God, no doubt is the great evidence to the believer himself, for that which is known in consciousness cannot be denied. We stand firmly on scriptural grounds that every individual who is baptized in the Holy Ghost will and does speak in tongues.

Baptism means a degree of the Spirit upon the life sufficient to give the Spirit of God such absolute control of the person that He will be able to speak through him in tongues. Any lesser degree cannot be called the baptism or submersion, and we feel could properly be spoken of as an anointing. The life may be covered with deep anointings of the Holy Ghost yet not in sufficient degree to be properly called the baptism.

The Baptism of the Holy Ghost

Sermon 3

The Baptism of the Holy Ghost is a most difficult subject to discuss with any degree of intelligence, for though we may not care to admit it, the fact remains that the density of ignorance among the people and the ministry on this subject is appalling. To view this subject with any degree of intelligence we must view it from the standpoint of progressive revelation. Like Christian baptism, the operation of the Holy Ghost must be seen (comprehended) in its various stages of revelation. Otherwise we shall be unable to distinguish between the operations of the Spirit in the Old Testament dispensation and the Baptism of the Holy Ghost in the New Testament.

As we approach the threshold of this subject it seems as if the Spirit of God comes close to us. A certain awe of God comes over the soul. And it is my earnest wish that no levity, satire, or sarcasm be permitted to enter into this discussion. Such things would be grievous to the tender Spirit of God.

In the beginning of this revelation after the deluge it seems as if God was approaching man from a great distance, so far had sin removed man from his original union with God at the time of his creation. God seems to reveal Himself to man as rapidly as man by progressive stages of development is prepared to receive the revelation. Consequently we see that as baptism was a further revelation of God's purpose in purifying the heart from sin than was the original ceremony of circumcision, so the Baptism of the Holy Ghost is a greater, more perfect revelation of God than were the manifestations of the Spirit in the Patriarchal or Mosaic dispensations.

Three distinct dispensations of God are clearly seen, each with an ever-deepening manifestation of God to man. A preceding dispensation of God never destroys a foregoing one. On the contrary it conserves its spirit and broadens its scope in a deeper and richer revelation of God. This is manifestly seen in looking at the Patriarchal, Mosaic and Christian dispensations. In the Patriarchal dispensation we see God appearing to man at long intervals. Abraham furnishes the best example, for to him God appeared at long intervals of 20 and 40 years apart; so with the other patriarchs. Under the Mosaic dispensation there is a deeper and clearer manifestation of God. God was ever-present in the pillar of cloud and the pillar of fire. He was present also in the tabernacle where the Shekinah Glory overshadowed the Mercy Seat. This is a continuous, abiding revelation of God. It was God with man, not to man, as was the Patriarchal dispensation. God was leading, guiding, directing, forgiving, sanctifying and abiding with man. But the revelation of God under the Christian dispensation is a much deeper and truer revelation of God than this. It is God in man. It is the actual incoming of the Spirit of God to live in man. This brings us then to where we can see the purpose of God in revealing Himself to man in progressive steps of revelation.

Man by progressive stages through repentance and faith is purified, not alone forgiven his transgressions, but cleansed from the nature of sin within that causes him to transgress. This cleansing from inbred sin, the nature of sin, the carnal mind, the old man, et cetera, is the actual taking out of our breast the desire for sin, and all correspondence with sin in us is severed. The carnal life is laid a sacrifice on the altar of Christ in glad surrender by us. This inner heart cleansing that John and the disciples of Christ demanded is the work of the Holy Spirit by the blood and is necessary if maturity in Christ is to be achieved. A holy God must have a holy dwelling place. Oh wondrous salvation, wondrous Christ, wondrous atonement, man born in sin, shaped in iniquity, forgiven, cleansed, purified outside and inside by the blood of Jesus and made an habitation (dwelling place) of God. It was that man, once created in the likeness of God, should again become the dwelling place of God. That is what the atoning blood of Christ provided.

Galatians 3:13-14: *"Christ hath redeemed us from the curse of the law, being made a curse for us: for it is written, Cursed is every one that hangeth on a tree: That the blessing of Abraham might come on the Gentiles through Jesus Christ; that we might receive the promise of the Spirit through faith."* This reveals to us God's purpose by the blood of Jesus Christ for us now to become the habitation of God:

Ephesians 2:22, *"In whom ye also are builded together for an habitation of God through the Spirit."*

Again in 1 Corinthians 6:19 we see Paul in astonishment says, *"What? know ye not that your body is the temple of the Holy Ghost...?"* Let us now see where we are and we will better understand how to go on.

The Holy Ghost is the Spirit of God. His purpose is to dwell in man after man's perfect cleansing from sin through the blood of Jesus Christ. His coming was definite, just as definite as was the advent of Jesus. When Jesus was born His birth was proclaimed by an angel voice and chanted by a multitude of the heavenly host praising God (Luke 2:9, 13-14). Equally so was the Holy Spirit's advent attested to by His bodily form as a dove (Luke 3:22) and by His sound from heaven as of a rushing mighty wind and by cloven tongues of fire upon each of them (Acts 2:2-3). Heavenly dove, tempest roar, and tongues of fire crowning the hundred and twenty were as convincing as the guiding star and midnight shout of angel hosts. The coming of the Holy Ghost upon the hundred and twenty is found in Acts 2.

At the last supper when Jesus addressed the disciples, He said to them, *"Nevertheless I tell you the truth; It is expedient for you that I go away: for if I go not away, the Comforter will not come unto you; but if I depart, I will send him unto you. And when he is come, he will reprove the world of sin, and of righteousness, and of judgment"* (John 16:7-8).

As the disciples were together at Jerusalem after the resurrection, when the two who had walked with Him to Emmaus were conversing with the eleven disciples, Jesus Himself stood in their midst. He saith unto them, *"Peace be unto you"* [Luke 24:36]. They were affrighted believing they had seen a spirit. Jesus addressed them and said, *"And, behold, I send the promise of my*

Father upon you: but tarry ye in the city of Jerusalem, until ye be endued with power from on high" (Luke 24:49). Then in Acts 1 we find that the one hundred and twenty tarried in prayer in the upper room ten days. Thus between the crucifixion of Jesus and Pentecost is 53 days.

There was a crucifixion day. It was necessary. And now, we the children of God, must be crucified with Christ and freed from sin, our old man nailed to the cross. We die to sin, a real act, a genuine experience; it's done. So we are made partakers of Christ's death. But there was a resurrection day. He arose as a living Christ, not a dead one. He lives. He lives. And by our resurrection with Him into our new life we leave the old sin life and the old man buried in baptism (Romans 6), and are made partakers of His new resurrection life. The life of power, the exercise of the power of God, is made possible to us by Jesus having elevated us into His own resurrection life by actual spiritual experience.

Then comes His Ascension, just as necessary as the Crucifixion or the Resurrection. Jesus ascends to heaven and sits triumphant at the right hand of the Father. And according to His promise, He sent upon us the Holy Ghost. This experience is personal and dispensational. The Holy Ghost descends upon us, entering into us, for the Baptism of the Holy Ghost is the Holy God, the Spirit of Jesus, taking possession of our personality, living in us, moving us, controlling us. We become partakers of His glorified life, the life of Christ in glory. So it was with the hundred and twenty. See Acts 2:2-4:

> **And suddenly there came a sound from heaven as of a rushing mighty wind, [Suppose we heard it now. What would this audience think?] and it filled all the house where they were sitting. And there appeared unto them cloven tongues like as of fire, and it sat upon each of them. And they were all filled with the Holy Ghost, and began to speak with other tongues, as the Spirit gave them utterance.**

Not as they liked, not when they liked. They spoke as the Spirit gave them utterance. It was the Spirit that spoke in other tongues. What spirit? The Holy Ghost Who had come into them, Who controlled them, Who spoke through them. Listen: Speaking in tongues is the voice of God. Do you hear God's voice? They spake as the Spirit gave them utterance.

Now we have advanced to where we can understand God's manifestations.

Not God witnessing to man.

Not God with man.

But God in man — the Holy Ghost in man. They spake as the Spirit gave them utterance. [Please note: At this point the Spirit of God fell on Brother Lake causing him to speak in tongues in an unknown language. The audience was asked to bow their heads in silent prayer for the interpretation of the words spoken in tongues. As they prayed the interpretation was given as follows:]

"Christ is at once the spotless descent of God into man and the sinless ascent of man into God. And the Holy Spirit is the agent by which it is accomplished."

He is the Christ, the Son of God. His atonement is a real atonement. It changes from all sin. Man again becomes the dwelling place of God. Let us now see one of the most miraculous chapters in all the Word of God, Acts 10. A man, Cornelius, is praying. He is a Gentile centurion. An angel appears to him. The angel speaks. The angel says to send to Joppa for Peter. Peter is a Jew and he is not supposed to go into the home of a Gentile. He has not learned that salvation is for the Gentiles. God has to teach him. How does God do it? Peter goes up on the housetop to pray, and as he prays he is in a trance. Think of it! A trance. He falls into a trance. Suppose I was to fall on the floor in a trance, nine-tenths of this audience would be frightened to death. They would instantly declare that my opponent had hypnotized me. Why? Because of the ignorance among men of how the Spirit of God operates. But listen, listen! As he lays on the roof in a trance he sees a vision, a sheet let down from heaven caught by the four corners full of all manner of beasts and creeping things. And a voice, — what voice? — the Lord's voice said, *"Rise, Peter; kill, and eat. But Peter said, Not so, Lord; for I have never eaten any thing that is common or unclean."*

But the Voice said, *"What God hath cleansed, that call not thou common"* [Acts 10:13-15]. Peter obeyed. He went with the messengers.

Now see the result. As he spake the Word, the Holy Ghost fell on all them that heard the word. *"And they of the circumcision which believed were astonished, as many as came with Peter, because that on the Gentiles also was poured out the gift of the Holy Ghost"* [Acts 10:45].

How did they know? They heard them speak with tongues and magnify God.

Then answered Peter, *"Can any man forbid water, that these should not be baptized, which have received the Holy Ghost as well as we?"* [Acts 10:47]. And so it all ended in a glorious baptismal service in water of all who had been baptized in the Holy Ghost.

In Acts 22:12-13, Paul tells of Ananias coming to see him, but how did Ananias know Paul was there? See Acts 9:10-19, *"And there was a certain disciple at Damascus, named Ananias; and to him said the Lord in a vision... go into the street which is called Straight, and inquire in the house of Judas for one called Saul, of Tarsus."*

Now let us see that as we would see it today. The Lord said, *Ananias, go down into Straight Street to the house of Judas and ask for a man named Saul of Tarsus for behold he prayeth.*

And now the Lord tells Ananias what Saul had seen (Acts 9:12), *"And hath seen in a vision a man named Ananias coming in, and putting his hand on him, that he might receive his sight."* Here Ananias talks with the Lord. Do you know anything of such communion or talks with God? If not, get the Baptism of the Holy Ghost like the early Christians and their knowledge and experiences afterward can be yours, and you will see as we do the operation of the Lord upon saint and sinner by the Holy Ghost. Men say to us, "Where do you men get your insight into the Word?" We get it just where Paul and Peter got it—from God by the Holy Ghost (Galatians 1:11-12).

Beloved, read God's Word on your knees. Ask God by His Spirit to open it to your understanding. Read the Word with an open heart. It is a lamp unto our feet and a light unto our path.

Ananias went as the Lord had directed him and found Paul. And Paul was healed of his blindness and was baptized in the Holy Ghost and was also baptized in water and spoke in tongues *"more than ye all"* (1 Corinthians 14:18).

Now we see again Acts 22:14-15. Ananias is speaking to Paul, *"And he said, The God of our fathers hath chosen thee, that thou shouldest know his will, and see that Just One, and shouldest hear the voice of his mouth. For thou shall be his witness unto all men of what thou hast seen and heard."* Say, what about the people who say, "Don't tell these things to anyone"? *"And now why tarriest thou? arise, and be baptized, and wash away thy sins, calling upon the name of the Lord"* [Acts 22:16]. You see as with Peter at Cornelius' house all this work of the Spirit ended in salvation and baptism.

Now God through Ananias promised Paul that he should know *"his will, and see that Just One, and shouldest hear the voice of his mouth"* (Acts 22:14). When did that come to pass? Three years after when Paul returned to Jerusalem. *"Then after three years I went up to Jerusalem"* (Galatians 1:18). *"And it came to pass, that, when I was come again to Jerusalem, even while I prayed in the temple, I was in a trance"* (Acts 22:17).

Think of it, the intellectual, wonderful Paul, the master theologian of the ages, the orator of orators, the logician of logicians in a trance. Bless God for that trance. It was the fulfillment of what Ananias had said to him three years before: *"And saw him [Jesus] saying unto me, Make haste, and get thee quickly out of Jerusalem: for they will not receive thy testimony concerning me"* [Acts 22:18].

Now what is a trance? A trance is the Spirit taking predominance over the mind and body, and for the time being the control of the individual is by the Spirit; but our ignorance of the operations of God is such that even ministers of religion have been known to say it is the devil.

Let us see where Paul got his commission to preach and instructions about what he was to preach, and what his condition and attitude were when Jesus gave him his commission. See Acts 26:16-18. He was lying on the road on his way to Damascus. Now if we were to see someone lying on the road talking to an invisible somebody, no doubt in our ignorance we would send for an ambulance or for the police. But this is where the glorified Christ spoke to Paul and gave him definite instructions about what he should preach; and the purpose of his preaching was to be the salvation, not the entertainment, of others.

"But rise, and stand upon thy feet: for I [Jesus] have appeared unto thee for this purpose, to make thee a minister and a witness both of these things which thou hast seen, and of these things in the which I will appear unto thee" (Acts 26:16). Jesus promised to appear to Paul again and that was fulfilled while he lay in a trance in the temple three years later.

Now the object of his preaching was:

> **To open their eyes, and to turn them from darkness to light, and from the power of Satan unto God, that they may receive forgiveness of sins, and inheritance among them which are sanctified [present experience]**

> **by faith that is in me [Jesus]. Whereupon, O king Agrippa, I was not disobedient unto the heavenly vision (Acts 26:18-19).**

From this we see and are able to understand the operations of God by His Spirit. And now, is the Holy Ghost in the church today? Verily, yes; but you say, "We do not see Him work in this way." Why is it? Because you say all these things were for the Apostolic days. You cannot take the Word of God and find one place where the gifts of the Holy Ghost were withdrawn.

The nine gifts of the Holy Ghost are found in 1 Corinthians 12:8-10:

> **For to one is given by the Spirit the word of wisdom; to another the word of knowledge by the same Spirit; To another faith by the same Spirit; to another the gifts of healing by the same Spirit; To another the working of miracles; to another prophecy; to another discerning of spirits; to another divers kinds of tongues; to another the interpretation of tongues:**

Oh, praise God for the discovery of the gifts of the Holy Ghost and especially for the gift of healing. May we all learn to know Christ not alone as our Savior but as our sanctifier and healer, too.

Now I will go over these gifts on my fingers:

1st, wisdom
2nd, knowledge
3rd, faith
4th, healing
5th, miracles
6th, prophecy
7th, discerning of spirits
8th, divers kinds of tongues
9th, the interpretation of tongues

We have seen that the Holy Ghost came into the Church at Pentecost and the gifts are in the Holy Ghost; consequently, if the Holy Ghost is in the Church, the gifts are, too. Because of the lack of faith we do not see them exercised in the ordinary church. We stand for the obtaining of the gifts of the Holy Ghost through our personal baptism in the Holy Ghost and the enduement of the Holy Ghost power as promised by Jesus, yea, commanded by Him, *"Ye shall receive power, after that the Holy Ghost is come upon you"* (Acts 1:8).

People ask, "What is tongues?" Tongues is the voice (or operation) of the Spirit of God. In Acts 2:4, the one hundred and twenty spoke in tongues, the external evidence of the Spirit of God within. When the Holy Ghost came in, He spoke. Again, in Acts 10:44-48 when the Holy Ghost fell on them, Peter demanded the right to baptize them in water, saying, *"Can any man forbid water, that these should not be baptized, which have received the Holy Ghost as well as we?"*

How did they know they had been baptized in the Holy Ghost? See verse 46: *"For they heard them speak with tongues, and magnify God."* Tongues is the evidence of the Baptism of the Holy Ghost by which Peter claimed the right to baptize them in water. Again in Acts 19:1-7, Paul at Ephesus met 12 men whom John had baptized unto repentance, but now Paul re-baptized them by Christian baptism. In verse 5 we read that when they heard this, they were baptized (water baptism) in the Name of the Lord Jesus. And when Paul had laid his hands on them, the Holy Ghost came on them and they spoke with tongues and prophesied. Tongues are for a sign, not to them that believe, but to them that believe not (1 Corinthians 14:22).

Put Off "The Old Man"

In order to "put off the old man" it must have been something that was added to man when he fell. Otherwise God created man with something wrong with him. Adam was a perfect man. There were no flaws in him. God looked on His creation and declared it was very good. So the term "old man" cannot refer to the spirit, soul, body, mind, affections, self or will of a man. It is that thing that made Paul do what he did not want to do when he tried to keep the law by his own efforts (Romans 7:15-16, 23, 25). It is sin, the law of sin: some call it the principle of sin. It might also be termed the spirit of rebellion.

God says, *"Put off the old man."* The term "put off" in the Greek has the same force as when one puts off his coat. Jesus came to destroy the work of the devil. He came to rid man of all that was added to man at The Fall. He wants man to get rid of that detestable thing that has controlled man since The Fall.

How do you put off the old man? Our "old man" is crucified with Christ. When Jesus rose from the dead He did not bring up our old man or our sins with Him. He left them behind. You must reckon yourself to be dead to sin and alive unto God. You can reckon on the crucifixion of the "old man" with Christ. Reckon in the Greek means to take inventory, i.e. to estimate. Watchman Nee put it this way: "And now the good news is that sanctification is made possible for you on exactly the same basis as that initial salvation. You are offered deliverance from sin as no less a gift of God's grace than was the forgiveness of your sins. For God's way of deliverance is altogether different from man's way. Man's way is to try to suppress sin by seeking to overcome it; God's way is to remove the sinner."[1] God pulls you out of the river of sin and then must get the river out of you.

Crucifixion involves suffering. *"But the God of all grace, who hath called us unto his eternal glory by Christ Jesus, after that ye have suffered a while, make you perfect, stablish, strengthen, settle you"* (1 Peter 5:10). Jesus' crucifixion took but a very short time. If you make a complete surrender, the act of applying the finished work of Calvary to your heart will take but a little while. Putting off the old man is not a growth, it is a death (Romans 6:6-12).

Can I sin after the old man is put off? Colossians 3:9 warns against lying after the old man is put off. It will be willful sin. Can the old man reenter my life? Yes, if you give place to the devil, he is going about as a roaring lion seeking whom he may devour.

You have put off the old man. Now you can say with Jesus, *"for the prince of this world cometh, and hath nothing in me"* [John 14:30]. *"Who hath delivered us from the power of darkness, and hath translated us into the kingdom of his dear Son"* (Colossians 1:13).

[1]Nee, Watchman *The Normal Christian Life, 38.*

The Baptism of the Holy Ghost

(Chicago Pentecostal Convention July 16, 1920)

Sermon 4

There are as many degrees in God in the Baptism of the Holy Ghost as there are preachers who preach it. Some people are born away down weeping at the foot of the cross. They are still on the earth plane with Christ. They are still weeping over their sins, still trying to overcome sin and be pure of heart.

But there are other people who are born away up in the blessed dominion of God, like our Mother Etter. They have resurrection power. All power is given, and it is in our soul.

And beloved, one day there are going to be Christians baptized in the Holy Ghost who are away up in the throne of God, away up in the consciousness that is breathed out of His holy heart. Somebody is going to be born a son of God, and be baptized in the Holy Ghost where Jesus is today, in the throne-consciousness of Christ—where they can say, like Jesus said, where they can feel like Jesus feels: *"I am he that liveth, and was dead; and, behold, I am alive for evermore, Amen; and have the keys of hell and of death"* [Revelation 1:18]. Absolute overcoming consciousness!

You dear folks listen who are trying to pump up a Pentecost that has worn out years ago. God let it die. God had only one way under heaven to get you to move up into God, and that way is to let you become dissatisfied with the thing you have. And if you have not the consciousness you once had, God Almighty understands the situation. He is trying to get you hungry, so that you will commit your body and your soul and your spirit to God forever, and by the grace of God you will be baptized in the Holy Ghost over again, at the throne of God-consciousness, in the power of Jesus Christ, as Jesus is today. *"As he is, so are we in this world"* [1 John 4:17].

Why, with most of you, when you were baptized in the Holy Ghost, the Lord had to baptize a whole dose of medicine, and pills, and everything that was in you. Well, God never had to baptize that kind of stuff in the Lord Jesus. Jesus came down to the River Jordan, and gave His BODY and His SOUL and His SPIRIT to God forever, and He never took a pill or a dose of medicine. He never went to the Spirit of the world for assistance or to the devil for help. His SPIRIT, His SOUL, and His BODY were God's from that minute, forever.

Beloved, God is calling men and women to a holier consecration, to a higher place in God, and I am one of God's candidates for that holy place in God. I want to get to the throne of God. Oh, Yes, God baptized me in the Holy Ghost with a wondrous baptism, according the understanding I possessed ten or fifteen years ago. But I am a candidate today for a new baptism in the Holy Ghost that comes out of the heart of the GLORIFIED Christ, in the lightnings of God; everlasting overcoming on the throne with Jesus.

And that is the experience that is going to make the sons of God in the world. That is the reason they will take the world for Jesus Christ, and the Kingdom will be established, and they will put the crown on the Son of God, and declare Him *"King of kings and Lord of lords"* [Revelation 19:16] forever. Amen

---

> Therefore, fear not, for God is able to perform in you even that which He performed in Jesus, and raise you likewise in union with Christ Jesus, and make you reign in dominion over sin, instead of being dominated by the powers of evil and darkness.

Tongues and Interpretation
Battle Creek, Michigan
September 1913

44

Adventures in Religion

Radio Sermon 1

June 24, 1935

This is the first of a series of articles on the general subject of *Adventures in Religion.* I want to remind you for a few moments of some of the old mystics who were given glimpses into the unseen that it has not been the privilege of the ordinary man to understand.

The first and foremost was St. Francis of Assisi, whom the world has conceded to be one of the most Christ-like characters who has ever lived in the world. At a later period came St. John of the Cross, who for ten years seemed to live detached from the world. Today he is discovered to be one of the most practical men.

At a later period Madam Guyon appeared on the scene, and most every library contains one of her books. The molding of her character was so amazing that it has caused much discussion in the religious world of our day.

We have only, however, to look over the records of our own land to see many others. Such men as Charles G. Finney, founder of Oberlin College, and its first president. He was a practicing lawyer. He was seized with a conviction for sin so pungent that he retired to the woods to pray, and the Spirit of the Lord came upon him so powerfully, so divinely and took such amazing possession of him that he tells us he was compelled to cry out to

God to cease lest he should die. His wonderful ministry in the land is so well known, his books so frequently found in our libraries that it is not necessary to discuss him further.

On this list I wish to mention one who is not usually mentioned so lovingly as Finney. He was a Scotch boy, educated in the University of Australia, John Alexander Dowie. In addition to this, the Lord came to him in his own tabernacle one morning as he sat at his desk. Jesus was accompanied by His mother, the Virgin Mary. He advised Dowie concerning his ministry. Jesus laid His hands upon him and from that period his ministry was marked by the supernatural.

It is a matter of public record and one of the most astonishing facts that on one occasion he invited all persons who were healed under his ministry to attend a meeting at the auditorium in Chicago. Ten thousand people attended the meeting. At the psychological moment they all arose and gave testimony to the fact that they were healed. Those who were not able to attend were asked to send in a card, three and a half inches square, telling of their healing. Five bushel baskets were filled with these cards, representing the testimony of 100,000 people. At the psychological moment these five bushel baskets of cards were spilled over the stage, to emphasize the extent and power of God's ministry and blessing to the people.

Again, I want to call your attention to another marvelous life, that of Hudson Taylor, founder of the China Inland Mission. To him the Lord came, not only in personal presence, but in prophecy concerning the future. It was Hudson Taylor who prophesied the great revival in Wales ten years before it came to pass, giving almost the very day on which it would begin, and its power and extent. All this came to pass just as he had outlined it, while he was in the heart of China.

The Welsh revival was one of the most remarkable revivals that was ever produced. It was apparently prayed out of heaven by a single little church whose lights were never extinguished for seven years. This indicates that if a portion of that congregation was continually in prayer to God, that God would send a revival. And thus it came, the most astonishing and intensely powerful revival. In small churches which would hold perhaps 500 people, in one corner fifty people would be singing praises of God, thirty-five people would be down praying, another group would be praising God and testifying of His power.

It was not produced by evangelism, but it was the descent of the Spirit of God on the people. Conviction for sin was so powerful men knelt in their stores or wherever they were to give themselves to God. Sometimes while men were drinking in the public houses at the bar, they would cry out to God and give their hearts to Him.

Beginning with that revival there was a movement of God that spread throughout the world. In our own land we were particularly and wonderfully blessed by a movement that began New Year's Eve, 1900, which was accompanied by the Baptism in the Holy Ghost, and multitudes were baptized in the Holy Ghost.

After that revival there arose a phenomenal group of men and women. I am going to mention a few. The first I am going to mention is Aimee Semple McPherson. She was a young girl on a farm in Ontario, Canada. She attended a meeting by a young Irishman, Robert Semple, who was preaching under the anointing of the Holy Ghost. She became convicted of sin, opened her heart to God, and found Him, and was baptized in the Holy Ghost. Finally they were married and went as missionaries to China, where he died of fever. She was left a widow, and soon with a newborn baby. Some friends provided the funds that brought her back to the United States. Later she formed the acquaintance of a fine young businessman, and decided to settle down and forget all her burning call to the Gospel. This she tried to do. Two children were born to them. And then one day God came to Aimee in a meeting at Berlin, Ontario, conducted by Rev. Hall. Her ministry for a period of about fifteen years surpassed everything that we have ever seen in any land since the days of the apostles. (A multitude was healed under her ministry.)

Again, I want to call your attention to another unusual man, Raymond Ritchie, who belonged to Zion, Ill. His father was mayor of Zion City at one time. This boy was tubercular. They did not seem to understand his difficulty. He had no ambition; he could not work like other boys. He was in a state of lassitude. Eventually he found God. We speak of finding God as the old Methodist Church spoke of being saved, getting religion, meaning one and the same thing. When he has a consciousness of his salvation, he has found God.

Young Ritchie after his salvation was so absorbed in prayer, and the family got sort of worried. The father finally told him he had to get to work and help earn his living. But some woman who understood the boy said, "I have a room you can have." Another said she would provide him with food to keep him alive.

The great war came on, and the epidemic of the flu followed, when men died by the thousands throughout this United States. He became stirred, and began to pray for people and they were healed. The medical department presently took notice of it, and they sent him to pray for sick soldiers, and they were healed. Very well, he has continued in the ministry from then until now, and some of the most wonderful healing meetings that have ever taken place he has conducted.

Another man God has marvelously blessed and used is Dr. Price. He belongs to our own locality. Price used to live in Spokane. Dr. Price was baptized in the Spirit. Right away he began to manifest a most amazing ministry of healing. I attended one of his meetings at Vancouver, B.C. He had four audiences a day and 15,000 people in each, and people for a block around who could not get inside. All the churches in Vancouver I think united with him in that meeting. It was the most amazing meeting I ever saw. The sick people stood in groups of fifty and he would anoint them with oil according to the fifth chapter of James, and then pray for them. They were so overpowered by the Spirit they would fall to the floor, and a great number were healed.

Radio Sermon 2

June 25, 1935

No greater book has ever been given to mankind than the Bible. The amazing things recorded there that men experienced and that men wrought in the Name of Jesus Christ through faith by the power of God stand forever as an incentive to every man who enters and labors where they did. There is a place in God into which the soul enters and that makes it possible for the Spirit of God through you as His agent to register in the hearts of others.

Harry Fosdick says, "Until the New Theology can produce the sinless character of the old theology, it stands challenged." We believe that. We believe that the old-fashioned salvation through the blood of Jesus Christ and the Baptism of the Holy Ghost make possible an experience that no other religious experience in the world has ever been able to produce.

In the year 1900, there came a new wave of heavenly experience to this land and to the world. It began in Topeka, Kansas. It was in a Bible School conducted by Charles Parham. The founding of that school was an amazing thing. He was moved of God to go to Topeka, Kansas. He obeyed the promptings of the Spirit and went to the city. After looking all around for a building suitable for a Bible School and finding none, one day a gentleman told him of a residence on the outskirts of the city. It contained about twenty-two or more rooms and it was unoccupied. The owner lived in California. He went to see the building, and as he stood looking at it the Spirit of the Lord said, *I will give you this building for your Bible School.* And he said to himself, "This is the house."

As he stood there a gentleman came up to him and said, "What about the house?" Parham told him what the Lord had said to him, and the man being the owner of the house said, "If you want to use this building for a Bible School for God it is yours," and he handed him the key without any more ado.

The next day he went to the train and met a young woman of his acquaintance. She told him that when she was praying the Spirit of God told her there was going to be a Bible School here and that she should come. She was the first student. Thirty-five students came, all correspondingly directed by the Spirit of God.

This group began a study of the Word of God to discover what really constituted the Baptism of the Holy Ghost. After a month of study they became convinced that there was one peculiarity that accompanied the Baptism of the Holy Ghost—speaking in tongues.

They went to seeking the Baptism of the Holy Ghost. Parham was not present at the time. On New Year's night at twelve o'clock, 1900, one of the group, a Miss Osmand, a returned missionary, was baptized in the Holy Ghost and began to speak in tongues. In a few days the entire group, with a couple of exceptions, was baptized in the Spirit. When Parham returned and found that the students in his school had been baptized in the Holy Ghost, he himself went down before the Lord, and God baptized him in the Holy Ghost, too.

I want you to keep this story in mind for it forms the basis of the wonderful experience I want to relate in my next talk.

Radio Sermon 3

June 26, 1935

For a moment I want to call attention to a challenge that has been distributed widely through the ministry of Henry Fosdick, as I mentioned yesterday. Fosdick has said, "Until the New Theology can produce the sinless character of the old theology, it (the New Theology) stands challenged."

That is our position. We are reminding you, friend, that God is a miracle God. God is a miracle; Jesus Christ is a miracle; His birth was a miracle; His life was a miracle; His death was a miracle; His resurrection from the grave was a miracle; His Ascension was a miracle; His reception at the Throne of God by the eternal Father was the greatest of all miracles. Because of that God then gave Him the gift of the Holy Ghost, and made Him the administrator of the Spirit forever.

Some things can be better taught by relating experiences than in any other way. I might try to impress you with the beauty and wonder of the Baptism of the Holy Ghost, but dear friends, I think the relating of a few experiences will make it clearer to our minds than any other way.

I am reminded of an incident that took place on a railway train. Father Neiswender was stricken with a paralytic stroke. He had not been able to sleep for weeks. When they got him on a train to bring him to Spokane, the motion of the train temporarily soothed him and he fell asleep and dreamed. In his dream an angel came to him and said, "When you get to Spokane, inquire for a man by the name of Lake. He will pray for you and God will heal you." He was directed to our place, and when we prayed for him he immediately began to use his paralyzed arm and side, but was not completely delivered. The third time I went to pray the Lord showed me a blood clot in the spinal cord as large as bead. I prayed until the blood clot disappeared. No one could explain an incident like that by any natural law. Consequently we must classify it in the line of miracles IN OUR DAY—not a thousand years ago.

One more incident of this order. A family by the name of Bashor had a lovely boy who became dissatisfied at home and ran away. He went to a farmer where he was not known, gave another name, and worked for him a year. In the meantime the family with the aid of the police searched everywhere for the boy, but he could not be found. One day the mother came to me brokenhearted and told me the story. We knelt and prayed and asked God that He would cause that boy to get in touch with his parents.

Two days later she received a letter from the boy. He told her that on the night we had prayed he went to bed and had an unusual vision. Jesus appeared and talked to him. Jesus said, *I forgive your sins, but I want you to write to your mother, and get home to your folks.* The boy was greatly moved, got up and told the farmer the incident, and the result was the farmer hitched up his team and brought the boy in to his home. That boy is now married and has a nice family, and still lives in Spokane.

The part of that incident that might interest young folks is this. I was preaching at Mica, Washington where I related this incident. A young lady in the audience listened to the story, and after the meeting she said to me, "I would like to get acquainted with that young man." She did, and he is her husband.

Dear friends, these are some of the things that show us that there is a work of God's Spirit different from what we are ordinarily accustomed to, and these are the things that make religion real to New Testament Christians. Different ones in the Scriptures were guided by dreams. Joseph was guided by dreams. Some were guided by a voice from heaven. Now we are contending and bringing to your attention that there was an experience provided by the Lord Himself that made that intimacy a possibility. That is, the Baptism of the Holy Spirit. I wish I might say that with such emphasis that it would penetrate the deep recesses of your spirit.

One more incident. Over in the woods back of Kellog, Idaho lived a family by the name of Hunt. I visited in their home just a little while ago. The aged father was given up to die; the son was very anxious about him. The father kept saying, "Son, I ought not to die." The son had been much in prayer about this matter. One day he stood on a log road and presently he said a man appeared a little distance ahead, and as the gentleman approached he addressed Mr. Hunt saying, "I am Mr. Lake. I have Healing Rooms in Spokane. If you will bring your father there, the Lord will heal him." He was so impressed, that he got his father and brought him to me for prayer, and the Lord healed him gloriously and he lived many years.

1916

The value of the ministry of healing is not in the mere fact that people are healed. The value of healing is more largely in the fact that it becomes a demonstration of the living, inner, vital power of God, which should dwell in every life and make us new and mighty men in the hands of God.

Radio Sermon 4

June 27, 1935

When the German army started their famous march on Belgium and France with an army of three million men, they came to the borders only to find that they were met with such a tremendous opposition that for ten full days they were compelled to stay back until they could bring up their heavy artillery. Statesmen of Germany declare that that ten days' delay resulted in their losing the war. France and Belgium were prepared in the meantime to meet the assault.

Jesus Christ, the Son of God, said to His disciples: *"Behold, I send you forth as lambs [in the midst of] wolves"* [Luke 10:3], but He did not send them out without being prepared. They were commissioned and empowered by God, for that is what constitutes the Baptism of the Holy Ghost. Jesus Christ gave His disciples a big program before He left them. He told them they were not only to preach the Gospel to the whole world, but that they were to demonstrate its power.

> **Go ye into all the world, and preach the gospel to every creature...And these signs shall follow them that believe; In my name shall they cast out devils; they shall speak with new tongues; They shall take up serpents; and if they drink any deadly thing, it**

> **shall not hurt them; they shall lay hands on the sick, and they shall recover (Mark 16:15-18).**

These signs shall follow them that believe—those who accepted their work.

Dear friends, men who were going to put a program like that into effect needed heavy artillery from heaven. That is what Jesus undertook to give from heaven. So He said they were not to go out right away unprepared. Instead He said: *"Tarry ye in the city of Jerusalem, until ye be endued with power from on high"* (Luke 24:49). That endowment from on high is the equipment of every child of God who follows the biblical pattern. We are trying to impress upon the minds of men that one of the greatest Adventures in Religion that this world ever has found was when men dared to step across the usual boundaries and dared receive from His hand the Baptism of the Holy Ghost, which equips them with the power of God to bring blessings to other lives.

Just for one moment I want to bring you this fact. That the first thing Jesus said would be manifested in the Christian's life was: *"In my Name shall they cast out devils"* [Mark 16:17]. It was the first thing in Christian experience, and the exercise of Christian power that Jesus said would follow the Christian's life. They had power to cast out devils.

Jesus first gave that power to the twelve, then He gave it to the seventy, then He gave it to the Church at large on the day of Pentecost, when the Baptism of the Holy Ghost descended upon 120 at Jerusalem. Jesus gave the equipment from heaven.

In our day, within the past thirty years, we have seen such a manifestation of God from heaven as no other century in the world's history ever saw with the exception of the first four centuries of the Christian era. Beginning with 1900, the Spirit of God began to be poured out in power upon the world so that every country in the world has received this amazing power of God. Men who were ordinary businessmen, men who were scholars and teachers, students, and men from every walk in life found this equipment from heaven by the grace of God, and stepped out into a great life and ministry for God. This preparation, friends, is not for preachers only, but for the people. Jesus said, *"These signs shall follow them that BELIEVE"* [Mark 16:17].

Friends, there is an adventure for your soul, the most amazing adventure in all the world. It takes a brave soul to step into the light of God and receive the equipment He provides. That is no place for a coward. A cowardly spirit, a spirit that is always hiding, always apologizing for his faith, will never enter there. That is the gate of God. That is the gate into His Spirit. That is the gate into a life of effectiveness for every one who wants to serve God aright. Friends, you need this equipment to meet the demands of this day.

Sanctification is the cleansing of a man's nature by the indwelling power of the Spirit of Christ, for the purpose of the transformation of the mind and nature of man into the mind and nature of Jesus Christ.

I like John Wesley's definition of sanctification: "Possessing the mind of Christ, and ALL the mind of Christ."

Radio Sermon 5

June 28, 1935

This afternoon I want to talk to you on the subject of MIRACLES. From the year 400 until now the church has assumed the attitude that the days of miracles are passed without any scriptural evidence whatever. They have taught that miracles were to demonstrate the divinity of Jesus, and therefore the divinity of Jesus being demonstrated there was no longer any need for miracles.

We had a local incident that demonstrates the effect of this teaching I think. My convictions on the matter is that it has done more damage to the Christian faith than any other teaching that has been promulgated. There is a gentleman who works at the Devenport Hotel in Spokane, O.A. Risdon, who is one of the engineers there. He had a son with a deformed head. The top of the head raised up like the ridge of a roof, the forehead and back of the head also were forced out in similar manner, giving the head the appearance of the hull of a yacht upside down. He was born with what the physicians call a closed head. The boy was always slobbering; the pressure on the brain caused the right side to become paralyzed, and the boy was dumb. He was five years old at this time.

The physicians said there was nothing they could do. Then in desperation he appealed to his pastor. The pastor told him the days of miracles were past; that the Lord did not heal now;

that miracles were given to demonstrate the divinity of Jesus. The father replied, "If Jesus would heal my son, I would be convinced that He is divine now. If He is divine, He could lift this damnation from our house."

Finally, he came to us seeking help. We began to minister to the child. In a few days we observed that the paralysis began to depart; instead of walking on one side of his ankles he began to walk on the foot, and that indicated that the pressure was relieved on the brain. In seven weeks the child was perfectly well. The bones of the head softened and came down to normal. The paralysis disappeared and the child began to talk. In three months he was in the public school. He is a young married man now.

Dear friends, if we had continued to believe that the days of miracles were past that boy would be in the insane asylum. But we believed that Jesus Christ was the same yesterday, today and forever, and the boy was healed. It is a delight to believe the *Words of Jesus.* I have used this rule in my study of the Scriptures. If there is any question on any scripture I settle it with the *Words of Jesus.* I consider all the scriptures are a common court of the Gospel, but the Words of Jesus are the supreme court of the Gospel. When I want a supreme court decision, I appeal to the Words of Jesus.

You can read all the Words of Jesus in two hours or less in a Red Letter New Testament. Make a practice of seeking the Words of Jesus on any subject that troubles you, and make a compilation of what He says. He ought to be sufficient authority on any question for the heavenly Father called attention to the fact that He is the Son of God, and that we are to hear Him. He said:

"This is my beloved Son, in whom I am well pleased; hear ye him" (Matthew 17:5).

Radio Sermon 6

July 2, 1935

Jesus Christ came on the scene as a challenger. We have almost come to believe in our day that He was a sentimentalist and an easy type. He was King. He was the Prince of God. He was the Glory of Heaven! He was the representative of the Eternal Father! He had a mission. He declared the Father. He stepped among the religions of the earth as the challenger.

Jesus said there was real sin, that there was real sickness, that there was real death. He was not dodging the issue. He met it foursquare, and He said, I am bigger than it all. I am the Prince of Life. He destroyed sin and obliterated it from the souls of men. He blasted sickness and dissolved it from their system. He raised the dead to life. He challenged the devil, who was the author of death, to destroy Him if he could. He went into the regions of death and conquered and came forth triumphant so that it became necessary for the Lord to have a new vocabulary. He said after coming forth from the grave, *"All power is given unto me in heaven and in earth. Go ye therefore, and teach all nations, baptizing them in the name of the Father, and of the Son, and of the Holy Ghost"* (Matthew 28:18-19).

Sin and sickness and death, the triumvirate of darkness, that Jesus met and overcame were the original forces of evil in the world—the manifestation of the kingdom of darkness. There never will be a heaven, there never could be one, where these exist. Their destruction is necessary. That is one of the reasons why men cannot save themselves. All the good works that man may perform from now to the day of his death will not save him. Sin is of the heart. It is in the nature. Jesus came to reconstruct man's nature and give him instead of his own evil nature, the nature of God. Sin has made the nature of man vile. Christ came to give him deliverance from this nature and give him a new nature, the divine nature.

Through sin death entered into the world [see Romans 5:12].

Death is not a servant of God, nor a child of God, nor a product of God. Sin is the ENEMY of God. The New Testament declares that *"The last enemy that shall be destroyed is death"* [1 Corinthians 15:26]. Not the last servant or friend, but the last enemy. Death is doomed to destruction by the Lord Jesus Christ. Sin and sickness are incipient death.

That is the reason we do not speak of the things of the Lord and His salvation in moderate tones. We are shouting them to mankind. The spirit of a real child of God challenges darkness, challenges sin, challenges sickness. The Lord Jesus came to destroy sickness and wipe it out of the lives of men, to make possible the heaven of God in their hearts and lives now. There could be no heaven where disease and sickness are found. Sin and sickness and death must be blotted out. That is the reason, dear friends, that Christianity is always a challenger. Christianity is a thing of strength. Real religion is a source of power. It is the dynamite of God. The Holy Spirit gives the overcoming grace and strength essential to destroy sin, to destroy sickness, to overcome death.

Radio Sermon 7

July 3, 1935

I am pleased to greet you today, dear friends, with a real account of one of the marvelous adventures in God. Jesus said, *"Heal the sick, cleanse the lepers, raise the dead, cast out devils: freely ye have received, freely give"* (Matthew 10:8).

Christianity was not to be stinted in her giving. She was not to be a beggar. She was to be a giver. She had something from heaven to give that the world did not have. She had something to give that would bring deliverance to the world. Jesus was putting His program of deliverance in force through the Church.

The man is a bold man who undertakes to carry out this program of Jesus. The Christian who never has faith enough in God to undertake it, I fear, is of the cowardly type. I am afraid that modern Christianity stands indicted at the bar of God for cowardliness because of fear to undertake the program of Jesus.

Friends, that is why we urge upon men the necessity of the Baptism of the Holy Ghost. It is the only thing that brings the heavenly equipment to the hearts of men, that makes them equal to this program and the possibility of carrying it out.

I want to talk to you today of a bold soul, and in my judgment a very extraordinary one indeed. I refer to a gentleman who lives in this city, a preacher of the gospel from the days of his youth, Rev. C.W. Westwood. His home is on Nora Avenue.

A number of years ago there was born at one of the great hospitals of the city a little child (a girl) from healthy parents, Mr. and Mrs. Young. Mr. Young for many years had a stall in the Westlake Market. Mrs. Young has been a nurse for many years and also is well known. When this baby was born it weighed six and a half pounds. Because of some strange difficulty the child could not assimilate its food. When she was nine months old she only weighed four and a half pounds. The child looked more like a little dried up alligator than it did like a human being. She finally fell into a state of death and remained in a dying condition. In the meantime we were called to minister to the child.

Mr. Westwood was assigned to the case. One day when he went to the hospital as usual to minister to the child, they explained that the child was not there. It had died that morning and was in the dead room. He asked if he might see the child, and went into the dead room, and took the child down. He sat down on a chair with the baby on his knees. He opened his heart to God, turned the spirit of faith in his heart loose in behalf of the little one. In a little while (and I am saying this with all reverence before God, because I expect to meet this matter when I stand before the great Judgment Throne), the child revived. He sent for the parents, they took the child from the hospital and put her in the hands of an elderly lady by the name of Mrs. Mason, who nursed her for six weeks. At the end of that period she was as well as any other child. Her name is Agnes Young.

About a year ago I received a telephone call from Agnes Young asking me if I would perform a marriage ceremony for her and her fiance. This young couple lives at Eugene, Oregon now.

And so I want to leave this testimony, that God is as good as His Word. That faith in Almighty God brings to pass the very same things today that it always did.

Radio Sermon 8

July 5, 1935

The climax of all adventures was the adventure of Jesus in delivering men from sin and sickness and death. One cannot measure the Man of Galilee with any tapeline or yardstick that comes from human reasoning. Jesus is outside of the realm of reason. In the first place, His history was written by the prophets ages before He was born. Man can write a better history of Jesus from the Old Testament than they can from the New Testament. In the New Testament we have simply a little fragment about His incarnation and birth and then thirty years of silence, except for a little glimpse of Him when He was twelve years of age. All the books that have been written of Jesus have been written almost entirely about His three years of public ministry that began with His baptism in the Jordan and closed with His resurrection. Now men try to write on His pre-existence. Here and there one has caught a glimpse of His ministry seated at the right hand of the Majesty on High.

I want you to see another fact. That every prophecy that was written before His time was all in the miracle realm. His incarnation was a real miracle. He was not born under the natural laws of generation. He was conceived of the Holy Ghost. He was a true incarnation—God uniting Himself with humanity. The scenes surrounding His birth—the angelic visitation, the coming of the wise men were all miracles. The angel's warning to Joseph to flee with the child to Egypt was miraculous. The very silence of those thirty years is considered most miraculous. The divine silences represent the most marvelous elements in the Book we all love. The descent of the Spirit at His baptism was a miracle. From that day until Mount Olivet was a period of miracles. His life among men was a miracle. The new kind of life that He revealed to the world was a miracle. Jesus' mental processes were miraculous. Our libraries are full of books written by great thinkers, like Thomas Edison, and others, who were incessant thinkers. With Jesus there is something different. He speaks out from the Spirit that dominated His spiritual faculties. Jesus' spirit ruled His intellect. Gems of divine truth dripped from His lips as honey from the honeycomb. The sermon on the Mount, great portions in Luke and John are as untouched as when they dropped from the lips of Jesus. Men's writings grow old and out of date. God's truth is ever fresh. Yes, Jesus words and life and contact with men was miraculous. It is still miraculous.

It would be uncharitable if we were to criticize the man of reason, who knows nothing about the spiritual realm. Christianity is not the product of human reasoning. Christianity is a divine intervention. Christians are those who have been "born from above." They have been recreated. This life of God that comes into their spirit nature, dominates the reason so that they have the "mind of Christ" to think God's thoughts and live in God's realm of miracles.

Friends, when a Christian tries to live by REASON he is moving out of God's country into the enemy's land. We belong in the miraculous or supernatural realm.

Christ was a miracle. Every Christian is a miracle. Every answer to prayer is a miracle. Every divine illumination is a miracle. The power of Christianity in the world is a miraculous power. God help us to realize that ours is a High and Holy Calling.

Radio Sermon 9

July 9, 1935

I want to talk to you concerning some of the purposes of God. Among them is God's amazing purpose to baptize men in the Holy Spirit. I think that even among the deepest Christians in our day little is understood of the real purpose of God in this wonderful experience.

We say to one another that the Baptism of the Holy Spirit is God coming into man; that it is God manifesting Himself in man, and other expressions of this type, but it fails to convey to the mind anything like the great purpose of God in His incoming in us.

The Baptism of the Holy Spirit has among its wonderful purposes the swelling of God in us, the perfecting of His life in us through His Word in our spirit, through His power in our life. Tongues is the peculiar manifestation of God accompanying the coming of God the Holy Spirit into our life. This was the evidence when the Holy Spirit of God descended on the day of Pentecost at Jerusalem. The Scripture is given in these wonderful words:

> **Suddenly there came a sound from heaven as of a rushing mighty wind, and it filled all the house where they were sitting. And there appeared unto them cloven tongues like as of fire, and it sat upon**

> **each of them. And they were all filled with the Holy Ghost, and began to speak with other tongues, as the Spirit gave them utterance (Acts 2:2-4).**

What is the real purpose? What is God doing? Is He giving to the individual certain powers to demonstrate and to convince the world? I do not think that is the real reason. There is a deeper one. God is taking possession of the inner spirit of man. From the day that Adam sinned the spirit of man was a prisoner. This prison condition continues until God releases the spirit of the individual in the Baptism of the Holy Ghost. The spirit remains dumb, unable to express itself to mankind, until God through the Holy Ghost releases the spirit, and the voice of the spirit is restored.

You understand man is a triune being—spirit, soul and body, and these departments of our life are very different. God manifests Himself to the spirit of man; and the experience of real salvation is the coming of God into the spirit of man—the infusion of the spirit of man and God.

In the olden days the church used to discuss the subject of sanctification but was somewhat hazy in its explanation of what it was. Sanctification is God taking possession of our mental forces, just as He took possession of our spirit when He bestowed on us eternal life. Your mind is brought into harmony with God, even as your spirit was brought into harmony with God. Following the example of Jesus we dedicate not only our spirit and soul (or mind) to God, but also our body to God. That is the reason we left doctors and medicine behind.

I want to talk to you about speaking in tongues by relating this experience, and reciting a poem God gave me, when I was a missionary in South Africa and had my residence there. There was a dreadful epidemic of African Fever and within thirty days about one-fourth of the population of some sections of the country of both white and black died. I was absent from my tabernacle on the field with a group of missionaries and we did the best we could to get them healed of God, and help bury the dead. I returned to my tabernacle after about three week's absence to discover that the same thing was taking place there. I was greatly distressed. My pianist was gone; my chief soloist was gone—the only daughter of an aged mother. I went to her home to console her and comfort her. As I sat by her table she reminded me that just four weeks before I had been present when the pianist and the soloist were practicing music in that home. My soul was very sorrowful. As I sat meditating I began to pray: "My God, I would like to know what sort of reception such a soul as that gets when they arrive on the other side." Presently God spoke to my soul and said, "Take your pen and I will tell you about it."

The first thing that came was the name of the poem in tongues. Then the Lord gave me the interpretation. It was called "The Reception." Then the first verse came in tongues, then I received from the Lord the interpretation, and then the next verses likewise, and so on. In the meantime something transpired in my own spirit. I felt as if I was being elevated into the presence of God, and I could look on the folks on earth, and it was described in these verses:

The Reception

List! 'Tis the morning hours in Glory.
A shadow through the mists doth now appear—
A troop of angels sweeping down in greeting.
A "Welcome Home" rings out with joyous cheer!

A traveler from the earth is now arriving;
A mighty welcome's ringing in the skies!
The trumpets of a host are now resounding
A welcome to the life that never dies.

Who is the victor whom the angels welcome?
What mighty deeds of valor have been done?
What is the meaning of these shouts of triumph?
Why welcome this soul as a mighty one?

She's but a woman, frail and slight and tender,
No special mark of dignity she bears:
Only the Christ light from her face doth glisten:
Only the white robe of a saint she wears.

She's but a soul redeemed through the blood of Jesus.
Hers but a life of sacrifice and care;
Yet with her welcome all the Heaven's ringing,
And on her brow a victor's crown she bears.

How come she thus from sin's benighting thraldom,
The grace and purity of heaven to obtain?
Only through Him Who gave His life a ransom,
Cleansing the soul from every spot and stain.

See! As you gaze upon her face so radiant,
'Tis but the beauty of her Lord you see;
Only the image of His life resplendent;
Only the mirror of His life is she.

See with what signs of joy they bear her onward;
How that the Heavens ring with glad acclaim!
What is the shout they raise while soaring upward?
"Welcome! Thrice welcome, thou, in Jesus' Name!"

Rest in the mansion by thy Lord prepared thee,
Out of the loving deeds which thou hast done,
Furnished through thoughts and acts which have portrayed Me,
Unto a lost world as their Christ alone.

Hear how thy heavenly harp is ringing!
Touched are its strings with hands by thee unseen.
Note that the music of thine own creating
Heaven's melodies in hearts where sin has been.

See how the atmosphere with love is laden,
And that with brightness all the landscape gleams!
Know 'tis the gladness and the joy of heaven
Shed now by rescued souls in radiant beams.

Oh, that here on earth we may learn the lesson
That Christ enthroned on our hearts while here,
Fits and prepares the soul for Heaven,
Making us like Him both there and here.

Doing the simple and homely duties
Just as our Christ on the earth has done,
Seeking alone that the Christ's own beauties
In every heart should be caused to bloom.

Showing all men that the blood of Jesus
Cleanses our hearts from all sin below,
And that the life of the Christ within us
Transforms the soul till as pure as snow.

When we thus come to the dark cold river,
No night, no darkness, no death is there,
Only great joy that at last the Giver
Grants us anew of His life to share.

Given to John G. Lake
in Tongues and Interpretation
while in Africa

Radio Sermon 10

July 10, 1935

Today I want to talk to you concerning one of the remarkable and outstanding incidents in the Word of God. You will find it in Acts 19:11-12. It reads: *"And God wrought special miracles by the hands of Paul: So that from his body were brought unto the sick handkerchiefs or aprons, and the diseases departed from them, and the evil spirits went out of them."*

The people brought their handkerchiefs or aprons to the Apostle Paul that they might touch his person. They were then carried to the sick and laid on them; the demons went out of them, and the sick were healed.

An examination of this incident discloses one of the most wonderful facts I know. First, that the Spirit of God is tangible. We think of the air as tangible, of electricity as tangible and we register the effects of it. And I want to say to you, friends, that the Spirit of God is equally as tangible and can be handled and distributed—He can be enclosed in handkerchief or apron and sent as a blessing to the one who needs it.

Get this scripture and read it for yourself and secure from heaven the blessing it contains. And remember when you are in a struggle and doubts and fears assail you that God is not far away in the heavens. His Spirit is right here to bless, here to act in your life for a blessing.

Along with this line I want to present this testimony of Mrs. Constance Hoag, who is dean of women at the state college, Pullman, Washington. She was visiting her son at Fairfield, Washington. They were going for a motor ride. When she stepped on the running board, her son thinking she was already in the car, started the car. She fell and broke the knee-cap and the bone protruded through the flesh. They carried her into the house, then called us on the long distance and asked that we pray and send her a handkerchief as soon as possible by messenger. We sent the handkerchief and in fifteen minutes after she received it the bone had gone back into place. In forty-five minutes the knee was entirely well.

However, her friends began to challenge this healing and she found herself in the midst of a strange debate. A little later almost the same accident happened again. She was thrown to the pavement and the other knee cap was broken and protruded in two sections through the flesh. Once again we prayed over a handkerchief and sent it to her, and once again the power of God acted, but this time not so quickly as the first time. The second time she said the pain was gone in half an hour; in an hour the bone had gone back in its place and in an hour and a half the knee was healed and she was well. Friends, the Spirit of God is as tangible today as it was in the days of the Apostle Paul.

Radio Sermon II

July 11, 1935

This morning I was out on the extreme east side of the city. I ran across a strange thing. A man was coming down the street with a pack on his back. The pack was in a cowhide which was only about half cured. In the sack he had a cow's leg. As I came up to him he said, "Excuse me, sir, but this is my Christian cross."

I said, "Excuse me, but it looks like just the opposite to me." He went down the street and as far as I could hear him he was scolding me.

Then I went to the home of a woman who had been ill a long time. She had lain in bed and was gradually growing worse, and all the time she was accepting this sickness as from God. So I told her this foolish incident and I said, "Dear woman, if you knew the Word of God you would never accept a thing like that as the will of God, because Jesus most emphatically declared that sickness was not the will of God but the devil's."

She had accepted that rotten, nasty business as God's will and had lain in bed for eight months. It is as offensive to God as the man with his "Christian cross." I want you to know, dear friends, that the Word of God is the foundation upon which our faith is to be built.

Jesus said that He came *"to destroy the works of the devil."* Acts 10:38 declares: *"How God anointed Jesus of Nazareth with the Holy Ghost and with power: who went about doing good, and healing all that were OPPRESSED OF THE DEVIL; for God was with him."*

You do not find "if it be Thy will" in the teaching of Jesus. He never suggested in word or deed that sin, sickness and death were the will of God. The leper who came to Jesus for healing in the eighth [chapter] of Matthew did say, *"Lord, if thou wilt, thou canst make me clean."* I suppose he, too, was accepting the dirty leprosy as the will of God.

Jesus instantly said, *"I will; be thou clean."* The answer of Jesus to the leper is Jesus' answer to you, to every sick man. "If it be Thy will" was never suggested in any of Jesus' teaching concerning sickness and disease. Friend, Jesus had declared His will in the most emphatic manner. His will is always to heal if you but come to Him.

Dr. John G. Lake, 1909

Every student of the primitive Church discerns at once a distinction between the soul of the primitive Christian and the soul of the modern Christian. It lies in the spirit of Christ's dominion.

The Holy Spirit came into the primitive Christian soul to elevate his consciousness in Christ, to make him master. He smote sin, and it disappeared. He cast out devils (demons); a divine flash from his nature overpowered and cast out the demon. He laid his hands on the sick, and the mighty Spirit of Jesus Christ flamed into the body and the disease was annihilated. He was commanded to rebuke the devil, and the devil would flee from him. He was a reigning sovereign, not shrinking in fear, but overcoming faith.

It is this spirit of DOMINION, when restored to the Church of Christ, that will bring again the glory-triumph to the Church of God throughout the world and lift her into the place where, instead of being the obedient servant of the world, the flesh, and the devil, she will become the divine instrument of God. She will minister Christ's power in salvation, in healing the sick, in the casting out of demons, and in the carrying out of the whole program of Jesus' ministry as the early Church did.

Radio Sermon 12

August 22, 1935

I want to tell you the story of an unusual family. I am going to call this story, "Following the Trail of Jesus." A number of years ago I felt as if I wanted to do something out of the ordinary to call attention to the subject of Divine Healing. So I went to the newspapers and posted $500. Then I announced that if anyone who was sick or diseased would come to the Healing Rooms and be ministered to for thirty days, and if at the end of that time they were not substantially better or healed, they could have the $500.

Over at Monroe, Washington, was a man by the name of Paul Gering, who had got to fooling around with spiritualism. That dear fellow was an open, splendid man. He was a hard-working business man. After he got to fooling with spiritualism nobody could live with him. He was more like a raging lion than a human. He went all over the United States seeking deliverance from all kinds of folks who were praying for the sick.

He read my announcement and became interested. He sent me a telegram asking me to come to Monroe and put on a meeting, and, of course, pray for him. He met Mrs. Lake and me at our hotel and drove us out to his home on the outskirts of the city. He walked into his home and stopped in the middle of the dining room and fell on his knees saying, "Mr. Lake, I am waiting for you to pray for me that I may be delivered." We laid hands on him and prayed, and, bless God, the power began to go through him. He was completely delivered, the demons were cast out, and he was baptized in the Spirit. From that time on hundreds of people have been saved and healed and baptized in the Holy Ghost under his ministry. Now he is a great wheat farmer in the Big Bend country. Last night I spent the evening at his home and conducted a public service for his relatives and neighbors.

Just let me follow the trail of Jesus with you in that family for a few minutes. His sons were unsaved, his daughters were unsaved. One by one, after the father's deliverance, the faith of God in his heart laid hold on God for his family. They became converted and baptized in the Spirit until his entire family, including his beloved wife, was saved and baptized in the Holy Ghost.

Mr. Gering had a brother, Joe, a hard fellow and a heavy drinker. He owned a farm down in the country. His wife was distressed for she saw he was gradually losing his grip on his affairs and squandering his money, and they were getting into financial difficulty. She was a woman of prayer and was praying for him. Finally one day he came to visit Paul Gering. Paul said, "Joe, I am going to Spokane to attend Mr. Lake's meeting, come and go with me."

We were conducting meetings in our tabernacle. When they came, we were in the prayer room. The meeting went through without anything unusual occurring until we were practically ready to dismiss. This man, Joe Gering, was sitting on one of the back seats. A lady turned to me and asked, "Who is that man on the back seat?"

I said, "That is Paul Gering's brother."

She said, "The Lord told me to go and lay hands on him and pray, and he would be saved and baptized in the Holy Ghost."

I said, "Then you had better go and do it, sister."

She went back to him and engaged him in conversation and finally asked if she might pray with him. He said he had no objection to her praying for him. So she laid her hands on him and began to pray, and as she did, the Spirit of God from heaven came down on him, and in a few minutes he yielded his heart to the Lord and prayed through until he got a real witness from heaven and began to rejoice in the Lord. After he rejoiced for a while she said, "Now you ought to be baptized in the Holy Ghost." He knelt down again and began to pray, and after a few minutes Joe Gering was baptized in the Holy Ghost. That man's soul was so full of rejoicing that he spent the entire night singing and praying and rejoicing and talking in tongues and sometimes in English. In a few days he was out among the sinful and sick and getting folks saved and healed.

Here is another portion of the story. These men had a sister who lived at Palouse, Washington. She was unfortunately married to a very wicked man. She developed a tumor, and he insisted on her being operated on. She tried to tell him that in their family the Lord always healed them. He would not listen and insisted she be operated on. They brought her to St. Luke's Hospital in Spokane and she was operated on. A dreadful infection developed and they wired to the family that she was going to die, so the family began to gather here to see her. I knew nothing of these circumstances.

I was riding up Monroe Street when the Spirit of the Lord said, "Go to St. Luke's Hospital and pray for Paul Gering's sister. She is dying." I went immediately and inquired at the office and was directed to her bedside. I laid my hands on her and began to pray, and the Spirit of the Lord came upon the woman, the infection was destroyed, and in ten minutes she was sound asleep and the next day was on the highway to a blessed recovery. These are some of the things that take place when folks get into the line of God.

Their old mother was a godly woman who lived at Palouse. She had been notified that her daughter was likely to die, and when she got the word she went into her closet and interceded with God and prayed for the daughter's deliverance. I believe before God that when God spoke to me it was the answer to that mother's prayer. He sent help through me, and the Lord made her whole.

Gerber Girl's Healing

One day Mrs. Lake and I were present in a gathering of Christian people where these Gering people were and some of their neighbors. A family by the name of Gerber had a girl 17 or 18 years old. She stood up with her back to us, and I remarked to Mrs. Lake, "Did you ever see such a perfect form? That girl would do for an artist's model." But when she turned around I was shocked at her appearance; I never saw anyone so cross-eyed. It was a dreadful sight.

Later I talked to the father and he told me that surgeons would not undertake to straighten her eyes. They said it was impossible, and if they undertook it she was likely to lose her eyesight. Presently the young girl came over our way and I said, "Sit down, little woman, I want to talk to you." After talking a few minutes I stood up and laid my hands on her eyes. The Spirit of God came upon her and in three minutes' time those eyes were as straight as they were supposed to be. She is now married and has a beautiful home and lovely babies. Her eyes and heart are straight.

> Christ is at once the sinless descent of God into man, and the sinless ascent of man into God. And the Holy Spirit is the Agent by which this is accomplished.

Tongues and Interpretation
Somerset East Cape Colony, South Africa, June, 1910
Dr. John G. Lake

Bibliography

"A Strong Man's Gospel"

Books:

Burgess, Stanley M. and McGee, Gary B., eds. *Dictionary of Pentecostal and Charismatic Movements.* Grand Rapids, Mich.: Zondervan, 1988.

Lake, John G. *Adventures in God: A Living Classic Book.* 1981. Reprint. Compiled by Wilford H. Reidt. Tulsa, Okla.: Harrison House, 1991.

Lake, John G. *The Astounding Diary of Dr. John G. Lake.* Dallas: Christ For The Nations, 1987.

Lake, John G. *The John G. Lake Sermons on Dominion over Demons, Disease and Death.* Edited by Gordon Lindsay. 1949. Reprint. Dallas: Christ For The Nations, 1976.

Lake, John G. *Spiritual Hunger and Other Sermons.* Edited by Gordon Lindsay. Reprint. Dallas: Christ For The Nations, 1987.

Lindsay, Gordon. *John G. Lake—Apostle To Africa.* Reprint. Dallas: Christ For The Nations, 1987.

Lindsay, Gordon. *The New John G. Lake Sermons.* Reprint. Dallas: Christ For The Nations, 1986.

Reidt, Wilford H. *John G. Lake: A Man Without Compromise: A Living Classic Book.* Tulsa, Okla.: Harrison House, 1989.

Wyatt, Brett A. *Anointing Fall on Me: John G. Lake: The 1924 Healing Revival in Spokane.* A paper compiling articles published in *The Spokane Press* and a personal letter from John G. Lake and his church in Portland, Ore., in 1924. Spokane, Wash.

Newspapers:

The Spokesman-Review. Newspaper articles. Spokane, Wash.: 17, 19 September 1935.

Audio/Video Tapes:

Lairdon Ministries, Roberts. *God's Generals: John G. Lake.* Audio cassette/video tape. Vol. 3.

Prayer for Salvation and Baptism in the Holy Spirit

Heavenly Father, I come to You in the Name of Jesus. Your Word says, "*...whosoever shall call on the name of the Lord shall be saved*" (Acts 2:21). I am calling on You. I pray and ask Jesus to come into my heart and be Lord over my life according to Romans 10:9-10. "*If thou shalt confess with thy mouth the Lord Jesus, and shalt believe in thine heart that God hath raised him from the dead, thou shalt be saved.*" I do that now. I confess that Jesus is Lord, and I believe in my heart that God raised Him from the dead.

I am now reborn! I am a Christian—a child of Almighty God! I am saved! You also said in Your Word, "*If ye then, being evil, know how to give good gifts unto your children: HOW MUCH MORE shall your heavenly Father give the Holy Spirit to them that ask him?*" (Luke 11:13). I'm also asking You to fill me with the Holy Spirit. Holy Spirit, rise up within me as I praise God. I fully expect to speak with other tongues as You give me the utterance (Acts 2:4).

(Begin to praise God for filling you with the Holy Spirit. Speak those words and syllables you receive—not in your own language, but the language given to you by the Holy Spirit. You have to use your own voice. God will not force you to speak.)

Now you are a Spirit-filled believer. Continue with the blessing God has given you and pray in tongues each day. You'll never be the same!

Books by Kenneth Copeland

* A Ceremony of Marriage
A Covenant of Blood
Faith and Patience—The Power Twins
* Freedom From Fear
From Faith to Faith—A Daily Guide to Victory
Giving and Receiving
Honor—Walking in Honesty, Truth & Integrity
How to Conquer Strife
How to Discipline Your Flesh
How to Receive Communion
Love Never Fails
* Now Are We in Christ Jesus
Our Covenant With God
* Prayer—Your Foundation for Success
Prosperity Promises
Prosperity: The Choice Is Yours
Rumors of War
* Sensitivity of Heart
Six Steps to Excellence in Ministry
Sorrow Not! Winning Over Grief and Sorrow
* The Decision Is Yours
* The Force of Faith
* The Force of Righteousness
The Image of God in You
The Laws of Prosperity
* The Mercy of God
The Miraculous Realm of God's Love
The Outpouring of the Spirit—The Result of Prayer
The Power of the Tongue
The Power to Be Forever Free
The Troublemaker
The Winning Attitude
* Welcome to the Family
* You Are Healed
Your Right-Standing With God

*Available in Spanish

Books by Gloria Copeland

* And Jesus Healed Them All
  Build Yourself an Ark
  From Faith to Faith—A Daily Guide to Victory
  God's Success Formula
* God's Will for You
  God's Will for Your Healing
  God's Will Is Prosperity
  God's Will Is the Holy Spirit
  Harvest of Health
  Love—The Secret to Your Success
  Pressing In—It's Worth It All
  The Power to Live a New Life
* Walk in the Spirit

*Available in Spanish

For more information about KCP and a free catalog, please write:

Kenneth Copeland Ministries
Fort Worth, Texas 76192-0001

World Offices of Kenneth Copeland Ministries

Kenneth Copeland
Post Office Box 58248
Vancouver
BRITISH COLUMBIA
V6P 6K1
CANADA

Kenneth Copeland
Post Office Box 15
BATH
BA1 1GD
ENGLAND

Kenneth Copeland
Post Office Box 830
RANDBURG
2125
REPUBLIC OF SOUTH AFRICA

Kenneth Copeland
Locked Bag 1426
Parramatta
NEW SOUTH WALES 2124
AUSTRALIA